THE SCIENTIFIC STUDY OF RELIGION

THE SCIENTIFIC STUDY OF RELIGION

J. Milton Yinger *OBERLIN COLLEGE*

The Macmillan Company
Collier-Macmillan Limited : London

THE MACMILLAN COMPANY
866 Third Avenue, New York, New York 10022

COLLIER-MACMILLAN CANADA, LTD., Toronto, Ontario

Library of Congress catalog card number: 75–95188

Third Printing, 1971

To S, J, N, C, and C

PREFACE

It is interesting and a bit puzzling that in this day of disenchantment, of attacks on the Establishment (whether governmental, educational, or religious), and of presumed secularization, the study of religion is flourishing. Many studies, to be sure, document the decline of traditional beliefs; but their findings will be misinterpreted unless they are seen in the context of the rise of new systems of belief. If it is a period of disenchantment, it is also a period of longing. To me, the evidence is decisive: Human nature abhors a vacuum in systems of faith.

This is not, then, a period of religious decline but is one of religious change. During times of relative stability in religious matters, scholars tend to take patterns of belief for granted; but when traditional faiths are put under severe strain and new faiths appear with promises of salvation and enlightenment, it is not only theological thought that is stimulated. Philosophical study of religion is encouraged, and, in our time, the scientific study of religion prospers.

Since World War II there has been a sharp increase in the number of journals, particularly in Europe, Japan, and the United States, devoted to the science of religion—a reflection of the steady growth of research. Scholarly associations have been founded that bring workers from several disciplines into close interaction. University courses dealing with religion from the perspective of science have increased significantly in number. All this expansion multiplies both the need for and the possibilities of a theory of religion—a theory that will tie the study of religion into the sciences of human behavior as they are developed around other substantive areas and around general concepts.

In my judgment, the scientific study of religion must be simultaneously anthropological, psychological, and sociological; that is, it must deal with the individual forces, the cultural systems, and the social structures that, in interaction, shape religion and are shaped by it. My aim in this book is to establish as powerfully as I can a frame of reference that expresses this judgment and a method of study appropriate to it that the reader can carry with him as he explores questions of particular interest to him. Although we shall examine a large number of specific issues in the scientific study of religion, issues drawn from many times and places, we shall not try to "cover the field." We shall try to sharpen the tools necessary for the science of religion and to use them in dealing with some of the major problems. If the theory we develop is useful, it will help us interpret the data to which we refer and it will generate explanations of other religious phenomena that are not explored here.

When I began to make plans for this book, about five years ago, it was my intention to undertake an extensive revision of *Religion, Society, and the Individual*, Part 1, which appeared in 1957. (A separate edition included, as a second part, a reader containing a number of articles and book excerpts.) I had no doubt that somewhat drastic revision would be required, for several reasons: The scientific study of religion was developing rapidly, so that I could draw on increasingly rich resources; I wanted to bring under analysis more material from Eastern religions and from the study of primitive societies; and I wanted to tie the discussion of religion more closely to the general theoretical perspectives with which I had recently been concerned, particularly as expressed in *Toward a Field Theory of Behavior* (1965). As I got into the writing, it became apparent that it would require a very nice distinction indeed to separate the idea of revision from the idea of a new book. And when the opportunity arose for a full year's work on the manuscript, allowing me to undertake studies not at first envisioned, the new rapidly exceeded the old. It seemed wisest under these conditions to give the present work a new title. Nevertheless, about a third of it comes from the older book, revised and updated. I hope that whatever may have been of value in my essay *Religion, Society, and the Individual* has been included here.

I am deeply grateful to the Guggenheim Foundation and to the East-West Center for fellowships that allowed me to concentrate on this work over a period of twelve months. Much of this time I was in residence at the Center and found there among the scholars from Asia and America, my colleagues in the Senior Specialist program, the kind of stimulation, encouragement, factual information, and correction (gently urged and not always heard) that a work of this kind so strongly needs. I also express my sincere thanks to Dr. Everett Kleinjans, Chancellor of the East-West Center, and Dr. Minoru Shinoda, Director of its Institute of Advanced Projects, for their support, to Mrs. Hazel Tatsuno and her staff for skilled translation of rough manuscript into legible copy, and to Mr. Dan Burhans, my assistant, who performed innumerable feats of library detective work that saved me many hours. Most of all, I thank my wife for her unfailing belief—expressed in endless ways—that what I was doing was significant.

Oberlin, Ohio   J. Milton Yinger

CONTENTS

Chapter One

ON THE DEFINITION OF RELIGION

In a recent symposium on the religious situation, Reinhold Niebuhr asked: "Why has religious faith persisted for three centuries after the first triumphs of modern science?" And he answered his own question by a functional interpretation: Basic trust is born from the security given to a child by his parents. "But life is full of ills and hazards, of natural and historical evils, so that this childlike trust will soon be dissipated if maturity cannot devise a method of transmuting the basic trust of childhood, based on obvious security, to a faith which transcends all the incoherences, incongruities, and ills of life." [1] Religious faith, he affirmed, is such a transmutation.

In this book I shall ask the same question in a different way: Has religious faith persisted? If it has, in what forms, old and new, does it express itself? And does it persist because of the functions it fulfills for individuals?

No one can doubt that religion *survives*—in the villages of Burma or the slums of New York or the cathedrals of Rome. But that is not what Niebuhr meant. Religion, he affirmed, is continually renewed out of the incongruous situation of man—he is a child of nature who yet transcends nature, a creature who experiences disorder and incoherence but who also thinks about it and struggles with it.

Can this proposition be examined by the methods of scientific inquiry? It is the conviction of many thoughtful men that the objective study of religion is at best impossible, and at worst dangerous. How is it possible, they may ask, to see a stained-glass window from the outside? Its whole meaning is apparent only as the light shines through, just as the true meaning of religion is visible only to one on the inside. Moreover, must not the consequence of an objective study of religion, which is itself based upon

---

[1] Reinhold Niebuhr, in *The Religious Situation: 1968*, Donald Cutler, ed., p. x.

faith, be the weakening of that faith? And many would add: At a time when mankind so desperately needs courage to face the crises that beset us, is not the weakening of faith disastrous?

For generations, many social scientists have either disregarded these questions or treated them lightly. It has often been assumed that everything of importance about religion could ultimately be learned by objective study. And weakening of faith was variously regarded as desirable, unnecessary, or of no concern to the scientist.

In the contemporary scene, however, easy assumptions about the problems associated with the objective study of religion are gradually being dispelled. Social scientists no longer assert that everything important about religion is available to the objective observer. This is, after all, an extra-scientific assumption, which is not itself demonstrable by scientific study. No one would claim that the analysis of paint, painter, and patron exhausts the meaning of art; and we are becoming cautious about making equivalent claims for the analysis of religion. The scientist must realize that his propositions, derived from objective study, do not exhaust the meaning of things.

In my judgment, the scientific study of religion will gain by the adoption of this more modest conception of its role. This does not mean, however, that the objective study of religion is unimportant. Nor does it mean that the scientist should refrain from the complete examination of his topic. Indeed, it is only a part truth to say that one can see a stained-glass window only from the inside. One can see the *inside* of the window only from the inside. To press the analogy a little farther: From the outside one can see the outside, and one can find out who built it, who put it in, who keeps it in repair, and who goes inside to see it from that perspective. Judgments will vary concerning the importance of analogous questions about religion. Though the writer thinks they are very important, for reasons which I hope to make clear, this is not a position that can be demonstrated or argued meaningfully with one who disagrees.

I think it an error to assert that "only someone who knows religion because he practices some form of it can be expected to say something meaningful about it." [2] Some things can be said about a religion only by the practitioner, other kinds of observations can be made by one who holds another faith, and still further study can be made by the doubter. The scientist must not prejudge any of these observations, for each approach may furnish him with data valuable for the development of his theory of religion.

The question of the desirability of an objective study of religion is even more controversial than the question of its possibility. There are few major subjects about which men know so little, yet feel so certain. The educated man is often more provincial in his religious views than in almost any other part of his thinking. At one extreme it is held that one's received religion has all the necessary thinking already embodied in it. At the other,

2 Joachim Wach, in a review of Joseph Fichter's *Southern Parish*, Vol. I, *Journal of Religion*, April, 1952, p. 139. Helmuth Schelsky takes a somewhat similar position, but emphasizes the need for distinguishing between a sociological and a theological approach. See his "Religionssoziologie und Theologie," *Zeitschrift für evangelische Ethik*, 1959, pp. 129–145.

religion is dismissed as insufficiently important to command the resources of scholarship.

I do not want to dismiss this issue lightly. One cannot hope to demonstrate that the analysis of religion by science is beneficial in its consequences for all people in all times and places. My own position is a *belief* —which is probably part of my religion, as we shall come to define the term —that the total, long-run consequences of scientific study are beneficial. In the words of Ducasse: "To inform one's self, however, and to exercise intelligence, is a risky business—for skeptics, let it be noted, no less than for bigots. But then, risky too and probably more so, are conceit of ignorance and allegiance to bias." [3]

We shall come back to this topic briefly later in the discussion. When we have explored some aspects of the sociology of religion, we shall be in a better position to judge its consequences. It may be that part of that knowledge men of science ought to seek is knowledge of the consequences of their own work. Let us turn, then, to the analysis of religion without timidity or hesitation, but with full regard for its significance in the total human enterprise.

THE PROBLEM OF DEFINITION

Many studies of religion stumble over the first hurdle: the problem of definition. Though I am by no means certain of being able to leap over this difficulty, I have some hope of doing so, based on my conviction that the problem is less one of communication than a matter of disagreement over the nature and functions of definition. The disagreements, to be sure, are often substantial ones, based both on different values and on different conceptions of the nature of the universe in which we live. Once their causes are recognized, the disagreements will not be eliminated, but they will no longer rest on a failure of communication. One may be able at least to say: I can understand how a person, starting from those particular premises, would define religion in that way.

What are some of the disagreements over value and premise that have complicated the definition of religion? A devotee of a particular faith is likely to believe that a definition ought to describe the *true quality* of religion. He is not happy with the concept that a definition is a heuristic device, useful for one purpose, but of no value for another. He knows what religion *is* (it is belief in and activities toward the supernatural, for example) and he is impatient with a definition that may seem to be a subtle evasion of an obvious truth. A related difficulty stems from the fact that some people divide the phenomena of the world into sharply distinct categories, mistaking the labels they attach to things and events for those things and events themselves. The scientist is more likely to look upon the world as a flowing continuum. He considers his definitions to be dividing marks placed arbitrarily between phenomena that cannot be sharply distinguished. Thus religion-nonreligion is a continuum; we must recognize that there are some patterns that are marginally religious, according to any criteria that one may select.

3 C. J. Ducasse, *A Philosophical Scrutiny of Religion*, p. 16.

Definitions, then, are tools; they are to some degree arbitrary; they lay stress on similarities *within* a delimited area and on the differences *outside* it, thus giving emphasis to one aspect of reality. They are abstract, which is to say that they are oversimplifications. In dealing with a subject so complex and concerned with such a broad range of data as religion, a topic approached for many different purposes, we must relinquish the idea that there is any one definition that is "correct" and satisfactory for all. We readily grant that the definitions of a tree offered by a botanist, a lumberman, and an artist might vary widely, yet each definition would be appropriate to a specific interest. Such variety is equally appropriate in definitions of religion.

Types of Definitions. We need not undertake a history or a catalogue of definitions. A hundred or more can be gathered in the space of a few hours; for our purposes three kinds of definition will suffice. One type expresses valuation; such definitions describe what religion "really" or "basically" is in terms of what, in a given writer's judgment, it *ought* to be. Clearly such definitions are inappropriate for the tasks of science. Other definitions are descriptive or substantive. They designate certain kinds of beliefs and practices as religion but do not evaluate them, on the one hand; nor, on the other hand, do they indicate their function or seek to discover whether other beliefs and practices perform similar functions. Thus, in Edward B. Tylor's words, religion is "belief in Spiritual Beings." This kind of definition has the advantage of being clear-cut and reasonably easy to apply.[4] One can proceed from it to a classification of the kinds of Spiritual Beings and the kinds of practices and organizations that are found in various societies. Such a definition naturally draws attention to the differences among religions as distinct historical entities. The emphasis is placed primarily on religions as *cultural* systems. Their doctrines, rites, sacred texts, typical group structures, and the like, are described, contrasted, and compared. This is what religion *is*, such definitions say, and these particular patterns indicate what Buddhism, Judaism, and the religion of the Arunta *are*.

Substantive definitions can be of great value, particularly for those who are concerned with religions as historical and cultural facts rather than with religion as a panhuman phenomenon.[5] They are of greater value in the study of stable societies, where distinctive and coherent religious systems are likely to develop, than they are in the study of changing societies; for in the latter, religion itself is also in the process of changing, which continually complicates any attempt to define what it is, but equally suggests new efforts to study what it does.

4 In recent years a number of writers have expressed the view that Tylor's definition was essentially sound. See Jack Goody, "Religion and Ritual: The Definitional Problem," *British Journal of Sociology*, 12, 1961, pp. 142–164; Robin Horton, "A Definition of Religion, and Its Uses," *Journal of the Royal Anthropological Institute*, 90, Pt. 2, 1960, pp. 201–226; and M. E. Spiro, "Religion, Problems of Definition and Explanation," in *Anthropological Approaches to the Study of Religion*, Michael Banton, ed., pp. 85–126. I will indicate later why I do not share this judgment.

5 For a useful substantive definition that refers primarily to individual religiousness, see J. Paul Williams, "The Nature of Religion," *Journal for the Scientific Study of Religion*, 2, 1962, pp. 3–14.

A Functional Definition

For many problems, the functional kind of definition suggested in the previous sentence is the most useful. Some may prefer to define religion in terms of value or in terms of essence, but for analytic purposes the need is for a definition that focuses on process. A comparative science of religion, which must perforce be involved not only in the vast range of differences in belief and practice, but also in the similarities that justify the use of a common term to refer to this whole range, has to be concerned with function.[6] This is particularly true if the kinds of questions one is interested in refer not only to religion as a cultural fact, but to religion as a manifestation of character and as one aspect of society. It is widely believed that for many purposes it is a mistake to separate the analysis of culture (the system of norms and usages designating "right" behavior to the members of a society) from the analysis of character (the organized system of tendencies of an individual); and it is equally a mistake to separate these from the analysis of social systems ("networks of interactive relationships," as Talcott Parsons calls them). Special studies of culture, character, and society are appropriate, of course; but their theories must remain on a highly abstract level. To come nearer to the understanding of concrete action we must study their mutual influence.

It is paradoxical that in order to focus attention more closely on religion as concrete behavior, a definition must be more abstract. To define religion, for example, simply as "belief in God" (a definition that can be interpreted as either valuative or substantive or both) is to give it a fairly sharp referent; but such a definition raises no question of the relationship between personal anxiety or concern for one's salvation, for example, and belief in God; and it poses no problems of the relationship between the efforts to maintain social order and religion as defined. The more abstract definition that we shall develop holds an implicit concern for the analysis of actual behavior. It points to major questions of human action; and thus, in our judgment, is more fruitful for the study of a science of human behavior. We need not say that it is *truer*—only that it will serve the needs of current scientific work more fully than valuative or substantive definitions.[7]

The person who seeks to define religion in functional terms, to be sure, faces a number of difficulties. He must avoid a definition that is tied specifically to his own religious experience or to cultures similar to his own. He must recognize that the intense specialization of modern societies gives him a perspective on religion very different from that obtainable in less highly differentiated societies, where the infusion of religious elements into all phases of life is more obvious. Perhaps the most serious difficulty is related to the ease with which one can drift into a valuative position in his

6 We shall reserve for Chapters Five and Six the task of examining and criticizing the functional explanation of religion. Perhaps it will suffice here to define function as the full range of consequences of a pattern for the system of which it is a part, and to call attention to the fact that a functional definition is not a functional explanation.

7 We can be instructed by the study of analogous problems of definition in other areas. See, for example, Walter Goldschmidt's comments on the definitions of marriage, *Comparative Functionalism*, pp. 16–26.

definition without intending to do so. If religion is defined by what are thought to be its functions, then one should not be surprised to find it functional, that is, having only supportive consequences. And this may lead, in turn, to a circularity of reasoning. If it can be shown that a given system of beliefs and practices that is generally thought to be a religion is not performing the functions by which religion has been defined, then one can declare that such a system is not really religion at all. This error can be avoided by indicating that religion is an *effort* to perform certain functions for man. This does not imply that it always succeeds, nor that systems that do not succeed are therefore not religions. Nor does it necessarily imply that one desires those functions to be performed.

To solve or reduce this problem, however, may only serve to create another. Is every effort to perform certain functions, however wide the range of differences between them—in content of belief, in number of persons involved, or in degree of historical continuity—to be called religion? Is there no place, in other words, for functional alternatives, because every possible alternative must, by definition, also be considered a religion? We shall deal with this question at several points later in this book, so it is only necessary to say here that we shall define religion as a certain kind of effort to perform various functions. We shall identify it by the intensity or ultimate quality of the attempt, and by the interconnection of several related functions. Thus there is a great deal of room for functional alternatives. Because we are dealing with several continuous variables, the problem of more or less inevitably arises; we shall therefore need to describe some systems of belief and action that are only marginally religious, in our sense, in order to indicate that there is no sharp dividing line.

What, then, are the functions that distinguish religion as a human activity? To try to answer this question fully is essentially the task of this book; hence the highly condensed statement appropriate to a definition can only hint at problems that will receive fuller treatment in later chapters. Paul Tillich has said that religion is that which concerns us ultimately. Robert Bellah has expressed the same idea: ". . . religion is a set of symbolic forms and acts which relate men to the ultimate condition of his existence." [8] This can be a good starting point for a functional definition. Though there are important disagreements concerning the ultimate problems for man, a great many people would accept the following as among the fundamental concerns of human societies and individuals: How shall we respond to the fact of death? Does life have some central meaning despite the suffering and the succession of frustrations and tragedies it brings with it? How can we deal with the forces that press in upon us, endangering our livelihood, our health, and the survival and smooth operation of the groups in which we live—forces that our empirical knowledge cannot handle adequately? How can we bring our capacity for hostility and our egocentricity sufficiently under control to allow the groups within which we live—without which our life would indeed be impossible—to be kept together?

Put in this way, these questions appear to be both rational and self-conscious. They are more appropriately seen, however, as deep-seated

8 Robert Bellah, "Religious Evolution," *American Sociological Review*, 29, 1964, p. 358.

emotional needs, springing from the very nature of man as an individual and as a member of society. The questions appear first of all because they are felt—the death of a loved one wrenches our emotions; the failure to achieve what we yearn for saddens and bewilders us; the hostility between ourselves and those around us infuses our social contacts with tension and prevents the achievement of mutual values. Religion may develop an intellectual system to interpret and deal with these questions, but they must be seen first of all not as a group of rationally conceived problems, but as expressions of an underlying emotional need.

Religion, then, can be defined as a system of beliefs and practices by means of which a group of people struggles with these ultimate problems of human life. It expresses their refusal to capitulate to death, to give up in the face of frustration, to allow hostility to tear apart their human associations. The quality of being religious, seen from the individual point of view, implies two things: first, a belief that evil, pain, bewilderment, and injustice are fundamental facts of existence; and, second, a set of practices and related sanctified beliefs that express a conviction that man can ultimately be saved from those facts.

All men experience these wrenching difficulties to some degree. For some persons, however, they stand out as the most significant experiences of life. These individuals are impelled to try to discover some meaning in what seems to be senseless suffering, some road to salvation through the obstacles of human life. The beliefs and rites that make up a religion as a more or less coherent system are the expressions of those who have felt the problems most intensively, who have been most acutely sensitive to the tragedies of death, the burdens of frustration, the oppression of failure, the disruptive effects of hostility. Powered by the strength of their feelings, such religious innovators have created "solutions" appropriate to the enormity of the problems—solutions that frequently have burst the bonds of man's senses and of nature, but have brought their adherents some relief. Thus religions are built to carry the "peak load" of human emotional need.

This variation in intensity suggests another problem of definition. Whose religion will serve as the basis for the description? Religion as practiced by the average member of society, with his particular level of concerns and his particular talent for handling them, is different from the religion of specialists, virtuosi, and those who feel most acutely the discrepancies between the actual human condition and human experience as they dare to envision it—in history or beyond. The degrees of consistency, intensity, capacity for mystical experience, and other aspects of religion are unequally distributed. We must make clear, therefore, in any context, whether we are referring to a formal system, or to the life of an intensely religious person, or to the beliefs and practices of the average member of society.

By their emphasis on tragedy and frustration the definitions we have suggested may seem to leave out a vital aspect of many religions. Where, we might well ask, are the joyful celebration, the aesthetic experience, the serenity, the positive affirmation, the ecstasy, and the simple thanksgiving for the goodness of life that are found in many religious systems? Our understanding would be incomplete if we did not recognize that religion is expressed in many efforts to maximize joy as well as in efforts to handle tragedy. Inevitably, however, these terms are comparative. The most positive affirmations achieve their power in the context of the defeat of tragedy by faith. The ode to joy—whatever cultural form it takes—is a celebration of this ultimate victory. Glory is tragedy seen through a religious prism. They are part of the same fundamental facts of human existence.

Once they become part of a religious system, to be sure, the joyful and aesthetic expressions may develop to a certain degree on their own. They even become the focus of attention for some adherents. The cultivation of art and of elaborate forms of celebration, in fact, under many conditions can turn into sources of tension, appearing to some as primary sources of religious expression, but to others as disconcerting or even corrupting practices that endanger the true faith.[9]

The Persistent Functions of Religion. Defined in these various ways, religion is—and seems likely to remain—an inevitable part of human life. Although the ways of struggling with these ultimate problems are enormously diverse, and seem destined for continuous change, the problems themselves are universal. A society that did not furnish its members with beliefs and practices that gave them a means of dealing with these ultimate problems would have to struggle along with an enormous burden of tragedy unallayed and hostility unrestrained—if indeed it could survive at all. This is only to make the point that some effort to deal with these questions is essential to human life as we know it, not to say that any given religious system adequately answers these questions.

Religion, of course, is not alone in attempting to deal with the ultimate problems of human life. Rational efforts are important in all societies. Moreover, insecurity and the problem of evil arouse many individual emotional responses in addition to the religious one. Even in the healthiest and wealthiest and most rational of societies, however, secular responses cannot eliminate the problems of suffering, evil, and hostility. Realizing the gap between their hopes and the realities of their existence, men everywhere seek to close it by a leap of faith that says: This need not, this will not, be true; sometime, some place, somehow, suffering and evil will be defeated. (The enormous variation in conceptions of time, place, and method measures the range of religious expressions.)

In this sense, religion can be thought of as a kind of residual means of response and adjustment. It is an attempt to explain what cannot otherwise be explained; to achieve power, all other powers having failed us; to establish poise and serenity in the face of evil and suffering that other efforts have failed to eliminate. "When other helpers fail, when comforts flee," man can give himself over to despair, or he can seek relief by the leap of faith. Most people have chosen the latter, and have preferred, in Reinhold Niebuhr's words, "a citadel of hope built on the edge of despair," to acceptance of ultimate defeat.

Dunlap uses the concept of "residual" in his definition of religion, which he describes as "the institution, or feature of culture, which undertakes, in the service of mankind, those functions for which there is no other institution or for the undertaking of which no other institution is as yet

9 See Max Weber, *The Sociology of Religion*, especially pp. 242–245.

adequately prepared." [10] This definition, although it is helpful, seems to me to require further attention to the *persistent* functions of religion. Is there no core of functions that seems likely to be a continuing source of religious activity? Or are science, philosophy, art, government, medicine, and the like chiseling away at religion so steadily that it has become a "suicidal institution," as Dunlap calls it? I myself find it difficult to envisage a society in which no major problems of the ultimate variety we have discussed remain unresolved. We reduce the amount of premature death only to discover the tragedies of senescence. We begin to conquer poverty only to realize that the knowledge behind that achievement is part of a larger knowledge that brought the hydrogen bomb. I suspect—and here I run the danger of an attempt to prove by definition, which is a very unsatisfactory kind of proof—that the belief that man can devise secular processes for performing the functions now served by religion is itself a "citadel of hope," and not an empirically validated proposition. It is an emotional and intellectual closing of the gap, which is more congenial to the cultural training and personality tendencies of many people today, and thus has at least a quasireligious function for them.

The word *residual* need not carry the connotation of "unimportant final item" or "gradually disappearing." It might better be thought of as "that which always remains." Malinowski writes:

To us the most essential point about magic and religious ritual is that it steps in only where knowledge fails. Supernaturally founded ceremonial grows out of life, but it never stultifies the practical efforts of man. In his ritual of magic or religion, man attempts to enact miracles, not because he ignores the limitations of his mental powers, but, on the contrary, because he is fully cognizant of them. To go one step further, the recognition of this seems to me indispensable if we want once and for ever to establish the truth that religion has its own subject-matter, its own legitimate field of development; that this must never encroach on the domain where science, reason, and experience ought to remain supreme.[11]

This is not a wholly satisfactory statement, from the point of view of science. That religion "never stultifies the practical efforts of man," is subject to grave doubt. Malinowski shifts easily into a value assertion when he declares that there is an area "where science, reason, and experience ought to remain supreme." But Malinowski implies, in contrast to Dunlap, that religion as a residual mode of adjustment is unlikely to disappear. This is an empirical question for which we have only inadequate evidence. What evidence we have inclines me toward the view that religion as I have defined it is a permanent aspect of human society, which is no more likely to disappear than the family (however much it may change) or government (despite the enormous range of variation).

William James, in one of his acute observations, notes that in the responses to life that "fall short of religion" we may come to accept the suffering and frustrations of life, but we regard them as impositions of necessity, and at best we accept them without complaint. In religious life, however, surrender and sacrifice are positively espoused; and in this attempt to conquer our problems, we may even add "unnecessary givings-up"

10 Knight Dunlap, *Religion: Its Function in Human Life*, p. 321.

11 Bronislaw Malinowski, *The Foundations of Faith and Morals*, p. 34.

in order to increase our happiness. "Religion thus makes easy and felicitous what in any case is necessary. . . ." [12] If we tamper with James's statement by adding that "religion is an *attempt* to . . . ," we might be led to another definition of some value: Religion is an organized effort to make virtue of our ultimate necessities.

Are Individual Systems of Belief to Be Called Religion? A primary difficulty with a functional definition is that there is no obvious point at which one may draw a line and say: "Here religion ends and nonreligion begins." In a religiously heterogeneous and changing society, the question of "private" systems of belief and practice arises. Are these to be called religions? Are they not attempts to fulfill the same functions that shared and historically identified faiths seek to perform? In my view, one should answer this question in the negative. There is, to be sure, some truth in the statements "his work is his religion," or "he has dedicated himself to the discovery of a cure for cancer," which carries the implication that this is his religion. There can be religious *aspects* of private systems of belief and action. A complete religion, however, is a social phenomenon: it is shared, and it takes on many of its most significant aspects only in the interaction of the group. Both the feelings from which it springs and the solutions it offers are social; they arise from the fact that man is a group-living animal. The ultimate questions that we have identified as the center of the religious quest are ultimate primarily because of their impact on human association. Even death is not fundamentally an individual crisis but a group crisis, which threatens to tear apart the fabric of family and community.

Joachim Wach holds that all religions, despite their wide variations, are characterized by three universal expressions: the theoretical, a system of belief; the practical, a system of worship; and the sociological, a system of social relationships. Until all of these are found, one may have religious tendencies, religious elements, but not a full religion. Although the first of these expressions—the system of belief—is the one that modern man is most likely to think of as the heart of religion, both ethnological and etymological evidence suggests that religion as worship and religion as a system of social relationships may be the more basic aspects, belief coming in later as an attempt to give coherence and meaning to worship and associations, that have developed out of deeply felt needs. The word *religion* may have derived from the Latin *religare,* meaning to bind together, or from *religere,* meaning to rehearse, to execute painstakingly, which suggest both group identity and ritual. The testimony of most anthropologists gives support to the proposition that it is the acts of religion and the associations, more than the beliefs, that give it a vital place in the life of preliterate societies. This may well be less true in a literate society, where the practice of seeking out explanations is more fully established and where religious specialists seek to relate religion to the social complex from which it has become organizationally separated.

The growing importance of the "belief" aspects of religion, however, should not lead us to misinterpret the nature of a religious intellectual system. It is a group of "mighty hypotheses," of "over-beliefs," of deductions

---

12 William James, *The Varieties of Religious Experience,* p. 51.

that leap beyond those admissible by a calm appraisal of the facts. Man is not calm in the face of the needs from which religion springs. As Durkheim says: "Science is fragmentary and incomplete; it advances but slowly and is never finished; but life cannot wait. The theories which are destined to make men live and act are therefore obliged to pass science and complete it prematurely." [13]

Are Non-Theistic Systems of Belief to Be Called Religion? If we take the functional approach to the definition of religion, it is not the nature of the *belief*, but the nature of the *believing* that requires our study. Even a quick glance over the vast range of phenomena that we call religion reveals an enormous variety. The only justification for referring to such diversity of belief, of worship, and of organization by one term is the assumption that the many forms represent different attempts to deal with the same problems. In Paul Tillich's words: "We are all laboring under the yoke of religion; we all, sometimes, try to throw away old or new doctrines or dogmas, but after a little while we return, again enslaving ourselves and others in their servitude." [14] Many "nonreligious" persons object to such a statement. They explicitly reject beliefs, forms of worship, and group associations that they identify as religious. It is unwise to argue this point, for from the perspective of the definition they use they are correct in claiming to be nonreligious. It is highly likely, however, that such individuals, having left some traditional religion, will nevertheless affirm their faith in some "over-beliefs," will get emotional support from various symbols, acts, and ceremonies (worship), and will join with others in groups that seek to sustain and realize these shared beliefs. This point of view is seldom argued when it refers to some of the intense political movements of our time. Communism is now considered by many observers to have a religious quality.[15] Few deny the religious element in nationalism. In multireligious societies (in the traditional sense) or in societies where an established religion has lost much of its appeal, nationalism as a religious force is particularly likely to appear. Faith, symbols, worshipful acts, and organizations built around the nation all appear. This is not simply the nationalization of religion (*Gott mit uns*), but the religionization of nation (*Vaterland über alles*).

Many modern intellectuals, particularly perhaps among the writer's fellow social scientists, will agree that many modern political and other secular movements might appropriately be regarded as religions, but they see no parallel in their own lives. A supernatural view of the world has become meaningless to them; they are repelled by a boastful and worshipful nationalism; they feel comfortable with a quiet kind of scientific secularism, motivated by idle curiosity with perhaps a nudge from a desire to help solve some human problem. Certainly, a definition of religion that attempts to include such phenomena strains our imaginations. Yet a term that already includes, by common consent, the contemplations of a Buddhist

13 Emile Durkheim, *The Elementary Forms of the Religious Life*, p. 431.

14 Paul Tillich, *The Shaking of the Foundations*, p. 98.

15 This view is expressed, for example by Tillich, ibid.; by Erich Fromm, *Man for Himself;* by Reinhold Niebuhr, *Christianity and Power Politics;* by Jacques Maritain, *True Humanism.* See also the discussion of "functional alternatives" in Chapter Six.

monk and the ecstatic visions of a revivalist cult member, human sacrifice and ethical monotheism, may have room in it for science *as a way of life* (not as a method or as a group of tested propositions about nature). Not all scientists, in the methodological sense, accept science as a way of life. Many feel that the answers to man's ultimate problems are to be found in a humanist faith or in the traditional religions. But some turn to science even for faith. If they do not require the ritualistic trappings and elaborate organization of a Comte, with his "positivistic religion," they certainly manifest many over-beliefs that, to repeat Durkheim's words, are "obliged to pass science and complete it prematurely." Few scientists doubt that the best way to grapple with human problems is to extend our knowledge of nature. Hydrogen bombs and the mass manipulation of people by propaganda may have given us pause, but they have not destroyed our faith. That the gap between knowledge and action can be closed by knowledge itself is a mighty hypothesis that few of us would care to deny. A careful reading of the story of man in the era of science, however, would scarcely lead to the conclusion that the evidence on that question is complete. Our belief in the hypothesis has more of the quality of sanctity than of a proposition logically derived from established theory or a generalization based on empirical study. "Sanctity is the quality of unquestionable truthfulness imputed by the faithful to unverifiable propositions." [16] Knowledge of the unquestioned value of science is sanctified knowledge.

It is doubtless true that emotion-evoking symbols, rituals, elaborate group organizations for the purposes of reinforcing science as a way of life are rudimentary; but anyone who has attended a convention of scientists or has observed their actions when "freedom of research" is threatened by overzealous regents or parsimonious legislators will hesitate to say that they are entirely lacking.

These sentences are not written to criticize science. Many of the author's own over-beliefs stem from science. They are written rather to show that few men can avoid the problem of struggling with questions of salvation (how can man be saved from his most difficult problems?), of the nature of reality, of evil (why do men suffer?), and the like. Science as a way of life is an effort to deal with these questions.

Nor should this point of view be taken as a support for what we may call "religion in general." Some writers are happy with functionalist theory, as contrasted with earlier studies of religious origins, because they somehow find in it support for a belief that *religion* is true, and often also a belief that the traditional religions have won scientific support. But the problem is more complicated than they recognize. Important problems of value inevitably arise from the use of a functional definition. If almost any system of beliefs and actions can be religious, it is clear that one cannot regard religion in general as a "good thing." There are questions of choice. From the perspective of certain stated values, a given religion may be good, or it may be evil, or it may be a mixture of good and evil. The idea widely current in the United States that one ought to be religious, with no reference to the nature or the consequences of various religions, is not a logical inference from the position developed here. Abraham Maslow has sug-

16 Roy Rappaport, "Systems and Sanctity," unpublished manuscript, 1968, p. 23.

gested that a line dividing the "concerned" from the "unconcerned" is more valuable in defining religion than a line separating natural and supernatural.[17] This is a valuable lead if one avoids the implication that being concerned is self-evidently good. It seems probable that religious intolerance, conflict, and rigidity can result from our most deeply felt concerns, just as easily as can the brotherhood envisaged by Maslow.

General Problems of Distinguishing Religion from Nonreligion. Our words almost inevitably divide experience into sharper categories than the seamless web of history permits. We cannot cognitively handle all experience at once. We break it up, the better to contrast and compare. By our words we emphasize what we think are important differences hidden beneath superficial similarities, and highlight important similarities that are disguised by minor differences. Unhappily for purposes of communication, the criteria for determining what is important and what is minor are often not agreed upon. I have suggested that individual beliefs and actions, however much they resemble shared systems of rites and symbols, are in fact critically different, and ought not, therefore, to be labeled religions. On the other hand, I have taken the opposite position that some nontheistic systems of belief and action share so much in common with theistic ones that we do well to call them religions. In making these judgments, I have been considering contemporary mankind. Our problem of definition is complicated by the fact that the most appropriate lines of distinction for purposes of understanding may well be drawn at one point in some circumstances, but at another point when different evidences are being examined. If one is dealing with societies within which supernatural conceptions are universal, there is little reason to wonder whether naturalistic conceptions may not have a similar place in the lives of some people. If one is dealing primarily with contemporary urban societies, however, within which definitions of the supernatural have become vague for some individuals, and "ultimate belief and practice systems" (I need to avoid the use of the term *religion* at this point) grow out of older religious traditions by gradual steps, the use of the supernatural as a defining criterion becomes problematic. The difficulty becomes even more serious if one is seeking to develop a theory of religion that encompasses both types of societies.

Let me anticipate some of the questions that will be dealt with in Chapter Four by suggesting that most conceptions of religion give answers, implicitly or explicitly, to two questions: Is religion limited to ultimate concerns? Is it limited to supernatural modes of action? Let us start with an excellent functional definition by Clifford Geertz: ". . . a religion is: (1) a system of symbols which acts to (2) establish powerful, pervasive, and long-lasting moods and motivations in men by (3) formulating conceptions of a general order of existence and (4) clothing these conceptions with such an aura of factuality that (5) the moods and motivations seem uniquely realistic." [18] This definition is highly abstract; its referent is not specified; it does not answer the two questions suggested above. If we put them into a simple matrix, however, we can picture the

17 Abraham Maslow, *Religions, Values, and Peak Experiences*, pp. 54–57.

18 Clifford Geertz in *Anthropological Approaches to the Study of Religion*, Michael Banton, ed., p. 4.

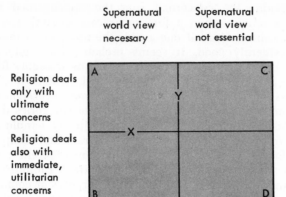

Supernatural
world view
necessary

Supernatural
world view
not essential

Religion deals
only with
ultimate
concerns

A

Y

C

Religion deals
also with
immediate,
utilitarian
concerns

X

B

D

FIGURE I–I. *Necessary items in a definition of religion*

various ways in which different persons might choose the referent for
Geertz's definition (see Figure I–I).

Perhaps most commonly, particularly among laymen and more conservative theologians, religion would be limited to the upper left quadrant, to
cell A. Many anthropologists, however, have studied the infusion of the
supernatural view throughout the lives of the members of primitive societies. In practice it is very difficult to draw a conceptually sharp line
between religion and magic. Hence many think it unwise to attempt to
make the distinction. Supernaturalism becomes the essential criterion
variable in defining religion or "religiomagical" systems. Line X is erased,
or cells A and B are both included. Anthony Wallace, for example, writes:
". . . religion is a set of rituals, rationalized by myth, which mobilizes
supernatural powers for the purpose of achieving or preventing transformations of state in man and nature." [19] By "transformations of state," Wallace refers to day-by-day changes in life conditions, important and unimportant, large-scale and small-scale. He sees little value in distinguishing
between religion and magic.

Sociologists have devoted most of their attention to religion in urban
industrial societies, where magic, at least in its supernatural forms, has
receded, and where the supernatural view generally has become more
abstract. Consequently, they are faced less with the difficulty of drawing a
line between religion and magic than with that of drawing the line between
natural and supernatural. They substitute other terms which, if they do not
actually erase line Y, make it a wide boundary instead of a sharp division.
They speak of the holy, transcendental, or sacred, words that are not
synonyms for supernatural yet carry some of the same connotations.[20]
Thus they open up for investigation the ways in which some men today
struggle with problems of ultimate concern that are not easily encompassed
by the concept of supernaturalism.

Definitional problems seldom arise in dealing with cell D—sanctified

19 Anthony Wallace, *Religion: An Anthropological View*, p. 107.

20 The three terms, as I hear their tones, become progressively less synonymous with
supernatural.

beliefs and rites relating to the naturalistically conceived immediate concerns of a group. A group of sportsmen may *know* that the Green Bay Packers are the best football team in the world. They may celebrate that fact with calendrical rites each Sunday afternoon throughout the autumn. But only so far as these beliefs and practices become connected with their deepest concerns—that is, move toward C—or become infused with supernatural qualities—moving toward B—do they take on a religious quality. (I use the adjectival form here to stress the fact that religion is probably better understood as a quality, present at greater or lesser levels of intensity, rather than as an attribute.)

There is no way of avoiding these problems of delimitation and conceptualization if we seek to develop a general theory of religion, which has wide applicability in time and space. Most of our attention, to be sure, will be focused on A; at least that will be our point of departure. In many instances, however, our interest will swing in an arc that includes both B and C, when our understanding of man's behavior in relation to sacred things promises thereby to be enhanced.

We have looked at the problem of definition from several points of view. Perhaps our approach can be summed up in these words: The human individual, who is blessed (and sometimes cursed) with the power of language, is capable, therefore, of anticipating the future, including a foreknowledge of his own death; he is also able to verbalize ideal states, and to create standards; yet he is continually threatened with failure, with frustration, with lack of fulfillment of his conception of justice. These problems tend to loom up as overwhelming or *absolute evils*. Religion is man's attempt to "relativize" these difficulties by interpreting them as part of some larger good, some conception of the absolute that puts the individual's problems into new perspective, thus to remove or reduce their crushing impact. At the same time, man's social relations, his societies, are threatened by these same problems. Fear and frustration can lead to disrupting hostilities, unless they can be reinterpreted as part of a shared experience. In addition, there is the tendency of each individual to think only of himself, to make his personal joys and desires into *absolute goods*, thereby threatening the patterns of mutual adjustment that social life requires. Religion is the attempt to relativize the individual's desires, as well as his fears, by subordinating them to a conception of absolute good more in harmony with the shared and often mutually contradictory needs and desires of human groups.

Certain kinds of belief and action commonly, if not universally, develop from this double rooting of religion in the fundamental individual and group needs. First, failure and frustration are symbolically reinterpreted: failure is only apparent; death is not what it seems. Second, religion brings each individual into a fellowship that emphasizes shared experiences. This has two aspects: it spreads the burdens of one's fears and frustrations, and thus is a kind of psychic insurance policy; and it lays emphasis on shared and universally available values—the scheme of salvation—rather than upon the scarce values, which makes the inevitable failures with regard to the latter seem less important. This leads to a third element in religion. At least some of the values that it upholds are superempirical. This does not necessarily mean that they are supernatural, but rather that they are beyond the reach of constant refutation by the facts of immediate experience.[21] It is a likely hypothesis that the more punishing the actual experience of a society—the more uncertain its food supply, for example, and the heavier the hand of death—the greater is the likelihood that its religion will emphasize supernatural means and/or supernatural goals. Members of a society more favorably situated, or a group that forms part of such a society, may make their leap of faith by projecting the trends they see around them in the natural world. In either event, men believe more than the facts would allow, in an effort to sustain life and hope and to give more meaning to existence.

Such a definition of religion is, of course, highly abstract. It is an attempt to isolate, by analysis, a common factor that is embedded in enormously diverse religious systems. Another point of view might isolate different common elements that we have overlooked and obscured. Moreover, any abstract definition must be seen simply as a starting point for the study of religion, a point from which religions, as concrete systems of belief and action, depart in varying degrees and in many directions. These departures and the forces behind them must be of vital concern to the student of religion, as we shall see.

Categories of Religious Behavior

As we have noted, functional definitions of religion are abstract. What one sees when he studies religion, however, are not the purposes or consequences, but concrete behavior and physical objects related to behavior. Although the range is wide, it is not infinite, and it can be classified. We can suggest, therefore, as our concluding way of defining religion, the specification of basic categories of religious behavior. Wallace gives thirteen categories as the minimal list. These types of behavior are found almost everywhere. His list is influenced by the focus of attention on anthropological materials, by the inclusion of magic within his definition, and by the restriction to supernatural systems. With some modification, nevertheless, it serves as a valuable outline of types of religious behavior:

1. Addressing the supernatural (prayer, exorcism).
2. Music (dancing, singing, chanting, playing instruments).
3. Physiological exercise (physical manipulation of psychological states through drugs, deprivation, and mortification).
4. Exhortation (addressing others as representative of divinity).
5. Reciting the code (use of the sacred written and oral literature, which contains statements regarding the pantheon, cosmology, myths, and moral injunctions).
6. Simulation (imitating things for purposes of control).
7. Mana (touching things possessed of sacred power; laying on of hands).
8. Taboo (avoiding things to prevent the activation of unwanted power or undesired events).
9. Feasts (sacred meals).
10. Sacrifices (immolation, offerings, fees).

21 See Kingsley Davis, *Human Society,* pp. 518–531.

11. Congregation (processions, meetings, convocations).

12. Inspiration (pursuit of revelation, conversion, possession, mystical ecstasy).

13. Symbolism (manufacture and use of symbolic objects).[22]

These are not tight analytic categories of religious behavior, but they serve well to indicate the range. Perhaps they treat religion too much as a static and isolated system, and therefore we might extend them in two directions:

14. Extending and modifying the code (in connection with category 5).

15. Applying religious values in nonreligious contexts (what later, following Charles Glock, we will call the consequential dimension).

Both ritualistic and belief aspects are found in each of these activities. There is a tendency among contemporary students of religion to over-emphasize belief aspects and to overlook ritual elements in religious behavior. This may be a result of the frequently observed falling away from the practice of many traditional rites, so characteristic of urban civilizations, without an equivalent falling away from the beliefs to which the rites were formerly tied. In connection with this observed disjunction, I am inclined to say: Look for rituals first, then for the beliefs connected with them; there you will find the operating religion of an individual or of a group. For example, in a later chapter we will examine America's "civil religion"— an amalgam of traditional faiths, shaped by and focused on the country's historical experience. In the lives of many people there is no lack of ritual in connection with this religion. Most of the categories listed above are represented in the civil religion, in fact, by both ritualistic and belief elements. By contrast, some of those who share the beliefs of a traditional faith are seldom involved in its rites. Insofar as this is true, it is the civil rather than the traditional faith that can be designated as the operating religion, or as the most basic level in a multileveled religion.

THE FIELD THEORETICAL APPROACH TO THE STUDY OF RELIGION

Although the definition of religion we have proposed has been developed from a scientific orientation, it can be used from various perspectives. It does not contain within it a definition of what for the moment I will call the sociology of religion. Here again comes the temptation to avoid brief denotation and to say: this book is the author's attempt to define the sociology of religion. As a starting point, however, we may sketch its mode of approach.[23]

Claude Levi-Strauss has written: "Man is a social animal interacting in an idiom of culture." A science of man must deal with all the elements in this statement and with their influence upon each other. As one branch of that study, the science of religion must recognize that religious behavior is the combined result of man's biological and learned tendencies (including elements of character that are shared among all men and those that are variant), the structures of interaction through which men influence

22 Anthony Wallace, op. cit., pp. 52–67.

23 For the statement of the field approach as a general theory, without reference to religion, see J. Milton Yinger, *Toward a Field Theory of Behavior*.

one another, and the cultural systems, the "blueprints for action" as Clyde Kluckhohn called them, that guide interaction.

The field theoretical approach to religion is thus an application of the position, most thoroughly developed in the work of Talcott Parsons, that complete analysis of human action requires the study of social, cultural, and character facts, both as separate systems and as mutually influencing parts of a larger system.[24]

All of the behavioral sciences have been interested in each of these elements, but in selective ways that place the focus of attention on one of the elements. That is, each has tended to develop a synthesizing science of religion, but more by spreading out from the chosen "basic" element to the others than by explicit efforts to integrate all of them into a common theory. With calculated exaggeration, one can say that anthropologists, who are mainly interested in the study of primitive peoples, have developed a theory of religion built around the study of ritual and myth—that is, around religion as culture. Psychologists, who are often concerned with the isolation of the properties and processes within individuals, without reference to group settings, have developed theories of religion around the study of individual needs and tendencies. Social psychologists have focused on interaction as the key element. Sociologists, who are interested primarily in social structure, have given attention mainly to a theory of religious organizations. And historians have sought to describe past events by paying such attention to the full range of religious facts and to the nonreligious setting as to enable us, in some measure, to re-experience them.

Academic structure and compelling demands for specialized competence have kept the several social sciences interested in the study of religion from the close interaction that adequate research and theoretical work require. The distinction frequently drawn, for example, between anthropology, as the study of culture, and sociology, as the study of society, seems to me to have a limited usefulness. It is difficult to study a society (an interacting group of human beings) without continuous reference to their culture (the system of norms and usages) by which their interaction is so strongly affected. (Even their departures from the cultural norms are highly significant.) And it is equally difficult to study a culture without constant attention to the people who are its bearers, the groups through which it is communicated, the societal processes by which it is changed. That is not to say that an analytic distinction cannot be drawn between society and culture; such a distinction, indeed, is a necessary one. But a theory of religion that does not encompass both societal and cultural facts is partial and likely to be misunderstood.

Kroeber, while indicating that anthropology and sociology are very close, pointed to the anthropologists' emphasis on culture and the sociologists' emphasis on society. Take the study of churches, for example. Sociology is concerned with these primarily "as operating systems of interacting people." Anthropology, however, is concerned *also* (n.b.) with their culture. Are their beliefs trinitarian, unitarian, or dualistic? What are the types of baptism? The precise doctrines and details of ritual, Kroeber wrote, are

24 See especially Talcott Parsons, *The Social System;* and Talcott Parsons and Edward Shils, eds., *Toward a General Theory of Action,* pp. 47–275.

not very important if one is studying the structure and function of religion as a social institution (the sociological task, in his view).

The relations of the communicants to one another are likely to be the same whether they are all trinitarians or all unitarians. On the contrary, if it is the doctrines or rituals or other cultural features, and the changes going on in them, that are the specific subject of study, the organization of the church somehow cannot properly and permanently be left out of consideration. At any rate, anthropologists so feel.[25]

To the present writer it seems very unlikely indeed that the "relations of the communicants" are independent of the beliefs they share in common. What Kroeber admitted for the anthropologist—that he must study social systems in order to understand cultural systems—is equally true for the sociologist—he cannot comprehend society without analysis of the facts of culture. There can profitably be a difference in emphasis, but we must avoid theoretical separation.

It is equally true that a theory of religion as an expression of individual needs and tendencies (the social-psychological question) is less likely to be misunderstood if it is part of a larger theoretical scheme that encompasses social and cultural facts as well. Individual tendencies are in part a product of social processes and cultural norms; in turn, they condition social interaction and affect the ways in which cultural requirements are carried out and are changed. We need, therefore, to pay attention to tendencies as they relate to a theory of religious behavior.

It is a matter of empirical observation that most, if not all, religions combine group and individual elements. They are generally concerned with both individual salvation and with group integration and conflict. This dual reference may derive from the fact that each of these functions of religion is carried on most effectively within a religious system that contains the other also. Individual needs may be more adequately met by a *shared* system of beliefs, by a religion that furnishes some measure of the integration of society or of smaller groups necessary for individual life. And the group functions may be adequately performed only by a religious system that seems to satisfy at least some measure of the needs of individual adherents. To be sure, the various functions will not always be found together within a single religious tradition. Confucianism paid scant heed to questions of individual salvation, for example; but this may account for the spread and the direction of development of Taoism and Buddhism, with which Confucianism learned to live in a somewhat uneasy combination. If a tendency toward a duality of functions, either in a complex of religions or in a more unified pattern, is the rule, we have an additional reason for a theory of religion that is simultaneously anthropological, psychological, and sociological.

Even such a broadening of the way in which we shall ask the questions still leaves us with an abstraction. Our theory will explain religious behavior only insofar as that behavior is related to social, cultural, and character facts. We shall need to be on our guard to avoid "the fallacy of misplaced concreteness," as Alfred North Whitehead has called it. Such questions as

25 A. L. Kroeber, *Anthropology* (new edition, revised), pp. 846–847.

how, in the psychological sense, one learns religious ways of behavior or the effects of man's inherited nature on religious tendencies, for example, will for the most part be disregarded.

To understand religion, then, we must study the cultures that embody it, the characters that internalize it, and the social structures that carry it. When David Mandelbaum described a new set of gods, shrines, and ceremonies that appeared in a Kota village in India after an epidemic had killed more than half its population, he observed that to understand how this came about, and how some villagers adopted the new religious forms though others did not, required not only knowledge of the religious traditions available, but of the disrupted interactions, and of the variation among the individuals.[26] That is, he examined the whole field.

Even a quick glance shows us that behavior is heavily influenced, although not determined, by the system of norms, those prescriptions and proscriptions that characterize every human society. No society is without a culture; nor can there be a culture, of course, that is independent of the individuals who sustain it through their actions. Culture as a system of norms is inferred from the patterned actions of the members of the society. Behavior in conformity with culture is secured, not so much by external social controls as by internal tendencies that are the result of socialization. Character, however, is not simply the *result* of culture: the needs and tendencies of individuals have played a part in cultural development and change; moreover, deviations from the norms are important to study.

A second fact that emerges from the study of human behavior is that a society is a complex system, not a collection of unrelated parts. There are incoherences and inconsistencies to be sure, especially in times of rapid change, but this should not lead us to overlook the interconnections. The element of system, in fact, is often made apparent as a result of change. It can readily be observed that changes in the economy of a society, for example, are accompanied by changes in politics, in family patterns, and, as we shall see, in religion. The conception of system is particularly important for the student of religion. If one tries to study religion apart from the social and cultural systems in which it is embedded, he will miss most of the sociologically important points.

Thirdly, it is widely held by students of society that there are certain functional prerequisites without which a society could not continue to exist. At first glance, this seems to be obvious—scarcely more than to say that an automobile engine could not exist, as a going system, without a carburetor. No one will quarrel with the fact that a human society cannot exist that does not provide for the reproduction and protection of infants, or for the satisfaction of economic necessities. What is not so self-evident is that these functions are normatively governed everywhere. The processes followed for the satisfaction of these prerequisites of human life are culturally patterned. Mating is a necessity for the biological survival of a group, but the family, according to this view, is necessary for its survival as a society. The

26 David G. Mandelbaum, "Social Trends and Personal Pressures," in *Anthropology of Folk Religion*, Charles Leslie, ed., pp. 221–255.

family must fulfill, as a minimum, the functions of protection and socialization of the young and the reduction and control of sexual jealousies. Most writers list religion among the functional prerequisites.[27] The kind of religion, like the kind of family, can vary within extremely wide limits; but the absence of any religion, or the presence of sharply conflicting religions, imposes severe strains that a society cannot long sustain.

If this basic proposition concerning the functional prerequisites of society is correct, as I believe it to be, the study of religion must be recognized as one of the central concerns of students of human behavior.

What Shall the Science of Religion Be Called? Studies of religious institutions, beliefs, and behavior are seldom as purely anthropological, psychological, historical, or sociological as the disciplinary starting point might seem to indicate. Our interest in understanding human behavior encourages each of us to move out from our starting point to incorporate other perspectives. Our need is to do this explicitly, with full awareness of the importance of each of the elements and paying particular attention to the results of their interaction. In the chapters to follow, we will examine some psychological theories and studies that connect religion with individual motives and needs. Our interest will be in relating them to a larger field theory. We will explore a great many anthropological studies and concepts, once again with the aim in view of seeing how they contribute to a general theory. In connection with some problems we will use historical materials, for the light they can throw on the context of religious action. Sociological studies of the structure of religious organizations and of their relationships to the society of which they are a part will also command our interest; but we shall seek to be alert to the ways in which structural elements are affected by variations in culture and the diversity of individual needs and motivations. When our attention is given to the study of religious *behavior* —which is always the product of the interaction of structural, cultural, and character elements—we shall need to be most acutely aware of the multidimensional system from which religious behavior emerges.

If I label this multidisciplinary approach *the sociology of religion,* it is partly out of a lack of a satisfactory general term to replace it and partly out of belief that in usage, if not with full logic and clarity, the phrase "sociology of religion" is emerging as the most commonly acceptable title for the discipline dealing with the scientific study of religion. The German term *Religionswissenschaft* carries somewhat the same connotation, but is rather too closely tied to the classical and historical traditions to be fully adequate. Comparative religion and the history of religion are coming to be thought of more and more as general disciplines with wide-ranging interests. Mircea Eliade suggests, indeed, that the mission of the history of

27 See David Aberle, and others, "The Functional Prerequisites of Society," *Ethics,* 60, 1950, pp. 100–111; Chandler Morse, in *The Social Theories of Talcott Parsons,* Max Black, ed., pp. 109–152; Talcott Parsons, *The Social System;* Talcott Parsons, Robert Bales, and Edward Shils, *Working Papers in the Theory of Action.* A. R. Radcliffe-Brown uses the phrase "necessary conditions of existence" to avoid possible teleological connotations of "functional prerequisites." See his *Structure and Function in Primitive Societies.* I will discuss problems associated with the use of the concept of functional prerequisites in Chapter Six.

religions "is to integrate the results of ethnology, psychology, and sociology." [28] Although this seems to be a generous extension of the mission of history, and one uncongenial to many historians, I myself would not be inclined to discourage it.

Thus I hold no brief for using the label *sociology of religion* to refer to this book, and would as readily accept, for example, *anthropology of religion, social psychology of religion, comparative religion,* or some reasonably felicitous neologism, if it served to emphasize the total field within which religious behavior develops.[29] Understanding sociology of religion in this sense, I shall mean by it the scientific study of the ways in which society, culture, and character (or, in another sense, societies, cultures, and characters) influence religion—influence its origin, its doctrines, its practices, the types of groups that express it, and their kinds of leadership. But it is also the study of the ways in which religion affects society, culture, and character—the processes of social conservation and social change, the structure of normative systems, and the satisfaction or frustration of needs. One must keep continuously in mind the interactive nature of these various elements.

Objections can well be raised to such a broad definition of the field. It is sometimes contended that a distinction should be drawn between the sociology of religion and the sociology of churches and religious institutions. The difficulty with this distinction is not simply that the one shades off imperceptibly into the other, but also that the sociology of religion, thus delimited, tends to become an ideology. Religion is defined as a cultural system only, and its effects are spelled out, free from the influences of its institutional development, or, from a different value perspective, free from the various distortions or inadequate expressions with which it may become associated. From our point of view, we must be concerned with the whole range of structures and functions that become associated, under various circumstances, with the religious core. The elaborations, or if one will, the distortions of religion defined in cultural terms are part and parcel of religion as it is lived and used, and are essential to its comprehension. The sociology of democracy may be an interesting exercise, but the sociology of democratic societies is a far more important task. So it is with the study of religion. We must be alert to the distinction between what a religion, ideally or culturally conceived, *might* do and what religious systems, embedded in societies and in individuals, *actually* do. Not only theologically oriented scholars, but many functional theorists fail to make this distinction, with consequent injury to their analyses.

A further problem in the delineation of the field of the sociology of religion concerns the level of abstraction most useful for a science of religion. On the most abstract level, the theoretical propositions of the sociology of religion will apply to all societies. There are obvious difficulties in trying to develop a theory that will apply to religions and societies of widely different types—ranging from those in which supernaturalism pervades almost everything to others where much of life is given natural explanation;

28 Mircea Eliade, *Shamanism. Archaic Techniques of Ecstasy,* p. xiii.

29 I have commented on this question of names among the behavioral sciences in more general terms in *Toward a Field Theory of Behavior,* pp. 26–31.

from those threatened continually with hunger, drought, or pestilence to those where these dangers have been brought substantially under control; from small, relatively stable and homogeneous societies, bound in "the cake of custom," to large, mobile, heterogeneous, and rapidly changing societies. What we need, therefore, are generic propositions, applicable to all religions, and specific propositions, applicable to religious systems under certain stated conditions. We need a sociology of religion, but also a sociology of the Ghost Dance, of Sōka Gakkai, of Theravada Buddhism. Needless to say, propositions on each level of analysis should be consistent with those on other levels.

Chapter Two

THE MEASUREMENT OF RELIGIOUS BEHAVIOR

Problems of definition and description merge with problems of measurement. This has become sharply apparent in recent years as students of religion have sought a sounder empirical basis for their work. If one seeks to discover, for example, the ways in which religion affects politics, or vice versa, it is essential to specify the operations by which these two critical terms are defined. Most measurements to date, unfortunately, are simply nominal; that is, they specify the category to which someone or something belongs, often by the indication of one attribute only. In the United States, one is Democrat, Republican, or Independent, and one is Catholic, Protestant, Jew, or Other, as indicated by membership or self-identification. Using such "measurement by attribution," one can proceed to discover various broad relationships. Catholics are more likely to vote Democratic, to live in cities, or to attend private schools than are Protestants. Sometimes, indeed, the discoveries go beyond those readily observable through common sense to give a needed precision. In his study of a Detroit area sample, for example, Lenski found significant differences between Catholic and Protestant in their interpretations of freedom of speech, a difference that was especially sharp when the clergy were compared (see Table 2–1).[1]

METHODOLOGICAL PROBLEMS IN THE MEASUREMENT OF RELIGION
These data not only make observations explicit that are often quite imprecise, but refine them in such a way that important problems for study are revealed, such as the relative similarity of Catholic and Protestant laymen, for example, or the sharp contrast between the clergy. As given here, however, the facts must be treated with caution. The categories used are quite heterogeneous, with the possibility that internal variations are hidden within them. Had Lenski been able to subclassify the data by educational

1 Gerhard Lenski, *The Religious Factor*, p. 308.

Table 2–1. Percentage of Detroiters expressing belief that American Constitution provides various forms of freedom of speech

Issue	White Protestant Clergy	White Protestant Laity	Catholic Laity	Catholic Clergy
Right to attack religion	94	51	44	41
Right to advocate fascism	79	43	36	29
Right to advocate communism	75	39	32	16

level, ethnicity, and other variables, the observed relationship might have disappeared or it might have been increased. Moreover, different relationships might have appeared. I shall refer briefly to several methodological procedures by means of which we can strengthen the inferences we draw from the examination of individual religious behavior. In a later chapter, we will deal with problems of measurement in relation to religious groups.

Exposing Spurious Relationships. A minimum requirement in the use of nominal data is to determine the extent to which those identified with different religious groups are similar in other regards. Lenski, for example, repeatedly subclassifies his data, particularly by social status, but also by race, age, educational level, and other variables. The size of his sample, however, and the nature of his data did not always permit him to take account of critical variables. Ethnic background, for example, was seldom used. The ideal is to make certain that comparisons are made only between individuals who are alike in all regards except religion *and other characteristics that adhere closely to religion.* This last phrase is difficult to use in research because there is no general agreement on what are those characteristics that so closely adhere to the quality of religiosity that to control for them (that is, to eliminate their effects) would be to create an artificial comparison. Yet the principle must be stated. If several Catholics and Protestants are so perfectly matched that each pair is exactly alike in education, occupation, age, ethnic origin, length of time in the country, residence, secular group memberships, individual motives and tendencies, and so on, and is different only in religious identity, the researcher may have produced such a "pure" comparison that some of the impact of being Catholic or being Protestant in a given setting may be lost.

The opposite difficulty, however, is still by far the larger one: comparisons between members of different religious groups too often overlook major secular differences between them, leaving unresolved the question of the degree to which observed variations are spurious—the product of uncontrolled differences in class, education, or other variables rather than in religion.[2]

The Several Dimensions of Religion. The need to avoid interpretations based on purely spurious relationships is well understood, even if it is often overlooked in research. Two additional problems of measurement have received less attention in the scientific study of religion. Only in the last

2 See Andrew Greeley, "A Note on the Origins of Religious Differences," *Journal for the Scientific Study of Religion,* 3, 1963, pp. 21–31.

few years has attention to them begun to influence research procedures. The first problem has to do with the assumption that the quality of being religious can be adequately measured by a single characteristic. Attempts to treat religion as either an independent or a dependent variable which are based on one measure only, such as group membership or self-stated identity, classify together individuals who are in fact quite diverse. We need to pay attention to the several dimensions of religiosity, even if we continue to treat each one as an attribute that is present or absent. In dealing with the physical world, we readily classify objects by size, shape, material, texture, color, and other attributes. Now we are beginning to get measures of the several dimensions of religion.

Charles Glock and Rodney Stark have emphasized, in a series of documents, the need for distinguishing among religious belief, practice, knowledge, experience, and consequences.[3] In their most recent formulation they define these dimensions in the following terms:

> 1. The *belief* dimension comprises expectations that the religious person will hold a certain theological outlook, that he will acknowledge the truth of the tenets of his religion. . . . 2. Religious *practice* includes acts of worship and devotion, the things people *do* to carry out their religious commitment. . . . 3. The *experience* dimension takes into account the fact that all religions have certain expectations, however imprecisely they may be stated, that the properly religious person will at some time or other achieve a direct, subjective knowledge of ultimate reality; that he will achieve some sense of contact, however fleeting, with a supernatural agency.[4] . . . 4. The *knowledge* dimension refers to the expectation that religious persons will possess some minimum of information about the basic tenets of their faith and its rites, scriptures, and traditions. . . .

3 For a variety of studies of the dimensions of religion, see Charles Glock and Rodney Stark, *Religion and Society in Tension*, ch. 2; Rodney Stark and Charles Glock, *American Piety: The Nature of Religious Commitment*, ch. 1; Yoshio Fukuyama, "The Major Dimensions of Church Membership," *Review of Religious Research*, 2, 1961, pp. 154–161; Joseph Faulkner and Gordon DeJong, "Religiosity in 5-D: An Empirical Analysis," *Social Forces*, 45, 1966, pp. 246–254; Morton King, "Measuring the Religious Variable: Nine Proposed Dimensions," *Journal for the Scientific Study of Religion*, 6, 1967, pp. 173–190. Gerhard Lenski, op. cit., uses a different series of measures, mainly two pairs which he calls orthodoxy and devotionalism, associational and communal involvement. Although he does not make extensive use of these distinctions, they potentially serve the same function as do the "dimensions" of emphasizing the variety of ways of being religious. Snell Putney and Russell Middleton have shown that at least one of the dimensions, the belief or the ideological, can usefully be conceived in terms of subdimensions that may vary independently. See their "Dimensions and Correlates of Religious Ideologies," *Social Forces*, 39, 1961, pp. 285–290. Although the widely used "scale of values" designed by Gordon Allport, Philip Vernon, and Gardner Lindzey (*Study of Values*, 3rd ed., 1960) deals primarily with the belief dimension, it includes some items on experience and practice. They are used together, however, to form one scale of religious values. Richard Hunt has isolated five factors from the scale questions dealing with religion, and has shown that failure to identify them can lead to false inferences concerning the relationship of religion to various items of behavior, from prejudice to vocational choice. See Richard Hunt, "The Interpretation of the Religious Scale of the Allport-Vernon-Lindzey Study of Values," *Journal for the Scientific Study of Religion*, 7, 1968, pp. 65–77. Glenn Vernon has shown that the religious "nones," usually a residual category, require subclassification. See his "The Religious 'Nones': A Neglected Category," *Journal for the Scientific Study of Religion*, 7, 1968, pp. 219–229.

4 As I shall note later, this definition seems to me to be unnecessarily restrictive.

5. The *consequences* dimension . . . identifies the effects of religious belief, practice, experience, and knowledge in persons' day-to-day lives.[5]

Our language habits have probably blocked the development of this concept of dimensions. We think of religion as a coherent "thing" with rather sharp boundaries, rather than as a somewhat imprecise bundle of rites, beliefs, knowledge, and experiences. For primitive societies, the unitary way of looking at religion is more nearly adequate. There is probably greater coherence among the various aspects of religion, so that knowledge of one is likely to be a good index of the others. Even in regard to such societies, however, we would be wise to consider the likelihood of variation. Seldom do we have the individual or subgroup information that permits us to measure the range of belief or the variation in ritual practice in tribal societies. As knowledge grows, however, we are likely to find, matching the development of ideas with regard to other aspects of life, that there is far more variety in religion than had at first been imagined.

However that may be, it is clear that in multireligious, mobile, and urban societies religious systems tend to become less coherent. The five dimensions suggested by Glock and Stark may prove, in fact, to be insufficient. By means of factor analysis, Morton King has isolated nine dimensions that seem to vary independently in the religious responses of a group of Southern Methodists.[6] Several of these are similar to those proposed by Glock and Stark (for example, "creedal assent and personal commitment," "participation in congregational activities," "personal religious experience"); but several are different. The kinds of dimensions that emerge out of factor analysis, particularly from the use of a limited sample, are doubtless too *ad hoc* to be used with confidence. Replication with other samples and guidance by theoretical formulations are needed to bring us to a list of dimensions that are valuable over a period of time and in a variety of religious traditions.

Thus we are left with tentative but valuable formulations. A strong beginning has been made in the specification of the several dimensions of religion, making possible more subtle research on the nature of interactions between religion and other influences on human behavior.

Scaling the Dimensions of Religion. An additional methodological problem is closely related to the matter of dimensions, but takes us a step farther. It is one thing to take account of several attributes, rather than just one. It is something else to conceive of each of the attributes as a variable with a specified range, to design ways of measuring points along the range, and thus to be able to develop an ordinal scale for the comparison of individuals and groups. We assume too easily, for example, that *church member* and *nonmember* are meaningful categories. There are intensities of membership that can be put into an ordered scale, as Joseph Fichter has

---

5 Stark and Glock, op. cit., pp. 14–16. They recognize that the consequences dimension is of a different order from the other four, and state that "we will assume that the initial four dimensions provide a complete frame of reference for assessing religious commitment" (p. 16). It is perhaps unfortunate that they reduce the clarity of their list by putting what is primarily a dependent variable into a list of independent or intervening variables.

6 King, op. cit.

done in a study of a Catholic parish. He describes points along the range by the words *nuclear, modal, marginal,* and *dormant,* indicating progressively weaker attachments to the parish church.[7] Glock, Ringer, and Babbie have built on Fichter's idea by designing a more complex index of church involvement, taking into account three types of activity: participation in rituals of the church, involvement in church organizations, and use of church publications and ideas for meeting problems. The three measures, which were highly correlated, were then combined into a composite index of involvement. Since the data used were drawn from a sample of one American denomination, it is not clear how widely applicable this index might be. Moreover, it seems to cut across several of the dimensions of religion—the ritualistic, intellectual, and consequential—in a somewhat unsystematic way. The procedure for designing a scale of involvement, nevertheless, is highly instructive.[8]

There have been additional efforts to scale a religious dimension, and then to study the relationship between scale position and some other item of belief or behavior. Putney and Middleton, for example, used an ideological scale (skeptic, modernist Christian, and conservative Christian) in a study of conformity and rebellion among 1,200 American college and university students.[9] Unfortunately, they used the answers to only one question, having to do with belief in God, to determine ideological position. Any peculiarities in response to that question, therefore, make it difficult to interpret the findings. In another study of college students, Jack Sawyer used a game theory approach to isolate tendencies toward cooperation, individualism, and competition. The "altruism scale" that he derived from responses to a hypothesized seminar situation involving, in turn, a friend, a stranger, and an antagonist, can be seen as a measure of one element in the consequential dimension of religion.[10] Because it is based on a limited sample and employs a somewhat specialized instrument, we cannot yet judge the general usefulness of his procedure for scaling altruistic tendencies.

The value of these studies is not that they have produced finished scales. It is unlikely that any one of them will remain unrevised as they come to be used in different contexts. But the work of these authors does help to jar us out of the tendency to view religion as a unitary phenomenon; or if we think of various dimensions, to see them simply as attributes that are present or absent. Let me cite one further illustration of the need for more refined measures. I have recently suggested that the study of interfaith marriage would be strengthened if the phenomenon were redefined from an attribute to a variable. That is to say, persons can be more or less inter-

7 Joseph Fichter, *Social Relations in the Urban Parish.*

8 Charles Glock, Benjamin Ringer, and Earl Babbie, *To Comfort and To Challenge,* ch. 1.

9 Snell Putney and Russell Middleton, "Rebellion, Conformity, and Parental Religious Ideologies," *Sociometry,* 24, 1961, pp. 125–135.

10 Jack Sawyer, "The Altruism Scale: A Measure of Co-operative, Individualistic, and Competitive Interpersonal Orientation," *American Journal of Sociology,* 71, 1966, pp. 407–416.

married.[11] At first it strains our imaginations to transform a long-held dichotomy into a variable. If individuals can be different or alike on several religious variables, however, then the fact that they belong to different religious groups does not inevitably indicate that they differ in other ways. They may attend the same church, yet have different religious experiences and hold different beliefs; or they may go to different churches and still share many religious values and tendencies. An adequate study of intermarriage must take account of the possibility that the former are just as heterogamous as the latter.[12]

The use of several dimensions, particularly when each dimension has been defined not as an attribute but as a variable with several possible values, permits us to move beyond nominal scales to ordinal scales, albeit of a fairly crude variety. This permits one to determine, for example, not simply that 60 per cent of Catholics as opposed to 40 per cent of Protestants favor candidate X, but that Catholics as measured by a series of indicators vary along a stated range, as compared with Protestants measured by the same series.[13] Thus we might find that those Catholics and Protestants who rate high on four scales (IV) that measure religiosity differ more sharply than those rating high on only one (I), thus giving evidence, if we have controlled for secular variables, that the religious influence is stronger than the original 60–40 split might indicate. The imaginary data in Table 2–2 illustrate that kind of situation.

Table 2–2. Percentage favoring Candidate X

	Catholics 60	Protestants 40
Total		
By intensity of religious identity		
IV	70	30
III	65	35
II	55	45
I	50	50

If the opposite variation appeared—that is, if the more religious members of the two groups were more alike than the average members—we would suppose either that secular factors were producing the result or that the quality of being religious, regardless of the particular church involved, was the critical factor. The series would then appear as in Table 2–3.

To discover whether nonreligious differences were involved, we would have to classify individuals on each level of religious identity by secular characteristics. As an illustration, let us use social class only, assigning

11 J. Milton Yinger, "On the Definition of Interfaith Marriage," *Journal for the Scientific Study of Religion*, 7, 1968, pp. 104–107.

12 For a more complex statement of this point, see ibid.

13 Lenski found systematic differences among "activists," "regulars," "irregulars," and "marginals" on several issues. Since he could not simultaneously control for such other variables as class or ethnicity, however, it is not easy to interpret these differences. See Gerhard Lenski, op. cit., pp. 185, 186, and 194.

Table 2–3. Percentage favoring Candidate X

Total	Catholics 60	Protestants 40
By intensity of religious identity		
IV	50	50
III	55	45
II	65	35
I	70	30

each person to A, B, or C on the basis of income, occupation, and education. If in fact there were secular differences helping to produce the distribution of support illustrated in Table 2–3, the breakdown by class might produce the following results as shown in Table 2–4.

Table 2–4. Percentage favoring Candidate X

Total	Catholics 60	Protestants 40
By intensity of religious identity and by social class		
IV (total)	50	50
A	40	40
B	50	50
C	60	60
III (total)	55	45
A	45	40
B	55	50
C	65	60
II (total)	65	35
A	35	25
B	65	55
C	75	65
I (total)	70	30
A	40	20
B	70	50
C	80	60

In these hypothetical figures, although the totals for those having an intensity of religious identity marked by I are 40 points apart, the subtotals, broken down by class, show each pair of comparisons to be different by only 20 points. This indicates that the proportions in A, B, and C are different in the Catholic from those in the Protestant column. The effect of class was obscured by giving only the combined percentages.

These illustrations of a multivariate approach to analysis may indicate the importance of going beyond the classification schemes so frequently used in studies of religious behavior. The ordinal scales suggested by these procedures are fairly crude, however. They are derived from the assumption that a person who scores high on both a belief and a practice dimension, for example, is more religious than one who scores high on belief only. A more adequate ordering can be obtained by the Guttman technique.[14] This is a process for discovering a series of questions or statements of such a nature that if individuals agree with the first, they will, within a small margin of error, also agree with all the others. If they agree with the second, but not with the first, they will nevertheless agree with all but the first. If there were four questions, the pattern, were there no "errors," would be as follows:

Individuals	Statements			
	1	2	3	4
A	yes	yes	yes	yes
B	no	yes	yes	yes
C	no	no	yes	yes
D	no	no	no	yes
E	no	no	no	no

The appearance of such a pattern, Guttman argues, reveals an underlying variable, or a undimensional property of social space. Rose Goldsen and her associates discovered that four of the five measures of religiosity they had used with students in a representative group of eleven universities fell into such a scale. It is suggested, although not fully documented, by the percentage totals of four measures (see Table 2–5).[15]

Table 2–5. A scale of religiosity

	Percentage of students giving "religious" responses (Total = 2975)
Need for religious faith	80
"I believe in a divine God"	48
Church or religion "has its own personality" (something over and above individual members)	38
Religion is expected to be a major source of satisfaction in life	17

Virtually all students who answered in the affirmative to the last statement agreed also with the other three. They can therefore be regarded as the most religious, within the limits of the aspects of religion deemed important in this study.

If the ordinal scales we have been discussing are a long way from the interval and ratio scales that an advanced science of religion will require, they nevertheless represent a necessary first step. Only when we have so reconstructed the ways in which we think about religion that measure-

14 A brief statement can be found in "A Basis for Scaling Qualitative Data," by Louis Guttman, *American Sociological Review*, 9, 1944, pp. 139–150.

15 Adapted from Rose Goldsen, and others, *What College Students Think*, p. 159.

ment and scaling form standard parts of our modes of approach shall we be in a position to design more sophisticated and powerful methods of study.

TOWARD CROSSCULTURAL MEASUREMENT OF RELIGION

A serious difficulty associated with virtually all efforts to measure religion is the limitation of the dimensions or scales to one or to a few closely related religious traditions. This puts serious limits on any efforts to develop generalizations about the relationships of religion and society that are capable of being applied across cultural lines and across time periods. Measurements having crosscultural validity must abstract from specific social and cultural systems those qualities that are intrinsic to the phenomenon of religion whatever the form of their expression.[16]

This requirement is not difficult to state in principle, but it is difficult to apply. What information are we going to examine? By what criteria are we going to determine that we are dealing with religious data? The simplest procedure is to measure those phenomena labeled religious by the individuals or societies in question. Most current research on religion follows this pattern; it is clearly a necessary and valuable procedure. It has serious limitations, however, for the development of comparative measures through space and through time. The word religion or cognate terms are by no means universal among the world's languages.[17] More importantly, if one's measurements use as a criterion the degree of acceptance of traditional forms of belief and practice, one is confronted with a serious problem of distinguishing between religious change and religious decline.[18] And one is likely to miss completely the more ephemeral, the emergent, or the poorly institutionalized expressions of ultimate concern.

In modern societies particularly, institutional specialization has produced readily identifiable religious organizations—the churches, which come to be regarded as the fundamental religious facts by participants and students alike. But such "official" structures, as Luckmann has pointed out, get "frozen" into particular texts, doctrines, and rites in such a way that they cannot persuasively deal with chaos for many people. This does not mean that religion disappears; it appears in disguised, unexpected, new forms.

16 The next several pages are adapted from my paper, "A Structural Examination of Religion," *Journal for the Scientific Study of Religion*, 8, 1969, pp. 88–99.

17 Werner Cohn develops this point in an effective way. I find puzzling, however, his conclusion that those who do have such a word should not apply it to different cultural contexts where no cognate exists. I should suppose the test of the wisdom of such extension would be, Can one, by use of such a concept, bring together a series of phenomena that have many important characteristics in common? The question is, Have we tended to classify together actions and experiences that have only superficial similarities, while labeling with different terms experiences that are superficially different but significantly similar? See Werner Cohn, "What Is Religion? An Analysis for Cross-Cultural Comparisons," *Journal of Christian Education*, 7, 1964, pp. 116-138.

18 See Talcott Parsons' discussion of this point. He argues that recent developments in the United States are not secularization, nor are they indications of a falling away from religion. *Sociological Theory, Values, and Sociocultural Change*, Edward Tiryakian, ed., pp. 60–65. See also James Dittes, "Secular Religion: Dilemma of Churches and Researchers," *Review of Religious Research*, 10, 1969, pp. 65–81.

Luckmann argues with a great deal of cogency that we find today only a sociology of "frozen" forms of religion, a sociology of churches rather than of religion. Much of contemporary religion remains invisible, in the words of his title, because we are trained to look only for the traditional manifestation.[19]

Is there any way for us to reduce these difficulties? I would propose that we set aside questions of who is religious and who is not, how far secularization has proceeded, whether there is a return to religion, and the like. In my judgment, examination of such questions has been carried about as far as is profitable. I suggest that we adopt a research model analogous to that of structural linguistics. Rather than asking *if* a person is religious, we ask *how* he is religious. What concerns him most fundamentally? What actions follow as a result of these concerns? How widely shared are they? What groups form around them? We may discover that there are many hidden religions around us that haven't been apparent because we expected all religions to look like the most familiar ones. I find it helpful to think of everyone—or nearly everyone—as being religious, just as nearly everyone speaks a language. This is an assumption, not a demonstrated truth. The question is: What can one do with such an assumption that will advance our understanding of human action? It does not imply that all persons are equally interested in or involved in religion, just as not all persons find language equally important. Some are highly lingual, others inarticulate.

In structural linguistics, the various elements or dimensions of language have been identified—phonology, semantics, grammar, and so on. One determines whether or not any given system of sounds is a language by the presence or absence of these constituent elements. We can observe the shifts from *Beowulf* to Chaucer to Shakespeare to Tennyson to Eliot without saying that the latter forms are a nonlanguage, that they have been "secularized." In the same manner, let us design measures of continuity and change in religion without presupposing that some efforts to deal with man's ultimate problems—those that are new, for example, and only slightly institutionalized—can be disregarded. Let us ask our respondents to "speak their religion" to us, uninstructed by our own preconceptions.

Those who have pointed to and begun the measurement of the several dimensions of religion have taken an important step toward a structural examination of religion. I am suggesting another step, which involves the search for more analytic categories that are less closely identified with the major institutional systems we have labeled religions. In such a search we might profitably use the following operational definition: Where one finds awareness of and interest in the continuing, recurrent, *permanent* problems of human existence—the human condition itself, as contrasted with specific problems; where one finds rites and shared beliefs relevant to that awareness, which define the strategy of an ultimate victory; and where one has groups organized to heighten that awareness and to teach and maintain those rites and beliefs—there one has religion.

Each of the three parts of this definition is a variable, not an attribute. We will do well, I think, to speak in terms of a religious quality, present

19 See Thomas Luckmann, *The Invisible Religion.*

to greater or lesser degrees in many situations, rather than of religions. What I have described is a three-level definition combining an individual character aspect (awareness and interest), a cultural aspect (shared rites and beliefs), and a social structural aspect (groups).[20] Each is vital in my judgment. Where one is lacking, religion is not present in the full meaning of the term.

Following this line of argument, one does not start out by identifying the highly visible religious traditions present in a group, and then measuring individuals' relationships to them in terms of belief and participation. Important work has been done in this way, but it misses, as we have already noted, the emergent and the invisible religions, and gets seriously caught on the problem of distinguishing between religious change and religious decline. In many ways, such measures of religiosity as those designed by Glock and Stark, for example, are better able to determine the religious views and practices that are *not* performed than those that are. Some standard is set—usually a conservative one—as a benchmark from which departures are recorded. Those who share fewer of the traditionally stated beliefs or practice fewer of the designated rites are "less religious."

From the benchmark, however, one can move in at least three directions. The measures being used indicate only whether one has left point A, not where he has gone. We can, by these procedures, say that certain individuals are still close to point A, and that others have departed significantly from it. But where have they gone? One traditionally trained and formerly practicing Presbyterian may drop out of all religious groups, become individual- and family-oriented, play golf on Sunday, and drift a long way from the beliefs he once shared. Another joins the Unitarians or the Quakers. Measured against his Presbyterian background, he too gets a low score. He engages in few of the established rites. If he is asked whether "miracles actually happened," "the devil actually exists," "there is life beyond death," [21] he answers No, as does the first person. Measured positively, however, in terms of their ultimate concerns, they are quite different. Still another person drops out of the Church but joins the American Civil Liberties Union, supports the National Association for the Advancement of Colored People, gives to CARE, and develops strong faith in the possibilities of the United Nations and the long-run potentials of science as the way to solve man's problems.

If we are to understand religious trends, it is not enough that these three individuals all be recorded as having moved from point A. The need is to determine positively what the beliefs and practices of various segments of a population *are*, not simply what they are not. It would be better if the range of religious beliefs and actions were allowed to *emerge* from research, rather than being imposed upon it, by letting individuals and groups speak for themselves. Let us approach them "blind," and inquire about the ways they view the human condition in its most fundamental aspects, and what responses they make to that viewing. After such data have been collected from a wide range of persons, we can look for patterns and rela-

20 For a general theoretical statement of this tripartite approach to behavior, see J. Milton Yinger, *Toward a Field Theory of Behavior.*

21 Statements from Stark and Glock, op. cit.

tionships. We can compare different times and places. We can chart the changes in religion during a person's life. College students, for example, are often identified as irreligious. I propose that we examine *their* ultimate concerns, the groups that form around them, and the activities that flow from them. We may discover that they are simply differently religious.

Illustrative Questions for Crosscultural Study. The first research task in the preparation of a crosscultural measure is to design ways of eliciting religious statements that will be comparable from group to group. I offer the following suggestions; because they have not been widely used, they are tentative and subject to extensive revision. I have recently asked several groups of respondents to answer the questions and respond to the statements noted below. The respondents were given a minimum of instructions. The word *religion* was not used in the introduction and in some versions of the questionnaire did not appear until the last page. I did not explain what I was trying to do until after they had completed the task. These were some of the questions and statements, the questions having been used only with Group A:

1. In your most reflective moments, when you are thinking beyond the immediate issues of the day—however important—beyond the headlines, beyond the temporary, what do you consider the most important issue mankind has to face? Or, to put the question another way, what do you see as the basic, permanent question for mankind?

2. What do you believe with regard to the issue stated above? By belief, I mean not simply something you can clearly support by evidence, but statements you are ready to affirm as almost certainly true even if evidence is lacking?

After these and other questions there followed seven statements, preceded by the following instructions: "Please record the degree of agreement or disagreement with the following statements by placing a check in the appropriate column." Table 2–6 summarizes the answers of two sets of respondents. The first, a pretest group, is broadly representative of one college student body, but is not a formal sample. The second and larger group is a carefully drawn sample from the student bodies of ten Middle Western liberal arts colleges.

What I shall define as a "religious" response requires disagreement with questions 1, 3, and 5, and requires agreement with the remaining four questions. In calculating totals, I have followed the procedure in each instance of labeling an uncertain response as nonreligious, a conservative procedure in view of my thesis.

Responses to the seven statements were strongly in the religious direction, with over two thirds of the choices indicating support for the religious position.

Turning to one of the open-ended questions given above, I shall draw on data from the smaller sample from whom answers were obtained. It may be of interest to note that the students were strongly interested in the problem; they responded to the questions seriously; they left few of the items blank. Every respondent indicated at least one "permanent" question. Only half, however, stated that they were members of or participated in a group that was primarily concerned with that question (and only 15 per cent indicated a church). Although the first question asks for their

Table 2–6. Responses of two samples of college students to nondoctrinal religious questions in percentages

Sample A, N = 96 Sample B, N = 1325		Fully Agree	Partly Agree	Partly Dis-agree	Fully Dis-agree	Un-certain	Percent-age "Re-ligious"
1. Efforts to deal with the human situation	A	6	16	44	30	4	74
by religious means, whatever the content of the beliefs and practices, seem to me to be misplaced, a waste of time and resources.	B	5	22	37	33	4	70
2. Suffering, injustice, and finally death	A	26	41	15	15	4	67
are the lot of man; but they need not be negative experiences; their significance and effects can be shaped by our beliefs.	B	39	39	10	8	3	78
3. In face of the almost continuous conflict	A	13	25	29	23	11	52
and violence in life, I cannot see how men are going to learn to live in mutual respect and peace with one another.	B	16	32	27	23	3	50
4. There are many aspects of the be-	A	44	32	14	7	3	76
liefs and practices of the world's religions with which I do not agree; nevertheless, I consider them to be valuable efforts to deal with man's situation.	B	46	37	10	4	3	83
5. Somehow, I cannot get very interested	A	3	12	11	73	2	83
in the talk about "the basic human condition," and "man's ultimate problems."	B	9	17	22	48	4	70

		Fully Agree	Partly Agree	Partly Dis-agree	Fully Dis-agree	Un-certain	Percent-age "Re-ligious"
6. Man's most difficult and destructive ex-periences are often the source of in-creased understand-ing and powers of endurance.	A	32	42	9	8	8	74
	B	40	38	10	5	7	78
7. Despite the often chaotic conditions of human life, I believe that there is an order and pat-tern to existence that someday we'll come to understand.	A	23	32	8	13	24	55
	B	27	35	17	12	9	62
Percentage of "re-ligious" answers, Total				Sample A Sample B			69 70

view of the most important, permanent issue, some gave two responses. I tabulated them all, a total of 118 from the 96 respondents. The answers can be classified into eight varieties, which in turn might be consolidated, in an informal way, into four categories.

The lines drawn in the columns of Table 2–7 indicate what seem to me to be a clustering around four basic themes:

1. Major social issues

Table 2–7. Ideas of "the basic, permanent question for mankind" as seen by students

	Separate themes N	Categories of themes N
1. Establishing peace; insuring survival	35	
2. Overcoming poverty; reducing population pressure	19	54
3. Removing barriers between people; understanding others	24	24
4. Promoting individual creativity and happiness	9	
5. Balancing needs of individual freedom and social order	4	20
6. Using technology creatively	7	
7. What is the meaning of life; what are basic purposes; where are we going	17	
8. What is the relation of man to God; what is the soul of man	3	20

2. Interpersonal relations
3. Individual creativity and development
4. Questions of meaning, purpose, and relationship of man to God.

It is highly problematic, of course, whether a formal factor analysis of more adequate data would reveal such a clustering; but the pattern revealed here can serve the purpose in hand, namely, to indicate the basic religious issues for the respondents. They emerge from the students' ultimate concerns. In developing crosscultural measures, the responses given here could be compared with those given by persons of different age, class, cultural training, and religious tradition, much as a linguist might compare the phonemes of a series of languages to see how much they overlap and the ways in which they differ. The relationship of these themes to beliefs, knowledge, and action could be studied on both individual and group levels.

From a Natural History to a Natural Science of Religion. The results of this study should be treated lightly; they are reported in this preliminary form only to illustrate problems of measurement. The approach used is patterned, in an analogous sense, more after structural linguistics than institutional sociology. I believe it may yield measurements of greater validity, through space and time, than more traditional approaches. Validity, of course, means that one is measuring what he thinks he is measuring; or, in another sense, is measuring something that will give him predictive power. I am expressing it as my judgment that if I had a choice between the following two bodies of knowledge, I would select the latter:

1. Knowledge of the range of beliefs in a population with reference to the traditional or institutionalized or established religions, with knowledge of memberships, participation in rites and other activities, and extent of individuals' information about these religions, with knowledge of changes in these items through time and comparative information about other such cultural systems.

2. Knowledge of the range of perceptions concerning man's most fundamental problems, the beliefs related to those perceptions, the groups that form with reference to them, and the activities that flow from the perceptions, beliefs, and groups, with knowledge of changes in these items through time and comparative information described in terms of structural categories.

There is no need, of course, to choose between these bodies of information. I am simply suggesting that we have been pursuing the relatively less valuable part. Or perhaps it is enough to say that we have been giving most of our attention to one approach, and we need a better balance. We shall move more rapidly toward a comparative science of religion when we move beyond the study of unique cultural traditions and begin to explore structural categories.

Let us suppose that the four themes emerging from the questionnaires I have reported on (those referring to the "basic, permanent question for mankind") proved to be inclusive and universal categories. (This is unlikely to be the case; but I would guess that such a list would not be long and that there would be common elements in many societies.) We could then ask: In what various combinations do we find concern for (1) major social issues, (2) interpersonal relations, (3) individual creativity and development, and (4) questions of meaning, purpose, and relationship of man to God? How are these blended in the beliefs of the adolescents of society, compared with those of the middle-aged, or the old? How do middle-class persons in one country view these matters as compared with those in another? Are the various combinations associated with different group structures?

All this is to say that in religious studies we are still at the "natural history" level of research, trying to describe all the wonderful beasts of the jungle. Only by isolating analytic categories of religious facts that permit comparisons and contrasts, despite the variations in cultural expressions of those categories, can we move from basically descriptive natural history to analytic natural science. I think we shall discover, for example, that knowledge of the distribution of a belief in some fundamental orderliness of the universe, as a religious category, is a more important datum for a science of religion, more predictive of behavior, than knowledge of the several forms by which such a belief can be expressed.

There is always a feeling of impoverishment of our materials when we move from examination of their concrete expression to a more abstract level, where we are searching for similarities that lie hidden in their diverse contexts. In some fields we have become accustomed to this abstracting process, and recognize its value. When the biologist classifies the bat, the lion, and the whale together, we recognize that he does so because of the importance of the characteristics they share in common, despite their obvious differences. We realize that the analytic concepts that permit him to see their similarities greatly increase his understanding of their life processes.

Our task, as students of religion, is to isolate the analytic categories that will permit us to compare religions in all their diverse forms. Some will ask: Why not reserve the word *religion* for the species (lion) and select or invent another term for the class (mammal)? This takes us back to the problem of definition. In part, I am willing to accept this as a satisfactory decision, but it then follows that we must shift our attention to the sociology of "ultimate belief systems" (or whatever term we decide to use to label the class rather than the species) because, in my judgment, most of the important scientific problems related to belief systems appear at that level. By studying only religions at the species level, we miss the analytically similar processes at the class level.

My preference, however, is to use the word *religion* to refer to the class, not the species. This preference is perhaps partly valuative and partly strategic. Such a usage may help to smooth mankind's way from declining "ultimate belief systems" that have become irrelevant or uncommunicative to the contemporary ear, toward those that can more successfully maintain our concern for the permanent problems of the human situation. My preference is also based on a scholarly judgment: We are less likely to overlook the invisible, the emergent systems of ultimate beliefs and actions, and therefore less likely to overlook their analytic similarities with older, more visible systems if we place them all within a major category labeled by a word already possessing a wide range of connotations— namely, religion. If we do this explicitly, using our words as tools of analysis, not as blinders on our ability to see relationships, we will more rapidly advance in our efforts to develop a science of human behavior.

Throughout nature, species change more rapidly in their characteristics than do classes; but their change is in minor, adaptive ways. Hence they form a poorer base for a theory of the underlying processes of development than do class changes. Knowledge on the class level is also easier to generalize from. Study of the relatively unique processes of a species is of less value to scientific growth than study of the processes that are shared by many species.

Chapter Three

THE RELATION OF RELIGION TO MORALS

In the description and analysis of religion, one is inevitably confronted with the task of stating its relationship to other modes of belief and action. Its connections with the moral codes of a society, with science and other intellectual activities, and with magic are especially important. In each case there are innumerable views, many of them part of a general philosophy of religion or expressions of a particular theological orientation. It would be an oversimplification to state that there are two types of conceptions, one stating what the relationships between religion, morals, science, and magic ought to be, and the other attempting to describe what the relationships actually are; for the *is* and the *ought* are usually found together in each conception. It is possible, however, to differentiate between those descriptions of the relationship that start from a value position, although they may bring many empirical observations to support it, and those that start with the hope of objective statement, although value propositions may be mixed with it. For the purposes of this book, our need is clearly for an objective analysis. We shall not, therefore, undertake a survey or critique of the many different views, but shall simply point out a few approaches, by way of comparison and contrast with an approach that seems consonant with the sociology of religion.

In this chapter, our attention will be focused on the relationship of religion to morals; and in Chapter Four upon science and magic, along with a discussion of the whole complex of interactions among these several forms of belief and action.

TYPES OF RELATIONSHIP BETWEEN RELIGION AND MORALS

There are four logically possible relationships between religion and morals. Although these are seldom propounded in pure form, they can be described separately for purposes of analysis.

Morality Seen As Part of Religion. To a great many theologians and perhaps to a majority of the adherents of the world religions, morality is an inseparable part of religion. "The moral teaching of Muhammadanism . . . is an integral part of a practical code designed to instruct the true believer concerning the path he must follow to win the approval of Allah and the reward of Paradise." [1] That the Ten Commandments, most of which are moral prescriptions and proscriptions, or the Golden Rule, are "part of my religion" would seem to be obvious to most Jews and Christians. They are part of the laws of God, no more to be challenged than are sacred rites and the beliefs associated with them. In Hinduism, "the karma doctrine is grounded in a moral view of the universe, and . . . it therefore commits man to the obligation of a truly moral life . . . the doctrine presupposes the possibility of moral growth; and the rewards and punishments, which it signifies, are not therefore ends in themselves but only the means to bring about such growth. They are thus really more than retributive; they also constitute a discipline of natural consequences to educate man morally." [2]

Several refinements are needed to comprehend fully this idea that morality may be part of religion. In some settings, first of all, this conjuncture of religion and morality is on a rather abstract ideological level. Religion as practiced in a given tradition may be largely concerned with individual salvation, leaving to other social structures the statement and enforcement of moral themes. This has often been true, for example, in societies where Buddhism has flourished alongside other religious and ethical systems. Its ethic of brotherhood has been pushed into the background. In China, and only to a slightly lesser degree in Japan, the influence of the Confucian ethic has been to inhibit the development of a strong emphasis on morality within Buddhism. On the other hand, when Buddhism is the dominant formal religion, existing alongside folk beliefs and magical cults, its moral elements are more apparent. In lands of Theravada Buddhism the myth— and to some degree the fact—of devout lay kings has provided a model of the ethical man. It is primarily through the *nat* cults in Burma, for example, that individuals seek health and other personal, mundane ends. Although Buddhism in this context remains, for the most part, a religion of salvation, a moral code is integral to it, even if in a muted way. As Spiro has put it: "Morality (including acts of charity) is not only required by Buddhism, but it is the only Buddhist means by which one's future lot can be improved. It is through morality that one increases one's store of merit; it is one's merit that determines one's karma; and it is one's karma that determines one's rebirth. . . . Morality, then, is inextricably associated with Buddhism." [3]

The way in which a moral code is related to religion, then, is not purely

1 Reuben Levy, *The Social Structure of Islam*, p. 192.

2 Mysore Hiriyanna, *The Essentials of Indian Philosophy*, p. 49. As Max Weber put the same idea: "*Karma* doctrine transformed the world into a strictly rational, ethically-determined cosmos. . . ." (*The Religion of India*, p. 121.)

3 Melford Spiro, *Burmese Supernaturalism*, p. 258. The strong dependence of a moral code on a religious theodicy, shown particularly in Hinduism and Buddhism, raises in an acute form a question relevant to all the world religions: What are the consequences for morality of a loss of religious faith?

a function of the religious ideology, but varies with the social structure, including the structure of opportunities. In every situation, the "religion of the common man," however closely associated with brotherliness it may be in theory, tends to be shaped into an instrument for dealing with individual problems and attaining personal salvation. We must be attentive, therefore, both to the exalted expressions of the tradition and to its actual manifestations, with special regard for conditions that maximize or minimize the distance between the two.

One may agree with Yang: "From an early date in Chinese culture, the major role of religion was not as the fountainhead of moral ideals but the magical one of inducing the gods and spirits to help bring happiness to man, to ward off evil, to cure sickness, to obtain rain in a drought, to achieve victory in war and peace in a crisis." [4] At the same time, Suzuki's description of Buddhism gives a sense of the moral foundation it helps to build even if it does not create the superstructure:

The doctrine of Nirvana is doubtless more intellectual than the Christian gospel of love. It first recognises the wretchedness of human life as is proved by our daily experiences; it then finds its cause in our subjective ignorance as to the true meaning of existence, and in our egocentric desires which, obscuring our spiritual insight, make us tenaciously cling to things chimerical; it then proposes the complete annihilation of egoism, the root of all evil, by which, subjectively, tranquility of heart is restored, and, objectively, the realization of universal love becomes possible. [5]

Where Buddhism is relatively unalloyed with other religious traditions, as in the Singhalese parts of Ceylon, it strongly incorporates the moral implications of Suzuki's statement, a situation that is in rather sharp contrast with that of China. Thus the enormous range of Buddhism produces not only a variety of relationships between morality and religion, but also a variety of interpretations of those relationships. Weber stresses the "cool" quality of Buddhist brotherliness, for example, thus minimizing its influence, as compared with Suzuki. [6]

Can we reconcile these varying interpretations by seeing the whole range? Almost everywhere, the Buddhist tradition involves attention to mundane, individual problems (such as health), to salvation, and to morality. But these three elements are mixed in widely varying proportions. Nowhere is the central concern for salvation lost. Combinations with the other two elements, however, depend upon interaction with other religious and ethical systems in a society. Figure 3-1 indicates three possibilities in a schematic way. Since each of the three Buddhist traditions has within itself many variations, the designations can at best be regarded as broadly representative.

Similar comparisons and contrasts can be made for other complex religious traditions, although it might not be true that the central place should be assigned, in each instance, to salvation.

4 C. K. Yang, *Religion in Chinese Society*, p. 279.

5 D. T. Suzuki, *Outlines of Mahayana Buddhism*, p. 58.

6 Max Weber, *The Religion of India*, p. 208. In contrast, see not only Suzuki, op. cit., on the Mahayana tradition, but E. Sarkisyanz, *Buddhist Backgrounds of the Burmese Revolution*, dealing with a Theravada land.

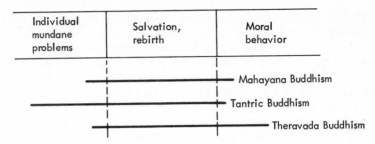

Individual mundane problems	Salvation, rebirth	Moral behavior

FIGURE 3–1. *Varieties of religious concern with mundane problems, salvation, and morality*

A second necessary refinement to the idea that morality is part of religion is to note that in many societies there are several layers in the religious structure, with a large share of the population participating in each of the layers. (This is distinct from the existence of several separate religious traditions.) Thus many Japanese are at the same time Buddhists, Shintoists, and participants in a family cult with Confucian overtones. Any discussion of the degree to which morality is part of a religious system must make clear whether it is referring to only one of these layers or to all. It is one thing to say that moral elements have been pushed far to the background in the Buddhist tradition in many lands. It is something else to say that the total religious complex, which is what the individual experiences, is lacking in moral concerns. This latter situation is much less common.

There is a third necessary refinement of the belief that morality is an inseparable part of religion. Among those who take this view there is wide variation in the importance assigned to the moral dimension.[7] To some it is a small part of religion; correct belief and correct performance of ritual mark the religious man more certainly than does correct conduct. Religion is fundamentally the relation of man to God, and if moral behavior—the right relation of man to man—is religiously significant, it is only as a sign of the relation of man to God. In the history of Christianity, this assertion that morality is merely a subsidiary part of religion has often been made in reaction against the "overinvolvement" of the church in secular affairs. It is a protest against the "loss of religion," the loss of primary concern for man's salvation, which is felt by many acutely religious people to be the central problem of existence. One phase of Luther's protest, for example, was the emphasis on "justification by faith alone." Logically and consistently developed, this not only had implications for the entanglements of the Roman Catholic Church with the feudal social structure, but it also led to the belief that concern with the affairs of this world, attention to good works and problems of justice, were not fundamental religious questions.

7 In a study of a large sample of church members in four Northern California counties, Rodney Stark and Charles Glock found that half of their respondents believed that "doing good for others" and "loving thy neighbor" were "absolutely necessary" for salvation. Most of the others thought these actions would "probably help"; but nearly 10 per cent rejected them as irrelevant to salvation. There were important denominational differences in the responses. See *American Piety: The Nature of Religious Commitment*, pp. 71–76.

The moral aspect of Christianity was not repudiated, but it was made wholly subsidiary. One could hope that justice would be the *result* of a religious life, but it was scarcely a direct religious concern.

Kierkegaard made something of the same response to what he considered the drift of the churches away from the basic religious task. It was not so much that they had lost their focus by direct involvement in almost every aspect of secular life, as was the case in Luther's day. But in their growing optimism and concern for making this life a happy one, the churches had forgotten the fundamental tragedy of human existence, a tragedy from which man could be rescued only by God, by a purely religious, not a moral effort. To Kierkegaard, faith came first, morality second; and yet, it must be added, it was "a real second," for if religion dethrones morality, it does not eliminate it.

The Monistic Approach to Morals and Religion. The position we have just described shades off into a second conception of the relation of religion and morals. This is the belief that the two are not only inseparable, but in a very real sense identical, that the effort to draw a distinction between a moral life and a religious life is an error. To some interpreters, Luther is nearer this position than the first. His work is seen as a protest against the separation of the concerns of this world from religious questions. Many would consider this to be the classic Christian view, contending that Jesus sought to eliminate any dualistic approach to life: "Inasmuch as ye have done it unto the least of these"; and particularly his declaration, following the statement of the first Commandment, that "the second Commandment is like unto it." Jacques Maritain and John MacMurray, writing from what today seem fairly conservative theological perspectives, have been able proponents of this view. Many would characterize Reinhold Niebuhr in this way also, on the basis of his intensive moral concerns. Others, however, would identify him more closely with Kierkegaard.

It is interesting to examine the radical theology of the last decade in connection with the relationship of morality to religion. There are many facets to this work, of which reference to problems of morality is only one. Seen from this perspective, however, the dominant view seems to be monistic. Involvement with the crushing problems of the secular world is intrinsic to religion. There are wide differences, of course, among such writers as Rudolf Bultmann, Dietrich Bonhoeffer, John Robinson, William Hamilton, Harvey Cox, Thomas Altizer, and Paul Van Buren.[8] They differ theologically in important ways (which I shall not attempt to spell out); but what is of more interest to us here, they draw different lessons from their theological work in connection with moral problems. If the common tendency among them, disregarding their differences, is to define God in more immanent, less transcendental terms and to restate Christianity in what are seen as more contemporary ways (that is, perhaps, their least common denominator), there is no equivalent shared tendency in moral

8 See, for example, Rudolf Bultmann, *Jesus Christ and Mythology;* Dietrich Bonhoeffer, *Letters and Papers from Prison;* John Robinson, *Honest to God;* William Hamilton and Thomas Altizer, *Radical Theology and the Death of God;* Harvey Cox, *The Secular City;* Paul Van Buren, *The Secular Meaning of the Gospel.* Gabriel Vahanian, though he precipitated a great deal of discussion with his book *The Death of God,* does not fit readily into this list. He takes a more conservative position.

theory. Without trying to identify particular writers with various positions, I shall sketch a range along which they can be placed. A few share some of the emphasis on meditation and mysticism characteristic of Zen Buddhism. Immanence interpreted in this way is associated with withdrawal, with concentration on problems of salvation, with reduced attention to moral problems. Some middle- and upper-class American college students may be attracted to "radical theology" of this type because of a combination of qualities. It is tolerant of, indeed actively interested in, other religions; it is anti-church, and therefore can be seen as anti-establishment, giving one a sense of exhilarating protest; it tends to be anti-intellectual (tough-minded scientism and intellectuality can be quite a drag to some students on the highly academic campuses); and it downgrades the importance of social issues, which have won a near-monopoly on the label of relevant radicalism on campuses, a monopoly challenged by this variety of new theology.

This mystical quality, however, is not dominant in the work of most of these writers. A more important theme is the insistence that religion be relevant to the secular world, that moral concern be regarded as fundamental to the religious life. Some of the radical theologians, indeed, may fit the description offered by Langdon Gilkey: From deep involvement in the civil rights movement, ". . . much of America's most recent radical theology has understood its religion solely in the ethical terms of love and service, commitment and self-giving, and creative and hopeful action." [9] Insofar as this characterization is correct, they belong in the fourth group we shall describe. More frequently, in my judgment, they are identified with the monistic approach to morality and religion, well expressed in Bishop Robinson's statement: "Prayer and ethics are simply the inside and outside of the same thing." [10]

Affirmations of the integral quality of religious and moral values, in opposition to a dualistic view, are found not only in Christianity, but also very strongly in Judaism, in Buddhism in some contexts, and in Islam. In the classical Islamic view, both civil and moral law are expressions of divine revelation, however much in fact they have been shaped by particular circumstances.[11] Without love of his fellow man, ritual and belief do not make a religious man. "Piety," wrote Muhammad, "is not that ye shall turn your faces towards the east or the west, but the pious man is he who believes in God and the last day and the angels and gives his wealth for his love of kinsmen, orphans, the poor and the wayfarer." [12]

In some societies, the integral quality of religion and morals takes the form, not simply of ideological fusion, but of detailed prescriptions of "right" behavior. The extent of continuity or change in societies is strongly influenced by the degree to which this is true. Although we shall reserve for a later chapter a full discussion of social change, we need to distinguish here between those "prescriptive" religious systems, within which detailed

9 Langdon Gilkey, "Sources of Protestant Theology in America," *Daedalus*, 96, 1967, p. 95.

10 John Robinson, op. cit., p. 105.

11 See Noel Coulson, "The Concept of Progress in Islamic Law," in *Religion and Progress in Modern Asia*, Robert Bellah, ed., pp. 74–92.

12 Cited by Reuben Levy, op. cit., p. 196.

rules are laid down for the guidance of behavior, and "principled" religious systems, wherein only broad guidelines, not detailed requirements, are indicated.[13] The contrast is an expression of a dilemma: detailed prescription may mean rigidity in the face of changing conditions; [14] general principles may entail irrelevance because of the tendency of different individuals and groups to interpret the principles in their own ways. Prescriptive codes may become legalistic; principled codes may support anarchy, or, in Fletcher's terms, move from situationalism to antinomianism. Prescriptive codes are likely to be accepted only under rather stable conditions, wherein detailed rules produce predictable results and fit into the total system. Under conditions of change and in heterogeneous populations, those who experience the stress of change will be least likely to accept the prescriptions. Indeed, under conditions of severe and continuous stress, even principled codes may seem inadequate and restrictive, leading some to an existential view. Life is seen as too incoherent, too absurd, too filled with nausea, as we experience the massive discontinuities, to permit us to postulate any general principles at all.[15]

Religion and Morals Viewed As Separate Systems. A third belief concerning the relation of religion and morals holds them to be separate and quite unrelated. This position can be taken by persons with widely different orientations. Early anthropologists, many of whom regarded religion as an archaic survival, tended to emphasize its sharp separation from morality. Moral codes were found everywhere, of course, but their statement and enforcement were found in "tradition and public opinion," as Edward Tylor put it, not in religion. This view is still widely held among anthropologists, although the current tendency is to see the separation as a matter of degree—sharper in tribal societies than in more complex societies, but seldom total; ". . . even the most primitive peoples often regard violation of the moral code as entailing the threat of supernatural punishment." [16] Norbeck did not imply an ideological blind spot, but I believe he might appropriately have done so when he wrote: "It is possible that the relative scarcity of reported supernatural sanctions for ethical behavior in the beliefs of primitive peoples reflects in some degree failure on the part of ethnologists to inquire into every aspect of supernaturalism." [17] Even those more recent ethnological reports that emphasize the absence of moral sanctions in religion are likely to cite exceptions. "On balance," Nadel writes, "Nupe religion is amoral," but in a few instances there are ritual supports for ethical requirements.[18] Evans-Pritchard stresses

13 This distinction is suggested by Howard Becker, in his *Through Values to Social Interpretation.* It is helpfully applied by Robert Bellah, "Religious Aspects of Modernization in Turkey and Japan," *American Journal of Sociology,* 64, 1958, pp. 1–5. In a less neutral sense, Joseph Fletcher draws a similar distinction between "legalistic" and "situation" ethics in his book *Situation Ethics.* A theological approach to the "principled" position is taken by Harvey Cox, *On Not Leaving It to the Snake.*

14 For some comments on the ways in which an overly close identification of religion and morals may create rigidity in both, see Sigmund Freud, *The Future of an Illusion,* especially pp. 70–73; see also my *Sociology Looks at Religion,* pp. 152–158.

15 See Jean-Paul Sartre, *Nausea* and *Being and Nothingness: An Essay on Phenomenological Ontology.*

16 Anthony Wallace, *Religion: An Anthropological View,* p. 193.

17 Edward Norbeck, *Religion in Primitive Society,* pp. 171–172.

18 See S. F. Nadel, *Nupe Religion,* p. 268.

the need to avoid imposing Western ideas of sin and immorality on the Nuer, whose lives he has reported in such rich detail. He also describes, however, the subtle interplay between sinful acts, punished only by God, and possible dangers to the community.[19]

Others who emphasize the separation of religion and morality may do so on ideological grounds. To some, the religious quest, in the sense of union with God or eternal salvation or nirvana, may so dominate their lives that moral issues—what happens to man on earth—are utterly unimportant. To relate them to the religious effort is to obscure that effort, to prevent its development in purest form. There are others who protest against moral emphasis in religion because they do not want religious sanctions to become involved in the secular struggles of the day. Usually these are persons who are fairly well satisfied with the existing social structures. They are fearful that if the conflicts became defined as religious questions, they could not possibly gain and might well lose. Many American clergymen who have become concerned over questions of race relations or industrial conflict or poverty have been told that they ought to mind their own business, which presumably does not include attention to such moral problems. Much of the return to religion, so much discussed in the United States in the 1950's, had, and perhaps we can say *has,* only slight moral implications, particularly with regard to the complex and impersonal contacts of human beings in a mobile society—contacts that are becoming increasingly important and raise many new moral questions. This is more true of laymen than of the clergy. Although over 90 per cent of American adults identify themselves with one of the major religious groups, many of them believe that their religion does not affect their ideas of politics and business. In 1955, interviewers for the American Institute of Public Opinion asked those who considered religion to be something "very important" in their lives, "Would you say your religious beliefs have any effect on your ideas of politics and business?" Fifty-four per cent said No.[20] A somewhat different but related question was asked by the Institute in 1957 and again in 1968: "Should the churches keep out of political and social matters—or should they express their views on day-to-day social and political questions?" In 1957, 47 per cent thought churches should express their views, with 44 per cent saying that they should keep out. By 1968, however, the percentage in favor of expression had fallen to 40, and those wanting churches to keep silent had increased to 53 per cent.[21] These proportions are doubtless somewhat influenced by the wording, particularly by the inclusion of the word *political.* The general results, however, are indicative of substantial support for the belief that moral issues are not religiously relevant.

These two groups, which one might label the "pure religionist" and the "comfortable layman," despite their wide differences are in a sense religious colleagues, because each finds some support in the other for their common belief that religion must be purged of "merely moral" interests. The comfortable layman actually holds a different position, however. His desire to

19 See E. E. Evans-Pritchard, *Nuer Religion.*

20 American Institute of Public Opinion, "Public Opinion News Service," March 20, 1955.

21 *New York Times,* April 12, 1968, p. 21.

"keep religion out of politics and business," which seems to be a call for sharp separation of morality and religion, may usually be interpreted as a desire to maintain religious sanction for his particular moral views.

Still another group agrees that religion and morality are—or at least ought to be—entirely separate, but for a very different reason. To the "secular moralists," powerful and absolute religious sanctions can only serve to make rigid and nonrational what needs to be flexible and rational. Morality requires, in their view, continuous adaptation to a changing situation on the basis of constant study and knowledge of consequences. Their lament is not that concern over moral questions obscures the religious quest, but rather that a connection with religion obscures the moral quest.

Religion As an Agent of Morality. Those who take a fourth position agree with the proponents of the first two that religion and morality are closely related, but they differ in their emphasis on morality as the "senior partner." Those who take this orientation, as well as the others, frequently mix their conceptions of what is with their beliefs concerning what ought to be. When Kant interprets religious observances simply as means for directing the will toward the achievement of moral law, it is not clear whether he is asserting that this is indeed the case or declaring that it ought to be true.

The adherents of this view differ among themselves. Some believe that even if religion is to be defined, as Carlyle defined it, simply as "morality touched by emotion," it is a necessary component of a moral system because of the motivational force it supplies. Some contend that a supernatural religious sanction is required to obtain a changeless frame of reference that cannot be upset by variable human experience. Others believe that eventually morality may be quite free of religion, at least of the traditional varieties, and will find its motivation and sanctions in the expanding knowledge of the consequences of human behavior. This view is well represented in Julian Huxley's *Religion Without Revelation* and John Dewey's *A Common Faith.* Both stand close to what we have called the secular moralist position.

Despite these differences, there is agreement among the various proponents of this view in their tendency to apply a pragmatic criterion to religion: its consequences for the moral life are the central test to which it should be put. This approach finds its most complete expression in the religious philosophy of Confucianism, which holds that the quality of a religion is to be judged, in the words of Kenneth Latourette, "by its power to produce worthy character and a just social order." There are other interpretations of Confucianism, of course. It is a complex movement, with a long history, making diverse emphases inevitable; but there is little disagreement concerning its dominant theme. In the words of Hu Shih: "Teaching a moral life is the essential thing; and the ways of the gods are merely one of the possible means of sanctioning the teaching. That is in substance the Chinese concept of religion." [22]

In the history of Christianity, it has usually been marginal movements of various kinds that have upheld the position that ethical questions are the central questions. One thinks of Comte's positivistic religion or of contemporary "Ethical Culture" and "Humanist" groups more as offshoots from, than as manifestations of, the Judaic-Christian tradition. Yet their

22 Quoted by Wing-tsit Chan, *Religious Trends in Modern China,* p. 246. See also C. K. Yang, op. cit., pp. 255–257.

relationship to that tradition is close. This is made explicit in a recent work by Erich Fromm. Although he states that he is a "radical humanist" rather than a theist, he sees the concept of God as having been a major force in freeing man from "the incestuous ties to nature and clan." The idea that man has been created in the image of God leads to the humanist conviction "that every man carries within himself all of humanity." Thus God is a poetic expression, not a reality in itself, "of the highest value in humanism." [23]

Even in the mainstream of Christian movements, the contention that religion is mainly to be judged by its contributions to the moral life is not without vigorous defenders. These are found not only in such sectarian developments as those led by Winstanley and the Anabaptists, but in some of the classic doctrinal and theological struggles, including those led by the British monk Pelagius in the fifth century and by Arminius, an early Dutch Protestant. It was a strong emphasis in the "social gospel" movement. And as we noted earlier it is important in the work of some of the contemporary radical theologians.

The history of a religion is sometimes written as a struggle between the priestly and the prophetic tendencies, usually by those who believe that moral questions, which should be central, are too easily obscured. They see the controlling power of religion being used by a priestly class, in their own behalf or to serve the ruling elite, the emphasis being placed on ritual and dogma in order to protect secular structures. Into this scene come "prophets," who declare that true religion is concerned with justice and righteousness, not with rite and belief. They may accomplish a reformation that gives fresh emphasis to morals, until the pendulum swings back again toward priestly religion. Some view the process as one in which the moral concerns are gradually, even if waveringly, winning.[24]

From one perspective, the history of Christianity can be read as the interplay of these four points of view concerning the possible and the desirable relationships between religion and morality. In the struggles among them before the time of Luther and probably up to the eighteenth century (perhaps one ought to say, even up to the present), the first position has won most of the official victories, with strong emphasis on some aspects of the third position. This view can perhaps be summed up in these words: moral questions insofar as they are religious questions at all, are part of revealed religion. The second and fourth positions have had eloquent spokesmen but have never become the established and dominant doctrines. At several points in the chapters that follow we shall try to discover some of the social forces that help to explain the predominance of one view of the relation of religion and morals over the others.

A SOCIOLOGICAL REVIEW OF RELIGION AND MORALS

Each of the preceding conceptions mixes statements of value with statements of fact. In the development of a scientific theory of religion, however,

23 See Erich Fromm, *You Shall Be As Gods: A Radical Interpretation of the Old Testament and Its Tradition.*

24 See for example, L. T. Hobhouse, *Morals in Evolution* and L. L. Bernard, *Social Control in Its Sociological Aspects*, p. 483 ff.

the need is first for an examination of crosscultural data to describe what the various patterns of relationship between religion and morals *are,* and then for an exploration of the conditions in which the various patterns occur. The first requirement is much easier to fulfill than the second. We have extensive materials on many different societies that permit us to outline some of the diverse connections of religion and morality. As we deal with various questions in the sociology of religion, we shall hope also to untangle some of the variables that influence this relationship.

From the perspective of science, several generalizations emerge in the study of the relationship of religion and morality. It is possible and desirable to define them in independent terms and to separate them analytically. Their origins, their causes, their internal variations, and their relationships to society and culture can be studied separately. At the same time, it is perfectly clear that they are interdependent in most times and places. There are many types of relationship, with widely varying consequences. There is no clear-cut line between moral codes and religious prescriptions, for they may be identical, mutually reinforcing, entirely distinct, or antithetical. The religious idea of *sin* is not synonymous with the moral idea of *wrong,* for the former implies a suprasocial norm (as well, perhaps, as a social norm) while the latter implies only evil social results.[25] Yet a given act may fall under both proscriptions.

One cannot clearly establish an evolutionary line leading from a religion without moral concern to one where moral questions are found, although subsidiary, to a situation where morality is the central question of religion, then to a supposed final situation where religion has vanished and only a moral system remains. This pattern overlooks their separate quality, which stems from distinctive needs and problems. In theological terms, religion is concerned with "is-ness," morality with "ought-ness." Morality seeks, for example, to control conditions that lead to death—to prohibit cruelty and murder, to reduce sources of illness and hunger. Religion seeks to help one to adjust to the fact of death. Morality is concerned with the relationship of man to man; religion is concerned with the relationship of man to some higher power or idea, sometimes, but not always, in addition to a moral concern. Even a purely naturalistic and humanistic religion is not to be equated with a moral code, although it doubtless will have fewer norms that are unrelated or antithetical to existing moral codes, for it is still basically concerned with the development of a satisfying response to that which *is* in human existence.

These statements are largely, of course, matters of definition. It is the contention of the author that such analytic separation of religion and morals, however much they may be empirically related, is necessary for the adequate study and particularly for the explanation of the wide variety of relationships. The distinction cannot be based on differences in prescribed rules of conduct, for religion, morality, and law may require the same acts, although some deeds may involve only one of the sanctions. The distinction is in terms of the authority and the sanctions that are attached to the codes.[26]

25 See Robert MacIver and Charles Page, *Society: An Introductory Analysis,* pp. 169–170.

26 See ibid., p. 168.

Disagreements over the relationship of morality and religion have arisen from the failure to see that we need not choose between two opposite theories. It is not necessary to say either that they are aspects of one system or that they are entirely separate. The evolutionary theorists, in their belief that there was a progressive development toward ethical monotheism, tended to describe the religious and moral codes of primitive societies in separate terms. As knowledge of primitive regions grew, it became clear that there were many types of relationship with morals. In particular, the belief that they were always sharply distinct, that only the "higher religions" had an ethical content, was shown to be inadequate. Ruth Benedict wrote: "Nor are all the cultures that use religion as a sanction for ethical conduct found upon the plane of complex civilization. The Manus people of the Bismarck Archipelago have an ethical religion, and it would be hard to imagine a culture that more consistently used all their supernatural concepts to back a puritanical code of morals." [27]

Weston LaBarre has shown that confession—a rite peculiarly effective in connecting religion with a moral code—is fairly widespread among American Indian societies.[28]

Malinowski and other functionalists swung the pendulum to the other extreme from the conception that morality and religion are separate. Speaking of the Trobriand Islanders in particular, but seeking for conclusions concerning "the nature of religion in general," Malinowski declared: "Myth, ritual, and ethics are definitely but three facets of the same essential fact. . . . Take away from the natives the belief in the reality of their sacred lore, destroy their sense of the spirit world as it exists and acts upon them, and you will undermine their whole moral outlook." [29]

It is highly desirable to call attention to the functional interconnections of morals and religion, but the evidence does not support the proposition that one type of relationship is characteristic of the nature of religion in general. In a broad sense, since they are aspects of a sociocultural *system*, they can be thought of as "facets of the same essential fact." They cannot exist together in society without mutually influencing each other. The morals of a society are often reinforced by the claim that they are supported by divine sanctions; and the conceptions of the gods are frequently affected by associating them with the moral qualities most admired. This should not obscure, however, the separate needs, patterns, and functions that may be involved.

Two Illustrations of the Relation of Religion and Morals

A glance at Judaism and at ancient Greece reveals the possibilities of different patterns of relationship. The law of Moses, in early Hebraic religion, is a combination of rules of ritual, prescribed beliefs, and moral requirements. In this tradition, religion is a source and a sustainer of morality. "We see that even in its rudest form Religion was a moral force, the powers that men revered were on the side of social order and moral law; and the fear

27 In *General Anthropology*, edited by Franz Boas, p. 663.

28 Weston LaBarre, "Primitive Psychotherapy in Native American Cultures: Peyotism and Confession," *Journal of Abnormal and Social Psychology*, 42, 1947, pp. 294–309.

29 *The Foundations of Faith and Morals*, pp. 25–26.

of the gods was a motive to enforce the laws of society, which were also the laws of morality." [30] This relationship became ever closer in the later development of Judaism. In the work of the eighth-century prophets, and afterward, the dualism was reduced to a minimum. The religious life and the moral life became as nearly identical as in any major religion. This is, of course, the primary source of the Christian approach to this question.

Judaism became so consistently and thoroughly a communal affair that it was less capable of struggling with more personal needs. In the words of Robertson Smith:

It was a national not a personal providence that was taught by ancient religion. So much was this the case that in purely personal concerns the ancients were very apt to turn, not to the recognised religion of the family or of the state, but to magical superstitions. . . . There was therefore a whole region of possible needs and desires for which religion could and would do nothing.[31]

It is perhaps fair to say that Christianity, faced with this problem, has incorporated far more attention to individual salvation. In most times and places it has brought personal needs into the religious system more thoroughly than Judaism. This reintroduces the tendency toward dualism; and it increases the likelihood that magical elements will become entangled with religion. At the same time, as a somewhat more complicated religio-moral system than Judaism, it has often been concerned with a broader range of human needs.

In ancient Greece, there was a sharper separation of morality and religion. When Socrates, Plato, Aristotle, and most of the other philosophers sought to discover the nature of moral obligation, the source of the distinction between right and wrong, they did not relate their answer to a religious system. The differences among them are less important in this connection than the common perspective that morality is to be discussed in human and social terms. Greek religion, on the other hand, was primarily concerned with the frightening aspects of individual life and death, not with moral obligation and community need. This is seen in the sacrifice at the Diasia, for example. This was a holocaust, in the original meaning of that word: every shred of the victim was burned. As Gilbert Murray says:

We know quite well the meaning of that form of sacrifice: it is a sacrifice to placate or appease the powers below, the Chthonioi, the dead and the lords of death. It was performed, as our authorities tell us . . . with shuddering or repulsion. . . . The Diasia was a ritual of placation, that is, of casting away various elements of pollution or danger and appeasing the unknown wraths of the surrounding darkness.[32]

One might find similar sacrifices and ceremonies among the ancient Hebrews, purges and incantation formulas by which they sought cleansing from sin. By the eighth century, however, these had been sharply reduced. Yahweh had become a God of righteousness rather than of wrath. "Yea, though ye offer Me your burnt offerings and meal offerings, I will not

30 W. Robertson Smith, *Religion of the Semites*, p. 53. Max Weber's *Ancient Judaism* is a rich source on this issue.

31 Ibid., pp. 263–264.

32 Murray, *Five Stages of Greek Religion*, p. 29.

accept them: neither will I regard the peace offerings of your fat beasts. . . . But let judgment roll down as waters, and righteousness as a mighty stream." Greek religion, to be sure, underwent some of this same transformation. In its early stages, it pictures the world as one of caprice and terror. This is well described in Murray's account of the Anthesteria, said to be the oldest of the feasts to the Olympian Dionysus:

On the surface there is a touch of the wine-god, and he is given due official prominence; but as soon as we penetrate anywhere near the heart of the festival, Dionysus and his brother gods are quite forgotten, and all that remains is a great ritual for appeasing the dead. All the days of the Feast were *nefaste,* ill omen. . . . On it the Wine Jars which were also Seed and Funeral Jars were opened and the spirits of the Dead let loose in the world. Nameless and innumerable, the ghosts are summoned out of their tombs, and are duly feasted, each man summoning his own ghosts to his own house, and carefully abstaining from any act that would affect his neighbours. And then, when they are properly appeased and made gentle, they are swept back again out of this world to the place where they properly belong, and the streets and the houses cleaned from the presence of death.[33]

Only gradually within this setting of dread and appeasement do the Olympian gods become prominent. The overwhelmingly fearsome quality of Greek religion takes on a new appearance. In the "reformation," led perhaps by Homer, the great mass of rites concerned with food supply and human fertility was swept away. Much of the worship of the dead was eliminated; and the confused pattern of spirits and deities was gradually fused into a pantheon. At least, these trends could be seen in the thinking of those who lived in the centers of culture contact. The majority of the people, isolated from the urban and commercial developments, moved far less significantly in this direction. And in the last analysis, the "Homeric reformation" failed. In Murray's judgment, the isolation of most of the people, the inertia of the ancient traditions, the inability to remove the personal, human qualities from the gods of the pantheon, and the confusion associated with the collapse of the Greek city-state were among the forces involved in "the failure of nerve."

The response of the philosophers to culture contact and to the collapse of the *polis* was a group of brilliant intellectual systems. They saw the situation not so much in terms of individual tragedy as of social disorganization, and were led, correspondingly, to the search for ethical propositions more than to religion. Plato, for example, dismayed by the confusion and disorganization of his time, held that there were transcendental and universal norms of right, which could be discovered by philosophical study, if only the disorder of life could be reduced by a rationally ordered society. He would achieve that order by cutting off the disrupting influences of outside cultures, of commerce and riches, by isolating one's group from the world, from the "bitter and corrupting sea." Aristotle was far less nostalgic. A life guided by reason and virtue would lead to happiness, which was the true aim. The philosophers who followed them saw disorganization lead to collapse. They often maintained their faith in reason, but it was a kind of

33 Ibid., pp. 31–32.

negative faith: reason could help one to adjust to the world, but scarcely to solve the problems of the world.

None of these systems of thought was able to take hold of the imaginations of the great majority of people. When the Olympian gods fell, fate, unpredictable and overwhelming Destiny, came in to take their place. This religious successor to the pantheon gave no higher place to moral questions than had the earlier stages of religion.

Thus the Greek situation developed very differently from the Hebrew. In some measure, Christianity may be seen as an attempt to blend the two. It shares the Judaic concern for the community, for problems of morality as religiously significant; but it is also a response to the overwhelmingly fearful problems of the individual, with which the mystery cults and religions of Greece were largely concerned. This is not to imply that it is a successful blend. An informed value judgment on this intricate question would scarcely be meaningful "in general." Judaism clearly suffered, perhaps because of its very lack of magic and mystery, from an inability to appeal to the great majority of distraught individuals, more concerned with their own salvation than with ethics. Once it moved beyond the borders of a small and fairly unified society, this was a barrier to its growth. Greece, for all its intellectual achievements, its brilliant ethical theories, failed to develop a system of belief that grappled simultaneously with morals and salvation. The sharp separation tended to allow the search for salvation to march unrestrainedly in the direction of mystery and superstition and to leave the ethical codes unsupported. Christianity, maintaining the two in an uneasy alliance, has often exhibited a rigid and parochial adherence to the customs and morals of a given group—part of a heritage that Judaism has never been able completely to eliminate. This is one of the fruits of a close identity of morality and religion. Equally often Christianity has followed the "Greek" line, with problems of morality becoming obscured in the search for individual salvation. This is one of the fruits of sharp separation of morality and religion.[34]

Altogether, what we see is a wide variety of possible relationships between morality and religion. The task of sociology is to describe the range, to attempt to isolate the conditions under which the various patterns emerge, and to analyze the consequences.[35] Some attempts to deal with small segments of this task will be found in the chapters that follow.

34 In *Oedipus and Job in West African Religion*, Meyer Fortes has noted that this contrast between the Greek and Judaic views of the relationship between morality and religion may have general analytic value in the study of societies. He finds that the Oedipal principle of fate and the Jobian principle of supernatural justice interweave in the religious systems of West Africa.

35 In recent years, several studies of the relationship between religious views, typically measured by degree of agreement with rather conservative statements, and various forms of moral behavior have been reported. See, for example, Jack Sawyer, "The Altruism Scale: A Measure of Co-operative, Individualistic, and Competitive Interpersonal Orientation," *American Journal of Sociology*, 71, 1966, pp. 407–416; and Russell Middleton and Snell Putney, "Religion, Normative Standards, and Behavior," *Sociometry*, 25, 1962, pp. 141–152. Although these studies suffer from rather rough-hewn measures of both religion and morality, they are useful extensions of the empirical emphasis.

Chapter Four

RELIGION, SCIENCE, AND MAGIC

For a century, the complex relationships among religion, science, and magic have attracted the attention of students of human behavior. It was a topic of great interest to Spencer, Tylor, and Frazer, for example, who applied an evolutionary interpretation to such relationships. And it was the subject of a well-known essay by Malinowski, who opposed the evolutionary doctrine with a functionalist explanation.[1] We can learn a great deal about religion by continuing this study of its relationships to science and to magic.

RELIGION AND SCIENCE

The wide variety of views concerning the existence and the desirable relationship of religion and morals is matched by the conceptions of the relationship between religion and science—or more broadly, religion and the intellectual life. There are the same four logical possibilities: they may be considered harmonious, or, indeed, ultimately identical; they may be thought to be entirely distinct, and thus not engaged in any fundamental conflict; religion may be considered a "higher truth," superior to science in any area where they may conflict; or science may be considered the only certain road to truth, thus effectively refuting any religious prosposition that its evidence contradicts.

From the examination of these views, the sociologist of religion is confronted with a number of questions: What are the conditions of society and culture under which these various interpretations of the relationship between science and religion emerge and become dominant? How has science affected religious beliefs? Does it prove or disprove such beliefs? Do religions vary in the degree to which they inhibit or promote the appearance and growth of science? Is there a sense in which science itself is believed in as a faith, with functions similar to those of religious faiths? If so, are its

[1] I will comment later on this controversy.

own ultimate values and allegiances established by the processes of empirical research? That is, can science determine not only the efficiency of means but also the validity of ends? Or are the basic premises of science as a faith superempirical, no more to be confirmed or refuted by scientific study than are the ultimate values and premises of other religions?

All of the logically possible relationships between science and religion can be illustrated in the history of Christianity, which has experienced most deeply, along with Judaism, the impact of science. The view that religion and science are fundamentally harmonious, that they are dual roads to truth, or indeed an identical road, is an ancient one. To St. Thomas there could be no contradiction betwen religion and science, if man knew enough, because both stem from God. Hegel, referring to philosophy and reason rather than to science *per se,* was close to St. Thomas: the true content of the Christian faith would be justified by philosophy.

A similar position is taken in modern terms by MacMurray, when he writes: "We may say that in Jesus the Jewish religious consciousness has reached the point in its development at which the law of human history has been formulated and *prediction, on a basis of knowledge,* becomes possible."' [2] Since the eighteenth century, at least, many people have come to this same conclusion, that science and religion are harmonious, from a position directly opposite to that of MacMurray. To them, it is not that religion is good science but that science is good religion. The rational religion of the enlightenment, Comte's positivism, and contemporary views that science is not only a method but a way of life all express this view.

Those who take this position, whether they approach it through religion or through science, are not unaware of the sharp conflicts between science and religion. But they can explain these conflicts, with St. Thomas, on the grounds that we do not know enough; or they can contend that it is only in incidental and unimportant matters that conflict arises. Thus Andrew Dickson White declared in *A History of the Warfare of Science with Theology in Christendom* that the conflict was not between science and religion but between science and dogmatic theology. Science, he contended, inevitably contributed to the health of religion.

Another way to try to resolve the conflict between science and religion is to hold that they are quite unrelated, that science is based on reason whereas religion is based on faith. Or one may declare that the grounds for proof of religious knowledge are entirely distinct from the processes of validation of nonreligious knowledge. Religious proof comes from inner experience. Or, as Pascal said, "The heart has reasons which reason does not know." Some would even hold, with William of Occam, that it is foolish to try to establish the "truth" of religion, for if one fails, the foundation of religion is broken. Science cannot, of course, refute this position. It is quite possible, however, that in a society where science had become crucial in the life perspective of many persons, such a view would become irrelevant and meaningless. This statement is put in the conditional, for such a society is certainly not yet to be found.

2 John MacMurray, *The Clue to History,* p. 59 (Italics mine). See also Pierre Teilhard de Chardin, *The Phenomenon of Man,* pp. 291–298; and Gabriel Vahanian, *The Death of God,* pp. 165–180.

For a great many people, any conflict between science and religion is resolved in favor of religion, which is conceived to be a higher truth. If scientists contend that the earth is round, or that man is an ancient and changing species, or that miracles can be explained by natural laws, refutation comes, not from an appeal to evidence, but by reference to established religious doctrines.[3] This position in Islam is well expressed in the legend of the Caliph Omar. Arguing that the learning encompassed in the library at Alexandria either was or was not in the Koran, he ordered the library destroyed, for "in the one case it was superfluous and in the other harmful."[4] This legend, of course, captures only part of the truth, for as Islam developed it became clear that many things were not in the Koran nor yet forbidden by the scriptures. The law—and knowledge—was interpreted and expanded.

A subtle development of this point of view, so foreign to the dominant perspective in the Western world, is found in the work of Lev Shestov, the Jewish philosopher. He decries "the fruitless efforts of the Middle Ages to reconcile the revealed truth of the Bible with the Hellenistic truth. . . ."[5] Knowledge assumes and creates a deterministic world in which, Shestov affirms, freedom is lost. Reason has taken away "the sovereign right to participate in the divine 'let there be'—by flattening out our thought and reducing it to the plane of the petrified 'it is.' "[6] He does not deny that reason can create a science, an ethical system, even a religion; ". . . but to find God one must tear oneself away from the seductions of reason with all its physical and moral constraints and go to another source of truth. In Scripture this source bears the enigmatic name 'faith,' which is that dimension of thought where truth abandons itself fearlessly and joyously to the entire disposition of the Creator."[7] Although this shares some of the quality of Kierkegaard's thought, Shestov is critical of Kierkegaard for having failed to see the source of the horrors he experienced—his own belief in a final capacity to know, his wish to understand.[8]

Among the world religions, however, it is doubtless in Christianity that this kind of conflict is most likely to arise. Precisely because the dominant tradition in Christianity seeks to encompass the whole of life, and because, therefore, it contains an intellectual system, it cannot remain indifferent to changes in scientific views. Thus to some, "theology is the queen of the sciences"; or on a more common-sense level, religion is "a scientific methodology for thinking your way through problems." Those who hold that religious truth is of a different order of truth from science are less disturbed by changes in the scientific view of the world. This dualistic view, however, is not common, particularly in a society where science is highly developed. Allport wrote: "For most people, even for primitives, it is not

3 On the history of the conflict of science and religion see, in addition to White's book just mentioned, Clifford Kirkpatrick, *Religion in Human Affairs*, chs. 12 and 13; Homer Smith, *Man and His Gods*.

4 Reuben Levy, *The Social Structure of Islam*, p. 459.

5 Lev Shestov, *Athens and Jerusalem*, p. 66.

6 Ibid., p. 70.

7 Ibid., p. 41.

8 See ibid., pp. 226–266.

hard to assign to science that which is science's and to religion that which is religion's." [9] He might better have written, "particularly for primitives," for a frank dualism is much more congenial to societies in which there has been only a small development of science and technology than it is to a society in which increasing knowledge has led to the belief that the world is of one piece. In fact, there is a great deal of doubt whether Allport was correct when he said that "most people" do not find it hard to separate religious from scientific questions. He referred to Weber's conception that science is concerned with problems of empirical causation whereas religion is concerned with problems of meaning. But these are the conceptions of a scientist. Data from one of Allport's own studies [10] indicate that in 1946 a large minority among 386 Harvard students believed that there was substantial conflict between science and religion. When I repeated this question, in 1968, to carefully drawn samples from ten Middle Western colleges, the range of answers was quite similar. When asked, "How do you feel about the frequently mentioned conflict between the findings of science and the principal (basic) contentions of religion?" they answered as shown in Table 4–1.

Table 4–1. Science and religion among college students

	1946 (n = 386) %	1968 (n = 1325) %
Religion and science clearly support one another	21	22
Conflict is negligible (more apparent than real)	32	34
Conflict is considerable but probably not irreconcilable	17	15
Conflict is considerable, perhaps irreconcilable	14	11
Conflict is definitely irreconcilable	16	6
Don't know	n.a.	11

It would be unwise to assume that the conflict is thought to be less severe by those with less education, yet a dualistic view of the world may be more acceptable to such people.

A number of studies conducted in the United States in recent years have attempted to measure the degree of compatibility of religion and science by examining the beliefs and behavior of those presumably most affected by a scientific world view—graduate students and scientists themselves. These studies have often suffered from inadequate measures of religion and presuppositions regarding the nature of its relationship to science. Thus Rodney Stark writes: "Religion, because of its ultimate commitment to a non-empirical system, *must take* the position that man's reason is subordinate to faith as a means to truth." [11] This is to disregard the wide variety

9 Gordon Allport, *The Individual and His Religion*, p. 20.

10 Gordon Allport, James M. Gillespie, and Jacqueline Young, "The Religion of the Post-War College Student," *The Journal of Psychology*, January, 1948, p. 18.

11 Rodney Stark, "On the Incompatibility of Religion and Science: A Survey of American Graduate Students," *Journal for the Scientific Study of Religion*, 3, 1963, p. 4 (italics mine).

of positions that religious thinkers have in fact taken. Stark's study, indeed, explores a more limited problem than the title implies. The limits are indicated by his statement: "By religion, I am referring here to traditional beliefs and institutions of Christendom." [12] His data, based on a sample of American graduate students taken in 1958 by the National Opinion Research Center, show that graduate students are less likely to be affiliated with churches than the total population, that the more prestigious the school the lower the level of involvement with religious organizations, and that those religiously affiliated are less likely to think of themselves as intellectuals. A person who takes a scientific perspective, it is reasonable to infer (although there are no direct measures of that perspective in the study), is less likely to be affiliated with a traditional religious organization than is an average member of the population.

On the other hand, data from students enrolling in twelve top graduate schools in 1961 lead to a different interpretation. Andrew Greeley found affiliation rates highly similar to those in the NORC sample; but he also inquired about church attendance. About one fourth of the students were weekly churchgoers, and nearly one half attended at least once a month. "Thus a Catholic or Protestant in the top arts and science graduate schools is no less likely to go to church on Sunday than is a coreligionist in the general population." [13]

In a sample drawn from the 1960 edition of *American Men of Science* (642 out of 850 responding), more than three fourths indicated that they were affiliated with a religious organization, and more than half attended services at least once a month. In response to the question, "Do you believe in life after death?" 31.8 per cent answered Yes, 38.5 per cent answered No, 25.4 per cent were undecided, and 4.4 per cent did not respond.[14]

No easy generalization emerges from these various studies; but perhaps it would be fair to say that about half of these respondents, all closely in touch with science if not active participants in it, find traditional religion compatible with it, as indicated by the behavioral measures used. How much this figure might be expanded if religion were defined and measured in less traditional terms is suggested by the data given in Chapter Two.

The fourth position, that science is the road to truth and that its propositions refute any religious doctrines with which they may conflict, is also held by persons with widely differing value stands. Some, seeing specific religious beliefs brought into serious question by scientific developments, have projected this trend and concluded that all of religion will one day be proved false. This is likely to be the conclusion of those who adopt a substantive definition of religion. Howells, for example, despite a basically functional approach, is not content to dispense with a substantive definition

12 Ibid.

13 Andrew Greeley, "The Religious Behavior of Graduate Students," *Journal for the Scientific Study of Religion*, 5, 1965, p. 36.

14 Ted Vaughan, Douglas Smith, and Gideon Sjoberg, "The Religious Orientation of American Natural Scientists," *Social Forces*, 44, 1966, pp. 519–526. See also David P. Rogers, "Some Religious Beliefs of Scientists and the Effect of the Scientific Method," *Review of Religious Research*, 7, 1966, pp. 70–77.

entirely, with the result that he sees a sharp conflict between science and religion:

everything religious has been founded upon the supernatural, the unseen. Now our whole culture fights tooth and nail every weekday to see the unseen, to drive the supernatural and the mystical back at every point. This can have only one effect, which is to gnaw away religious belief. Philosophers and others try desperately to hush up this conflict of science and religion, and suggest various kinds of adjustments and refurbishments of belief, but these are not promising because they are generally reduced to a set of ethics and a highly abstract idea of the divine, and could hardly serve as a religion that people at large could get their teeth into.

There is the dilemma. Can civilization retain enough of the supernatural to constitute a base for religion? [15]

Others, observing these same trends but seeing them in the perspective of a functional definition, believe there is no dilemma. To be sure, the impact of science is to require drastic changes in religion. There is a "strain toward consistency" in society that makes it impossible for a religion that developed in a prescientific situation to remain unaffected by the growth of science. Specific beliefs and practices inevitably lose their appeal. In a functional view, however, this is no more a destruction of religion than the transition from an absolute monarchy through a limited monarchy to a democracy is the destruction of government.

Does Science Disprove Religious Beliefs?

What is the position of the sociology of religion concerning these four ways of responding to the question of the relation of religion and science? The answer emerges from three propositions, each supported by a wealth of empirical observation: 1. There has, in fact, been a long series of sharp conflicts between science and specific religious beliefs and practices. 2. The result of these conflicts has been the drastic and continuous modification of religious systems of belief and practice. One is tempted to write that in the long run 100 per cent of the adjustment has been made by religion. This would result, however, in a dispute over the meaning of "the long run," for certainly religion has prevented, and is preventing, the spread of scientific propositions for substantial periods of time. Let us be content, therefore, with the statement that most of the adjustment is made by religion. 3. Despite these drastic and continuous changes, religion remains a vital part of the life of human societies.

If each of these propositions is correct, the answer to our question is clear: Science disproves specific religious beliefs, but it does not disprove religion. There may be conflict between science and a given religion, if part of its total system is a series of propositions about the nature of the world, but there is no general conflict between science and religion defined in functional terms. A particular religion may be destroyed by science, because the speed of change and the sharpness of the conflicts with its beliefs and practices may be too great to permit the necessary adjustment; or the interpreters of the religion may for various reasons prevent the adjustment. If

15 William Howells, *The Heathens, Primitive Man and His Religions*, p. 287.

the religion of a society is seriously weakened or destroyed, however, new religious and quasireligious movements tend to appear. Indeed, if the functionalist view is correct, such movements *must* appear if the society is to survive. We shall hold in the next chapter that a society that did not furnish its members with a system of beliefs and actions for handling the endemic anxieties of human existence, and a system for modifying its interhuman conflicts, would collapse from the load of personal anxiety and group tension.

In taking this position, however, the sociologist of religion does not contend that the lack of any basic or ultimate conflict is the only important fact. Indeed, the presence of continuous and pervasive conflict between science and religion, in terms of specific beliefs, is highly significant in its influence on human behavior.[16] This is undoubtedly a point at which modern societies are not of a piece. Change has been too rapid to allow the "strain toward consistency" on the societal level or cognitive dissonance on the individual level to work themselves out, to produce an integration between science and religion. The student of religion who disregards this fact and instead lays emphasis on the absence of *ultimate* conflict is unable to understand a great deal of modern life. When a particular belief is brought into question by a scientific discovery, the person whose system of faith includes that belief as one of its sustaining elements is not likely to be made comfortable by the proposition that, in the long run, religious systems have absorbed a great many scientific ideas without being weakened. Even in societies where science and religion have developed side by side for many generations the conflicts may be sharp. They are vastly sharper in societies, or among those groups in a society, that feel the impact of modern science abruptly. When the growth of science is rapid and pervasive, several responses are possible: a given religious system may deteriorate rapidly, a rigorous dualism may develop or be reinforced, or a strange hybrid may appear in which a superficial integration of science and religion is accomplished, which actually hides deeper conflicts. Each of these responses may be seen in contemporary America.

Thus there is no simple answer to the question: "Does science disprove religious beliefs?" On the one hand, modern social science emphasizes the functional importance of *some* religious system for society. It also grants that a great part of religion has to do with nonempirical propositions that are not subject to scientific proof or disproof. Science can neither validate nor refute them. On the other hand, specific religious beliefs about the world may be refuted by science. More importantly, tension between religion and the life of the intellect may be persistent because of a fundamental clash of perspectives. Much has been made of the observation that scientific discoveries are less easily adjusted to by Christianity than, for example, by Buddhism. This may be true. Christianity has not been content to leave questions of truth concerning the world of nature to secular thinkers. Yet there may well be a sense in which all religions hold to the belief that they stand for the highest truth and the conviction that their beliefs can be proved. Without such a belief and conviction it is difficult to fulfill the function of giving meaning to an existence that is burdened with frustration,

16 See Harold Schilling, *Science and Religion: An Interpretation of Two Communities.*

injustice, unequal rewards, and puzzling contradictions. Weber writes that sharp tension between religion and the intellectual sphere comes to the fore whenever rational and empirical knowledge has

consistently worked through to the disenchantment of the world and its transformation into a causal mechanism. For then science encounters the claims of the ethical postulate that the world is a God-ordained, and hence somehow *meaningfully* and ethically oriented, cosmos. . . . For the tension rests on the unavoidable disparity among ultimate forms of images of the world.

There is absolutely no "unbroken" religion working as a vital force which is not compelled at *some* point to demand the *credo non quod, sed quia absurdum*— the "sacrifice of the intellect." [17]

Even if one holds, however, that there is a basic clash between science and religion, because of the disparity in their images of the world, this need not be seen as an unhappy fact. One can see it with Alfred North Whitehead as an opportunity, not a disaster. He would look upon religion, not as a rule of safety, but as an adventure of the spirit.[18] Part of this adventure, certainly, is the continuing tension between science and religion, a tension that challenges religion to try to achieve a more adequate view of nature, and challenges science to try to achieve more relevant and valid knowledge concerning the total human situation.

Influences of Religion on Science

It is scarcely necessary to document the fact that in many times and places, religions have opposed the discoveries of science and have censored its conclusions, exhorting the faithful to hold fast to the established beliefs. One must also point out, however, that religion may promote science, both directly and as an indirect consequence of its influences on society. In many societies, men of learning are also men of religion. Their learning may be narrowly circumscribed by religious tradition, but these boundaries are difficult to maintain. By encouraging a contemplative life, a religious order may set in motion a process of observation and study that leads far beyond the existing traditional views.

Religions that are concerned not only with salvation, but with the quality of human life on earth, may give encouragement to science to support that concern. Those who observe that there have been many sharp conflicts between Christianity and scientific discoveries might observe also that science has developed most rapidly in Christian societies. The cause-effect sequence is not clear. It may be that science has developed in spite of Christianity due to an otherwise favorable situation. It seems more likely, however, that Christianity, and Judaism too, to an even greater degree, are driven to try to understand the world in order to control it, to a degree not found in many other religions. Science is probably primarily a product of

17 *From Max Weber: Essays in Sociology*, edited by Hans Gerth and C. Wright Mills, pp. 350–352.

18 A similar position has been taken by John Compton, "Some Contributions of the History of Science to Self-Clarity in Religion," *Journal for the Scientific Study of Religion*, 3, 1964, pp. 147–157.

nonreligious forces; a religious approach to it is ambivalent; but it would be a mistake to consider science and religion wholly antithetical.

In indirect and unintended ways, moreover, religion may help to stimulate scientific work. The influence of Protestantism illustrates this situation well. The Reformation certainly did not directly sponsor a situation of religious tolerance and openmindedness; but the momentum of the protest against the medieval patterns of authority and the conflicts among the Protestant churches helped to break the cake of custom and facilitated thought. Preserved Smith describes this latent function well:

the chain of authority was broken and each Christian taught to acknowledge no interpreter of Scripture but his own conscience. This led, rather as a consequence than as a design, to toleration, to indifference and to skepticism.[19]

Protestantism helped to break the intellectual monopoly of the clergy, it encouraged the masses to read, it established colleges and universities in greater abundance, and thus, in Smith's phrase, "made way for greater emancipations than its own."

To account for the degree of support for science in a religion, it is clear, one must go beyond the study of its doctrines. Structural and characterological as well as cultural factors must be examined. On the basis of doctrine and the absence of fixed theories concerning the nature of man and the universe, Buddhism is undoubtedly more open to science than is Christianity. Alan Watts persuasively argues, in fact, that Buddhism is peculiarly congenial to contemporary relativity and field theories.[20] But the advancement of science requires not only a culture or ethos to sustain it, but individuals motivated to pursue it and structures within which it can be carried on. In his well-known study of "Puritanism, Pietism, and Science," Merton describes influences from all three levels. On the level of culture, he notes: "Perhaps the most directly effective element of the Protestant ethic for the sanction of natural science was that which held that the study of nature enables a fuller appreciation of His works and thus leads us to admire the Power, Wisdom, and Goodness of God manifested in His creation." [21] A favorable cultural environment, however, is insufficient. Merton describes the beginnings of the Royal Society and the schools created by Puritans, showing how they contributed to the development of science.[22] A Buddhist monk may also seek salvation through the study of nature; but if this is done in serene isolation from a structure designed to expand knowledge, it will not lead far down the road of science. Character elements are equally important; ". . . the mere fact that an individual is *nominally* a Catholic or a Protestant has no bearing upon his attitudes toward science. It is only as he adopts the tenets and implications of the

19 *The Age of the Reformation*, p. 711; see also Ernst Troeltsch, *Protestantism and Progress*, pp. 155–161; and Robert Merton, *Social Theory and Social Structure*, rev. ed., especially Ch. XVIII.

20 See his Prefatory Essay to *Outlines of Mahayana Buddhism*, by D. T. Suzuki, pp. ix–xxix. He deals, however, with an intellectualized conception of Buddhism. There is, in fact, a wide range of responses to science among Buddhists. See Winston King, *A Thousand Lives Away*, Ch. 4.

21 Robert Merton, op. cit., p. 580.

22 Ibid., pp. 583–587.

teachings that his religious affiliation becomes significant." [23] There are ambiguities regarding science in every religious tradition. To know the effect of that tradition on the scientific endeavors of an individual, or the lack of such endeavors, one must know not only the level of cultural support and the availability of structured opportunities, but also the values and motives he has internalized. Thus a field approach is essential to the comparative study of the influence of religions on science.

Religion and Education

The study of the relationships between religion and science is part of a larger topic—the study of the relationships between religion and education. The subject is perhaps too specialized for our purposes here, which are to attempt to state a general theory of religion; but a few references to it will indicate more clearly the range of patterns relating religion to the intellectual life.

In most of the world religions, there has traditionally been direct and powerful involvement of churches and of priests in education. Schools were attached to mosques in Islam; the rabbi has been central to Jewish thought and education; among the Hindus, the Brahman priestly caste was dominant in education and learning; and within Christendom, monasteries have been centers of learning, universities have been founded and supported by churches, and parochial schools have been of continuing importance. Societies within which Buddhism is important have varied more widely. In China, for example, priests have generally played only a small role in education; religion has been a minor subject of study.[24] In lands of the Theravada tradition, however (such as Burma, Ceylon, and Thailand), Buddhism has been of greater significance in education.

Religious values do not directly determine the extent and variety of religious involvement with education. Those values are strongly influenced by the social, political, and economic context within which they are expressed. In Christendom, the near-monopoly of the church in matters of education was broken in the late medieval period, as a result of competition in religious values, of urbanization, industrialization, and the demand for secular skills, of mobility and culture contact, and of the growing power of the state. These forces have more recently influenced India and to a lesser degree Islam, modifying their traditional patterns of religiously influenced education.

The Effects of Parochial Education Among American Catholics. Empirical study of the interrelationships of religion and education is somewhat scarce. The most extensive work has been done on the education of American Catholics, in both parochial and secular schools, which enables us to use it as an illustrative topic. Firm generalizations, however, are difficult to formulate. These are among the questions under investigation: To what degree do Catholic values affect the types and amount of education? How much is the influence of these values filtered through secular factors— class, ethnicity, occupation of parents, and the like? Does training in a

23 Ibid., p. 587.

24 C. K. Yang, *Religion in Chinese Society,* pp. 337–339.

parochial school produce significantly different religious views and secular choices? In what ways are parochial schools affected by the environment within which they work—the presence or absence of public support, the degree of homogeneity of the communities in which they are found, the secular values of their constituency?

In the United States, enrollment in private schools has gone up from 8 per cent in 1900 to 15 per cent in 1960, with Catholic parochial schools accounting for over four fifths of the total.[25] In the early 1960's more than half of Catholic elementary school children and nearly a third of Catholic secondary school students were in parochial schools.[26] The 417,000 college and university students in Catholic schools over the academic year 1965–66 also represent about a third of the Catholic students at that level.[27]

The effects of parochial education are difficult to sort out. Some Catholic schools are quite selective in their admissions policy; the cost of tuition discourages lower-class families from enrolling their children; and families that are "more Catholic" may be more likely to send their children to church-supported schools. On the other hand, continuous interaction between adults who did and those who did not attend such schools blurs their impact. Lenski, who observed several moderate differences between adults who had attended parochial schools and those who had not, hoped that these two opposing influences might cancel out, thus supporting the validity of his findings; but there are no measures indicating whether this hope is justified.[28]

Greeley and Rossi, in what is perhaps the most adequate study of the effects of parochial education on adult belief and action, found that among a randomly selected national sample there were significant differences, which distinguished in particular those who had all their schooling in parochial schools from those who did not. The influences were especially strong in matters pertaining directly to church practice and doctrine. Greeley and Rossi are careful to note, however, that the impact of schools is significant mainly among those who come from strongly religious families, particularly those where the parents also have had parochial education. Thus they emphasize the interdependence of Catholic schooling and the religiosity of parents, operating with a multiplier effect.[29] Although they give no direct measure of the "readiness" of children from the highly Catholic homes to be positively oriented toward the school's influence (a character measure), we can probably safely infer that it was higher, on the average, than the readiness of children from less religious homes. When this is combined with the strongly supportive culture of the home and the structured interactions in the schools, maximum influence is produced.

Brief references to other studies may indicate the complexity of the interactions that determine the effects of parochial education. Peter and Alice

25 See Burton Clark, *Educating the Expert Society;* and Rolfe Hunt, "Religion and Education," *Annals of the American Academy of Political and Social Science,* 332, 1960, pp. 89–100.

26 George Shuster, *Catholic Education in a Changing World,* pp. 55–56.

27 Ibid., p. 237.

28 Gerhard Lenski, *The Religious Factor,* pp. 267–280.

29 See Andrew Greeley and Peter Rossi, *The Education of Catholic Americans.*

Rossi found a few differences in faithfulness to Catholic teachings and rites but almost none in other beliefs and practices that could not be accounted for by differences in the class and ethnic origin of parochial school students, as compared with Catholics attending public schools.[30] Bressler and Westoff found few differences either in economic success or in values relating to economic activity between parochially and secularly trained Catholics.[31]

On the other hand, Fichter sees significant even if rather small influences coming from parochial education, as does Lenski. It should be noted that the former supports these differences in the name of pluralism whereas the latter tends to wonder if they are not potentially divisive.[32] The evidence seems to justify Greeley's cautious generalization that "the Catholic experiment in value-oriented education has been a moderate (though expensive) success, giving us some reason to think that value-oriented education can affect human behavior and attitudes in matters that are invested with heavy symbolic importance." [33]

There is room for debate, of course, over the meaning of the success. Some evidence indicates more anti-intellectualism and authoritarianism among Catholics.[34] Data from Lenski's study might be interpreted as support for anti-intellectualism among Catholics. They were more likely than Protestants and Jews to value obedience over autonomy; more highly educated Catholics in particular saw conflicts between religion and science as more serious than did their Protestant and Jewish counterparts. Lenski does not view the material in this way, however: ". . . it appears to me that Catholics are not anti-intellectual. Rather, they have adopted a variant form of intellectualism—one which lays unusually heavy emphasis on revealed truth and the importance of individual assent to this truth." [35]

Any contemporary assessment of the influence of parochial school education must recognize the changes that are taking place, both in the schools and among those who attend them. In the United States, there has been an increase in secular control of Catholic schools, particularly in higher education; there are more lay teachers than in the past; and the goals have become more nearly equivalent to those in public schools, except for the

30 Peter and Alice Rossi, "Parochial School Education in America," *Daedalus*, 90, 1961, pp. 300–328. A somewhat stronger influence on religiosity is reported in Reginald Neuwien, ed., *Catholic Schools in Action*, but there is a lack of control groups for comparison.

31 Marvin Bressler and Charles F. Westoff, "Catholic Education, Economic Values, and Achievement," *American Journal of Sociology*, 69, 1963, pp. 225–233.

32 Joseph Fichter, *Parochial School: A Sociological Study*; Gerhard Lenski, op. cit., Ch. 6.

33 In Andrew Greeley and Peter Rossi, op. cit., p. 74.

34 See James Trent and Jenette Golds, *Catholics in Colleges: Religious Commitment and the Intellectual Life*.

35 Lenski, op. cit., p. 283. See also Thomas O'Dea, *American Catholic Dilemma: An Inquiry into the Intellectual Life*. One wonders how much this same interpretation of intellectualism might be applied to fundamentalist Protestantism, as described, for example, by Larry King in "Bob Jones University: The Buckle on the Bible Belt," *Harper's*, 232, 1966, pp. 51–57.

specifically religious content of the training.[36] The recent Vatican Council states the goals of Catholic education to be "that young men and women will be helped to learn what it means to be a Catholic, a cultivated person, and a citizen of a democratic society committed to its welfare." [37]

The schools are changing; so are those who enter them and support them. In the United States, Catholics and Protestants are becoming more nearly alike in class and occupational distribution. Catholics are less set apart than formerly by recency of immigration, by language, and by degree of urban residence. The results will probably be that differences between parochial school graduates and others will be reduced, while at the same time the significance of such differences as do remain will increase, because they will more nearly be accounted for by the effects of the schools themselves.

Religious Values and Educational Performance. Any study of the interaction of religion and education must pay attention not only to church-sponsored schools but also to the effects of religious values on educational choices and performance, whatever the kind of school attended. Continuing to use studies of American Catholics to illustrate the problems involved, we must note again the difficulty in getting matched samples. Comparisons of Protestants and Catholics must, as a minimum, control for the facts that higher proportions of Protestants are Negro and more come from rural and small-town backgrounds, whereas Catholics are more likely to be of recent immigrant status and, at least until recently, to be of a lower class, on the average, than white Protestants. Only after such controls can we speak with confidence about the effects of the religious values themselves on educational and occupational aspirations and attainments.

Earlier data show quite unmistakably that Catholics have been underrepresented among the ranks of scientists and scholars in the United States.[38] But since lists of scientists and scholars are cumulative and are seldom subclassified by class origin of the parents, it is difficult to use them to see trends or to isolate the influence of religious values *per se.* More direct measures of family values, with the effects of class at least partially controlled, are found in the researches of Rosen and of Lenski. In these studies, Catholic families were found to be less achievement-oriented and less supportive of education than class equals among Protestants.[39]

More recent studies, however, qualify these views. Reporting on a sample of 35,000 graduates from 135 colleges and universities in 1961, Greeley states: "Catholics were as likely to go to graduate school, to choose an aca-

---

36 For a discussion of current changes, recommendations for further changes, and valuable international comparisons, see James M. Lee, *Catholic Education in the Western World.* See also Erik Von Kuehnelt-Leddihn, "How Catholic are American Catholics?" *Catholic World,* 203, 1966, pp. 42–47; Robert McNamara, "Catholics and Academia," *Review of Religious Research,* 8, 1967, pp. 81–95; and Andrew Greeley, *The Changing Catholic College.*

37 Cited by George Shuster, op. cit., p. 13.

38 See Robert H. Knapp and H. B. Goodrich, *Origins of American Scientists.*

39 See Lenski, op. cit., pp. 252–254, 262–266; Bernard Rosen, "Race, Ethnicity, and Achievement Syndrome," *American Sociological Review,* 24, 1959, pp. 47–60.

demic career, to specialize in the physical sciences, and to plan a life of research as Protestants, even under a battery of socioeconomic and demographic controls." [40] Unhappily the battery of controls was not altogether adequate. Graduates of Catholic schools, particularly the stronger ones, tended to be over-represented; full controls for race and residence were not possible with the data in hand; and, as Donald Warwick pointed out, there was no measure of the quality of school and extent of graduate study being planned.[41]

Thus we are left with somewhat contradictory findings. It seems probable, on the basis of present evidence, that most of the differences between Catholics and Protestants with respect to scientific and educational attainments were the result of differences in class, ethnic background, and other secular differences. Now that the secular differentiation has been sharply reduced, most of the educational variation has disappeared. Some differences in occupational choice and in attitudes toward work may remain. It should be added that after all possible controls have been applied to comparisons between these two groups and Jews in the United States, the Jews attain a higher average level of education. It is not clear, however, that a purely religious influence is at work, since the specifically religious element of being a Jew is seldom used as a test variable.

RELIGION AND MAGIC

Religion's relationship to magic has been a major question in the development of a theory of religion. Some writers have emphasized the similarities, others have stressed the differences. This disagreement stems in part from the tendency to describe the numerous connections between magic and religion in actual cultural and social systems, on the one hand, and the tendency, on the other hand, to define them in analytically separate terms. To the present writer, it seems necessary to do both of these things: in the first place, to define religion and magic separately, and then to describe their relationship in concrete social systems—the religiomagical complexes of various societies. Both of these tasks are necessary because the patterns of relationship vary widely. Only by analytically separate definitions can we describe the wide variety of relationships adequately. Perhaps this point can be illustrated by an analogy. If a chemist were so impressed by the frequency of the hydrogen-oxygen complex that he failed to define the two elements independently, he would be unable to deal with them when they occurred separately in pure form, or, more commonly, when they appeared in compound with other elements. To define them separately, however, would in no sense be a denial of the phenomenon *water*. It is, to be sure, quite unusual for magic or religion to appear in "pure" form; but it is very common for them to be found in "compound"

40 Andrew Greeley, "Influence of the 'Religious Factor' on Career Plans and Occupational Values of College Graduates," *American Journal of Sociology*, 68, 1963, p. 658. See also his *Religion and Career: A Study of College Graduates;* Seymour Warkov and Andrew Greeley, "Parochial School Origins and Educational Achievement," *American Sociological Review*, 31, 1966, pp. 406–414; and Greeley and Rossi, op. cit.

41 See Donald Warwick, "To the Editor," *American Journal of Sociology*, 69, 1963, p. 295.

with other systems. Magic and technology, for example, and religion and politics are frequently interrelated in complex systems. For an adequate theory of religion, therefore, one must define it separately, yet must stay thoroughly alert to its frequent close tie to magic.

Even on the level of abstract definition, there are recognizable similarities between religion and magic. Most important is the fact that both are nonempirical, based on faith in processes and powers whose efficacy cannot be established simply by observation. Both are attempts to struggle with the frustrations, the fears, the imponderables of life, and to achieve a larger share of the positive values. They can be distinguished, however, both by the kinds of goals that are primary, and by the attitudes associated with the efforts to achieve these goals. In Malinowski's words, "religion refers to the fundamental issues of human existence, while magic always turns round specific, concrete, and detailed problems." [42] Religious rites are often described as ends in themselves. Insofar as they are associated with further consequences, it is with fundamental questions—with salvation, with death, with the meaning of existence. Magic is concerned with immediate goals—control of the weather, assurance of a good crop, victory in battle, good health. The devotees of magic and of religion tend to differ in their attitude toward the nonempirical or the supernatural. The religionist prays and sacrifices, the magician manipulates and controls. But the utility of this distinction, even for abstract definitions, breaks down if it is pressed very far. The modern theory will go only part way with Frazer when he holds that religion emphasizes a belief in the elasticity of nature, because of the power of a personal supernatural, whereas magic believes in impersonal law, or in personal forces subject to impersonal law.[43] Prayer for rain in the midst of a disastrous drought, a supplication for help, can certainly be distinguished from a rain-making ceremony, in which it is believed that the proper incantations and formulas can produce the desired result. Despite the difference in attitude, however, one must recognize that there may be an element of coercion in the religious approach and a continuing feeling that the world is full of caprice in the magical approach.[44]

Mischa Titiev, after examining the range of criteria used in distinguishing magic and religion, suggests that many of them cohere quite closely around one distinction, that between calendrical practices and what he calls critical practices. The former take place at a specified time; they cannot, therefore, be related to specific, practical problems; they almost invariably involve a group; and are generally carried out by officially sanctioned priests. Critical rites, on the other hand, are designed to deal with immediate, pressing needs; they may well be individual needs; there is no necessary "church" setting; and performance may be carried out by a rather wide variety of seers, diviners, fortunetellers, and medicine men. The communal nature of the calendrical rites and the more individualistic elements in the critical rites are shown by the fact that when a society loses its identity (or when individuals move into a new setting) the former ordi-

42 *A Scientific Theory of Culture and Other Essays*, p. 200.

43 *The Golden Bough*, pp. 48–60.

44 William Goode, in *Religion Among the Primitives*, pp. 50–54, has summarized the variety of possible distinctions in a helpful way. See also Rosalie Wax and Murray Wax, "The Magical World View," *Journal for the Scientific Study of Religion*, 1, 1962, pp. 179–188.

narily disappear though the latter may persist for a long period of time. Like the more complex efforts to distinguish, on an analytic basis, between religion and magic, this criterion suggested by Titiev leaves us with the difficult problem of drawing a line, for there are many marginal phenomena, as he recognizes, and some that do not easily fit into his classification. It does, however, serve as a valuable index of many of the variables frequently used to draw the distinction.[45]

When one turns from definitions to empirical systems, he finds that magic and religion are often very closely tied together. The degree to which magical elements are found in close relationship to a religious complex varies widely, of course, in time and place; but there is scarcely a religion that does not have some magical aspects mixed with it. It is in this empirical sense that one can agree with those, as, for example, Herskovits, who hold that "magic . . . is actually an integral part of religion." In treating the two as functional equivalents, Robin Horton very nearly eliminates the distinction. "Thus, from the point of view of instrumental analysis, whether a fighter pilot setting out on a hazardous mission prays to a god or packs a luck charm is a matter of chance." [46] The balance between a "communion" and a manipulative quality, Horton suggests, is not so much a measure of the comparative use of religion and magic as an indication of the whole social system within which superempirical processes develop. Societies that furnish men with many ways to control their environment, for example, will exhibit low degrees of manipulation with high degrees of communion in their religions. Social situations within which low degrees of secular communion are possible will also tend to support communion elements in religion.[47]

This emphasis on the social context within which the religiomagical system develops is of critical importance. It is found also in Weber's work, although he notes the difficulty in drawing a line between religion and magic rather than stressing their essential unity. "In prayer, the boundary between magic formula and supplication remains fluid." [48] It is difficult to draw the line whether one is dealing with prayer or with other rites and beliefs. "Nonetheless, in general the distinction is fairly clear. We may say that the realm of magic is that in which human beings believe that they may directly affect nature and each other, for good or for ill, by their own efforts . . . as distinct from appealing to divine powers by sacrifice or prayer." [49]

Magic and Science
An examination of the relationships of magic to science can help us to understand its connection with religion. Here again, the early concepts of Tylor and especially of Frazer can be instructive, even though they are

45 See Mischa Titiev, "A Fresh Approach to the Problem of Magic and Religion," *Southwestern Journal of Anthropology*, 16, 1960, pp. 292–298.

46 Robin Horton, "A Definition of Religion and Its Uses," *Journal of the Royal Anthropological Institute*, 90, Part 2, 1960, p. 218.

47 See ibid., especially pp. 218–223.

48 Max Weber, *The Sociology of Religion*, p. 26.

49 John Middleton, *Magic, Witchcraft and Curing*, p. ix.

inadequate. They came to their view that magic was "primitive science" or pseudoscience on the basis of a particular conception of magic. They held that it was rooted in the belief that man could control nature by supernatural means if he used the proper formulas. The formulas of magic were not empirically derived, of course, but Tylor and Frazer held that primitive men drew no clear-cut distinction between procedures that were based on observation and those derived from tradition. Magic, like science, is governed by a body of "principles" that indicate how one should proceed if he wishes to accomplish a given result.

These interpretations, based on an evolutionary perspective, are developed most explicitly in *The Golden Bough*. There Frazer describes the three stages of human intellectual development—from magic to religion, and from religion to science. Frazer saw each as a rational effort, in its own way, to struggle with man's problems, but magic and religion were hampered by inadequate empirical study and by faulty logic. Evans-Pritchard summarizes this thesis well: "Eventually, says Frazer, the shrewder intelligences probably discovered that magic did not really achieve its ends, but, still unable to overcome their difficulties by empirical means and to face their crises through a refined philosophy, they fell into another illusion, that there were spiritual beings who could aid them. In course of time the shrewder intelligences saw that spirits were equally bogus, an enlightenment which heralded the dawn of experimental science." [50]

This interpretation illustrates the view, so succinctly stated by Herbert Spencer, that social development is gradual, uniform, and progressive. One can imagine that this neat evolutionary formula yielded a great deal of intellectual satisfaction to its proponents. As evidence accumulated, however, it proved quite unable to account for a wide variety of acts, such as the existence of rather complex religious systems among peoples who were deeply imbued with a magical world view as well, or the persistence of magical ideas among urban and educated populations.

Although evolutionism itself was sharply attacked for a generation or more, it has now, in restricted and perhaps chastened form, regained its credentials as one among several ways of examining human behavior. What the nineteenth-century evolutionists failed to see adequately was that religion, and in my judgment magic as well, goes through its own developmental process. It is not a matter of evolution from magic to religion to science, but of parallel evolutionary streams, each influenced by the others but subject to its own laws of development. [51]

This point of view could not be developed so long as magic and religion were seen as primitive survivals, destined for extinction. One of the major contributions of functional theory has been to make possible the reappearance of a more adequate and differentiated evolutionary theory. This was not, however, its first fruit. Using Malinowski's work as an illustration, we can see that the first result of functionalism was to require the formulation of distinctions that were obscured by the evolutionary formula. A second major influence was to focus attention on magic and religion as

50 E. E. Evans-Pritchard, *Theories of Primitive Religion*, pp. 27–28.

51 For an acute interpretation of religious development, see Robert Bellah, "Religious Evolution," *American Sociological Review*, 29, 1964, pp. 358–374.

contemporary facts, to see how they worked in the lives of men, and how they were related to the whole complex of experiences that men faced.

The fact that magic and science are somewhat alike in their use of formulas, cannot hide the far more important differences. Magic is sustained by belief and emotion; science rests on experience and reason. When the formula of the scientist does not work—when it fails to give him control and prediction—he willingly revises it; the magician adduces counter-magic or error in the sanctified routine to explain his failure. In Malinowski's words:

similar as they appear, science and magic differ yet radically. Science is born of experience, magic made by tradition. Science is guided by reason and corrected by observation, magic, impervious to both, lives in an atmosphere of mysticism. Science is open to all, a common good of the whole community, magic is occult, taught through mysterious initiations, handed on in a hereditary or at least in very exclusive filiation. While science is based on the conception of natural forces, magic springs from the idea of a certain mystic, impersonal power, which is believed in by most primitive peoples.[52]

Malinowski insisted that primitive peoples were well aware of the distinction between their magical practices and their technology (they can scarcely be said to have a science). Magic was no substitute for technology, but a supplement, a kind of second line of defense to protect them from dangers for which their knowledge was inadequate. He found a clear-cut distinction in the minds of the Trobriand Islanders between natural causes and other events for which there seems to be no accounting. "They know quite well what effects can be produced by careful tilling of the soil and these effects they try to produce by competent and industrious labour. They equally know that certain evils, such as pests, blights, bush-pigs, drought or rain, cannot be overcome by human work however hard and consistent." [53] They see gardens thriving despite expectations of failure, and other gardens that fail despite the application of techniques on which they had come to count. It is to control these mysterious variations that they resort to magic.

It always appears in those phases of human action where knowledge fails man. Primitive man cannot manipulate the weather. Experience teaches him that rain and sunshine, wind, heat and cold, cannot be produced by his own hand, however much he might think about or observe such phenomena. He therefore deals with them magically.[54]

Malinowski has made a major contribution by correcting the picture of primitive man as a magic-ridden, pre-logical person with no true knowledge of the world around him, quite unable to distinguish between a natural cause and a magical one. Without a great deal of empirically tested knowledge—of techniques, materials, foods, implements—he could scarcely exist. Yet Malinowski may have carried his argument too far in emphasizing the distinction in men's minds between their technology and their magic. It is one thing to say that every human society possesses a great

52 In Joseph Needham, ed., *Science, Magic and Reality*, p. 23.
53 Malinowski, *Coral Gardens and Their Magic*, p. 77.
54 Malinowski, *A Scientific Theory of Culture and Other Essays*, p. 198.

deal of knowledge that derives from experience; it is something else to hold that this knowledge is readily disentangled from magical beliefs in their minds. Primitive medical therapies often contain practices deemed rational by contemporary standards—massage, bloodletting, use of poultices—thoroughly mixed with magical practices.

In a study of the responses to an epidemic in "West Town," China, Hsu observed that there were rational responses and there were magical responses, but they were so closely linked together that it was only in the mind of an outside observer that they appeared to be separate. Hsu contends that this kind of mixing of responses is characteristic of all societies. One who lives in a society where science is highly developed will be science-oriented; but his approach to it, his use of it, will not be sharply different from the magic-orientation of one from a society in which magic is widely used.

But in either case there is hardly any question of rationality, for a science-oriented people do not always differentiate magic with a pseudo-scientific wrapping from science, just as magic-oriented people mix real knowledge in their magic. In either instance there can be correct as well as erroneous belief. . . .

It is not fantastic to say that, to achieve popular acceptance, magic has to be dressed like science in America, while science has to be cloaked by magic in West Town, [China.] [55]

To this writer it seems likely that one would find, with Malinowski, some clear-cut distinctions between technology and magic in every society, and that one would find, with Hsu, other situations in which they appeared almost as a unit. One might further expect to find variations in the degree to which these tendencies occurred.

The Functions of Magic

To the scientific observer, the magical way of thinking is invalid and ineffective. Based as it is on crude analogies and false inference, magic certainly does not "work." Why, then, is it not quickly dismissed because of its failure? The answer to that is twofold: to the believer it *seems* to work; and to some degree, in an indirect sense, it does work. This question is interesting to the student of religion, not only because of the frequency with which magical elements are found in religious systems, but also because some of the same reasoning applies to religion.

To the believer, magic often seems to work. It is well known that a person's perceptions, the observations that he considers to be evidence, the premises on which his logical processes are based, and other cognitive acts are not independent of his personal tendencies and his cultural training. A person trained to believe in magic can "see" its success. One instance of a positive correlation between the aims of a magical process and the results may outweigh many negative instances. This is particularly true when failures can be explained by counter-magic or by inexpert use of the formula. Moreover, many kinds of magical practice have an impressive record of "success": most medical cures "work," thanks to the recuperative

55 Francis L. K. Hsu, *Religion, Science and Human Crises*, p. 8 and p. 114.

powers of the human body; a rain-making ceremony that is performed when it is most needed—at the end of a long period of drought—is likely to precede a rainy season.

The most ardent rationalist can accept such an argument to explain the efficacy of magic. Those who take a functionalist view, however, have made a more dramatic claim: magic does work, in a sense. It appears in human societies as one way of struggling with disruptive emotional forces that arise as a result of man's helplessness in certain situations. In the magical rite, man feels that he is doing something, not succumbing to a paralysis of fear. When he reaches an impasse, when knowledge fails him, man responds with spontaneous gestures and rudimentary beliefs. In Malinowski's well-known words:

Magic fixes upon these beliefs and rudimentary rites and standardizes them into permanent traditional forms. Thus magic supplies primitive man with a number of ready-made ritual acts and beliefs, with a definite mental and practical technique which serves to bridge over the dangerous gaps in every important pursuit or critical situation. It enables man to carry out with confidence his important tasks, to maintain his poise and his mental integrity in fits of anger, in the throes of hate, of unrequited love, of despair and anxiety. The function of magic is to ritualize man's optimism, to enhance his faith in the victory of hope over fear. Magic expresses the greater value for man of confidence over doubt, of steadfastness over vacillation, of optimism over pessimism.[56]

This rather extreme functionalist view has raised many questions. If magic is used to defeat a rival it may bring hope to one but despair to another. How, then, does it help to establish optimism over pessimism? If at one time it gives an emotional release and a sense of confidence, does it not at other times promote delusions of fear that can lead to a paralysis of effort? There are few who would argue any longer with Malinowski's point that magic is not an unimportant and aberrant item in a culture, but a functioning part of a complex system. This does not, however, entitle one to slip easily into the position that accepts it as functional in a value sense, with little attention to all of its long-run consequences, many of which may be dysfunctional for the achievement of stated ends. If magic becomes established as a mechanism of adjustment to situations where knowledge is inadequate, it may become a barrier to the acceptance of new knowledge, thus entrenching a problem that might be reduced.

Radcliffe-Brown, though he accepts the functionalist view, has criticized Malinowski for his excessively individualistic emphasis. A magical rite performed at the occasion of a childbirth, for example, is not necessarily a way of gaining confidence in a situation fraught with danger. Without the rite, the individual might feel no anxiety: the rite is the cause, not the result of the anxiety. Its function, according to Radcliffe-Brown, might more appropriately be seen, not as a device to maintain the poise of the individual, but as an effort to ease the group through a crisis situation, to contribute to the survival of the society, by reinforcing the sense of group identity, and making a solemn occasion of an important event.

Although we must avoid an uncritical functionalism, it is equally an

56 In Needham, op. cit., p. 83.

error to study the question from the perspective of one's own cultural situation and then to generalize to other situations. The concept that magic may have some positive functions for the individual is less likely, in fact, to be exaggerated by the educated member of an urban society than it is to be disregarded. The key to the analysis is the question of available alternatives. Those among whom magic is most deeply embedded are caught in a situation for which their knowledge is wholly inadequate. The choice is not between magic and a tested medical or agricultural technology, for example, but perhaps between magic and complete resignation. Magic is a culturally furnished defense against fear and the sense of powerlessness. It may provide, as does witchcraft, according to Kluckhohn, a channel for otherwise disruptive aggression and an affirmation of the solidarity of the group "by dramatically defining what is bad."

Witchcraft belief allows the verbalization of anxiety in a framework that is understandable and which implies the possibility of doing something. Witches (who are living individuals) are potentially controllable by the society; the caprices of the environment are not. Likewise, it is important for the adjustment of the individual that witchcraft is a focus of anxiety which the culture recognizes as valid.[57]

Kluckhohn was well aware that there are dysfunctional elements in Navaho witchcraft. "The informant's remark, 'If the white people hadn't stopped us, we'd have killed each other off' has more than a grain of truth in it." [58] By interpreting witchcraft in the context of the total Navaho situation, however, he was also able to see it as an effort to struggle with severe problems for which other mechanisms of adjustment were lacking.

There has been a growing recognition in recent years that religious and magical therapies can deal effectively with some of the causes of illness. These causes are now seen as much more complex than a strictly physio-chemical theory of disease indicates. Illness is not simply a pathology of cell, tissue, and organ, but also of the self, and indeed of interpersonal relations. Religious action may heighten the sense of self-worth, increase hope, and create a dependence upon others who are seen as supportive. Magic may define chaotic experience in such a way that it no longer seems beyond comprehension and control. Jerome Frank, viewing these facts as a psychiatrist, writes: "The ideology and ritual supply the patient with a conceptual framework for organizing his chaotic, mysterious, and vague distress and give him a plan of action, helping him to regain a sense of direction and mastery and to resolve his inner conflicts." [59]

There is now ample evidence that various magical and religious healing practices do in fact deal with important causes of illness.[60] Indeed, part of the success of modern medicine is based on processes similar to those in magical and religious acts of healing. A culturally supported definition of the problem, giving it limits; confidence in the skill of the medical prac-

57 Clyde Kluckhohn, *Navaho Witchcraft*, pp. 60–61.
58 Ibid., p. 62.
59 Jerome Frank, *Persuasion and Healing*, p. 63.
60 For a variety of materials documenting this, see Ari Kiev, ed., *Magic, Faith, and Healing: Studies in Primitive Psychiatry Today*. See also Melford Spiro, *Burmese Supernaturalism*, especially pp. 194–203.

titioner; designation of a sick role that helps to relate a person, despite his pathology, to those around him—these are elements in cure, whether of a magical or a scientific variety. Frank states the issue clearly: "In industrial as well as in primitive societies, illness may create noxious emotions, raise moral issues, disturb the patient's image of himself, and estrange him from his compatriots. Barred from the front door, these intangibles sneak in at the back, and, unless the physician takes them into account, he will often fail." [61] The continuing importance of magical and religious healing in modern societies is testimony that contemporary medical practices frequently do not take into account these problems of self-image and interpersonal relations.

Nonscientific medical practices, in short, can cure some illness and reduce some of the causes of many others. Their theories of illness may be uncongenial to modern men, but this does not eliminate their consequences. Their therapy depends upon faith. And we may be wise to recognize that there is a faithful quality to medical practice everywhere.

Magical Beliefs in Modern Society

Cultures vary widely in the degree to which magic is found. If the functionalist approach is correct, one of the reasons for this variation (but not, however, the only reason) is the difference in control over life events. In a society in which scientific agriculture has greatly increased the yield and reduced the fortuitous and unpredictable aspects of farming, magical practices lose much of their meaning. Those who are in closest touch with scientific medicine are usually least likely to resort to magical cures, or at least to accept magical theories. Those who, for economic, educational, or personal reasons are alienated from modern medicine, however, continue to rely on magical practices in part. This is particularly likely to occur in connection with those diseases about which scientific knowledge is least adequate. The magical treatment may, as Hsu has noted, be blurred with science, little distinction being drawn between the use of a doctor's prescription and a patent medicine.

Attempts to control the world by analogy—a prime characteristic of magic among primitives—is matched to some degree by what we might call word analogy today. Millions of dollars are spent annually in the United States for completely untested mixtures that carry the word *medicine*. It is not clear that a man from Mars would find a great difference between love potions or magical herbs and contemporary man's belief that the correct facial soap or cigarette guarantees one's vivacity and the presence of charming companions. The religious systems of modern urban people have lost many magical elements, but some certainly remain. The efficacy that is felt to reside in sacred objects, the feeling of well-being that comes from a rite duly and correctly performed, are close to a magical view.

In international diplomacy, in the punishment of criminals, in education, modern men carry out activities that may allay their fears and feelings of helplessness, but such activities can scarcely be shown to be technically competent to achieve their avowed aims.

61 Jerome Frank, in ibid., p. viii.

There is always the danger that we will define magic as "a superstitious idea in which I do not believe." It is someone else's false inference or untested formula. The functional view tries to remove this error, by paying attention to the conditions in which magic thrives. This point has been difficult to convey, for two reasons. It has often been exaggerated, to make it appear that magic was as much a part of the world view of the contemporary urban society as of the Dobu; but the increasing control that man has over many aspects of the world reduces magic's importance.

A more important problem is that much of modern urban magic is not supernaturalistic. It is of the same genus, perhaps, but of a different species from the magical views of earlier times; and we need to note both the differences and the similarities. Interest in the witches of Salem, for example, may have been stimulated in Arthur Miller's mind (as dramatically expressed in his play *The Crucible*) by the "witch trials" of the Joseph McCarthy period. There were differences, of course. The world view of those frightened by "Communist witches" did not involve a supernatural interpretation; their actions were perhaps more ambivalent. Yet there were some fascinating similarities. In both periods powerful, poorly understood, and potentially destructive forces were loose in the world. By lodging them in individuals, who were potentially subject to control, some found them less threatening. How the nation should respond to its new environment was highly problematical; the population was divided; but the presence of "witches," by "dramatically defining what is bad," to repeat Kluckhohn's phrase, might help to re-establish group solidarity. (In a heterogeneous society, this effort cannot work, because the reality and the interpretations of threat vary too much. "Witchcraft," therefore, can only be divisive, although it might be cohesive in a society more homogeneous in belief and experience.) Perhaps the United States, in the mid-1950's, needed its political deviants (and if it did not have them, manufactured them) to help set the boundaries of a fluid and changing national and international political scene, to give some sense of understanding and control in an environment being abruptly transformed, particularly by the increasing strength of a nuclear-armed Soviet Union. The witches of Salem were believed to be possessed of supernatural power, but their identification and trials were used, as Kai Erikson convincingly shows, for similar purposes.[62] The social *use* of deviation to reconfirm and re-establish boundaries, a theme so powerfully developed by Durkheim, is, I suspect, a prime source of magical beliefs and practices among contemporary people.

Some of modern magic is the series of rather trivial superstitions that urban people half believe and half joke about—the broken mirror, the lucky and unlucky number, the dangers of walking under a ladder. Among the less well educated, however, and a few of the educated too, magic goes far beyond such survivals. In every large city one finds clairvoyants, palmists, and soothsayers of many varieties. A recent headline declared: "Witchcraft Is Going Big Time." The story suggests that "the next witch you see . . . may be your neighbor," that perhaps 20,000 persons in the United States belong to covens, that in New York "groups of disenchanted

62 See Kai Erikson, *Wayward Puritans*, pp. 137–159 and 185–205.

young people try to use the power of magic to create a new consciousness and a new community." [63]

In a recent celebrated case, the late Bishop James Pike reported that he talked to his dead son in a number of sessions with a medium. The son had died by suicide; the grieving father experienced thereafter a number of puzzling events that made him wonder if his son was trying to communicate with him. He believed that in the séances he established communication. [64]

Faith healing continues to be the biggest realm of magic in the modern world. In the East, whether in the cities of Japan or the villages of Indonesia, it has seen little abatement. In the West, it is found not only in marginal cults and sects but in some measure in the major churches. Its continuing importance demonstrates the double source of magical belief: when an issue is important and when a satisfactory resolution is far from certain, magic prospers. This has been nicely demonstrated by Vogt and Hyman in their study of water-witching. They estimate that 25,000 water dowsers are practicing their divination in the United States, despite its demonstrated failure to improve upon sheer chance as a way of locating a water supply. It continues to be tried precisely in those areas where uncertainty is greatest and the need for new sources of water high. [65]

One is struck here by the similarity to situations wherein rumors spread. Gordon Allport designed the formula $R = a \times i$. The likelihood of rumor is a function of the ambiguity of a situation multiplied by its importance. Neither ambiguity nor importance by itself produces rumor; nor, we suspect, does it produce tendencies toward magic. If we are to use the same formula to describe conditions conducive to both magic and rumor, however, we need some additional evidence to indicate when one or the other will occur. This evidence lies in the nature of the needs related to the two activities. Where a practical problem must be solved, magic is likely to be found; where individuals are struggling with problems of meaning or with guilt which would seem lighter if projected, rumor is likely to occur. One does not find rumors indicating where water will be found; he finds water-witching.

SUMMARY OF THE RELATIONSHIPS OF RELIGION TO SCIENCE, MORALITY, AND MAGIC

It is not surprising that the relationships between religion and science, morality, and magic have been the subject of a great deal of discussion and disagreement, for these relationships are complex and highly variant. I have suggested that the four concepts can profitably be defined separately. Religion is often empirically mixed, however, with the other three, the patterns of relationship varying widely, depending upon the religious tradition and on the social situation in which it is found. Can we now draw these ideas together in more systematic form?

To Talcott Parsons, the basic features of social action are ideas, values, and desires. Expressed in terms of his vocabulary of motivation, these are

63 *Cleveland Plain Dealer*, Nov. 5, 1967, p. 32E.

64 James Pike, with Diane Kennedy, *The Other Side: An Account of My Experiences with Psychic Phenomena.*

65 See Evon Vogt and Ray Hyman, *Water Witching in the U.S.A.*

cognitive, evaluative, and cathectic orientations.[66] These may be expressed in many forms, but in terms harmonious with our interest in the analysis of religion, we may think of these orientations in connection with efforts to establish truth, justice, and salvation; or, expressed negatively, activities designed to avoid error, injustice, and suffering. These are indeed the critical orientations of human life; and most of what we do can readily be interpreted, in either the positive or the negative way, as efforts to cope with their import. Our efforts often fail, however. Our knowledge fails just at those points where we need it most—in our efforts to make sense of existence. Our efforts to establish justice through law and custom fail us continually; for we know that the ungodly prosper. We manage to reduce some forms of suffering only to discover that our capacity for creating new forms seems almost unlimited. Continually, therefore, our scientific systems (or more generally, our intellectual efforts), our ethical systems, and our magical systems (those attempts to reduce suffering that we adopt when knowledge fails us), must all somehow be "lifted up" beyond the reach of our own failings, beyond the crushing impact of experience. Religion, in this sense, is the ultimate science, morality, and magic. It is designed, not only "to pass science and complete it prematurely," but in the same sense to pass our ethical systems and our efforts to reduce suffering in an effort to complete them also—to give them an ultimate formulation.

I hope that all the necessary qualifications will be read into the previous paragraph. Empirical systems of religion draw these various processes together in different ways, with one or more of the three processes being quite absent from some traditions. As human creations (no other point of view is appropriate to a scientific treatment such as this, however much other approaches to religion must adopt different perspectives), religions are as much subject to human failings as the patterns they complete. Religion is an *effort* to establish a final justice, to conquer perpetual suffering, to solve the eternal mysteries, or at least to give meaning to them. As a scientist, one must sometimes stand in awe at the majesty of the effort, considering the enormity and the intractability of the problems with which it deals. At other times one could weep at the inadequacy of the attempt. At all times, I suspect, one participates in the religious quest, whether under a traditional label or not; for ignorance, injustice, and suffering surround us, and we cannot be content with partial systems for dealing with them.

The threefold quality of the religious effort is well stated by Clifford Geertz:

> There are at least three points where chaos—a tumult of events which lack not just interpretations but *interpretability*—threatens to break in upon man: at the limits of his analytic capacities, at the limits of his powers of endurance, and at the limits of his moral insight. Bafflement, suffering, and a sense of intractable ethical paradox are all, if they become intense enough or are sustained long enough, radical challenges to the proposition that life is comprehensible and that we can, by taking thought, orient ourselves effectively within it—challenges with which any religion, however "primitive," which hopes to persist must attempt somehow to cope.[67]

66 See *The Social System.*

67 In *Anthropological Approaches to the Study of Religion,* Michael Banton, ed., p. 14. See also Mircea Eliade, *Cosmos and History* and Peter Berger, *The Sacred Canopy* for valuable discussions of "sacred" as a category opposed to "chaos."

The nature of the coping varies widely. It is never, of course, a simple *solution* to the problems with which it deals. Nadel and others have criticized Malinowski's "theology of optimism" in which religion is interpreted as a declaration that "hope cannot fail nor desire deceive." "Over its career," Geertz writes, "religion has probably disturbed men as much as it has cheered them; forced them into a head-on, unblinking confrontation of the fact that they are born to trouble as often as it has enabled them to avoid such a confrontation. . . . there are few if any religious traditions, 'great' or 'little,' in which the proposition that life hurts is not strenuously affirmed and in some it is virtually glorified." [68]

Religion, seen from this perspective, shows men not how to eliminate suffering, but how to suffer. It does not give them final knowledge; it shows them how, through faith, to deal with the inadequacies of knowledge. It does not promise justice, but affirms that injustice is not the central fact. This point of view, however, must be qualified in two ways. It is much more descriptive of the thought and feeling of religious virtuosi and of the intensive systems they develop than of the average man. Malinowski's interpretation may be closer to the religious life of most laymen. Secondly, even those religious forms within which tragedy is viewed unblinkingly contain in their design the promise of an *ultimate* victory—escape from the wheel of rebirth, nirvana, paradise.

Geertz, indeed, comes back part way toward Malinowski, in my judgment, and accepts at least the second of the qualifications I have made, when he writes:

The effort is not to deny the undeniable—that there are unexplained events, that life hurts, or that rain falls upon the just—but to deny that there are inexplicable events, that life is unendurable, and that justice is a mirage. . . . What is important, to a religious man at least, is that this elusiveness be accounted for, that it be not the result of the fact that there are no such principles, explanations, or forms or that life is absurd and the attempt to make moral, intellectual or emotional sense out of experience is bootless.[69]

In summary of the theme of this chapter and the previous one, then, religion lives in tension between two forces. On one side, the tragedy of the human condition presses it toward a magical utilitarianism, toward a man-made and therefore partial moral code, and toward a cognitive system that explains the world to man in terms of existing or traditional knowledge. On the other side, the failures of efforts to deal with suffering, injustice, and ignorance leave men unprotected. If religion is tied closely to empirical systems of magic, ethics, and thought, it will fail when they fail. There is pressure, therefore, to formulate some "ultimate solution," more abstract, less ephemeral, and in the last analysis, "beyond tragedy."

---

68 See Geertz, op. cit., pp. 17–18.

69 Ibid., pp. 23–24.

Chapter Five

A FIELD THEORY OF RELIGION

In Chapter One we noted, in a definitional sense, the field approach to the study of religion. Now we shall examine that approach with greater care, giving particular attention to its relationship to functional and conflict models of society. Our aim is to contribute as fully as our understanding permits to the development of a general theory of religion, one that is capable of dealing with the cultural, structural, and character elements in religious behavior and with their interaction. There is a close connection, of course, between the problems of definition, which have been our main concern so far, and the development of a theory. The task of definition and the task of stating a systematic theory must, indeed, be carried on together.

We need scarcely point out that no one approach to the examination of religion is adequate for all purposes. Every approach starts from assumptions that are neither demonstrable nor provable. A scientist starts from the point of view that something interesting and useful (for the tasks of science) can be said about religion if one assumes that it is part of the world of nature, subject to the laws of causation, and capable of analysis according to the methods of science. The adequacy of his statement is to be judged by its contribution to the systematic analysis of observations of an empirical, objective sort, and by the degree to which it aids further such observations. Persons asking theological, aesthetic, or moral questions may find the scientific statements irrelevant (or perhaps impudent). This need not be the case, however, if they do not attempt to use those statements for purposes of nonscientific investigations. It is equally incumbent on the scientist to avoid "intellectual imperialism": he should not mistake his theories for a theology, a philosophy, an ethical, or an aesthetic study of religion.

Scientific theories are frequently confused with philosophies of religion, with which, indeed, they have much in common. Yet it is well to recognize the differences. Philosophies of religion are usually specific expressions of a general philosophy—attempts to study reality as a whole, as well as to isolate its basic categories or structure. Philosophical observations may derive from intuition, revelation, logic, observation, and other modes of cognitive response to experience, for philosophy is not sharply limited in methodology, as science is. These two facts—the tendency toward a theoretical synthesis (not abstraction) and methodological diversity—make the philosophical approach to religion different from the scientific. That does not mean, however, that the scientists can disregard the observations of the philosophers. Indeed to do so is to forego a great wealth of hypotheses, sharp observations, fruitful discussion of concepts, and theoretical insights. Awareness of the philosophical quest can also help prevent the scientist from forgetting the nature of his abstraction—and the fact that he *has* abstracted—from a more complicated total reality than his theory can encompass. We shall draw on the philosophers wherever their observations would seem to help us to develop a sociological theory of religion; but we shall not try to develop a philosophy of religion.

We have been using the term *theory* in a broad sense. It is too much to say that what follows is a scientific theory in the sense of a group of inter-related propositions, fully tested by empirical study, pertaining to the inter-action of religious behavior with other phases of social life. Our theory, instead, will combine propositions on several different levels, in the belief that systematic statements are essential at every stage of scientific development. They are efforts to draw together what is known and to guide research that tests and extends the existing generalizations. Propositions will range from what we may call prehypotheses (insightful guesses about the relationship of variables that have not yet been posed in a manner that permits empirical tests), to hypotheses (propositions capable of testing, but not yet sufficiently explored), to statements that have been quite adequately tested by research. We do not know how well the theoretical structure will carry the weight of continuing research and theoretical elaboration. Its adequacy is partly tied to the adequacy of the more general theories in sociology, anthropology, and psychology, of which it is a specific application. Because these more general theories of human behavior have received more adequate testing in their application to other specific questions, however, there is reasonable ground for the belief that this theory will be substantiated as our knowledge of religious behavior grows. Such a theory of religious behavior may help in turn to indicate research necessary for further development of some of the major propositions in contemporary social science.

THEORIES OF THE ORIGIN OF RELIGION

We shall be primarily concerned with the development of a field theory of religion. Our approach is systematic, not historical or biographical. Some attention to the history of theories, however, may help us to reach toward a systematic statement. Perhaps this can be done most effectively by stating briefly some of the theories of the origin of religion, for they indicate the way in which many social scientists first structured their questions about religion. It is now generally agreed, to be sure, that a scientific theory of the origin of religion is impossible. It seems clear that religious beliefs and practices reach back tens of thousands of years in the history of man; and

the story of their origins has to be built out of the flimsiest of archaeological, philological, and anthropological evidence, filled out with psychological
and sociological guesses. These guesses have by no means been fruitless,
however, for the development of a scientific theory of religion. They have
raised a number of fundamental problems, and some of them have posed
theoretical ideas from which valuable leads can be drawn.

The observations of the early scientific students of religion were based
largely on data drawn from living preliterate societies. Although these data
could scarcely support a theory of origins, because these societies had had
religions for thousands of years, and could not solve the problem of "how
religion arose out of a life not religious at all," as T. H. Grafton put it, they
could, as a by-product of their search for origins, throw light on the nature
and variety of religious behavior and on the functions it serves.

A further caution, not always observed by the students of the origin of
religion, is necessary if we are to avoid the misuse of our data. Just as we
need to withhold conclusions concerning religious origins that are drawn
from the study of living societies, so too we need to be cautious not to
assume that the study of preliterate societies is an adequate guide to the
study of modern, complex, and literate societies. A general theory will be
able to explain religion in the whole range of types of societies, but will
indicate also the differences in religion and the variables related to those
differences.

Two Types of Explanation of Religious Origins

In briefest outline, social scientific theories of the origin of religion may be
classified into two types, each with some elements of a field analysis implicit within it or explicitly developed.

Psychological Theories of Origins. This group of theories has two vari-
ants, one emphasizing the cognitive aspects of religion, the need for
an explanation of mysterious and awesome events, the other stressing
emotional sources. The former can be characterized as basically intellectu-
alistic, individualistic, and evolutionary. Religion, according to this interpretation, springs from the efforts of primitive men to explain the
phenomena of dreams, echoes, visions, and above all of death. The key
element in the explanation, in Tylor's famous formulation, is the concept
of the soul. Such a concept gives to "the savage mind" an explanation of
many puzzling bodily and mental conditions—they are the "effects of the
departure of the soul." This animistic view of the world, the basis of
religion in Tylor's view, represents a "fairly consistent and rational primitive philosophy."

This rationalistic conception of religion was easily related to the evolutionary doctrine. If animism is a primitive effort to explain the puzzling
facts of a complicated world, it will undergo step-by-step modification as
man's knowledge of the world increases. Presumably the final result will be
the disappearance of religion when its basic function—explanation—is
taken over by other elements of culture, particularly by science.

It is unnecessary for our purpose to undertake a lengthy critique of this
conception of the origin of religion. It seems obviously inadequate as a
total explanation, although the swing of the pendulum away from such
rationalistic interpretations of human behavior may have traveled too far.

But the failure to explore fully the deep-seated emotional qualities of religion makes the work of Spencer and Tylor seem strangely anachronistic today.

"Let us recall how religion actually operates. Our reaction to the death of a deeply loved friend or relative is not simply one of cognition. We are not satisfied merely with knowing how he died. We want something more satisfying than this cold knowledge. Our emotional equilibrium has been upset, our hopes and desires frustrated. We need, in short, an interpretation in terms of sentiments and values." [1]

The animistic theory of religious origins is inadequate also in its disregard of the social and group elements in religious life. How can one account for the obligatory element in religious belief, and for its continuation in modern life despite the growth in our knowledge of the naturalistic causes of the events on which animism presumably rested? An adequate theory must deal with the social aspects of religion. [2]

The assumption of unilineal evolution has proved to be equally unsatisfactory. It was criticized both by those who, with Lang and Schmidt, believed that conceptions of "high gods" can be found at very early stages in the development of religion, and by those who believed, with Codrington, Marett, and others, that belief in an impersonal supernatural force—*mana* —preceded the appearance of belief in spirits. These criticisms represent an increase in attention to the emotional and to the functional aspects of religion, but they still accept a great deal of the evolutionary approach. A sharper criticism, particularly of the assumption that religion was gradually being destroyed by the evolutionary increase in knowledge, stems from a fully developed functional theory. [3]

The second variant of the individualistic approach to the question of the origin of religion places great emphasis on man's emotional needs. This view is readily translated into a concern for functions and an interest in the sources of the continuing influence of religion, as contrasted with efforts at historical reconstruction. We shall examine this question in a later chapter. Some of the writers, however, use the study of needs as the basis for a theory of the origin of religion as well. In *Totem and Taboo* and elsewhere, for example, Freud develops his version of "the elementary forms of the religious life," to use Durkheim's well-known title. It is a vastly different conception from that of Tylor. In Freud's interpretation, a primeval slaying of the father by the sons, primarily because the tyrannical father had monopolized the females of the horde, and the guilt and repression attendant on this, are the source of totemism. Out of this emerge the later forms of religion and the whole pattern of culture. In Chapter Ten we shall examine the way in which Freud uses the basic Oedipus conflict as the key to his

1 Kingsley Davis, *Human Society*, p. 517.

2 See W. J. Goode, *Religion Among the Primitives*, pp. 243–246.

3 On this whole approach to a theory of the origins of religion and some of the controversy that it generated, see Sir James G. Frazer, *The Golden Bough;* Irving King, *The Development of Religion;* Andrew Lang, *The Making of Religion* and *Magic and Religion;* R. R. Marett, *The Threshold of Religion;* P. W. Schmidt, *The Origin and Growth of Religion;* Herbert Spencer, *The Principles of Sociology*, Vol. I; Edward B. Tylor, *Primitive Culture.* E. E. Evans-Pritchard's *Theories of Primitive Religion* is an excellent summary and critique.

theory of the functions of religion. The propositions that he develops in that connection are at least partially subject to testing, as his theory of origins is not.

Paul Radin interprets the origin of religion in a way that ties it closely to a functional theory. He asks, "What is it that originally led man to postulate the supernatural?" To answer this question, we must try to visualize the conditions under which man lived at the dawn of civilization. With wholly inadequate technological preparation, he was helpless before the powerful capricious forces of the environment.

His mentality was still overwhelmingly dominated by definitely animal characteristics although the life-values themselves—the desire for success, for happiness, and for long life—were naturally already present. . . . No economic security could have existed, and we cannot go far wrong in assuming that, where economic security does not exist, emotional insecurity and its correlates, the sense of powerlessness and the feeling of insignificance, are bound to develop. . . .

It is but natural for the psyche, under such circumstances, to take refuge in compensation fantasies . . . the main goal and objective of all his strivings was the canalization of his fears and feelings and the validation of his compensation dreams.[4]

Thus religion springs primarily, according to Radin, from man's emotional responses to a threatening situation.

Sociological Theories of Origins. The second line of argument concerning the origin of religion emphasizes interpersonal sources rather than individualistic ones. Those who take this point of view see religion as primarily a product of social interaction and group life. Once again, since we have no direct interest in a complete survey of origin theories, we shall be content with a brief mention of only a few writers who make social factors the focus of their attention. These ideas are also easily transposed into functional terms, without attention to the question of historical origins at all. Simmel, in fact, who emphasizes the human-relations source of religion, indicates that he is not trying to describe the historical origin, but what he calls its "psychological origin," as one of many sources. And Durkheim is primarily important not for his speculations about origin but for his functional analysis.

Simmel develops the thesis that one of the sources of religion is human relations which themselves are nonreligious. "I do not believe that the religious feelings and impulses manifest themselves in religion only. . . ."[5] Religion is the heightening and abstracting from their particular content of certain human relations—of exaltation, devotion, fervency, and the like— that are found widely in social life. Faith, for example, is first of all a relation between individuals; we do not base our relations with others on what we know conclusively about them. "The social role of this faith has never been investigated; but this much is certain, that without it society would disintegrate. . . . In faith in a deity the highest development of faith has become incorporate, so to speak; has been relieved of its connection with

4 Paul Radin, *Primitive Religion, Its Nature and Origin*, pp. 6–9.

5 Georg Simmel, "A Contribution to the Sociology of Religion," *American Journal of Sociology*, November, 1905, p. 360.

its social counterpart." [6] Thus, in Simmel's view, religion is an outgrowth of human relations.

Noting the persistence of religious faith despite three centuries of growing scientific predominance, Reinhold Niebuhr and Erik Erikson both take a position similar to Simmel's: Faith is first of all a product of the trust a child learns from loving parents. Religion raises that trust to a social principle that helps man deal with all the tragedies and incongruities of life.[7]

Durkheim's emphasis on the social origin of religion is more extreme than that of Simmel. For Durkheim, society is the object of religious veneration and the basic source of "the sacred." The primary function of religion is the preservation of social unity. "So everything leads us back to this same idea: before all, rites are means by which the social group reaffirms itself periodically." [8] Thus he calls attention to aspects of religion that had previously been given inadequate attention—rite, cult organization, and its relationship to the social structure. It is in such a context that he interprets totemic cults, which he considers "the elementary forms of the religious life."

From this, we may be able to reconstruct hypothetically the way in which the totemic cult should have arisen originally. Men who feel themselves united, partially by bonds of blood, but still more by a community of interest and tradition, assemble and become conscious of their moral unity . . . they are led to represent this unity in the form of a very special kind of consubstantiality: they think of themselves as all participating in the nature of some determined animal. Under these circumstances, there is only one way for them to affirm their collective existence: this is to affirm that they are like the animals of this species, and to do so not only in the silence of their own thoughts, but also by material acts.[9]

Meyer Fortes makes skillful use of the Durkheimian perspective in his interpretation of West African religion. The basic religious institution of the Tallensi is an ancestor cult. It cannot be accounted for by belief in immortality of the soul or by fear of ancestors, origins Frazer might have given, for neither is found among the Tallensi. They have an ancestor cult, Fortes writes, "because their social structure demands it." "It is the religious counterpart of their social order, hallowing it, investing it with a value that transcends mundane interests. . . . The ancestor cult is the transposition to the religious plane of the relationships of parents and children; and that is what I mean by describing it as the ritualization of filial piety." [10]

Although adopting something of Durkheim's point of view, Fortes is dealing with religious processes, not religious origins. The importance of Durkheim's theory, in fact, does not rest on its interpretation of origins, which are beyond demonstration. It is significant because of the attention it focuses on the group aspects of religion. Like the individualistic theories, it

6 Ibid., pp. 366–367.

7 See *The Religious Situation*, Donald Cutler, ed., pp. ix–xv and 711–733.

8 Emile Durkheim, *The Elementary Forms of the Religious Life*, p. 387.

9 Ibid.

10 Meyer Fortes, *Oedipus and Job in West African Religion*, pp. 29–30.

is basically a functional theory, not an explanation of origins in the historical sense. When they are put together, exposing their mutual exaggerations, they form the basis for a contemporary interpretation.

Before attempting this integration, let me call attention briefly to a different approach to the study of religious origins, an approach less likely to be a covert interpretation of continuing religious sources and more likely to examine actual historical relationships. I refer to studies of the origins of particular religious ideas. Students of the Mediterranean area, for example, have argued that the development of monotheism may be accounted for by reference to all-powerful monarchs and the irrigation systems developed under their rule.[11] Although direct causal relationships are clearly impossible to establish, some authors do not hesitate to assert them. Weber, for example, writes: ". . . the personal, transcendental and ethical god is a Near-Eastern concept. It corresponds so closely to that of an all-powerful mundane king with his rational bureaucratic regime that a causal connection can scarcely be overlooked."[12] Swanson has submitted this kind of proposition to a much sterner empirical test by examining fifty representative societies. Following Durkheim's lead, he asks whether in these societies the beliefs about God and the supernatural are related, in consistent ways, to aspects of their social structures. One of his major conclusions is that monotheism occurs most commonly in those societies where at least three levels of fairly independent or sovereign groups (such as family, clan, and tribe) are found, each with distinguishable areas of power. Swanson is well aware that his multivariate survey design requires great caution in imputing a causal connection between complexity of social structure and presence of monotheistic beliefs. In going beyond the case-study method, however, he adds strength to such a hypothesis.[13]

FROM A SEARCH FOR ORIGINS TO A SEARCH FOR CAUSES

As this brief review of some of the efforts to describe the origins of religion may indicate, they are more likely to be a search for causes than statements of the historical sequence. Although intriguing pieces of the picture can be reconstructed, the story of origins is probably lost, even to the most intensive archaeological and historical study. What we see before us in the archaeological, historical, and contemporary records are hints concerning the *continuing* sources of religion in the lives of individuals and in group processes. We cannot, in any strictly causal sense, say that religion emerged, along with many other patterns of behavior, from the interaction of these individual and group forces, which, being in existence before religion, may properly be studied as possible causes of it. In other words, it seems useless to posit some prereligious state of man in an effort to establish a temporal sequence that would permit causal inferences regarding the origin of religion. Small-scale causal series involving particular religious forms can be analyzed; but for a general theory, it is more plausible

11 James Breasted, *The Dawn of Conscience;* Henri Frankfort, *Ancient Egyptian Religion.*

12 Max Weber, *The Sociology of Religion*, p. 56.

13 See G. E. Swanson, *The Birth of the Gods: The Origin of Primitive Beliefs.*

to think of the sociocultural and individual forces as emerging *with* religion. To visualize the interactions, however, we can picture religion as an intervening variable in a continuous process (Figure 5–1).

A strictly causal interpretation treats religion either as the dependent variable, produced by some combination of the forces mentioned in column L, or as an independent variable, which produces various individual and group effects.[14] Typically, in the area of our interest, students have cut into the process at point M, as compared with theories of origin or, in recent years, more standard causal theories, which have cut in at point L. (It is no doubt apparent that I have used middle-of-the-alphabet designations to indicate that in a sense each approach "begins in the middle.")

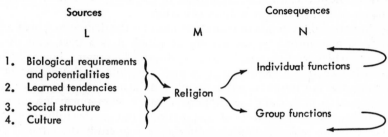

FIGURE 5–1. *The field context of religion*

Functional theories, insofar as they are causal theories, are based on more complicated models. The most sophisticated versions deal with causal *processes,* in which consequences feed back into the system out of which they came, modifying them in various ways. Lest there be any doubt about it, let me state here, in advance of the fuller discussion to follow, that functional theory is, or can be, a causal theory in a completely naturalistic, non-teleological sense. There has been a great deal of confusion on this point in recent years, caused perhaps equally by careless statements made by those adopting functional explanations and by lack of methodological and theoretical subtlety on the part of some of the critics of functionalism. Those functional statements with which we shall be concerned are not, for the most part, of the simple mathematical variety that X varies with Y. These may be interesting starting points for analysis; but until various causal loops are described, functional explanation is not very powerful.

Field Theory and Functional Theory. I have given this chapter the heading, "A Field Theory of Religion." A fully developed and carefully stated functional approach is harmonious with a field approach and in some usages nearly synonymous with it. I shall use the language of functionalism in connection with some problems. There are several advantages, however, in using the more inclusive field theory as our basic point of reference:

14 For the most part, I will combine levels (1) and (2), and frequently levels (3) and (4). Although some information is lost in this way, there is some gain in clarity. On this question of condensation of levels, see J. Milton Yinger, *Toward a Field Theory of Behavior,* Chap. 2.

1. It more readily combines attention to individual and group elements, to part-whole relationships, thus reducing such disagreements as those between Malinowski and Radcliffe-Brown, which we have commented on. Because in field theory individual and situation cannot even be defined fully, independently of each other, there is no chance that their mutual influences will be disregarded.

2. A field approach can use both one-directional and feedback causal models, as contrasted with an emphasis on the latter in functional theory. In this I disagree with Kingsley Davis, who sees functionalism, if anything, as simply another name for sociological theory in general.[15] I see it as the study of those particular patterns of behavior where system qualities and feedback processes are involved. The more "standard" cause-effect processes, however, are also important, in the study of religion as in other branches of the science of human behavior.

3. Functionalism tends to focus attention on the degree to which a given pattern is determined by the system of which it is a part, and then the degree to which that pattern helps to maintain the system. Logically, attention to the *degree* of mainenance is also attention to the degree of non-maintenance, but in practice this double emphasis is not easy to sustain. A field approach makes no assumptions about system normalcy, and is as prepared to study the effects of disjunctions among the influences of the social structure, culture, and character as it is to study the effects of their conjunction.[16] It therefore incorporates attention to change and to intra-individual, inter-individual, intragroup and intergroup conflict more readily.

The Need for Combining Functional and Conflict Theories. This last point requires further examination. What is functional for one unit, seen as a system, may be dysfunctional for a larger or smaller unit to which the first is related.[17] Shifts in our perspective, therefore, may focus attention on conflict or on integration. "A way of seeing is always a way of not seeing." [18] Realizing this, we need at least to treat functional and conflict elements as, alternately, figure and ground. Looking at the same design, one person may see a goblet, united into one piece; the other sees two faces frowning at each other. Functional theory tends to minimize attention to conflict and to handle changes in a system with difficulty, although when properly qualified it can avoid these problems. Conflict theory tends to overlook reciprocity and to handle the very fact of society with difficulty, although when carefully stated it can leave room for integration.

15 Kingsley Davis, "The Myth of Functional Analysis as a Special Method in Sociology and Anthropology," *American Sociological Review*, 24, 1959, pp. 752–772.

16 For a penetrating examination of the effects of such disjunction, see Clifford Geertz, "Ritual and Social Change: A Javanese Example," *American Anthropologist*, 59, 1957, pp. 23–54.

17 For valuable statements of the part-whole problem in functional theory, see N. J. Demerath, III, "Synecdoche and Structuralism-Functionalism," *Social Forces*, 44, 1966, pp. 390–401; Alvin Gouldner, "Reciprocity and Autonomy in Functional Theory," in *Symposium on Sociological Theory*, Llewellyn Gross, ed., pp. 241–270; Pierre L. van den Berghe, "Dialectic and Functionalism: Toward a Theoretical Synthesis," *American Sociological Review*, 28, 1963, pp. 695–705; and George E. Simpson, *The Shango Cult in Trinidad*, esp. p. 129.

18 Kenneth Burke, *Permanence and Change*, p. 70.

It is not enough, however, that we try to reduce these problems by viewing society alternately as an integrated system and a coercion system. An adequate view of society, and of its parts, will see function and conflict together.[19] They are not opposites. If we shift from the examination of a highly integrated system to study of some larger system of which it is a part, we may discover that the very fact of its internal integration helps to account for conflict in the larger unit. On the other hand, conflict that under some circumstances breaks a group apart may, in a different situation, serve adaptive and even integrative functions. Some kinds of conflict, often those most visible and with definable limits, may serve to prevent other kinds of conflict wherein the goals are unspecified and the limits unknown. Among the functions of religious conflict may be the focusing of attention on critical problems, promoting adaptation of a social system to changed circumstances, or the support of religious development itself. Conflict is often not functional for a given system, however, and it is important not to blur the distinction between integration and disruption even as we study their interdependence.

We need to be alert to both integration and conflict in small-scale interpersonal relationships as well as in large-scale, institutional contexts. Because the former are less likely to be underlined by ideology and ritual they are less visible to us. We tend to take daily occurrences of mutual adjustment and of conflict for granted until they are pointed out by perceptive observers. An intricate and subtle network of understandings and expectations affects even our fleeting encounters and temporary gatherings, so vividly described by Erving Goffman. We demonstrate that we are members of society in good standing by the way we ride an elevator, greet a friend, or overlook a mistake. We stand at "civil inattention" while unavoidably overhearing a personal conversation.[20]

These patterns are based on the nearly universal desire for social order. They serve to maintain that order, to reinforce its more formal structure. From another perspective, however, they are experienced as coercive. In heterogeneous societies and those experiencing rapid change, many individuals may be poorly socialized to these subtle norms. They protest, not only against the major constraints of the institutional, bureaucratic order, but also against the patterns of etiquette, the rules of deference and civility of polite society. In one way or another they join in the early morning shout of the man in Herb Gardner's play, *A Thousand Clowns*: "O.K., all you rich people. Everybody out for volleyball."

Thus the polite order of integration is sometimes experienced as coercive. There is also a more direct and continuous element of conflict and competition in interpersonal relationships. I refer not only to the obvious hostilities, but to those latent forms of self-seeking that are disguised by symbols of civility. Matching Goffman's keen observations of the informal understandings that smooth social interaction are other observers' descriptions of small-scale coercions and competitions. They may be disguised as

19 I will examine the problem of bringing functional and conflict theories together more fully in the next chapter.

20 See, for example, Erving Goffman's *Presentation of Self in Everyday Life, Encounters,* and *Behavior in Public Places.*

etiquette or play, but they nonetheless express tension and conflict.[21]

The importance of religion for integration and conflict is usually examined with reference to major institutional processes. We will be wise, however, to be alert also to the ways in which it enters into small-scale interpersonal relationships, smoothing our encounters or serving as an instrument of coercion in them.

It is difficult, in the study of religion, to maintain consistent attention to both conflict and integration. There is little by way of research based on a conflict perspective. Marxism has yielded numerous ideological statements, but little by way of objective study.[22] In the West, most intellectuals seem to alternate between a vague feeling that religion lends some support to brotherhood and equally vague notions that it is irrelevant. In this context one finds support for an imprecise functionalism, which we might illustrate by paraphrasing a well-known statement of Davis and Moore in a paper [23] on stratification: Sects are thus unconsciously evolved devices by which societies insure that deprived individuals will carry their burdens with maximum grace while acquiring motives and skills necessary to lessen those burdens. I would not want so much to argue against this statement— indeed, I think it contains a great deal of truth—as to place it in a larger context by noting two qualifications. First, the statement cannot be used as a direct explanation of the causes of sects. Their causes are to be found among the cultural, structural, and character conditions that preceded them. Once created, to be sure, these groups and movements have certain consequences that may *reinforce* the causes. As we shall note in the next section, an effect, through conscious or unconscious learning or through social selection, may lead to increased support for the pattern that produced that effect. Functionalism may short-circuit this full explanation; but carefully framed it can, instead, be a shorthand statement of it. Second, other statements about the consequences of sects are also needed, including statements about their conflict-producing potential, along with descriptions of possible feedback of those consequences for the system out of which they came. This is done in an intriguing way by Kai Erikson, in his discussion of conflict between the dominant Puritan church (and political leadership) and the antinomian and Quaker groups in seventeenth-century Massachusetts. There was bitter controversy; but the deviant groups also served to define the limits for a rapidly changing social situation. Thus, in Erikson's interpretation, the deviant groups were needed; they performed an important functon; but they were also sources of conflict.[24]

A theory adequate for our needs will see the patterns under study as consequences *of* the system as well as examining their consequences *for*

21 See, for example, Thorstein Veblen, *Theory of the Leisure Class;* and Eric Berne, *Games People Play.*

22 There may be some small reason for optimism in the reports on two conferences held in Eastern Europe in 1965 anod 1966. See Olaf Klohr, ed., *Religion und Atheism heute. Ergebnisse und Aufgaben marxistischer Religionssoziologie;* and the chapters by Max Stackhouse and Norman Birnbaum in *The Religious Situation: 1968,* Donald Cutler, ed., pp. 887–930.

23 Kingsley Davis and Wilbert Moore, "Some Principles of Stratification," *American Sociological Review,* 10, 1945, pp. 242–249.

24 See Kai Erikson, *Wayward Puritans.*

the system. A good rule, in order to avoid misstating the functionalist type of causal sequence, is to look outward to the larger system for the sources (in our instance, of religious phenomena) before looking beyond one's interest for consequences, particularly for those that support the causal process. In looking outward, moreover, we will be wise to seek for separate indicators of structural, cultural, and character elements in the system. Research into religious change that is guided by field theory will examine, for example, new patterns of interaction created by industrialization, new values emerging from affluence or added by diffusion from one group to another, and new motives resulting from instabilities in socialization. A religious movement may begin in a situation described in these terms; it will have certain functions; these functions may help to determine whether the movement will grow or decline, and thus they will be part of the causal circuit in which they are embedded.

THE NATURE OF FUNCTIONAL ANALYSIS

In light of its importance in studies of religion and the strength of the controversy surrounding its use, I shall examine functional theory rather fully. In the next chapter, I shall discuss its weaknesses in connection with a discussion of conflict theory.[25]

Functional investigation focuses on those intrasystem processes in which a product of the system helps to maintain it by reducing or eliminating otherwise destructive processes. Or perhaps it would be better to say that functional investigation is a study of *the degree to which* a product of the system serves to maintain it, full attention being paid to the balance of support and costs.

Assumptions and propositions concerning the consequences of religion for societies and individuals were implicit in much of the earlier work devoted to the study of origins. It is the virtue of more recent studies, however, that they have made the functional question explicit, thus being able to use it more effectively while at the same time pointing up its limitations and its hidden assumptions. As Kingsley Davis has pointed out, social theory has often been inadequate to interpret religion, because it has asked the wrong, or the relatively less important, questions. Viewing religion primarily from a cognitive standpoint, it has asked, "Do religious ideas represent reality?" This leads to questions concerning the nature of reality and the reasons for any errors that religious beliefs may be said to contain. There is value in this approach but there is also a great weakness, for it tends to reduce religion to a system of beliefs or statements of purported facts.[26] Whether religious ideas are true or not hinges on one's definition of the truth, and hence becomes a metaphysical rather than a scientific problem. The virtue of functional analysis is that it avoids the metaphysical debate (which, for problems other than those of empirical study, may be an important one) and states instead: Religious beliefs and

25 The literature on functionalism is massive. See the end of this chapter for a bibliographical appendix of works that explicate or criticize functional theory from a variety of points of view.

26 See Kingsley Davis, *Introduction to Goode*, op. cit.

practices do exist; they have consequences for human behavior. How are they used?

A functional interpretation rests upon several related ideas. Perhaps most important is the conception, discussed briefly in Chapter One, that societies are systems of interdependent parts. The religious patterns, therefore, cannot be understood in isolation from the whole structure in which they are embedded. For example, Fortes and Evans-Pritchard, in their discussion of African political systems, describe the ways in which religious symbols, rites, dogmas, and sacred places unify the social systems of which they are a part. They give each whole system a mystical value that promotes acceptance far beyond the obedience that the secular sanctions could bring.

The social system is, as it were, removed to a mystical plane, where it figures as a system of social values beyond criticism or revision. . . . The African sees these ritual observances as the supreme safeguard of the basic needs of his existence and of the basic relations that make up his social order—land, cattle, rain, bodily health, the family, the clan, the state. . . . Periodical ceremonies are necessary to affirm and consolidate these values because, in the ordinary course of events, people are pre-occupied with sectional and private interests and are apt to lose sight of the common interest and of their political interdependence.[27]

Closely linked to the concept of system is the proposition that there are some "invariant points of reference," in the nature of man as a biological type, in his psychology, in the structure of social systems, and so on, which pose certain necessary conditions for the existence of any society. These are perhaps best stated in the form of questions, to indicate the tentative quality of many of the propositions: What is the significance of man's biological patterns—the long infancy, the length of the life span, the relative lack of "instinctual" responses, and the like—for human interaction? Are there panhuman responses to extreme stress and frustration that are manifest in every social system? Do groups as such have basic isolable properties that set limits to the kinds of developments possible in a society? Do these lead to certain "functional prerequisites" in all societies, to patterns that are essential for the very existence of a society? [28]

To some degree, these concepts are in opposition to the extreme relativism that characterized earlier anthropology and sociology. They do not deny the wide variation in specific cultural content, but regard many of the specific forms as alternative ways of meeting functionally similar requirements of social life. The earlier point of view, supported by the impressive range of culture (and also by a methodology that emphasized intensive

27 M. J. Fortes and E. Evans-Pritchard, *African Political Systems*, p. 16 ff. Fruitful use of the system concept in studies of religion is widespread, particularly in anthropological research. See, for example, Susan Tax Freeman, "Religious Aspects of the Social Organization of a Castilian Village," *American Anthropologist*, 70, 1968, pp. 34–49; and Roy Rappaport, "Ritual Regulation of Environmental Relations among a New Guinea People," *Ethnology*, 6, 1967, pp. 17–30.

28 See the excellent discussion by Clyde Kluckhohn in *Anthropology Today*, A. L. Kroeber, ed., pp. 507–523. This whole question is treated with the greatest care by Talcott Parsons in several works. See also David Aberle and others, "The Functional Prerequisites of Society," *Ethics*, 60, 1950, pp. 100–111.

study of separate societies) saw man as almost infinitely inventive in cultural matters. All categories of culture were regarded as artificial and unduly constrictive. The concept of functional prerequisites, however, states that there are a limited number of necessities for social life. Since these necessities must be satisfied, inventiveness is more in manner than in substance. Walter Goldschmidt points out, for example, that food-sharing practices are universal among hunters and gatherers. The mechanisms of sharing—institutionalized generosity, kinship obligations, and the like— vary widely. Were we to study societies singly or observe only the variation, we would miss the universal element. He calls, therefore, for a comparative functionalism.[29]

In What Sense Are Functional Statements Causal Statements?

Although problems connected with the concepts of system and functional prerequisites have been commented on frequently, it is a third element in functional theory that has proved most controversial. This is the proposition, implied or directly stated, that a system exists because of what it does —that in a sense it has been caused by its own consequences. We need to examine this proposition with care. It is in a special sense that functions may be interpreted as part of a causal sequence. When the nature of this sequence has not been carefully stated, functional theorists have blurred the distinction between direct and functional causation, and critics have been unnecessarily sweeping in their condemnation. It is necessary, in the beginning, to distinguish among structural causes, purposes or goals (individual causes), and consequences or functions. There are intricate linkages among them, but because these linkages can be of many varieties, they require careful specification.

It is clear that a simple two-step, one-direction causal sequence, of the form A → X → C (cause A results in situation X which has certain consequences, C) has no room for functional interpretations. If one studies only the sequence given, there is no sense in which it can be said that C causes or influences the level of A or the continuation of X. We can call this sequence an *event-unit*. Frequently, however, we are interested in an ongoing *event-process*. Having been caused, C enters a field in which A is still operative. It can enhance, retard, or deflect A; it can help to sustain or to change situation X.

Perhaps an illustration outside the field of religion can help us to clarify the operation of a functional-causal sequence. In 1924 the United States Congress passed an immigration law; it was slightly revised in 1952; and then more drastically changed in 1965. Without attempting a full argument (the validity of my interpretation of immigration policy is probably not crucial here), let me state that among the causes of the 1924 Act were these: the tensions of World War I, the closing of the frontier, the large number of immigrants entering the country between 1880 and 1910, cultural contrasts between the new immigrants and the native-born popula-

29 Walter Goldschmidt, *Comparative Functionalism: An Essay in Anthropological Theory*. I shall examine some of the problems associated with the concept of functional prerequisites in the next chapter.

tion, religious prejudice, racialist views based on extrapolation of evolutionary and other biological theories, the dismay of some New England aristocrats at being overrun by newcomers, and economic insecurity. These sociocultural causes were refracted through the purposes and motives of the members of the Congress and their constituents. These purposes and motives were partly shaped by the causes, but came also from other sources, ranging from deep-seated values to desire for re-election (these might in some cases be identical). Figure 5–2 shows how structural forces (A) and character forces (B) combined to produce the 1924 law (X).

Many consequences (C) flowed from the law, some of them directly in line with the stated purposes (manifest functions) and some quite unexpected (latent); some contributed to the health of the society, some injured it, and some had mixed effects. Immigration from the quota countries was reduced from about 500,000 to about 100,000 a year—a manifest consequence. The proportion from Northwest Europe increased, also as planned. On the other hand, there were several unintended effects. International relations with countries of the Far East, particularly Japan, were worsened; the 1929 depression may have been made more intense; migration from Mexico and Puerto Rico increased; and Negro migration out of the South became a flood, probably speeding up the appearance of desegregation and the civil rights movement.

Now immigration policy, as contrasted with the immigration law of 1924, is an event-process, not an event-unit. (When we speak of religion, it should be noted, we almost always have an event-process in mind.) Consequently we need to examine the ways in which it fed back into the system from which it came. The process can be described in a schematic way (Figure 5–2).

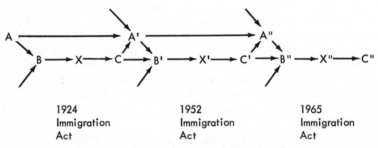

FIGURE 5–2. *Developmental functionalism*

The consequences of the 1924 Act (C) in no way caused that Act (X). The consequences did, however, influence some of the ongoing causes that shaped immigration policy, as shown by the diagonal arrow running from C to A'. Other forces also bore upon A'—continuing influences from A and new forces (the other diagonal arrow). C also influenced the purposes and motives of individuals (C → B'), which were affected as well by forces from A' and from other sources (the two diagonal arrows pointing toward B'). Out of this complex of forces came the 1952 Act, X'. Some of its consequences (e.g., a small increase in immigration from Asia and Africa, without the dire consequences implied for such immigration in the 1924 Act) affected the sociocultural environment and the goals and purposes of individuals (A″ and B″), from which further developments in immigration policy took place, culminating in the 1965 Act, X″. Thus the later manifestations of a developing immigration policy have been partly caused by the consequences of earlier manifestations.

Functional explanations of this type are appropriate when one is interested in developmental processes, rather than in unitary cause-effect sequences. If one thinks of a religion as having been founded at a particular time, or defines it in static terms, then its functions cannot be seen as causes of its development. Viewed as an ongoing series of events, however, a religion can appropriately be interpreted as being partly a product of its functions. It is what it is now partly because of what it has done in the past.

In addition to this sequential model, there is a much tighter sense in which a functional-causal model is appropriate. In time, let us say at the time of X″ in Figure 5–2, a causal pattern may become relatively stabilized. It has become what it is partly because of what it has done. And it goes on because of what it continues to do. Had it not had certain consequences, it would not have been modified and then established as a system. In another form, the original cause is not changed as it becomes established; it is selected, from among various competing patterns, because of the functions it performed. Or, in psychological terms, the pattern is reinforced because of its consequences. These consequences do not need to be understood in order to be rewarding and therefore reinforced. Or they may be understood by some, who promote the learning process and help to establish the pattern in culture. In all of these cases, had this particular pattern not had these effects, another pattern would have been selected and reinforced. We can express these relationships in diagrammatic terms (Figure 5–3).

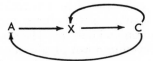

FIGURE 5–3. *A feedback model of functional analysis*

Pattern X did not come about originally because of what it produced; but it survived and exists in the current situation partly because of its consequences. This is indicated by the arrow running from C back to X. Indeed, the original causes, which are the individual needs and tendencies and the social sources of religion, signified by A in Figure 5–3, may also be affected by the consequences of a pattern produced by those causes. Thus we have an arrow running from C back to A. Religion and its consequences are not only a result of human need, they partly cause human need. Even biological causes are modified by their own effects: a consequence that gives adaptive advantage selects those most capable of it. Culture did not develop solely because of man's inherited intelligence; but his inherited intelligence has grown because he was cultural.[30]

30 See, for example, J. N. Spuhler, ed., *The Evolution of Man's Capacity for Culture;* and S. L. Washburn and F. C. Howell, "Human Evolution and Culture," in *The Evolution of Man,* Sol Tax, ed., pp. 33–56.

In my view, these evolutionary and cybernetic models of causation are naturalistic and non-teleological. They may employ, to be sure, such concepts as those of goal-directed behavior, memory, and other selective processes within the individual as parts of causal cycles. Critics of functionalism are sometimes given to mechanical analogies that hide as much as they inform because they disregard these aspects of human behavior. Thus Ernest Nagel writes: "It would surely be an oddity on the part of a modern physicist were he to declare, for example, that atoms have outer shells of electrons in order to make chemical unions between themselves and other atoms possible." [31] Without getting into the debate over behaviorism, I think it can be stated that human beings remember, plan, and evaluate, as atoms do not. These processes have to be taken into account in purely naturalistic description of cycles of causation.

As Nagel himself noted in another place, there is a difference between systems with self-maintaining processes vis-à-vis the environment and those without such processes. The temperature of a physical object, for example, will fluctuate with the temperature of its environment; but an organism with homeostatic capabilities can maintain a constant temperature despite rather wide variation in the environment.[32]

A related way to describe this difference is the contrast between open and closed systems. In the latter, the final state of the system is the inevitable product of the original conditions. This is not true of open systems, however, due to the operation of what Ludwig von Bertalanffy has called the principle of equifinality. Because there is interaction between the system and its environment, "the same final state may be reached from different initial conditions and in different ways." [33] How a cluster of cells will develop, for example, is not determined by their internal properties alone, but also by the tissues that surround them, the levels of various nutriments available to them, and the like. The final result is a product of a transaction between the cells and their environment.[34] The contrast between open and closed systems is sometimes expressed in terms of the differences between evolution and entropy. The second principle of thermodynamics describes the leveling down of differences, but the principle of evolution describes development and growth, perhaps "towards states of increased order and organization," because of the import of material high in free energy.[35]

Functional theory, then, deals with open systems, with evolution, with the study of transactions between a consequence and the cluster of conditions out of which it emerged. To judge it by reference to a mechanical cause-effect model is to disregard important developments in contemporary science.

31 Ernest Nagel, *The Structure of Science*, p. 401.

32 See Nagel's *Logic Without Metaphysics*, p. 251.

33 Ludwig von Bertalanffy, in *System, Change, and Conflict*, N. J. Demerath, III and Richard A. Peterson, eds., p. 121.

34 I have developed this concept by use of the phrase "the principle of multiple possibilities." See *Toward a Field Theory of Behavior*, especially pp. 43–45.

35 See Bertalanffy, op. cit., p. 122.

BIBLIOGRAPHICAL APPENDIX ON FUNCTIONALISM

The reader interested in examining further the issues regarding functionalism that are raised in this chapter and the next will find the following titles of value. I cite here only fairly recent criticisms and explications.

Gabriel Almond and James Coleman, *The Politics of Developing Areas,* pp. 3–64; Max Black, ed., *The Social Theories of Talcott Parsons;* Harry Bredemeier, "The Methodology of Functionalism," *American Sociological Review,* 20, April, 1955, pp. 173–180; Walter Buckley, ed., *Modern Systems Research for the Behavioral Scientist;* Walter Buckley, *Sociology and Modern Systems Theory;* William Catton, Jr., *From Animistic to Naturalistic Sociology,* Chap. 3; Ralf Dahrendorf, *Class and Class Conflict in Industrial Society;* Ralf Dahrendorf, "Out of Utopia: Toward a Reorientation of Sociological Analysis," *American Journal of Sociology,* 64, 1958, pp. 115–127; Kingsley Davis, "The Myth of Functional Analysis as a Special Method in Sociology and Anthropology," *American Sociological Review,* 24, 1959, pp. 752–772; N. J. Demerath, III, "Synecdoche and Structuralism-Functionalism," *Social Forces,* 44, 1966, pp. 390–401; N. J. Demerath, III and Richard Peterson, eds., *System, Change, and Conflict;* Allan Eister, "Religious Institutions in Complex Societies: Difficulties in the Theoretic Specification of Functions," *American Sociological Review,* 22, 1957, pp. 387–391; Walter Goldschmidt, *Comparative Functionalism: An Essay in Anthropological Theory;* James Gregor, "Political Science and the Use of Functional Analysis," *American Political Science Review,* 62, 1968, pp. 425–439; Alvin Gouldner, "Reciprocity and Autonomy in Functional Theory," and Carl Hempel, "The Logic of Functional Analysis," both in *Symposium on Sociological Theory,* Llewellyn Gross, ed., pp. 241–270 and 271–310; George Homans, "Bringing Men Back In," *American Sociological Review,* 29, 1964, pp. 809–815; George Homans, *The Human Group;* Clyde Kluckhohn, *Navaho Witchcraft;* Marion Levy, Jr., *The Structure of Society;* John G. Kennedy, "Mushahara: A Nubian Concept of Supernatural Danger and the Theory of Taboo," *American Anthropologist,* 69, 1967, pp. 685–702; David Lockwood, "Some Remarks on the 'Social System,' " *British Journal of Sociology,* 7, 1956, pp. 134–146; Don Martindale, ed., *Functionalism in the Social Sciences;* Don Martindale, *The Nature and Types of Sociological Theory,* Pt. Six; Robert Merton, *Social Theory and Social Structure,* rev. ed., pp. 19–84; C. Wright Mills, *The Sociological Imagination,* pp. 25–49; S. F. Nadel, *The Theory of Social Structure;* Ernest Nagel, *Logic Without Metaphysics,* pp. 247–283; Ernest Nagel, *The Structure of Science,* pp. 520–535; Talcott Parsons, *The Social System;* Talcott Parsons and Edward A. Shils, *Toward a General Theory of Action;* Talcot Parsons, Robert F. Bales, and Edward A. Shils, *Working Papers in the Theory of Action;* Talcott Parsons in *Theories of Society,* Talcott Parsons, Edward A. Shils, Kaspar Naegele, and Jesse Pitts, eds., pp. 30–79; A. R. Radcliffe-Brown, *Structure and Function in Primitive Society;* Louis Schneider, "The Role of the Category of Ignorance in Sociological Theory: An Exploratory Statement," *American Sociological Review,* 27, 1962, pp. 492–508; M. E. Spiro, "Religion; Problems of Definition and Explanation," in *Anthropological Approaches to the Study of Religion,* Michael Banton, ed., pp. 85–126; Pierre L. van den Berghe, "Dialectic and Functionalism: Toward a Theoretical Synthesis," *American Sociological Review,* 28, 1963, pp. 695–705; Anthony Wallace, *Religion: An Anthropological View.*

Chapter Six

FUNCTIONAL AND CONFLICT MODELS OF SOCIETY:
A Field Perspective

Functionalism, properly qualified, furnishes a valuable perspective to the social analyst. Unfortunately, its potential value is sometimes obscured by careless use and by its transposition from theory into ideology. This is especially likely to occur when functional analysis is not carried on in full awareness of the questions and evidences raised by other approaches to human behavior. Its relationship to conflict theory is particularly instructive in this regard.[1] In this chapter, therefore, I shall examine some of the limits and weaknesses of functional theory, and discuss conflict theory as an alternative perspective. This will lead us back to a problem we raised in Chapter Five: Can we overcome not only the neglect of major elements of human behavior, but the figure-ground alternations that leave us with a succession of partial views?

DIFFICULTIES IN THE FUNCTIONAL APPROACH

We have already examined some of the difficulties associated with functional analysis in our study of its premises and methods. Additional problems, however, should be noted. It is sometimes used to "prove" the ultimate

1 The interactions of functional and conflict interpretations are important in many areas. They have been particularly critical in stratification theory, where the problem of separating ideology from analysis is as difficult as it is in the study of religion. Study of the controversy and the tendencies toward a synthesis can be highly instructive to the student of religion. See, for example, Ralf Dahrendorf, *Class and Class Conflict in Industrial Society;* Kingsley Davis and Wilbert Moore, "Some Principles of Stratification," *American Sociological Review,* 10, 1945, pp. 242–249; Talcott Parsons, "A Revised Analytical Approach to the Theory of Social Stratification," in *Class, Status and Power: A Reader in Social Stratification,* Reinhard Bendix and S. M. Lipset, eds., pp. 92–128; Edward Wiehn, *Theorien der Sozialen Schichtung;* J. Milton Yinger, *A Minority Group in American Society,* chs. 2 and 3. Gerhard Lenski, in *Power and Privilege: A Theory of Social Stratification,* is explicitly concerned with bringing functional and conflict theories together.

validity, or inevitability, or changelessness of some specific practice or belief. These nonempirical statements are unwarranted. Durkheim's famous proposition that social facts cannot be explained by psychological theories might be matched here by the formulation: Do not try to support nonempirical statements (this religious practice is good and true because it is universal) by empirical generalizations (religion is universal). Some people have used Heisenberg's principle of indeterminancy in physics to support theological ideas. Others have jumped, reluctantly or enthusiastically, from "the mores can make anything right," (an overly simple empirical generalization) to the moral—or if you prefer, the immoral—conclusion that the culture of one society is as good as that of any other. Partly because it tends to be an orientation to problems more than a tightly formulated theory, functionalism is liable to various distortions, particularly of the variety that equates purposes or goals of a system with its consequences; often manifest results alone are observed.

One of the sources of functionalism is a teleological approach to explanation that is often, although it need not necessarily be, non-naturalistic in perspective. "Historically speaking, functional analysis is a modification of teleological explanations, *i.e.*, of explanation not by reference to causes which 'bring about' the event in question, but by reference to ends which determine its course." [2] One can only share Hempel's view that traditional teleological statements lack the "minimum scientific requirement of empirical testability." In fact they are congenial to some observers because they represent a non-naturalistic affirmation of order.

Assumptions that Hamper Functional Analysis. Even if one escapes the problems associated with a teleological approach, unexamined assumptions can distort one's observations. Robert Merton has shown that three interconnected postulates often used by the more extreme functionalists are not necessary to functional analysis and tend to make it into an ideology:

1. The postulate of the functional unity of a society—that every standardized activity or belief is functional, that is, necessary and useful, for the whole social system.

2. The postulate that every social form has a positive function—universal functionalism: ". . . *no* culture forms survive unless they constitute responses which are adjustive or adaptive, in some sense. . . ." (quoting Clyde Kluckhohn).

3. The postulate of indispensability—that certain functions are necessary to the survival of a society and/or that particular cultural or social forms are indispensable in carrying out these functions.[3]

So long as these postulates are assumptions rather than propositions to be tested by empirical study, functional analysis will be inadequate. In the contrast that he draws between manifest and latent functions, in his attention to functional alternatives, and in his emphasis on the need to study dysfunctions and functionally irrelevant patterns of behavior, Merton develops concepts that help us to avoid these assumptions. The study of

2 Carl Hempel, "The Logic of Functional Analysis," in *Symposium on Sociological Theory*, Llewellyn Gross, ed., p. 277.

3 See Robert Merton, *Social Theory and Social Structure*, pp. 25–37.

latent functions (and dysfunctions) is particularly likely to add significantly to our knowledge of a social process, for these, by definition, are not common knowledge; their consequences are unintended and unrecognized.

research which uncovers latent functions very often produces 'paradoxical' results. The seeming paradox arises from the sharp modification of a familiar popular preconception which regards a standardized practice or belief *only* in terms of its manifest functions by indicating some of its subsidiary or collateral latent functions.[4]

This is particularly true, perhaps, of the study of religion, for the analysis is likely to be carried on in terms of what religion does for society or the individual only as expressed in the prevailing ideology. Or, on the other hand, in various debunking studies, attention is given only to manifest and latent dysfunctions, with little or no attention paid to possible latent functions. Preconceptions of either sort will block our ability to explore religion fully.

Goode summarizes the situation well by indicating the six questions that need to be raised if one is to develop an adequate functional analysis:

Positive Function		Negative Function		Irrelevant	
Manifest	Latent	Manifest	Latent	Manifest	Latent

Functional anthropologists have concentrated upon those *positive functions* which are *not usually known* to the members of the society, i.e., the positive, latent functions. The rebels and debunkers among modern economists and historians have concentrated upon the *negative latent functions*. It is clear that much exploration remains to be done among the remaining cells.[5]

Some of the needed exploration is blocked by various analogies used to support or refute functionalism. We have noted that some critics use mechanical analogies, thus tending to overlook the questions related to feedback processes. Supporters, on the other hand, often employ organic analogies, dealing with relatively changeless systems, with clear boundaries and well-established homeostatic processes. The analogies can be helpful descriptive devices, if they are used with great caution. To say that the heart, as a blood-circulating pump, carries nutriment to all the cells of a body and removes wastes is to state clearly its functions for the whole system. Its functions having been specified, it is justifiable to state that a heart is a functional prerequisite for various kinds of organisms and that, in the sense described in Chapter Five, it exists because of what it does. We cannot afford an easy transfer of functional language from organic systems to superorganic systems, however, which are nowhere nearly so stable and have boundaries that are far less clearly marked.[6] We shall note below that part-whole and part-part conflicts are of great importance to

4 Ibid., p. 68.

5 Goode, *Religion Among the Primitives*, p. 33. See also Harry C. Bredemeier, "The Methodology of Functionalism," *American Sociological Review*, April, 1955, pp. 173–180.

6 Societies vary in these respects, however. Relatively smaller, more isolated, more stable societies are nearer the organic model. It is not by accident that students of primitive societies are more often favorable to a functional view, whereas critics are often students of intergroup conflict in urban societies.

the study of human groups. There is no direct analogue in organic systems. The criteria for health or effective functioning are also more readily specified for organisms than for societies. It is difficult to state that a given structure is essential to the good working order of a system if we do not know what good working order is. This contrast, of course, is a matter of degree. Organic health is not easy to define; and on the other hand there is probably sufficient agreement on the nature of social order that investigation can proceed, provided that the tentative and incomplete quality of the analysis is recognized.

Functionalism versus Ethnocentrism. Functionalism developed in anthropology partly out of opposition to the tendency to disparage primitive societies and their cultures, a tendency characteristic not only of laymen, when they heard about the strange ways of other people, but of eminent scholars. Evolutionary dogma and ethnocentrism often combined to govern the perspective of the first anthropological students of religion. Tylor, for all his contributions to the study of preliterate peoples, did not hesitate to speak of "this farrago of nonsense" in describing primitive beliefs. Cultural relativism, not as an empirical generalization about the range of practices but as a value (treat all cultures as dignified efforts to deal with life's problems), and functionalism (do not judge these practices by your own criteria; look carefully and you will see that they serve their participants well under the conditions *they* face) are well designed to reduce the distortions produced by ethnocentrism.

The pendulum can swing too far, however. An anti-ethnocentric conviction that affirms the existence of goodness in all practices can blind one to the total range of consequences almost as surely as cultural bias can.

Noting the tendency, in some functional studies, to assume that what exists is good, Leslie comments:

it is refreshing to read in Ralph Barton's *Ifugao Religion:* "The Ifugao religion is a distorted reflection of the Ifugao himself—distorted because it reflects his ignorance and not his knowledge, his slothfulness and not his industry, his fear and not his assurance, his wishful thinking and not his resourcefulness, his credulity and not his investigativeness, his helplessness and not his strength.". . . It may be necessary, if one is to grasp the historical reality of Iatmul religion, to speak as Gregory Bateson does of the "mass of fraudulent heraldry" that is their totemic system, or the "spirit of irresponsible bullying and swagger" with which they conduct their initiation ceremonies. Alfred Metraux tells us that we have to face the fact that in the Voodoo cults of Haiti the sacrament of communion is "a counterfeit." [7]

Criticism of functionalism, in turn, can be equally ideological. There is little to be gained by returning to earlier ethnocentric positions. The ideological quality can be avoided only by clear specification of the goals for which a given pattern is deemed functional.

Attempts to control ethnocentrism have been bound up, in an interesting way, with the fate of the concept of functional prerequisites. For several reasons, this concept has been difficult to incorporate into the study of society. We have noted that once the ethnocentric bias was exposed, and

7 Charles Leslie, *Anthropology of Folk Religion*, pp. xvi–xvii; see also Thomas O'Dea, *The Sociology of Religion*, pp. 100–101, on dysfunctions.

perhaps partly overcome, the idea of cultural relativity became congenial to both humanists and students of society (or to the humanistic and scholarly tendencies in each of us). It is a sign of respect for the cultures of other peoples that we examine them in all their wholeness and uniqueness. I certainly do not want to oppose such an attitude. We need to be aware, however, that it can stand as a barrier to the examination of the concept of functional prerequisites, with its analytic approach to culture. Common qualities can be seen only by abstracting from the range of empirical expressions those elements that are related to similar functions. The need, of course, is not to set aside the gains made possible by reduction of our ethnocentrisms, but to keep open for empirical study the question of the limits to social and cultural variability.

Problems that derive from ideological anti-ethnocentrism, as we might call it, are heightened by the fact that it is difficult to demonstrate empirically that a given pattern is essential to social life. Without a heart, a man dies. Would a society die without religion? Leaving aside the problem of definition for the moment, it is clear that a definitive answer to that question would require information on many societies, some of which lived although others did not despite conditions that were similar save for the presence or absence of religion. In fact, the very notion of the death of societies is problematic. Those few that we know have become extinct, as opposed to having evolved into different forms, have been destroyed from the outside. We have to rely instead on much softer evidence. Virtually all societies (let us leave it slightly open-ended) have religions. Even those that have gone through decisive institutional changes, perhaps involving an antireligious ideology (a communist revolution, for example), exhibit, often after a period of confusion, the same range of institutional structures as the regime that was replaced. As Talcott Parsons has pointed out, widespread alienation and strain may permit a revolution to succeed in the name of a utopian dream. Once the task of organizing a society is faced, however, the limits of utopianism are revealed; requisite structures reappear.[8] We should not be comfortable, as Goldschmidt notes, with refutations of the notion of requisites to society based simply on the citation of one or two exceptions.[9] These presumed exceptions must be examined with care, and even if finally demonstrated to be true, cannot be used to refute the importance of an almost universal pattern.

This last point is made difficult by the problem of determining when an exception has been found. The concept of functional prerequisites does not specify the particular structures through which a function must be performed. *Some* way to care for and train infants, for example, and to protect the mothers of young children may be required; but it need not be the monogamous family. There are alternative arrangements, which we do not hesitate to call families.[10] Criticism of the postulate of the functional indis-

8 See Talcott Parsons, *The Social System*, especially pp. 528–532.

9 Walter Goldschmidt, *Comparative Functionalism*, pp. 134–139.

10 I will not explore here the debate regarding the minimum cluster of functions relative to the control of sex, the protection and socialization of children, the protection of women, the placement of a child in the social structure, and the like, which are variously regarded as essential to the definition of the family. In a treatise on the family, this problem would require careful examination.

pensability of certain structures hinges on the degree to which functional equivalents or alternatives are designated by the same term. When is an alternative in fact an alternative, and when is it another form of the same item? Hempel warns against the risks of falling into a covert tautology—proving indispensability of a given structure by giving any possible alternative to it the same label.[11] He suggests that only rather weak conclusions can be based on the procedure, to cite his statement in abbreviated form: Some variety of I is essential for the adequate functioning of S. "This kind of inference, while sound, is rather trivial, however, except in cases where we have additional knowledge about the items contained in class I." [12] I would suggest that whether or not the inference is trivial depends upon what is already known, how sharply a finding challenges received knowledge, and how successfully it reorganizes the study of a problem. To establish that the existence of some form of shared system of superempirical beliefs is essential to the adequate functioning of a society and of its individual members would be far from trivial, even if the phrase "some form" left serious problems of definition unresolved. Beyond that, of course, one can only underline Hempel's observation of the value of additional knowledge about the items in class I—that is, about the range of alternatives and the conditions in which they operate. This may call for a form of research not tied to a functional definition of the problem, yet complementary to it.

The same tendency to over-correct represented by the shift from ethnocentrism to anti-ethnocentrism is found in another problem connected with functionalism. Examine the consequences of the shift in theoretical interest from the question of the origin of religion to the question of its functions. The student of the origin of religion tended to ask, How does a society (or, as Durkheim might say, the very fact of society) influence the development of religion? Or, How do individual intellectual and emotional needs affect religious origins? Religion was treated primarily as a dependent variable. The functionalist, taking religion as an established fact, is more likely to ask, What does religion do for societies and individuals? He tends to deal with religion as the independent variable. A theory that maintains a continuous and systematic interest in the *interaction* of religion and society seems to be difficult to develop. Just as questions concerning origins *tend toward* an ideology that religion is an archaic survival, destined gradually to be outgrown (as suggested by Spencer and Tylor, for example), so questions concerning functions *tend toward* a conservative ideology. A broad enough functional theory, one that includes latent and dysfunctional processes, can encompass the questions raised by the concept of interaction. To encompass them, however, we must avoid the assumption that society, or personality, or religion is always to be treated as the independent variable, with the others as dependent.

To What Degree Is Religion an Integrator of Society?

Many of the potentialities and problems associated with functional analysis are found in the discussions of religion's influence on social integration.

11 Carl Hempel, op. cit., pp. 284–287.

12 Ibid., p. 287.

It is immediately apparent that it is difficult to find a neutral vocabulary by means of which one can express the "function-dysfunction" of religion in its relationship to social integration. (The lack of an objective vocabulary doubtless indicates the absence of objective study of these phenomena.) Most people probably assume that to integrate a society is good, purely and simply. No distinction is raised in their minds between integration as a general fact and a specific pattern of integration. Religion, in this view, as the primary source of integration, is good and necessary; and the particular religious beliefs and practices of the moment are therefore defended.

To others, religion is a necessary ingredient of a well-integrated society because of the passions and lack of intelligence of the "masses," who must be protected from their own inadequacies. This is an ancient view, at least as old as Confucius, who declared that rites bind the multitudes together and "serve as dikes against excesses to which the people are prone." It was expressed also by Polybius, the Greek historian. Commenting on the honesty of the Romans, because they feared their gods, he admits that his own countrymen:

if entrusted with a single talent, though protected by ten checking-clerks, as many seals and twice as many witnesses, yet cannot be induced to keep faith. However, the Romans have managed to forge the main bond of social order out of something which the rest of the world execrates: I mean, out of Superstition. . . . In my opinion, however, the Romans have done it with an eye to the masses. If it were possible to have an electorate that was composed exclusively of sages, this chicanery might perhaps be unnecessary; but, as a matter of fact, the masses are always unstable and always full of lawless passions, irrational temper and violent rage; and so there is nothing but to control them by 'the fear of the unknown' and play-acting of that sort.[13]

E. A. Ross gives a modern version of the same thesis:

The genius who is to impress the mind of coming generations as the hand impresses the waxen tablet, does not commend his ideal on the ground that it is good for society. He does not advertise it as a means of securing order. He knows that men will not do as they would be done by, or forgive injuries, or subject their impulses to reason, for mere utility's sake. The genius that succeeds takes high ground from the first. His way is not merely a better way of getting along together. He declares it the one possible path of life. It is the God-ordained type of living. It is prescribed by man's nature. It is the goal of history. It is the destiny of the race. So it comes to pass that the inventors of right and wrong, the authors of ideals, not only disguise their sociology as ethics, but often go farther and disguise their ethics as religion.[14]

Ross's interpretation is similar to that expressed by Schopenhauer in *Dialogue on Religion* and by Freud in *Future of an Illusion*. Integration is also seen to be an important product of what Henri Bergson calls the static religion of the closed society. In his view, "religion is then a defensive reaction of nature against the dissolvent power of intelligence." Individual intelligence, unregulated, would lead primarily, Bergson says, to egocentric behavior. "Primitive religion, taken from our first standpoint, is a precau-

13 Quoted by Homer Smith, *Man and His Gods*, pp. 166–167.
14 E. A. Ross, *Social Control*, pp. 358–359.

tion against the danger man runs, as soon as he thinks at all, of thinking of himself alone." [15]

Many others would agree with this doctrine that religion gives support to social order, but would not see it as a matter of conscious manipulation by an elite; they would treat religion, as Plato does, somewhat more piously.

Other writers, starting from different value premises, while agreeing that religion may hold a society together, would call this not integration but rigidity. According to this view, the explosive tensions of a society are kept in check by its religious beliefs and practices, but this is done for the benefit of the dominant few, while the creative energies of the great majority are bottled up. This, of course, is the interpretation given by Marx in his proposition that "religion is the opiate of the people," but a similarly critical view of traditional religion may be taken by others who strongly disagree with Marx in their judgment of how to meet the situation. Thus a wide diversity of proposals for new ways to achieve the integration of society, ranging from "scientific" humanism to "scientific" Marxism, has been developed. It is paradoxical that Marxism, despite the vigor of its attack on religion, can itself readily be interpreted as a religious movement. Far from destroying the idea of the need for an integrating system of values, it simply offers itself as a substitute.

In studying these various approaches to the question of the integrating effects of religion, we must make a necessary distinction. The concept that *some* integrating system of beliefs and practices is necessary to the survival of society—a proposition that has strong empirical support (whether society ought to survive is itself, of course, a value judgment, but one that few care to deny)—cannot be equated with the idea that a particular system, as it is operating, contributes to social integration. We will note below the argument that society can also be conceived as a system of tensions. It has come to be observed that the "spaceless and timeless generalizations about the 'integrative functions of religion' are largely, although not of course entirely, derived from observations in non-literate societies." [16] But what, Merton asks, are the consequences when different religions coexist in the same society? This need not always produce disharmony, as Merton seems to imply, but it often does. And how does religion make for integration in the larger, more complex societies if it defends values that contradict other values of those societies? Can Hindu defense of caste purity help to integrate a society in which value is gradually coming to be attached to efficient industrial production, with an accompanying demand for rational organization of the work situation? Whether one of these values is "better" than another need not concern us here. We are simply asking whether Hinduism can integrate a society into which the other value is intruding.

The Problem of Order. Before we explore in more detail this question of relationship between religion and social integration, we need to take a brief look at a more general question concerning social order. One need not agree entirely with Hobbes that human life, before the establishment of strong

15 Henri Bergson, *The Two Sources of Morality and Religion,* pp. 112–113.

16 Merton, op. cit., p. 28. See also Allan Eister, "Religious Institutions in a Complex Society: Difficulties in the Theoretic Specification of Functions," *American Sociological Review,* 22, 1957, pp. 387–391.

governments, was "solitary, poor, nasty, brutish, and short," in order to realize that man's egocentric tendencies place great difficulties in the way of smoothly running social groups. Even the smallest and most stable of human societies faces the problem of distributing scarce values. The economic means of livelihood, power (a person's ability to influence others in directions he desires more than they can influence him), and prestige (comparative by its very nature, so that if one has more, another has less) are all, by definition, in scare supply. How can a society prevent individual and subgroup pursuit of these values from disrupting the network of agreements and accommodations that social life requires? And how do social groups prevent the hostility that is generated by frustration, by a sense of injustice, by guilt, from constantly tearing the fabric of society? Pushed back further, the question becomes, How can we account for the fact that societies manage to exist at all, when the tendencies toward self-aggrandizement are so strong and hostile feelings so abundant?

Aristotle raised this question, and gave us the answer: "Man is by nature social" (political), a theory picked up in the twentieth century in the McDougallian idea of "gregarious instincts." In a day when man's antisocial potentialities loom so large, however, we are not much impressed by these doctrines, nor by the whole attempt to explain behavior by putting something "in" man, which is then pointed to as a simple "explanation" when questions arise. We are perhaps more likely to be persuaded by Hobbes' doleful belief in an ever-threatening "war of all against all," and its twentieth-century variant, the Freudian doctrine that every individual has a reservoir of hostility, partly (and here we leave Hobbes) because of the very fact of society.

An adequate view, it would seem, must recognize that man has potentialities both for social life and for hostility and the self-centered pursuit of values. How do societies manage to keep the latter at a minimum (or at least aimed in directions not likely to injure the social order) while strengthening the potentialities for social life? One may guess that those societies that did not learn to do this were simply torn apart and disappeared (and that this process continues). This does not tell us, however, what surviving societies learned.

There are probably several related social processes that can be understood in this context, and some of them are distant from our conception of religion. The hostility may be directed toward other societies. It may be focused on socially approved scapegoats within a society. (It is interesting here to note that the term *scapegoat*, which originally had a specifically religious meaning, has now acquired a broader referent.) There may be processes whereby the hostility and egocentricity are sublimated into activities that are not socially disruptive. (*Sublimation* is a slippery concept, capable of about as many nonscientific distortions as *instinct*. We cannot discuss its weaknesses here, but will use it in the minimal sense of accepting a substitute activity for a blocked one.) And finally, coming to the function of religion in these processes, intragroup hostility and egocentricism may be prevented from reaching destructive force by religion's organized system of rites and beliefs. The last requires more careful explanation.

If a society is to exist at all, it must find some means for distributing its scarce goods and values in such a way that the great majority accept the outcome or protest against it only in ways that are approved by the social system itself. And it must find a method of controlling the expression of hostility that is inevitably generated by frustration, pain, and guilt. That even complex and mobile societies succeed in these tasks is a matter of daily observation. Although it is the violations that make the headlines, this may be related to a society's need to make the deviant highly visible as a means of emphasizing the norms. The headlines should not lead us to forget the number of times we count on, and receive, normatively prescribed behavior even from strangers. Most of us, most of the time, use means that are approved by our society, and do not use other means which, although perhaps more technically efficient in helping us acquire scarce values, are forbidden. We do not steal money, but work for it at a socially approved task; instead of destroying our competitor or spreading malicious gossip about him, we compete against him. Even when we buy goods and services from strangers—a much more common occurrence in urban societies—we generally get full measure and quality. Despite our tensions and fears, we accept the "strait-jacket of culture" (as Freud might call it), at least on the conscious level.

No strictly egocentric theory of man can explain these facts. How can we account for this order?

Certainly, one level of explanation is the fear of punishment: fear of ridicule, isolation, and public censure in the simpler societies, and, added to those, the power of explicit political authorities to coerce and punish in "civil" societies. We abide by the normatively approved means for acquiring scarce values, we express our hostility only in socially designated ways, because violations threaten greater loss than gain. Obviously this fear of punishment or loss is only partially successful. In the larger, more mobile societies the amount of effort necessary to enforce the norms must be increased. Moreover, this does not solve the problem of integration and social order, because there is the continuing danger that the enforcement authorities themselves—those who have been assigned the task of upholding the normative system of the society—may use for their own advantage the coercive means that have been given them. This is the eternal political problem. Every society must have a pattern of control "beyond politics" that will reduce the necessity for coercion and keep the authorities themselves within bounds. This final basis of social order rests on what Davis calls the "common-ultimate ends," which are socialized into the individual members of that society as their basic values. These values are shared, noncompetitive values, against which all other derivative goals are judged: ". . . these ends can refer not so much to a future state of the individual himself as to the future state of other individuals and, in the last analysis, to the group itself. . . . As between two different groups holding an entirely different set of common-ultimate ends, there is no recourse. But within the same community this type of ends constitutes the integrating feature." [17]

Putting these various influences together, we can summarize them in these field theoretical terms: Insofar as order exists, it is the product of the interaction of structural control (the network of interacting persons), cultural control (shared norms), and self-control (socialized tendencies toward order).

17 Kingsley Davis, *Human Society,* pp. 141–143.

How does religion come into this picture? The answer is much clearer for static and isolated societies than for changing ones. Insofar as it is accepted, and where there are no conflicting traditions, religion gives emotional support to the fundamental values of a society; it softens the hardness of the struggle for scarce values by emphasizing values that can be achieved by all (as, for example, salvation); and by emphasizing supramundane values it lessens the tensions of those who have failed to achieve a desired level of a society's values by the approved means. Beyond the integration that comes from socialization and social control in their secular aspects, beyond economic and political integration, beyond the focusing of disruptive hostilities onto socially designated scapegoats within the society or enemies without, every viable society has a transcendent system of unifying values, beyond politics and, indeed, in most cases, beyond history.

This is not to say that any particular religion is, therefore, good. The statement above is empirical, not valuative. A religion may give support to a society based on principles that one considers bad, such as the acceptance of slavery; the rites it employs may, from the value stand of the outsider, seem barbarous, as, for example, the custom of human sacrifice; the lowering of the sense of frustration may, in some circumstances, cut the nerve of effort that many would regard as essential. On another level, in connection with the relations between societies that have a different kind of religious integration, strong barriers to intersociety cooperation and accommodation may be erected. One's value judgment concerning the integrative function of religion, therefore, can most profitably be based on the analysis of *all* the consequences, both manifest and latent.

Difficulties in the Emphasis on Integration. How can this approach to religion be brought into an adequate theory? Several problems need to be solved before this long-established insight into the role of religion as "integrator of society" can take its place in a scientific theory of religion:

1. A great deal of empirical observation, in different types of societies, is still needed to discover how generally the proposition applies; to discover where, if at all, it does not apply (where religion serves as disintegrator of society, or appears unimportant in this regard); and to specify the *conditions under which* these various possibilities occur. Did religion "integrate" Russian society in the period between 1915 and 1917? Would Taoism and Buddhism, independent of Confucianism, have held Chinese society together? Although this insight is perhaps three thousand years old and has taken its place in dozens of philosophies of religion, the task of isolating the conditions in which it applies has yet to be carried out adequately.

2. A statement of the integrative function must be united with statements of religion's other functions and dysfunctions, and this broader statement tested by widespread empirical observation. Is there a changeless core of functions without which one should not speak of the existence of a religion, or are some of these functions performed primarily by other kinds of social structures in certain kinds of societies? (Here again, the problem of definition is not easily solved.) Is there an inherently interrelated group of functions that one finds always embodied together in religion because one cannot be carried out effectively in the absence of the other? It is a plausible hypothesis that the functions for the individual, which we shall discuss in

the next several chapters, are better served by a religious system that also integrates, and that the group function is more adequately performed by a religion that also satisfies various individual needs. By contrast, societal integration is less likely to be accomplished, according to this hypothesis, by a pattern of beliefs and practices that fails to satisfy important needs in the lives of individual adherents (remembering how exceedingly various such needs, many of which are defined by the religion itself, may be). Finally, in this regard, a religious system that for the moment satisfies individual needs but fails to hold together the society within which those satisfactions are achieved, is unlikely to be able to continue to carry out even its individual functions. This hypothesis must receive further exploration before the observation that religion contributes to social integration can become part of an adequate scientific theory of religion.

3. The proposition also needs to be related to broader theories of society and personality. If it is true that a system of religious beliefs and practices supports social integration, under stated conditions, what is there about the nature of society and of personality that makes this true? Is this proposition congruent with other statements about society and personality? Can it be reduced to a more general theory of human behavior, following the principle of parsimony, thus bringing it more solidly into the framework of sociology?

We are slowly making headway in answering these questions; and it is my hope that this book, drawing on today's increasingly rich resources, can contribute to the process of bringing such ancient insights as we are discussing into the framework of an adequate theory.

Variables Influencing the Integrative Function of Religion. The growth of the comparative study of religions, both of preliterate and literate societies, and the study of how a religion changes as the society in which it is embedded changes are our primary sources of information. On the basis of that material, some of which will be discussed in other connections in later chapters (empirical material will be kept at a minimum in this systematic statement), the following propositions concerning religion and social integration seem justified. These propositions are not mutually exclusive, because each one deals with part of an interacting group of forces— where one is present, several others are also likely to be found. The statements are put negatively, reversing the usual emphasis, in order to point up the need for indicating the conditions in which religion will tend to produce social cohesion. The integrative function of religion is at a minimum—other things being equal—in the situations that follow.

1. In societies where more than one religion is practiced.

2. When the "established expectancies" of the members of a society are frustrated. This refers, not to some absolute level of need, but to the satisfactions that the members of a society have come to expect. When these are denied, those who feel frustrated may become more religious, in the manner of the Old Believers in Russia, or that of the Black Muslims of the United States or of the explosive Kitiwala movement in the Congo, which is a politico-religious sect built around Christian symbols. But becoming more religious, in these cases, does not mean embracing more strongly a unifying religious tradition. Members of such sects are likely to use religion as a means of expressing their sense of separation and even as a weapon to

fight for the re-establishment of their "rights." This is illustrated by the way in which nominally Christian Indians used the Ghost Dance against white Americans.

3. When social change reduces the appeal of the ritual and belief systems. What will give one generation a sense of a unifying tradition may alienate parts of another generation who have been subjected to different social and cultural influences.

4. When mobility from society to society is greatest; and the corollary, when a society is composed of members who were socialized to different patterns of behavior. Even when the mobility is among societies sharing the same basic religious system, there are bound to be local variations in the religious tradition, and the heterogeneous society will have a wider range of personality systems to integrate.

5. When a society is sharply divided into classes, or other hierarchical divisions, and this is strongly felt as an oppressive fact. Religion itself may help to *prevent* a stratification system from being felt as an oppressive fact, as in the case of classic Hinduism or medieval Christianity, but it may not be able to do so in the face of competing value systems derived from nonreligious sources or from some aspects of the religion itself. If a religion cannot "explain away" the differences in income, power, and prestige on the basis of its own principles, it is less able to serve the function of integrating a society. Those who are most disadvantaged are particularly likely, under these circumstances, to desert the dominant religion and to accept some new religion, or protoreligion as the way to solve their problems. In such a situation, the religious forces are as likely to express and even to accentuate the internal tensions of a society as they are to integrate that society. Thus the lower classes were those most likely to desert the emperor worship of Rome in favor of Christianity. In the nineteenth and twentieth centuries, the lower classes and alienated members of the middle and upper classes have been the most likely to leave Christianity for the secular salvation of communism. And in India today, most converts from Hinduism to Buddhism and Christianity are drawn from the highly disadvantaged groups. The proponents of a religious system might argue that "true" Buddhism, Christianity, or Hinduism could not thus be involved in social conflict rather than social integration; only "corrupt" versions could permit that. This is a point on which debate is likely to be fruitless. Let us say simply that, whatever may be the basic ideology, religion as it is lived and used becomes, under certain circumstances, an important factor, as symbol and cause, of social conflict.

6. When outside pressures split a society. Perhaps this is only to say that when outside forces are sufficiently strong or of a particular kind, the cohesive effects of religion may be inadequate to maintain the unity of a society. Thus many American Indian tribes are divided into reactionaries (those who want to reaffirm the validity of their original culture) and liberals (who would prefer recognition simply as individual Americans), with many positions in between. Religious differences usually match these differences and perhaps intensify them. We must state, of course, that in other circumstances outside prsssure can have an exactly opposite effect: It may revivify a religious system and greatly increase the internal solidarity of a society. Judaism is often cited as the classic illustration of this process.

It is well to recognize that often both tendencies—the unifying and the disrupting—may be present in an ambivalent relationship. Thus there have been continual divisions among Jews, showing that religion is unable to resolve all the differences that may occur as a result of the outside situation; by contrast, some of the religious movements among American Indians served to express their unity against the white man.

These are among the conditions that can reduce the integrative effects of religion. This discussion perhaps serves to make clear why we cannot accept the simple assertion that "religion produces social integration." When the tendencies that we have discussed run in the opposite direction, of course, they will serve to strengthen the integrative aspects of religion. It should also be noted that we have used a society as our unit. When one is concerned with some subdivision of a society—a class or minority group, for example—some of the limitations on the power of social cohesion through religion do not apply, although several of them are relevant even to the question of the integration of such groups.

Many students of religion might accept these qualifications with respect to the integrative function of religion, but then ask: Is it not true that there is a *tendency* in a society, in the face of these disintegrative influences, to recover or discover a unifying religious theme? If we define religion broadly enough, the answer would seem to be Yes. These tendencies, however, may not have time to work themselves out before new disintegrative influences enter the scene—thus maintaining a continuously mixed situation. Here we are in the realm of prehypothesis, but the speculation may be worthwhile. When religious integration is weakened, other types of integration for subdivisions of a society or the whole society tend to emerge because of the need for a unifying system of values. Nationalism is an outstanding example in our time. (The causal sequence may, of course, be the other way around. Nationalism, as a unifying system of values, may have come about as a result of causes independent of the presence or absence of a unifying religious tradition and then *caused* the weakening of the religious view. It is more likely, however, that the various influences continuously interacted.)

It may be true, however, that subsocietal religions or secular systems of value integration *tend toward* a full-fledged religious pattern because such a pattern serves the individual and group functions more successfully. Religion may tend to spread to the boundaries of a society (and in our time, beyond), because the existence of conflicting systems weakens these functions. Most secular systems of value integration, moreover—what we may call incipient or protoreligions—tend to prove inadequate because of their inability to achieve their proclaimed goals. Religion, by making extra-empirical goals (salvation) most important (though not necessarily all-important), by transvaluing the meaning of human failure and suffering, by dealing in shared, not scarce and therefore competitive, values, may reduce this difficulty.

These propositions are to some degree illustrated by Warner's description of the half-patriotic, half-religious ceremonies of Memorial Day in the United States. In this description, one sees a complex and heterogeneous society struggling toward a group of cohering, unifying beliefs and practices, building the unifying theme out of materials from the society's own experience—the widely shared and emotionally significant experiences of death in war.

It is the thesis of this chapter that the Memorial Day ceremonies and subsidiary rites (such as those of Armistice Day) of today, yesterday, and tomorrow are rituals of a sacred symbol system which functions periodically to unify the whole community, with its conflicting symbols and its opposing, autonomous churches and associations. It is contended here that in the Memorial Day ceremonies the anxieties which man has about death are confronted with a system of sacred beliefs about death which gives the individuals involved and the collectivity of individuals a feeling of well-being. Further, the feeling of triumph over death by collective action in the Memorial Day parade is made possible by re-creating the feeling of well-being and the sense of group strength and individual strength in the group power, which is felt so intensely during the wars when the veterans' associations are created and when the feeling so necessary for the Memorial Day's symbol is originally experienced.

Memorial Day is a cult of the dead which organizes and integrates the various faiths and national and class groups into a sacred unity. It is a cult of the dead organized around the community cemeteries. Its principal themes are those of the sacrifice of the soldier dead for the living and the obligation of the living to sacrifice their individual purposes for the good of the group, so that they, too, can perform their spiritual obligations.[18]

THE COERCION THEORY OF SOCIETY

Many of the qualifications we have suggested regarding the functional view of society imply the contrasting view—society conceived as a product of force and constraint applied by some to others. It may be useful to make this "coercion theory of society," as Dahrendorf calls it,[19] the direct object of our study for a moment, rather than relying on criticisms of the integration theory. This will permit us to examine their relationship more explicitly. Now the scowling faces become figure and the goblet becomes ground, as we focus on the fact that force, conflict, and violence are significant aspects of human life. To suggest that the study of religion need not be concerned with this dimension would be to deny many of the important facts of religious behavior. At many points in the chapters that follow we shall study the ways in which religion enters into conflict.

To those who emphasize the place of coercion in society, it is not enough to see coercion as an intrusion into normally integrated systems. In these days of turmoil, it is easy to see that a picture of smooth-running societies is inadequate. The presence of disorder, conflict, unfulfilled desires, and long-run cycles of deterioration in systems must be accounted for by any theory. The dedicated functionalist is likely to see them as bothersome strains on the system, and to assign them to a residual category of dysfunctions, rather than viewing them as intrinsic elements of the system. To a conflict theorist, however—for example, Marx—the very structure of society involves coercion. This is a natural starting point for change, as also are disrupting influences from outside.

18 Lloyd Warner, *American Life: Dream and Reality*, pp. 2–3.

19 Ralf Dahrendorf, *Class and Class Conflict in Industrial Society*, particularly pp. 157–173.

Even in dealing with a fairly stable structure, we can think in terms of a system of balanced tensions rather than of an order based on shared values. This is a perspective not easily developed, however, in the context of a coercion theory. That conflicts and pressures toward change are a natural product of the power and authority relations of a society is easily recognized; but continuity and equilibrium are more difficult for conflict theory to take into account. Emphasis on shared values and functional interdependence is more readily able to do this.

It should be emphasized that coercion and integration theories are not alternative but complementary ways of viewing society. "We cannot conceive of society unless we realize the dialectics of stability and change, integration and conflict, function and motive force, consensus and coercion." [20] It is not enough, indeed, to see the items in each of these pairs alternately, for the strategic facts have to do with the limitations they mutually impose on each other when seen together. When the problem is seen in this light, we ask a different set of questions, not, How does religion function to maintain a system? but, What is the degree to which and the conditions in which religion functions to maintain the system; and to what degree and in what ways is it involved in the coercion patterns of the society? To measure the degree to which a pattern supports a system is also to measure the degree to which it disrupts the system. To measure the conditions in which a pattern contributes to system adaptation and integration is simultaneously to suggest the need for study of the conditions in which it does not do so. Dahrendorf believes that social science, with its alternate ways of viewing society—as a system of coercion or a system of integration—may have to be content with stressing their mutual limitations and their separate advantages for different kinds of problems. He notes that the wave theory and the quantum theory of light exist side by side in physics, each apparently equipped to handle certain problems better than the other. I am unable to judge the aptness of this analogy; but I do not see the need for adopting either an integration or a coercion model of society, once we surmount ideological and temperamental predilections. Why not an integration-coercion model, with major effort devoted to the analysis of those conditions that maximize the one or the other in various patterns of human behavior? Dahrendorf himself notes: "It is evidently virtually impossible to think of society in terms of either model without positing its opposite number at the same time. There can be no conflict, unless this conflict occurs within a context of meaning, i.e., some kind of coherent 'system.' . . . Analogously, the notion of integration makes little sense unless it presupposes the existence of different elements that are integrated." [21]

In my judgment, continuous attention to the analytically distinct categories of social structure, culture, and character, with the possibilities that they may converge in their support of a given pattern or diverge, producing change and/or conflict, can reduce the weaknesses associated not only with neglect of one perspective but even with their alternate use.

20 Ibid., p. 163; see also David Lockwood, "Some Remarks on the 'Social System,'" *British Journal of Sociology*, 7, 1956, pp. 134–146.

21 Ralf Dahrendorf, op. cit., p. 164.

The Sociology of Conflict

There is, of course, a vast literature dealing with the importance of conflict and competition in the life of man. For Heraclitus, "conflict is the father of all things." Not many have taken such an extreme position; but I think it would be fair to say that until the twentieth century, not only the inevitability but also the positive contributions of conflict have been stressed more than has functional integration. I shall not discuss the extensive literature on conflict, but the mere listing of a rather diverse series of names—Ibn Khaldun, Machiavelli, Hobbes, Adam Smith, Marx, Spencer, and Gumplowicz, for example—may suggest the importance attached to conflict by thinkers through the centuries.[22] In recent years, a less ideological, more empirically and theoretically based literature has begun to translate insightful but problematic statements into questions for research. Along with other specialties, the sociology of religion will profit by this development.[23]

Many themes run through the literature on conflict and competition. Four of these are significant to the student of religion.

1. Perhaps the dominant theme is the emphasis on conflict as the major source of change. In Marx's famous statement in the *Communist Manifesto:* "The history of all societies up to the present is the history of class struggles." The command-obey relationships characteristic of all societies (until utopian communism is achieved) meant for Marx that conflict was endemic, the inevitable product of society, not an exceptional disturbance of it. Set against a vocabulary of functional ideology, conflict theory affirms that a structure-culture-character "match" sufficiently perfect to handle all fluctuations by means of homeostatic processes is an illusory model.

2. Another theme emphasizes conflict and competition (which is distinguished from conflict by the inclusion in the dispute of appeals to a third party) as a *source* of integration rather than as its disturber. To Adam Smith, competition was necessary to the "natural harmony" of social processes. To the social Darwinists, competition and conflict strengthened a society by selecting the stronger, the more intelligent, the "fittest." In a related theme, deviation, often involving conflict, has been interpreted as functional for a group. Thus Durkheim noted that crime furnished society with an opportunity to underline and reaffirm its standards. More recently, even violence has been acclaimed, not only as a source of change, but also of affirmations of personal identity and productive involvement in the social order, when other avenues are blocked. It also serves, according to

22 See Don Martindale, *The Nature and Types of Sociological Theory*, Pt. Three.

23 The work of George Simmel, *Conflict*, is a good starting point. See also Lewis Coser, *The Functions of Social Conflict*, and *Continuities in the Study of Social Conflict;* Raymond Mack and Richard Snyder, "The Analysis of Social Conflict—Toward an Overview and Synthesis," *Journal of Conflict Resolution*, 1, 1957, pp. 212–248; Joseph Himes, "The Functions of Racial Conflict," *Social Forces*, 45, 1966, pp. 1–10; Pierre van den Berghe, "Dialectic and Functionalism: Toward a Theoretical Synthesis," *American Sociological Review*, 28, 1963, pp. 695–705; and John Horton, "Order and Conflict Theories of Social Problems as Competing Ideologies," *American Journal of Sociology*, 71, 1966, pp. 701–713, followed by commentaries from Bert Adams and Robin Williams, Jr., pp. 714–721.

this interpretation, as a warning flag that integration and adaptation processes have been inadequate.[24]

3. A third theme in the literature on conflict we have already commented on: Conflict and cohesion are best studied together, in terms of man's complex of allegiances. Both processes are intrinsic to society. Indeed, every allegiance implies something one is aligned against as well as something one is for; every social conflict implies colleagues as well as opponents.[25]

4. Some students of conflict emphasize its destructive and disruptive qualities. Perhaps few would counter Heraclitus with the statement that integration, consensus, and stability are the father of all things, although Peter Kropotkin approaches that view in *Mutual Aid.* There are, however, many who would emphasize the vicious cycles of distrust, the sacrifice of values, and the suffering associated with conflict. It is seen as illness in the organism or as disruption of a value-achieving stable equilibrium. This theme in extreme form brings us back, of course, to functionalism as an ideology. As a hypothesis, however, it directs our attention to the study of the conditions in which the coercive, conflictful, and violent aspects of human behavior block the attainment of stated goals.

Each of these themes, we will find, has relevance to the study of religion.[26] Religious conflict is often deeply involved in social change. The sharp challenges offered by sectarian movements to prevailing religious views may point unmistakably to serious social problems; and the competition they offer to established religious groups may help to preserve some autonomy in religious organizations. Religious conflict that seriously splits one group may be a source of powerful unity for the subgroups. And, finally, religious conflict may be associated simply with hostility, prejudice, and social disorder. To the simple proposition that religion serves to integrate a society, therefore, we must answer: "It may. But it may also arm those in conflict with absolute convictions. It may emphasize brotherhood; or designate the antichrist." In the sociology of religion, we shall need to keep fully in mind an integration-coercion model of society if we are to do full justice to the range of the facts before us. Our task is to discover "the con-

24 Much of the literature on violence, from George Sorel's *Reflections on Violence* to Frantz Fanon's *The Wretched of the Earth,* is highly ideological. But there are also more analytical treatments. See, for example, Bayard Rustin, "The Watts 'Manifesto' and the McCone Report," *Commentary,* 41, March, 1966, pp. 29–35.

25 This theme is well developed with respect to specific societies in Max Gluckman, *Custom and Conflict in Africa.* Edward Norbeck interprets some of the data used by Gluckman differently, but takes a similar position with respect to conflict. See his "African Rituals of Conflict," *American Anthropologist,* 65, 1963, pp. 1254–1279. See also the works of Coser, van den Berghe, Mack and Snyder, and Dahrendorf, cited earlier. In his more recent writing, Dahrendorf seems to have moved toward a more one-sided conflict orientation. See his *Gesellschaft und Freiheit.*

26 There will be attention to conflict under many topics in the chapters to follow. Any doubt that the student of religion must be a student of conflict is erased by such studies as those of Norman Cohn, *Pursuit of the Millennium,* and Vittorio Lanternari, *The Religions of the Oppressed.* For a variety of studies dealing primarily with the United States, see Don Hager, Charles Glock, and Isidor Chein, eds., "Religious Conflict in the United States," *Journal of Social Issues,* 12, No. 3, 1956; Robert Lee and Martin Marty, eds., *Religion and Social Conflict;* Earl Raab, ed., *Religious Conflict in America;* and Kenneth Underwood, *Protestant and Catholic: Religious and Social Interaction in an Industrial Community.*

ditions under which varying systems of beliefs and values allow for toleration, compromise, insulation, partial incorporation and the like, or else eventuate in conflict, domination, and persecution." [27]

Summary of the Field Perspective of Religion

Our discussion of the functional and conflict models of society, as they relate to a theory of religion, can be summarized in the following propositions:

1. Social order involves a unifying value scheme, specifying approved means and ends, that facilitates interaction and helps to hold in check the conflict involved in the individual pursuit of scarce values and the hostility generated by frustration and disappointment.

2. Social order involves "authority relations," structured patterns of dominance and subjection. These partly reflect and partly challenge the values.

3. Under stable conditions, the value scheme is largely self-enforcing, built into the characters of the members of the society by socialization.

4. Changes in the social structure, however (as a result of mobility, technical innovation, or other causes), often lead to "inadequate socialization." When this occurs for substantial numbers, the conflict of interest implicit in the authority relations becomes more explicit.

5. Political enforcement—designation of legitimate authorities who may use force, taxation, and other coercive measures, which are widely variant from society to society—becomes more and more important as societies become more heterogenous and mobility more common. This source of order, however, continues to rely on the self-enforcing source of order; and it raises the new problem of the use of political authority for individual gain.

6. Religion may, under some circumstances, help to solve the problem of order, both as a designator of goals (with particular emphasis on shared goals), and as an enforcer of means. By ritual, by symbol, by its system of beliefs, its doctrines of rewards and punishments, religion may help to produce the socialized individuals who accept the dominant values as to legitimate means and ends. This aids the political authorities, but also has an influence upon them.

7. Certain conditions weaken, or even reverse, the place of religion in social integration. In some places it becomes involved, as symbol and cause, in social conflict and the reduction of order.

8. None of these points implies a value judgment concerning the desirability or undesirability of any particular system of social order. Religion may help to preserve a social order that from stated value premises is bad or it may help to destroy a social order that from given values is good.

9. The balance of integration and coercion is not necessarily the same for all social structures. Political and economic structures, for example, may imply a larger share of coercion than do religious and educational structures, despite mutual influences. Although the distinction is certainly only one of degree, the latter structures may deal with values that are not

27 Robin Williams, Jr., "Religion, Value-Orientations, and Intergroup Conflict," *Journal of Social Issues,* 12, 1956, p. 13.

scarce in significantly higher proportion. One person's salvation and knowledge need not be achieved at the cost of another's. Power and income, on the other hand, are in scarce supply. Power, in particular, may be a "zero-sum" commodity, so that one person's gain is another's loss—a characteristic likely to increase the use of coercion. Income is technically not of the zero-sum variety; but granted the relative quality often associated with it, one person's high income may imply another's low income, regardless of the absolute level of both. Between groups already separated by economic and political contrasts involving coercion, to be sure, religious variation may also be associated with scarcity: salvation belongs only to the elect. Thus the suggestion that there may be variation in the balance of coercion and integration among the major institutions must also be read as a suggestion that both qualities can be found in all institutions.

10. Adequate attention to integration-coercion processes requires information about structures of interaction, systems of culture, and the predispositions of individuals. Only under conditions of great and prolonged stability can one of these serve as an adequate index of the others, permitting a simpler system of analysis. In the modern world it is their disjunction that sets the stage for most religious events: Individuals develop new needs in the face of old structures and values; new values intrude into ancient structures, engulfing people trained to older forms; drastically revised patterns of interaction are experienced by people who share older values. It is from the permutations of these complex processes that we must seek to increase our understanding of man's religious behavior.

POSTSCRIPT

Since writing Chapters Five and Six, I have come across Arthur Stinchcombe's book *Constructing Social Theories*, which contains a valuable, systematic statement of functional theory.[28] Although he may underestimate the risks involved in functional analysis, I believe that a person following the procedures he outlines can effectively heighten the power of functional interpretations. Since Stinchcombe's position is, so far as I can see, harmonious with the point of view developed in this chapter, I will cite only a brief section of his summary, while encouraging the reader to examine the full statement:

Functional theories explain phenomena by their consequences. They are very generally useful in explaining social phenomena because there are many chains of reverse causation which select patterns of behavior by their consequences: biological evolution; social evolution; individual and collective planning to achieve the consequences; satisfaction to the actor from the consequences with consequent operative conditioning; satisfaction to others who reward the actor; and satisfaction to others combined with social selection in a market system. Each of these common processes selects out and reinforces behavior or social structures according to their consequences. This means that it is always a good bet, in trying to explain a social phenomenon, to look at its consequences.[29]

28 Arthur Stinchcombe, *Constructing Social Theories*, pp. 80–101.

29 Ibid., pp. 98–99.

Chapter Seven

RELIGION AND CHARACTER

The field theoretical approach to religion emphasizes the need to examine both individual and structural elements. It also stresses the need to study each of these in context with the other. In discussing the character aspects of religion, therefore, as we shall be doing in the next several chapters, we shall attempt to keep in mind their interrelationships with structural aspects. And later, when we turn to the examination of social structures and culture, we shall seek to study their *range* of significance, depending on the individuals involved.

I shall use the term *character* to mean all those tendencies and potentialities that a person brings into a behavioral situation. We can avoid confusion if at the start we clearly distinguish several different questions that are involved in the study of religion and character: (1) To what degree and in what ways is religion the product of various individual needs and tendencies? Religion examined in this way is the dependent variable. (2) What are the varieties of religious experiences? These are sometimes related analytically to needs, but are often treated descriptively, as types of behavior. (3) What are the individual consequences of religion—as, for example, on motivation, health, or interpersonal behavior? From this perspective, religion is the independent variable. (4) How do these consequences feed back into the system from which they came? Is there any sense in which these individual functions are causes of religion as well as its consequence? Having examined this question in some detail in the preceding two chapters, I shall refer to it here only where misunderstanding might otherwise occur. (5) In what ways are the needs, the varieties of religious experience, the consequences, and the reciprocal functions affected by the sociocultural environment within which they occur; and how do they affect that environment? The structural elements will be in the background at this point, but if we forget them, our analysis will be inadequate.

These five questions do not constitute an outline of the discussion to follow, for several of them may be raised in connection with specific subjects. They do, however, represent major theoretical problems for the scientific study of religion viewed from the perspective of the individual.

INDIVIDUAL TENDENCIES AND NEEDS AS A SOURCE OF RELIGION

In each of the preceding chapters, we have implied various ways in which individual tendencies and needs are among the sources of religion. Few would want to quarrel with the general proposition that individual factors should be taken into account. There are important problems involved, however, in stating exactly which needs and tendencies, and under what conditions they are operating, before this general proposition can be of much value in a scientific theory of religion. As Gordon Allport has pointed out, virtually every human desire finds expression, at one time or another, in one individual or another, in religious belief and behavior. The complex and varying conceptions of the deity are projections of the multiplicity of the human needs involved in religion. God is omnipotent, the embodiment of power; He is the source of security and strength; He is cosmic perfection. "When we need affection, God is love; knowledge, He is omniscient; consolation, He granteth peace that passeth understanding. When we have sinned, He is the Redeemer; when we need guidance, the Holy Spirit. Divine attributes plainly conform to the panorama of desire, although the individual is seldom aware that his approach to his deity is determined by present needs." [1]

"Determined" is certainly too strong a word in Allport's last sentence. And his statement is better designed to refer to monotheistic religions than to religion generally; hence we would do well to extend it. Man's projected needs may lead, not to belief in a powerful and benevolent god, but to belief in malevolent and harmful, or potentially harmful, spirits, ghosts, and witches. Spiro argues persuasively, for example, that nat worship in Burma—a system of rituals and beliefs related to supernatural beings who are able to affect man, for good or for evil—can be accounted for, on the perceptual and motivational levels, by early socialization. After a period of "warm nurturance and free indulgence," Burmese children enter a situation that they experience as one of parental rejection and hostility. They develop anxieties around their feelings of rejection and around their own resulting sadistic and malevolent tendencies. By projecting their perception of hostile and rejecting parents onto the nats, Burmese children protect themselves from the likelihood of an anxiety-laden observation. "By means of this culturally constituted defense mechanism the original threatening perception, 'my parents are hostile,' is converted into the nonthreatening perception, 'it is the nats (not my parents) who are hostile.' The latter perception, of course, is also threatening: The Burmese rightly fear the nats. But the threat-value of the nats is small compared to the threat-value of rejecting and hostile parents." [2]

[1] Gordon Allport, *The Individual and His Religion*, pp. 10–11.

[2] Melford Spiro, *Burmese Supernaturalism*, pp. 77–78. Something of this same interpretation is found in Clyde Kluckhohn, *Navaho Witchcraft*.

Whether we are dealing with an urban, a village, or a tribal population, the underlying idea that human need is one of the roots of religion is scarcely to be questioned. The contemporary problem is to specify which needs, to design adequate ways of measuring them, and to relate them to religion in ways that permit sound deductions.[3]

It may be useful to draw two distinctions to describe the range of observations about individual needs and religion. The first is a contrast between universal or general needs, those that are found among all human beings, and variant needs, which may be present or absent, or present in differing amounts. The second is a distinction between normal and abnormal needs and tendencies. Putting these two contrasts together, as shown in Figure 7–1, we have four varieties. Illustrative problems and authors who have dealt with them are indicated.

	General	Variant
Normal	How handle the fact of death? (Malinowski)	How deal with persistent loneliness? (Fromm)
Abnormal	How deal with repressed hostilities? (Freud)	Does religion help control neurosis? (Boisen)

FIGURE 7–1. *Individual tendencies and needs relevant to religion*

Both distinctions are difficult to make in practice.[4] If we neglect them, however, we will not understand the differences in interpretation to be found among those who have examined individual sources of religion. The four categories are not mutually exclusive, to be sure. Variation in the intensity and direction of religious expression may result partly from the fact that all four categories are relevant to one person's experience although only the two general ones are relevant to other persons. Or, to put the matter in what I believe is a more adequate way: Needs of all four varieties influence everyone, but in widely varying amounts.

3 Fortunately we are beginning to get more empirically oriented work to complement the more qualitative observations. See, for example, Timothy Brock, "Implications of Conversion and Magnitude of Cognitive Dissonance," *Journal for the Scientific Study of Religion*, 1, 1962, pp. 198–203; Bernard Spilka and J. F. Reynolds, "Religion and Prejudice: A Factor-Analytic Study," *Review of Religious Research*, 6, 1965, pp. 163–168; Sam Webb, "An Exploratory Investigation of Some Needs Met Through Religion," *Journal for the Scientific Study of Religion*, 5, 1965, pp. 51–58; William Wood, *Culture and Personality Aspects of the Pentecostal Holiness Religion;* and Leon Gorlow and Harold Schroeder, "Motives for Participating in the Religious Experience," *Journal for the Scientific Study of Religion*, 7, 1968, pp. 241–251.

4 For a discussion of the problem of defining abnormality see J. Milton Yinger, *Toward a Field Theory of Behavior*, pp. 269–273.

Religious Interpretations of Death

The most significant of the tendencies with which religion everywhere grapples is fear of death. Bergson believed it to be the second major source of "static religion" (control of selfishness being the first). "Looked at from this second standpoint," he wrote, "religion is a defensive reaction of nature against the representation, by intelligence, of the inevitability of death." [5] Malinowski, in his well-known analysis of primitive religion, brings the problem of death into his theory not only of the functions, but also of the origins of religion:

The savage is intensely afraid of death, probably as the result of some deep-seated instincts common to man and animals. He does not want to realize it as an end, he cannot face the idea of complete cessation, of annihilation. The idea of spirit and of spiritual existence is near at hand, furnished by such experiences as are discovered and described by Tylor. Grasping at it, man reaches the comforting belief in spiritual continuity and in the life after death. Yet this belief does not remain unchallenged in the complex, double-edged play of hope and fear which sets in always in the face of death. To the comforting voice of hope, to the intense desire of immortality, to the difficulty, in one's own case, almost the impossibility, of facing annihilation there are opposed powerful and terrible forebodings. The testimony of the senses, the gruesome decomposition of the corpse, the visible disappearance of the personality—certain apparently instinctive suggestions of fear and horror seem to threaten man at all stages of culture with some idea of annihilation, with some hidden fears and forebodings. And here into this play of emotional forces, into this supreme dilemma of life and final death, religion steps in, selecting the positive creed, the comforting view, the culturally valuable belief in immortality, in the spirit independent of the body, and in the continuance of life after death. In the various ceremonies at death, in commemoration and communion with the departed, and worship of ancestral ghosts, religion gives body and form to the saving beliefs.[6]

This statement is not without serious weaknesses. The use of the term *instinct* to explain the source of the fear of death scarcely does more than give a name to a phenomenon that needs more careful explanation. A second difficulty is that Malinowski has given inadequate attention to the variation in concern for and fear of death among individuals, societies, and religious systems. It is doubtful that one can afford to disregard the differences between the conceptions of nirvana and of heaven as a physically located place with golden streets (even if, by stretching the meaning a great deal, one defines them both as demonstrations of a belief in immortality). And thirdly, the *assumption* that belief in immortality is "positive" and "culturally valuable" needs exploration and not simply assertion. If it brings poise and serenity to some, does it not also, on occasion, arm an Inquisition and justify its brutality (for who can afford to let an antichrist endanger the immortal souls of thousands)? Is it not possible that belief in immortality may help to produce resignation in the face of suffering and injustice—a resignation that according to certain value standards is sometimes good, sometimes bad?

5 Henri Bergson, *The Two Sources of Morality and Religion,* p. 121.
6 Bronislaw Malinowski in *Science, Religion and Reality,* Joseph Needham, ed., pp. 49–50.

In the light of these difficulties in Malinowski's statement, it may be more accurate simply to state that religious systems everywhere are *involved in* the way individuals and societies grapple with the problem of death. This does not imply an instinctive origin for the fear of death (or even that fear of death is a universal emotion); it does not imply that a belief in immortality is universally the way in which religions meet the fact of death; it does not assume that the system of beliefs and practices of any particular religion is entirely functional for the total value system of the individuals and groups involved.

This much, then, remains: Everywhere, the ways in which men meet the problem of death lie within the realm of the sacred. Cults of the dead are among the primordial expressions of religion. Ancestor worship, "basically a device to cope with the emotionally shattering and socially disintegrating event of the death of an intimate member in the family group," as Yang says of China, is one of the most widespread forms of worship.[7] One of the most fundamental of the *efforts* of religion is to rescue individuals and societies from the destructive force of death. Whether these efforts are successful will depend on the degree to which they are congruent with other tendencies of the individuals involved and on other forces at work in the society. In a stable and homogeneous society, a coherent body of rites and beliefs may emerge which function "as well as might be expected"—in face of the stubborn fact that death remains. But in a mobile, heterogeneous society, individual personalities will be developed for whom the existing system of rites and beliefs proves to be unsatisfactory. Here can be seen a continuous struggling with new solutions, new formulas that will permit one to exclaim, with St. Paul, "Death, where is thy sting!"

We do not say, therefore: "One of the functions of religion is to solve the personality needs that come from the fact of death," but rather, "Religions everywhere struggle, sometimes partially successfully, sometimes unsuccessfully, with the problem of death." The particular religious system may not work for some individuals; it may tend to break down for a whole social group that has been drastically changed by some intrusive force (industrialization or great mobility or outside invasion); it may produce unintended consequences (latent functions and dysfunctions) that a complete analysis must explore.

The traditional view of death in a religion may require such an ascetic and demanding belief that the average person cannot hold to it, at least not without supplementary beliefs and rites. Thus the Buddha did not hold out what he believed were false hopes about immortality, but stressed instead that satisfaction could come only from realization of a common hopelessness. "From the world view of countless births and deaths that a human being experiences, *sub specio sansarae,* so to speak, the span between one single birth and death is but a speck of sand on the limitless shores of time. The contemplation of such vastness and one's littleness in the face of it cannot help but reduce the intensity of one's suffering." [8] In the face

7 C. K. Yang, *Religion in Chinese Society,* p. 29.

8 E. R. Sarachandra, in *Religion and Progress in Modern Asia,* Robert Bellah, ed., p. 113.

of such a stern interpretation of death, it is not surprising that ancestral and national cults have often developed that soften its message.

Our discussion has implied that the way in which a religion meets the fact of death has consequences for the society as well as for the individual members. The close interaction of these effects indicates again why an adequate theory of religion must combine the analysis of societal and personality systems. Parsons indicates this when he writes:

No ritual observances will bring the deceased back to life. But precisely for this reason, the problem of emotional adjustment is all the greater in importance. The significance both practically and emotionally of a human individual is of such a magnitude that his death involves a major process of readjustment for the survivors. Malinowski shows that the death of another involves exposure to sharply conflicting emotional reactions, some of which, if given free range, would lead to action and attitudes detrimental to the social group. There is great need for patterns of action which provide occasion for the regulated expression of strong emotions, and which in such a situation of emotional conflict reinforce those reactions which are most favorable to the continued solidarity and functioning of the social group.[9]

Some writers, following Durkheim, would stress this group function of rituals and beliefs about death almost to the exclusion of the individual function (the countering of individual fear and dismay). Radcliffe-Brown, for example, would say that the rites create the individual anxiety, rather than growing from it and expressing it. They represent primarily an effort on the part of society to reaffirm its solidarity. To the present writer, the interaction of the individual and group aspects seems to be the fundamental fact.

The wide range in the ways in which religions interpret death can perhaps be illustrated by contrasting the traditional Christian view of personal immortality with selections from a funeral address used by the Ethical Culture Society. If one were to ask a Christian layman to give his religious interpretation of death, he might well cite one or more of these passages from the Bible:

Yea, though I walk through the valley of the shadow of death, I will fear no evil: for thou art with me; thy rod and thy staff they comfort me. (Psalm 23:4)

For God so loved the world that he gave his only begotten Son, that whosoever believeth in him should not perish, but have everlasting life. (John 3:16)

So when this corruptible shall have put on incorruption, and this mortal shall have put on immortality, then shall be brought to pass the saying that is written, Death is swallowed up in victory. (I Corinthians 15:54)

Contrast these views, with their emphasis on the individual and his needs and fears, with brief selections from the Ethical Culture Society's funeral address, with its primary emphasis on the group and on moral problems. Yet note also that in both, despite the contrast, the effort is to make death somehow meaningful, to place it in a larger context, and to rescue the mourner from despair.

9 Talcott Parsons, *Essays in Sociological Theory Pure and Applied,* pp. 58–59.

Death brings us into closer communion with each other. We are not singled out for a special judgment when we give up our dead; we but enter into a common sorrow that visits the proudest and humblest, that has entered into unnumbered hearts before ours, and will enter into innumerable ones after us; a sorrow that tends to make the world one by dissolving all other feelings into sympathy and love.

. . . And when death speaks to us, what does it say? It does not speak of itself. It does not say: Fear me. It does not say: Wonder at me. It does not say: Understand me. It bids us think rather of life, of the privileges of life, of how great a thing life can be made. In the presence of death we are awakened to think of the meaning of life. And when we thus reflect, we see that there are things that are mightier than death. Honor is mightier than death, for men and women have died to escape dishonor. Justice is mightier than death, for men and women have chosen death rather than countenance or do injustice. Love is mightier than death, for men and women have oftimes died for those they loved.

. . . Let us commit ourselves with a new consecration to living in the spirit of human love and service. For it is only thus that true peace can be won. We would that out of this our sorrow may come a deeper sense of the worth of that love which prompts to self-forgetfulness, and finds solace in doing justice and in being ever more kind in our relations one with another. . . .[10]

Religious Responses to Frustration and Suffering

Death is the most difficult and serious problem with which religions attempt to deal. It cannot be separated, however, from other tension-creating difficulties that weaken social order and threaten the unity of personalities. Men carry the constant burden of earthly frustration and failure and of guilt, as defined largely by the cultural system they share. They face the fact that the highest earthly rewards manifestly do not always go to those who most closely follow the codes of a society; the just and the righteous may suffer and fail while "the ungodly" may prosper. Why do men suffer? Why is there evil in the world? This is a central religious question. Tension may also arise from the need for some explanation of the mysterious, awesome, and sometimes frightening facts of nature. Early students of the origins of religions doubtless gave too much emphasis to this cognitive problem, just as they defined religion too largely in terms of belief. But it would be equally unwise to disregard the partly emotional, partly intellectual questions that press in on us from nature. If we are no longer disturbed by echoes and shadows or even the awesome movement of the sun and stars, a large part of mankind still is puzzled by dreams, by visions and hallucinations, by the great mystery of how the universe, and man, came to be.

Seen from the perspective of the individual, religion is an effort to deal with the anxiety that springs from the sense of helplessness and frustration. Modern man is confronted by almost as many dangers and tragedies—the "tremendum" of experience, as Otto and Goodenough have called it—as were his forebears.[11] Insofar as religion reduces anxiety, as Malinowski noted, it releases action.

10 Quoted by James H. Leuba, *The Reformation of the Churches*, pp. 213–215.

11 Rudolf Otto, *The Idea of the Holy*; Erwin R. Goodenough, *The Psychology of Religious Experiences*.

The problems to which we have referred not only threaten the individual but are also potentially disruptive of the social order. A society that does not develop some system for dealing with them places a great burden on its members and risks its own disintegration. Samuel Klausner observes that worship helps to increase faith—which is the capacity to act. Since we want our fellows to live up to expectations, we seek guarantees of their motivation. Worship, a group act, can increase the courage of faith.[12]

Individuals will, of course, vary widely in the degree to which they experience these difficulties and in the meaning they attach to them. Some will have a great deal of frustration, others much less; but, in addition, some will have a higher tolerance level for frustration than others. Some will be relatively indifferent to the "injustice" in the distribution of rewards, while others will be acutely sensitive to the fact that "sinners" sometimes prosper while "saints" suffer. Few men, however, can escape the problem of evil entirely. Why do I suffer so? What can be the meaning of an existence in which so much suffering is found? It is to answer these questions that the religions of the world offer their roads to salvation.

Not only are there wide individual variations in frustration, tolerance for frustration, and sense of injustice, but there are also wide variations in the degree to which social systems produce these tendencies. For that reason, among others, there are many differences in the types of religion and the extent of religious interest in various societies. In every society, however, the total reservoir of need is large. Those who feel it most acutely may struggle with it in religious terms, making articulate what others sense only dimly. These struggles will have meaning for most individuals, if not at one time, then at another; and for a few—the mystics, the ascetics, the prophets—they become the dominant preoccupation of life.

Consequences of Religious Efforts to Deal with Frustration and Suffering. To say that religions are *attempts* to help individuals face frustration, failure, and injustice is not to say that any given religion succeeds. In rapidly changing societies, particularly, systems of belief and practice that once were effective in helping individuals deal with critical problems of life may prove to be ineffective. They are not thus proved to be false, any more than they were proved to be true when they were effective; they simply become irrelevant, meaningless. Only new religious patterns (usually built directly on the old, for the break is not sharp) that are congruent with the new societies and their members are likely to be effective. Thus a doctrine of transmigration may seem to ease the suffering and explain the lowliness of a Hindu peasant in a static society. None around him ever improves his status in life and no new methods for the reduction of pain and powerlessness are to be found. Such a doctrine, however, is proving to be less satisfying to the urbanized peasant who comes in contact with ideas and facts of social mobility, who acquires new needs for this life, and who sees that various means for struggling to satisfy those needs are in fact being used. In these circumstances Hinduism tends to change, and some of its adherents leave it for other religions or for secular systems of belief and practice that seem to them to be more relevant to their needs. The Communist Party in India exploits feelings of resentment among the

12 Samuel Klausner, "The Social Psychology of Courage," *Review of Religious Research,* 3, 1961, pp. 63–72.

members of lower castes and is particularly effective when these combine with regional and economic interests.[13] Dr. B. R. Ambedkar led perhaps 2½ million untouchables in a mass conversion to Buddhism,[14] and most of the converts from Hinduism to Christianity are drawn from the lowest castes.

Part of this emphasis on the need for study of actual consequences is the attention to *latent* functions and dysfunctions. Untouchables converted to Buddhism "experienced a sudden sense of release, a psychological freedom." They are "filled with a new spirit of self-confidence." [15] One sees similar results among converts to the Black Muslims in America. They feel a sharp break with old, unwanted selves; they acquire self-confidence and self-control.[16] Calvin's doctrine of predestination, essentially a religious doctrine, also had many latent consequences. The effort to prove to themselves and to others that they were of "the elect" may, as Weber declared, have driven men on to unusual thrift and industry. (We shall discuss Weber's thesis in a later chapter.) Most people would regard this as a latent function, a desirable but unexpected consequence of religious belief. It may also, however, have encouraged fanaticism, a desire to make certain that no sinners invaded the community of the elect, an arrogance, a lack of an ability to enjoy this life while proving oneself chosen for heavenly success—effects that most people would regard as dysfunctional. And in other circumstances, the doctrine of predestination leads to a defeatism that may carry undesired consequences. It is the total results that must be analyzed.

The comments of William James are highly interesting and instructive on this matter. In his discussion of "saintliness" he asks, What are its fruits? On the one hand, "The highest flights of charity, devotion, trust, patience, bravery to which the wings of human nature have spread themselves have been flown for religious ideals." [17] And yet, devoutness may lead to fanaticism; purity may lead to utter withdrawal; tenderness and charity may preserve the unfit and breed parasites; asceticism, carried to an extreme, repudiates life. It is clear that James considered these to be unhappy results. Regardless of value judgments, however, adequate analysis requires that we explore the conditions in which these various possibilities come about, before we can understand the total functions and dysfunctions of religion for personality and society. James also emphasizes, of course, what he considers to be the creative aspects of saintliness. Our soft age cannot appreciate the hard life of the ascetic, he writes. We have become afraid to be poor, and we are thus subject to slaveries from which the poor are free. We are less able to achieve the prophetic view of

13 This does not mean that communism seriously challenges the caste system; indeed it often bows to caste influence. See Taya Zinkin, *Caste Today*, p. 22. Other religions continue to be influenced by caste also.

14 From the *Census of India*, 1963, cited by Eleanor Zelliot, in *South Asian Politics and Religion*, Donald E. Smith, ed., p. 191.

15 See Zelliot in Smith, op. cit., chapter 9.

16 See E. U. Essien-Udom, *Black Nationalism;* and C. Eric Lincoln, *The Black Muslims in America.*

17 *The Varieties of Religious Experience*, p. 254.

the world that the ascetic contrives to grasp.[18] The task of analysis is to discover the conditions that maximize and those that minimize the various consequences of "saintliness."

With these qualifications in mind concerning the function of religion in serving human needs, it may be well to summarize the way in which religion is an *effort* to reduce tension, allay fear, and give a sense of unity to one's life. Howells describes the situation well:

Man's life is hard, very hard. And he knows it, poor soul; that is the vital thing. He knows that he is forever confronted with the Four Horsemen—death, famine, disease, and the malice of other men. And because he can speak and so frame ideas for himself and his mercurial imagination, he is nature's great and only worrier; he can worry alone and he can worry in unison, always with justice. It is among people living a primitive existence, however, that this should be particularly true.[19]

The last sentence is perhaps open to doubt. Howells may give too much attention to the physical problems of survival and too little to the tensions that come from a sense of failure to achieve socially learned goals, a feeling of justice (as defined by a person or society) left unserved. Moreover, in the day of hydrogen bombs, the power of science to grant life and health is brought into question. But his basic point is sound, and he weaves it into his very definition of religion, which he conceives to be something that is

used to piece out the ground between what man can attend to himself and what his imag'nation tells him must be attended to. It is the extension of his wishes and beliefs beyond the edges of what his senses grant him; it is what lies outside the light of the campfire. It is the notions he feels he must accept if life is to be satisfactory, or even safe. In other words, religion is composed of all the serious things man feels obliged to take for granted. . . . More than anything, it seems to reflect the refusal of man's whole being, physical and psychic, to accept a block to his aspirations or a menace to his peace of mind.[20]

Few human beings are able to avoid all the things they have learned to dread or able to achieve all the things they have been taught to desire. Religion is the effort to make the dreaded fact seem less dreadful, the failure less important or part of a larger, ultimate success; "for *all things* work together for good, for them that love God." Moreover, religion furnishes goals that all may share. "These are goals that transcend the world of actual experience, with the consequence that no evidence of failure to attain them can be conclusive. If the individual believes that he has gained them, that is sufficient. All he needs is sufficient faith, and faith feeds on subjective need." [21]

So it is that the religious person, acutely aware of man's finitude and of the tragedies and frustrations of life, may declare, with Isaiah:

> The foundations of the earth do shake.
> Earth breaks to pieces,

18 See ibid., pp. 254–369.

19 William W. Howells, *The Heathens, Primitive Man and His Religions*, p. 17.

20 Ibid., p. 19 and p. 293.

21 Kingsley Davis, *Human Society*, p. 532.

Earth is split in pieces,
Earth shakes to pieces,
Earth reels like a drunken man,
Earth rocks like a hammock;
Under the weight of its transgression earth falls down
To rise no more!

Lift up your eyes to heaven and look upon the earth beneath:
For the heavens shall vanish away like smoke.
And the earth shall grow old like a robe;
The world itself shall crumble.
But my righteousness shall be forever,
And my salvation knows no end.   (Isaiah 24: 18–20)

Variation in Religious Tendencies and Needs

The fact of death, the sense of injustice and of failure, the feeling of helplessness—in sum, the problems of suffering and evil—are universal in one form or another. A science of religion must deal not only with such shared experiences, however, but also with variations in character and experience as they relate to religious behavior. Individuals in modern societies differ widely in the strength and form of their religious interest. Is this simply a manifestation of differences in training, or does it also indicate the influence of differences in basic character structure and of variation in other personal tendencies? Is it related to different social roles, with their various requirements and influences?

The sacred books, the rites, the basic beliefs of a religion almost certainly spring from the intensely religious persons, from those who have felt the problems of suffering and evil most acutely. They also develop during the critical periods of history—the times of disorder and maximum stress. Thus religions are equipped to carry the "peak load" of human need. For many people, however, suffering and evil are less acute. It is a mistake to assume that only the intensive religious experience of the mystic or the ascetic or the person overwhelmed by the problem of evil needs explanation. The more casual beliefs and actions of the mildly religious are also important. This requires some attention to normal socialization and to the cultural norms that are transferred to most members of a society in the process of growing up.

There are several aspects to this question: (1) The need for religion is partly a culturally learned need and will vary, therefore, with the nature of one's training. (2) Variation in religion is partly related to different social roles; one's place in the social structure influences the extent and direction of religious interest. (3) Differences in experience beyond those that derive directly from culture and role affect personal tendencies and therefore religious inclinations. The basic attitude toward oneself, for example—a product in large measure of the experiences of the first decade of life—is an important influence on one's religious inclinations.

Social Learning as a Source of Religious Need. Intensive analysis of the place of religion in the struggle for individual adjustment sometimes causes us to overlook the rather prosaic fact that those persons who are most interested in religion, who express the strongest need for religion, are drawn, although not entirely, from those groups that are most concerned about training their members to be religious. On the basis of his study of a sample of university students in Australia, Brown warns against reductionist interpretations of religious beliefs—namely, that they are expressions of such underlying needs and tendencies as authoritarianism, extraversion, neuroticism, rigidity, and the like. "The results from this factorial study are inconsistent with the assumption that a person's religious beliefs depend upon personality attributes. . . . The religious belief factor is quite clearly involved with social variables operating within a religious context, including a family tradition of churchgoing, the social support provided by a religious denomination, and acceptance of the church as a significant institution." [22] Brown's data most strongly support a social learning theory. One learns his religion from those around him. This is not inconsistent with the idea that individual needs are among the sources of religion; but what is learned, and to some degree the intensity of religious interest, are carried along on a social stream. Fundamentalist parents tend to bring up children who share the fundamentalist tradition; liberal religious views are found most often among those who have been trained to such views. Liberal and conservative may be manifesting no deep-seated character differences; perhaps they were simply taught different religious beliefs. And later change in such beliefs is often group-supported. College students move away from orthodoxy in response to norms of an academic setting and in interaction with their fellows.[23]

More individual changes in belief and practice, to be sure, as well as variations among those brought up in the same tradition, indicate that cultural training alone does not account for religious attitudes and behavior. We are indicating simply that it is important not to overlook the influence of normal socialization. This is obvious when one takes a cross-cultural view; it should be given full attention in the explanation of religious variation within a society as well.

In a study of 412 Harvard and 85 Radcliffe students, Allport, Gillespie, and Young found a marked relationship between the extent of religious influence in a person's upbringing and the feeling of need for religion. Among the men, 82 per cent of those who reported a "very marked" religious influence in their early training indicated a need for religion; only 32 per cent among those who answered "none at all" to the training question reported such a need. The percentages among the women were 96 and 44. Clearly the felt need for a religious orientation is in part a product of one's training; yet it should not be overlooked that a third or more of those who had no early religious training still expressed a need for religion.[24] And we might inquire further whether those who declared that they felt no need for religion may not express a need for some alternative,

22 L. B. Brown, "The Structure of Religious Belief," *Journal for the Scientific Study of Religion*, 6, 1966, p. 268. See also R. M. Dreger, "Some Personality Correlates of Religious Attitudes, as Determined by Projective Techniques," *Psychological Monographs*, 66, 1952.

23 See Joseph Havens, "The Changing Climate of Research on the College Student and His Religion," *Journal for the Scientific Study of Religion*, 3, 1963, pp. 62–69.

24 Gordon Allport, James Gillespie, and Jacqueline Young, "The Religion of the Post-War College Student," *The Journal of Psychology*, January, 1948, p. 11.

some system of faith and devotion that does not bear the name religion but functions for them in many of the same ways.

In 1955 and again in 1967 I put the same questions used by Allport to random samples of Oberlin College students (total n = 532). The results, which are tabulated in Table 7–1, were similar to the Harvard-Radcliffe study. Among men and women and for both years, the more marked the respondents' religious training, the more likely were they to express a need for a religious orientation to life.

Table 7–1. Relationship between strength of religious training and felt need for religious orientation

	Felt need for religious orientation	Strength of religious training						
		Very marked		Moderate		Slight or none at all		Total by felt need
		%	n	%	n	%	n	%	n
1955 males	Yes	76	(22)	70	(30)	46	(17)	63	(69)
	No or doubtful	24	(7)	30	(13)	54	(20)	37	(40)
	Total by strength of training	27	(29)	39	(43)	34	(37)	100	(109)
1955 females	Yes	93	(40)	85	(40)	50	(13)	80	(93)
	No or doubtful	7	(3)	15	(7)	50	(13)	20	(23)
	Total by strength of training	37	(43)	40	(47)	23	(26)	100	(116)
1967 males	Yes	84	(41)	57	(36)	40	(23)	59	(100)
	No or doubtful	16	(8)	43	(27)	60	(34)	41	(69)
	Total by strength of training	29	(49)	38	(63)	34	(57)	100	(169)
1967 females	Yes	77	(34)	71	(39)	54	(21)	68	(94)
	No or doubtful	23	(10)	29	(16)	46	(18)	32	(44)
	Total by strength of training	32	(44)	40	(55)	28	(39)	100	(138)

In these four series there is not a single exception to the statement that the more marked the religious training, as judged by the persons questioned, the stronger the felt need for a religious orientation. Whatever other influences are involved, it is clear that a substantial proportion of the variation in felt need for a religious orientation can be accounted for by the perceived strength of religious training. It should be noted, to be sure, that we have no direct measure of the religious training received by these students. We rely instead on their memories and perceptions. It is conceivable that those with the strongest need selectively remember and those with the weakest need selectively forget their training. To whatever extent this may be true, the inference that training creates need must be reversed. Although this seems unlikely to be a major factor, its possible presence in these data and in the Allport study suggests that character influences cannot quickly be set aside in favor of a "social learning" theory.

Role Influences on Religious Need. The interrelationship of the personality aspects of religion with the sociocultural influences is further shown by variation in religious interest among those who occupy different social roles. The concept of *role* is one of the key meeting places of personality theory and sociocultural theory, for it represents an internalized style of life for the individual and at the same time a cultural blueprint of approved behavior for certain designated members of a society. Although our evidence is not precise, there is little doubt that the extent and nature of religious interest varies significantly among persons occupying different social roles. One illustration may serve to make this point: Women in the United States are known to be "more religious" than men; they make up a larger proportion of church membership, take a larger part in religious-group affairs, and express more interest in religion when asked about their beliefs than men do. Allport found that 82 per cent of the women students whom he studied reported need for a religious orientation, as compared with 76 per cent of nonveteran men and 64 per cent of veterans.[25]

When I repeated Allport's question in 1955 and 1967, I obtained similar results; but the differences in attitude between men and women were smaller, particularly in the latter year. Among women students, the percentages expressing a need for a religious orientation were 80 in 1955 and 68 in 1967, as shown in Table 7–1. Among the men the percentages answering Yes in the two years were 63 and 59.

This tendency toward convergence of attitudes of men and women was not found in a study of National Merit Scholarship winners in a variety of colleges. Differences between men and women students were rather small at the time of their entrance to college, with 88 per cent and 91 per cent indicating a personal need to believe in some sort of religious faith. Those asked the question at the end of their junior year were less likely to give an affirmative answer and the contrast between men and women was larger—51 per cent as opposed to 69 per cent.[26]

Despite their differences, these various studies all support the observation that men and women in American society differ to some degree in the strength of their religious interest, a contrast that should neither be exaggerated nor overlooked. How can the facts be accounted for? They can partly be explained, in my judgment, by reference to differences in social role. Women occupy a more important place in the socialization of the young. The rights and duties embodied in their role expectations in American society give them less latitude and choice. They are expected to abide more closely by the traditional standards of the culture than are men. In addition to these cultural facts—the normative influences on their behavior—there are certain effects of their place in the social structure. Women in general have narrower contacts and have therefore experienced somewhat less secularization than men. There are strains that derive from their roles in a situation where there is an equalitarian ideology, but many non-

25 See Gordon Allport, *The Individual and His Religion,* p. 37.

26 Harold Webster, Mervin Freedman, and Paul Heist, "Personality Changes in College Students," in *The American College,* Nevitt Sanford, ed., p. 826. See also Gerhard Lenski, "Social Correlates of Religious Interest," *American Sociological Review,* 18, 1953, pp. 533–544.

equalitarian facts of life—a situation that produces some minority-group influences on their religious behavior. Women in American society wield less secular power than men, they have fewer secular-group contacts. Religious-group associations and religious interests, therefore, seem to fill a more important place in their lives. This is not true of all women, of course. For a full explanation we would need to introduce evidence of individual character variation which, along with the cultural and structural facts, influences the extent of religious interest.

This contrast between men and women does not apply to many societies. Because of different cultural expectations and the different influences of their place in the social structure, it is often the men who are "more religious." The effects of roles are deeply imbedded in the patterns of specific societies. Kiyomi Morioka, for example, in his study of Japanese farm families found more male than female participation in religious rites.[27] This is a study of behavior, not of belief, which was the focus of the American studies cited above. Among Muslims, Buddhists, and Jews, it is generally true that men predominate in public acts of worship. Role requirements may not be the same for the several dimensions of religion. American data, however, generally show that women are more religious than men in several dimensions.[28] We need, however, to examine less traditional forms of religion than the reported studies emphasized. Men may be more involved in the "invisible" and unconventional forms, to which the term religion may not be attached.

Interactions Between Character and Religious Need. Social learning and role variation help to account for variation in religious behavior and values. To such structural and cultural factors, however, we need to add attention to individual character. Our brief references to sociocultural influences may help us to avoid the implication, which is not uncommon in discussions of religious experience, that religious interests are found only among the more anxious and insecure members of society. But they should not lead us to neglect the fact that individual needs and inclinations vary.

The relationship between religion and character is highly complex, as the following questions may suggest: Which is the independent variable? What dimensions of religion and of character shall be studied? And how shall they be measured? Reference to a few empirical studies will document this complexity and indicate some fruitful lines of inquiry for understanding it.

In a factor analysis of responses to fifty-six items measuring religious orientation, Robert Monoghan found three distinct patterns among the members of a fundamentalist church. He identified the patterns as "authority-seeker," "comfort-seeker," and "social participator." [29] Among the mem-

27 See *The Sociology of Japanese Religion*, Kiyomi Morioka and William Newell, eds., pp. 25–43. Morioka declines to use the term *role*, because he has evidence, based on household time budgets, only of religious participation, not of the normative agreement denoted by the term *role*. This is a wise caution; but he recognizes that independent role measures might yield similar results.

28 See Charles Glock, Benjamin Ringer, and Earl Babbie, *To Comfort and to Challenge*, p. 42. See also David Moberg, *The Church as a Social Institution*, pp. 396–401, for a discussion of various interpretations of the greater religiosity of American women.

29 Robert Monoghan, "Three Faces of the True Believer. Motivations for Attending a Fundamentalist Church," *Journal for the Scientific Study of Religion*, 6, 1967, pp. 236–245.

bers of this church, different needs were expressed by their participation. These needs are treated as independent variables which produce, despite their differences, a similar result.

In their study of Catholics and Protestants in a Midwestern county, Schroeder and Obenhaus think of religious membership as the independent variable and ask: Can one, by knowledge of church membership, predict such personal characteristics as family emotional attitudes, peer identification, relationship to authority, sexual adjustment, and intellectual functioning? Using the Thematic Apperception Test to measure these dependent variables, they found few differences across denominational lines. This result could be due, as the authors note, to a common lack of influence by the churches on the characteristics measured, or to the fact that the Catholic and various Protestant denominations have a similar influence on those characteristics. They are inclined toward the latter interpretation.[30]

These studies deal with religion as a unitary phenomenon, measured either by participation or membership. James Keene undertakes a more complicated task by relating several dimensions of religion to several dimensions of personality.[31] Although his respondents are not a formal sample, he was able to match fifty from each of five groups on the basis of age, sex, education, and socioeconomic status. This strengthens the possibility that observed relationships are due to the religion-personality interaction and not to uncontrolled variation in other variables. The results are too complex to report in detail; but the main finding can be stated. There are several significant personality-religion interactions. Knowing which of the five religious groups to which a person belongs (Jewish, Catholic, Protestant, Baha'i and nonaffiliates), we know something of his scores on the four personality factors (neurotic-adaptive, spontaneous-inhibited, worldminded-ethnocentric, and self-accommodating–group-accommodating). That is, the group means and variances are significantly different. We also know something about his scores on the four dimensions of religion that emerged from a factor analysis of the questions used. More importantly, various interactions among the dimensions appeared. "For example, participation in religion (Salient) is correlated with Worldmindedness in the Baha'i group and with Ethnocentrism in the Jewish group." [32] Keene also found that the orthodox experience of religion was related to adaptive behavior. This lends support to the importance of Allport's distinction between extrinsic and intrinsic religion; or, as Keene suggests, it may help to account for the different interpretations of Freud and Jung. Religion for Freud was orthodoxy; for Jung it was an inner, personal experience.[33]

These brief references to social learning, role, and character may suggest the several factors governing variation in religious tendencies and needs. Only when we have learned to bring them together in a common framework of analysis, however, will we be able to speak with some confidence about the sources of that variation.

30 W. W. Schroeder and Victor Obenhaus, *Religion in American Culture: Unity and Diversity in a Midwestern County*, Chap. 5.

31 James Keene, "Religious Behavior and Neuroticism, Spontaneity, and World-mindedness," *Sociometry*, 30, 1967, pp. 137–157.

32 Ibid., p. 154.

33 Ibid., p. 153.

Chapter Eight

RELIGION AND CHARACTER (Continued)

In the preceding chapter we treated religion as a relatively undifferentiated fact, while examining its relationship to general and variant individual characteristics. Here we will reverse that perspective by focusing attention on the variation among religious traditions and in types of religious experience, with little attention being given to character differences.

THE VARIETIES OF RELIGIOUS INTERPRETATIONS OF NEEDS

It is not enough to examine individual needs as sources of religion. We could not thereby account for the wide variety of ways in which religions interpret those needs. This variation doubtless reflects the different circumstances human beings face, and have faced. Once formulated and institutionalized, however, various religions' interpretations of the need of or the essence of the human condition affect the ways in which need is experienced. They also affect the actual level of some needs, by their influence on values and motivations. We shall sketch, therefore, the various ways in which religions define man's fundamental needs and design ways to satisfy or handle them.

The Problem of Evil

What we have been discussing becomes, in theological terms, the problem of evil and the question of religious efforts to save man from evil. In one way or another, religions declare that though the "earth breaks to pieces," "my salvation knows no end." It is the sociologist's task to inquire: How do different societies, or separate groups in a society, interpret suffering and evil? What different ways to salvation do they find meaningful and satisfying? Are these differences related to their total social situation?

One may describe a broad continuum along which religions are ranged in their interpretation of evil. The world may be considered basically good, evil and suffering being thought of, not as the ultimate essence of the world but as specific problems with which men can hope to grapple successfully. The Homeric interpretation of Greek religion, classic Confucianism, and modern humanism are close to this position. Or, the world may be thought to be filled with evil and yet "sanctifiable." This is the ambivalent position of the classic Muslim and Christian traditions. They are pessimistic about the present state of the world, but the pessimism is conditional. One need not surrender to despair or resignation, for with God's help man may struggle with evil and suffering with enough success to make the struggle worthwhile, even if ultimate success is not likely to be achieved on earth. The third position is more radically pessimistic. Evil and suffering are the inevitable lot of man on earth; they can be dealt with only by rejection of the world, by detachment from this life. This is the dominant view in Hinduism and more especially in the more pristine forms of Buddhism.

There are various possible modes of orientation to evil and suffering in addition to religion. One might take each problem as it came along and try to reduce it, without trying to find some ultimate meaning. One might examine it objectively, trying to find out how it came about. Religion, however, which offers itself as a road to salvation from man's ultimate problems, must try to furnish an answer to the question of *why*: Why is there evil; why do men suffer? And more than that, Why is there such wide variation among men in the extent of suffering and of evil?

It is not the concern of the sociologist of religion to judge among the various answers to these questions, but rather to ask: In what kinds of societies and among what groups do the various interpretations of evil arise? And what are their various consequences? The evidence does not suggest any clear and easy formula that answers these questions. There is no clear development, for example, from religions that make a thoroughly pessimistic response to the question of evil and suffering, through religions that take an ambivalent position, to those that tend toward "this-worldly optimism." The religions of primitive peoples, which we assume, perhaps unwisely, to be very ancient, seldom if ever adopt a radically pessimistic view, devaluing this world, counseling resignation to suffering, and projecting hopes outward to another world. The idea of heaven, if it is conceptualized at all, is likely to be thought of as a continuation of the good of this life, for the religions of primitive peoples describe no dichotomy between the evil of this world and the peace and happiness of the next.

However a given conception of the problem of evil may have developed (and we shall see in the chapters on social change that one may sometimes regard religion as the dependent and sometimes as the independent variable) it has great implications for the whole social system. It is functionally interdependent with many secular values and structures. Thus a society overwhelmed by pestilence and suffering may nourish a religious view of the world that is highly pessimistic. Once established, however, such a religion helps to shape the values which its adherents pursue in their secular as well as their religious activities.

To the orthodox Hindu, for example, the evil experienced by an individual is a result of his conduct in an earlier life. "An orthodox Hindu confronted with the deplorable situation of a member of an impure caste would only think that he has a great many sins to redeem from his prior existence. . . . The reverse of this is that a member of an impure caste thinks primarily of how to better his future social opportunities at rebirth by leading an exemplary life according to caste ritual." [1] That is, he accepts the definition of the sources of evil, and seeks only to relieve its crushing burden on him by strict fulfillment of his caste obligations. As Weber noted, this is the most consistent theodicy ever produced, a very "tough" system within which those who had the most to gain by change were least motivated to do so, for fear their lot would become even worse in the next life. "So long as the *karma* doctrine was unshaken, revolutionary ideas or progressivism were inconceivable." [2]

Within a society, to be sure, there are often different interpretations of the meaning of evil by those on whom suffering has fallen in unequal amounts. Where there are class differences, those who are successful need to feel justified in their success, and consequently seek, by religion as well as by other means, for ways in which they can protect themselves against the claims of the less successful and against their own doubts. Thus if suffering and evil befall the poor, this is a sign of their odiousness, their unworthiness. Those on the lower status levels, on the other hand, seek support for their violated sense of justice and an assurance that their present state is a meaningful part of a total career (here and beyond) that promises ultimate success. Suffering, indeed, may become a mark of virtue, and lowliness of status a condition for greater rewards to come. The evil that befalls them is not a sign, in this view, of their own previous failings, but of injustice or the accident of birth. Challenges to the social order can stem from such belief.

The religious view of a society or of a class in a society is by no means perfectly correlated with the existing level of suffering, but social circumstances are among the factors that influence the ways in which the problem of evil will be handled.

In addition to class variation, another factor affects definitions of and responses to evil. A large share of the world's people are participants in more than one religion, or in a syncretist faith that carries diverse elements within it. They may accept and act upon quite contradictory beliefs. The sanctified beliefs of the "high" tradition regarding evil may carry with them one set of interpretations and obligations, although the workaday beliefs carry other interpretations and obligations. Most Burmese, for example, think of themselves as Buddhists. If they interpret Buddhist doctrines strictly, the suffering they experience is a result of the balance of merits and demerits they have accumulated in earlier existences. One can affect his future existence by meritorious behavior on earth, but he cannot change his lot in the present. This is a severe doctrine, however, for the average person to accept with all his heart. He is confronted here and now with a great many ills that threaten to overwhelm him. He deals with them by rational means, of course; but he also tries to appease the nats—

1 Max Weber, *The Religion of India*, p. 121.

2 Ibid., p. 123.

the troublesome spirits that abound. And he calls in exorcists and shamans to help him control the sources of his suffering. "As Buddhists we should not propitiate the nats, but out of fear, we must."[3]

The meaning of evil, therefore, is not defined solely by the religious culture, influential though it may be. It is defined also by the social structure and one's location in it, by an individual's experience, and by his tendencies to interpret that experience in given ways. We will not get very far if we are content to say: Buddhism, or Hinduism, or Judaism, seen as a coherent and intellectualized system, interprets evil in such and such way, and therefore its adherents respond to it accordingly.

Religious Roads to Salvation

Not only do conceptions of the nature of evil vary widely, both in terms of what are man's deepest problems and how ineradicable they are, but the ways of salvation are also extremely diverse. On this, most religions agree: Man can be saved; suffering and injustice are not his final lot. There is wide disagreement on *how* and *when* salvation will be achieved; but every religion, by definition, offers itself as a road, and many claim to be *the* road, to salvation. Many human endeavors, of course, are concerned with salvation in some sense, again indicating that religion is not sharply cut off from other aspects of life. King expresses this well when he writes:

Art would save man from ugliness and boredom; philosophy from the unexamined life and the incoherent intellectual world; science, as the epitome of all practical disciplines, would save us from ignorant slavery to natural forces and the more severe physical threats to life and welfare; politics would provide a bulwark against social chaos, anarchy or civil war within, and against aggression from without; ethics would save us from unprincipled and unregulated conduct.[4]

Thus religion, as King says, enters a somewhat crowded field. A line can be drawn between the religious and the nonreligious approaches to salvation, however, on the basis of the ultimate quality of the religious attempt. Within various religious systems, one may find ways of protecting the believer against almost every threat—sickness, hunger, childlessness, false pride, malevolent spirits, and on through a long list. These are concerns that religions share with—and perhaps tend to hand over to—other techniques of human adjustment. The core that remains to religion, however, is the attempt to save man from meaninglessness, from despair when his partial efforts at salvation fail, from the sense of final annihilation, or, in the most pessimistic formulation, from the inability to obtain annihilation.

The idea of salvation raises many questions for the sociologist. How do religions vary in proposed roads to salvation? When and where will man be saved according to the various conceptions? Are there systematic differences among types of societies and among individuals in terms of the approaches to salvation that they are likely to find satisfying? What are the

3 Melford Spiro, *Burmese Supernaturalism*, quoting one of his informants. Spiro's discussion of this doctrinal conflict is full of insights. See especially pp. 253–257.

4 Winston L. King, *Introduction to Religion*, p. 122.

consequences for human interaction of the adoption of different patterns? In the chapters that follow, we shall be exploring such questions as these in some detail, with reference to specific groups and situations. Here we shall simply sketch the broad outlines of the range of answers.

Conceptions of salvation vary enormously among, and indeed within, the world religions. One can think of a range—it is probably too Western a notion to describe it as a pessimism-optimism range—along which the many beliefs can be placed. On the one hand are the conceptions that salvation means the surcease of desire, the absence of earthly pain, a merging of self into the absolute, or the final annihilation that brings release from the recurrent rounds of birth and death. At the other extreme are those conceptions of salvation that see man's final state as the purest expression of all his joys; it is paradise, heavenly bliss, an experience that is not only free from pain and death but that offers positive and supreme happiness. Without paying attention to the wide variation through time and place (variations that permit interpreters to find the "true" belief at many different points), we can say that the former conception characterizes the Hindu and Buddhist traditions, whereas the latter expresses the Judaic, Christian, and Muslim traditions.

One can immediately note exceptions to this generalization. In some expressions of the Hindu tradition, for example, nirvana is a state of bliss; indeed, through perfect knowledge, it may even be attained on this earth. Such a belief, as Weber noted, has given encouragement to independent mystical movements of great intensity. Such heterodox sects have challenged the influence of orthodox priests and the more traditional interpretations.[5] On the other hand, sectarian movements in the Christian tradition sometimes carry a tone of nirvana—Free us from pain, from fear, from desire, they beseech God.

These exceptions are important, and the science of religion must not only explore the conditions that promote them but also study their consequences. But the presence of exceptions should not obscure a fundamental difference in outlook that develops among most of those immersed in the Eastern or the Western tradition. To a dedicated Buddhist, even one for whom secular opportunities are quite abundant, salvation is the attainment of serene composure and liberation from desire. To the dedicated Christian, even one for whom secular opportunities are minimal, salvation is the attainment of positive joys. As the plantation Negro sang: "I gotta shoes, I gotta robe, I gotta crown . . . and I'll shout all over God's heaven." This contrast in the meaning of salvation has shaped experience and activity in powerful ways.

Despite these differences, however, it would be a mistake to forget the sense in which the world religions are alike in their beliefs about salvation. All offer radical solutions to human ills: What one sees, hears, and experiences, what one's people have seen, heard, and experienced for as long as the memory of man goes back, is not the true meaning of existence. In the last analysis it is unimportant. This radical doctrine must be viewed against man's primordial condition. Illness, injury, and hunger are endemic. At what we might call the natural death rate, half of a community

5 See Max Weber, op. cit., pp. 178–179.

dies before reaching ten years of age. And if an individual manages to avoid these evils for a time, many of his fellows are ready to contribute to his malaise in some other fashion. With problems as deep as these, only a most dramatic way of salvation can command man's allegiance. The way must not be vulnerable to constant refutation—it must be super-empirical; and it must be demanding on the believer—it must strain his endurance, his income, his credulity. Without such strains he will not believe it sufficient to deal with the grievous condition in which man finds himself. Those for whom some of the problems have receded, to be sure, modify the severity of these doctrines. Projection of salvation into a different life is unnecessary, for one can imagine such a condition existing on earth simply by extrapolating from his own experiences and those of others. Since such a man's problems are less overwhelming, he can be convinced of the truth of doctrines that are less demanding—of energy, time, resources, and intellect. But this contrast is one of degree. Who can say that even the most prosperous and fortunate residents of the twentieth century have an easy existence? Some of the primordial problems have been reduced, but mankind has shown extraordinary talent for inventing new ones. The faith of a few has become naturalistic, but it is still super-empirical. With apologies to Kierkegaard, we must still *leap* onto the road to salvation. No path of facts and observation will take us there.

There are, of course, sharp value disputes involving contrasting doctrines of salvation. If one believes that some measure of salvation is possible within the limits of human societies, projection of all hope into another existence is unfortunate. However, if one believes that the fundamental fact of human life on earth is tragedy, religious efforts to alleviate what are seen as minor ills in this life may seem to endanger the wholehearted search for salvation beyond.[6]

There is another sense in which the world's religions are more alike than they are different. They face a common problem: Their radical, classical descriptions of the road to salvation are so demanding that few can follow them to the end. Even if we are convinced that only the ultimate salvation is worth striving for, we cannot escape the burdens of every day. It is all right to talk about nirvana several existences from now, but today I suffer. Only the few can dedicate themselves to ultimate salvation in face of the need for little pieces of salvation in the present. Confronted by these needs, the classical traditions are bent to include them, or they are joined by more magically oriented traditions, or both. Thus once again, as with the problem of evil, the student of religion must be aware of the complex structure of beliefs about salvation, and not be satisfied with idealized versions.[7]

The central task of the sociology of religion in dealing with this problem is to see what societies, what groups, and what individuals take various views of salvation. Niebuhr suggests a thesis—although it is an oversimple one:

Evolutionary millennialism is always the hope of comfortable and privileged classes, who imagine themselves too rational to accept the idea of the sudden

6 See Talcott Parsons, *The Social System*, pp. 367–379.

7 See Winston King, *A Thousand Lives Away*, Chap. 2.

emergence of the absolute in history. For them the ideal is in history, working its way to ultimate triumph. They identify God and nature, the real and the ideal, not because the more dualistic conceptions of classical religion are too irrational for them (though they are irrational); but because they do not suffer as much as the disinherited from the brutalities of contemporary society, and therefore do not take as catastrophic a view of contemporary history.[8]

Class position, as Niebuhr suggests, is no doubt one of the factors influencing the view of salvation that will be adopted, but its impact will vary with the religious tradition, with the nature of leadership, with the personal development of a given individual, with the total social situation in which class identity is experienced. There are times when the "disinherited" support religious movements that conceive of salvation in history; and members of the "privileged classes" may project their religious hopes wholly into a future life. Such circumstances do not contradict the thesis that schemes of salvation are related to social facts; but they do indicate the need for exploring complicated series of social facts.

The Means to Salvation. We have referred to the various ways in which salvation is defined by the world religions and the time patterns that they envisage. Doctrines of salvation also prescribe the means. Beliefs about the appropriate ways vary, of course, among those who have different conceptions of the basic human problem, because the ways must be designed to deal with the major obstacles. We have referred to three fundamental points of tension for mankind: his limited insight and knowledge, his limited power of endurance in the face of continuous suffering, and his limited ability to achieve justice. It is around these three points that the answers to the question, How shall man achieve salvation, are formulated. By knowledge, by devotion, by works—these are the roads.[9] They correspond closely, although not perfectly, with mysticism, asceticism, and prophecy, as we shall see.

No religion is likely to give emphasis exclusively to one of these approaches, although particular groups and individuals may do so. "Love alone is blind, knowledge alone is lame." [10] Such versions of desirable mixtures are important clues to the nature of a religion and its subdivisions. With good methods of measurement we might compare the "salvation profiles" of different groups. Similarity of profile—that is, matching emphasis on knowledge, devotion, and works—may be as significant as similarity or difference in the content of religious beliefs.

Differences in status and other secular facts are often related to differences in emphasis and the attendant controversies over the best roads to salvation. Salvation through action has many different varieties: full and correct performance of the religious law may be considered most important, which is a strong element in both the Muslim and Jewish traditions; partaking of sacraments may be emphasized, as in Roman Catholicism; or morality, right behavior toward one's fellows, in the manner of Puritanism, may be given primary attention.

8 Reinhold Niebuhr, *Moral Man and Immoral Society,* p. 62.

9 For excellent discussions of this topic, see Winston King, *Introduction to Religion,* Pt. III; and Max Weber, *Sociology of Religion,* Chaps. 10–12.

10 D. T. Suzuki, *Outlines of Mahayana Buddhism,* p. 361.

To seek salvation through devotion is often the way of the untrained layman, the religiously illiterate. Unskilled in the law, unmoved by the established forms of worship, he seeks salvation by the ardor of his belief. If he cannot follow the mystic's pursuit of direct knowledge of the universe, or win reassurance from his priest by the punctilious performance of correct action, he can give a fervent and emotional demonstration of his faith in the efficacy of his religious patterns, and thus seek to insure his salvation.

To seek salvation by knowledge in the religious sense is not to follow the prosaic and severely limited methods of the scientist. To pursue knowledge through controlled observation may be accepted and even encouraged, but it is almost never considered to be the fundamental source of truth for religion. A much higher place is given to intuitive knowledge achieved through meditation, to knowledge derived directly from God, to the insight of the mystic into the "ultimate reality." This approach to salvation is found in its most intensive form in Hinduism and Buddhism, but it is not lacking in the religious life even of "secularized" urban people in Western societies.

One further question concerns the *consequences* for human behavior of various approaches to salvation. Emphasis on works promotes the development of elaborate ecclesiastical structures for the interpretation of the laws and the administration of the sacraments. This has very different effects upon the social order than those that result from an emphasis on mysticism, on the individual pursuit of religious understanding, or on devotion. A highly structured Roman Catholicism, with its emphasis on works, is very differently related to the societies of which it is a part than fundamentalist Protestantism, which lays primary emphasis on devotion as the road to salvation. An even sharper contrast can be drawn between Catholicism and Hinduism, where the mystical approach is of great importance. The mystic's search for direct contact with the ultimate reality of the universe can be carried on in almost complete indifference to the situation existing around him. This is not to say that it does not affect that situation; but it does so indirectly. Catholicism, on the other hand, becomes directly and immediately involved in the total social structure.

We must be thoroughly aware, therefore, that however the different approaches to salvation may have developed, once they become established they have a direct effect upon the social situation and must therefore be seen as important forces influencing human life.

THE VARIETIES OF RELIGIOUS EXPERIENCE

Although they are closely connected, we can distinguish between the definitions of evil and salvation found in a religion and the individual experiences through which those definitions are interpreted. This distinction is needed because the experiences are products, not only of the religious values and structures, but also of the full range of tendencies of the individuals involved and the social situations in which they find themselves. Therefore, we need a field perspective: Individuals are culturally prepared for certain experiences, both by specifically religious values and by relevant secular norms. They are also affected by the situation, particularly by the kinds of support they are getting from others. And their religious experiences are influenced by their values, needs, and motives, both those that spring directly from their religious training and those that result from the full range of their socialization.

We can define religious experience as a general term, following Joachim Wach, as a response to what is seen as ultimate reality.[11] The variety of religious experiences is extremely wide, ranging from the relatively prosaic reaffirmation that comes from performance of an accustomed rite to the loss of self or the enormous heightening of self in trance or ecstasy. The range was made vivid a half-century ago in William James's classic distinction between the religion of "healthy-mindedness" and the religion of "the sick soul." The weakness of his explanation was his tendency to rely on a vague concept of temperamental differences to account for the range, rather than to explore the differences in personal experience and the differences in social environment that lie behind individual variation. The healthy-minded are inclined to view life optimistically; they do not linger over the darker facts of human existence. In contrast to this deliberate minimization of evil is the tendency of the sick soul to maximize evil, ". . . based on the persuasion that the evil aspects of life are of its very essence, and that the world's meaning most comes home to us when we lay them most to heart." [12] There are those who cannot easily throw off the burden of evil and guilt but suffer constantly from its presence. The sense of failure, pain, and helplessness may come even to the successful and the powerful. Such individuals resist what they consider to be the superficiality of the healthy-minded view of life. Those in whom awareness of sin and sorrow and suffering is most acute reason that:

To ascribe religious value to mere happy-go-lucky contentment with one's brief chance at natural good is but the very consecration of forgetfulness and superficiality. Our troubles lie indeed too deep for *that* cure. The fact that we *can* die, that we *can* be ill at all, is what perplexes us; the fact that we now for a moment live and are well is irrelevant to that perplexity. We need a life not correlated with death, a health not liable to illness, a kind of good that will not perish, a good in fact that flies beyond the Goods of nature.[13]

To those who hold this view, an individual who is not thoroughly aware of suffering and evil is simply shortsighted. If *he, now*, does not suffer and does not need their radical scheme of salvation, in time he will.

There is a substantial literature, much of it stimulated by James's work, dealing with particular varieties of religious experience—conversion, ecstasy, possession, and revelation; experiences of joy, terror, wonder, mysticism, and prophetic power; along with less exuberant experiences of contentment, enlightenment, and expansion of self.[14] The rich descriptions have not always been matched by attention to the range, which would lead to a useful system of classification, nor by concern for a theory powerful

11 Joachim Wach, *Sociology of Religion.*

12 William James, *The Varieties of Religious Experience*, p. 128.

13 Ibid., p. 137.

14 A bibliographical postscript at the end of the chapter lists representative works dealing with religious experience.

enough to make use of the variety of explanations that have been offered. I shall attempt a tentative classification and a theoretical statement in the hope that they may carry us beyond the descriptive level in dealing with religious experience.

Variables Affecting Religious Experience

A useful system of classification is generally based on the combined use of several important characteristics. Three such characteristics seem to me to be of special significance in classifying religious experiences: intensity, temporal referent, and attitude toward the surrounding social order. I will examine each of these briefly and then explore ways in which they may be combined into a taxonomic system.

There is general recognition that experiences vary in intensity, from the moderate feeling of contentment from performance of an accustomed rite to ecstasy. We have no adequate scales, however, on which to measure this variation; hence we employ a rather diverse group of adjectives, counting on connotations to achieve an informal placement along the scale. Perhaps the most useful aspect of a taxonomy developed by Rodney Stark is an implied scale of intensity of religious experiences. He describes four varieties: confirming, responsive, ecstatic, and revelational experiences, which represent increasingly greater "intimacy with divine power." They are defined briefly in these terms:

1) the human actor simply notes (feels, senses, etc.) the existence or presence of the divine actor.
2) mutual presence is acknowledged, the divine actor is perceived as noting the presence of the human actor.
3) the awareness of mutual presence is replaced by an affective relationship akin to love or friendship.
4) the human actor perceives himself as a confidant of and/or a fellow participant in action with the divine actor.[15]

What Stark describes in terms of degree of intimacy with divine power may be correlated with the degree to which, in religious experience, one loses self-identity and self-awareness. Described in this latter way, which is less culture-bound, the intensity dimension of religious experience ranges from the moderate sensation of a break with everyday life and one's mundane self to states of trance in which all conscious self-awareness is temporarily lost.

A second variable by which religious experiences may be classified has to do with the time referent of the experience. Probably the most common (and paradoxically, therefore the most neglected) are those experiences, of whatever intensity, that affirm one's contemporary religious views. Performing a daily ritual and going to church are religious experiences, even though they are usually of a low level of intensity. Past-oriented experiences are suggested by the story of the Prodigal Son and the revival meeting: They reconfirm a lost faith. Future-oriented experiences imply conversion

15 Rodney Stark, "A Taxonomy of Religious Experience," *Journal for the Scientific Study of Religion*, 5, 1965, p. 99.

to a new faith, whether it be an existent one or an emergent one. These three analytically separate types are often mixed, of course; but the distinctions are essential, for the individual and structural conditions that promote affirmation, revival, and conversion are not identical.[16]

A third variable is difficult to separate clearly from the time referent, and is probably correlated with it. I think it stands as analytically separate, however, and that it can profitably be used to classify religious experiences more precisely. Religious experiences variously involve escape or withdrawal from, acceptance of, or attack upon the social order. We can refer to these as ascetic, mystical, and prophetic experiences, although this involves sharper typological denotation of those terms than is usually found. Disregarding his various qualifications for the moment, we can follow Weber in his use of these terms:

Asceticism: "Concentration upon the actual pursuit of salvation may entail a formal withdrawal from the 'world': from social and psychological ties with the family, from the possession of worldly goods, and from political, economic, artistic, and erotic activities—in short, from all creaturely interests." [17]

Mysticism: "The contemplative mystic minimizes his activity by resigning himself to the order of the world as it is, and lives incognito, so to speak, as humble people have always done, since god has ordained once and for all that men must live in the world." [18]

Prophecy: "The genuine prophet . . . preaches, creates, or demands *new* obligations." [19] Or as Talcott Parsons has stated it: "The prophet is above all the agent of the process of breakthrough to a higher, in the sense of more rationalized and systematized, cultural order. . . ." [20]

These terms, when seen as varieties of individual religious experiences, can be defined in the following way:

Ascetic experience: the sense that one has, by withdrawal from the demands and values of the secular world and by mastery of self, achieved contact with what is seen as ultimate reality.

Mystical experience: the sense that by disregarding and accepting the world around one, by purging oneself of mundane interests, or by abandoning self and concentrating on ways to illumination, one has achieved union with the divine. The distinction between ascetic self-mastery and mystical self-abandon is difficult to draw in practice.

---

16 Albert Gordon distinguishes between "ecclesiastical conversion"—shifting allegiance to a different faith—and "inner conversion"—the experience of having regained a sense of unity and purpose. The former usage is the object of his study; it is close to the dictionary meaning. We shall also use the term in that sense. The latter usage was employed by William James, who emphasized the renewal aspects of many religious experiences. The term *revival* seems more appropriate for the renewal experiences, however. See Albert Gordon, *The Nature of Conversion*, Chap. 1.

17 Max Weber, *The Sociology of Religion*, p. 166.

18 Ibid., p. 174.

19 Max Weber, *The Theory of Social and Economic Organizations*, p. 361.

20 In his Introduction to Weber's *The Sociology of Religion*, p. xxxiii.

Prophetic experience: the sense that one is serving as the agent for a challenge to an evil social order in the name of ultimate standards.[21]

Or, in oversharp typological terms: The ascetic struggles with individual suffering, the mystic with ignorance, and the prophet with injustice.

As usual, empirical mixture of these experiences relating to the social order has made it difficult to arrive at a clear usage of terms. One author emphasizes the shading off in one direction, another a different modification. We may start, then, with the three-part system represented by the triangle depicted in Figure 8–1, but almost at once we have to add the qualifications, represented by subtypes along the sides of the triangle, that empirical mixtures require.

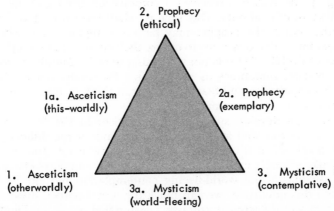

FIGURE 8–1. *Religious experience as types of response to "the world"*

Weber was not satisfied with his own distinctions among the three major types, and added subtypes that appear to me intermediate, although they are not stated in these terms by Weber. They suggest that we would be wise to move beyond the idea of types, to a recognition that religious experience may fall anywhere along the perimeter outlined in Figure 8–1. Dealing only with Weber's subtypes, however, I suggest that *this-worldly asceticism,* while still involving withdrawal from the world in one sense, contains also an impulse to control the world in another sense—and thus shares qualities with *ethical prophecy.* In Weber's words, as he distinguishes between Occidental and Oriental asceticism: "In the rules of St. Benedict, still more with the monks of Cluny, again with the Cistercians, and most

21 An individual who has a succession of religious experiences, particularly if they are intense and of the same variety, is often identified by the name for that experience. Thus we speak of prophets, ascetics, and mystics. This is useful if we do not reify the terms, if we remain aware that *mystic,* for example, refers to a person who has fairly frequent and fairly intense mystical experiences. It does not describe the total person. The nouns are often used as well to describe religious leaders. It is important to note that when thus used, the terms imply not only an individual's experience, but also his relationship with others. To say that a person is a prophet, in the sense of having frequent and intense prophetic experiences, is not identical with saying that he is a prophetic leader.

strongly the Jesuits, it has become emancipated from planless other-worldliness and irrational self-torture. It had developed a systematic method of rational conduct with the purpose of overcoming the *status naturae*, to free man from the power of irrational impulses and his dependence on the world and on nature." [22] Other-worldly asceticism, on the other hand, is an extreme withdrawal from the world, and denial of it. This experience is most intensively cultivated in orthodox. Hinduism.[23]

The valuable distinction drawn by Weber between ethical and exemplary prophecy indicates the need for a subtype between mysticism and prophecy. Weber contrasts the two types in these terms: "The prophet may be primarily . . . an instrument for the proclamation of a god and his will. . . . Preaching as one who has received a commission from god, he demands obedience as an ethical duty. This type we shall term the 'ethical prophet.' On the other hand, the prophet may be an exemplary man who, by his personal example, demonstrates to others the way to religious salvation, as in the case of Buddha." [24] It is not surprising that the Buddha is sometimes seen as a mystic, sometimes as a prophet.[25] By emphasizing this or that aspect of his experience and teaching, one can think of him as an ethically oriented mystic or as an exemplary prophet.

Weber did not develop subtypes of mysticism in the form of explicit concepts; but he was well aware of the range, and of the difficulty, on the empirical level, of distinguishing between asceticism and mysticism: ". . . we may strongly emphasize here that the distinction between world-rejecting asceticism and world-fleeing contemplation is fluid." [26] Using a phrase from this quotation, we can mark the area between mysticism and asceticism as *world-fleeing mysticism* (designated as 3a in Figure 8–1), contrasting it with *contemplative mysticism,* which is associated with resignation and acceptance of the world.

Having suggested three variables that seem crucial in distinguishing among types of religious experience, we are faced now with the question, Can they be put into one system, giving us a picture of the full range of possibilities? The resulting matrix disregards, of course, the fact that in the empirical world the types are mixed. And in suggesting only three positions for each variable, I am using crude scales. More subtle shading, however, is unwarranted with the data available.

Figure 8–2 can be "read" in the following way, using the first three types as illustrations: A person experiencing a revival of interest in a religious tradition, of a fairly low level of intensity, may express it in several ways. The reaffirmation may come through various ascetic acts of withdrawal from the social order (Protestant revivals have emphasized ascetic self-control and the need to escape from a world of sin). It may be sought through a mystical search for reunion with the divine, while accepting the

22 *The Protestant Ethic and the Spirit of Capitalism,* pp. 118–119.

23 See Weber, *The Religion of India,* especially Chap. 5.

24 *The Sociology of Religion,* p. 55.

25 See ibid., p. 55; and Isidor Thorner, "Prophetic and Mystic Experience: Comparison and Consequences," *Journal for the Scientific Study of Religion,* 5, 1965, pp. 85–86.

26 *The Sociology of Religion,* p. 170.

world as it is (Buddhist laymen may enter a "meditation center" for several days of contemplation). Or it may be expressed in a prophetic demand for reform of the social order in the name of ancestral religion (contemporary Jews supporting the civil rights movement are the heirs of Amos).

Such confirming, low-intensity experiences, are identified as types 1, 2, and 3 in Figure 8–2. In actual practice, of course, the experience of particular individuals may be a mixture of ascetic, mystical, and prophetic elements. The proportions of the mixture rather than the nearest type may be the critical defining characteristic of a person's experience.

Time orientation vis-a-vis religious tradition	Attitudes toward the social order	Intensity of religious experience		
		Confirming (low)	Responsive (medium)	Ecstatic (high)
Revival (past)	Asceticism (escape)	1	10	
	Mysticism (accept)	2		20
	Prophecy (oppose)	3		21
Affirmation (present)	Asceticism (escape)			
	Mysticism (accept)	5		
	Prophecy (oppose)	6		24
Conversion (future)	Asceticism (escape)			
	Mysticism (accept)			26
	Prophecy (oppose)			27

FIGURE 8–2. *Varieties of religious experience classified by three variables (On the intensity variable, I have used the terms suggested by Rodney Stark, but have omitted "revelational," which he sees as the most intensive. It seems to me this term introduces a second dimension, having to do with the quality of experience. "Revelational" may be close to the meaning of prophecy, as we are using it.)*

With twenty-seven possible types, this matrix is quite complex; but two comments may make it seem somewhat less so. By thinking of nine types, each with different levels of intensity, the series becomes more manageable. Implied in this remark is the idea that there are "low-intensity prophets" and "medium-intensity ascetics," for example. I am suggesting that average laymen, as well as religious leaders, have various inclinations relating to opposition, resignation, and withdrawal in their religious experiences. In this way we can perhaps begin to make better use of Weber's repeated suggestion that religious virtuosi be compared and contrasted with the religiously less intense.[27]

A second way in which the matrix can be seen as less complex than at first appears is to note that not all of the possible types are likely to be empirically important; and some may even be logically inconsistent. With reference to prophecy, for example, Weber writes: "No radical distinction will be drawn between a 'renewer of religion' who preaches an older revelation, actual or suppositious, and a 'founder of religion' who claims to bring completely new deliverances. The two types merge into one another."[28] Thus he shows the possibility of a distinction between the position I have designated 21 in Figure 8–2 and that numbered 27; but the prophet who opposes the world around him in order to affirm the existing religious situation is difficult to imagine. The prophet can say, "Return ye, return ye," or he can say, "But I say unto you." He seems unlikely to cry, "Continue ye." This may be in contrast with the less intensive layman who is inclined toward a reformist view of society, that is, to have the confirming, prophetic kind of religious experience. He may more readily associate such an experience with the affirmation of his religious tradition than with conversion or revival. (Such an experience would be indicated by Position 6 in the matrix of Figure 8–2.)[29]

In light of the usually vivid quality of the descriptions of religious experience, this discussion of critical variables for classifying the full range seems flat. It is unfortunate that the exuberant, the newsworthy events have received much more attention than the more common events. Perhaps by introducing this more prosaic approach, although we reduce the drama, we can take a step toward more systematic formulations of religious experience and strengthen our ability to accumulate knowledge in this area.

When adequate measures have been designed, the matrix can be used to compare the religious "profiles" of different groups. The modal response for an American middle-class suburban congregation may be a low-intensity

27 One of the unfortunate results of typological work in the social sciences is that we have become used to rather simple schemes. The physical and biological sciences have long since learned to live with complexity. In my judgment, that part of nature with which the social sciences deal is particularly complex, and our classificatory and analytical devices will have to recognize that fact.

28 *The Sociology of Religion*, p. 46.

29 Although the focus of attention in this chapter is on individual factors in religious experience, their full interpretation requires attention to the ways in which individual experiences are cumulated. Because religious groups will be the subject of attention in later chapters, however, I shall only refer here to terms that indicate the relationships between the individual and group level. When religious experiences are shared by two or more individuals, we have a religious event. These two can be classified, particularly by the degree of homogeneity or heterogeneity among the participants when measured by the three scales discussed above. They can also be classified by the degree of continuity with other such events. A series of new events is a religious movement; a series of relatively repetitive events is a religious tradition.

affirmative mysticism (Position 5 in Figure 8–2); [30] that of lower-class rural migrants to a city may be medium-intensity, revivalistic asceticism (Position 10); [31] while that of upwardly-mobile but insecure middle-class Japanese city dwellers may be high-intensity, revivalistic mysticism (Position 20). [32] Description of the full profiles, by indication of the distribution around the modes, would yield us rich information about the religious situation of a group, whether a society or a smaller unit within it.

The Field Sources of Religious Experience

The contrast drawn by James, to which we have referred, is concerned as much with varieties of individuals as with varieties of religious experience. Indeed, it is difficult to keep the two ideas separate, for the kind of experience is strongly influenced by the motives, fears, hopes, and values of the individuals involved. These characteristics do not determine the experience, however. Certain individuals are more susceptible to particular kinds of religious experience, but unless that susceptibility is supported by the surrounding situation, the experience cannot occur. The compound cannot occur in the presence of one element only. If persons in the Orient are more likely to obtain a mystical experience, whereas those in the Occident are more likely to obtain a prophetic experience, [33] cultural supports rather than individual needs are the key variables in explaining the difference. Yet the presence of Eastern prophets and Western mystics shows the incompleteness of a cultural interpretation.

The need to take several levels of influence into account is well shown in Alexander Alland's discussion of "possession." "Our analysis," he writes, "centers upon the external (physical and socio-cultural) circumstances and the internal (individual psychological and physiological) states which elicit trance." [34] He notes the combination of the following influences: heat; high level of CO_2; loud, rhythmic music with a simple repetitious beat, leading to sensory deprivation; "the presence of strong models for trance in significant others who set the pattern for behavior in the church"; lack of information; isolation. In addition, "receptivity to the trance is most certainly influenced by personal differences such as: range of experience, needs of the individual, and tolerance for various physiological stresses." [35]

30 See Peter Berger, *The Noise of Solemn Assemblies;* Pierre Berton, *The Comfortable Pew;* Frederick Shippey, *Protestantism in Suburban Life;* Gibson Winter, *The Suburban Captivity of the Churches.*

31 See Liston Pope, *Millhands and Preachers;* Bryan Wilson, ed., *Patterns of Sectarianism.*

32 See H. N. McFarland, *The Rush Hour of the Gods;* The Seiko Press, *Sōka Gakkai.* Although referred to frequently as "new religions," the sectarian developments in Japan are in many ways strongly traditionalist. Nevertheless, there are some new qualities that help to carry their adherents over into the dramatically new world they are experiencing. To the degree that this is true, they are better represented by Position 26.

33 See Thorner, op. cit.

34 Alexander Alland, Jr., " 'Possession' in a Revivalistic Negro Church," *Journal for the Scientific Study of Religion,* 1, 1962, p. 205.

35 Ibid., pp. 212–213.

It is the combination of physiological, characterological, cultural, and structural forces that produces the mild convulsions, the semistuporous condition, and the loss of voluntary control that Alland defines as the trance state.[36]

Most studies of religious experience tend to emphasize one or another of its sources—in the individual, in culture, or in patterns of interaction. So long as these are recognized as analytic works, focusing attention on one part of a causal complex, they contribute to our understanding. When they treat one part as causally sufficient, however, or when they blur different causal levels, they are less valuable. It is useful to study the source of religious experience in cultural beliefs and rites, as most anthropologists do.[37] Under conditions of relative stability, attention to the cultural source may furnish a good *index* of the structural and characterological sources as well. Since the several sources co-vary, measurement of one yields good approximations of the others. Under conditions of culture contact and change, however, and in heterogeneous societies, a specialized cultural approach is less adequate. In the study of messianic movements, for example, it is much more necessary to pay attention to individual variation. Specialized psychological study of individual variation is also valuable, but it does not explain religious experience. Erwin Goodenough's examination of "types of religious experience" (legalism, supralegalism, orthodoxy, supraorthodoxy, aestheticism, and so on) is treated as an analysis of individual experiences.[38] It could as easily be read, however, as a description of types of cultural systems. To speak of these as descriptions of "the psychology of religious experiences," is to fail to make necessary distinctions.

Students of comparative psychiatry have emphasized that the behavioral significance of individual anxiety is a function not only of its intensity and form but of the cultural interpretation given it and by the responses of others. Consequences as diverse as acute schizophrenia and shamanism may result from the same underlying psychological events, depending upon the way they are responded to by others. As Julian Silverman has stated: "in primitive cultures in which such a unique life crisis resolution is tolerated, the abnormal experience (shamanism) is typically beneficial to the individual, cognitively and affectively; he is regarded as one with expanded consciousness. In a culture that does not provide referential guides for comprehending this kind of crisis experience, the individual (schizophrenic) typically undergoes an intensification of his suffering over and above his original anxieties." [39]

36 For another valuable study that combines attention to cultural elements, group support, and individual receptivity—i.e., takes a field approach—see George E. Simpson, *The Shango Cult in Trinidad.*

37 Many anthropological studies, of course, introduce both cultural and individual variables. See, for example, Ruth Benedict, *The Concept of the Guardian Spirit in Native North America;* Clyde Kluckhohn, *Navaho Witchcraft;* Anthony Wallace, *Religion: An Anthropological View;* Clifford Geertz, "Ritual and Social Change: A Javanese Example," *American Anthropologist,* 59, 1957, pp. 23–54.

38 *The Psychology of Religious Experiences.*

39 Julian Silverman, "Shamans and Acute Schizophrenia," *American Anthropologist,* 69, 1967, p. 21.

When urban Catholics, members of the Cursillo movement, become part of a group of thirty or forty persons "who talk, eat, pray, think, laugh and, sometimes, cry together from Thursday sunset to Sunday sunset," their religious experiences are quite different from those achieved by participation in liturgically oriented church services.[40] There is group support in seeking and interpreting the experience. Group dynamics, not individual needs and tendencies alone, influence the result.

Group factors can, of course, inhibit as well as support various forms of religious experience. Maslow hypothesizes that persons who participate regularly in conventional religious practices may be less likely than others to be open to religious experiences in other contexts.[41] This may be true in some conditions. Under other conditions, however, group influences may inhibit both conventional and extraordinary religious experiences, even among those who, in the character sense, are "ready."

This is well shown in the study of "conversion, proselytization, and maintenance of faith" in a small cult examined by John Lofland. There were some "seekers" who came in contact with the cult, but were not attracted to its particular beliefs and practices; others who came in contact with the group lacked the predisposing qualities for membership in any widely deviant movement. Some might have been drawn in had they heard about the cult earlier or later; and doubtless there were possible converts, persons with appropriate tendencies, who knew nothing of the movement. The few who joined, then, were those who were predisposed to its message, who came in contact with the group at a time in their lives when it was most likely to be appealing to them, and who lacked other group attachments that might serve as barriers. In Lofland's words:

For conversion it is necessary that a person:
1. experience enduring, acutely felt tensions;
2. within a religious, problem-solving perspective;
3. which lead to defining himself as a religious seeker;
4. encountering the cult at a turning point in his life;
5. wherein an affective bond to adherents is formed (or pre-exists);
6. where extra-cult attachments are low or neutralized;
7. and where, to become a 'deployable agent,' exposure to intensive interaction is accomplished.[42]

The conversion experience, in other words, is a product of both tendency and opportunity. It cannot be explained by psychological analysis alone. This is equally true of the other varieties of religious experience.

BIBLIOGRAPHICAL POSTSCRIPT
Representative works dealing with religious experience:

Gordon Allport, *The Individual and His Religion;* William James, *The Varieties of Religious Experience;* Max Weber, *The Sociology of Religion;* Melford Spiro, *Burmese Supernaturalism;* Winston King, *Introduction to Religion;* Joachim Wach, *Types of Religious Experience, Christian and Non-*

40 See *The New York Times,* Jan. 8, 1966, p. 60.

41 *Religions, Values, and Peak Experiences,* pp. 30–31.

42 John Lofland, *Doomsday Cult,* pp. 7–8.

Christian; Henri Hubert and Marcel Mauss, *Sacrifice: Its Nature and Function;* Hervé Carrier, *The Sociology of Religious Belonging;* Anton Boisen, *The Exploration of the Inner World. A Study of Mental Disorder and Religious Experience;* Godfrey Lienhardt, *Divinity and Experience;* William Wood, *Culture and Personality Aspects of the Pentecostal Holiness Religion;* James Leuba, *The Psychology of Religious Mysticism;* Marghanita Laski, *Ecstasy;* Abraham Maslow, *Religions, Values, and Peak Experiences;* Rodney Stark, "A Taxonomy of Religious Experience," *Journal for the Scientific Study of Religion,* 5, 1965, pp. 97–116; Isidor Thorner, "Prophetic and Mystic Experience: Comparison and Consequences," *Journal for the Scientific Study of Religion,* 5, 1965, pp. 82–96; John Lofland, *Doomsday Cult;* Mircea Eliade, *Shamanism: Archaic Techniques of Ecstasy;* Erwin Goodenough, *The Psychology of Religious Experiences;* Albert Gordon, *The Nature of Conversion;* Philip Ennis, "Ecstasy and Everyday Life," *Journal for the Scientific Study of Religion,* 6, 1967, pp. 40–48; Ari Kiev, ed., *Magic, Faith, and Healing;* Evelyn Underhill, *Mysticism: A Study in the Nature and Development of Man's Spiritual Consciousness;* Anthony Wallace, *Religion: An Anthropological View,* Chap. 3; William Braden, *The Private Sea: LSD and the Search for God.*

vary from society to society, from time to time. We can scarcely say with any confidence that this is a period of greater loneliness, of stronger feelings of individual isolation, than were other periods of rapid change; but there are clear evidences of the strength of such feelings today, whatever their comparative measurement might show. The Harris poll reported that 52 per cent of an American sample declared "they are lonely and depressed" some of the time.[6] It is not only the youth who feel a sense of kinship with the Beatles' "Eleanor Rigby":

Ah, look at all the lonely people!
Eleanor Rigby picks up the rice in the church where a wedding has been, lives
    in a dream.
Waits at the window, wearing the face she keeps in a jar by the door.
Who is it for? [7]

If many of us today live in "the lonely crowd," we would expect to find "cults of re-assurance." [8] It is not surprising that the title of a prominent Protestant family magazine is *Together*, or that the "new religions" in Japan have spread most widely among recent migrants to the city who have been cut off from regular contacts with their families and villages. In the last several years, to be sure, the somewhat self-centered emphasis on the pains of loneliness has been modified by greater activism among some groups. This may only change the way in which isolation is dealt with, however, and not indicate its abatement. One can observe, without in any way criticizing programs of social action by religious groups, that joint efforts in "good works" can produce a powerful effect of communion, of attachment to others.

The more common experience in the urban world, however, continues to be the service or meeting without direct reference to action. Across a wide range of classes we find religious themes and movements that declare: You are not alone. Even this is an ancient theme, but it has particular relevance to mobile societies. As Paul Tillich pointed out, the sense of our separation from others is heightened today by our growing knowledge of the hidden streams of hostility within us. We know, with Immanuel Kant, that there is something in the misfortune even of our best friends which does not displease us. "Are we not almost always ready to abuse everybody and everything, although often in a very refined way, for the pleasure of self-elevation, for an occasion for boasting, for a moment of lust?" [9] The feeling of separation is increased by ambivalence toward ourselves. It is difficult to avoid a mixture of self-love and self-hate in a time of mixed systems of social norms, in the presence of large gaps between aspirations and achievements.

The Oxford Group Movement. In such situations, the religious theme, "You are accepted," is likely to be a dominant one. We shall see later that this is one aspect of the religious movements of minority groups and of the recently urbanized lower classes. It is an important part of the appeal of

6 *Honolulu Advertiser*, Nov. 20, 1968, p. A3.

7 From the lyric of the song "Eleanor Rigby," by the Beatles.

8 For a discussion of this theme, see Peter Berger, op. cit., pp. 90–104.

9 Paul Tillich, *The Shaking of the Foundations*, p. 157.

the Oxford Group movement to some members of the middle and upper classes. The movement is not formally a church, but an effort to revitalize religious life. Frank Buchman, the founder, came to believe that the "up-and-outers," the high-status persons of modern society, were religiously neglected.[10] By its doctrine of individual "right-living," by the sharing of doubt and guilt in small, congenial groups, by its assumption that the world's ills can be solved by "getting right with God"—with no need for change in the social structures in which its members have found privileged positions—in these ways the Oxford Group movement tells its adherents that they are "accepted."

The fact that many adherents are drawn into the movement for a few months or years and then drift away may indicate that the prescriptions of the Oxford Group movement are too easy. They demand little intellectual effort, little personal sacrifice or discipline, little change in style of life. There is good evidence that in what we might call the economy of the personality, a system of salvation that is bought too cheaply—with little sacrifice or effort on the part of the adherent—soon wears out; it does not work. Somehow—the personality processes are not clear—the individual comes to believe, consciously or unconsciously, that if a "solution" to his fundamental problems requires so little of him it cannot be of much value.

This need for a "difficult" religion is not equally shared by everyone, however, and is perhaps relatively unimportant with many of those who are attracted to the Oxford Group movement. Its appeal has been primarily to educated, well-to-do persons whose early training typically has been in a fairly conservative Protestant church. They are mobile, urban people without many community roots, worldly, and somewhat sophisticated. The influence of earlier conceptions of religion, however—the idea of sin, the belief in a personal relationship to God, and the like—is still strong. The nature of the religious appeal of the Oxford Group movement may thus be seen as an attempt to tie together a conservative background and a partially sophisticated present that has left many persons uncertain and insecure.

The movement illustrates Weber's conception of a "theodicy of good fortune." Although its membership is largely drawn from among the "successful," their self-confidence has been weakened by a succession of crises in the society in which they have won high status. Depression, war, and the power of communism have aroused many anxieties. The program of the Oxford Group reassures them that their way of life is good. Its conservative political leanings (which are sometimes, in the literal sense, reactionary) correspond with their inclinations. Its emphasis on individual "moral rearmament" harmonizes with their need to find the source of their difficulties not in a social system that has treated them well, but in individual perversity. Its "house-party" approach brings them together with a congenial group, which reduces their sense of alienation, reassures them about the validity of their status, and gives them an exciting sense of

10 See Hadley Cantril, *The Psychology of Social Movements*, Chap. 6; W. H. Clark, *The Oxford Movement: Its History and Significance*; Allan Eister, *Drawing Room Conversion. A Sociological Account of the Oxford Group Movement*; Peter Howard, *The World Rebuilt* (an uncritical, laudatory account of the work of Frank Buchman).

"doing something" about the world's problems in precisely the way best calculated to reduce their own self-doubts.[11]

Guides to "Confident Living"

We have suggested that the Oxford Group movement is a fairly cosmopolitan and somewhat "elitist" religious development, appealing to a high-status but doubt-ridden group. It may be seen as a "guide to confident living," but one that has attraction for people with a particular combination of needs and tendencies. Other groups appeal to those with a different constellation. There is wide variation in the degree to which the members of society feel its tensions and are equipped to deal with them. There is also great variety in the kinds of cultural preparation for various "solutions." These differences in personality are reflected in the kinds of religious movements that appeal to different people. The widespread influence of Norman Vincent Peale is found primarily among the urban middle classes who have been attuned to his message by their cultural training and their personal problems. His appeal is partly to those afflicted, in his words, with "fear, inferiority, tensions and kindred troubles," those who want to know how they can succeed, and why, indeed, when success surrounds them they themselves should be only moderately successful. His appeal is also to the less sophisticated among the "fully" successful. Despite their occupational and monetary accomplishments, they feel continually off-balance in a rapidly changing world. People whom they half fear and half admire, particularly the intellectuals, keep telling them that their values are shoddy, their conceptions of the world inadequate, and their accomplishments mediocre. This message is made visible to them partly in a form that strengthens their natural inclination to repudiate it—the protesting college student or the long-haired hippie. By attacking the form of these protesters' "deviation" from society rather than the substance of the critique thus implied, such people can deflect the challenge it offers to their definition of the good life.

The solution that Dr. Peale puts forward for their problems is one that middle-class Americans, trained to the optimism of a bountiful environment, but "temporarily" confused and anxious, are ready to accept: Your problems are not deep; your critics are unacceptable; solutions to your difficulties are ready at hand. "Think your way to success"; "forget failures and go ahead." All that is needed is contact with God, so that his power can come into you. Fear breaks that contact, but faith restores it. Peale quotes the prescription sometimes given by "a young and highly trained physician" to persons suffering from fear and inferiority: "Go to church at least once a Sunday for the next three months." [12]

If you will utilize the principles of faith stated in this book, you, too, can solve the difficult problems of your personality. You, too, can really learn to live.[13]

[11] For a useful discussion of the social psychological processes in intimate (T-group) encounters, of value to the study of Oxford Group influences, see Philip Slater, "Religious Processes in the Training Group," in *The Religious Situation: 1968*, Donald Cutler, ed., pp. 765–798.

[12] Norman Vincent Peale, *A Guide to Confident Living*, p. 1.

[13] Ibid., p. 17.

In a recent book, Peale quotes two professional golfers whose games were strengthened by reading his works. The first wrote: "I used to think negatively about my game. . . . I don't have that complex any more. I play offensive golf. I think positively." The other described a match on a course that was better suited to the style of his competitors. Few gave him a chance to win. "But I wasn't concerned about the opinion of the press or public, because I knew that I could 'do anything through Jesus Christ Who strengthened me'—one of the quotes from the Bible that Dr. Peale uses. When I won the U.S. Open, many of the quotes from his book were a great help. Let me say that the one that says 'visualize, prayerize, actualize,' helped me very much." [14]

Dr. Peale's message appeals to many people. *The Power of Positive Thinking* has sold more than three million copies; in the late 1960's, he was receiving between five thousand and eight thousand letters per week; his church is filled to overflowing each week; and he is in great demand as a lecturer, writer, and guest minister.

Through the years his dominant theme has remained steady: By self-confidence, enthusiasm, positive thinking, and with the help of the Lord, you can solve your personal problems. His sermon topic on one occasion when he served as a guest minister in 1969 was "The Sovereign Cure for Worry." The text, from John, "I have come that ye might have life and have it more abundantly," was congenial to the large congregation of middle- and upper-class parishioners, who numbered some 1,600, instead of the church's more usual 400–600. It was, with few exceptions, "the Conservative Party gathered for prayer." They were assured that the problems they faced were good for them; that by Christian faith the problems were transformed into challenges that made life meaningful. Dr. Peale told the story of one of Winston Churchill's last speeches, given when he was nearly ninety years of age to an assemblage of students at Harrow, the school he attended as a boy. The speech was six words long: "Never, never, never, never give up." (I wondered if it made no difference what one was doing.) In recounting the courage of a young woman who believed herself threatened by a group of men in the subway late at night, Dr. Peale raised the congregation to feelings of righteous anger and even of hatred by his description of the long-haired young punks, with their pointed shoes, black leather jackets, skin-tight pants, and sneering faces. If these young men had problems of their own or were deserving of sympathetic study, if the institutions of the country that had treated his congregation so well were in need of criticism and revision, if one's worry might extend beyond oneself to the state of the nation and of the world, no hint of such considerations was heard in the sermon. It was designed to allay the anxieties, to quiet the self-doubts, and to strengthen the faith of his listeners that what they stood for was good and what obstructed them could be overcome.

Perhaps I may be permitted an aside here, in the hope of avoiding misunderstanding. The preceding paragraphs are not intended as a critical evaluation of the work of Dr. Peale. I know people who are sensitively aware of the possible functions of cruel practices in medicine and magic

14 Norman Vincent Peale, *Enthusiasm Makes the Difference*, pp. 57–58.

among mountain tribesmen in South America, or who are ready to support extravagant distortions and hostile rites among the Black Muslims in the belief that these distortions and rites may contribute to the development of those who adhere to them. These same people quite lose their objectivity when they examine the beliefs and rites of their suburban neighbors. Any adequate critique must be based on a careful study of all the consequences for everyone affected by a given doctrine, judged against carefully stated values and in the light of available alternatives. Lacking that, one should limit himself to description and analysis.

I realize that we no more like to be analyzed than we enjoy being criticized. In some ways analysis can be read as an even sharper attack, for criticism may at least imply that one is worthy of opposition, while the aloofness of analysis can be read as disdain. I know of no sure way to avoid this difficulty, and can only reaffirm that my intent is to try to understand the religious phenomena before me, treating them with all the sympathy and objectivity I can muster. (I regard sympathy and objectivity as complementary.) Critical evaluation is properly reserved for another time.

Sociocultural Sources of Belief in "Positive Thinking." What are the sources of support for the basically optimistic and individualistic approach represented by Peale? They abound in the American environment. It is not surprising that persons who are brought up hearing claims that a change to the correct soap can revolutionize your chances for marital happiness, or reading implications that if you improve your vocabulary by twenty words a day you may become a "big" executive, should respond favorably to "the power of positive thinking." But that is only a small part of the environment that has created persons favorable to the religious views of Dr. Peale. It would be a mistake to forget the factual reinforcements of the attitude that "salvation" (the reduction of fear and inferiority feelings, an increase in worldly success) comes fairly easily. We can find all around us many individuals (probably a small minority, but a highly visible one) who, by a combination of hard work, self-confidence, luck, and some ability have achieved fame and fortune. Peale's formula, moreover, is plausible to those trained to values of individual initiative. There is little reference to possible social causes of human problems, and no need to criticize or tamper with the social structure, which is an uncongenial task to many members of the middle class.

Peale's work appeals to a generation trained to think that "science" is important and a valuable aid in the solution of problems. It is doubtless fair to say that no religious movement could attract the contemporary American urban middle classes to any extent that did not try to show its harmony with science. The harmony may be on a fairly superficial level; there may be no intensive effort to analyze the relation of science to religion (some psychiatrists, indeed, think that Dr. Peale has retarded their work); but at least at the level of slogans, there must be accommodation.

There are other elements in the cultural preparation of individuals for such religious developments as those represented by Peale. His adherents have been raised in an atmosphere of "liberal" theology, with its optimistic view of man and relative lack of concern with tragedy and the "sinfulness of man," and with little insistence upon dogma, yet with a general feeling that the "good man ought to be interested in religion," which is perhaps a kind of residue from an earlier piety. Thus Peale has no dogma or ritual; he can appeal to people "whatever your church." And he makes little of the traditional and the neo-orthodox emphasis on sin, an emphasis that makes little sense to people reared in optimism, to belief in moral man in moral society, as one might put it.

To persons with different personality tendencies, trained to a different pattern of cultural values, and living in a different social situation, there is no power in "positive thinking" as it is preached by Peale. Some are simply unmoved by him; others are vigorously opposed. It is the latter who express themselves and thus allow some assessment of the personality factors involved in his acceptance or rejection. Some of his critics oppose him because of his theological views. They believe that his approach to salvation shows far too little awareness of the depth of human suffering and evil. His religious views, therefore, according to these critics' conception of life, are shallow and unsatisfying. Despite Dr. Peale's active cooperation with psychiatry, his "bootstrap" approach is also thoroughly unsatisfactory to many scientists, both in its analysis of the source of human difficulties and its attempts at therapy. In their judgment he solves few problems, for human problems lie deeper than he knows. He harms as well as helps when he declares that a man needs only faith to solve his problems; those who continue to suffer, therefore, accuse themselves of lack of faith, and thus increase their sense of guilt. His approach demonstrates that "the battle of the Renaissance" is still far from won. He has, in fact, retarded the development of efforts to find solutions to problems of personal anxiety by the systematic application of human intelligence, by his attention to such "magic formulas" as "energy-producing thoughts," "seven simple steps," and "eight practical formulas."

Needless to say, some psychiatrists work actively with or support Dr. Peale, either because they accept his formulas, or because they believe his religious approach has pragmatic value for certain kinds of emotional disturbances.[15] We shall comment in due course on this larger question of the relation of religion and psychiatry.

A Catholic Guide to Peace of Soul. Although some people are led to seek confident living by positive thinking (we have suggested that they are largely urban middle-class people, of an average educational level, with conservative political leanings, from nonliturgical Protestant backgrounds —a characterization that is impressionistic), others, with different personality tendencies, find this approach unsatisfactory. It is not too gross an oversimplification to say that Bishop Fulton Sheen represents a contemporary Catholic approach to the same constellation of problems of urban middle-class people that Dr. Peale tries to handle for "standard" Protestants. Drawing on a different tradition, however, Sheen offers a guide to "peace of soul," not "confident living," and the people to whom he appeals have had different cultural training in what constitutes an effective and valid religious adjustment to their problems. Thus, though many of the problems are the same, the religious efforts to deal with them are different.

---

15 For a discussion of the clinic established at Dr. Peale's church, see Samuel Klausner, *Psychiatry and Religion*, Pt. II.

Persons of Catholic training, and some Protestants too, of course, have been taught to need a method of religious expression with a complex doctrinal and dogmatic system. The writings of Bishop Sheen have an elaborate intellectual framework and a philosophical cast that is foreign to the work of Dr. Peale. Intellectuals (of humanistic rather than scientific leanings) may be drawn to the former, but almost certainly not to the latter.

The writing of Sheen also emphasizes the traditional doctrine of the "sinfulness of man," in a way congenial to those trained to Catholicism and to "twice-born Protestants" (those in whom the sense of tragedy, sin and guilt is particularly acute). Such an emphasis only alienates those who respond favorably to an optimistic and liberal view of man.

> *Nice* people must see themselves as nasty people before they can find peace. When they exchange their proud and diabolical belief that they never did anything wrong to hope for a Divine remedy for their mistakes, they will have attained to the condition of normality, peace, and happiness. . . . The *nasty* people are the convertible people; aware of their own imperfections, they sense within themselves an emptiness. . . . This sense of sin in them does not beget a forlorn despair, but a creative despair, when once they know that they can look beyond themselves for loving relief.[16]

Just as Peale attempts to help men escape from anxiety by affirming the optimistic Protestant creed (to an important degree the product of American middle-class life), so Sheen seeks to help by affirming the classic Christian theology and dogma: There is a natural law, and feelings of guilt are inevitable when this law is broken. The solution of men's problems, if they will recognize their guilt and give up their pride, is to turn to God, who forgives and understands.

Sheen makes a substantial attack on some aspects of psychoanalysis, claiming that what is true in it has long been known by the Church, and that its efforts to remove the sense of guilt are destructive.[17] The attack is not frivolous or shallow but elaborate and reasoned (although not necessarily *reasonable*). This appeals to those who require careful argument, if not substantial evidence, who are trained to the Catholic doctrine of guilt or show some residues of Calvinist feeling, and who feel alienated from a world of secular liberalism and science.

Opium is the Religion of the People

By the mid-1960's, Christian Science and the Oxford Group movement, as well as the more churchly activities discussed above, seemed somewhat bland. It was not so much that their appeals, as religiously inspired efforts to deal with confusion, loneliness, and anxiety, no longer attracted the kind of urban middle-class Europeans and Americans who originally were

16 Fulton J. Sheen, *Peace of Soul*, p. 85.

17 Other Catholic writers are more sympathetic to psychoanalysis and scientific psychiatry generally. James Van der Veldt and Robert Odenwald, for example, take the Thomist position that since truth is one, there can be no essential conflict between the valid teachings of psychiatry and Christian ethics. See their *Psychiatry and Catholicism*. Pope Pius XII attacked Freudian psychoanalysis—no Catholic was free to undergo it, no Catholic doctor to practice it—but he did not condemn all of psychoanalysis.

drawn to them. It was rather that they had been replaced in public attention by more exuberant movements. A new constellation of conditions and tendencies among a few, mainly young, mainly college-trained, urban middle- and upper-class persons, has led to the search for self-discovery and meaning through the use of drugs.

Marx's formula has often been reversed before, of course. The use of opium or, more commonly, other drugs in the search for revelation, mystical encounter, and ecstasy has been widespread among some Oriental religious movements, some Muslim mystical orders, practitioners of yoga in pursuit of ecstasy, and various Siberian and American Indian tribes.[18] There has been little support, however, for the use of drugs in predominantly Christian societies. When Thomas de Quincey exclaimed, "Eloquent opium . . . thou hast the keys of Paradise," he was regarded as entirely heretical.

This attitude undoubtedly still prevails. Whatever religious use of drugs can be found in the United States and Europe runs strongly against many norms, and in a numerical sense, at any rate, the use of drugs is probably not very important among the religious movements of the day. Because of the very sharpness of its deviation from standard practices, however, examination of the use of drugs for religious purposes can be a useful case study, highlighting the forces at work in creating new religious developments.

From the perspective we have adopted, we must ask: What combination of structural, cultural, and character sources supports the use of drugs in religious activities? For a number of reasons, this is a difficult question to answer. First, it is difficult to specify with any confidence when drug use is in any sense a religious act. It is probably true that most use of drugs today in Western societies has no more (and perhaps we should say no less) religious significance than the Saturday night "beer bust." It is related to the primordial search for "kicks," to protests against an authority that has lost its legitimacy, to boredom, to a desire to shut out the confusion and lower the anxiety promoted by a world in constant turmoil. Some of these can also be sources of a religious quest, however, so it is difficult to draw the line. It is perhaps not too fanciful to suggest that some of the hippies are involved in a kind of secular "mendicant" protest, although they are closer to St. Anthony fleeing into the desert than to St. Benedict with his vows of poverty and service. It seems likely that they may also be subject to St. Anthony's temptation—self-centered attention to one's own problems and a heightened interest in gratification—but Benedictine elements may not be entirely lacking. Aldous Huxley, although applauding the "cleansed perception" and the growth in powers of contemplation that are promoted by drugs, also wondered how these were "to be reconciled with a proper concern with human relations, with the necessary chores and duties, to say nothing of charity and practical compassion?" [19]

18 See Mircea Eliade, *Shamanism: Archaic Techniques of Ecstasy*, pp. 402 and 416–417; and Aldous Huxley, *The Doors of Perception*. Among American Indians, the peyote cult has been most studied. See, for example, David Aberle, and others, *The Peyote Religion among the Navaho;* Weston LaBarre, *The Peyote Cult;* and J. S. Slotkin, *The Peyote Religion: A Study in Indian-White Relations.*

19 Op. cit., p. 40.

A second problem springs from the extraordinary difficulty in maintaining some objectivity in the study of drug use. In those societies where it is illegal and generally regarded as immoral, it is mainly persons with unusually strong feelings of resentment against authority, or who have problems of self-discovery, or feelings of anxiety who are motivated to take the risks involved in using drugs.[20] What appear to be consequences, therefore, are based on a highly selective sample, a situation that compounds the problem of objectivity. In addition, relatively little is known about the physiological, psychological, and social consequences of the wide variety of drugs—"hard" and "soft," addictive and nonaddictive—that are employed. These factors create a vast ambiguity into which values flow.

Leaving aside the committed members of Timothy Leary's "League for Spiritual Discovery" and other such groups, and their committed opponents, who find examination of the question too painful, we still find room for wide disagreement. Aldous Huxley expresses a doubt that humanity will ever be able to dispense with various "artificial paradises." "Most men and women lead lives at the worst so painful, at the best so monotonous, poor and limited that the urge to escape, the longing to transcend themselves if only for a few moments, is and has always been one of the principal appetites of the soul." [21] He wonders if some of the newer drugs—or some drug as yet unsynthesized—are not superior to alcohol, tobacco, and other artificial paradises. They may be superior both because they lead to less harm, and because they are more nearly compatible with religion—with contemplation and a sense of unity with others.

Michael Novak speaks of the " 'pelagian' prejudice that spiritual achievement is proportionate to personal effort. Those who share this prejudice cannot conceive of the possibility that the Creator may have graced his creation with drugs which, discovered in due time, might be instrumental in preparing people to understand the gentleness, brotherhood, and peace of the gospels. Spiritual achievement is not won only through will and effort; often it is grace." [22] Those who approach religion through mysticism are most likely to accept this point of view.

Those closer to an ascetic tradition, on the other hand, suspect that those who see religious possibilities in drug use are not so much emphasizing some message of gentleness found in the gospels as expressing their extensive secular training for "instant success." If we can have instant romance, instant beauty, instant wealth, why not instant religion? No self-sacrifice, no steady period of service, no intensive study of the human condition is needed. There's a religious genius—or at least a religious experience—in each of us, waiting to get out, if we can only learn how to pry off the lid. Seen from this perspective, the use of drugs in the supposed service of re-

20 This is probably not true of the large number who have used drugs, primarily marijuana, only once or a few times. There are some estimates that perhaps a third of college students, for example, have tried pot at least once. Curiosity and group pressure probably motivate more of them than does anxiety. Most of them find reality as they have learned to define it and their accustomed selves more satisfactory than the "reality" and the new feelings produced by drugs. Hence they do not repeat the experience.

21 Op cit., p. 62.

22 Michael Novak in *The Religious Situation: 1968*, Donald Cutler, ed., p. 206.

ligion is basically a contemporary variant—for all its superficial differences —of earlier "optimistic" movements among the middle class that promise salvation by "seven simple steps." It is partly the heir of an environment that produced Christian Science and "positive thinking," although a number of new elements have been added, as we shall see.

These two interpretations are a modern form of the ancient clash between ascetic and mystic. It is well expressed by Reinhard Bendix, although without reference to drugs:

From the standpoint of "innerworldly asceticism" . . . contemplation appears a lazy and religiously sterile indulgence. A Puritan theologian would say that the mystic does not think of God but only of himself. To be consistent, the mystic would only live on what is freely available to him: alms and the berries in the forest. . . . For Hinduism and Buddhism, on the other hand, the active asceticism of the Puritan is a constant violation of the Divine. Ancient Buddhism viewed action with a purpose as a dangerous form of secularization. "He who wants to do good deeds should not become a monk," is a Buddhist saying. To be a tool of God is incompatible with being a "vessel" that is ready to receive God.[23]

A third difficulty faced by one seeking to discover the structural, cultural, and character sources that support drug use grows largely from the other two; there has been little empirical study. Thus all we have to offer are highly tentative observations, designed more to define the problem as a field of study than to answer questions related to it.

On each level we can distinguish between those influences that permeate the environment and those that affect relatively few people. We are dealing, of course, with a range, involving many possible positions. Speaking only of the extremes, however, we see that general influences can support a wide variety of social movements, while the specific influences focus on particular modes of expression. Knowledge of both is essential to understanding.[24] Schematically, we can describe these multiple influences in this way:

CONDITIONS SUPPORTING A DRUG CULT

I. Structural Conditions
   A. General. The major social changes, tragedies, and upheavals of our time. Relative failure of societies based on faith in science and reason. The cornucopia of goods alongside massive destruction. Mass media, making tragedies of the world quickly visible.
   B. Specific. The relative availability of drugs in some settings. The networks of communication indicating how one obtains them and indicating group support in their use. Availability of knowledge of Eastern religions.[25] Group support for selective cultural elements (see II B).

23 Reinhard Bendix, *Max Weber. An Intellectual Portrait*, p. 214.

24 Such perceptive interpretations of social movements as Eric Hoffer's *The True Believer* give attention mainly to the general conditions, thus leaving problematic the question of which social movements particular individuals will support.

25 Unorthodox religious movements in the United States have often turned to the East for inspiration. See William Braden, *The Private Sea. LSD and the Search for God.*

II. Cultural Conditions
   A. General. Norms that support a religious search. Approval of mystical religious experience (not strong in the West, but an "alternative," in the Linton sense). Normative support for quick, "magical" solutions to problems, an extension of the romantic tradition. (In Irving Babbitt's words, an event is romantic when it is "wonderful rather than probable.") If love or business success require only an appropriate cosmetic or cigarette, may not salvation be as readily found? Various "subterranean" values—the thrill, the easy mark—are given cultural support, even if not complete approval.[26]
   B. Specific. Subcultural norms alien to, in part hostile to, general cultural supports are found in some groups. Such groups may also draw *selectively* from the general culture, being differentiated by emphasis as well as by norms. Under certain characterological and structural conditions, norms of some groups tend to become *reversals* of, not simply variations of or exceptions to, the dominant culture; they are contracultural.[27] Among the relevant values are these: independence from the "system," from the establishment; the value of self-discovery; desirability of trying everything for oneself, to measure the range of human experience; emphasis on the mystical unity of mankind, the repugnance of lines that divide; a tendency toward a "Zen" distrust of reason in favor of intuition and individual experience; value placed on turning inward, away from a confusing and repelling world, in a search for existential meaning. Thus selective use of the dominant culture plus subcultural and contracultural norms give support of a more specific variety to religious movements involving drugs.

III. Characterological Conditions
   A. General. A fairly large number of persons in Western societies have experienced the volatile mixture of affluence and tragedy. Having achieved "success," or been reared in families that experienced success, and found it wanting, they no longer seek confident living; they seek self-discovery and meaning. Their aspirations may be more fully developed than their disciplines, hence they are not fully prepared for the hard training that maintenance of success usually demands. In Freudian terms, there has been little development of a superego. Donald Barr suggests a thesis in the sociology of knowledge when he observes that such conditions support contemporary trends in radical theology. "One would hardly expect a boy or girl without a Superego to experience God the Father." [28] With the weakening of traditional views, the shift to mysticism and the use of drugs is made easier.

26 David Matza and Gresham Sykes, "Juvenile Delinquency and Subterranean Values," *American Sociological Review*, 26, 1961, pp. 712–719.

27 For a discussion of the processes involved, see J. Milton Yinger, "Contraculture and Subculture," *American Sociological Review*, 25, 1960, pp. 625–635.

28 Donald Barr, "What Did We Do Wrong?" *New York Times Magazine*, Nov. 26, 1967, p. 137.

Many affluent and relatively permissive homes are also of liberal persuasion. Children have been made aware of other cultures, made sensitive to injustice, and informed about the disparities around the world; thus they are peculiarly sensitive to the value contradictions they see around them. They may have experienced a special type of deprivation—the lack of affection and stability in their closest personal associations—and thus are alienated, even though more sophisticated than the children of earlier affluent eras.[29] Even among those who have no lack of affection, problems of self-identification arise: How does one differentiate himself from successful and loving parents; how does one push away from unfailing affluence?

B. Specific. Some of those who have the tendencies mentioned under general characterological influences, which can lead to a wide variety of actions, have other tendencies that encourage *experimental, religious* behavior.[30] Both adjectives are essential qualifiers. Were they effectively socialized to traditional Western religious forms— that is, were not experimental—they would not be ready to challenge such Judaic-Christian ideas as the transcendence of God and the belief that salvation comes, not by being absorbed in the infinite, but by maintaining one's identity and entering into a self-conscious relationship "of mutual love with God and other men." [31] But some are ready for such a challenge. Their experiences have prepared them for an "Eastern" religious approach, for mysticism, and for the use of drugs as an appropriate agent.[32] Others, with many of the same tendencies, may not at the same time be religiously oriented; that is, these tendencies are not focused on questions of ultimate significance.

What we have sketched, then, is a series of six clusters of conditions, *all of which* are essential to persons trained in the West before participation in a religious cult that involves the use of drugs can occur. Were we able to measure these clusters of conditions well enough to assign each a "score"—for each is a variable, with many possible scale values—we

29 It is not clear how much self-alienation and anxiety are also general character conditions; but in my judgment they play quite an important part. This is clearly the case in the life of Timothy Leary. See his book, *High Priest.*

30 This is true of some of the young British aristocrats who have joined the hippie world. One seeks to found a utopian commune, others believe that "drugs are part of the divine plan," some see a millennium at hand. See "Hippies at the Top," *Newsweek*, January 27, 1969, pp. 46–47.

31 See William Braden, op. cit.

32 This is similar to what Havens calls "set"—expectations and general state of a person just before an experience. He reports: ". . . the administration of LSD to a group of religious volunteers (Mennonites) in an experimental setting dealing with mental illness led to uniformly unpleasant experiences and, so far as reported, no religious experiences. In contrast, Dr. Timothy Leary, whose main concern in drug research is 'transcendental experiences,' summarizes his results: 'Less than ten per cent of our original sample were believers or church goers, yet such terms as "god," "divine," "deep religious experience," "meeting the infinite" occurred in over half the reports!' " Joseph Havens, "Memo on the Religious Implications of the Consciousness-Changing Drugs," *Journal for the Scientific Study of Religion*, 3, 1964, p. 223.

could speak more precisely of the *product* score [33] necessary to produce a particular form of religious behavior. Lacking those measures, we have outlined a paradigm for interpreting the results. The illustration we have chosen—the use of drugs for religious experience in the West—may be relatively unimportant; but as a new and dramatic development, it serves well to illustrate the complex interaction of many forces.

The Search for Confident Living in Japan

When one compares American religious movements with those in Japan, one is struck both by the cultural variations—the beliefs and practices in one society that would seem bizarre in the other—and by the similarities. The similarities are perhaps the more remarkable, for it is scarcely surprising that persons who until recently were governed by an emperor and trained in a rather complex blend of Buddhist, Shinto, Confucian, and folk religious elements should differ from those raised in a democracy and trained in a perhaps equally complex blend of Christian-Judaic, civil, and folk religious traditions. Alongside these differences, however, we must put the similarities of experience that come from rapid urbanization, mobility, and the pressure brought to bear by contemporary experience on received values and beliefs.

The "new religions" of Japan, which are almost entirely a product of the twentieth century and particularly of the period since World War II, differ in membership from the predominantly middle-class American groups we have discussed.[34] A few of the Japanese groups are largely middle-class, but the adherents of most of them are drawn from the urban proletariat, recent migrants to the cities, and from the lower middle class. When one examines the individual feelings and tendencies that support these new religious movements, he finds the same combination of old and new that characterizes recently urbanized populations in many lands: the desire for success, for health, for an end to loneliness and value confusion. They are not, typically, sectarian movements for social reform. They tend to be politically conservative, to emphasize the elimination of individual suffering and the attainment of individual success. Although young workers comprise most of the members of Sōka Gakkai, for example, which is the largest of the "new religions," there is little hint of proletarian class struggle notions in their doctrines. The political party with which the sect is allied is highly conservative in tone; its policies are based on an ideology of "Buddhist democracy." Participants in Sōka Gakkai are success-oriented; their aspirations have been sharply raised by their move to the cities and by Japan's industrial accomplishments. Although fairly well off economically, com-

33 In a product or multiplicative model, any score of zero will yield a product of zero, whatever the other scores, thus expressing mathematically the idea that all of the variables must be present.

34 For valuable studies of these movements, see H. Neill McFarland, *Rush Hour of the Gods;* Ichiro Hori, *Folk Religions in Japan,* Chap. 6; Joseph Kitagawa, *Religion in Japanese History,* Chap. 6; Fujio Ikado, op. cit.; James A. Dator, "The Sōka Gakkai: A Socio-Political Interpretation," *Contemporary Religions in Japan,* 6, 1965, pp. 205–242; and Earl Babbie, "The Third Civilization. An Examination of Sokagakkai," *Review of Religious Research,* 7, 1966, pp. 101–121.

pared with their situation in the past, many Japanese have fallen behind relatively, as disparity of income grows in the nation as a whole. At the same time they are lonely, confused in values—as a result both of urbanization and the breakup of the empire—lacking in self-confidence, and uncertain about the roads to success.

After World War II, the established religious organizations had been at least partly discredited by their association with the defeated empire. The Japanese government's efforts to keep tight control over all religions, expressed in the 1939 Religious Organization Law, were completely removed by a directive from General MacArthur in October, 1945. All restrictions on religious liberty were removed. Various statutes codified this directive in the next several years, the most important being the Religious Juridical Persons Law in 1951.

Significant cultural influences are closely related to the individual motivations that predisposed many Japanese to new religious movements and to the changed structures that were brought about by industrialization and warfare. On the one hand, the effect of the simultaneous influence of urban migration, war, defeat, and occupation has been a great increase in anomie—normlessness. The sense of a shared cultural system of values is difficult to maintain in these circumstances. On the other hand, the new religions offer themselves as antidotes to anomie. "The primary concern of the new religions is how to protect their adherents, especially those who belong to the rapidly growing urban lower middle class, from such evil influences of Western civilization as a high crime rate, juvenile delinquency, an increase in the divorce rate, a lack of discipline at home and in the schools, the irresponsible behavior of the youths who waste their newly found leisure either in moral dissipation or extreme political activities." [35] This view of the world is not unlike that shared by urban migrants to American cities, many of whom support fundamentalist Christianity as a source of stability and coherence in a situation that threatens their basic values.

It is in this context of rapid social change, cultural confusion, and personal bewilderment, then, that several million Japanese have joined the new religious organizations. They are in search of strengthened convictions that their values are the right values and are widely accepted; and they are in search of happiness and success. It is not surprising that many, perhaps more than five million people in the late-1960s,[36] support a movement that declares:

> The purpose of the sokagakkai lies, first of all, in teaching the individual how to redevelop his character and enjoy a happy life through the supreme religion. Through this supreme religion, a person can escape poverty and live a prosperous

35 Joseph Kitagawa, op. cit., p. 335.

36 Professor Fujio Ikado gives the number as 5,600,000 in 1969 (personal conversation). The sect's own estimate nine years earlier was four million. (See The Seikyo Press, *Sokagakkai*, p. 17.) James Dator, op. cit., p. 205, gives the much higher figure of 5,500,000 households. And by 1969 the movement claimed the support of 6,800,000 households for its political agency Komeito; but if elections are used as an index, this is an unreliable claim. (See *The Mainichi Daily News*, Tokyo, June 9, 1969, p. 8.) One leader stated that there were 40,000 members in the United States. (*The New York Times*, March 3, 1968, p. 3.)

life, if only he works in earnest; a man troubled with domestic discord will find his home serene and happy; and a man suffering from disease will completely recover his health and be able to resume his former job. By the power of the Gohonzon [object of worship], a mother worried with her delinquent son will see him reform, and a husband who is plagued with a neurotic wife can see her return to normalcy. We often hear of a man whose business is bad and who, after becoming a convert to Nichiren Shoshu, has a brilliant idea, makes a contact with an unexpected customer and begins to prosper again.[37]

It is not surprising that such a movement should be called by one of its chief leaders a "happiness-manufacturing machine." Other sects also emphasize the avoidance of suffering and the achievement of happiness, although there are variations in style that match some variation in constituency. P L Kyōdan, the "Perfect Liberty" association, places its emphasis on the achievement of self-expression. Its first precept is, "Life is art." To its basically middle-class membership it declares: ". . . each individual is a unique personality who by right ought to be happy. Happiness is achieved when the individual is able to express perfectly that which he is, basically and uniquely, as a person." [38] This message would be received readily in the more conservative Catholic, Jewish, or Protestant youth meetings in the United States, although others would object to its lack of a social-action emphasis.

Altogether, these new religious developments in Japan express the same search for confidence, success, fellowship, health, and guidance that one finds in other rapidly urbanized populations.

RELIGION AND HEALTH
In the preceding pages we have made several references to the ways in which contemporary religious movements are related to the anxieties of modern men. One important aspect of their work is the search for health and emotional poise, thus bringing religion inevitably into contact with the medical profession, either to oppose or to work with it. The relationship between religion and medical practices is, of course, primordial. From the manipulations of the "medicine man"—near the magical end of the pole— to the prayers and sacrifices and appeals to faith—near the religious end of the pole—the religiomagical complex has everywhere been concerned with problems of ill-health. The relationship between religion and medical practice has become problematic, however, in societies in which extensive scientifically based medical organizations are found and among groups that are generally unsympathetic to magical elements in their religion. We can think of a continuum, relative to the association of religion and medical practice, based on three elements:
 1. The extent of empirical knowledge of health and illness and the existence of independent medical structures based on that knowledge.
 2. The degree of acceptance of medical concerns in the religious culture of various groups.
 3. A series of individual characteristics and experiences, particularly the

37 The Seikyo Press, op. cit., pp. 14–15.
38 H. Neill McFarland, op. cit., p. 130.

following: the level of health and of anxiety, attitudes toward science, especially its medical branch, and the degree to which a person has been socialized to view healing as a legitimate religious concern.

Through most of man's history technical medical knowledge was rudimentary—as it is in many areas even today. Religious values included a central concern for healing, and most individuals, faced by the experience of uncontrollable illness and premature death, were socialized to religio-magical systems in which curing was of vital importance.[39] At the other extreme, there are some, probably a small minority of mankind, who have ready access to scientific medicine, who share a religious culture that is oriented toward ethics, and who are predisposed as a result of their experience to support the scientific approach to medicine and to oppose magical elements in religion.

Probably the most interesting situations for analysis are those in which these three variables are split apart. The religious culture, for example, may include a salvation religion in which the healing message is marginal or even opposed, but also a folk religion built around curing techniques and beliefs. Sometimes these are blended into a syncretist cult;[40] sometimes they exist side by side, organizationally distinct, even though blended in the lives of most adherents.[41] In other settings, elaborate facilities for scientific medicine develop among groups whose traditional religion has contained a continuous, if not central concern for sickness. This is the situation of many urban Protestants and Catholics today. They take modern medicine for granted; only the bare rudiments of direct magical practice remain in their search for health; yet it would be a rare church service in which they did not hear a prayer for the return to health of some member of the congregation. In their study of church members in the San Francisco area, Stark and Glock found that 42 per cent had prayed "to ask God to restore my health," and 79 per cent had prayed "to ask God to restore someone else"s health." [42]

There is a sharper contrast in the lives of recent migrants to Japanese cities. Modern medicine is technically but not culturally (or perhaps financially) available to them. Part of the success in recruitment of such move-

---

39 This is the situation described by most anthropological studies of curing. See for example, Claude Levi-Strauss, *Structural Anthropology*, Chap. 9 and 10; Erwin H. Ackerknecht, "Problems of Primitive Medicine," in *Reader in Comparative Religion*, rev. ed., William Lessa and Evon Vogt, eds., pp. 394–402; George E. Simpson, *The Shango Cult in Trinidad*, pp. 61–79; E. E. Evans-Pritchard, *Witchcraft, Oracles, and Magic among the Azande;* Clyde Kluckhohn, *Navaho Witchcraft;* John Middleton, ed., *Magic, Witchcraft, and Curing;* Mircea Eliade, op. cit.

40 See Alfred Metraux, *Voodoo in Haiti.*

41 See Melford E. Spiro, *Burmese Supernaturalism: A Study in the Explanation of Suffering*, Chap. 14. Spiro argues that the existence of shamans and exorcists permits Buddhism to concentrate primarily on salvation, rather than on rites and beliefs designed to deal with immediate and pressing problems of this world. Not all students of Burma agree with this interpretation, however. Some see a much closer relationship between nat worship and Buddhism, even if not a syncretist blending. See, for example, Winston King, *A Thousand Lives Away: Buddhism in Contemporary Burma.* Chap. 2; and Donald E. Smith, *Religion and Politics in Burma*, pp. 172–177.

42 Rodney Stark and Charles Glock, *American Piety*, p. 118. There were rather large denominational differences, it should be noted.

ments as Tenri and Sōka Gakkai has been based on their attention to ill-ness.[43]

I shall not undertake to examine all the ways in which structure, culture, and character can become separated in the matter of religion and health, but will comment briefly on one type of pattern, to illustrate the need for keeping the three elements in mind when studying particular situations.

The Social Psychology of Christian Science. Even in the modern city, the search for health is a basic concern for some religious groups; it is in the background of the work of others; nowhere is it entirely lacking. Few clergymen are healers of physical ills, but psychological therapy, in the form of counseling, is an important part of the work of many of them. Although the primary theme in Dr. Peale's work, for example, is the elimination of fear and the development of faith and self-confidence, he has long paid attention to "the healing power of enthusiastic faith," to quote a heading from a recent book. In the next chapter I shall comment on the relationships between religion and psychiatry in terms of certain efforts to bring medical and religious structures and values, as well as individual tendencies, into greater coherence. In Christian Science, however, we have an urban, middle-class movement that resists this effort at integration. Although the facilities of scientific medicine are technically available to its members, they are not attracted to them. That part of the Christian culture which emphasizes healing appeals to them; their experience has led them to mistrust scientific medicine. Thus they are different to some degree from their neighbors.[44]

As contrasted with the development of interest in psychiatry and medicine in the established denominations, the approach of Christian Science is *sectarian*, not *churchly*. We shall define those terms at length in a later chapter and therefore shall distinguish them here only briefly, with reference to the immediate question: The churches attempt to absorb modern medicine into their framework, to adjust to it, and to use whatever aspects of it they can in their work. The sectarian approach of Christian Science is to challenge the claims of secular approaches to health and to offer itself as a substitute. It should be emphasized that this is becoming less and less true, that Christian Science is following the familiar road "from sect to church," [45] and in many ways it can now scarcely be distinguished in modes of worship, church organization, and even in its approach to health, from the more standard middle-class denominations. The trend is illustrated by the growth in the importance of church services, as contrasted with an earlier greater emphasis on practitioners. Middle-class sects, as we shall see, are particularly likely to be short-lived, to be absorbed quickly into the

43 See William Newell and Fumiko Dobashi, in Morioka and Newell, op. cit., p. 99; H. Neill McFarland, op. cit., pp. 79–80.

44 The contrast should not be drawn too sharply. Because developments in the standard denominations and in the more eccentric movements are affected by some of the same sociocultural conditions, they share some tendencies. See, for example, Charles S. Braden, *The Rise and Development of New Thought.*

45 This shift is frequently accompanied by internal tensions in a movement. They are carefully described for Christian Science by Charles S. Braden in *Christian Science Today: Power, Polity, Practice.*

mainstream of the churches, with only residues of special emphasis, tradition, and a separate literature remaining.

Without trying to assess how far this process has gone in Christian Science (there is doubtless wide variation from congregation to congregation), we shall speak of its earlier more sectarian approach to religion and health.[46] Not only does it set itself up as a substitute for secular medical practices (accepting only those aspects that harmonize with its own teaching, rather than the churchly approach of accepting what medical men affirm, and harmonizing its teaching to coincide with that); it also offers a metaphysical doctrine and a mysticism in the guise of science that are more congenial to the needs of some people than a simple attempt to apply secular psychiatry under church auspices.

In the basic document of Christian Science, Mary Baker Eddy writes:

> How do drugs, hygiene, and animal magnetism, heal? I venture to affirm that they do not heal; they only relieve, and exchange one disease for another. I classify disease as error, that nothing but Truth, or Mind, can heal, and this Mind must be divine, not human. Mind transcends all other power, and will ultimately supersede all other means in healing. . . . What are termed Natural Science and Material Law are laws of mortal mind. The physical universe expresses the conscious and unconscious thoughts of mortals. Physical force and mortal mind are one. Drugs and hygiene oppose the supremacy of the Divine Mind, and act against it. Drugs and inert matter are unconscious. Certain results, supposed to proceed from them, are really caused by that faith in them which human consciousness is educated to feel.[47]

This passage may suggest something of the tone of the "Science of Divine Mind," in some ways a deeply fundamentalist interpretation of Christianity, but in other ways a mystical and messianic deviation that seeks to absorb the word *science* into its special theology and doctrine.

To whom does such a movement appeal? The range of persons is wide, and doubtless has become wider in recent years, as Christian Science has modified the mysticism of its founder and moved toward a "standard middle-class denomination." Yet we can perhaps describe a modal type that indicates some of the functions of this religious group. R. W. England [48] has made an interesting analysis of a sample of five hundred letters drawn from the columns of the *Christian Science Journal* in various years from 1929 to 1946. Letter-writers are probably not a good sample, in the statistical sense, of readers of the Journal, who in turn are not a statistical sample of Christian Scientists. They are underrepresentative of the more casual members, overrepresentative of the more intense and perhaps the more disturbed members. Yet if one recognizes this, he can use the data from the letters to highlight the approach of Christian Science to illness and other problems. The letters suggest that perhaps half of the writers were drawn to Christian Science because of specific, chronic troubles: ill-health, financial problems, bereavement, family worries, or "undesirable" personal

46 See Bryan Wilson, "The Origins of Christian Science," *The Hibbert Journal*, 57, 1959, pp. 161–170.

47 Mary Baker Eddy, *Science and Health*, pp. 414–415.

48 "Some Aspects of Christian Science as Reflected in Letters of Testimony," *American Journal of Sociology*, March, 1954, pp. 448–453.

traits. The largest group of adherents are urban, middle-class, married women with bodily disorders. Many of their letters are testimonials to remarkable cures, often from vague and emotionally toned illnesses.

Christian Science is supported by the fact that it undoubtedly reduces the illness and anguish of many of its adherents. In Chapter Four we discussed the way in which illness is an attribute of the self and of interpersonal relationships, as well as of the body. Cultural definitions and group interactions are crucial in its incidence and cure. Shamanism can prevent psychopathology; exorcism can promote healing among those who believe.[49] The healing power of faith is an established part of Christianity, existing in a fairly easy alliance with scientific and folk medicine. Christian Scientists are different in that this alliance, as a result of their particular training and experience, is unacceptable.

Like every other system of medicine, from that of the primitive witch doctor to modern scientific practice, Christian Science also profits from the self-validation that follows from the fact that most illnesses "cure themselves." There are very few other fields in which one may have such a good "batting average" just by not making too many mistakes. This is one of the reasons why it is difficult to prove the inadequacy of many approaches to health: almost any method works for a great many people. And only secular science lacks an additional advantage: If a cure is not forthcoming, one can attribute the failure to improper application of the formula or to lack of faith. Secular medicine imposes upon itself the requirement that the formula itself be continually investigated.

England effectively summarizes the basic doctrine of Christian Science:

Briefly, Christian Science teaches that the power of Divine Mind can manifest itself at the behest of believers by curing ills, harmonizing interpersonal relationships, providing material needs, and by otherwise ameliorating one's lot upon the moral plane of existence. The only "reality" is the reality of God; all else is illusion. Traditional Christian virtues are identified with God. Inharmony, such as sickness, poverty, war, is the illusory product of mortal mind and error.[50]

As a phase of the contemporary religious search for "peace of mind," Christian Science shares some tendencies with such religious developments as those epitomized by Dr. Peale, but it differs in other respects. They are similar in appealing primarily to persons of the middle class who respond favorably to the "individual" approach. This requires no examination of the fact that some human ills may find their source in the structure of society. Most of *their* ills, indeed, are not in society, at least in a direct sense, for they are persons of moderate or even large success. The adherents of both groups have come largely from what might be called standard Protestant backgrounds, but had lost interest in their traditional churches. Both groups appeal to those with a smattering of knowledge of modern science. Those in whom the orientation of science has become a crucial life perspective—whether for good or ill—can scarcely be attracted to either movement.

49 See Melford Spiro, op. cit., Chaps. 9–11; Ari Kiev, ed., *Magic, Faith, and Healing: Studies in Primitive Psychiatry Today;* Joseph Eaton and Robert Weil, *Culture and Mental Disorders.*

50 Op. cit., p. 449. See also Walter Wardwell, "Christian Science Healing," *Journal for the Scientific Study of Religion*, 4, 1965, pp. 175–181.

There are other ways in which Christian Science differs rather sharply in its social psychological meaning from a religion of confident living. We have suggested that it is a sect more than a church—or was, at any rate, in its earlier days. As a sect it involves a great deal of the thought and energy of its members, penetrating into many areas of their lives. It appeals to people with mystical tendencies, those who might be discontent with the fairly pat and unimaginative formulas of Peale, but who are drawn to the fairly elaborate and mysterious formulas of Mary Baker Eddy. These require that one be able to set himself somewhat apart from traditional American views, for many hard-headed, practical, middle-class people feel little attraction to doctrines of the power of "Divine Mind." And finally, as contrasted wiith the use of modern medicine invoked by Peale, Christian Science opposes many of its premises. It attracts people who, for different reasons, distrust doctors—perhaps because the vague, emotional difficulties that they so frequently face are at present substantially beyond the reach of medicine.

It is perhaps not too wide of the mark to suggest that the doctrines of positive thinking represent an absorption of Christian Science into the framework of the church, as many another sectarian movement has been absorbed. In the transition, many aspects have been changed, particularly those that represent separation from society; but many of the personality needs from which Christian Science springs are expressed in such churchly developments as those of Peale.

In the search for health through religion, lower-class, poorly educated people, who are close to the fundamentalist Christian tradition, find little need to try to adjust to science and to use it, as Peale does, or to prove that one's doctrines are a kind of superior science, as does Christian Science. As heirs of a tradition that includes miraculous cures, who have stayed closer to the ancient stream of medical magic, they can appeal more frankly to the religio-magical complex in their search for health. The distinction is not sharp, of course, for it is a question whether such an approach is essentially less scientific than many of the middle-class movements. It is more openly nonscientific, however, for the training of its adherents has not presented them with so many problems in reconciling science and religion. They have fewer inhibitions in the use of magical healing cults and formulas. This does not prevent such people from using scientific remedies as well, for these can easily be thought of as alternative means to the same end—a kind of dualistic thinking that is characteristic not just of the Trobriand Islanders, but probably of most of mankind.

Chapter Ten

RELIGION AND INDIVIDUAL NEED:
Interactions with Secular Movements

Religious efforts to deal with individual need seldom proceed in isolation from parallel secular efforts. The nature of the interactions between the two approaches is of great interest to the student of religion. These interactions can be examined from two related perspectives. In the first, secular efforts are studied in terms of the extent of cooperation or conflict with religion; in the second, they are studied as substitutes for religion. I shall illustrate both of these perspectives, first by examining some aspects of the relationships between religion and psychiatry, and then by commenting on several contemporary movements that are basically secular in outlook but which, nevertheless, can be seen as organized efforts to deal with ultimate questions.

RELIGION AND PSYCHIATRY

For some religious leaders, problems of reconciliation between religion and medicine, particularly psychiatry, have become acute. They cannot disregard the scientific approach to health, with the cultists, nor be content with adding the word *science* to the name of their group. As religious leaders, they are heirs to a tradition that contains a good deal of insight into the nature of mental anguish, rooted as it is in sorrow, guilt, hostility, and a sense of aloneness. From the point of view of modern science, these insights, which concern both diagnosis and therapy, are mixed with magic and a miraculous view of the universe that is unacceptable; yet the insights themselves should not be underemphasized. These religious leaders are also strongly affected by the developments of modern science. Many are highly educated men who are aware of the ways in which psychiatry is struggling with the emotional problems with which religion has so long been concerned. Can the efforts of religion and science be united? That is the question they are asking.

The answers they give range over a long continuum, from situations where a few easy propositions drawn from psychiatry are added to the traditional insights (which themselves are variously understood), to the serious study of psychiatry, including a recognition of the conflicts in theory and in premises as well as of the harmony between religion and psychiatry. The majority of ministers probably incline toward the former end of the continuum, since few of them have more than a minimal training in the various disciplines relevant to psychiatry. There are also some deep conflicts between the two traditions that are generally resolved in favor of their primary training. Yet it would be a mistake to overlook the growing interest and training of many religious leaders in psychiatry.[1]

Some psychiatrists and clinical psychologists, in turn, are reaching toward religion. A very little observation reveals that many deeply religious people have a poise and an ability to withstand emotional strain that must command the psychiatrists' professional admiration. It inevitably occurs to some of them to ask: Can I, by giving my patient a "dose of religion," develop in him some of that poise? The question is put in this rather impudent fashion to indicate the utilitarian and pragmatic interest in religion that frequently characterizes the medical man. He too is likely to make use of a few pat formulas. The fact that the religious leader is likely to have an equally pragmatic view of psychiatry reveals the basic differences in assumptions and first premises from which men in the two traditions often proceed.

Our interest here is to show how the personality tendencies of some contemporary religious leaders pose for them serious problems of adjustment or of reconciliation with science. We shall not explore the very extensive literature, along the whole continuum, which represents the many efforts to relate religion to psychiatry.[2] We shall note only briefly that the efforts range from statements that what is true in secular psychotherapy has long been religious knowledge, to the development of clinics and seminary courses for the training of ministers in psychotherapy.

Those who emphasize the traditional role of religion in psychotherapy hold that modern medicine is refining and rediscovering truths that are part of the religious view of man. Effective therapy, they hold, requires the development of a religious faith. They do not oppose the secular developments, though they often criticize their premises, but contend that these developments are true insofar as they harmonize with religious conceptions.

1 For a careful account of the "religio-psychiatry" movement seen through its literature, see Samuel Klausner, *Psychiatry and Religion.*

2 See, in addition to Klausner, op. cit., O. H. Mowrer, *The Crisis in Psychiatry and Religion;* Philip Rieff, *The Triumph of the Therapeutic;* Seward Hiltner, "Freud for the Pastor," *Pastoral Psychology,* 5, 1955, pp. 41–57; A. T. Mollegen, "A Christian View of Psychoanalysis," *Journal of Pastoral Care,* 6, 1952, pp. 1–14; Henry Guntrip, *Psychotherapy and Religion;* A. T. Boisen, *The Exploration of the Inner World;* Albert C. Outler, *Psychotherapy and the Christian Message;* David E. Roberts, *Psychotherapy and a Christian View of Man;* James H. Van der Veldt and R. P. Odenwald, *Psychiatry and Catholicism.*

This is the view taken by Misiak, with special reference to psychosomatic medicine:

The value of religion in psychosomatic medicine becomes evident when we consider the following points: 1. Religion furnishes man with a philosophy of life and gives to his intellect the necessary enlightenment. It becomes to a man what a mariner's compass is to a ship, offers him direction and guidance on the sea of life. 2. Religion assists the will of man, strengthens it, and helps him to carry out the orders of the intellect. 3. Religion fulfills the most basic spiritual needs and yearnings of man, especially that for love and immortality.[3]

From these contributions, Misiak holds, come "peace of mind," internal harmony, and the ability to resist moral dangers. Some psychiatrists agree with this appraisal in a general way, but their utilitarian view of religion leads them to see it as one of various alternative modes of adjustment—a position that the dedicated religious person cannot accept. Allport points out that religion and therapy are alike in stressing the need for unity and order in personality.

But from the point of view of psychotherapy sentiments dealing with family, art, sports, business, would be equally good if they succeeded in marshaling energy and bestowing order in the life. Religion is bound to disagree at this point, asking whether such sentiments are adequate to sustain personality. Can a person ever really attain integration until he has likewise signed and sealed a treaty of peace with the cosmos? [4]

Many medical men may answer No to this question, and thus support the view that religion is fundamentally related to emotional health. The extent of the agreement should not be exaggerated, however, for virtually all psychiatrists take a very tolerant and undogmatic view of religion that is not likely to be satisfactory to those who defend specific religious beliefs and practices as the fundamentally valid ones—however much they may tolerate the "partial insights" of other religions. Thus Christian ministers who turn enthusiastically to Jung (as they may not to Jünger) perhaps do not see the full implications of his views. His support of religion is well known:

Among all my patients in the second half of life . . . there has not been one whose problem in the last resort was not that of finding a religious outlook on life. It is safe to say that every one of them fell ill because he had lost that which the living religions of every age have given to their followers, and none of them has been really healed who did not regain his religious outlook.[5]

Religious liberals, who look upon the continuous modification of ritual and doctrine as a natural and desirable process, can find strong support in Jung. Those who "know" unchanging religious truths, however, can find in him little defense of *the* way.

Those who stress the extent to which modern psychotherapy reaffirms religion often refer not only to their agreement on the individual's need for

3 Henry Misiak, "Psychosomatic Medicine and Religion," *Catholic World*, February, 1953, p. 343.

4 Gordon Allport, *The Individual and His Religion*, p. 79.

5 Carl G. Jung, *Modern Man in Search of a Soul*, p. 284; see also his *Psychology and Religion*.

a unifying scheme of values, but also to similarities in therapy. William Roberts, for example, points to several common aspects: Psychotherapy re-enacts the process of justification by faith; both religion and psychoanalysis stress the "sinful" powers of man; clinicians perform many priestly functions, such as ministering to suffering and awakening hope.[6] Those who have seen the way in which a recently analyzed person defends his "faith" and uses it for explanation and adjustment will not doubt that psychoanalysis has a religious quality for him. One might add that the current attention to group therapy builds on, or at least matches, a religious pattern of long standing. Indeed, organized religious worship is easily regarded, from the perspective of traditional religion, as a "healing of the soul." And some current religious practices, from "underground" Catholic groups to the Oxford Group movement, make explicit use of small groups for mutual confession and support—a development that has probably been virtually unaffected by secular group therapy. Needless to say, any emphasis on the similarities between psychotherapy and religion must pay full attention to the differences. Both may emphasize man's capacity for "sin," for example, but the concept fits into their total schemes in very different ways.[7]

Toward the other end of the continuum are those who are not so concerned to prove that modern psychiatry is only an adaptation of ancient religious theories and methods as they are to learn from psychiatry all that they can, recognizing in it something at least partially new. They look upon psychotherapy as a valuable ally in the struggle to deal with man's age-old problems of anxiety. Some of these religious leaders pay little attention to possible points of contention between the allies, whereas others are more alert to the conflicts in premises and in theories, despite the consensus on many aims. Rabbi Joshua Liebman's popular *Peace of Mind* illustrates the former position and Albert C. Outler's *Psychotherapy and the Christian Message* the latter. Such writers agree, however, that the cooperation of religion and science is valuable and necessary in the search for harmonious individual lives. The extent of the agreement with this idea is seen in the great increase in emphasis on "pastoral psychology." Some ministers look upon this as their central function today, and few escape "clinical" demands upon their time. It is shown in the flood of writings concerning religion and psychotherapy,[8] in the development of specialized periodicals,[9] and in the increase in seminary curricula of courses in the psychology of religion and counseling. It is shown most dramatically, perhaps, by the fact that, in the

6 See "Analysis and Faith," *New Republic*, May 16, 1955, pp. 16–22, where the statement by Roberts is followed by replies from several psychiatrists and clergymen.

7 For a broadly psychoanalytic view of religious development and evolution based on studies of small groups, see Philip Slater, *Microcosm: Structural, Psychological, and Religious Evolution in Groups*, pp. 219–233.

8 Under the direction of Samuel Klausner, the Bureau of Applied Social Research at Columbia University has prepared a bibliography of over 1,300 items. See "Annotated Bibliography and Directory of Workers in the Field of Religion and Psychiatry," mimeographed, 1960. See also W. W. Meissner, *Annotated Bibliography in Religion and Psychology*.

9 See, for example, *Journal of Religion and Health* and the less specialized journals *Lumen Vitae* and *Pastoral Psychology*.

last few years, hundreds of clergymen have been given clinical training in hospital centers where special institutes have been established for them.

Thus on the contemporary religious scene we can see a wide spectrum of psychiatric activity, ranging from faith healing to active cooperation between religious leaders and psychiatrists.[10] The search for health and for peace of mind continues to be a vital part of the religious complex, and as such it is pursued by various people in ways that reflect the differences in the urgency of their needs, their educational level, the extent of their acceptance of the *ethos* of modern science, the nature of their religious training, and the many other aspects of their personality systems.

Psychoanalysis and Religion

When one looks at the religion-personality complex from the point of view of the clinician, the question raised is not, How can the efforts of religion and science be united? (which is a question that assumes that they *can* be) but rather, Does religion contribute to mental health? Among the various aspects of psychiatry, psychoanalysis has been most influential in exploring this question. Both directly, as an effort to develop a complete system of theory and therapy, and indirectly, by its impact on other personality theories and upon clinical practice, psychoanalysis has strongly affected the social psychology of religion. From a brief examination of psychoanalytic ideas—both of the Freudian school and of other approaches —one can learn a great deal about the ways in which religion and personality are related. Both the errors, from the point of view of the theory we are developing, and the insights of psychoanalysis can be instructive. The various schools of psychoanalysis are likely to be very sensitive to their differences; but we must be equally alert to the similarities—particularly their agreement on the way in which the question should be posed: What is the function of religion in the total "economy" of the individual? How is it related to his search for happiness? From what needs does it spring? Does it help to satisfy or does it block the satisfaction of those needs?

The Freudian Theory of Religion. We shall be primarily concerned with Freud, whose sharp propositions can be very instructive, even when they are most in error.[11] It is paradoxical that Freud is attacked for his view that religion is an illusion, and yet his analysis of the nature of man is sometimes cited to support conservative religious doctrines.[12] A brief examination of his theory of religion may help to explain this paradox.

Freud never relinquished his view that the norms of culture were somehow unnatural. The proscriptions and prescriptions that everywhere accompany communal life have to be imposed on the majority of men; they are built upon coercion and instinctual renunciation; they stand in opposition

10 This cooperation is not limited to Christianity or other world religions. See, for example, Judith Randal, "Witch Doctors and Psychiatry," *Harpers*, 231, December, 1965, pp. 56–61.

11 See particularly the following works of Freud: *Civilization and Its Discontents; The Future of an Illusion; Moses and Monotheism; Totem and Taboo.*

12 See David Riesman, *Individualism Reconsidered*, pp. 388–408; and Philip Rieff, *Freud: The Mind of the Moralist*, pp. 272–273.

to the destructive antisocial tendencies in all men. Most men "accept" culture, despite its required renunciations, because of the narcissistic satisfactions it brings, based primarily on the right to despise outsiders. "True, one is a miserable plebeian, tormented by obligations and military service, but withal one is a Roman citizen, one has one's share in the task of ruling other nations and dictating their laws." [13] If the prohibitions of society were removed, one would take his instinctual pleasures as he wished—killing, robbing, sexual satisfactions without confine. That is, one would until he discovered that others acted in the same way (a kind of Kantian categorical imperative, it would seem, which Freud implies would lead men back to the restrictions of culture). "Indeed, it is the principal task of culture, its real *raison d'être*, to defend us against nature." [14]

Needless to say, this is scarcely an adequate view of culture from the perspective of modern sociology and anthropology. Culture creates and expresses needs; it does not simply repress "nature." Group life is also "natural," and the manifestations of society and culture in the personality cannot adequately be interpreted as intrusions from outside. Yet the attention to the inhibitive aspects of culture is legitimate, provided one avoids trying to build a total theory from them. How does religion become involved in this "defense against nature"? It is, says Freud, a key cultural tool: "The gods retain their threefold task: they must exorcise the terrors of nature, they must reconcile one to the cruelty of fate, particularly as shown in death, and they must make amends for the sufferings and privations that the communal life of culture has imposed on man." [15]

Such a statement brings Freud close to a functional theory—which, indeed, he helped to build. Had he brought the phenomena of society (culture in particular) into his analysis of nature, and had he conceived in less narrow terms of the individual needs with which religion is connected, he would have been less inclined to interpret religion simply as an attempt to fashion an illusory shield against the severe blows of individual fate. He would have seen it on occasion as a sword, used to oppose one's fate. Few scientists will quarrel with his proposition that to understand religion one must understand man and his total situation. The controversies concern his interpretation of the nature of man and of group life.

The strength of religion, according to Freud, derives from the power of the wishes that it reflects. It is impossible to establish the truth of the illusions from which religion is built, but these illusions grow from man's most persistent wishes, and "the secret of their strength is the strength of these wishes." [16] Helplessness, demands for justice unfulfilled, the desire for the prolongation of life—these are the forces out of which religion is constructed. It may or may not be true, for illusion is not demonstrably error, but it is always tied to a wish.

Basic to this view of religion is Freud's emphasis on man's helplessness.

13 Sigmund Freud, *The Future of an Illusion*, p. 22.

14 Ibid., p. 26.

15 Ibid., p. 30.

16 Ibid., p. 52. This thesis was not original with Freud. It had been powerfully developed by Ludwig Feuerbach, who saw God as a projection of man's greatest and most pressing desires. See his *The Essence of Christianity*.

Religion is an effort to deal with that helplessness by personifying forces, the gods and spirits, who are not helpless and on whom one can depend, who, in fact, one can under some circumstances control. Freud sees religion, then, as a powerful projective system springing from family experience— the helpless child and the powerful father, who is sometimes terrifying, sometimes consoling, but always necessary. Where Durkheim located the sources of religion in generalized experience with society, Freud saw it as a product of family experience. These are not, to be sure, contradictory ideas. There is no reason why both cannot be true.

Meyer Fortes, for example, finds both explanations necessary in his account of the religion of the Tallensi. Their beliefs are "extrapolations of the experiences generated in the relationships between parents and children"; but they also bind the family to the political society, investing both parenthood and society with sacredness.[17]

Religion to Freud is consolation for a shared anxiety, an anxiety that springs not only from human experience but also from religion itself. Rieff expresses this idea well: "Religion may have been the original cure; Freud reminds us that it was also the original disease. And the cure is doubtful. Appeasement feeds what needs to be fought. Were it not for religious encouragement of anxiety, the individual would feel less anxious; and the effect of this palliative is to remind the patient that he is ill." [18] At times, Freud was ready to accept religion as a necessary illusion, by which he recognized the fact that however much religion may be implicated in man's anxieties, it is not the primordial source of anxiety. Remove the projective systems, as he interpreted them, and the human condition that necessitated them does not change: It simply expresses itself in other ways.

Freud interpreted religion as one of several ways in which men seek to avoid the pains of life and to increase its pleasures. To avoid pain—and it is significant that Freud emphasizes this negative view of the problem —a man may create powerful diversions, which lead to his caring little about his misery, or he may seek substitute satisfactions, which lessen misery, or he may take intoxicating substances, which make him insensitive to it. This suggestion of functional alternatives is an important lead; unfortunately, Freud did not follow it up. Nowhere does he adequately discuss the conditions in which one or another of the roads to happiness will be taken; but without such an analysis, he cannot develop a theory of the interrelationship of personality tendencies and religion. Freud suggests that one may seek happiness by voluntary loneliness to avoid the unhappiness that comes from human relations, by intoxication to ward off misery, by "annihilation of instincts," by sublimation in mental work, by a positive search for pleasure (especially for love, but we are defenseless against suffering when love is not returned), by flight into neurotic illness, and by the "illusions" of art and religion.[19]

When will one or another of these paths be taken, and what are their various consequences? Although Freud gives little attention to the former question, he is not hesitant about giving his judgment concerning the

17 Meyer Fortes, *Oedipus and Job in West African Religion.*

18 Philip Rieff, *Freud: The Mind of the Moralist,* p. 290.

19 See *Civilization and Its Discontents,* pp. 23–42.

latter: Religion has not done its job; it has performed some services for men, but not enough. It is comparable to a childhood neurosis, built on the admiration and fear of one's father. Freud expresses a very guarded optimism that man may outgrow this childhood phase and develop responses to his situation that are based on reason, not illusion.

> Religion circumscribes these measures of choice and adaptation by urging upon everyone alike its single way of achieving happiness and guarding against pain. Its method consists in decrying the value of life and promulgating a view of the real world that is distorted like a delusion, and both of these imply a preliminary intimidating influence upon intelligence. At such a cost—by the forcible imposition of mental infantilism and inducing a mass-delusion—religion succeeds in saving many people from individual neuroses. But little more. There are, as we have said, many paths by which the happiness attainable for man can be reached, but none which is certain to take him to it. Nor can religion keep her promises either. When the faithful find themselves reduced in the end to speaking of God's "inscrutable decree," they thereby avow that all that is left to them in their sufferings is unconditional submission as a last-remaining consolation and source of happiness. And if man is willing to come to this, he could probably arrive there by a shorter road.[20]

This severe judgment was rooted in a theory of the origin of religion that blocked the development of an adequate functional theory, toward which Freud was moving, almost in spite of himself. His ingenious attempt at anthropological reconstruction, however plausible and convincing to "the faithful," cannot be the basis for a scientific theory of religion; yet it set the framework within which his later conceptions were formulated. Fortunately, his acute powers of observation prevented his analysis of the function of religion in personality from being quite as bad, from a scientific point of view, as his attempts to reconstruct the origin of religion. It is the Oedipus myth, of course, which he uses as his version of the Garden of Eden. Man's "fall" occurred when the brothers, who had been expelled from the "primal horde" in which the father monopolized all the females, joined forces, "slew and ate the father, and thus put an end to the father horde." But after they had satisfied their hate "the suppressed tender impulses had to assert themselves." Remorse and a sense of guilt made the dead father more powerful over them than he had been when alive. The slaying of the father and the remorse that followed are specifically, to Freud, the source of totemism. (The totem animal is a father substitute, who may not be killed; and the men deny themselves the women of the totem group, a further recognition of their guilt.)

> The totemic system was a kind of agreement with the father in which the latter granted everything that the child's phantasy could expect from him, protection, care, and forbearance, in return for which the pledge was given to honor his life, that is to say, not to repeat the act against the totem through which the real father had perished.[21]

This imaginative account of the origins of totemism could be set down more readily as interesting speculation if Freud had not used it as a general theory of the origin of religion.

20 Ibid., p. 42.

21 Sigmund Freud, *Totem and Taboo*, p. 238.

All later religions prove to be attempts to solve the same problem, varying only in accordance with the stage of culture in which they are attempted and according to the paths which they take; they are all, however, reactions aiming at the same great event with which culture began and which ever since has not let mankind come to rest.[22]

This kind of historical and psychological reductionism serves only to obscure the complex of forces that lead to religion. Few, aside from convinced Freudians, will be persuaded of the validity of these observations by the claim that they "harmonize" with the conception of personality that emerges from psychoanalytic treatment. Most will demand firmer evidence. One can imagine that Freud himself was not entirely happy with his solution. He came back to the Oedipus relationship in *Moses and Monotheism* and opened the door, at least a crack, to some other kind of explanation than "racial memory." The primeval experience of family conflict, he writes, was such an important one that "I cannot help thinking, it must have left some permanent trace in the human soul—something comparable to a tradition." [23]

Despite its weaknesses the Freudian analysis of religion can contribute a great deal to a functional theory.[24] Even the Oedipus account, if not taken literally, can lead one to a study of the ambivalent feelings, the aggressive impulses, the sense of guilt, the helplessness that are among the forces that sustain the religious quest. The serious weaknesses of Freud's interpretation derive from the narrowness of his general theory and the selective nature of his evidence. His description of the consequences of religion— that it sustained inadequate institutions, prohibited critical thinking, prevented the continuing development of an adequate morality, and fostered an infantile fixation—is based primarily on the religious expressions of neurotic people. This duplicated his tendency to elaborate a total psychological theory on the basis of evidences drawn from the study of upper-middle-class, neurotic, Viennese women in 1900—to state the case a little too severely. Because he tended to assume that all religions were alike in their consequences, he could leap from a fanciful anthropological reconstruction to a contemporary religion without being concerned with major social and cultural differences.

Freud's sweeping generalizations about religion are not readily subjected to test; but some efforts have been made to do so. The most ambitious efforts have been those of John Whiting and his associates to examine childhood experience crossculturally, to see if there were systematic relationships with religious belief. If religious institutions are projections of the emotional conflicts of childhood, they ought to vary with the nature of childhood experience. Freud was himself unconcerned with variation in socialization practices, seeing a kind of universal experience epitomized by the Oedipus conflict. Less bound by biological presuppositions, modern anthropology can examine the varieties and range of infant training and

22 Ibid., p. 239.

23 *Moses and Monotheism*, p. 167.

24 For a valuable comparison of Freudian with functionalist theories of taboo, see John Kennedy, "Mushahara: A Nubian Concept of Supernatural Danger and the Theory of Taboo," *American Anthropologist*, 69, 1967, pp. 685–702.

other socialization patterns. Differences in punishment and reward should, if projective processes are operating, be related to differences in religious belief and practice. The results of these relationships are somewhat ambiguous. Whiting and Child found that socialization processes that produced severe anxiety in children were associated with belief in sorcery as the source of illness. They were not associated, however, with beliefs regarding supernatural sources of illness other than sorcerers.[25] It seems reasonable, on the basis of their evidence, to continue to regard as worthy of further investigation the hypothesis that a relationship exists between man's projective and displacement processes and his beliefs and actions concerning the superempirical world. The hypothesis, however, as Whiting and Child are careful to note, has not been definitively supported.[26]

Modification of the Freudian View of Religion
Freud decisively posed the question, as Rieff has put it, ". . . whether our culture can be so reconstructed that faith—some compelling symbolic of self-integrating communal purpose—need no longer superintend the organization of personality." [27] Freud himself was not sure. He had an aristocratic distrust of the masses—those who "have no love for instinctual renunciation" and do not understand its necessity. But he also had an intellectual's disdain for many of the religious myths and other cultural constraints on man. "Freud maintained a sober vision of man in the middle, a go-between, aware of the fact that he had little strength of his own, forever mediating between culture and instinct in an effort to gain some room for maneuver between these hostile powers. Maturity, according to Freud, lay in the trained capacity to keep the negotiations from breaking down." [28] Freud sought to give men insight that he believed would furnish a wider range of choices; he did not propose to specify the choice.

It is not surprising that critics of Freud, including some who were at first his disciples, pushed away from his position in two directions. Some criticized him for not carrying through in his campaign for freedom; they did not share his distrust of impulse nor his conviction that culture is the fruit of renunciation. A thorough-going individualism, with the self as the center of things, has become a dominant theme today. In modern interpretations of Rousseau's vision of the noble savage, Wilhelm Reich, D. H. Lawrence, and others have seen beneath the cruel and repression-filled unconscious that Freud described, a good and beautiful instinctual unconscious, which needs only to be freed of the coercions that surround it.

Other critics, Jung, Adler, and Fromm being among the most prominent,

25 John W. M. Whiting and Irvin Child, *Child Training and Personality*, Chap. 12.

26 In a study of a sample of American college students, Aron Siegman found little support for three hypotheses derived from Freudian theory, namely that the more religious will project more, that feelings toward God and father will be similar, and that males will be more likely to perceive God as punishing. There was some support for the second hypothesis, but the opposite of the third was more nearly true. See Aron W. Siegman, "An Empirical Investigation of the Psychoanalytic Theory of Religious Behavior," *Journal for the Scientific Study of Religion*, 1, 1968, pp. 74–78.

27 Philip Rieff, *The Triumph of the Therapeutic*, p. 5.

28 Ibid., p. 31.

sought to correct Freud from the opposite side. In his wholly undifferentiated interpretation of religion, as they saw it, he released impulse not only from rigid and irrational controls but from control. They modified his negative judgment of religion, despite their own opposition to traditional forms of religion. With Jung, for example, the analytic process itself became an object of faith. "Against the disenchantment of the world Jung proposes therapeutic commitment. This reverses Freud's analytic attitude. . . ." [29] Jung's approach to more standard religions was wholly unorthodox, to be sure; he gave no support to formal religious organizations or to doctrines; and he did not blur the distinction between religion and medical practice: "The cure of souls as practised by the clergyman or priest is a religious influence based on a Christian confession of faith. Psychoanalysis, on the other hand, is a medical intervention, a psychological technique whose purpose it is to lay bare the contents of the unconscious and integrate them into the conscious mind." [30] Viewed from this perspective, analysis is seen as a valuable adjunct to religious efforts. Jung also stressed, however, the positive functions that he believed religion served in helping one to achieve "individuation" or self-realization. He declared that man stands in need of mystery and symbols, that he has a natural desire to submit to powers higher than himself. Such submission may lead to the infantilism and uncritical thinking that Freud described, but it can also, Jung held, contribute to self-realization.

Among the "neo-Freudians," Erich Fromm is outstanding for his interest in religion and his contributions to a functional theory. Unlike Freud, he differentiates sharply among varieties of religion, in terms of their relationship to what he calls full self-realization. And from the point of view of contemporary social science, his analysis is much more adequate than that of Jung, because he explores the kinds of sociocultural conditions in which various types of religious patterns are most likely to appear. Fromm defines religion broadly: "I understand by religion any system of thought and action shared by a group which gives the individual a frame of orientation and an object of devotion." [31] The very conditions of human existence, he believes, create in man a need for a common system of orientation and an object of devotion. Religion, therefore, is an inevitable aspect of any culture.

The question for Fromm as a therapist is not whether there will be a religion, but what kind of religion man will have and with what consequences for human life. Many traditional religionists will applaud this statement. They may not agree, however, with his instrumental approach, nor with his comments on the kind of religion that he considers necessary for the full realization of human potentialities (a goal, indeed, that they may not accept as the primary one). Fromm, to be sure, indicates that there are aspects of major world religions that contribute to full human development; but he stresses the ease with which they regress toward more "primitive" forms that are "incompatible with the essential teachings of monotheism." Ancestor worship, totemism, fetishism, compulsive ritualism,

29 Ibid., p. 137.

30 Carl Jung, *Psychology and Religion: East and West*, p. 348.

31 *Psychoanalysis and Religion*, p. 21.

in his judgment, lie just beneath the surface of most contemporary religions, and are frequently encouraged by institutional forms.

A religion that contributes to the full realization of human powers will, according to Fromm, be sharply different from the traditional varieties. It will, in his terms, be "humanistic" not "authoritarian." The analytic distinction is sharp, although particular religious complexes may contain both tendencies. The usual conception of religion, he believes, inclines strongly toward the authoritarian type. The very definition of the word *religion* in the *Oxford English Dictionary*, for example, does not describe religion as such but "is a rather accurate definition of authoritarian religion." It states that religion is the "recognition on the part of man of some higher unseen power as having control of his destiny, and as being entitled to obedience, reverence, and worship." It is not alone the emphasis on a controlling, higher power outside man himself that makes this an authoritarian conception, according to Fromm.

What makes it so is the idea that this power, because of the control it exercises, is *entitled* to "obedience, reverence and worship." I italicize the word "entitled" because it shows that the reason for worship, obedience and reverence lies not in the moral qualities of the deity, not in love or justice, but in the fact that it has control, that is, has power over man. Furthermore it shows that the higher power has a right to force man to worship him and that lack of reverence and obedience constitutes sin.[32]

Why is authoritarian religion dysfunctional, according to Fromm's analysis of personality? Because it alienates man from himself. In humanistic religion, God is the image of man's higher self, a symbol of what he might or ought to be; "in authoritarian religion God becomes the sole possessor of what was originally man's: of his reason and his love. The more perfect God becomes, the more imperfect becomes man. He projects the best he has onto God and thus impoverishes himself." [33]

Religion can serve man only when it encourages love and the assertion of one's own powers, not fear and submission. Fromm declares that early Christianity and the mystic thinking in many religions are strongly humanistic. "Jesus' precept that 'the kingdom of God is within you' is the simple and clear expression of non-authoritarian thinking." [34] In emphasizing this aspect of early Christianity, Fromm doubtless minimizes the paradoxes and the complexities, indeed even the contradictions, that it contained. His tendency to make of Jesus a kind of early-day neo-Freudian and a full supporter of humanistic religion seems wide of the mark. It does emphasize in a dramatic way, however, the insights into personality that Christianity contains. The Oedipus complex, Fromm declares, can be understood in its full significance only when it is translated from the sphere of sex into that of interpersonal relations. The "incestuous" craving for the parents is not sexual, as Freud believed, but is an expression of the "much more profound" desire to remain a child, to remain attached to protecting figures.

When Jesus said, "For I am come to set a man at variance against his father, and the daughter against her mother, and the daughter in law against her mother in

32 Ibid., p. 35.

33 Ibid., pp. 49–50.

34 Ibid., p. 48.

law," he did not mean to teach hatred of parents but to express in the most un-equivocal and drastic form the principle that man must break incestuous ties and become free in order to become human.[35]

One can imagine the many responses to this interpretation. Our concern is only to describe it as part of Fromm's attempt to define a religion that in his view is positively functional for human personality. The attachment to parents, although it is the most fundamental form of incest, is not the only form. The tribe, the nation, the race, the class may serve as protecting "homes." "Here are the roots of nationalism and racism, which in turn are symptoms of man's inability to experience himself and others as free human beings." [36]

Thus Fromm does not share Freud's categorical judgment that religion is an infantile fixation that man may someday be able to afford to discard. Although he stresses the ease with which it serves selfish interests and neurotic trends in the individual, Fromm also declares that religion can help men to achieve their highest potentialities. Under what conditions is this most likely to occur? Fromm gives no detailed answer to this question, but he shows his full awareness of the fact that the kind of personality capable of humanistic religion will emerge in certain kinds of sociocultural situations. He who would make man religious, in Fromm's sense, must work to create the kind of conditions in which character structures capable of mature religious experience will develop.

What people think and feel is rooted in their character and their character is molded by the total configuration of their practice of life—more precisely, by the socio-economic and political structure of their society. In societies ruled by a pow-erful minority which holds the masses in subjection, the individual will be so imbued with fear, so incapable of feeling strong or independent, that his religious experience will be authoritarian. . . . On the other hand, where the individual feels free and responsible for his own fate, or among minorities striving for free-dom and independence, humanistic religious experience develops.[37]

Such a hypothesis—one can scarcely say that it has been fully dem-onstrated—is pertinent only to an instrumentalist approach to religion which asks: How does religion affect the quality of human life? To those who seek to establish or defend "the truth" and to those for whom the rele-vance of religion to the quality of adjustment to this life is quite unimpor-tant, Fromm's observations have little significance. To those who share his orientation, the key question remains: Does humanistic religion merely reflect mature personalities, which in turn are the product of favorable sociocultural conditions? Or does such a religion, once established, help to create mature persons and a nonauthoritarian society? Fromm strongly implies that the latter is true, but does not adequately describe the process by which the influence is conveyed. The ease with which religions became authoritarian shows that man has not yet learned how to prevent religion from becoming an accumulating reservoir of his projected needs. But there

35 Ibid., p. 81.

36 Ibid., p. 81.

37 Ibid., p. 52.

are also evidences of close connections between religion and personal growth and "individuation," to use Jung's term. The full picture must include both tendencies.

SECULAR ALTERNATIVES TO RELIGIOUS ACTION

There is no sharp break that distinguishes religious behavior from other kinds of behavior; only a shading off, as various criteria in one's definition become less and less applicable. It is possible, of course, to pay so much attention to a few similarities among phenomena that the large differences are obscured. Neurosis may be described as a private form of religion, or a man's job may be called his religion. These are not so much wrong as they are intriguing part truths that require careful qualification. The opposite difficulty, however, is perhaps more common: Differences among phenomena are so heavily stressed that the important similarities, in terms of function, are overlooked. At the extreme is the assertion that nothing is religion except one's own system of beliefs and practices. In a day of widespread culture contact, this is less likely than the contention that, although there may be many forms of religion, no phenomenon should be admitted to this category unless it bears the *name* religion. But this word *religion* is without cognates in many languages. It draws a line through reality at places uncongenial to some usages. We are concerned, however, not with names but with processes. If nationalism, for example, performs some of the same individual and group functions as religion, this is an important fact that must be explored, despite differences in name.

There are two primary questions to keep in mind in the analysis of functional alternatives: What are the conditions under which one alternative rather than another will be followed? And what are the similarities and differences in their consequences? These are difficult questions, to which we shall refer at various points in the chapters that follow, in connection with specific situations. In a general answer, one may only say that social, cultural, and character facts set limits to the kinds of alternatives that may be selected. A contemporary American may develop such a faith in the power of science, may make it so much an object of devotion, that it can fairly be said that science is his religion. Clearly this would not be an available alternative in many other sociocultural situations. Nor is it available to persons of different tendencies. Those in whom a love of mystery is strong; those who have been taught to distrust reason; the "twice-born" torn by doubt and a sense of sin—all these are people unlikely to adopt such an alternative.

The consequences of having adopted one alternative rather than another also vary from situation to situation and from individual to individual. One cannot say that the results of infusing nationalism with a religious fervor will be everywhere the same. To respond to a sense of powerlessness by joining a Nazi movement does not have the same consequences as a universalist religious response to the same feeling. Clearly there are important value questions involved, as well as problems of analysis, for one response may be far less effective than another in achieving stated goals and may produce more unintended dysfunctions.

Almost every need that we have mentioned in connection with religion finds expression in a wide variety of secular movements. This is particularly true in modern society, in which traditional religious symbols and forms have lost force and appeal. The needs with which religion is connected are still with us. If we are not trained to look to a religious system in our attempts to satisfy them, we will tend to infuse secular patterns with a religious quality. We may seek to overcome a sense of aloneness by joining a lodge, rather than (or in addition to) joining a church congregation. We may struggle with a feeling of powerlessness by imbuing our nation with an absolute quality, rather than identifying with an all-powerful God. We may attempt to rid ourselves of guilt by projecting our weakness onto a minority group, instead of going to confession. We may try to reduce a sense of confusion and doubt by adopting rigid "all-knowing" secular formulas to explain the world's ills, holding to them with a desperation born more of uncertainty than of conviction. We may attempt to reduce our sense of meaninglessness in life, of boredom on our job, by avid pursuit of entertainment or by alcohol, trying to capture on a weekend what is denied us in the course of our work. (It is in such a situation that "the lost weekend" takes on a tragic quality, for if the weekend is lost, what remains to a man alienated from his job?)

Such secular attempts to reduce our problems do not necessarily stand in the way of religious efforts. A person with a strong sense of guilt, for example, may be drawn to religion and at the same time express strong racial prejudices, as a result of a tendency toward projection. This does not necessarily show a causal connection between the two patterns of behavior, although they may be causally interrelated. On the other hand, a secular alternative may be quite incompatible with certain kinds of religious attempts to deal with the same problem. The chauvinist who exalts the state into a god may also support a parochial religion, but he can scarcely give full allegiance to a universalist religion.

Those on whom the pressures of life fall most heavily (either because of individual circumstances or because of the times in which they live) *and* for whom an established religious system is lacking, are the most likely candidates for a secular movement of a protoreligious variety. These are the discontented, alienated people who follow the "Prophets of Deceit," as Lowenthal and Guterman call them.

Movements that are very different in ideology or in proclaimed goals may satisfy many of the same needs—needs for direction, for a sense of belonging to a vital and significant group, for projection and displacement of one's guilt and doubt, for answers to the meaning of life. Since few social movements accomplish more than a minimum of what they promise, their adherents move restlessly in and out of them, propelled by their own unsatisfied needs. Eric Hoffer describes "the interchangeability of mass movements":

In pre-Hitlerian Germany it was often a tossup whether a restless youth would join the Communists or the Nazis. In the over-crowded pale of Czarist Russia the simmering Jewish population was ripe both for revolution and Zionism. In the same family, one member would join the revolutionaries and the other the Zionists. Dr. Chaim Weizmann quotes a saying of his mother in those days: "Whatever happens, I shall be well off. If Shemuel [the revolutionary son] is right, we shall all be happy in Russia; and if Chaim [the Zionist] is right, then I shall go to live in Palestine." [38]

In one sense it is a "tossup" whether a person will support one or another of social movements that have quite different ideologies and different consequences. Whether or not a given movement is available, in the sense of being carried along a communications network of which an individual is a part, may be as critical a fact as its ideology. It is a mistake, however, to disregard the values and tendencies of potential adherents. These serve as screens that filter out and change various messages. Only under extreme conditions are a person's predispositions irrelevant to the outcome. It is when we combine knowledge of the ideologies, the networks of interaction, and individual tendencies that we best understand the success and failure of various movements.

This is shown clearly in examinations of the relationship between religion and prejudice. An individual may seize upon a socially established system of discrimination and prejudice against minority groups to assuage his self-doubt or to try to reduce his sense of failure. Some studies, in fact, have found a positive correlation between prejudice and traditional religious views of the world. The correlation, however, requires careful examination and interpretation. Does the religious training cause the prejudice? Or does a prejudiced person find a traditional religious outlook congenial? Or does a self-doubting, frustrated person grasp at *both* prejudice *and* religion to try to reduce his difficulties?

The evidence is somewhat mixed. Putney and Middleton found a small but statistically significant correlation between religious orthodoxy and authoritarianism in a large sample of college students. The orthodox were also more likely to be highly concerned about their social status and to be conservative in political and economic matters.[39] These results must be interpreted cautiously, however. Since those with high scores in orthodoxy and authoritarianism were also more likely to be underclassmen, women, Southern, and Catholic, a functional relationship between variations in character (authoritarianism) and religious belief was not clearly established. Maranell, in a study of four undergraduate university samples, found a strong relationship between prejudice and religiosity only in the Southern groups.[40] Photiadis and Johnson introduced a number of personality and educational controls, by means of partial correlation analysis, and found that in a sample of three hundred church members, there was a significant relationship between prejudice and orthodox beliefs. Within the limits of the measures used, the relationship could show either that prejudiced persons retain orthodox beliefs or that they become orthodox believers. The

38 Eric Hoffer, *The True Believer*, pp. 16–17.

39 Snell Putney and Russell Middleton, "Dimensions and Correlates of Religious Ideologies," *Social Forces*, 39, 1961, pp. 285–290.

40 Gary Maranell, "An Examination of Some Religious and Political Attitude Correlates of Bigotry," *Social Forces*, 45, 1967, pp. 356–363.

causal direction cannot be established. They also found that both authoritarian and tolerant persons, orthodox and unorthodox, became more tolerant through extended church participation.[41]

This last finding points up the weakness of much of the work on this problem: It uses only one dimension of religiosity, most frequently a belief dimension. A high score on the scale of "being religious" usually implies that one takes a conservative or orthodox position. When other dimensions are introduced, such as Photiadis' and Johnson's measures of participation, we are able to develop a more differentiated interpretation of the relationship between religion and prejudice. Gordon Allport was working along these lines with his distinction between intrinsic and extrinsic religious beliefs, the former being a product of security and normal socialization and the latter a product of insecurity and self-interest. He suggested that extrinsic religious beliefs might be associated with prejudice whereas intrinsic beliefs were associated with tolerance.[42] Efforts to define and measure these terms precisely have not been entirely successful; and findings concerning the relationship between extrinsic beliefs and prejudice have been somewhat contradictory.[43] The need for differentiating among varieties of religious belief and adding attention to other dimensions of religion, however, is of continuing importance. When Allen and Spilka used multiple criteria for religiosity, they found a strong correspondence between prejudice and what they called consensual religion and a negative relationship between prejudice and committed faith, terms similar to Allport's extrinsic-intrinsic distinction.[44]

In the light of these several findings, we can no longer be satisfied with undifferentiated studies of "religion" and "prejudice."

Three "Secular Religions" of the Contemporary World

Individual prejudices may serve as the basis for groups with religious qualities; or more precisely, the needs underlying those prejudices, if they are shared by a number of persons, may provide that basis in certain supportive environments. The rites and doctrines of the Ku Klux Klan, for example, can be interpreted in this way. More substantial grounds for secular movements with religious qualities, however, are found in three international developments that express important aspects of the tensions

41 John Photiadis and Arthur Johnson, "Orthodoxy, Church Participation, and Authoritarianism," *American Journal of Sociology,* 69, 1963, pp. 244–248.

42 Gordon Allport, *Personality and Social Encounter,* pp. 257–267.

43 See Cody Wilson, "Extrinsic Religious Values and Prejudice," *Journal of Abnormal and Social Psychology,* March, 1960, pp. 286–291; and John Photiadis and Jeanne Biggar, "Religiosity, Education, and Ethnic Distance," *American Journal of Sociology,* 69, 1962, pp. 666–672.

44 Russell Allen and Bernard Spilka, "Committed and Consensual Religion: A Specification of Religion-Prejudice Relationships," *Journal for the Scientific Study of Religion,* 6, 1967, pp. 191–206. For further discussions of this question, see Frederick Whitam, "Subdimensions of Religiosity and Race Prejudice," *Review of Religious Research,* 3, 1962, pp. 166–174; and George E. Simpson and J. Milton Yinger, *Racial and Cultural Minorities,* 3rd ed., pp. 397–400.

and changes of the modern world. Brief comments on these three developments will be helpful in seeing the interplay of cultural, structural, and character elements. As Paul Tillich has noted, the encounters of the major world religions today are primarily with a series of what he calls quasi-religions—nationalism, communism, and humanism.[45] To fail to study such movements would be to leave a serious gap in the scientific study of religion.

In Chapters Three and Four I noted that science, morality, and magic were closely associated with religion because they dealt with issues of religious import—ignorance, injustice, and suffering. It is not surprising that in the last several generations, with traditional religions undergoing sharp challenge, substitute ideologies have appeared that offer themselves as new roads to salvation. What *is* perhaps surprising is that three of these substitutes, each proclaiming itself a science, have specialized around the three basic issues mentioned above, in an effort to save man from ignorance, injustice, and suffering. These are *Positivism, Marxism,* and *Freudianism.*

Religious Aspects of Positivism. This section might be called a comment on the religion of "reason and humanity," except that such a phrase calls up too specific an association with the Enlightenment. The religion might be called scientism, except that this term has a more cultist connotation than is intended. In *The Grammar of Science* Karl Pearson described the religion of science as "single-eyed devotion to truth," but that leaves aside the elements of worship and morality that need also to be kept in mind. Perhaps positivism, despite the variety of meanings associated with it, most nearly represents the range of ideas I wish to discuss.

The roots of positivism go deep, certainly back as far as the Renaissance and more particularly to the early forms of deism that developed along with seventeenth-century science.[46] Newton envisaged a kind God managing an orderly universe, or perhaps one should say viewing an ordered universe that he had created. For Newton and most of his contemporaries, reason could be combined with a fairly traditional faith.

The eighteenth century saw a great increase in belief in man's powers. At least we see such an increase in the thought of the most influential writers. They ranged from relatively conservative deists to secular nationalists, but their dominant emphasis was on reason and humanity, a belief in the possibilities of progress through the application of human intelligence and beneficence. To Condorcet, Diderot, Rousseau, Voltaire, and Paine, to mention some of the most influential among them, it was time for a religion of reason and humanity.[47] On the one hand, their work was oppositional and negative: traditional religion and clericalism must be destroyed —*Écrasez l'infâme.* On the other hand, however, there was a positive faith: By the combination of beneficence and reason mankind can achieve the heavenly city on earth.

45 Paul Tillich, *Christianity and the Encounter of the World Religions.*

46 Franklin Baumer, *Religion and the Rise of Scepticism* is an excellent study of the sources and varieties of positivism, as well as of other forms of departure from traditional religion.

47 This range of ideas is skillfully portrayed by Carl Becker in *The Heavenly City of the Eighteenth-Century Philosophers.*

For a brief period during the French revolution, the Cathedral of Notre Dame was known as the Temple of Reason. A succession of groups to propagate the "cult of reason" developed; but most were short-lived. For the most part, the religion of humanity, of progress, of reason, of posterity was an idea in the minds of intellectuals. It was with Saint-Simon and more particularly with Comte that this idea became the basis of a strong organizational effort.[48] Science was to replace theology as the source of ultimate values and perspectives. To his *System of Positive Polity*, Comte gave the subtitle *Instituting the Religion of Humanity*. By his religion of humanity, as Baumer remarks, he sought to become for his age what St. Thomas had been for his own. "A peace of unexampled duration," Comte wrote in 1852, "has thoroughly established the spontaneous extinction of the principle of War, and the manifest tendency of modern nations to form ultimately one vast family; the object of whose practical activity is to cultivate the earth, in the constant service of Humanity." [49] He saw the "true Religion, the final system of Sociocracy" toward which mankind was steadily converging, not as a revolt against traditional religions but an evolutionary development out of them. Voltaire could say that "to do good" was his worship; but Comte believed that the anarchy he feared would be avoided and the reasoned beneficence he sought could be obtained only by the full trappings of religion—by church and a hierarchy of leaders, by careful attention to the training of the young, by worship, and by regard for the emotional quality of human existence.

As an organized movement, Comte's religion achieved little success and survives only in a few small positivist groups and, in a more cultist form, in scientology. Many nineteenth-century intellectuals shared his belief in a religion of humanity based on reason, but could not accept the highly institutionalized and even authoritarian church that Comte envisaged. These views were perhaps most explicitly extended a generation after Comte by his countryman Ernest Renan, when he called for the institution of a religion of science.[50] But belief in the saving power of scientific knowledge has more commonly been mixed with nationalism or with ethical humanism. It is an aspect of secular religion rather than the very core of a faith. At least for many who take this view, science is a powerful instrument but is not itself the source of ultimate values. In terms that we shall develop later, belief in science is *diffused* through the structures and cultural values of some societies rather than *institutionalized* as a distinctive religious pattern.

We need to recognize that a religious attachment to science is no more immune from skepticism than are other faiths. For a century and a half, between the mid-eighteenth and the early twentieth centuries, it may have been possible to state, with Renan, that "science alone can solve" man's eternal problems or to predict, with Comte, the extinction of the principle

48 See Paul Arbouse-Bastide, "August Comte et la sociologie religieuse," *Archives de Sociologie des Religions,* 22, 1966, pp. 3–57, for a discussion of Comte's theory of religion and, to a lesser degree, his religion of humanity. For Baumer's discussion, see op. cit., pp. 162–186.

49 August Comte, *System of Positive Polity,* Vol. 2, p. 116.

50 Ernest Renan, *The Future of Science.*

of war. But today, such utter confidence in science requires more faithfulness than most men can manage, even those who regard themselves as
intellectuals, or perhaps I should say, especially among intellectuals. The
immediate past has been more "the age of longing" than an age of
positivism.[51]

In the sense of a diffused quality, nevertheless, faith in science is widespread in Western societies, even among the traditionally devout.[52] Its
victories over many of man's pressing day-by-day problems is too impressive to disregard in the formation of one's scheme of salvation. There is
something of Comte in Durkheim's vision of society reorganized by the
development of a scientific morality. Durkheim would have schools teach
morality, with society substituted for God—a kind of "functional equivalent of Catholicism." [53]

I shall not undertake here an examination of the various rationalist,
secularist, and humanist groups for whom science is a powerful object of
faith.[54] In some this has been a gradual development stemming from
liberal and radical expressions of a traditional religion. Julian Huxley's
Religion Without Revelation and John Dewey's *A Common Faith*, for
example, are extensions of "left-wing" Christianity, not sharp departures
from it.

Faith in science is commonly associated with a social movement built
primarily around some other dominant theme—it is an adjunct to the
movement rather than its source. Thus Weber speaks of the "almost superstitious veneration of science" as part of the "quasi-religious belief in the
socialist eschatology" among some of those in nineteenth-century radical
movements.[55] This leads us, however, to examination of faith of a different
kind; for if science has conditioned the beliefs of political radicals, it was
a secular millenarian prophecy that set the dominant tone.

Religious Aspects of Marxism. Prophetic condemnation of an evil
world has a long religious tradition. Marxism as an ideology and communism as a movement can be seen as a modern secularized, and highly
specialized, prophetic movement, proclaiming the road to justice. Where
positivism sees science as the road to salvation, communism sees the creation of new economic and political structures as the way. Its religious
quality is apparent in Western societies, where only a small minority of the
population have become adherents, as well as in societies where communism is dominant. In the former, the search for an "overwhelmingly strong
power" on which to rely, which may lead one person to give himself to God,
may under particular conditions of character and circumstance lead
another to "the party." It is a mistake to disregard the differences that these

51 See Franklin Baumer, op. cit., pp. 187–229; see also Arthur Koestler's *The Age of
Longing* for a novel that develops the consequences of being "dispossessed of faith."

52 See Samuel Klausner, "Images of Man: An Empirical Inquiry," *Journal for the
Scientific Study of Religion*, 1, 1961, pp. 61–73.

53 See Emile Durkheim, *Moral Education*. The quoted phrase is from Everett Wilson's
Introduction.

54 For a variety of observations on faith in science, see Martin Marty, *Varieties of
Unbelief*; Susan Budd, "The Humanistic Societies," in *Patterns of Sectarianism*, Bryan
Wilson, ed., Chap. 11.

55 Max Weber, *Sociology of Religion*, p. 135.

choices indicate, but equally a mistake to overlook some important similarities. There is ample evidence that some of the recruits to the Communist Party in the West during the 1930's were highly sensitive people, bewildered by the confusions of modern society, idealistic, and in need of a clear-cut program that claimed to be able to solve the problems they felt so deeply. They found in the authoritative program of communism and in its seeming dedication to justice an "escape from freedom" that gave them both a sense of belonging and a sense of power. They were no longer the alienated; they had a "home" and a program.

For many of them, of course, communism became "the God that failed," able to give them a sense of identity with an exciting movement but scarcely able to satisfy their idealism. As they became disenchanted with communism, they turned to other programs, propelled by the same burning need for a way to struggle with their bewilderment and sense of powerlessness. Some turned to vigorous anticommunism, investing it with the same energy and dedication they had formerly shown for communism. Others turned to classical religion, in several celebrated cases to Roman Catholicism. Such a dramatic change doubtless indicates a strong reaction against communism; but it also shows some personality continuity, for the Catholic Church more than any other in Christianity furnished its members with a fixed dogma, definitive rites, and an unchallenged structure of power that brought a sense of certainty to those torn by doubt—something of the same appeal that communism had for some people.[56] Because of significant changes in Catholicism, this may be less true now then in the 1930's. Those persons in the "new left" who become disenchanted may, if these processes in fact are operative, be less inclined to move into Catholicism.

Arthur Koestler describes the religious quality that communism had for him in vivid words:

By the time I had finished with *Feuerbach* and *State and Revolution*, something had clicked in my brain which shook me like a mental explosion. To say that one had "seen the light" is a poor description of the mental rapture which only the convert knows (regardless of what faith he has been converted to). The new light seems to pour from all directions across the skull; the whole universe falls into pattern like the stray pieces of a jigsaw puzzle assembled by magic at one stroke. There is now an answer to every question, doubts and conflicts are a matter of the tortured past—a past already remote, when one had lived in dismal ignorance in the tasteless, colorless world of those who *don't know*.[57]

Among the 221 former Communists studied by Almond, almost half came from homes where religious interests were important. He interprets

56 See Whittaker Chambers, *Witness;* and the highly insightful accounts in *The God That Failed,* Richard Crossman, ed.; see also Arthur Koestler's *The Yogi and the Commissar.* For attempts to explore some of the social and psychological factors in adherence to communism, see Gabriel Almond, *The Appeals of Communism* and Morris L. Ernst and David Loth, *Report on the American Communist.*

57 In *The God That Failed,* p. 23. Koestler's reference to Marx's *Theses on Feuerbach,* 1845, serves to remind us of the influence of the latter on Marx's theory of religion. Marx noted the value of being baptized in the "firebrook." He learned from Feuerbach to resolve "the religious essence into the human," but saw religion as a social product, not a product of the individual system of projection.

their opposition to the religion of their parents, not simply as antireligious development, but often as a redirection of interest to a movement that was embraced with religious fervor.

Contemporary radicalism in the United States is of many varieties. Our interest here is in those forms of it that are associated with extreme political deviation, with support for "Maoism" as an ideology and strategy, for example. Because this is mixed, more than was true of the radicalism of the 1930's, with other forms of protest—with attempts to change universities, increase Black Power, or simply to realize rather widely accepted but neglected goals—it is difficult to isolate the individuals and with them the tendencies that support it. There seems little reason to doubt, however, that the movement has its origins also in idealism and longing, heightened by social disorganization and by opposition to those in authority. Perhaps those under thirty who do not trust those over thirty might at least study them—to learn a great deal about themselves, and their probable futures.[58]

Within communist societies, of course, Marxism is not sectarian protest, but the Establishment. It is as vulnerable to schism, to be sure, as are other major faiths, so that one can see "denominational" variation within societies and major splits across societal lines. There is also sharp conflict, with varying degrees of accommodation, with older religions. In the Soviet Union, the fifty-year-long effort to destroy competing faiths has been only partially successful.[59] Mainland China's "cultural revolution," which is at least in part an effort by Mao's regime to break the hold of traditional values and to establish communist values, has also met strong resistance. Yet there is little doubt that in terms of belief, ritual, and organization, communism is the major religion of the Soviet Union and China.

The religious quality of communism was more readily visible in its sectarian period, when it took the form of utopian communities or a messianic movement.[60] Its relationship to the Judaic-Christian tradition is not entirely lost, however, even in its more explicitly political dimensions.[61] And now, after decades of sharp organizational separation and hostility, some slight movement toward encounter, if not reconciliation, is beginning.[62]

58 Unlike Marx, who advised baptism in the "firebrook," we must take our baptism without the cooling water: see Lewis Feuer, *The Conflict of Generations.* For vigorous expressions of revolutionary idealism, not lacking in a touch of utopianism, see Herbert Marcuse, *One Dimensional Man* and *An Essay on Liberation.*

59 On this struggle, see William Fletcher, *A Study in Survival: The Church in Russia, 1927–1943;* Walter Kolarz, *Religion in the Soviet Union;* Alexandre Bennigsen and Chantal Lemercier-Quelquejay, *Islam in the Soviet Union;* Moshe Decter, "The Status of Jews in the Soviet Union," *Foreign Affairs,* Jan. 1963, pp. 420–430; Peter Grose, "Religion Survives in Soviet Union Despite Regime's Hostility and Harassment," and "Soviet Union's Jews Pose Special Problem for the Kremlin's Nationality Policy," *New York Times,* Oct. 26, 1967, p. 28, and Oct. 27, 1967, p. 26. For a series of sociological studies of religion in Poland, see *Social Compass,* 15 (nos. 3 and 4), 1968.

60 See Henri Desroche, *Socialismes et sociologie religieuse,* pp. 35–194; and Norman Cohn, *The Pursuit of the Millennium,* pp. 307–319.

61 See Desroche's section, "'Engelianisme' et Christianisme primitif," op. cit., pp. 383–404.

62 See Harvey Cox, *On* NOT *Leaving it to the Snake,* chs. 6–8.

Leaving aside all these complexities, our brief reference here is to the ways in which communism (and indeed other forms of totalitarianism) functions as a religion. The injustices of the noncommunist world and the powerlessness of workers and peasants in it are described in rich detail in communist literature. But they are provisional facts, to be transformed by the movement. Problems of the present are interpreted in terms of a glorious future that gives those problems meaning. There are appeals to faith. A writer in *The New Masses* declared: "The loss of religious faith is good only if we can put in its place a faith in life so real and driving that it endows men's acts with an equal validity. . . ."[63]

Many despotic movements of the past have sought to use religion to reinforce their power, but in societies in which distinctive religious institutions have developed, despots have seldom been able to bring the religious forces completely under their control. Some element of restraint, some limit on their power was imposed by a partially competing religious system. Waldemar Gurian has distinguished such despotisms from modern totalitarianisms by the fact that the latter are not content simply to use or control the religious forces: they supplant them with their own creed, thus absorbing and using the religious interest to support their cause.

The totalitarian movements and their power replace God and religious institutions such as the Church; the leaders are deified; the public mass-meetings are regarded and celebrated as sacred actions; the history of the movement becomes a holy history of the advance of salvation, which the enemies and betrayers try to prevent in the same way as the devil tries to undermine and destroy the work of those who are in the service of the City of God.[64]

From contemporary evidence it is clear that Gurian should have written that totalitarian regimes *attempt to* supplant traditional religions. If they become reasonably secure, in fact, some processes of accommodation are undertaken, as has happened in the case of the Soviet Union and the Russian Orthodox Church. Moreover, in the second and third generations, liberal as well as reactionary opponents of the regime may begin to use religion of a traditional form as a mode of expressing their opposition, indicating further its staying power.

Keeping in mind these qualifications, we still must note that modern totalitarian systems serve as religions for many people. They attempt to make the grave problems of life more bearable by reference to a happier future, thus sharing the cosmic optimism of religion. The dictator becomes a living embodiment of a "supernatural" power, scarcely limited by the forces that have prevented other men from solving overwhelming problems. History is on the side of "the elect." Ritual, emotionally evocative music, and pageantry are used to heighten support for the cause. Sacred writings and official doctrines are recited and republished endlessly. (In Hitler's time a copy of *Mein Kampf* was given to every newly-wed couple.) Before the totalitarian parties have achieved power, there are many "sectarian" elements in their approach. After they have come to power, they become "churchlike." Altogether, the religious aspects of communism and other

63 Quoted by Reinhold Niebuhr, *Christianity and Power Politics*, p. 192.

64 Waldemar Gurian in *Totalitarianism*, Carl J. Friedrich, ed., p. 122.

totalitarian movements are important elements to the person interested in understanding their influence.[65]

Psychoanalysis as a Modern Faith. The alternative to religion may be, not some social movement with which one can identify, but a private pattern of belief and ritual used by an unhappy individual in his attempts to counter personal failure and isolation. In extreme cases, this private system will be identified by others as a neurosis. Many writers have noted the thin line that separates a moving religious experience from neurotic illness. James developed this point in his classic work. Freud, of course, tended to identify all religion as an expression of neurotic trends. Fromm adds that neurosis can be seen as a private form of religion—an attempt to struggle with the sense of isolation and powerlessness that overwhelms one. If reality is too painful to bear, one can redefine it with the schizophrenic, stand in opposition to it with the paranoic, or alternately run past it and hide from it with the manic-depressive. That each of these responses has its religious equivalent can readily be seen. In his detailed study of 173 seriously disturbed patients, Boisen observes the similarities between their efforts to struggle with their pains and religious behavior. He notes that many great religious leaders—George Fox, John Bunyan, and St. Paul, for example—had emotional disturbances comparable to those of acutely disturbed patients. Yet they were not simply neurotic individuals; ". . . the correct contrast is not between the pathological and the normal in religious experience but between spiritual defeat and spiritual victory." [66] Unfortunately, even if we accept his value judgment, Boisen does not explore the conditions in which one may hope for the visions of a Fox instead of the illusions and delusions of a disturbed person. The scientist must try to discover the social, cultural, and character factors that incline one toward a religious effort in dealing with his anxieties rather than toward a neurotic effort.

One of the conditions may be the degree to which an anxiety is "legitimized" by available cultural interpretations and to some degree "externalized" by the definitions of a group. A religious movement may help to transform an individual's suffering into an expression of the human condition—and thus furnish a means for dealing with it that is not caught in the ambivalences of the purely individual experience.

Freud was unwilling to accept such a compromise with his ideal of the free individual who governs his own fate to a maximum degree. Although he was ready to grant that, as a shared neurosis, religion had some advantages over the individual variety, he saw his task as the elimination of both. "He wanted merely to give men more options than their raw experience of life permitted" [67] by furnishing them with the power to interpret that experience. The zeal with which he defended this purely analytical approach, however, had something of a religious quality to it. It stimulated in his somewhat less tough-minded associates and followers faithfulness,

65 For additional discussions see Henri Desroche, *Marxisme et religions*; C. K. Yang, "Communism as a New Faith," in *Religion in Chinese Society*, Chap. 14; and Paul Tillich, op. cit., pp. 18–25.

66 A. T. Boisen, *The Exploration of the Inner World*, p. 79.

67 Philip Rieff, *The Triumph of the Therapeutic*, p. 87.

on the one hand, and zealotry for competing approaches on the other. In the context of the tragedies of the twentieth century, Freud's belief in the ability of the person to achieve mastery over both id and superego has been difficult to sustain. To some, the upwelling of violence and sexuality has demonstrated the strength of id forces. To others, the rigidity, injustice, and irrationality of existing institutions have documented the coercions of the superego. From either perspective one sees a need for a new community, through which not *the* individual but *all individuals in their interdependence* can find maturity.

Thus Freud has become, almost in spite of himself, ". . . the founder of a great religious sect," [68] or perhaps we should say, of a variety of related but competing sects. Jung and Adler, and many others after them, have elaborated the analytic experience as a source of commitment and community, through which suffering can be alleviated.[69]

Partiality of the Secular Alternatives. In these brief references to three major nontraditional, secular faiths I have tended, for purposes of sharpness of distinction, to exaggerate their special focus on the problems of ignorance, powerlessness, or suffering. We need to note further, therefore, the strong tendencies toward coalescence in some of the movements associated with one or another of these problems and in the writings of important adherents. There are many efforts, for example, to blend Marxian and Freudian principles, both of which, in turn, share elements of the positivist tradition. When the three lines converge, we have the basis for contemporary religious humanism, probably best represented in the work of Erich Fromm.[70] His chief concern is not that God is dead, but that *man* is dead—transformed into a thing by a depersonalized world of his own creation. He thus expresses the fear of existentialists, from Marx and Kierkegaard to Jean-Paul Sartre and Tillich, that a vast renewal of human purposes is needed. These existentialists vary widely, of course, and Fromm differs from each of them in his explicit formulation of a religious humanism.

At the same time, there have been some tendencies within the established religious organizations to reach out toward the secular movements, particularly Marxism and Freudianism, in an effort to enfold them and interpret them.[71] Religious efforts to make use of the insights yet to avoid the errors of the secular alternatives, as seen by religious adherents, often stress their incompleteness, their tendency to focus on one or another of

68 Erwin Goodenough, *The Psychology of Religious Experiences,* p. x. It seems likely, however, that if the Freudian doctrine is seen in this way—as a sanctified series of beliefs, supported by various rites and interactions—that Freud himself would have declared: "I am not a Freudian."

69 Philip Rieff, op. cit., has developed this point in a penetrating way.

70 In addition to Fromm's *Psychoanalysis and Religion,* see his *Sane Society* and *You Shall Be as Gods: A Radical Interpretation of the Old Testament and Its Tradition.* See also John Dewey, *A Common Faith;* John H. Randall and John H. Randall, Jr., *Religion and the Modern World.*

71 There is an extensive literature on this theme. See, for example, Paul Tillich, *The Courage To Be;* Michael Novak, "The New Relativism in American Theology," in *The Religious Situation: 1968,* Donald Cutler, ed., pp. 197–231; Harvey Cox, *The Secular City;* John Robinson, *Honest To God.*

the several basic elements of the human condition. More than that, however, from the perspective of the traditional religions, positivism, Marxism, and Freudianism fail to struggle with the truly ultimate questions: How does one deal with our lack of comprehension of the meaning of life, even after every effort to overcome ignorance has been made? How does one respond to the powerlessness and injustice that remain when every secular line of attack on them has been tried? How does one handle the suffering that our most dedicated efforts seem incapable of removing? From the perspective of religious thinkers, therefore, the secular alternatives, however fruitful and important they may be, are partial and incomplete. They do not deal with the ultimate questions.

In this discussion of alternatives, important value questions inevitably arise. The scientist cannot say simply that this is a better alternative than that; but he can declare: If this be one's aim, then choice A is better than choice B. Even Freud was willing to grant that in most cases, religion was better than neurosis, because it was a shared "illusion." The religious person, because he deals with others, finds his way to some part of reality —which to Freud was a basic goal. The neurotic is an isolated person; indeed, the most painful and difficult part of every neurosis is the overwhelming sense of isolation. But Freud grants very little, in fact. The religious person is likely to assert not only that religion will rescue man from the despair and isolation of neurosis, but that it will harness man's energies for positive achievements. Taking a leaf from the functionalist's notebook, he asks: If man cannot live without a "frame of orientation and an object of devotion," is not classical religion better than communism, or parochial nationalism, or positivism? Would we not have fewer social movements with narrow and limited goals, yet armed with convictions of absolute validity, and would we not have fewer distraught and bewildered persons, if men were to "return to religion"? Others, granting the force of this argument, will say: But classical religion is too loaded with the superstitions of the past and itself too easily twisted to support the aims of limited groups—of classes and nations—to make it clearly superior to its secular alternatives. What is in fact needed is a "new universalism," fully harmonious with modern science and the modern world. Still others believe that at least some of the functions formerly undertaken by religion are as well or better performed by secular alternatives. Few people now oppose secular medical practice, for example. Why should this development not fully include emotional disturbances as well as physical ailments?

We are not concerned here with exploring these highly significant value questions. It is our task to note the functional interconnections of different social and personal facts, secular and religious. But one need not deny the hope that a scientific statement may contribute to effective study and action in terms relevant to the facts of contemporary life.

Chapter Eleven

RELIGION, CULTURE, AND SOCIETY

In the next several chapters, the focus of our attention will be on culture and on society. More specifically we will examine the ways in which religion, as a major source and carrier of the values of culture, affects and is affected by its social context. At some points, religion will be treated as the independent variable, producing certain results; at other points, religion will be seen as a dependent variable, shaped by the sociocultural setting in which it is found; the overarching perspective, however, will be one of interaction. Religious systems are powerfully affected by the surrounding social structures, which means that Ceylonese Buddhism is not Japanese Buddhism, Spanish Catholicism is not American Catholicism. At the same time, these structures are modified by the religions they enclose, so that the impact of urbanization, for example, is different for a Japanese than for an Englishman. Individual tendencies were in the foreground in Chapters Seven through Ten. We shall not lose sight of them here, but they will be treated as limiting conditions, setting the boundaries within which the interactions of religion, culture, and society take place.

These interactions are now widely documented. Anthropological investigations, studies in religious history, the "higher criticism" of sacred writings, work in comparative religion, and sociological study of social structures have all demonstrated that we cannot understand a religion scientifically without relating it to society and culture. The task is to examine the interdependencies in connection with particular structures, and we shall study social stratification patterns, economic, and political institutions with some care. In preparation for that discussion, however, we need to state the problem in more general terms.

RELIGION AND CULTURE

Seen culturally, religion is part of the complex of prescriptions and proscriptions that guides the interactions of men in all societies. It furnishes major definitions of the meaning of ultimate things and interpretations of experience. Since the term *culture* is used in many different ways, let me note that I shall use it in the sense expressed by Clyde Kluckhohn and W. H. Kelly: "By 'culture' we mean all those historically created designs for living, explicit and implicit, rational, irrational, and nonrational, that exist at any given time as potential guides for the behavior of men." [1] I would modify this only by making explicit the idea that culture is shared; it refers to those designs for living that are widely accepted as appropriate by members of a society.

Religion is a cultural fact; but it is not only cultural. It is more than a design for living relative to sacred and ultimate things. It must be seen also as social organization, as Durkheim noted, uniting those who share a body of beliefs into a church. And from the standpoint of the individual, it is a series of tendencies—of beliefs and motives—that incline him toward various actions.

Under many conditions, religion as culture can be seen as an integral part of the total culture. It is a product of the forces that created the total design, interacts with other elements in that design, and changes—not without stresses and variation in timing—as the total pattern changes. Thus in traditional Chinese society, a strong kinship system, patriarchal authority, filial piety, and ancestor worship formed an interlocking group of sacred and secular values. In a democratic society, the inegalitarian doctrine of predestination is likely to lose much of its hold and to be replaced by such a doctrine as the Methodist "grace abounding to all."

It is important neither to exaggerate the degree of coherence between religious and other values nor to obscure the amount of value inconsistency that a society may express. Indeed, some range in the interpretation of cultural norms and some variation in values is not only inevitable but probably essential, at least to the functioning of heterogeneous societies.[2] Even relatively simpler and more static societies may exhibit incongruity between religious and other cultural values, or within the religious sphere itself. Ruth Benedict properly emphasized that societies with contrasting secular values are set apart religiously as well; [3] but she tended to overstate the case. The noncompetitive Zuni reject the pursuit of ecstatic visions, torture, self-torture, the frenzy of the Ghost Dance, and the hallucinations of the Peyote cult. Although the Zuni pueblos were near the Mexican plateau where the Peyote button was obtained and were in contact with the Apache, who were Peyote users, the practices of the cult made little headway among them. Their love of moderation, of poise, of calm stood as a barrier to religious forms that sought to break the bonds of ordinary sensory experience. On the other hand, their beliefs and practices relating to witchcraft qualify this picture. Their religion, narrowly defined, taught them to deny their hostility, but witchcraft allowed them to project it. The Zuni see themselves as peaceful, yet their murder rate is high and they are sharply divided by factionalism and gossip. "Cultural blinders permit the Zuni to believe that these events are not truly a part of their culture, but that they come

1 Clyde Kluckhohn, *Culture and Behavior*, p. 54.
2 See Robin Williams, *American Society*, Chap. 10.
3 See Ruth Benedict, *Patterns of Culture*.

from some outside, non-Zuni source, such as foreigners, or sorcerers, or bad Zuni who have been tainted by an external evil force. . . . Sorcerers in Zuni are executed with culturally sanctioned sadistic relish." [4]

Religion and Values

The concept of values overlaps that of culture, and we can properly devote some attention to it in this discussion of religion and culture. As goals, values are those states or objects toward which behavior is preferentially directed. They can often be identified by asking: What is an individual or a group willing to spend scarce resources (of effort, time, or money) to obtain? As guidelines for making decisions, values ". . . are the criteria in terms of which choices are made between alternative courses of action. . . ." [5] They are not purely cultural, for an individual's values may differ from and even contradict those normatively approved by his society. Yet they are substantially cultural, as comparative study of societies readily demonstrates. [6]

Religion is a primary source of a person's values. At the same time, the values embodied in a religion are affected by the social context and change to some degree when that context changes. Thus religion may be regarded for some purposes as the starting point: These criteria, states, and objects are valued because of a person's religious training. For other purposes the religious values themselves require explanation. Religious experiences that are eagerly sought by one generation, for example, may be of little consequence to another. We shall need to be continually alert to the interdependence of religion and values.

The scientific study of values has been undertaken by scholars from several disciplines. Brief reference to this work may help us to avoid some of the difficulties involved in the topic. There is, first of all, the problem of circularity. Values are sometimes used to explain behavior, having themselves been inferred from examination of behavior. Until this problem is solved, values should be treated as descriptive terms, not explanatory variables. [7] This requires the development of measures independent of any behavior for which explanation is sought, and a clear indication of the time orders involved. Even then, causal interpretations will be extremely difficult to demonstrate.

The study of values has moved through several stages, which parallel the points of view prevailing in the social sciences generally. Earlier ethnocentric judgments were partly, but only partly, displaced by evolutionary

---

4 John Whiting and others, in *People of Rimrock: A Study of Values in Five Cultures,* Evon Vogt and Ethel Albert, eds., p. 124.

5 Philip Jacob, Henry Teune, and Thomas Watt, "Values, Leadership, and Development: A Four-Nation Study," *Social Science Information,* 7, 1968, p. 53.

6 See Florence Kluckhohn and F. L. Strodtbeck, *Variations in Value-Orientations;* and Evon Vogt and Ethel Albert, op. cit. For studies of individual variation that also show differences in group means—suggesting the cultural influence—see Charles Morris, *Varieties of Human Value;* and R. B. Cattell, "The Principal Culture Patterns Discoverable in the Syntal Dimensions of Existing Nations," *Journal of Social Psychology,* 32, 1950, pp. 215–253.

7 See Robert Marsh, *Comparative Sociology,* pp. 28–29.

theory. The weaknesses of evolutionism were attacked by detailed ethnographic studies of particular cultures and value systems. These studies, however, by their emphasis on uniqueness, tended to obscure the question of possible shared or universal patterns. Functionalism continued the effort to eliminate ethnocentrism and correct the rigidities of evolutionism; and in its early stages it was scarcely different from ethnography in its emphasis on the distinctiveness of each culture. A configurational approach, represented by Ruth Benedict's *Patterns of Culture*, can be placed in this transitional position. Emphasis here was on the distinctiveness of cultures, but there was also attention to the total system. This opened the way to questions about system prerequisites and the search for possible general functions, necessary for the operation of social systems. Once this stage of functionalism was reached, more systematic comparative study was suggested. Comparative study of values leaves open the question of the degree to which they are universal or unique, and seeks rather to devise measures by which the range of uniqueness and universality can be determined.

I shall not undertake to review the many procedures designed to measure values comparatively.[8] Most of them refer to religion as a source of values or, somewhat more roughly, as a value in itself. From our point of view, it is important to distinguish between values as an aspect of character and values as an aspect of culture. It is also essential to examine the structural context in which they are expressed. Each of these, in turn, can be studied as a dependent or as an independent variable. Thus, in schematic terms, we have what is shown in Table 11-1.

Specialized study of each one of the six approaches to value is desirable and indeed necessary. It is also essential to recognize, however, that the results of such study can be used with only limited success to explain or predict behavior. To know which of the "paths of life" described by Charles Morris, or which of the six value clusters in the Allport-Vernon-Lindzey scale, is regarded mostly highly by an individual does not furnish knowledge of how that individual will behave. The extent to which those values are shared by other people around him—that is, have a cultural existence—and the extent to which those people with whom he interacts support or block him in the pursuit of various values must also be taken into account. Specialized studies of a purely cultural or purely structural approach must also be qualified in this way.

The Cultural Approach to Values. From the perspective of this section, our interest is primarily in values as part of culture. The states and objects an individual strives for are substantially affected by the culture that surrounds him and to which he has been socialized. The criteria he

8 Robert Marsh, op. cit., Chap. 7, has reviewed the literature carefully. In sociology, the work of Thomas, Znaniecki, and Weber is of continuing importance. Parsons' work is of major significance. A psychological approach is well represented by the work of Allport, Vernon, and Lindzey, by Cattell, and by Morris. In anthropology, perhaps the most systematic comparative work has been that of the "Harvard Comparative Study of Values in Five Cultures," with Clyde Kluckhohn, Florence Kluckhohn, Evon Vogt, Ethel Albert, and Fred Strodtbeck being among the central workers. There are few direct references to values in Walter Goldschmidt's *Comparative Functionalism*, but it has some useful leads. John Whiting and Irvin Child, *Child Training and Personality: A Cross-Cultural Study* and Beatrice Whiting, ed., *Six Cultures: Studies of Child Rearing* are valuable social psychological studies that make some use of the concept of values.

Table 11–1. The field approach to values

I. Values as a character fact. Those states and objects for which a person is willing to spend scarce resources; and those criteria that guide selection among alternatives.
   A. As a dependent variable, their sources are sought in socialization and other experiences, and in inheritance.
   B. As an independent variable, values are studied as criteria and as goals that influence behavior.
II. Values as a cultural fact. Those states and objects normatively approved by the members of a society as deserving of the expenditure of scarce resources; those criteria normatively designated as appropriate to decision-making.
   A. As a dependent variable, their sources are sought in the experiences of a people.
   B. As an independent variable, values are studied as influences on socialization, on other interactions, and on the formation and changes in social structures.
III. The structural context of values.
   A. As a dependent variable, social structures are studied in terms of the impact on them from values both as part of character and as part of culture.
   B. As an independent variable, the structural context is studied in terms of the ways in which it supports and inhibits the expression of particular values.

applies in selecting among alternatives to action are culturally defined to an important degree. Many of these values are imbedded in religion, so that they come to him with sacred support. We shall be examining with some care, for example, Max Weber's thesis that the peculiarly energetic and dedicated spirit of modern capitalism was powerfully influenced by the values of Protestantism. In terms of the outline above, he concentrated on levels I B and II B. In light of the earlier neglect of these levels (or their simple, unsupported affirmation), his analysis was a major contribution to our understanding. It is read most adequately, however, when its place in the full range of approaches is kept carefully in mind.

The continuous interactions with social structure and character make it extremely difficult to isolate the effects of cultural values. A sophisticated approach to the problem is found in the Harvard Comparative Study of Values in Five Cultures.[9] Five distinct societies (or perhaps we should say subsocieties, because of their interdependence with the national society) exist in a relatively small ecological area in New Mexico. "For two full generations four of the groups involved have been in continued face-to-face contact. They have also been subject to approximately the same historical process, influenced by the same streams of cultural diffusion. . . . Today all of these societies have available essentially the same technology." [10] Despite these shared influences, they differ widely in values and other cultural elements.

9 See Florence Kluckhohn and F. L. Strodtbeck, *Variations in Value-Orientations;* and Evon Vogt and Ethel Albert, eds., *People of Rimrock: A Study of Values in Five Cultures.* See also Clyde Kluckhohn, "Values and Value-Orientations in the Theory of Action: An Exploration in Definition and Classification," in *Toward a General Theory of Action,* Talcott Parsons and Edward Shils, eds.

10 Vogt and Albert, op. cit., p. 2.

Why these differences? And why do they persist? A fuller answer is given to the second question than to the first. Cultures persist because they contain "a ready-made and culturally acceptable set of defenses, rather than permitting each individual to develop and choose his own idiosyncratic defenses against the crisis-engendered conflict." [11] To give them up or to change them rapidly is to expose the individual and the group directly to the crises they were designed to cope with. The cultures were first differentiated by their different places of origin, by isolation from one another at an earlier period, and perhaps to some degree by conflict.

How do these cultures differ? I will give only that part of the answer which is of interest to us in terms of a general theory of values. They differ in their answers to five basic questions about nature, time, and human relationships that Kluckhohn and Strodtbeck affirm must be dealt with by all societies. (It is not clear why they must be dealt with. Perhaps it is enough to affirm that cultural answers to these questions can be found in

Orientation or question	Postulated range of variations					
Human nature	Evil		Neutral or mixture of good and evil		Good	
	mutable	immutable	mutable	immutable	mutable	immutable
Man–nature	subjugation-to-nature		harmony–with–nature		mastery–over–nature	
Time	past		present		future	
Activity	being		being–in–becoming		doing	
Relational	lineality		collaterality		individualism	

FIGURE 11–1. *Five value orientations and the range of variations postulated for each* (*Adapted from Florence Kluckhohn and F. L. Strodtbeck,* Variations in Value-Orientations, *New York: Harper and Row Publishers, Inc., 1961, p. 12.*)

an extremely wide range of societies, if not universally.) There is a limited number of answers to each of the questions, so that cultural systems are not infinitely variant at this level. They can be compared and contrasted in terms of a fairly small number of possibilities (see Figure 11–1).

Kluckhohn and Strodtbeck assume that each of the orientations is likely to be found in every society, but at different levels of preference. In their terms, one of the three possible answers to each question will be dominant, the others variant. This creates the possibility of a wide variety of

11 John Whiting and others, in ibid., p. 124.

"profiles" of response to the value orientations by which societies can be compared.[12] Not all the permutations are likely to be important empirically. An emphasis on individuality, for example, seems unlikely to be associated with a past time or a subjugation-to-nature orientation. There remain, however, a number of clusters of dominant and variant orientations from which within-culture and betweeen-culture comparisons can be made. Data from the "Values" study indicate the presence of significant regularities among the members of the five societies and of significant contrasts among the societies. The samples used were relatively small (20 to 23); the range of topics for comparisons is somewhat limited; and the assumption that the five orientations are basic and universal is open to further investigation. The total impact of the study, however, is to contribute notably to the comparative study of values.

Whatever the source of cultural variation with regard to these values, persons who are trained to accept one cluster will differ significantly from those trained to a different cluster. They will form different kinds of communities, pursue different goals, and respond to changes and pressures in the environment in different ways. We can postulate various combinations. Think first of a community whose members have been socialized to the belief that human nature is a mixture of good and evil, to feelings of subjugation-to-nature, to a present time orientation, to an emphasis on "being" rather than "doing," and to lineal (largely kinship) relationships with their fellows. Then think of a community whose members have largely been socialized to the idea that human nature is basically good, to mastery-over-nature as possible and desirable, to future time and to "doing" orientations, and to individualism. Confronted with the same environment, presented with the same challenges, threats, and possibilities, they will respond differently. What appeals to one will go unnoticed in another. What one regards as an opportunity, the other will see as a nuisance.

This is, of course, to argue against a Marxian interpretation of social process and social change. Few who emphasize the importance of values in the determination of behavior are inclined to disregard the "productive relations," the command-obey relationships, that Marx considered central. But they see them as severely qualified by the different value hierarchies and orientations that characterize societies.

If we keep fully in mind the need for locating the study of values in a larger system of analysis, as noted above, the comparative approach to values can be of great significance. Because religion is to a substantial degree the repository of a culture's orientation to these values (that is, they are part of its sacred heritage, not simply isolated and technical norms), the scientific study of religion must include analysis of value perspectives. A great deal has yet to be done, however, to study the ways in which structural and character facts interact with values. There is little warranty for treating values as first causes, and leaving their own origins and changes unexamined. Complexity of the interactions is shown by the contrasting findings of two careful studies. As part of the "Values" studies discussed above, Evon Vogt and Thomas O'Dea examined the approaches

12 For a summary table of these profiles for the five societies being studied in the "Values" research, see ibid., p. 351.

of a Mormon and a "general Protestant" community to various community needs and problems. They found that contrasting value orientations produced "two quite different community types," despite great similarity of environment.[13]

In a comparative study of Christian and Muslim villagers, however, George Fetter found few significant differences in their attitudes toward village life, farming, national leadership, education, the value of cooperation, and other issues. Those who were comparable in education, income, and length of residence in the area held strikingly similar attitudes, despite their religious differences and in the face of mutual hostility. "Differences in religion, insofar as they affect orientations and philosophies toward life in general, tend to be overridden and rendered insignificant by the wider impact of Arab culture generally and the historical-economic-geographical concomitants of rural Lebanese life in particular." [14]

Such contradictory findings make apparent the need for studying values in full context. We need to be especially alert to the quality of controls for other variables—the environment, the economic and educational levels, and the extent of outside contact, for example. It is possible that the different findings can be reconciled by examining the range of choices made possible by the surrounding sociopolitical and geographical environments. If there is very little "play" in the system, as was perhaps true in the Lebanese villages, different value orientations have no chance to make themselves felt. If the surrounding environment is open, however, if it presents greater opportunities and a wider range of possibilities, as may have been true of the American Southwest, then value differences can influence the outcomes. The lesson is clear: It is the *interaction* of values with the social structure that requires examination. And in a fuller analysis we would need to introduce character facts as well, to show how they modify the value-social structure interaction.

Pattern Variables: Universal Dilemmas in Goal Orientation. Talcott Parsons has powerfully influenced the study of values by describing five different pairs of perspectives that, in his judgment, universally affect social action.[15] These are the five pairs: *universalism-particularism; performance-quality; affective neutrality-affectivity; specificity-diffuseness;* and *self-orientation-collectivity-orientation.*[16] Parsons sees these as dilemmas con-

13 Evon Vogt and Thomas O'Dea, "A Comparative Study of the Role of Values in Social Action in Two Southwestern Communities," *American Sociological Review,* 18, 1953, pp. 645–654.

14 George Fetter, "A Comparative Study of Christian and of Moslem Lebanese Villagers," *Journal for the Scientific Study of Religion,* 4, 1964, pp. 48–59.

15 Harold Fallding states that these perspectives are not values in themselves, but "refer to the considerations involved in electing values." This reminds us again of the need to distinguish between values as goals and values as criteria. Fallding uses the former definition: "A value, then, is a generalized end that guides behavior toward uniformity in a variety of situations, with the object of repeating a particular self-sufficient satisfaction." ("A Proposal for the Empirical Study of Values," *American Sociological Review,* 30, 1965, p. 224.) Granted the amount of work given to the explication of values as criteria and values as goals, my inclination is to include both forms under the definition, while keeping in mind the necessary distinction.

16 The pattern variables have been explicated by Parsons and his colleagues in a number of places. See, for example, Talcott Parsons and Edward Shils, *Towards a General*

fronting individuals in interaction. The dilemmas can be noted in the form of questions: Should I deal with this person in terms of his particular relationships with me, or on the basis of universal criteria? Is an action to be judged by how it is carried out or by whom it is carried out? Is objectivity or is affective involvement the appropriate attitude? Are my obligations specific or are they diffuse, dependent upon the needs, desires, and requests of others? Can I appropriately pursue my own goals and desires or should the goals of the collectivity be governing?

Parsons emphasizes that culture is everywhere involved in determining the answers to these questions. They are built into role definitions and institutional norms. There would be little disagreement, in an urban situation, with the idea that a clerk-customer relationship should be universalistic, performance-oriented, affectively neutral, specific, and self-oriented; whereas the relationship of a father and son should be particularistic, quality-oriented, infused with affectivity, diffuse, and collectivity-oriented.

The sharpness of the dilemmas may be overstated by posing each of the variables as a dichotomy. Some blurring of the distinctions can be found not only in behavioral fact, but probably also in the cultural norms themselves. Thus a physician is supposed to be collectivity-oriented and affectively neutral; but at the same time some degree of self-orientation is expected and permitted, and a bedside manner that expresses some affectivity is approved. When an irreconcilable choice has to be made, however, the dilemma is exposed. In the last analysis, no sentiment should be allowed to interfere with the objectivity of the physician.

Cultural prescriptions are probably not so clear as this description seems to indicate. And even where they are clear, sharp conflicts can occur because of inconsistent role demands (as for example, when one is both a physician and a father). Nevertheless, the concept of pattern variables is a powerful organizing principle, making possible much more precise inter-role and intercultural comparisons.

Again, as the carrier and sustainer of many cultural norms, religion is involved in the designation of various applications of the pattern variables. It supports other cultural agents under some conditions and collides with them under different conditions. If all men are brothers, affective neutrality is never appropriate. Clearly this cannot be sustained (or, more empirically, it has not been). The scientific task is to study society and religion interactions to determine the conditions leading to various outcomes. Religions vary in their designation of appropriate choices relative to these dilemmas. Their various emphases are important facts in the comparative study of values.

RELIGION AND SOCIETY

The intricate connections between religion and other elements of culture are matched by the interdependencies of religion and other elements of social structure. By the term *social structure* I shall mean the network

---

Theory of Action, Chap. 3, Pt. II; Talcott Parsons, Robert Bales, and Edward Shils, *Working Papers in the Theory of Action*, Chaps. 3 and 5; Talcott Parsons, *Essays in Sociological Theory*, rev. ed., Chap. 2; Talcott Parsons and Neal Smelser, *Economy and Society*, pp. 33–38.

of interactions among the members of a group and among groups. Much of our attention will be directed toward societies, which are the largest of human groups, and the social structures that characterize societies. We shall try consistently to distinguish between societies as groups of people and cultures as normative systems, although these terms are used interchangeably in many works. It is understandable why the members of a society should be identified with their way of life. I think it is important to keep the concepts analytically separate, however, because they can vary independently. Patterns of interaction may change while values remain quite constant, as when a society experiences peaceful or violent contact with another society. Or new values may be imported or generated within a marginal segment of a society that redefine the meaning of existing social relationships. Only in the limiting case, in an isolated and quite static situation, can we afford to disregard the distinction between society and culture.

Turning from our references to the cultural system, then, to various aspects of the social structure, let us note that details of religious belief and practice vary with the size and mobility of a society, the nature of its economy, the type of stratification system, the kinds of contact it has had with other societies, the structures of political power, the organization of medical practices, and the other elements of the social structure. Even the religious innovator, the charismatic leader—although he is often thought to be a purely spontaneous new force in history—is not unaffected by the social interactions in which he is involved. When a society undergoes important changes, such as industrialization and urbanization, or when a religion is transported into a new society, the interactions of religion and society are made particularly visible.

To speak of religion and society separately in this way, let me emphasize, is to make an analytic distinction. It is a shorthand way of saying: Observe the relationships of that part of the social structure which is religious with other parts of the social structure. (Equivalent statements about culture and character are also appropriate.) It is clear that the devout Muslim does not think of a religion distinct from Islam. Hinduism as a religious term separate from Indian society is a Western idea. At an earlier time, if not today, Christendom and Judaism were socioreligious systems and not simply churches. Even where the ideology stresses the separation of religious structures from other structures, the reality of their close interdependence must not be disregarded.

Recognition of the analytic quality of the distinction between religion and the rest of the social structure, however, should not lead us to neglect that distinction. Our situation in this regard is precisely that of the student of economics or politics, who also abstracts from a complex whole the better to study some aspects of it. We speak, then, of religion *and* society in order to emphasize the partially distinct processes of one substructure in the context of the total structure in which it participates.

There are imperative factors in a society that set limits within which the religious development will take place. This is equally true, of course, of other social patterns. A tightly knit consanguine kinship system, for example, with close ties between generations, strong parental authority, and choice of marriage partner by parents, is almost certain to become less important in a society where there is a great deal of spatial mobility, emphasis on improvement of status, occupational specialization, and urbanization. Similarly, in such a society, a tightly integrated religious system, with a strong otherworldly emphasis is unlikely to survive. "The pattern of religious toleration and a diversity of denominations as in the American case seems to be the least disruptive structure." [17] Whether this is a happy or an unhappy fact, we need not try to determine, but there is strong support for it as an empirically valid statement.

These interdependencies may be of different orders of magnitude for different institutions. Knowing that a certain society has a high level of industrial development, for example, almost certainly involves knowing that it also has a complex educational system, although educational patterns may be quite variant culturally. The implications for religion, however, may be weaker. A wide variety of patterns may be consonant with industrial society; more alternatives are possible. Or it may be that the interactions are more indirect than in the case of education, so that mutual influences are less visible and more affected by intervening variables.

This contrast, however, should be treated somewhat lightly. Whatever the limits of influence, both religion and magic are clearly affected by the social structures with which they interact and by the experiences of individuals within those structures. We commented earlier on the functional interpretation of witchcraft. Seen from a different point of view, the level of witchcraft demonstrates the way in which social structure affects magical beliefs and practices. As Wallace puts it: "The prevalence of fear and accusations of witchcraft seems to be determined both by the natural cleavage lines in the social structure and by the success of the society in handling conflict by such secular means as court proceedings and arbitration." [18] He notes that in African societies where European administrators have interfered with native courts, witchcraft anxiety is likely to grow. Wallace interprets this as an effort to restore social control, in a context in which secular procedures for handling conflict have broken down or conflicts have outgrown the capacity of those procedures. With only small variations, this description fits Kai Erikson's account of the witchcraft conflicts in Massachusetts in the seventeenth century, despite the sharp contrasts in culture.[19] In *Navaho Witchcraft*, Clyde Kluckhohn gives somewhat more emphasis to cultural and personality elements. He notes the anxiety-producing effects of normal socialization in Navaho society, and the variation between individuals in susceptibility to those effects. Yet he also examines the effects of interpersonal conflicts, the disorganizing influence of contact with white American goods, power, and diseases, and the problems of social control.[20]

Two studies have demonstrated these relationships on a more quanti-

17 Talcott Parsons, *The Social System*, p. 189.

18 Anthony Wallace, *Religion: An Anthropological View*, p. 180.

19 Kai Erikson, *Wayward Puritans. A Study in the Sociology of Deviance*, pp. 137–159.

20 Kluckhohn's analysis is notable for the subtle interplay of cultural, structural, and character elements. Our attention here is drawn to the sources of witchcraft in the social structure; but a full account also requires information concerning individual predispositions and motivations as well as knowledge of cultural support.

tative basis. Using crosscultural comparisons, Guy Swanson and Beatrice Whiting have both shown that, with few exceptions (5 out of 54 in the two studies combined), witchcraft is strong in societies in which control by secular authorities is weak, and is weak in those societies where secular authorities are strong. The inference that witchcraft was prevalent *because* of the weakness of the authority structure is highly plausible if not definitively proved.[21]

It may not be difficult to accept the idea that aspects of the social structure affect the level of witchcraft. It is more controversial to observe that conceptions of God are not immune from this influence; but there is evidence to support such a view. We have noted that monotheistic beliefs developed in particular social contexts, those that involved strong political authorities and multileveled systems of decision-making (almost the reverse of the witchcraft setting). Monotheism does not allow, if an entreaty to God should fail, the explanation of another deity's intervention. This leads Robin Horton to hypothesize that "in a sample of world religions monotheism will be found highly correlated with the attribution of wide freedom of choice to the religious object, while polytheism will be associated with ideas of wide or total coercibility of the gods." [22] I am tempted to extend this hypothesis to suggest that only those people who have won some measure of control over their lives can "afford" monotheism—that is, can afford to allow their God freedom of choice. Those with some control give up the notion of coercibility because of the contributions of monotheism to their conceptions of salvation. In a monotheistic tradition, those groups will slip away from pure monotheism who most need, because of the harshness of their situation, the concept of flexibility and coercibility of deity.

It seems possible that the "death of God" as well as the "birth of God" is related to social structure. Michael Novak has pointed out that all the major figures among the radical theologians in America are teachers at secular institutions. "The inadequacy of the word 'God' was discovered in America when theologians ceased lecturing to captive audiences in churches and seminaries and began speaking both to the university community and to the mass media." [23]

Religious structures as well as beliefs are influenced by the social system of which they are a part. Horton observes that in "a system in which relations between the segments of a group at any level in the whole are markedly competitive, every level will have its own set of cults distinct from that of all other levels of the system. On each level, furthermore, there will be at least as many distinct, though mutually equivalent, cults as there are competing segments in it." [24] On the other hand, in social systems where relations between segments are predominantly harmonious, religious struc-

21 See Guy Swanson, *Birth of the Gods: The Origin of Primitive Beliefs,* Chap. 8; and Beatrice Whiting, *Paiute Sorcery.* See also Wallace, op. cit., pp. 180–187, for a valuable commentary on these studies and on the relationship of witchcraft to the social structure.

22 Robin Horton, "A Definition of Religion and Its Uses," *Journal of the Royal Anthropological Institute,* 90, Pt. 2, 1960, p. 210.

23 Michael Novak in *The Religious Situation: 1968,* Donald Cutler, ed., p. 200.

24 Robin Horton, op. cit., p. 214.

tures are likely to arch over the total group. This situation is probably rare. Horton notes that Benedict's description of Zuni religion sees it as uniting the whole community into one congregation. She stresses the lack of divisive cults "catering mainly for competitive aspirations at sectional or individual levels." This is in sharp contrast with the Guardian Spirit cults of the Plains Indians, with their strong individualistic emphasis. It is necessary to add, however, that more individualistic and competitive qualities are added to the Zuni scene by their beliefs and practices relating to witchcraft.

The competitive situation characterizes the religious structures of most societies. In complex societies, it frequently takes the form of sectarian movements, which we shall be discussing at length; but religious differentiation is not lacking among simpler societies in which social stratification is relatively unimportant. Horton notes that a Kalabari village, in the Niger delta, is divided into strongly competitive descent groups. Individuals also compete vigorously for positions of influence. "As we should predict on the basis of our assumptions, each of the three levels, village, descent-group and individual has its distinctive set of cults." [25]

VARIATIONS AMONG SOCIETIES AND THEIR RELIGIOUS EFFECTS

General statements and illustrations concerning the relationship of religion to society contribute to scientific development only when they are accompanied by systematic, comparative, and typological studies. These imply a search for differentiating variables, and exploration of the effects of their various combinations. Such a search is carried out effectively by S. F. Nadel in his study of the sources of difference between the religions of the Heiban and of the Otoro, two tribes of the southern Sudan. He deals with both cultural and structural facts, but he focuses attention on the interactions of religion and social structure. The two tribes live in a similar environment; in many ways their cultures are alike. But there are important differences. The Heiban are more magically oriented; they tend to be aggressive, emotionally tense, coercive, and pessimistic in their religious practices. The Otoro are calm, dispassionate, submissive, and optimistic in religion. Why the difference? After exploring other hypotheses (the effects of political integration, for example) and finding them inadequate. Nadel suggests that the social systems created continuous contexts for the emergence of these religious differences. The Otoro are much more skillful in regulating adolescence and accomplishing the shift to adult roles, by means of age-graded practices, competitive sports, and norms of etiquette and self-restraint, along with opportunities for the expression of aggression. Among the Heiban, on the other hand, adolescence is unregulated. Among the Otoro, wives join the husband's family completely; among the Heiban, incompletely. In the latter tribe, as a result, there are conflicts of loyalties, anxieties over marital success, and juridical ambiguities. In short, the Otoro reduce anomie and uncertainty; the Heiban increase them. And these qualities are manifest in their religious beliefs and practices.[26]

25 Ibid.

26 S. F. Nadel, "Two Nuba Religions: An Essay in Comparison," *American Anthropologist*, 57, 1955, pp. 661–679.

The interactions of religion and social structure in these groups are affected by a condition that has prevailed through most of man's history: the boundaries of the religious system are identical with the boundaries of the society. This affects both internal and external relations. John Dewey may have overlooked the internal religious differentiation found even in some tribal societies, but he helps us make a necessary distinction between greater and lesser degrees of religious homogeneity.

Each social group had its own divine beings who were its founders and protectors. Its rites of sacrifice, purification, and communion were manifestations of organized civic life. The temple was a public institution, the focus of the worship of the community; the influence of its practices extended to all the customs of the community, domestic, economic, and political. Even wars between groups were usually conflicts of their respective deities.

An individual did not join a church. He was born and reared in a community whose social unity, organization and traditions were symbolized and celebrated in the rites, cults and beliefs of a collective religion.[27]

Contrast that situation with the one that prevails in differentiated societies, where different religions may be found, where specialized religious practices and leaders emerge, where there is a measure of individual choice in matters of belief. Even if there is an established church that seems to unify the society religiously, that establishment is constituted by the state and can be dissolved by the state.

Joachim Wach emphasized the need for a distinction between a religion that is coterminous with a "natural group"—a society or tribe or kinship group—and what he calls "specifically religious groups." Although the correlation is not perfect, for there are some specifically religious groups to be found in primitive societies, the predominant tendency as societies become more complex is to move from an identity of social and religious groupings to specifically religious groups. The latter can be illustrated by "a special cultic group within a larger social or political unit (tribe or nation) or by a religion professed by ethnically or politically disparate adherents." [28] Thus the religiously specialized groups can separate members of one society or religiously bind together members of different societies. In either case, the identity of the religious and the social boundary is broken.

As Wach pointed out, it is not only the growing differentiation in the secular structure of a society that produces this transition, for changes in religion itself are also involved. These changes are perhaps not "autonomous," as Wach calls them, for they are set in motion at least partly by changes in the societal and cultural situation and by concomitant changes in personal tendencies; but once under way, as the result of a complex of causes, they develop in ways that cannot be understood simply by referring back to the secular environment. Particularly after the appearance of religious specialists and specifically designated religious practices, the religious system begins to undergo its own "inner dialectic," as Troeltsch calls it. This can profitably be studied as a closed system, if one does not forget the nature of his abstraction. The religious development then reacts back upon the society from which it grew.

27 John Dewey, *A Common Faith*, p. 60.

28 Joachim Wach, *Sociology of Religion*, p. 57; see also pp. 56–205.

Robert Redfield has shown how the functions and the management of religion change when folk society changes into civilization. In the first, classes are not separated by differences in knowledge or faith; there is no skepticism, no sense of a need to defend or to modify the basic ideals of the society. These things change as the society becomes larger and more differentiated. For example, among the Mayans, after about 320 A.D., there was a growth of shrine cities. Priests acquired the authority to manage the principal ceremonies on behalf of the whole community. They became specialists—writers, calculators, thinkers—who were separated from the mental world of the farmer to a significant degree. This concentration upon reflection and systematization brought new dimensions into the religious system. Thus civilization is not simply the development of the technical order; it destroys some moral and religious orders and creates others—for some ideas cannot be imagined until societies become complex and come into contact with each other. A religious conception of universal human brotherhood is possible only in civilization. Indian tribes that previously had known each other only as enemies were brought together and achieved a sense of common Indianness for the first time, under the attacks of the dominant whites.[29]

Thus any analysis of the relationship of society and religion must ask: What kind of society? Is it small and homogeneous or large and diverse? Is it isolated or in contact with other societies with different systems of value? Is it authoritarian in the distribution of power or based on democratic principles? Have religious specialists appeared who have developed an articulate system of beliefs, a tendency toward coherence and order in rite, and a specialized institution whose prestige and power they are eager to maintain and increase? (This last can be a source, as well as a result, of religious and social change, for it can set in motion competition for the title of *true interpreter* or for control of the institutional structure.) How far has the technical development of the society allowed it to bring hunger and disease under control? The great increase in the competence of the Western world to solve these difficulties has helped to create the idea that we can have "a brave, new world."

When man depends obviously and inescapably on forces outside himself, as he does in a primitive agricultural society, the Christian doctrine that pain and perplexity are sent by a loving Father at least makes sense. But when man begins to feel himself the master of his physical environment, and his awareness of a transcendent order becomes dim, then he begins to regard evil and suffering either as a technical problem (like the conquest of malaria) or as a political problem (like the defeat of the Communist Party).[30]

In the light of current religious trends, this statement requires qualification. The reduction of problems of hunger and ill-health does not mean that modern societies have reduced the sum of the difficulties with which men must deal. They may have aggravated the questions: Do I belong? Have I done right? Can I count on my neighbor? Can the species even survive its own discoveries?

29 See Robert Redfield, *The Primitive World and Its Transformations*, pp. 63–83.

30 K. S. Collier in *Religious Faith and World Culture*, A. W. Loos, ed., p. 25.

Many theologians regard human problems as perennial and inevitable, however they may seem to vary in their particular expression. In a day of intense internal and international problems, one is inclined to agree with this view and to grant that there is a great deal of force to the critique of "progressive" theories of history. This is not the kind of question one can answer definitively, however, for who can say that the weight of basic difficulties is the same or heavier or lighter for modern man than it was for his predecessors? And even if the perennial nature of human problems is assumed, it does not necessarily follow: (a) that a particular explanation of the cause, such as Reinhold Niebuhr's emphasis on man's fundamental egoism as a kind of "original sin," is a meaningful statement of the problem for a scientist; (b) that the differences in form that human problems take are unimportant for society or for religion (man's struggle for "acceptance" may prove to have very different consequences from his struggle for bread); or (c) that Niebuhr's theological solution must be accepted. The scientist, obviously, cannot answer the last question at all, nor is he under any obligation to accept the theological consequences that Niebuhr believes flow from the original proposition. To the sociologist, it is sufficient to note the existence of variations betweeen the ways in which religions empirically *do* struggle with individual and group problems and the ways in which they *may* struggle (not in a value sense, but in the sense of limits imposed by the social, cultural, and personality systems within which they work). An objective study of religion, therefore, must give careful attention to these variations.

Comparative Studies in Anthropology and Sociology

Systematic comparative work has had a long but somewhat uncertain career in both sociology and anthropology. Some of the greatest scholars have been concerned with it; yet comparative study has not become a standard procedure. Sometimes, in fact, it has not only been neglected but dismissed as impossible or irrelevant to the tasks of science. I will not review here the extensive methodological and theoretical literature dealing with comparative study.[31] Continuing the assumption, however, that the scientific study of religion must be developed as one expression of general social scientific theory and methodology (cognate with political science and economics), I will refer briefly to some of the issues and literature.

Interest in comparative work runs somewhat more deeply in sociology than in anthropolgy. Comte saw it as the basic method of science, although his own applications were rudimentary. Comparisons are implied, if not strongly developed, in the typologies that several early sociologists used to distinguish among societies. The contrasts between *Gemeinschaft* and *Gesellschaft*, status and contract, mechanical and organic solidarity, and folk and urban societies, for all the differences in shading that they carried, explored a common theme: the significance for societies and for human interaction of the decline of face-to-face, relatively unspecialized, particularistic, and stable relationships, and the rise in their place of indirect, contractual, performance-oriented, and rapidly changing relationships. In one sense, Weber's work can be read as a rich and multifaceted explora-

31 Robert Marsh, op. cit., is a valuable resource here.

tion of the same theme: the causes and consequences of the growth of rationalism, bureaucratic structures, and disenchantment. Parsons' pattern variables are a lineal descendant of this whole line of interest, indicating that the comparative study of societies and the comparative study of values must inevitably converge.

Although usually without assumptions of progressivism, these typological studies have been broadly evolutionary. Mankind is on a one-way street leading to differentiated, urban societies. This is seen as liberation by some, but others regard the trends with considerable trepidation. They wonder whether new bases of solidarity, consonant with norms of individualism and rationality, can be created to replace traditional social organizations; or whether anomie will become the chronic state of man; or if not anomie, new and coercive structures to which men seem willing to bind themselves. This is one of the grand themes of social and literary criticism of the twentieth century, as well as a topic for description and analysis.

Some social scientists have qualified the evolutionary element significantly. Even though he shared the interest in delineation of major societal types, Pitirim Sorokin wrote of "timeless and trendless fluctuations" from ideational to sensate societies, with only brief periods of idealistic synthesis. He saw the straight-line trends in technology and mobility, of course, but regarded these as less important than the fluctuations in mental styles, which were the critical facts in setting the tone of a society.

From earlier typological work, sociology has developed comparative studies in two directions. Some writers have focused attention on particular institutions rather than whole societies. At the same time they have given greater attention to systematic empirical methods. There has been significant comparative study of political institutions, stratification patterns, the family, and other institutions.[32] A substantial proportion of Weber's work was devoted to a comparative study of interactions between religion and social structure. His studies have inspired countless others, but only a few have gone beyond single-society interpretations to comparative analysis.[33]

Much of the work in comparative religion has been carried out by theologians and church historians, not by social scientists. Its purposes in the main tend to be evaluative and descriptive more than analytic. This is in no sense, however, to dismiss comparative religion, nor its sister discipline the history of religions, as of little importance for us. On the contrary, this work is one of the major sources of the developing science of religion, even

32 See, for example, S. N. Eisenstadt, *The Political Systems of Empires;* Seymour Lipset, "The Value Patterns of Democracy," *American Sociological Review,* 28, 1963, pp. 515–531; Seymour Lipset and Reinhard Bendix, *Social Mobility in Industrial Societies;* William Goode, *World Revolution and Family Patterns;* Gabriel Almond and Sidney Verba, *The Civic Culture;* Gabriel Almond and James Coleman, eds., *The Politics of the Developing Areas;* Talcott Parsons, Robert F. Bales, and others, *Family, Socialization and Interaction Process.*

33 See S. N. Eisenstadt, ed., *The Protestant Ethic and Modernization. A Comparative View.* The chapters by the editor, and by Robert Bellah, W. F. Wertheim, and Gino Germani are perhaps most explicitly comparative. Bellah's *Tokugawa Religion* makes effective comparative use of Weber's thesis. Wilhelm Muhlmann, and others, *Chiliasmus und Nativismus: Studien zur Psychologie, Soziologie und historischen Kasuistik der Umsturzbewegungen* offer many comparative observations on a variety of sects and cults. The studies by Guy Swanson and Beatrice Whiting to which we have referred are also excellent comparative works.

though it is seldom limited to scientific interests. Comparative students of religion are more likely to follow W. C. Smith in seeing their field as presenting an intellectual *and* a theological and moral problem. Some are only hesitantly comparative, preferring Max Scheler's dictum that we should let religious data speak for themselves. Others, however, are close to contemporary social science. These materials are variously useful, then, for analysis, interpretation, and description.[34]

The second line of development from earlier typological studies has been an emphasis on scaling and measurement. We have examined some aspects of this work with reference to religion in Chapter Two. It has been most systematically pursued, however, by those interested in scales that refer to general properties of societies. Freeman and Winch, for example, have found that "societal complexity," as measured by six variables, can be stated as a single dimension. The forty-eight societies they measured fell into a Guttman scale of complexity.[35] It seems likely that a six-step ordinal scale can prove to be much more valuable in research than a dichotomous nominal scale (folk-urban or *Gemeinschaft-Gesellschaft*).

Robert Marsh has developed an "index of differentiation" by which he has been able to range more than five hundred societies along a scale. He builds on George Murdock's work with the "World Ethnographic Sample." Murdock has classified societies into several levels of political integration (based on the size of the population in a political unit) and of degrees of social stratification.[36] To these variables, Marsh added measures of the percentage of males in the nonagricultural labor force and of per capita energy consumption. Combining the four items of information, Marsh assigns each society a score on an index of differentiation, thus making numerical, rather than simply typological comparisons possible.[37] Whether or not the particular variables used are adequate, the weights assigned to them in the index appropriate, and the data used to measure them reliable are questions that cannot yet be fully answered. Nevertheless, the process of scale and index construction is a highly valuable contribution to the comparative study of societies.

Comparative work in anthropology has developed over more serious disciplinary opposition. Frazer's *Golden Bough* and Tylor's *Primitive Society* were broadly but somewhat informally comparative. The work which followed, however, was often of a different style. One of the ways to avoid ethnocentrism is *not* to make comparisons, to examine each society and its culture as an entity in its own right. This perspective supports ideographic

34 An enormous amount of literature has appeared since Max Müller's *Comparative Mythology* was published more than a century ago. I have found the following books of value, and perhaps they are representative of recent work: Joachim Wach, *The Comparative Study of Religions*; Wilfred C. Smith, *The Faith of Other Men*; Joseph Campbell, *The Masks of God*, 3 vols.; R. C. Zaehner, *The Comparisons of Religion*; Mircea Eliade and Joseph Kitagawa, eds., *History of Religions. Essays in Methodology*; and E. O. James, *Myth and Ritual in the Ancient Near East*.

35 L. C. Freeman and R. F. Winch, "Societal Complexity: An Empirical Test of a Typology of Societies," *American Journal of Sociology*, 62, 1957, pp. 461–466.

36 See George Murdock, "World Ethnographic Sample," *American Anthropologist*, 59, 1957, pp. 664–687.

37 See Robert Marsh, op. cit., pp. 329–374.

ethnography rather than comparative ethnology. Classifications, however, could scarcely be avoided. Implicit in the schemes of culture areas and linguistic families are ideas of comparison and contrast. And in the last several decades, more explicit comparative work has been undertaken, particularly in linguistics, but with reference to total social structures as well. Much of this has drawn support from the work of Durkheim, who has been influential in both anthropological and sociological theory. In *Rules of the Sociological Method*, he stressed the comparative method as the very essence of a science of society. There have followed a number of significant works developing this theme. It would take us too far from our central interest to explore their various elaborations of the comparative point of view. However, they will furnish part of the background for our examinations of religion-society interactions.[38]

It should be noted that in much of the work we have cited, sociological as well as anthropological, cultural elements are mixed with structural elements in the designation of types, indexes, and scales. Although for some purposes we will need to re-emphasize the analytic distinction between society and culture, for other purposes we can profitably use the sociocultural environment as a more general variable.

Religion in American Society

At several points in chapters to follow we will discuss the fact, with reference to specific topics, that American religion is what it is partly because of its sociocultural context, and American society and culture are what they are in part because of their religious context. A brief general statement here, however, can serve to summarize our discussion of the religion-society-culture complex.[39]

I think it is important to recognize, as often is not done, that the American religious pattern is multileveled and in some sense syncretist. This is not to say simply that it is highly differentiated into churches, denominations, and sects, but that many *individuals* draw their beliefs and practices from several different levels. It is a commonplace to observe that the peasants in many lands share in both a "high" tradition and a "low" tradition, in one of the world religions but also in folk cults. Many Japanese are simultaneously Buddhists, Shintoists, and participants in a family cult. It is sometimes supposed, however, that the more closed ecclesiastical structures of Judaism, Muhammadanism, and Christianity make this impossible for their adherents. Yet we realize that from the earliest days of monotheism, golden calves and false gods have been decried. Without implying the value

38 See S. F. Nadel, *The Foundations of Social Anthropology;* A. R. Radcliffe-Brown, *A Natural Science of Society;* Meyer Fortes and E. E. Evans-Pritchard, *African Political Systems;* Claude Lévi-Strauss, *Structural Anthropology;* Walter Goldschmidt, *Comparative Functionalism;* John Whiting and Irvin Child, op. cit.; and Beatrice Whiting, op. cit. Specifically on religion, see William A. Lessa and Evon Vogt, eds., *Reader in Comparative Religion: An Anthropological Approach* (but only a few of the papers are explicitly comparative); Henri Hubert and Marcel Mauss, *Sacrifice: Its Nature and Function;* and William Goode, *Religion among the Primitives.*

39 For a variety of references, see the bibliographical postscript at the end of this chapter.

judgment contained in such terms, I would emphasize that most Americans are simultaneously participants in Christianity or Judaism, in a civil or national religion, and in various folk beliefs, magic, and assorted "pagan" notions. This last is a fairly miscellaneous list of beliefs and practices, ranging from astrology, spiritualism, and witchcraft, though a variety of superstitions, and to healing cults, to festivals that have become largely reduced to children's cults and highly secularized saturnalias. We have little information on how widespread or how deeply believed this third religious level is. It is not clear, however, that a naïve observer from afar [40] studying our behavior would find that we take this level any less seriously than our traditional religions. Where it has receded most fully, a cult of science has partially come in to take its place.

This American religious complex, and particularly the more traditional and institutionalized elements of it, have partly been shaped by the bountiful environment, by the democratic polity, by immigration, slavery, and conquest (the three sources of our diversity of culture and race), by the frontier (with its opportunities, problems, and isolation), by urbanization and industrialization, and by the particular form of America's stratification system. In recent years, religion has been increasingly influenced by science and technology, by bureaucracy, by mobility, by the mass media and mass education. These and other structural influences were all interpreted through the complex of values and individual tendencies brought to America.

Of course religion was not created *de novo*. The environment influenced and was influenced by often intense religious beliefs and tightly knit religious structures. Out of the interaction came the patterns, in some cases after generations of change, by which American religion is broadly categorized: formal separation from the state, great denominational variety, tolerance, revivalism and evangelism, and more recently ecumenism. These were not simply structural effects on religion; in part they were a product of religion. The separation of church and state, for example, was strongly supported—indeed, virtually made mandatory—by the diversity of religious organizations. The great emphasis placed in America upon education has doubtless influenced religion in many ways, but in the first instance, it was itself, to an important degree the result of religious interests.

This once again emphasizes the need to avoid any assumption that religion is always to be regarded as the independent variable, "causing" certain developments in society and culture, or that it is wholly a dependent variable, reflecting its social environment. I *do* assume that religion is a natural expression of man as an individual and as a member of society. (For other than scientific purposes, this may be an irrelevant or unhappy assumption.) But religious forces, once set in motion, become part of a complex system of interaction. The requirements of a cult ceremony may lead to efforts to get a more accurate calendar; the presence of a priestly hierarchy may prevent the breaking up of a feudal land-tenure system; trade may be stimulated by religious festivals; intense and almost ascetic economic activity may result from a desire to prove oneself of the elect;

40 One shudders to think that at times this might be an apt definition of the anthropologist—or at least of this writer—insofar as he assays to grasp the range of meanings among the members of other societies.

religious emotion may strongly affect an artistic style. For such questions as these, it is often useful to treat religion as the independent variable, keeping fully in mind the nature of one's abstraction. The influence of religion is sometimes facilitating, sometimes inhibitive; its functions may be manifest, or latent and unanticipated; its effects may be good or ill from the point of view of a stated value. However these may be, the scientist cannot disregard the influence of religion any more than he can overlook the ways in which religion is shaped and reshaped by its social environment.

BIBLIOGRAPHICAL POSTSCRIPT

There will be many references to specific patterns of religion-society interaction in America throughout the next several chapters. A few important titles of more general interest are these: H. Richard Niebuhr, *The Social Sources of Denominationalism*; Winthrop Hudson, *Religion in America*; Herbert Schneider, *Religion in 20th Century America*; W. W. Sweet, *The American Churches: An Interpretation*; W. L. Sperry, *Religion in America*; Will Herberg, *Protestant-Catholic-Jew*; T. Scott Miyakawa, *Protestants and Pioneers*; W. E. Garrison, "Characteristics of American Organized Religion," *Annals of the American Academy of Political and Social Science,* March, 1948, pp. 14–24; David Moberg, *The Church as a Social Institution. The Sociology of American Religion.*

There are a number of good sources for statistical information. See the annual issues of the *American Jewish Yearbook*, the *Catholic Directory*, and the *Yearbook of American Churches* (published by the National Council of Churches). See also the United States Bureau of the Census, "Religion Reported by the Civilian Population of the United States: March, 1957"; Bernard Lazerwitz, "A Comparison of Major United States Religious Groups," *Journal of the American Statistical Association*, 56, 1961, pp. 568–579; William Peterson, "Religious Statistics in the United States," *Journal for the Scientific Study of Religion*, 1, 1962, pp. 165–178; Edwin Gaustad, "America's Institutions of Faith," in *The Religious Situation: 1968,* Donald Cutler, ed., pp. 835–870; and Frank Mead, *Handbook of Denominations in the United States*, 4th ed.

Chapter Twelve

RELIGIOUS DIFFERENTIATION AND SOCIAL DIFFERENTIATION

In discussing the relationships between religion, society, and culture, I have largely disregarded the internal variation that characterizes each of them. For some purposes one can speak in such unitary terms. For other purposes, however, internal divisions of the population and subcultural variation are of central importance. Complexity of culture and of social structure is matched by complexity of religious structure. We need a perspective and a vocabulary that will permit a differentiated analysis.

We have a rich body of evidence that regional groups, classes, occupations, majority and minority groups, educational levels, persons of different ages, men and women, individuals of differing tendencies—to mention some of the ways in which a society may be divided—often show different religious inclinations and express themselves religiously in different ways. The analysis of only one of these divisions—classes, for example—is clearly inadequate, for in a multiple-variable situation, there is always the likelihood that the variables may offset each other to a greater or lesser degree. Persons of different class status may be religiously quite similar because of similar residence, educational level, and some shared personal needs. The fact that they are somewhat alike in their religious inclinations does not prove that class is unimportant; only that it is one of several factors. The influence of the variables may, of course, be cumulative, with the result that religious differences become large: a well-educated, urban, professional man can be sharply distinguished, in religious tendencies, from an illiterate peasant living in the same society and sharing "the same" religious tradition.

The degree to which religion is involved as a factor in the *reduction* of social differentiation has been much less adequately explored. To some degree this problem is implicit in the question of the integrative function of religion; but a new factor is added here, because there can be integration in a highly differentiated society. That persons who are socially very different, but who share a basic religious tradition in common, may have some similar beliefs, worship together, and embrace some elements of a common moral code can be amply demonstrated. This observation, however, does not establish the power of religion to reduce social differentiation. Even a concept of "equality before God" may prosper in a very inegalitarian society (indeed, some would say, precisely in such a society). It is clear that the degree to which, and the processes through which, the sharing of religion reduces social differentiation requires much more careful attention than it has had until now.

The related question, Does religious differentiation, once established, reinforce the lines of the social divisions out of which it grew? is also inadequately answered. We know that when some of the social factors involved in a religious division have disappeared, there may be a reunion, as has occurred in American Methodism, for instance. But was the process by which the social differentiation was reduced in fact slowed down by the religious split? Might Methodists of similar class and occupation in the South and in the North be somewhat more alike (in politics and in attitudes toward race relations, for example) if they had shared the same religious communion in the century after 1844? The fact that the Episcopalians, who were much less sharply split by the problem of slavery than were the Methodists, seem today to be more unified than the Methodists in their attitudes toward race relations gives us a hint—but only a hint—of the possible effects of religious division. (Class and educational differences between the two groups and the fact that a much higher proportion of Methodists were in the South are variables that prevent one from making any easy generalization.)

Approaching this same question from an individual point of view, one might ask: Does the experience of being brought up in touch with a "lower-class" religious group give a person values, levels of aspiration, motives, political and economic beliefs, and so on that tend to fix him in lower-class status? Or does it have the opposite result by giving him self-confidence, clear purposes, and a sense of support? There is some evidence that an affirmative answer should be given to the latter question. John Wesley observed that the virtues accompanying sectarian religious fervor helped one to climb the class ladder, and that piety led to riches. (Wesley was not at all certain that the reverse of this was true, and so regarded the situation as a serious dilemma.) The history of the Quakers in the United States is also often cited as evidence that religious differentiation does not fix the lines of class division. They came to do good, as the aphorism has it, and they did very well indeed. Benton Johnson has recently asked, in the words of his article's title, "Do Holiness Sects Socialize in Dominant Values?" [1] Do they, in other words, promote upward social mobility among their members? Johnson believes that frequently they do. The sect-to-church transition has been offered as further demonstration of the way

1 Benton Johnson in *Social Forces*, 39, 1961, pp. 309–316. See also C. Eric Lincoln, *The Black Muslims in America*.

in which lower-class sectarian movements may promote upward mobility.

There is evidence, however, on the other side as well. The transition from sect to church may be characteristic of the institutional structure only and may not be indicative of what is happening to the status of individual members. If churches become middle-class in values, doctrine, and ritual, lower-class members tend to drop out and to look for some other religious (or secular) expression more in keeping with their inclinations and desires.[2] A class-related religious movement may support motives and values congruent with the existing class experience of its members without there being strong latent contradictory effects.

In the discussion that follows, we shall be concerned at several points to examine the conditions in which religion supports and those in which it reduces social differentiation, the times when it serves as an opiate for its members and those when it serves as a stimulant. Before studying such questions, however, we need to explore the causes and the varieties of religious divisions. With that material in hand, we can turn to the study of the consequences of religious differentiation.

THE CAUSES OF RELIGIOUS DIVISIONS

It is commonly assumed that religious differences are the result of disagreements over doctrine, ritual, and church organization. Noting the differences between Mahayana and Theravada Buddhism, Suzuki asks: "How can there be two Buddhisms equally representing the true doctrine of the founder?" Although he notes the influence of "diverse needs, characters, and trainings," his answer mainly concerns religious interpretations and organizations: "It is due, on the one hand, to a general unfolding of the religious consciousness and a constant broadening of the intellectual horizon, and, on the other hand, to the conservative efforts to literally preserve the monastic rules and traditions." [3] The average participant would doubtless put the issue differently, but with essentially the same meaning: They are in a different church from ours because they prefer different rites and have different beliefs.

Social scientists, on the other hand, observe that a religious tradition is differentiated by nation, class, educational level, patterns of secular conflict, and other nonreligious variables. They suspect the correlations are not accidental but demonstrate the deep involvement of religion in the total pattern of life. For the most part, that will be the perspective of this chapter. There is no reason to insist, however, that the diversity of groups within a single religious tradition is wholly the result of social differences among its members. Wherever religious specialists are found, their "intrinsically religious" elaboration of the questions with which they are professionally concerned can lead to differentiation in doctrine, ritual, and institutional structure. Religious professionals are themselves strongly conditioned, of course, by their status, their audiences, and the secular problems and divisions of their time. The ways in which their religious observations are received and used are even more strongly conditioned by such forces. We

2 See Liston Pope, *Millhands and Preachers.*

3 D. T. Suzuki, *Outlines of Mahayana Buddhism,* p. 4.

shall pay some attention, however, following Weber, Troeltsch, Wach, and others, to that aspect of their thought which can profitably be viewed as the internal development of a religious system.

The secular impact on the differentiation of religious-group structure will be more apparent under some circumstances than others. It is commonly observed, for example, that the proliferation of religious divisions is far more extensive under Protestantism than under Catholicism. This does not mean simply that Catholicism shapes the religious needs of its members into a common mold. Although this may be partly true, it is also true that the structure of the Church permits a vast range of different needs and interests to be satisfied within it. Protestantism, with its greater emphasis on individual religious experience (and its greater development in mobile and individualistic societies), encourages the development of different religious structures. Catholicism reflects the variations in religious needs *within* its pattern: There are Catholic trade unions and support for large estates owners; monasteries and church supported festivals and bingo games; Catholic sociology and magical relics. Where Protestant polity is dominant, the wide range of personal inclinations is far more likely to be reflected in the proliferation of separate religious structures.

Religious Divisions Within the World Religions

The world religions are often seen as uniform traditions, each with a great deal of continuity through space and time. They are identified with their orthodox or classical expressions, as seen through certain dominant interpretations of their sacred literatures or manifest at certain dominant periods in their histories. Particularly when one sees a religion at a distance, its internal varieties disappear or are obscured. If one's purpose is evaluation, he may also disregard their range in favor of a statement of the religion's "pure," "true," or "integral" form.

For our purposes, however, study of the varieties of form within a major tradition is as essential as the study of the varieties of individual experience.[4] There is a substantial literature describing the contrasts between the crude Scandinavian peasant god Thor and Odin, the refined god of the nobility. There were wide differences between the intellectualized beliefs of the upper classes of Ancient Greece and the mystery cults of the masses. Perhaps such contrasts cut across religious lines more than they describe internal variation; but this distinction is not easy to draw, just as it is not always easy to determine when a major schism establishes a new religion and when it represents a variation within an existing tradition. In other cases, however, there is little doubt. From ancient days until the present

4 Examination of divisions within a religious tradition shades off into the study of interreligious relations, for the boundaries are not sharp. Weber noted that many religious variations occur because the average layman could not hold to the severe demands of Buddhist monkhood. Elements of Buddhism were therefore combined with more comforting beliefs among many laymen. He also noted that Hindu restoration, after the Buddhist challenge, meant compromise with various folk beliefs and practices. Spiro has similarly observed that there are many different ways in which the relationship between Buddhism and nat worship is regarded. See Max Weber, particularly *The Religion of India*; and Melford Spiro, *Burmese Supernaturalism*, pp. 247–280.

time Judaism has had its variations and denominations. There are many sectarian forms of Shinto. The history of Hinduism has been not only a story of major schisms, particularly that of Buddhism, but of significant internal contrasts.[5] The fact that Buddhism is found in many different societies has been particularly important in its differentiation; but there are important variations within societies as well.[6] Stretching from North Africa to Indonesia, Muhammadanism, for all of its emphasis on the Islamic quality of society and on Islamic law, has developed in several different directions.[7]

The varieties of Christianity are no less numerous than those of other international religions. It seems probable, in fact, that it has been associated with a wider range of societies, partly as the dominant faith and partly as a minority faith, than has any other religion; and we might therefore expect greater diversity in its expressions. Having no adequate measures of diversity, however, we must regard this as an impression. It is clear that early Christianity was capable of many interpretations, as were the early versions of other major religions. Christianity's success in becoming the dominant religion of the Roman Empire, in fact, was to an important degree based on the potentialities it had for being so many things to so many different kinds of people. This very diversity of appeal, however, made it vulnerable to schism, for as Christianity became more highly institutionalized, it began to give more weight to one emphasis rather than another, and thus encouraged the protest and perhaps the withdrawal of those who believed that the neglected aspect was the right one.

One well-known illustration of this tension concerns the relevance of Christianity for "social reform." It seems likely that a few of the immediate followers of Jesus looked upon him as a social reformer—or at least hoped that he would be—an emphasis that finds expression in Luke, as contrasted with the spiritual emphasis in Matthew. The dominant theme of the new religion, however, was certainly not social reform. The religious crisis that marked the end of the ancient world order was part of the vast social crisis —the destruction of the *polis*, the extinction of freedom under the military and bureaucratic power of the empire—in which, as Troeltsch shows, it had become clear that the social ideal of the Hebrew people was not to be realized by human thought and effort. The belief that the kingdom of God was to be of this world began to give way. This did not occur rapidly, nor was the process carried to its completion in Christianity. Nevertheless, after enduring centuries of frustrations and disappointments, culminating in the oppressions of Rome, religious thought lost much of its optimism con-

5 See Max Weber, *The Religion of India;* M. N. Srinivas, *Caste in Modern India.*

6 See, for example, Joseph Kitagawa, *Religion in Japanese History,* Chaps. 2 and 3; Winston King, *A Thousand Lives Away,* Chap. 2; Max Weber, op. cit., Chaps. 7 and 8; and Max Weber, *The Religion of China,* Chap. 7.

7 For a fascinating picture of the range of *views* of Islam among Westerners, as well as of its range of expressions, see Jean-Jacques Waardenburg, *L'Islam dans le miroir de l'Occident.* Waardenburg interprets the conceptions of Islam in the work of five Western scholars. See also Clifford Geertz, *The Religion of Java;* Noel Coulson, "The Concept of Progress and Islamic Law," in *Religion and Progress in Modern Asia,* Robert Bellah, ed., pp. 74–92; W. M. Watt, *Islam and the Integration of Society,* pp. 94–114.

cerning the possibilities of reordering the affairs of this world. The order established by the Roman Empire came to be accepted:

henceforth the conduct of external affairs was left to the rulers, while men sought and cultivated individual and spiritual freedom. This applies to the later development of Platonism and Stoicism; it applies to countless new religious movements, and in particular it applies to the establishment of Christianity as well as to the preparation for it within Judaism.[8]

Yet the implications of Christianity for the life of this world were there; the continuing hopes of man for justice and happiness and success on earth were not smothered. Tied together in primitive Christianity, as Troeltsch observes, are a thoroughgoing religious asceticism and an ethical-prophetic strain. They are not easily distinguished in the teachings of Jesus and the other sources of Christianity, which tended to view life monistically.[9] But followers could read into the teachings a reference to their own particular needs. Throughout the history of Christianity, one can see the emphasis, now on one, now on the other of these two themes. Hammond and Hammond describe the situation clearly:

The devout Christian, confronted with the spectacle of wrong and injustice, may draw either of two contrary conclusions. In the eyes of his religion the miner or weaver is just as important as the landlord or the cotton lord. Clearly then, one will argue, it is the duty of a Christian State to prevent any class, however obscure and trivial its place in the world may seem to be, from sinking into degrading conditions of life. Every soul is immortal, and the consequences of ill-treatment and neglect in the brief day of its life on earth will be unending. If, therefore, society is so organised as to impose such conditions on any class, the Christian will demand the reform of its institutions. For such minds Christianity provides a standard by which to judge government, the industrial and economic order, the life of society, the way in which it distributes wealth and opportunities. This was the general standpoint of such a man as Shaftesbury. But some minds drew a different moral from the equality that Christianity teaches. Every human soul is a reality, but the important thing about a human soul is its final destiny, and that destiny does not depend on the circumstances of this life. The world has been created on a plan of apparent injustice by a Providence that combined infinite power with infinite compassion. The arrangements that seem so capricious are really the work of that Power. But the same Power has given to the men and women who seem to live in such bitter and degrading surroundings, an escape from its cares by the exercise of their spiritual faculties. It is those faculties that make all men equal. Here they stand, in Marcus Aurelius's phrase, for a brief space between the two eternities, and no misery or poverty can prevent a soul from winning happiness in the world to come. Thus whereas one man looking out on the chaos of the world calls for reform, the other calls for contemplation: one says, Who could tolerate such injustice? The other says, Who would not rejoice that there is another world? One says, Give these people the conditions of a decent life; the other says, Teach them to read the Bible.[10]

These two differing interpretations are, indeed, possible. Our concern is to ask, Who will make the one and who the other? What are the circum-

<hr/>

8 Ernst Troeltsch, *The Social Teaching of the Christian Churches*, p. 47.

9 See Paul Tillich, *The Shaking of the Foundations*, pp. 24–28, on "The Paradox of the Beatitudes."

10 J. L. and Barbara Hammond, *The Town Labourer*, 1760–1832, pp. 223–224.

stances that will cause the one to be emphasized and not the other? What organizational forms will the different expressions take? Our task, in other words, is to discover the sources of religious differentiation.

The Sources of Schism

In his study of "schism in the early church," S. L. Greenslade discusses the causes of the splits that occurred frequently in the ranks of Christianity in the first few centuries of its existence. His research gives support to the thesis of Richard Niebuhr that variations in the ethics, polity, and theology among various denominations, have their roots "in the relationship of the religious life to the cultural and political conditions prevailing in any group of Christians. . . . The exigencies of church discipline, the demands of the national psychology, the effect of social tradition, the influence of cultural heritage, and the weight of economic interest play their role in the definition of religious truth." [11]

Greenslade gives somewhat more emphasis than does Niebuhr to the differences that develop as a result of personal conflicts among leaders; and he stresses the disputes that arises from the internal elaboration, by specialists, of the religious system. Both of these emphases can be related, in our judgment, to the personality factors of the leaders and to their social settings. It is useful, however, to see them on another level as well, for once set in motion, they become proximate causes of religious differentiation that it would be unwise to ignore.[12] Greenslade discusses five causes of schism in the early church, appropriately treating them as interactive and mutually reinforcing:

1. *Personal.* This category includes the pursuit of individual power, personal rancor, and so forth. Seldom were these the predominate cause of schism. (This influence may be seen today most clearly in the continual splitting up of sect and cult movements.)

2. *National, Social, and Economic Influences.* This is the major emphasis of Richard Niebuhr's important work and will receive documentation later.

3. *The Rivalry of Sees.* As a cause of schism, this is often difficult to distinguish from national and economic rivalries; but wherever separate ecclesiastical bureaucracies develop, the distinction is useful.

4. *Liturgical Disputes.* This category includes tensions between the opposing ideals of liturgical uniformity and freedom. Religious leaders, searching for the most effective ways of conveying their message, come to different conclusions about liturgy. We may explain this on the basis of

11 H. Richard Niebuhr, *The Social Sources of Denominationalism*, pp. 16–17.

12 Note the remark of Paul Hutchinson concerning the 1954 meeting of the World Council of Churches: "Evanston, we dare hope, could thus come to be remembered as the place where the World Council discovered how quickly the impulse to Christian unity in action could be sidetracked and reduced to impotence by a demand for prior theological agreement." *Christian Century*, September 22, 1954, p. 1125. Sociologists, who are often careful students of the internal forces in bureaucracies or of the patterns of control and development *within* an industrial plant or a university, sometimes fail to see the same processes at work in religious structures. Such developments are of no less interest to sociology than are the external forces that shape the patterns of religious groups.

their differing social experiences and individual tendencies; but the possibility of this relationship should not be allowed to obscure the further meaning that the disputes are the result of internal elaborations of a religious system. Liturgical disputes are not, in Greenslade's use of the term, serious doctrinal quarrels, in which theological differences lie behind a schism. They are seldom, in his judgment, sufficiently powerful to be the single cause of schism, but may combine with more powerful causes and often perpetuate separation after it has occurred.

5. *Problems of Discipline and the Puritan Idea of the Church.* The puritan spirit—with its emphasis on perfection and individual religious experience—has often caused men to break off from the main ecclesiastical group to set up a "congregation of saints." Reaction against the disciplines imposed by the hierarchy was a major source of such early schisms as Montanism, Novatianism, and Donatism. Intensification of the patristic doctrine of the church was, in turn, a response to these schisms. ". . . the tendency of Montanism was to repudiate the existing hierarchy altogether, and—by its emphasis on prophets under immediate inspiration—to deny the whole principle of order and authority which the bulk of the Church had welcomed, as well as the particular idea of apostolic succession which was at this time coming into prominence as the basis of episcopal authority." [13]

For the sociologist of religion it is necessary to pursue farther than does Greenslade, particularly with reference to his points 4 and 5, *why* some take this side in a liturgical dispute and some another, *who* defends most vigorously the need for church discipline and who the opposing doctrine of prophetic inspiration. Although these may partly be understood in terms of efforts to make a religious system as effective as possible, they must also be seen as manifestations of secular conflicts and of variation in individual needs. Whenever the institutional and authoritarian elements in the church have become predominant and the validity of its claim to religious leadership and holiness has been held "not to rest upon the achieved saintliness of its members," schismatic protests have arisen. Rigid insistence on the authority of the established structure and the exclusive validity of its system of rites and beliefs weakens the ability of the religious organization to fulfill the functions of religion for the weak and powerless, because, as we shall see, the highly institutionalized structure becomes adjusted to the needs and interests of the dominant elements in society. The "disinherited" are not simply those who are cut off from the predominant religious institution by economic and political differences. They are also alienated by the differences in belief, in form of worship, and in moral emphasis that their different needs demand. That is, they feel religiously disinherited as well.

It is significant for a functional analysis that the protests of the early schismatics, as expressed, for example, in Donatism, have recurred again and again, in much the same terms, in the religious movements of the disinherited.

13 S. L. Greenslade, *Schism in the Early Church,* p. 110; for his discussion of the causes of schism, see pp. 37–124; see also G. R. Cragg, "Disunities Created by Differing Patterns of Church Life," *Ecumenical Review,* April, 1952, pp. 276–281; and Reinhold Niebuhr, *The Nature and Destiny of Man,* Vol. 1, pp. 49–53.

They preferred enthusiastic movements of the spirit to humdrum official Christianity; they believed that the Holy Spirit can make His own ministers where he wills, apart from the authorised methods of the Church; they repudiated the ministrations of unworthy clergy; they held to the notion of the gathered congregation, the communion of saints, exercising a discipline which casts out the unworthy, and they believed that the Church can be infected by unworthy members to the point of corruption and death.[14]

Structural, Cultural, and Character Sources of Religious Divisions. These comments on schism can be brought into a larger system of concepts that summarizes the causes of religious differentiation. These are highly interactive and often mutually reinforcing:

1. Variations in personal religious needs and interests, because of differences in the strength of feelings of frustration and guilt, in level of intellectual development, in capacity for certain kinds of religious experience, in authoritarian tendencies, and so on. Individual tendencies by themselves are not enough, of course, to produce schism (or the related phenomenon of individual conversion and transfer). For religious variation to develop, tendencies must be shared by a number of interacting persons (a situation that suggests sociocultural sources for those tendencies); or at the least, mutually complementary and supportive tendencies must be present. Some catalytic agent must be operating as well, for individual problems, tensions, and needs can lead to a number of different patterns of action. When a charismatic leader proclaims the way, or when individuals sharing common concerns meet in a context that suggests and makes possible a religious response, schism develops.[15]

2. Variations in economic and political interests. It is a truism to note that the Reformation was supported by many of the German princes as part of their struggle with the Holy Roman Empire. Sectarian movements are to a substantial degree protest movements expressing alienation from society. "Marxists are, by and large, within their rights when they claim that sect movements are phenomena of an ongoing class struggle in societies within which the class conflict as such has not yet become conscious." [16] I shall interpret sectarianism in somewhat broader terms, but its roots in alienation, as Stark describes it, are of great importance.

3. Societal and national differences. We have noted that the world religions vary from society to society. This is documented by the fact that even into the third and fourth generation after migration into the same society, groups from "the same" religious tradition but different lands will manifest differences of doctrine, group structure, and patterns of belief. Although there have been significant mergers in recent years, Lutherans in the United States still exhibit some signs of their German, Swedish, Norwegian, and other national origins. Roman Catholics of Irish, Italian, Polish, German, Mexican, and Puerto Rican descent vary to some degree in their beliefs, their religious practices, and their attitudes toward the Church,

14 Greenslade, op. cit., pp. 114–115.

15 For careful statements of the interaction between individual tendencies and the situation, see Jon Lofland, *Doomsday Cult;* and Jon Lofland and Rodney Stark, "Becoming a World-Saver: A Theory of Conversion to a Deviant Perspective," *American Sociological Review,* 30, 1965, pp. 862–875.

16 Werner Stark, *The Sociology of Religion,* Vol. 2, p. 5.

even after language and class variations have been reduced in America. Such continuing differences emphasize the ways in which the religious lives of their ancestors had been influenced by their national settings.

Societal effects on religion are ancient. Specifically national effects (that is, those deriving from more centralized and politically unified societies) were probably not important until the modern era. "The nation was not yet born: *nacio* as yet meant merely 'place of birth.' After 1500 or so, all this changed, and there is no sharper division between medieval and modern times than precisely this, the all-importance of nationhood, or negatively expressed, the demotion and half-dissolution of neighborhood community and world unity." [17] In such a context, as Stark correctly observes, universalism is subjected to serious strains; national variation in religious loyalties grows.

4. Social mobility and social change. Movement up or down the class ladder is a powerful source of changing religious sentiments. When it is experienced by many persons in interaction with one another, new religious forms are likely to appear. Social change has the same effect. By upsetting established expectations, creating new patterns of interaction, making new values visible and subjecting old ones to strain, social change both challenges existing religious groups and creates a context in which new movements will arise.

Since we shall be concerned repeatedly with these four points in the next several chapters, I shall not discuss them further here. A fifth point, however, has perhaps been neglected in scientific studies of religion; so a somewhat fuller statement of it may be appropriate.

5. Differences that derive from internal development and internal strain of the religious system. This is akin to, but somewhat more inclusive than, Greenslade's argument that liturgical disputes and disagreements over the desirable amount of religious discipline are sources of schism independent of what are usually called the social sources. Certainly the elaboration of theological ideas, inventiveness in the field of ritual, and differences in judgment concerning the problems of continuity and authority produce sharp cleavages among religious leaders. These sources of religious differences are not outside the interests of a sociology and social psychology of religion, for they too can be seen as the results of the interaction of social, cultural, and personality factors. But it is well to remember that however caused, these variations become part of the cycle of interaction. It is not enough to reduce them to a supposed original cause.

Whether or not religious "inventions" lead to different religious groups is a question that leads us back to the other causes of schism. The influence of inventions depends in part upon the way in which laymen react to them. These reactions are much more dependent upon the differences outlined in the first four points I have listed, and upon the way in which new religious ideas and rites can be used to grapple with varying human needs, than upon some inevitable consequence of the new religious forces themselves. There is a level of analysis on which it is appropriate to study religious innovations as starting points of a series of events. The degree of

17 Werner Stark, *The Sociology of Religion*, Vol. 3, pp. 13–14.

acceptance of those innovations, however, and the direction of their spread, is vitally dependent on the needs and desires of potential audiences. In Weber's term, there is an "elective affinity" between certain religious ideas and the social circumstances of particular groups. We must not only pay attention, therefore, to the fact that a given group accepted a stated religious innovation—as if it forced itself upon them independently, without connection with their inclinations—but must also seek to discover what functions the religious idea served.

The Dilemma of Religious Leaders as a Source of Religious Differentiation

Another aspect of this question of the importance of internal religious development requires some attention. A religion almost inevitably requires many actions that its adherents would not perform without religious motivation. These actions would have no meaning in the context of purely egocentric, or economic, or hedonistic criteria. Certain ascetic restraints, taboos, self-torture, sacrifice, and so forth, can be understood only in relation to religiously motivated desires. Because they are tied, in the religious system, to the supposed achievement of the ultimate satisfactions, to the accomplishment of the greatest values, they are accepted or even enthusiastically espoused. To the nonbeliever in a given religion, however, these acts may seem irrational, immoral, and unpleasurable, as well as irreligious. Many modern Christians are revolted by the human sacrifices of the Aztecs, annoyed by the caste taboos of the Hindus, unconvinced that any value can come from vows of eternal chastity. They are baffled by the large-scale destruction of economic goods that is religiously prescribed in some societies; they cannot understand the devaluation of this life that is common in many religions. Yet these actions seem, or have seemed, absolutely essential to those who looked at them from the perspective of the believer.

Now we must ask: What happens when doubts begin to arise, when the efficacy of the religious restraints and sacrifices is brought into question, when the egocentric tendencies of man—never far away—begin to push for immediate satisfaction? Suppose that social change sets in motion various forces that undermine faith in the religious system, increase the desire for the satisfaction of immediate interests and needs, and make the rewards of religion seem uncertain, less important, or distant. Or suppose a competing faith promises surer rewards. Then those who still believe intensively in the first religious system as the right road to the supreme values, and are eager for others also to believe, are confronted with a difficult dilemma. If these religious leaders, as we may call them (those in whom religious interest is high and who are concerned about its meaning for others), demand too close allegiance to those aspects of the religious ideal that require the sacrifice of other values that have come into importance or reasserted themselves, they run the risk of being persecuted or neglected. On the other hand, if they do not insist on close allegiance to the religious values, or if they compromise drastically with secular interests, individual needs, or competing faiths, they will promote the neglect of the very religious values they revere.

There are also nonreligious aspects to this dilemma. In his discussion of modifications of ancient Hinduism during the "orthodox restoration"—

modifications involving concessions to folk beliefs—Weber noted that secular as well as religious interests of Brahmans were involved:

The driving motive of the Brahmans in this reception and accommodation process was in part quite grossly material. They wished to protect the many prebends and incidental fees which were available if one accepted the service of these ineradicable folk deities. As well, there was the force of competition against the powerful salvation confessions of Jainism and Buddhism which had managed to get into the saddle only through adaptation to the folk tradition.[18]

The dilemma of religious leaders, then, derives both from their own interests and from the strategic problems of their religious tradition. Thomas O'Dea concentrates on this latter source in his discussion of several dimensions of the dilemma of institutionalized religion. Perhaps these dimensions can be suggested by a series of questions that religious leaders might put to one another:

Shall we take account of the secular interests and motives of our members, running the risk of diluting the faith; or shall we disregard those interests and motives, running the risk of alienating many constituents? (The dilemma of mixed motivation.) Shall we objectify the sacred, to give it a communal and visible quality, running the risk of freezing it in symbolic forms that are meaningless to new generations; or shall we leave the sacred unsymbolized, to allow each individual to invest his own meaning in it, running the risk of loss of solidarity of the religious community? (The symbolic dilemma.) Shall we develop an administrative order capable of effective decisions, running the risk of bureaucratic rigidity, power concentration, and goal displacement; or shall we maintain an open, personal system, running the risk of inefficiency? (The dilemma of administrative order.) [19] Shall we translate the religious message into concrete rules and norms, running the risk of making them inflexible; or shall we state it as a guiding spirit, running the risk that it will not be understood or will be interpreted according to contradictory individual perceptions? (The dilemma of delimitation.) Because our faith is the repository of truth, shall we create structures to guarantee its acceptance (such as indoctrination, or opposition to other faiths), thus running the risk of a high level of coercion and of countercoercion; or shall we rely on persuasion and conversion, running the risk that religious freedom will mean loss of faith or the success of a competing religion? (The dilemma of power.) [20]

These dilemmas characterize institutional decisions generally, of course,

18 Max Weber, *The Religion of India*, p. 297.

19 There is an extensive literature on this subject, ranging from the overhasty generalizations of Pareto, Mosca, Michels, and others concerning an "iron law of oligarchy" (the phrase is from Michels and is used with reference to political parties) to more careful studies of specific organizations in which efforts are made to discover the conditions under which power concentration and goal displacement occur. See Alvin Gouldner, *Patterns of Industrial Bureaucracy; S. M.* Lipset, Martin Trow, and James Coleman, *Union Democracy;* David Sills, *The Volunteers.* Religious organizations are not free from the processes of bureaucratization; see Paul Harrison, *Authority and Power in the Free Church Tradition.*

20 See Thomas O'Dea, "Five Dilemmas in the Institutionalization of Religion," *Journal for the Scientific Study of Religion,* 1, 1961, pp. 30–39; and my own "Comment," pp. 40–41. See also my *Religion in the Struggle for Power,* where I made extensive use of the concept, "the dilemma of the churches."

and not simply those of religious institutions. Much of contemporary theory of administration and of bureaucratization deals with the dilemmas that confront complex organizations. This theory goes beyond O'Dea's discussion, however, which is concerned largely with internal processes, to examine dilemmas that are created by relationships with the external environment. As a group seeks to maintain or broaden its influence, it often has to win the support—or at least hold down the opposition—of other groups and persons who are only partly in agreement with its aims or even actively in disagreement with them. Shall it oppose them fully and directly, compromise with them, or try to co-opt them into its own program? Each strategy has its costs. Direct opposition may bring defeat; compromise may require yielding on significant values; co-optation raises the question of who will take advantage of whom.[21] Particularly in complex societies, religious organizations face these problems continuously.

If failure to win the support of powerful secular organizations means relative powerlessness, and if the effort to win their support runs the danger of co-optation, religious organizations face a serious dilemma. This dilemma is found most sharply, perhaps, in the relationships between churches and states. Those who believe that clear separation of church and state increases the power of the church emphasize the freedom from political domination, the freedom to criticize the political process and the secular power structure. There is the danger, however, that such freedoms are closely connected with powerlessness. On the other hand, close institutional connection between church and state scarcely avoids the dilemma, because the union raises the likelihood that the church will be used to lend sanctity to a secular power structure. The problem is to find a way to be simultaneously in politics (thus to influence it) and beyond politics (thus free to challenge it).[22]

Variation in how religious movements and leaders respond to these several dilemmas is one of the important sources of religious differentiation. Responses vary according to many factors: the nature of a particular religious tradition, the tendencies and needs of the leadership, the strength and nature of the secular values of the persons to whom the religion appeals, or is attempting to appeal. Interacting with the other causes of religious divisions that we have listed, they produce the various types of religious organizations discussed in the next chapter. Some react to this conflict between the demands of the religious ideal and the claims of competing interests by making strong concessions to the latter. This we shall call the church-type reaction. It is supported by strong secular interests; but, on our present level of analysis, it can be seen in part as the result of a religiously motivated strategic decision. Not to compromise is to alienate completely the people whom we hope to win or hold, says the churchman; to fail to recognize the impervious quality of man's secular interests is not to conquer them, but to be defeated by them. By accepting what in any event has to be accepted (war or great inequalities of station, for example) we can remain in a position of influence from which we can gradually undermine their causes. Not so, says the sectarian. Compromise is a one-way street down which the church moves, concession after concession,

21 For a valuable discussion of this dilemma of adjustment to outside powers, see Philip Selznick, TVA and the Grass Roots.

22 J. Milton Yinger, Sociology Looks at Religion, p. 177.

until it finally arrives at the place where the secular values are completely dominant. The only solution is to maintain the purity of the religious system of values in an uncompromised community of believers, and to hope that its light may become a beacon to the wayward.

Thus a religious strategic decision may promote differences in religious group structure. This cause, however, is never found in isolation from the other causes of religious differentiation. Since efforts to achieve the values of a religion require some kind of power over often recalcitrant human beings, organizations are developed. These organizations take on compulsions of their own, relative to their own order, control, and continuation, which are irrelevant to the religious quest. Moreover, other secular interests "invade" the religious organization, using it to support their claims for national independence or imperial dominance, land reform or the preservation of slavery, legitimization of their complaints against society or legitimization of their right to rule. Faced with these secular interests, which cannot simply be dismissed or overcome, the religious leader makes the religious strategic decision, with varying consequences for the relationship of his group to "the world."

Those in whom the *secular* interests are dominant may support him and his group, but as the result of asking a different question: What religious approach makes my view of the world, my claims and complaints, seem legitimate and right? The question is seldom if ever asked as baldly as that, of course; it is simply a matter of feeling the rightness of an approach that does justice to one's own view. A church that accepts the basic structure of a society, that has compromised with the secular powers, is likely to be supported by those who have fared relatively well in the distribution of goods and power in their society. They are likely to believe that the compromises are in any event not crucial, because they believe that there is nothing *basically* evil about a society that has treated them so well. There are, of course, important exceptions to this situation, for the needs of men are diverse, and for some the need to maintain power and station may be relatively unimportant. A sect that is based on a conviction that there are basic evils in society with which one must not compromise is most likely to draw support from the least privileged groups. A societal arrangement that treats them so poorly is clearly not one with which their most exalted ideals can make compromises; consequently they either oppose or withdraw from "the world." They support the leader who holds that the religious idea can be maintained only in freedom from the impact of the secular powers, in a "pure" religious community of believers. Thus the various causes of schism interpenetrate.

The concept of a dilemma, with its suggestion of a sharp polarity, must be used with care. Basically I agree with Kurt Lewin that "there are no dichotomies in science." Nevertheless, when it can be said that an individual or a group faces a dilemma, it is often profitable to *start out* with a dichotomous formulation as a way of examining the problem. This is a general principle, not limited to the study of religion. Its value for us may be increased if we apply it briefly to another problem. In American politics, for example, a person discontented with the dominant program and leadership of his party can decide—to oversimplify for a moment—either to participate in a "third party" movement or not to participate. That is, he can act like a sectarian or a churchman. He can argue: The only way to make the issues quite clear is to build a new party around them, a party unencumbered with compromises and contradictory policies. Or he can argue: It is no good making the issues quite clear if the result is to deprive me or my candidate of the power base necessary for election. A live politician is more effective than a dead statesman. By working within a coalition that brings various points of view together into a majority, even if this means mutual compromises, I will be in a position to achieve some of my goals.

In the American presidential campaign in 1968, only "churchmen" were prominent or publicly visible in the Republican Party; that is, all the leading candidates accepted the necessity for a coalition among diverse elements in order to achieve a majority. The Democratic Party exhibited a wider range of strategies. Vice-President Humphrey was a churchman; Senator McCarthy was ambivalent—hoping that there might be a majority of convention delegates and of voters in support of his sharp formulation of the Vietnam issue, but moving toward third-party sectarianism after the election. Governor Wallace was sectarian. Of course he also hoped that his point of view was shared by the majority of voters; but knowing that it was *not* shared by Democratic Party officials, he gave no thought to an effort to become the "manager of a coalition." His vocabulary and selection of issues were designed to polarize the electorate, not to piece together a majority out of disparate and partially conflicting groups. There were also a few sectarians on the left, forming around the Black Power and Vietnam issues. But these did not play a large role in the 1968 election. Only a few Black Power sectarians expressed themselves directly through the political process; most Vietnam sectarians were caught up in the campaigns of Senator McCarthy and Senator Robert Kennedy. That is, they became reluctant churchmen, as many sectarians will when there seems some little possibility that they can attain a majority with minimal compromise, with minor attention to the problems of putting together a coalition—in short, when the dilemma is not sharp. This is not to imply that Senator Kennedy was a sectarian, for it is quite clear he was not. He did not share the squeamishness of Senator McCarthy for the compromises of party building. My guess is that his convictions on the Vietnam issue and on problems related to the cities were deep; he thought that if there was a reasonable possibility of nomination and election, the risks involved in taking sharp stands on these issues were justified. Had he lived and been nominated, I should have expected him to carry out a "courageously churchly" campaign—one designed to deal critically with the difficult issues, yet to bring together a majority coalition. Indeed, I should have expected a somewhat similar campaign from Senator McCarthy, although with more public expressions of doubt about the compromises involved.

None of this should be read as an evaluation of the decisions involved. In politics or religion my own preference is for a group that contains two paradoxical mixtures: hard-headed sectarians and idealistic churchmen. Nor is this comment a judgment concerning the relative success of sectarian and churchly approaches. Both are right and both are wrong. The sectarian may keep a critical issue alive and visible; he may clarify it; he may win some marginal people to its support by the intensity of his views. But he may also activate the opposition, create antimovements, and polarize the group, thus blocking the very causes for which he stands. The churchman may achieve influence and the opportunity to move toward his goals. He may, however, compromise so unskillfully that he gives away most of the things for which he entered the contest; or he may be caught up in the process of goal displacement, whereby the pursuit of power becomes an end for its own sake.

Viewing the human scene, one can only emphasize that the dilemma is sharp.

THE DENOMINATIONAL SOURCES OF SOCIAL DIVISIONS

We have noted that religious differentiation is strongly influenced by social differentiation. Does the opposite relationship also occur? Does religious differentiation, however caused, reenforce social lines of division?

To give an empirical answer to these questions, with their strong value implications, we need first to discover the degree of association between religious divisions and other forms of division. This is insufficient, however, because the association may not be a result of religious influence. There may be a correlation between type of work and church membership, for example, because the members of various churches entered a community at different times. If the contrast remains when controls for length of residence, opportunity, and so on, have been applied, then one can speak more confidently of a religious influence on the work situation.

On a somewhat impressionistic basis, I would suggest that the associations between religious and social divisions can be put into a Guttman type scale. I will call this a scale of communality.[23] Economic and political separation from religious communality are most likely to occur. If the members of religious communities belong to different political parties and work in different places, therefore, we have evidence of particularly strong association. If even the most likely to change has not done so, the communal aspects of religion are shown to be strong. At the opposite end of the scale is the family situation. If it is only in the fact of *intra*marriage that the communal quality of a religious group is shown, religious divisions are not very strongly associated with social divisions. And if even that is changing, if the rate of intermarriage is fairly high, then the association between religious divisions and other divisions is minimal (see Table 12–1).

If in fact communality is most commonly supported by marriage patterns, we would expect societies to be more alike in rates of intermarriage than, to go to the other end of the scale, in rates of interoccupational and interpolitical association. There are probably few multireligious societies in which most marriages are not within the faith. Insofar as this is true, religious differentiation stands as a kind of final support, happily or un-

23 My usage is similar to, but somewhat more inclusive than, Gerhard Lenski's. He defines communality in terms of kinship and friendship patterns. See *The Religious Factor*, p. 23. Milton Gordon emphasizes these elements, but pays some attention also to education and residence. See *Assimilation in American Life*. For a valuable quantitative study, see Edward O. Laumann, "The Social Structure of Religious and Ethnoreligious Groups in a Metropolitan Community," *American Sociological Review*, 34, 1969, pp. 182–197. See also Rodney Stark and Charles Glock, *American Piety: The Nature of Religious Commitment*, Chap. 8.

Table 12–1. A scale of association between religious differentiation and social differentiation

Degree of religious group communality	Types of social separation of religious groups					
	Occupa-tional	Political	Residential	Educa-tional	Friendships	Marital
1. Low	no	no	no	no	no	yes
2.	no	no	no	no	yes	yes
3.	no	no	no	yes	yes	yes
4.	no	no	yes	yes	yes	yes
5.	no	yes	yes	yes	yes	yes
6. High	yes	yes	yes	yes	yes	yes

happily, for social differentiation of the communal variety. In some societies it is virtually unthinkable that one should marry a person of another religion. These are usually societies in which religious groups are high on the scale of communality; other forms of social separation reinforce marital separation. When these break down, rates of intermarriage may go up. In the United States, the level of communality varies from group to group. Lenski notes that it is strong for Jews, medium for white Catholics and white Protestants, and strong for Negro Protestants.[24] Although forms of measurement vary quite widely and it is not clear how we can compare the various adjectives and adverbs used (highly, predominantly, strong, and so on), many studies support this finding.[25] The evidence, however, is not unambiguous, as an examination of the rates of religious intermarriage shows. A special United States Census report for 1957, based on a sample of 30,000, indicated that 12.1 per cent of Catholics, 4.5 per cent of Protestants, and 3.7 per cent of Jews were intermarried.[26] These figures are not notably different from those in a survey taken in Holland, where communality is presumably much stronger. In 1960, 5.3 per cent of Catholics, 10.2 per cent of Dutch Reformed, and 6.4 per cent of Reformed persons were intermarried.[27]

Direct comparison of these figures must be made with care for several reasons. Comparative sizes of the groups are different, with Protestants outnumbering Catholics about 2½ to 1 in the United States, whereas in Holland the faiths have almost equal numbers. In Holland there is a large group without religious affiliation (18.4 per cent); but the United States

24 Op. cit., p. 41.

25 See, for example, Marshall Sklare and Joseph Greenblum, *Jewish Identity on the Suburban Frontier*, especially Chaps. 8 and 9; Will Herberg, *Protestant-Catholic-Jew*; Milton Gordon, op. cit.; Charles Anderson, "Religious Communality among White Protestants, Catholics, and Mormons," *Social Forces*, 46, 1968, pp. 501–508; Benjamin Ringer, *The Edge of Friendliness. A Study of Jewish-Gentile Relations*.

26 United States Bureau of the Census, "Religion Reported by the Civilian Population of the United States, March, 1957," *Current Population Reports*, Series P-20, No. 79, 1958.

27 Reported in Arend Lijphart, *The Politics of Accommodation*, p. 57. Separate figures for Jews are not given.

"no preference" group is scarcely one-tenth as large. Hence the marriage of an inactive with an active Protestant was often recorded as an intramarriage in the United States and an intermarriage in Holland. A further difficulty is related to the effect of the conversion of one partner to the religion of the other. This is not taken into account in the data cited; contemporary religious identity is used. But in the United States it is estimated that about half of all intermarriages lead to conversion. That is, the Census figures underestimate intermarriage by half. If the conversion rate is higher or lower in Holland, comparison of the census data from the two countries is inadequate.[28]

Various other factors complicate interpretation. Since most American Negroes are Protestants, obstacles to interreligious marriage are reinforced by obstacles to interracial marriage. Approximately 1.5 per cent of Roman Catholics and 17 per cent of Protestant church members are Negro. I know of no studies that examine the effects of this difference precisely, but there is no doubt that it reduces the rate of interreligious marriage among Protestants. The regional distribution of religious groups also affects marriage patterns. There is some regional separation in both Holland and the United States, but its effects are difficult to compare. From the Catholic South to the Calvinist Southwest of Holland is a short physical distance when seen beside the American situation, where we can contrast a Protestant South and Middle West with a Catholic Middle Atlantic or, to a lesser degree, New England. All regions are in fact mixed, however, and local patterns of residence with their effects on educational and other contacts, further qualify the picture.

Despite the need for these several qualifications, I believe we can say that intermarriage rates in the United States and Holland are approximately similar. When we go to the other end of the scale of communality, however, the situation is different. In both societies, political and occupational structures exhibit some religious element, but it is stronger in Holland than in the United States. In Holland there are explicitly church-associated political parties which draw most of their support from the separate religious communities. Lijphart gives us the data from a sample differentiated by the degree of regularity or irregularity of church identification—the latter group, presumably, being less likely to be associated with a church-related party (see Table 12–2).

Ninety-nine per cent of Catholic Party supporters are Catholics, with

28 For a discussion of various problems related to the use of intermarriage statistics, see my "Research Note on Interfaith Marriage Statistics," *Journal for the Scientific Study of Religion,* 7, 1968, pp. 97–103. And for a variety of studies of religious intermarriage, see Paul Glick, "Intermarriage and Fertility Patterns among Persons in Major Religious Groups," *Eugenics Quarterly,* 7, 1960, 31–38; Paul Besanceney, "On Reporting Rates of Intermarriage," *American Journal of Sociology,* 70, 1965, pp. 717–721; Hyman Rodman, "Technical Note on Two Rates of Mixed Marriage," *American Sociological Review,* 30, 1965, pp. 776–778; Paul Reiss, "The Trend in Interfaith Marriages," *Journal for the Scientific Study of Religion,* 5, 1965, pp. 64–67; Werner Cahnman, ed., *Intermarriage and Jewish Life: A Symposium;* Jerold Heiss, "Premarital Characteristics of the Religiously Intermarried in an Urban Area," *American Sociological Review,* 25, 1960, pp. 47–55; David Heer, "The Trend of Interfaith Marriages in Canada: 1922–1957," *American Sociological Review,* 27, 1962, pp. 245–250; Lee Burchinal and Loren Chancellor, "Survival Rates among Religiously Homogamous and Interreligious Marriages," *Social Forces,* 41, 1963, pp. 535–362.

Table 12–2. Religion and party preference in Holland, expressed in percentages
(Adapted from Arend Lijphart, *The Politics of Accommodation*,
Berkeley: University of California Press, 1968, p. 31.) *

	Catholic Party (328)	Anti-Revolutionary Party (143)	Christian Historical Union (147)
Catholics, regular	90	2	1
Catholics, irregular	9	0	1
Reformed	0	71	8
Dutch Reformed, regular	0	15	61
Dutch Reformed, irregular	1	8	22
Catholic bloc total, regulars only	90	2	1
Calvinist bloc total, regulars only	0	86	69
Others	0	4	7

* I have omitted reference to the Labor and Liberal Parties and to secularist voters in order to focus on the communal aspects of politics. Percentages are totalled by column.

90 per cent being regular or participant Catholics. The Calvinist parties are somewhat less concentrated religiously, drawing more support from "irregulars" and seculars, yet 86 per cent and 69 per cent of the supporters of the two parties are regular Calvinists.

There are also relationships between party preference and religion in the United States. Jews are substantially more likely and Catholics somewhat more likely to be Democrats whereas Protestants are somewhat more likely to be Republicans than one would expect either on grounds of sheer chance or on the basis of their class location. The data from Lenski expressed in Table 12–3 indicate the pattern in one city.

Table 12–3. Religion and party preference in the Detroit area, expressed in percentages (Adapted from Gerhard Lenski, *The Religious Factor*, Garden City, N.Y.: Doubleday & Co, Inc., 1961, p. 175.)

	Republican Party) (360)	Democratic Party (658)
White Catholics		
High involvement	22	31
Low involvement	3	10
White Protestants		
High involvement	29	10
Low involvement	39	26
Others	7	23

Again it is difficult to make a direct comparison of the information from Holland and the United States. I have transposed the percentages from Lenski's table to make them run down the column, as they do in Table 12–2, have consolidated the classes, and have given the data for white respondents only. I do not know to what degree Lenski's "high involvement-low involvement" distinction is equivalent to Lijphart's "regular-irregular" distinction. The ratio of Protestants to Catholics is slightly higher in the American study. In spite of these various ambiguities, it seems clear that the tendency toward communality in politics in this American community is considerably less than in the Dutch sample. To be sure, white Protestants, who represent only 47 per cent of the total sample, make up 68 per cent of the Republican group; but this is true only if we include those who are low in involvement as well as those high. The Democratic Party is less closely associated with Catholicism, because it has almost as many white Protestant as white Catholic adherents, and in addition, a large number of Negroes, most of whom are Protestants.

Perhaps these brief references to communal elements in marriage and politics will serve to illustrate the range in the degree to which religious differentiation matches social differentiation. I have suggested that occupational separation was perhaps the most likely to disappear, at least in urban societies. Where present it is most indicative of a strong communal pattern. It is significant, therefore, that in Holland even occupational separation by religion is readily visible, although by no means complete, whereas it is of less importance in the United States.[29] There is a similar contrast in educational communality.

With such data as we have, it is possible only to say that the United States falls perhaps in the middle of the scale of religious group communality while Holland falls near the upper end. Lacking adequately comparable data and a refined index, I will conclude this comment on the denominational sources of social divisions by suggesting two further critical questions: What conditions support religious communality? And what are its consequences for society. Wilensky and Ladinsky raise the former question in connection with occupations in a way that relates it to even broader questions:

under what conditions and in what groups and strata do occupational cultures (rooted in common tasks, work schedules, job training, and career patterns) and corporate cultures (rooted in the organizational context of work) overcome other sources of behavior? When does work shape social life more than ethnic-religious cultures (sustained by common descent and early socialization) or class cultures (sustained by common occupational stratum and similar levels of income and education) or "community" and "neighborhood" cultures (sustained by demographic and ecological features of the locality)? [30]

We can profitably ask similar questions in connection with each of the columns in Table 12–1. Only when we have fuller answers than now seem possible can we speak with confidence about the conditions that determine the level of religious group communality.

The consequences of various levels are also poorly understood. Two mutually limiting if not mutually contradictory values condition our judgments: Strong religious communality lends strength to a society by fur-

29 See Arend Lijphart, op. cit.; and Harold Wilensky and Jack Ladinsky, "From Religious Community to Occupational Group: Structural Assimilation among Professors, Lawyers, and Engineers," *American Sociological Review*, 32, 1967, pp. 541–561.

30 Ibid., pp. 541–542.

nishing groups with which an individual can identify and through which his interests and competing judgments can be expressed—the pluralistic argument. Strong religious communality weakens a society by dividing it along lines of maximum symbolic value to individuals, reinforcing the ever-present economic and political tensions—the conflict argument. American social scientists have generally tried to reconcile these two positions by accepting a kind of modified pluralism. On the one hand, well-organized groups with which individuals feel closely identified are regarded as the best ways to maximize freedom, create channels for the expression of interests, prevent alienation, and achieve some flexibility in the system. On the other hand, cross-cutting memberships that prevent the piling up of differences are considered necessary to safeguard society from splitting into such distinctive units that mobility, political compromise, and national action would be prevented. It is my judgment, although it would be difficult to defend in detail, that most observers are content with a level of religious communality that includes marital and substantial friendship supports (with most close friends chosen from one's own religious group), are ambivalent about educational and residential communality (parochial schools and religiously selective neighborhoods), and opposed to political and occupational communality.[31]

I would not want to quarrel with this appraisal; but perhaps it needs more specification. A high degree of religious group communality is associated in Holland with a stable democracy. In Canada it is not a major obstacle to social cohesion and stable politics, although there is probably a higher level of stress. It has been more divisive in Austria.[32] It is clear that additional factors are involved. Lijphart points to nationalism, the presence of national symbols, similar income profiles among religious groups, the relatively prolonged period of economic development, the fact that major problems of modernization occurred in a staggered fashion rather than all at once (a point strongly emphasized by Lipset), and other factors that moderate the possible divisive influence of strong religious communality in Holland. Many of these conditions doubtless have general significance.

In sum, the degree of religious group communality is an important element in a social structure. It enters into a variety of compounds, however, so that its consequences can be understood only in relationship to the history and present circumstances of the society under analysis.

SOCIAL SOURCES OF ECUMENISM

Our study of the interactions of religion and society would be incomplete if we paid attention to fission but not to fusion. The contemporary scene is filled with evidences of the reduction of lines of division among religious groups as well as with signs of continuing separation. Seen in terms of commissions and councils, the tendencies toward church unity appear to be the working out of religious ideas and values. Because these ideas and

31 See, for example, William Kornhauser, *The Politics of Mass Society;* and Seymour Lipset, *Political Man.*

32 See Alfred Diamont, *Austrian Catholics and the First Republic;* John Porter, *The Vertical Mosaic: An Analysis of Social Class and Power in Canada;* and Lijphart, op. cit.

values have been available for a long time, however, we must ask why they have become salient in the contemporary world. It seems likely that the "social sources of denominationalism" can be matched by the "social sources of ecumenism."

Not unexpectedly, various words relating to this topic are used to describe a series of overlapping ideas. From *encounter* and *dialogue* to *church integration* and *unity* we have a range that can be studied more adequately if we put it into some kind of order. I have found it helpful to use the term *ecumenical* in a rather literal sense: what binds the world together religiously. We can think of it as the limiting case or the most intensive expression of tendencies toward universalism which are also found in more moderate form. Thus ecumenism can be expressed as a variable, ranging from a minimum in the lower left of Figure 12–1 to a maximum in the

The extent of inter-religious unity		The range of interreligious unity			
		Interdenominational			Interfaith
		I	II	III	IV
Integration	5	Various Protestant unions			
Federation	4	National and World Councils of Churches			
Cooperation	3	World Fellowship of Buddhists	Various actions of Vatican II		
Conversation	2			Encounter of world religions	Christian-communist dialogue
Toleration	1				

FIGURE 12–1. *Ecumenism defined as a variable*

upper right. The vertical axis refers to the extent of interreligious unity, with different steps designated by familiar terms, while the horizontal axis refers to the range of religious differences being spanned by an ecumenical activity. Several varieties of ecumenical activity are included in the figure to illustrate the range.

I shall not undertake a review of the various forms of ecumenism. A few references, however, may create a context in which we can explore its sources and its limits, our purpose being to state some general principles of value in the scientific study of ecumenical activity in many settings.

A first glance at Japan reveals far more pressure toward proliferation than toward unity of church organizations. A restrictive Religious Organizations Law, passed in 1939, had required the consolidation of religious groups for purposes of stronger governmental control. The number of Buddhist denominations, for example, was reduced from fifty-six to twenty-eight. There was an abrupt shift in 1945, with proclamations of religious liberty and the separation of church and state in the midst of a chaotic environment. Many clergy were dead or wounded; thousands of temples had been damaged or destroyed; financial resources were meager; and the military defeat brought with it a severe challenge to all received ideas—religious as well as political and economic. Within a few years, two hundred and sixty Buddhist groups had registered themselves as corporations under a postwar ordinance.

Denominational splits and new religious movements were not the only products of those years, however. Referring again to Buddhism, we may note the growth of interdenominational agencies and committees, the founding of a weekly publication, and an annual All-Japan Buddhist Conference, sponsored by the Japan Buddhist Conference. At the same time Buddhism was being renewed in other countries; a World Fellowship of Buddhists was formed. The first conference, held in Ceylon in 1950, and subsequent biannual conferences have brought Buddhists together from Mahayana and Theravada lands, with Japan prominent among the former. Buddhists from mainland China visited Japan in 1955 and an organization was formed to promote interchange.[33]

Ecumenism has probably developed more fully in Europe and North America than in the East. It ranges from local community churches and federations, to the union of national denominations, to the National Council of Churches and the World Council of Churches, to various ecumenical implications of the Second Vatican Council.[34] On each of these levels there are strong forces at work. Where councils of churches have often spanned a fairly narrow range, they are now becoming more inclusive. In Texas, for example, a Conference of Churches has been formed that includes the ten dioceses of the Roman Catholic Church, the Greek Orthodox diocese of the state, and twenty-seven Protestant denominations.[35] Up to now the merger of Protestant groups has usually meant the bringing together

33 This material is drawn substantially from Joseph Kitagawa, *Religion in Japanese History*, pp. 290–295.

34 See Robert M. Brown, *The Ecumenical Revolution;* Walter Abbott, ed., *Documents of Vatican II*, particularly pp. 336–370 for the decree "On Ecumenism"; Augustin Cardinal Bea, *The Church and the Jewish People;* Lukas Vischer, ed., *A Documentary History of the Faith and Order Movement, 1927–1963;* Robert Lee, *The Social Sources of Church Unity;* Bernard Leeming, *The Vatican Council and Christian Unity;* Paul Crow, *The Ecumenical Movement in Bibliographic Outline.* See also *The Ecumenical Review* and *Journal of Ecumenical Studies.*

35 *The New York Times,* Jan. 28, 1969, p. 21. It should be noted that the largest Protestant denomination in the state, the Baptist General Convention, is not a participant in the Conference. Nor has its range of activities been defined.

of a few closely related denominations, but conversations are currently under way in the United States to explore the union of eight major groups. This was first proposed by Eugene Carson Blake in 1960; and by 1966 representatives had agreed on the general principles for ultimate merger.[36]

Part of the bringing up to date, which was a major goal of the Second Vatican Council, was an ecumenical emphasis, represented on the minimum level by recognition of the "ecclesiastical reality" of other churches and on a more organizational level by the presence of observers from other faiths and by the beginning of discussions about cooperation with the World Council of Churches. There were nonvoting Catholic delegates to the 1968 assembly of the World Council and Catholics have now become members of its Faith and Constitution Committee. Full membership of the Roman Catholic Church in the World Council seems unlikely in the near future, if for no other reason than the fact that Catholics would outnumber the 300 million Protestant and Orthodox members represented in the Council by about two to one.[37] But there has been a shift "from diatribe to dialogue," as Brown puts it, from toleration (and not always that) to conversation and cooperation. A few Catholic scholars teach and lecture at Protestant theological schools, and a few Protestants at Catholic theological schools. All of this is to say that there has been some movement up Column II of Figure 12–1.

There are also some beginnings of ecumenism that reach across major religious lines and even over to secular faiths. These are represented by Columns III and IV. In *Christianity and the Encounter of the World Religions*, Paul Tillich discussed both the difficulties and, as he saw it, the necessity for interreligious conversation. He noted the contrasts between Buddhism and Christianity—the essential detachment of the former, the impulse (often blocked) toward transformation of society in the latter. But even if the dialogue, when pressed far enough, comes to a "preliminary end," as Tillich believed, because of important differences in basic perspectives, there is room for a great deal of encounter before that point is reached.[38] His evaluation has begun to be matched by activity that goes beyond the long-established scholarly work in comparative religion; that is, there has been movement from level 1 to level 2.

Christian-Marxian encounter has also increased. If this is a fairly low-level ecumenism, it should nevertheless be recognized as a product of re-

36 The following churches are involved: Protestant Episcopal, United Presbyterian Church in the U.S.A., Presbyterian Church in the United States, United Methodist Church (which now includes the Evangelical United Brethren), United Church of Christ, Disciples of Christ, African Methodist Episcopal Church; African Methodist Episcopal Zion Church, and the Christian Methodist Episcopal Church.

37 As of 1968, there were 237 churches represented in the World Council. These are based in 80 countries. Most of the Eastern Orthodox Churches are members, including the Russian, which joined in 1961. Cordiality toward the idea of Roman Catholic membership varies, with churches from Europe and North America often favoring it, although some of those from former "mission" areas, where competition has sometimes been sharp, are more opposed.

38 See Paul Tillich, *Christianity and the Encounter of the World Religions*, especially Chap. 3, "A Christian-Buddhist Conversation."

ligious developments in both communist and noncommunist countries.[39]

The upper right quadrant of Figure 12–1 remains nearly empty, despite many fundamental ideas of the world religions, despite dreams of a religion of humanity, despite such efforts as those of Baha'i to blend traditional faiths into a new universalism.[40] For all the important ecumenical developments, the world is so divided by circumstance, citizenship, traditional outlook, race, and personal inclinations that religious differentiation is more strongly supported than religious unity.

The Causes and Functions of Ecumenism. No one can doubt the severe limits placed on religious unity; yet there have been significant developments in the last few decades. What has set them in motion? On the structural level, various differentiating factors have been reduced. In the United States, many "immigrant churches" lose their identity with the decline of distinctive languages, the fading of memories of national origin, and dispersal of the national group through the country and the economy.[41] Mobility and suburbanization have sharply reduced the sense of denominationalism for many Protestants.[42] Differences based on isolation, rural-urban contrasts, and regionalism have been reduced. Common problems have brought churches together.

Such structural changes would not produce tendencies toward unity if they were not given cultural support. A dedicated denominationalist may be made only more dedicated if he senses that his distinctive group is faced with erosion. For many groups, however, there has been a convergence of values. The salience of various differentiating beliefs and rites has fallen, while the salience of shared values has increased. This is partly because many groups have lost earlier sectarian qualities; it is also partly because the severe problems faced by nations and the world have tended to draw increased attention to the need for cooperation, tolerance, and brotherhood. Some observers put an opposite face on these cultural changes. They believe that ecumenism is made possible only by "indifferentism," by a decline of commitment. "If I held my values strongly," this seems to say, "I would not so easily reconcile myself to collaboration or union of my religious group with other groups whose values are in some measure different." I find this argument inadequate for two reasons: Indifference is more likely to lead to apathy than to ecumenical activity. And the concept of indifference itself is not very powerful. The salience of particular beliefs may rise or fall, but this is not a sign of loss of values. "Indifferentism" is usually

39 See the valuable comments by Harvey Cox, *On* NOT *Leaving it to the Snake*, Chaps. 6–8; and Roger Garaudy and Quentin Lauer, *A Christian-Communist Dialogue*. It is interesting to note that the Vatican Secretariat for Non-Believers, in a document issued in 1968, saw little prospect for conversations with communists, but called for wide-ranging dialogue with atheists. (Reported in Honolulu *Advertiser*, Oct. 2, 1968.)

40 For an interesting statement of a kind of humanist ecumenism, see Henry A. Murray, "A Mythology for Grownups," *Saturday Review*, Jan. 23, 1960, pp. 10–12.

41 See Nicholas Tavuchis, *Pastors and Immigrants: The Role of a Religious Elite in the Absorption of Norwegian Immigrants*. The original influence of immigration is shown clearly by Richard Niebuhr, op. cit.

42 In a national sample, between 51 and 57 per cent of Congregationalists, Episcopalians, Methodists, and Presbyterians shared the denomination of their fathers. The percentages for Lutherans and Baptists were somewhat higher (65 and 72). See Rodney Stark and Charles Glock, *American Piety*, p. 195.

a value-laden term that means "a regrettable drop in the salience of certain beliefs." Scientific study is better served by study of the conditions that influence the rise and fall of the strength of the full range of beliefs.

Not everybody who experiences these structural and cultural changes is equally likely to support church unity. The strength of attachment to a traditional group doubtless varies with normal socialization, some people being taught that membership in a particular church is vital, others being taught that many groups offer roads to salvation that are about equally acceptable. More general tendencies, however, are probably also involved. The insecure person, the possessor of a "closed mind," and the individual with authoritarian tendencies are all less likely to accept loss of group identity in favor of some larger pattern.[43]

Ecumenism emerges, then, out of a constellation of certain structural, cultural, and character sources. What are its probable consequences, and how far will it go? Those involved in the movement see it as a source of religious renewal, of ferment, of needed change. The unification of structures has often been accompanied by increased attention to international and racial conflict, by concern for the growing contrasts between the *haves* and the *have-nots*, and by vigorous debate over religious doctrine, practice, and organization. It rekindles the vision of a genuinely universal religion.

Others see a loss of pluralistic variety. They see various unions being hammered out by a political process that leaves the two extremes unrepresented. They see bureaucratization and the usual struggles for control of the mechanisms of influence. They see a great deal of energy being spent in trying to handle problems related to doctrinal and ritual differences that, viewed even from a short distance, seem quite small, and from a longer distance seem picayune. They see the intrusion of international political tensions, with national and class perspectives blocking the development of a religiously unified position. And even where substantial unity may be achieved, the dilemma of the churches, raised now to a higher power, cannot be avoided. This is not to say, however, that its sharpness cannot be reduced by skilled strategy.

We will best understand ecumenism, in my judgment, if we study it in context with forces that continue to support religious separation. "A Protestant congregation collapses when it cannot recruit a socially homogeneous membership."[44] This may be an excessively strong statement; but it expresses one of the influences at work, not only in suburban Protestantism but in sectarian and ecclesiastical groups as well. To some degree we see the paradox of ecumenical unity being sought by separated and internally homogeneous units.

The contemporary world is witnessing both more ecumenism and more separatism. On the one side we see the World Fellowship of Buddhists, Vatican II, and the World Council of Churches. On the other we see the proliferation of new religions in Japan, the presence of messianic sects in Africa, Cargo cults in Melanesia, Protestant fundamentalism in North and South America, experimental, underground groups in many parts of the

43 See Milton Rokeach, *The Open and Closed Mind;* Muzafer Sherif, *Intergroup Conflict and Cooperation: The Robbers Cave Experiment.*

44 Gibson Winter, *The Suburban Captivity of the Churches,* p. 69.

urban world, Black Muslims and other forms of black separatism, and various quasireligious groups that express deep ideological conflicts in the world more than an ideology of brotherhood. To put this last point in an oversharp way, it may be that various forms of ecumenism prosper because they are dealing with the shallow and unimportant divisions among men. As Robert Hoyt puts it: "There is a great deal more obvious relevancy and liveliness in the question whether the New Left will be able to come to terms with Black Nationalism than there is in the issue of whether intercommunion may perhaps come to be permitted on specific well-defined occasions some time in the next decade." [45]

A dedicated conflict theorist is likely to say: If there is ecumenism it is because the universalism it expresses is unimportant or because it is symbolically useful in some new form of conflict. (If I were to put this in its most cynical form, it would read: Ecumenism is the enlargement of the religious organization of the haves in order to deal more effectively with the have-nots at a time when the split has grown from a local or national to an international question.)

A dedicated functional theorist is likely to say: Interdependence having grown, and mobility and continuous contact having become facts of life in the contemporary world, religious forms expressive of these new facts have selectively evolved. They will function to give unity to larger, now highly interdependent groups by bringing them into one system of sacred symbols. Without such a system of shared sacred symbols, a world made suddenly and dramatically small will carry an enormous burden of tension; it might not be able to survive at all.

A field theorist (one says *dedicated* only with reference to someone else's theory) is likely to say: All of these things are true, but they are mutually limiting and must therefore be seen together. To some degree the ecumenical movement is irrelevant to the major conflicts of the day; it unites where union is easy. To some degree it is a movement of the prosperous: Comfortable people drive big cars to rather lavish villas and conference sites to think big thoughts about how to keep their combined churches influential. But to a significant degree, ecumenism represents an evolutionary development in religious forms in the context of a rapidly changing environment. Many of the religiously sensitive, wondering what will be effective in such a thoroughly interdependent world, are impelled toward more inclusive religious structures even though it means relinquishing various dearly held rites and symbols. How far this will go is dependent not only on their thinking and efforts, but on the direction of structural change and cultural evolution in the world. Ecumenism cannot create universalism, but it can contribute to other forces in that direction by giving them a superempirical perspective that challenges limited perspectives on the world condition.

45 In *The Religious Situation: 1968*, Donald Cutler, ed., p. 576.

Chapter Thirteen

TYPES OF RELIGIOUS ORGANIZATIONS

Discussion of the sources of religious differentiation leads naturally to examination of its various outcomes. One of the effects of the pressures toward schism, of the variations in religious interest and need among the members of differentiated societies, is the development of different religious group structures. These vary widely; but if our aim is a generalizing science we cannot be content simply to describe the individual forms—we must design a classification system.[1] Classifications are in one sense arbitrary. They oversimplify the data by disregarding what are held to be minor differences in order to emphasize what are thought to be major similarities. They are constructs of the mind, not descriptions of total reality. Moreover, classifications are specialized instruments, appropriate only to particular tasks. If one tries to use them for a different purpose, he will find the schemes inadequate. If, for example, one were studying the economic consequences of ill-health, he might classify illnesses according to the length of time they persisted and the costs of treatment. Such a scheme would be virtually useless, however, if one were concerned with the causes of sickness.

The system of classification of religious groups that I shall develop is an effort to describe typical relationships between religion and society. We have already described types of individual religious experience; and our discussion of the different interpretations of evil and of roads to salvation was concerned with types of religious organizations based on cultural distinctions. The types I shall describe here will cut across these distinctions and other lines of division such as those based on kinds of aesthetic activity or extent of supernaturalism. They will be completely inappropriate for

[1] There is an extensive literature dealing with problems of the classification of religious organizations. I will cite a number of relevant titles in a bibliographical postscript at the end of this chapter.

classifications based on valuational criteria. In the discussion that follows, we shall build on and extend the analysis of the causes of religious differentiation given in Chapter Twelve, and relate the variations in religious structure to the question of the functions of religion.

Church and Sect: The Heritage of Ernst Troeltsch

Most classifications of religious groups start from the basic distinction, first fully developed by Ernst Troeltsch, between the *church* and the *sect*, a distinction derived from an early one between *priest* and *prophet,* but used with more methodological sophistication and with reference primarily to group structure, not to leadership. The development of this instrument of analysis inevitably gives emphasis to the differences between church and sect, minimizing the similarities that all of the religious organizations within a particular sociocultural system share in common. The Jehovah's Witnesses and the Catholic Church, for example, appear to be very different when they are viewed from close range. On the basis of a wide culturally comparative study, however, their many similarities become apparent. Murray makes this point with regard to a temporal comparison:

Take three orthodox Christians, enlightened according to the standards of their time, in the fourth, the sixteenth, and the twentieth centuries respectively. I think you will find more profound differences of religion between them than between a Methodist, a Catholic, a Freethinker, and even perhaps a well-educated Buddhist or Brahmin at the present day, provided you take the most generally enlightened representatives of each class.[2]

In constructing a typology, we will do well to keep clearly in mind that it represents a deliberate stress placed on distinctions, in order to highlight various functions of religious groups. From a different temporal perspective or for different purposes other lines of division would appear.

The twofold scheme of classification developed by Troeltsch has proved to be a powerful concept for the analysis of Christian differentiation, particularly in the early modern period. As a general typology, however, it suffers from several weaknesses which I shall hope to reduce. It is difficult in any dichotomous typology to give an adequate picture of the full range of the data. The empirical world is filled with many mixtures and variations of degree which a system of classification must try to describe. If *church* and *sect* are designated as end points on a continuum, the description of intermediate positions can prevent misunderstanding. By his addition of the concept of *mysticism,* Troeltsch broadened the typology, but this served to point up a second difficulty in his classification: its failure to discuss adequately the conditions in which various types of religious organizations were most likely to occur. He notes that they all stem from fundamental Christian ideas and describes their relationship to social crises and historical movements; but he is more concerned with their variations as religious systems than in specifying sharply the social and personality factors involved in the various religious-group types. A third problem for our purposes was the explicit limitation to Christian organizations in Troeltsch's discussion.

2 Gilbert Murray, *Five Stages of Greek Religion,* p. 212.

The Church. Keeping these difficulties in mind, we may profitably describe the church and the sect in Troeltsch's terms. We shall then see what extensions might give a more adequate picture of the range of types of religious groups. The church as a type is a religious body that recognizes the strength of the secular world and, rather than either abandoning the attempt to influence it or losing its position by contradicting the secular powers directly, accepts the main elements in the social structure as proximate goods. (As we shall see, some churches have defended an existing power arrangement not simply as a proximate good, but almost as though it were an absolute good.) The church is built, therefore, on compromise; it is mobile and adaptive; "it dominates the world and is therefore dominated by the world." An individual is born into the church, which claims universality, by contrast with the voluntary membership of a select group in the sect. The church supports the existing powers in peace and war. It "utilizes the State and the ruling classes, and weaves these elements into her own life; she then becomes an integral part of the existing social order; from this standpoint, then, the Church both stabilizes and determines the social order; in so doing, however, she becomes dependent upon the upper classes, and upon their development." [3]

The emphasis of the church is on sacrament and creed, whereas that of the sect is on "right" behavior. Of the two primary functions of religion we have discussed, the one stressed by the church is the effort to insure social cohesion and order. The church must thus strive to be coextensive with society, to bring everyone within its "means of grace." To do this, however, requires a willingness to compromise with the wide ranges of behavior found in a society. "The moral demands are relaxed because salvation depends not upon ethical achievement but upon the reception of the sacraments and acquiescence in the creeds. . . . Discipline tends to be moderate and the ban may be more readily used to exclude those who question the faith than those who fail to realize the ethical standards." [4]

This "function-dysfunction" of social integration may well be latent in the church, for its manifest intentions are more likely to be the assurance of individual salvation. The fact that the support for "social order" is latent, however, makes it no less real or powerful. It creates the continuing possibility—indeed, the likelihood—that a religious system in which the church-type organization is predominant will serve to reinforce the power situation of the dominant classes of a society. In the logical extreme, the church-type lends itself to the support of an authoritarian pattern of order. This is the product of the compromises that are forced on a church when it tries to organize the whole of society.

A church, thus defined, is almost impossible in a mobile and heterogeneous society, particularly one that is based on democratic values. Such a church can be thought of as a limiting case, which actual situations approximate more or less closely. More empirically possible churchlike types will be described later, when we come to elaborate this typology.

The Sect. Astute religious leaders are aware of the possibility of capitula-

3 Troeltsch, op. cit., p. 331.

4 Roland H. Bainton, "The Sectarian Theory of the Church," *Christendom*, Summer, 1946, p. 382.

tion to secular powers; they realize the dilemma we have discussed and seek to reduce its sharpness by incorporating within the religious pattern some attention to the needs of the individual. But if some of these needs are—or are thought to be—a product of the very society which the religious system also supports, the church is unlikely to be successful with those who feel those needs most strongly. When, because of compromises with the secular powers, rigidity of ecclesiastical structure, the failure of doctrine and ritual to change as prevailing personality inclinations change (what are appealing symbols to one generation may lack meaning to another), the religious system loses some of its ability to satisfy various individual and group needs, sectarian developments are promoted.

As we shall see, the kinds of needs to which sectarian movements are related vary widely, as do the types of ways in which those needs are served. Study was first directed toward the sectarian movements of the lower classes—protests against the failures of the church to satisfy them emo tionally, to give them a sense of dignity, to challenge those aspects of society that the sectarians felt were unjust and sinful. Thus they rejected the church and frequently the society they identified with it. This is the primary emphasis in Troeltsch's discussion of the sect. It is a group that repudiates the compromises of the church, preferring "isolation to compromise"; in the Christian tradition it stresses literal obedience to the Synoptic Gospels. There is a small, voluntary membership, which stresses individual perfection and asceticism, and is usually associated with the lower classes.[5] It is either hostile or indifferent to the state, and opposes the ecclesiastical order. The sect is lay religion, free from worldly authority, and therefore able on the one hand to forget the world in asceticism, or on the other to fight it in radicalism. Troeltsch lists its traits:

lay Christianity, personal achievement in ethics and in religion, the radical fellowship of love, religious equality and brotherly love, indifference toward the authority of the State and the ruling classes, dislike of technical law and of the oath, the separation of the religious life from the economic struggle by means of the ideal of poverty and frugality . . . , the directness of the personal religious relationship, criticism of official spiritual guides and theologians, the appeal to the New Testament and the Primitive Church.[6]

Werner Stark has made perhaps the most intensive use of Troeltsch's concept of the sect, strictly defined. It is a one-generation conflict organization. "The last root of all sectarianism lies in the alienation of some group from the inclusive society within which it has to carry on its life. It is a kind of protest movement . . . ,"[7] distinguished by the fact that its opposition is expressed religiously. The fundamental cause of alienation in Stark's judgment is economic disprivilege. He is not entirely consistent in this emphasis, however, for he notes the part played by political and personal alienation as well, and he observes that now it may be the lonely more than the hungry who are attracted to sectarian movements.

Sectarian protests are not moderately in opposition to society; they are

5 See Russell R. Dynes, "Church-Sect Typology and Socio-Economic Status," *American Sociological Review*, October, 1955, pp. 555–560.

6 Troeltsch, op. cit., p. 336.

7 Werner Stark, *The Sociology of Religion*, Vol. 2, p. 5.

sharply in conflict with it. "The sect is typically a contraculture." [8] Stark describes three kinds of bifurcations of a sectarian protest movement to indicate the ways it contravenes the norms of society: It can be oriented to the glorious past or the glorious future (the present is repudiated); it can emphasize strict, ascetic morality or a licentious, indulgent morality (moderation is repudiated); it can respond passively or violently to the world around it (cooperation is repudiated). He believes that these are independent responses, so that all eight of the possible combinations may occur; but this must be regarded as a hypothesis requiring further demonstration.

By defining the term *sect* quite narrowly, as indeed Troeltsch did, Stark gains a sharp image of what it stands for: a short-lived religious protest against deprivation. Because he uses only two other concepts, however—namely, *universal church* and *established church*—either those terms must take on broader meaning or there are gaps in his classification. In fact, *universal church* is also defined quite strictly, so that *established church*, the "middle term" in Stark's system, has to cover the major part of the range of religious systems. This presents no problems if it is carefully subclassified and not used simply as a residual category. It is the latter, however, which tends to be the case in Stark's usage.

I shall broaden the meaning of the term *sect* somewhat, by relating it to several forms of deprivation and by leaving open the possibility that it may be prolonged past the first generation. By *sect* we shall refer to a religious protest against a system in which attention to the various individual functions of religion has been obscured and made ineffective by the extreme emphasis on social and ecclesiastical order. This emphasis often takes the form of primary attention to rite and dogma, with strong latent implications for the question of order. There can be no doubt that the need for some adjustment to the problems of poverty and powerlessness (age-old problems in every religion) should be given, as Troeltsch gives them, primary attention. This analysis does not explain, however, such middle- and upper-class developments as Christian Science or the Oxford Group movement, religious groups that represent protests against the failure of established churches to deal successfully with feelings of inadequacy, confusion, ennui, pain, and guilt. If these are included in the same concept, we may define a sect as a movement in which the primary emphasis is the attempt to satisfy various basic individual needs by religious means. It is usually seen as a revolt against a religious system in which these needs have been inadequately dealt with. *What* these needs are will vary from group to group. *How* they are treated in the sect will also vary, creating the necessity for subclassifying sectarian movements.

In the logical extreme, the sect emphasis on religious beliefs and practices that are efforts to deal with individual needs—with a minimum attention to the function of social integration—leads to anarchy. The sectarian associates order with the disliked order of the church and society in which he feels his needs are smothered. This may lead to the avoidance of any political claims over him, the rejection of some of the moral standards of

8 Ibid., p. 129. By this term, I have sought to distinguish norms that rather specifically reverse, rather than simply differing from, the dominant norms. See my paper "Contraculture and Subculture," *American Sociological Review*, 25, 1960, pp. 625–635.

the society (note the various experiments by extreme sectarians with new patterns of sexual morals or forms of marriage), and the repudiation of other aspects of the supposed wicked society—learning and art, for example. Seldom is this potentiality for anarchy carried to the extreme, but the tendencies are there, just as the tendencies for authoritarian rigidity are present in the church.

The sect cannot, however, avoid the problem of order. The problem begins immediately to reassert itself even in the isolated communities into which the sectarians sometimes withdraw. Moreover, the needs of the members may change—their socioeconomic level may improve, for example. The leadership tends to become established and to look for ways of assuring continuity of power. With the coming of a second generation, the problem of voluntary membership becomes acute, for parents are neither willing nor able to postpone the training of their children. Thus the sect may move back toward the church.[9] In mobile societies, where problems of order and the nature of human needs are undergoing continuous change, the dialectic between church and sect seems likely to continue. Even the syntheses of a St. Thomas and a Calvin were highly unstable, and there have been no approximations to a synthesis in the last three centuries. Indeed, the interactions between churchly and sectarian tendencies are among the most important processes of modern societies.

REFINEMENT AND EXTENSION OF THE CHURCH-SECT TYPOLOGY

Although the church-sect dichotomy can be a highly informative concept, it is not adequate to describe the full range of the data.[10] On the basis of three criteria, I will suggest a typology that may permit comparisons among a wide variety of religious groups. It should be treated as a series of abstract and constructed models against which particular groups can be measured, for purposes of contrast and comparison. Seldom will an existent group correspond in detail to one of the models. We shall note below some of the

9 See Walter G. Muelder, "From Sect to Church," *Christendom*, Autumn, 1945, pp. 450–462; H. Richard Niebuhr, op. cit., pp. 19–21 and throughout; Liston Pope, *Millhands and Preachers;* and J. Milton Yinger, *Religion in the Struggle for Power,* pp. 31–34.

10 There have been several efforts to design typologies, which the reader will wish to consult. Benton Johnson, noting the fact that a several-variable model would be complex, suggests that religious organizations be classified simply by their degree of acceptance or rejection of the values of society. Like all one-variable models, this has the value of clarity and the disadvantage of putting heterogeneous varieties into the same type. See his paper "On Church and Sect," *American Sociological Review*, 28, 1963, pp. 539–549. Paul Gustafson outlines a two-variable model, each variable having two values: universalism-particularism and objective-subjective means to grace. The resulting four types are based on the possible combinations of two cultural norms, hence leave unexamined the question of relationships to society—the central question in most typologies. See his "UO-US-PS-PO: A Restatement of Troeltsch's Church-Sect Typology," *Journal for the Scientific Study of Religion*, 6, 1967, pp. 64–68. Elmer Clark, *The Small Sects in America,* describes a classification of sects into seven types. The criteria are not entirely clear, but are largely normative, with less attention to society-religion interactions. We have noted Werner Stark's three-variable scheme for classifying sects. And we shall comment later on the work of Howard Becker, C. K. Yang, and Bryan Wilson.

qualifications necessary in the use of abstract types.[11] The three criteria are these:

1. The degree to which the religious group is inclusive of members of a society.

2. The extent to which the group accepts or rejects the secular values and structures of society.

3. The extent to which, as an organization, it integrates a number of units into one structure, develops professional staffs, and creates a bureaucracy.

Not all religious organizations fit readily into the paradigm I shall suggest, and it may be well to comment on two of the exceptions in advance of its description. These will create a frame within which the typology can be set.

The Universal Institutionalized Church. The universal church does not readily fit into a typology of religious organizations because it tends to include all types. Partly as an ideological vision, and approximated as a historical fact, it is a religious structure that is quite successful in supporting the integration of a complex society, while at the same time satisfying, by its pattern of beliefs and observances, many of the needs of individuals on all levels of the society. It combines both church and sect tendencies in a systematic and effective way. It is thus universal both in the sense that it includes all the members of a society and in the fact that the major functions of religion are closely interrelated. It also tends to be characterized by a complex ecclesiastical structure.

In heterogeneous societies, this balance is likely to be achieved only very rarely and is not likely to be maintained very long. The lack of flexibility of the system itself, the insistent demands of the ruling groups that the order favorable to them be maintained without the adjustments inevitable in a changing society, the variations in individual needs—these all lead to the tendency toward schism so common in the religions of complex societies. The Catholic Church of the thirteenth century is perhaps the best illustration of a universal church in Western civilization. It was relatively successful in finding a place (primarily the monasteries) for the individualizing tendencies in Christianity, its system of beliefs and rites was satisfactory to large numbers of people on all levels, and it reflected and helped to maintain a fairly well integrated social structure. In smaller compass, Calvinism approximated a universal church, as have some expressions of Islam.[12]

Werner Stark has argued strongly that the Roman Catholic Church has successfully enclosed its sects—primarily in the form of monastic movements—and has used them to preserve a substantial part of its universal characteristics. He notes that the founders of sects and the founders of religious orders are at first quite similar. "But there is a great—an all-decisive difference. The withdrawal of religious orders from the universal

11 For discussions of the uses and varieties of typologies, see John McKinney, *Constructive Typology and Social Theory;* and Howard Becker, *Through Values to Social Interpretation.*

12 See W. Montgomery Watt, *Islam and the Integration of Society;* Werner Stark, *The Sociology of Religion,* Vol. 3; Ernst Troeltsch, op. cit., pp. 617–625; and Arnold Toynbee, *A Study of History,* Vol. 7.

Church is never as total as the withdrawal of religious sects from an established church; and, above all, it is not as final. After retreat comes re-entry, after a turning away from their community, a turning back toward it." [13]

Unfortunately we have no clear measures by which we can state with certainty the comparative success with which various religious groups have enclosed their own protest movements. Since groups require not only integration, but modes of adaptation to changing circumstances, the long history of the Catholic Church is testimony to its skillful use of both internal and external critics. Perhaps these additional points, however, should be noted: There were many pre-Reformation sectarian protests, and not simply monastic orders, that sprang from Catholicism. Stark pays little attention to them.[14] There was the Reformation itself. The interaction between sects and major Protestant bodies has some similarities with the interaction between the Catholic Church and its monastic orders. In this regard I do not think one can speak of "an all-decisive difference." And there are processes within nonuniversal churches that serve to make use of their internal critics and radicals.[15] Not all are spun off to become sectarians.

Thus the contrast between the universal church and less inclusive groups should not be drawn too sharply. Even the most thoroughly universal church, moreover, can be described as only relatively capable of fulfilling the variety of functions associated with religion, for the intense problem of order, the continuing intrusions of man's egocentric tendencies, and the pervasiveness of the problems of suffering are not difficulties easily to be solved.

One needs to be aware, also, of the continuing possibility of dysfunctions. In this regard it is perhaps well to indicate again that a judgment concerning the church's ability to maintain itself as a "moving equilibrium" and to hold the allegiance of most of the members of a society is not at the same time a value judgment.

The Universal Diffused Church. What we have described is an inclusive religious organization capable of holding together the diverse strata of a complex society. This is an inherently difficult task in societies characterized by mobility, population change, and culture contact, as well as by extensive internal differentiation. One can scarcely speak of the universal institutionalized church in the contemporary urban world. In smaller, less differentiated, and more isolated societies, however, religious unity is more nearly the norm. A shared fate is manifest in a shared faith. In the Durkheimian sense, therefore, one can say that the members of small, homogeneous, often preliterate and tribal societies, are united into a church— "into one single moral community."

Although such a church is universal in one sense, it is different in many ways from what I have called the universal institutionalized church, and the grounds for this differentiation should be made explicit. In a relatively

13 Werner Stark, op. cit., Vol. 3, p. 250.

14 See Norman Cohn, *The Pursuit of the Millennium.*

15 This point is developed in an interesting way by Phillip Hammond and Robert Mitchell, "Segmentation of Radicalism—The Case of the Protestant Campus Minister," *American Journal of Sociology*, 71, 1965, pp. 133–143. Perhaps it is not too much to say that many campus ministers are members of a new kind of urban order.

undifferentiated and isolated society, there is unlikely to be any visible, distinct religious structure, separate from the kinship and political structures. Religious professionalization is at a minimum. Religion is a pervasive quality of the social system more than a separate institution. Building on Wach's contrast between a religion which is coterminous with a "natural group" and "specifically religious groups," Yang has developed a valuable distinction between diffused religion and institutionalized religion.[16] In a tribal society one does not belong to a church; he belongs to the society, which has religious qualities along with its other attributes. One does not need to speak of types of religious organizations, because there are no religious organizations. There are religious beliefs and practices which infuse communal life. The members of such a society are bound together by this shared system of sacred beliefs and practices. I shall call the religious qualities of a communal, undifferentiated society a universal diffused church. It is similar to the universal institutionalized church in its societal scope, but contrasts with it sharply in its organizational structure.

So long as we are dealing with them as analytic types, we need not speak of the varieties of religious organizations in societies characterized either by a universal institutionalized church or by a universal diffused church. There is simply the society's religion. The conditions that make either of these patterns possible, however, are becoming increasingly uncommon in the world. Partially conflictful heterogeneity is the rule in contemporary societies as it has been in many societies in the past. Religious differentiation is a reflection—and to some degree also a cause—of that fact. We shall use the institutionalized-diffused contrast, therefore, as a variable in the classification of differentiated religious systems rather than as an attribute by which societies can be divided into two types. Adding it to measures of inclusiveness and measures of alienation, we arrive at the typology of religious organizations in religiously differentiated societies that is set out in Figure 13–1. This system of classification is enclosed, so to speak, between the two varieties of universal churches.

Variables That Differentiate Types of Religious Groups
The first task of explication of this rather complex paradigm is to make clear the meaning of the three variables that constitute its sorting criteria. Variable I refers simply to the extent to which a religious system includes the members of a society within its constituency. The theoretical range is from an all-inclusive system to a small group with a handful of members. Variable II refers to the degree of accommodation between the values of the secular world and those of the religious group. This can range from the attitude that the economic, political, and other secular structures are natural, good, or even god-given, to the view that "the world" is an abomination. (We shall see that the reasons for this latter attitude, and the types of religious responses that flow from it are highly differentiated.) I have put

16 C. K. Yang, *Religion in Chinese Society*, Chapter 12. This distinction may help to deal with the problems raised in trying to apply a typology to a wide variety of religions. See, for example, G. S. Bhatt's discussion of the inapplicability of church-sect terms to Hinduism, "Brahmo Samaj, Arya Samaj, and the Church-Sect Typology," *Review of Religious Research*, 10, 1968, pp. 23–32.

I. Inclusiveness of the religious structures
High   Low

II. Extent of alienation from societal values
Low   High

A. Universal institutionalized church

	High			
III. Extent of organization, complexity, and distinctiveness of the religious structures	**C.** Institutional ecclesia	**E.** Institutional denomination	rare	null
	D. Diffused ecclesia	**F.** Diffused denomination	**G.** Established sect	null
	rare	rare	**H.** Established lay sect	**I.** Sect Movement
Low	null	null	null	**J.** Charismatic sect

B. Universal diffused church

FIGURE 13–1. *Types of religious organizations*

these two variables along the same axis, although with scale values reversed, because they are strongly inversely correlated. Except for the increase in complexity of the scheme, however, it might be preferable to think of Figure 13–1 in three-dimensional terms.

Variable III refers to the extent to which the religious structure itself has become organized and differentiated. I think it is likely, although it must be offered here as a hypothesis only, that on the basis of three criteria, this variable can be defined by a Guttman scale, representing progressively greater degrees of complexity of religious structure. The three criteria, stated as questions, are these: Are the separate religious organizations (for example, local groups or religious communities) integrated into larger structures; do they identify with one another across community lines, recognizing their religious kinship? Are there religious professionals whose knowledge and skills relative to sacred things set them apart from the laity? And have the religious groups and the professionals developed a hierarchical and bureaucratic structure for the performance of religious tasks and the strengthening of the church?

Since the small tribal society does not, typically, have distinctive religious groups, but only pervasive religious activities, the questions do not arise in this form on the level of what I have called the universal diffused church (B in Figure 13–1). I have placed it therefore as part of the frame for the paradigm of religious organizations. All three questions are answered Yes with reference to the universal institutionalized church (A in Figure 13–1), but because it spans the range of responses to society—from fully accepting to alienated (it institutionalizes ways for alienation to be expressed)—I have placed it too outside the paradigm, as part of the frame.

The questions can be put into a scale as shown in Table 13–1. It may

Table 13–1. Degrees of complexity of religious structures

	Are religious units integrated?	Are there religious professionals?	Is there a bureaucratic structure?
4. Most complex	yes	yes	yes
3.	yes	yes	no
2.	yes	no	no
1. Least complex	no	no	no

well be that these questions are not scalable, and that one should treat them simply as separate characteristics.[17] On the other hand, the scale may not be complicated enough, for it treats the variables in dichotomous fashion, when in fact each can be expressed as a matter of degree. On balance, however, I think this statement of the question allows us to see in an accurate way a critical variable that affects types of religious organizations.

The second task of explication is to examine each of the types that emerge from the paradigm. This is made somewhat simpler by the fact that some of the patterns are empirically unlikely or even impossible, because they involve mutually contradictory criteria. Thus, because we need not discuss a religious organization that is minimally inclusive, maximally alienated, and at the same time highly complex and bureaucratized, I have written "null" in the upper righthand corner. Nor is there any need to discuss a highly inclusive, minimally alienated group, with the lowest level of structural complexity, shown at the lower lefthand corner of Figure 13–1, and also labeled "null." This approximates the definition of the universal diffused church, but this latter type encompasses the whole society, including such alienative tendencies as are found, within its religious system. It thus includes a span across the bottom of the paradigm, just as the universal institutionalized church includes a span across the top.

Some other types seem likely to be rare. We will discuss them only insofar as we need to indicate that we are dealing with continua, with a gradual

17 For some observations on the relationship between professionalization and bureaucratization, which cast some doubt on the ordering I have suggested, see Richard Hall, "Professionalization and Bureaucratization," *American Sociological Review*, 33, 1968, pp. 92–104.

shading off from one type to another. The following types, then, should be regarded as measuring points against which empirical religious organizations can be placed for comparison and contrast.

The Ecclesia

I have borrowed this term from Howard Becker's adaptation of the work of Wiese.[18] Like the universal church, the ecclesia reaches out to the boundaries of the society; formal identification with the group is found on all levels of society. But the ecclesia is less successful than the universal church in incorporating the sect tendencies. It has become so well adjusted to the dominant elements that the needs of many of its adherents, particularly from the lower classes, are frustrated. It is more successful in reinforcing the existing pattern of social integration than in fulfilling the many individual functions of religion. There tend, therefore, to be widespread indifference, sectarian protests, and secular opposition.

The ecclesia, as we are using the term, might be called a universal church in a state of rigidification. Established national churches tend toward the ecclesiastical type, although they vary widely in the degree to which they incorporate sectarian elements. (Compare the contemporary state churches in the Scandinavian countries, which tend in the direction of the universal type, with the Russian Orthodox Church of 1915, which, when confronted with both religious and secular schism, only embraced the established order the more closely. This suggests again the close relationship between type of religion and type of society.) Becker describes the ecclesia in these terms:

The social structure known as the ecclesia is a predominantly conservative body, not in open conflict with the secular aspects of social life, and professedly universal in its aims. . . . The fully developed ecclesia attempts to amalgamate with the state and the dominant classes, and strives to exercise control over every person in the population. Members are *born into* the ecclesia; they do not have to *join* it. It is therefore a social structure somewhat akin to the nation or the state, and is in no sense elective. . . . The ecclesia naturally attaches a high importance to the means of grace which it administers, to the system of doctrine which it has formulated, and to the official administration of sacraments and teaching by official clergy. . . . The ecclesia as an inclusive social structure is closely allied with national and economic interests; as a plurality pattern its very nature commits it to adjustment of its ethics to the ethics of the secular world; it must represent the morality of the respectable majority.[19]

Becker's description of the ecclesia was strongly influenced by the work of Troeltsch. It is based primarily on Christian materials. When we try to apply it to other traditions, we find that some elements of the characterization fit, while others do not. I believe that by subclassifying ecclesia (types

18 In some ways this term has too Western a connotation for our purposes. But perhaps its Greek origins are sufficiently vague—and certainly clouded even in Western usage—to make *ecclesia* acceptable in a typology that I hope crosses traditional lines.

19 Leopold von Wiese, *Systematic Sociology*, adapted and amplified by Howard Becker, pp. 624–628; see pp. 624–628 of this work for a fourfold classification scheme; see also Harold W. Pfautz, "The Sociology of Secularization: Religious Groups," *American Journal of Sociology*, September, 1955, pp. 121–128, for a five-class typology based on the degree of secularization.

C and D in Figure 13–1) we can retain what is valuable while drawing a necessary distinction. The distinction is based on the degree of bureaucratization and hierarchalization of the religious structure, on one hand; or, oppositely, the degree of its diffusion through the society. Critics of commonly available typologies are likely to say: There is no *church* in Hinduism or in Buddhism. Church in this connection is generally close to the meaning of ecclesia, as defined above. In many ways this is a just criticism; in other ways it is not. It cannot well be argued that in India or in many Buddhist lands there are no inclusive religious structures, accommodated to the world around them, to which individuals are affiliated by birth rather than personal choice.[20] In this sense, there are ecclesias in the East. On the other hand, Hinduism and Buddhism *tend to be* more diffused, in the sense in which Yang uses this term. Religious belief and practice are more closely interwoven with kinship structures than is true in societies where Christianity predominates. They are also more local in outlook, so that ecclesiastical hierarchies and bureaucratic structures are less common.

I suggest that we give emphasis to both the similarities and the differences by speaking of institutionalized ecclesia and diffused ecclesia. The noun sets the limits of the type while the adjectives describe its range of variation.

Since each of the world religions has diverse forms, we cannot simply associate the institutionalized ecclesia with some (particularly Christianity) and the diffused ecclesia with others. By definition, all are at least at level 3 in Table 13–1; all have religious professionals and a religious structure that allows one to speak of a religious system in the society, not simply of a series of local religious expressions. And the major traditions vary through time and from society to society. Hinduism certainly tends to be diffused, not institutionalized. There is no Hindu *congregation* in the Western meaning of the term. Yet Brahmanism, in the sense of an organized and partly hierarchical priesthood, has waxed and waned in Indian history.

Buddhism furnishes clearer illustrations of both diffused and institutionalized tendencies. Where it is the dominant faith, as in the Theravada countries, the Sangha, the organization of monks, takes on many of the characteristics of Western ecclesiastical groups, particularly of those that are "established." This is seen particularly in Thailand. "The king of Thailand is the head of the order and appoints the Patriarch or Sangharaja and other high officers of the Sangha. The Sangharaja administers the affairs of the order with the assistance of a cabinet of ten ministers drawn from the Sangha. A state department headed by a civil servant carries out the decisions of the Sangharaja and undertakes the management of Sangha property."[21]

20 The inclusiveness, of course, is incomplete, because there are usually several religious traditions in each society. Where one is clearly dominant, however, we shall use the term *ecclesia*.

21 C. D. S. Siriwardane in *South Asian Politics and Religion*, D. E. Smith, ed., p. 536. Even among Theravada countries, however, there is variation. The Sangha is less structured in Burma than in Thailand. See D. E. Smith, *Religion and Politics in Burma*, Chap. 6. See also Hans-Dieter Evers, "The Buddhist Sangha in Ceylon and Thailand," *Sociologus*, 18, 1968, pp. 20–35.

Buddhism in Thailand is close to an institutional ecclesia. In Mahayana lands, however, it is both more diffused and less inclusive.

Anything more than informal distinctions among ecclesia can be made only when the defining criteria are made explicit and careful measurements carried through. Yang, although he does not use this terminology, offers a valuable list of criteria for determining the degree of institutionalization.[22] Translating his discussion into our terms, I would note that an institutional ecclesia exists when: 1) the size of the professional religious group is large as a ratio of the population; 2) there is a clear hierarchical structure among the professionals; 3) the religious organization has extensive financial resources, including places of worship and of study (as distinct from being diffused throughout the society, as, for example, in household shrines); and 4) there is an organized laity aware of its affiliation with religious structures larger than those of the community. Where the opposite conditions prevail, but in a situation where there is an inclusive religious pattern largely accommodated to the secular world, we will speak of a diffused ecclesia.

The Denomination or Class Church

This religious-group type is still less successful in achieving universality than the ecclesia, because it not only minimizes the sectarian tendency to criticize or withdraw from the social order, but it is also limited by class, racial, and sometimes regional boundaries. It may still be called a church, in the Troeltsch sense, because it is in substantial—though not perfect— harmony with the secular power structure. There are sectarian elements in all of them, however, and all class levels tend to be represented in their membership (although unequally, and to a lesser degree in positions of leadership). This sectarian quality is partly due to the fact that many denominations started out as sects and have not completely escaped their origins. It is also due to the variety of messages implicit in the universal religions. Perhaps most importantly, as an accommodated organization of a subsociety, a denomination is in a partially competitive situation. To put it in terms of our paradigm (Figure 13–1), because it is lower on scale 1, it is higher on scale 2.

One must note the range within this type. In American society, for example, Congregationalism, with fairly persistent sectarian tendencies, differs to some degree from Lutheranism, which is more thoroughly accommodated to the secular powers. In general, however, the denomination is conventional and respectable; it has gone somewhat far along the road of compromise. In a society of religious divisions, in contrast with the relative unity of the Middle Ages, the sect elements are much more likely to form their own institutions, instead of being incorporated into a universal church. Even during the Middle Ages, of course, sectarian and theological protests were evidence of the pressures toward religious diversity.

Denominations are characterized, whether out of necessity or out of conviction, by norms of tolerance. This applies both to their own members, who join voluntarily on the basis of relatively relaxed standards, and to

22 See Yang, op. cit., pp. 307–329.

other religious groups. Tolerance of other groups, as David Martin has observed, does not fall along a straight-line progression from church to denomination to sect. In this regard, the two extremes seem more nearly alike, while the "center" is different. One does not find much tolerance among the "Exclusive Brethren," nor in a church that seeks or claims to encompass the whole society. "It is therefore possible to speak of interdenominationalism, but hardly possible to speak of inter-sectarianism, or inter-ecclesiasticism." [23] This contrast, indeed, suggests a good test for determining whether or not an organization may appropriately be thought of as an ecclesia or as a sect: Does it participate readily in intergroup activities? A sect that does so has become an established sect, if not a denomination. An ecclesia that does so no longer sees itself in inclusive terms; it too has become a denomination. To a substantial degree this characterizes the Catholic Church in the United States. Because we are dealing here with matters of more or less, we cannot speak with precision, hence I shall leave "substantial" poorly defined.

The range among denominations is most visible when we make intersociety comparisons, for in such comparisons the "institutionalized-diffused" distinction we employed in our discussion of ecclesia becomes relevant. Christian denominations tend to be integrated, professionalized, and bureaucratized, that is, to be high on the scale of Table 13–1. Eastern religions are also subject to denominationalizing tendencies, and in some instances the organizations are highly institutionalized, that is, they also belong in Type E. Some of the "new religions" in Japan, for example, are not only quite traditional in doctrine and accommodated to the society around them; they are also highly organized and centralized. The four criteria for determining the degree of institutionalization of ecclesia are also appropriate for denominations; and when we apply them to "Perfect Liberty Kyōdan," for example, we find it on the institutionalized side.

There are both sect and cult tendencies (as we shall use these terms below) in the new religions, however. They do not so clearly represent institutional denominations in Japan as do the older divisions of Buddhism and Shinto. These are variously called schools, sects, cults, and religions, but I would judge the older Pure Land, Zen, and Nichiren divisions of Buddhism, for example, to fit our definition of denomination quite closely.[24] And as a result of urban life and of competition from new movements, they have tended to move significantly from the diffused toward the institutionalized category. (Only precise data would allow one to say they had "crossed the line.")

In other contexts, this shift has not taken place. The diffused characteristics more likely to be found in rural and less mobile societies still prevail. Thus Muslims in India are closer to the category of a diffused denomina-

23 David Martin, "The Denomination," *British Journal of Sociology*, 13, 1962, pp. 1–14. The quotation is from p. 214 of his book *Pacifism: An Historical and Sociological Study*, in which the paper is reprinted.

24 In societies where there is no dominant ecclesiastical organization, the terms *sect* and *cult* are often used to mean, not a movement protesting against society and the prevailing religious structure, but a small, often charismatically-based variant of dominant religious themes. I think we will avoid misunderstanding if these are identified as diffused denominations.

tion than an institutionalized one. Compared with the older Buddhist denominations in Japan, there are fewer Muslim professionals, a less hierarchical formation, and a lesser degree of organization among the laity. It is not their qualities as cultural systems, however, which determine this relationship, for in different societies this pattern is reversed, with Muslims being more institutionalized and Buddhists more diffused. In China, for example, during the modern period, the Buddhist priesthood has been small, without a strong central organization, and their economic resources have been meager. There have been periods in Chinese history when Buddhism was more structured and institutionalized; but as Yang observes, such periods have been the exception. He treats Buddhism as an institutionalized religion, as contrasted with the more diffuse magical cults and ancestor worship, even during the periods when it has been weakest. That is to say, it falls in the upper half of the scale in Table 13–1. I do not disagree with this judgment, but am simply indicating that through most of its history, it has been in the lower ranges of that half, perhaps at level 3.

In most societies where it is found, Islam is more nearly an ecclesia (and perhaps in some instances a universal church) than a denomination. It is technically inclusive, but exhibits a number of sectarian movements.[25] In a few countries, however, this inclusiveness is lacking, so that we can speak more accurately of a Muslim denomination or denominations. Either Muslims are divided into separate branches, each of numerical importance, as in Iraq and Afghanistan, or they live alongside non-Muslims in significant numbers, as in Lebanon.[26] In these conditions, the separate religious groups are made more aware of their individual identities and are more likely to develop institutional patterns.

Whatever the accuracy of these informal placements, I think it can be said that all the major religions contain tendencies for both institutionalization and for diffusion, although perhaps in varying amounts, and they can and do form ecclesiastical or denominational structures. The various outcomes are products of their cultural elements interacting with a variety of social conditions.

The Established Sect
This type of religious organization ought, perhaps, to be discussed after our further examination of sects, for the established sect is an outgrowth of these more ephemeral movements. I will reverse that order, however, in order to maintain the continuum relative to the criteria employed in our system of classification. The established sect is somewhat more inclusive, less alienated, and more structured than the sect, and therefore closer to

25 See Allan Eister, "Perspective on the Functions of Religion in a Developing Country: Islam in Pakistan," *Journal for the Scientific Study of Religion*, 3, 1964, pp. 227–238; Elaine Hagopian, "Islam and Society-Formation in Morocco Past and Present," *Journal for the Scientific Study of Religion*, 3, 1963, pp. 70–80; and Emile Marmorstein, "Religious Opposition to Nationalism in the Middle East," *International Affairs*, July, 1952, pp. 344–359.

26 See Dankwart Rustow, "The Politics of the Near East," in *The Politics of the Developing Areas*, Gabriel Almond and James Coleman, eds., p. 372.

the denomination. The small, uncompromising groups we have described as sects are, by their very nature, unstable. Either the group disintegrates when the members die, or it has been molded into a more formal structure with techniques for admitting new members and serving their common interests. Professional leaders may emerge, because the intense enthusiasm of the first generation which sustained the lay character of the movement tends to decline. The needs of "birthright" members are frequently different and their class status may be improved. Direct challenge or opposition to the social order subsides. Nevertheless, the full transition into a class or national church may not take place.

Certainly one cannot fully equate Methodism and Quakerism today, although both started out as sectarian protests and both have changed a great deal through the generations. Methodism has evolved into a denomination, as we have defined it, whereas Quakerism has developed into an established sect. An adequate theory must account for the difference. It does not seem that differences in status improvement can explain the contrast, because both Methodists and Quakers moved up the class ladder. Of the two groups, the Quakers were much more vigorously opposed and persecuted, which developed in them a stronger feeling of isolation and more intense group morale.[27] But this, in part, is only a proximate cause. Why were they more strongly persecuted? This seems to lead back to the nature of the sect in terms of its original protests. Those sects will tend to develop into denominations which, in the first instance, emphasized problems of individual anxiety and sin, those that are primarily efforts to reduce burdens of confusion and guilt. Middle-class sectarian developments usually fall into this group; they develop rather quickly into denominations. On the other hand, sects whose original concern was predominantly with the evils of society will tend to develop into established sects. Such groups make demands for social justice and reform, as did the Anabaptists and Levellers and to a lesser degree the Quakers; or they withdraw from the society by refusing certain obligations or by establishing isolated communities. The contrast between the two types of sects is well described by Richard Niebuhr:

Methodism was far removed in its moral temper from the churches of the disinherited in the sixteenth and seventeenth century. Briefly, the difference lay in the substitution of individual ethics and philanthropism for social ethics and millenarianism . . . the Methodist movement remained throughout its history in the control of men who had been born and bred in the middle class and who were impressed not so much by the social evils from which the poor suffered as by the vices to which they had succumbed.[28]

Niebuhr suggests that leadership is an important variable in setting the direction of a movement. One must add to that the process of selectivity that takes place in membership of different sects, as a result of varying

27 This is also true of the Mormons, who have maintained sectarian qualities for more than a century. There are strong denominational pressures today, including the pressure of success, both as a religious organization and in secular matters. Only precise measures would allow one to speak with confidence, but I am inclined to regard the Mormons as an established sect close to the denominational "line." See Thomas O'Dea, *The Mormons;* and Wallace Turner, *The Mormon Establishment.*

28 Op. cit., pp. 65–67.

emphases. Individuals who believe that the reform of the evils of a society are the primary problems will be drawn into the ethical-protest sects. Those who feel most strongly the burden of individual doubt and suffering will be drawn into sects that emphasize individual regeneration. This selectivity will, in turn, condition the development of doctrine.

Among the Mormons, separation, persecution, and migration were interacting factors that contributed to their survival as a distinct group. Just as many religious orders have concluded that the only way to preserve the clarity and purity of their religious beliefs and practices was to maintain independent communities, so many sects have followed the injunction to "come out from among them and be ye separate." This has sometimes entailed migration, which in many cases has contributed to the likelihood of sectarian survival. The Hutterites, for example, "have purchased an astonishing degree of perpetual self-identity by tactics of migration and cultural withdrawal since the sixteenth century. . . ."[29]

Migration does not always increase the solidarity of a sect, making it more likely to develop into an established sect than into a denomination. Phillip Hammond has argued that migration emphasizes the value base of a sect's cohesion, rather than its members' interdependence. On the basis of his examination of Norwegian immigration, he believes that schism and defection, not integration, are likely to result from this emphasis on values, because conflicts are defined in ideological terms.[30] Examined more comparatively, however, migration is seen to be associated with a variety of outcomes. Migration by itself was certainly not enough to maintain the sectarian qualities of many of the groups that came to America from Europe in prerevolutionary days. Several related variables interacting with migration determine its final influence: the reasons for migration, the extent of difference between a group and its new social environment, the amount of persecution, internal group processes, and the economic and political opportunities available in the new location. Thus one cannot state in general terms whether or not a migrating sect will become a denomination, an established sect, or will merge with other groups.[31]

In Figure 13–1 a distinction is made between "established sect" and "established lay sect." This is done to draw attention to the different degrees of organizational complexity among established sects. Some resist more strongly than others the tendencies toward a professional leadership and the development of a bureaucratic structure. It is rare that "the priesthood of all believers" is maintained in a full sense. Those sects with fewest tendencies toward denominationalism, however, are least likely to develop a complex organizational structure. If the original break with society was sharp, if the group is physically isolated, if it suffers severe persecution, then the pristine sectarian qualities are more likely to persist.

29 Donald Durnbaugh, *The Believer's Church*, p. 301; see also Victor Peters, *All Things Common: The Hutterite Way of Life*.

30 Phillip Hammond, "The Migrating Sect: An Illustration from Early Norwegian Immigration," *Social Forces*, 41, 1963, pp. 275–283.

31 See J. J. Mol, "Churches and Immigrants," *Research Group for European Migration Problems Bulletin*, 9, May, 1961, supplement 5; Bryan Wilson, "The Migrating Sects," *British Journal of Sociology*, 18, 1967, pp. 303–317; and J. T. Borhek, "Role-Orientations and Organizational Stability," *Human Organization*, 24, 1965, pp. 332–338.

Bryan Wilson has noted a number of additional conditions that influence the likelihood that a sect will become a denomination:

Thus it is clear that sects with a general democratic ethic, which stress simple affirmation of intense subjective experience as a criterion of admission, which stand in the orthodox fundamentalist tradition, which emphasize evangelism and use revivalist techniques, and which seek to accommodate groups dislocated by rapid social change are particularly subject to denominationalizing tendencies. These same tendencies are likely to be intensified if the sect is unclear concerning the boundaries of the saved community and extends its rules of endogamy to include any saved person as an eligible spouse; if its moral injunctions are unclearly distinguished from conventional or traditional morality; and if it accepts simple assertion of remorse for sin as sufficient to re-admit or to retain a back-slidden member. Denominationalisation is all the more likely when such a sect inherits, or evolves, any type of preaching order, lay pastors or itinerant ministers; when revivalism leads to special training for the revivalists themselves (and so leads to a class of professionals who cease to rely on "love-offerings" but are granted a fixed stipend); and when the members are ineffectively separated from the world, a condition enhanced by proselytising activities.[32]

In this statement, Wilson emphasizes the values of the sect itself and its internal structure as the critical variables in determining whether or not it will become a denomination, develop into an established sect, or possibly disappear. These internal qualities can partly be seen, however, as dependent variables. On one hand they reflect tendencies of the individuals attracted to a movement, tendencies that shape the sect in certain directions. On the other hand, internal development reflects the larger structural conditions within which the sect operates. Persecution, we have suggested, entrenches the sectarian qualities whereas tolerance denominationalizes. On a more impersonal level, expanding economic and political opportunities promote the shift from sect to denomination, whereas continued deprivation perpetuates sectarian tendencies. In time, to be sure, the members of an established sect may become prosperous; but if their sectarianism has been institutionalized, if it has been given a powerful cultural statement, it can persist through many generations of economic and political prosperity. This is particularly true if status discrepancies remain, or if some forms of persecution or disprivilege continue. For instance, in my judgment, Judaism in the United States is more nearly an established sect than a denomination, if we can disregard its own internal differentiation and view it as part of the total religious picture. There has been substantial accommodation to the American environment, of course, but there remains a strong element of alienation and marginality. Jews furnish substantial proportions of those who challenge existing patterns of race relations, conservative political, educational, and economic values, and traditional mores. Through many generations they have learned to "fight the system."[33] Values and

32 Bryan Wilson, *Patterns of Sectarianism, Organization and Ideology in Social and Religious Movements*, p. 44.

33 Most human systems are filled with qualities that need to be fought, as I view the world, so I am in no sense lamenting this element of alienation among Jews as an established sect, any more than I lament it among Quakers. Needless to say, there are points at which I might evaluate the pros and cons of the social order differently.

attitudes appropriate to that lesson are passed on despite changed circumstances. In a similar way, I expect various Negro religious movements to continue to be established sects long after full parity in economic, educational, and political matters has been achieved.

Werner Stark rejects the concept of established sect as a contradiction in terms. "There is no cause to doubt," he writes, that the Quakers are "a typical denomination. . . . Death, they say, waits for no man; it waits for no sect either." [34] Although he appropriately emphasizes the process of accommodation, Stark fails to see the extent to which an orientation in opposition to the dominant secular structure can itself become an established value, perpetuated by normal socialization and reinforced by various cycles of interaction between a sect and the larger society.

Not only can sects become established, but a church can become disestablished. I mean by this, not simply the loss of an official connection with government, but the loss of inclusiveness and of an organized, hierarchical structure, and an increase in opposition to the society of which it is a part. This is to say, there can be movement in both directions on each of the three scales we have used in classifying religious groups. Most attention has been given to movement from the sect to the church ends of the scales; but some conditions support the opposite shift. We cannot assume that a given group's location and the direction of its changes are permanently fixed by its own attributes.

Perhaps this point can be underlined by focusing on certain trends within Catholicism. To some small degree, the Catholic Church is becoming a sect in Europe and America, just as it has long been a sect in those lands where it includes only a small minority of the population. In the United States during the nineteenth century, the Catholic Church was something of an "established universal church," if I may use a somewhat paradoxical phrase. By that I mean that it continued to exhibit many of the characteristics of a universal church, or perhaps more appropriately an ecclesia, in a setting where it was in fact a minority group with at least some substantial value conflicts with the surrounding society. Thus it followed a pattern parallel to—but moving in the opposite direction from—that of an established sect, which continues to exhibit some sectarian tendencies after having become more inclusive and more structured. By the mid-twentieth century, the Catholic Church in the United States and in some countries of Europe had become denominationalized to a significant degree. There had been a growth in tolerance and a reduction in value differences, although the shift should not be exaggerated.[35]

Scarcely had the Catholic Church become a denomination in the United States—let us say in November, 1960—when it began to be apparent that it and many other religious groups were being severely challenged by contemporary trends in values. Despite membership figures that included per-

34 Werner Stark, *The Sociology of Religion*, Vol. 2, p. 305.

35 See, for example, the data in Gerhard Lenski, *The Religious Factor*, pp. 64, 166, 303, and 308; and Rodney Stark and Charles Glock, *American Piety: The Nature of Religious Commitment*, particularly Chap. 2. On the whole, differences between Catholic and Protestant are smaller in the latter study, whether due to differences in time, place, or methods of study.

haps 60 per cent of the adult population, the churches found that major value standards were set and value decisions made on the basis of secular criteria, by government, or in the context of a civil religion only partly harmonious with their own perspectives. It would be an exaggeration, but perhaps an instructive one, to suggest that the civil religion is now the church and most traditional religious bodies in the United States are now sects. In the case of Roman Catholicism, this sectarian quality is compounded of three elements: [36] 1) alienation from many of the values of the secular world; 2) some continuing opposition to norms of pluralism, tolerance, and the separation of church and state, an opposition that is reflected in the maintenance of separate structures, particularly schools, in which distinctive values can be taught; 3) some continuing protest against the lack of brotherhood, charity, and universalism in the economic and political orders. This last should remind us that the Catholic Church has always contained a sectarian quality obscured by an inflexible use of any typology. The contemporary situation has added other sect-forming tendencies to this intrinsic "explosive quality," as Troeltsch called it. The combination has set Catholicism, as well as many Protestant and Jewish denominations, more sharply at odds with the social order than has been true in recent generations. Needless to say, one should not exaggerate this trend. The intense participation, membership by individual choice, and other qualities of a sectarian organization are missing. The Roman Catholic Church is basically an ecclesia in lands where it includes the vast majority of the population; or it is a denomination in lands where it is one of several churches. Nor is my suggestion that in the United States today the Church has unusually strong sectarian tendencies in any way an evaluation. I would personally applaud some and lament others of these sectarian qualities.

To summarize the conditions that lead toward either denominationalism or an established sect, let me emphasize the interactions among the values of the group, the tendencies of its recruits, and the opportunities and restrictions that are brought to bear by the surrounding structure. Without attention to all of these, and their interdependence, we cannot understand why different courses of development occur.

It may be well to stress again that in describing types we are not creating a set of categories into which groups can readily be placed. Although we have selected a limited number of nouns and adjectives, and have drawn lines in Figure 13–1 as if there were clear marking points, we are in fact dealing with matters of degree. Actual religious organizations seldom correspond precisely to the types we are defining, but the type pictures should make comparison more accurate. Certainly there are many denominational elements in contemporary Quakerism: its opposition to the state has strongly subsided, professional leadership is common among some branches, and most members have been born into the group. Methodism is also a mixed case, as it has been from the beginning, for, despite the middle-

36 See Thomas Sanders, "Catholicism and Development: The Catholic Left in Brazil," in *Churches and States: The Religious Institution and Modernization*, Kalman Silvert, ed., Chap. 3; Benton Johnson, "On Church and Sect," *American Sociological Review*, 28, 1963, pp. 539–549; and N. J. Demerath, III, and Phillip Hammond, *Religion in Social Context*, pp. 69–77.

class and educated status of its top leaders, it was predominantly a lower-class movement with substantial lay leadership. Sectarian elements remain: pacifism among a small, but significant, minority; and a persistent interest in social reform. Yet the two must still be differentiated in terms of the degree of their accommodation to the secular world.

A sharper contrast can be drawn between a strictly middle-class sect that rapidly became a denomination and a sectarian movement that was even more pessimistic than the Quakers in its view of the world, a movement that, even after three centuries, has not developed into a denomination. We refer to Christian Science on the one hand and the Mennonites, an outgrowth of the Anabaptists, on the other. The difficulties that are expressed in the emergence of a middle-class sect are not primarily economic hardship or a sense of injustice in the secular world. They are more likely to be a feeling of inadequacy, confusion of standards in a highly mobile world, guilt, and physical pain. A religious movement that attempts to meet these difficulties has no need to make a sharp challenge to the society and the established churches; the pendulum swing away from them is much shorter and the return much quicker than with lower-class sects. Middle-class sects represent a protest against the lack of attention to illness, the burdens of guilt, and feelings of inadequacy. Since the churches can begin to pay more attention to these needs, however, without raising any serious questions about the structure of society, without any need for a basic reorganization of their views of the world, they can quickly absorb these new emphases from the sect. Thus churches "steal the thunder" of such sects very easily. This is part of the meaning of the development of "pastoral psychology," of attention to "peace of soul," of advice on "confident living." This too is christian science, if not Christian Science. The sect, in its turn, goes through the familiar process of institutionalization. We may say, then, that a sect will become a denomination instead of an established sect if the protest it represents can readily be absorbed into the dominant religious stream without a serious challenge to the secular social structure and without the necessity for a reorganization of the religious pattern.

The challenge of the Anabaptists was sharp: The society that makes us suffer and the churches that sanctify it are evil. Bear no arms, swear no oaths, accept the religious fellowship only of those who have proved themselves.[37] Such doctrines set a group on a different road from that traveled by the less uncompromising sects. Once set in motion, these influences may resist for many generations the disintegrating effects of improved economic status, mobility, persecution, and education.

The contemporary Japanese situation offers a valuable setting for further study of sect-denomination interrelationships. In general, the new religions are likely to denominationalize rapidly. In terms of their internal values and structure, they have most of the characteristics listed by Wilson, in the extract quoted earlier, as likely to be associated with denominational tendencies. The major exception is the lack of a democratic ethic; but I suspect that this criterion is culture-bound in any event. In a society where democratic processes are uncommon, a religious organization with a demo-

[37] For valuable background and commentary on the radical elements in the Reformation generally, see George H. Williams, *The Radical Reformation;* H. N. Brailsford, *The Levellers and the English Revolution;* and Donald Durnbaugh, op. cit.

cratic ethic may remain a sect. The dominant position of the leaders in the Japanese sects seems more likely to be associated with their evolution into denominations than with their development into established sects.

By speaking of them in general terms, I obscure important variations between them. Sōka Gakkai, for example, is more at odds with prevailing values than most of the other groups. It also draws a sharp line between its membership and the unregenerate. Other characteristics, however—its base in traditional religions, its professional and bureaucratized leadership, its membership drawn from among those experiencing rapid social change, its emphasis on individual success and happiness—all incline it toward denominationalism.

The ways in which these groups develop, of course, are dependent not only on their values, structure, and membership, but on the surrounding society. If individual problems related to change and urbanization increase, if hopes for social mobility are frustrated, if the gradual increase in participation in secular decision-making is retarded, then more sectarian tendencies will be promoted. Sharper polarization can develop, with oppression from the authorities matching alienative behavior from the members of religious sects. In such conditions new sects will form and older ones are much less likely to denominationalize.

In more favorable circumstances, the sects will serve a bridging function. They will help to carry the recently urbanized village population over into a drastically new kind of life. As McFarland puts it, they can serve as pressure chambers for the socially disadvantaged, faced with problems of adjustment to a new environment. They are confronted with the dilemma of two Japans: the old life, village- and tradition-oriented, unified by nationalism and the symbol of the emperor; and the new, urban, industrial, mobile world, divided by class interests, with an emerging democratic polity.[38] If conditions permit this transition without a major upheaval, the new sects are likely to become denominations. They may indeed reduce the likelihood of such an upheaval by helping to redefine symbols of identity and reshaping goals. If serious conflict develops, however, this accommodation process will proceed much less far. Current religious movements in Japan have few of the qualities of a reformation in them; but sharp conflict will encourage more radical religious responses to the urban world, along with radical political responses.

The Sect
After this lengthy discussion of the established sect as a type and of some of the processes by which it emerges, we need say little more about the sect. It can be described substantially in Troeltsch's terms, given in the basic dichotomy with which we started. We need to make, however, two modifications and extensions. The first is a distinction, suggested in Figure 13–1, between a *sect movement* and a *charismatic sect.* I use these terms to call attention to the fact that some sects, even from the beginning, develop a rather complex structure, a hierarchy of leaders, and extensive plans and programs for dealing with the outside world. That is, they can be distin-

38 H. Neill McFarland, *The Rush Hour of the Gods*, pp. 229–236.

guished from the small, often one-unit sects, on the basis of their placement on scale III of Figure 13–1. In one sense, the sect movement is simply the charismatic sect seen a few years later—on the road to establishment, one might say. It is more complicated than that, however, for the extent of early structuring may be a critical variable that influences the likelihood that a sect will become established. Ephemeral groups, lacking any structure, come and go. Their contemporaries may be aware of them, but they disappear from history. Those groups that come together into a movement, with at least a minimum level of organization, are probably no more influential over their individual members, but they play a more important role in society.

In a second extension of the concept of sect, I will make more explicit the subdivisions of this type that result from the differences in need from which they spring and the differences in response. This can be done in terms of the three possible responses to an undesired situation: One can accept it, one can aggressively oppose it, or one can seek ways to avoid it. All three of these responses are usually found in a sect movement, but one is likely to predominate. To use the terms of Kluckhohn and Strodtbeck, there are dominant and variant orientations, which can be combined in numerous ways. Although we will focus on the dominant orientations, to keep the scheme of classification within manageable proportions, it is important to remember that each variety has a range within it as a result of different combinations of variant orientations.

Karen Horney has noted that a neurotic may struggle with his anxieties by attacking their presumed sources, by withdrawing into a private world, or by seeking the shelter and protection of others.[39] These are basic strategies, indeed, that we all use in dealing with undesirable situations. Charles S. Johnson observed that these were also the choices available to the members of a minority group suffering from discrimination.[40] Lewis Killian and Ralph Turner have classified social movements in a way highly congruent with these criteria. They speak of power-oriented, value-oriented, and participation-oriented movements. While recognizing that these are analytic types, they see some movements as designed primarily for the pursuit of power in the larger society, others as focused on the realization of certain values, and others that are concerned with gratification of various desires of individual members.[41]

The same patterns are relevant to sectarian activities, on both the individual and group levels. We have followed Weber in defining the emissary prophet as one who propounds new obligations and sees himself as an agent of God in realizing those obligations. The ascetic is one who withdraws from the mundane world in an effort to achieve sacred values. The mystic accepts the world around him and strives for insight into ultimate reality by achieving union with the divine.

Thinking of them in sharply analytic terms (though in fact they appear only in mixed forms), these three religious styles correspond to three forms

39 See especially *The Neurotic Personality of Our Time.*

40 See his *Patterns of Negro Segregation.* This theme has been developed by George E. Simpson and J. Milton Yinger in *Racial and Cultural Minorities,* Chap. 7.

41 See Lewis Killian and Ralph Turner, *Collective Behavior.*

of deprivation. The prophet sees himself outside the structure of power; he feels alienated from the social structure. He has not given up on the world; he wants power over it. The ascetic sees himself outside the cultural system; he feels alienated from prevailing values. The values he most esteems seem beyond realization within the human communities he knows, so he is ready to withdraw to achieve them. The mystic sees himself outside the usual motivational systems; he feels alienated from himself and lonely; he lacks morale; he feels guilty and baffled. He may join with others, without reference to the world around them, to achieve poise, insight, and control over their spiritual and physical malaise.

In using nouns, we refer only to dominant tendencies. And if we speak of sects as being power-oriented (prophetic), value-oriented (ascetic), and participation-oriented (mystic), we are only taking a necessary first step toward an adequate classificatory scheme by isolating the analytic properties out of which various combinations are built. Some sects may develop values and activities with reference to all three forms of deprivation. A sect's own internal processes may reflect the struggle within the membership to give one a pre-eminent place. Both individuals and groups are likely to carry tendencies toward all of these orientations. I venture to suggest that many disagreements over taxonomy are based on the fact that some observers first isolate what they believe are the essential analytic elements, and then illustrate these by reference to organizations that approximate each one of them in relatively pure form; whereas others deal first with particular organizations, building their types out of empirical similarities and differences. I am inclined toward the former procedure, because I think it has greater usefulness in crosscultural and crosstemporal comparisons. In the last analysis, however, the two procedures pressed far enough should arrive at the same place.

The variety of sects that follow, then, are analytic types, which existing organizations will only approximate. They can serve, nevertheless, as valuable standards of comparison and contrast.

1. *Acceptance Sects.* These would be close to participation-oriented groups, in the terms of Killian and Turner, or Gnostic sects, as Bryan Wilson defines them. "The *Gnostic* sects accept in large measure the world's goals but seek a new and esoteric means to achieve these ends—a wishful mysticism." [42] The membership is predominantly middle class or upwardly mobile lower class. Although the members feel confronted with serious problems, which the dominant religious organizations are not helping them to solve, they do not interpret these in social terms. Society, on the whole, has been good to them and to those with whom they associate. The key difficulties, they believe, are lack of faith, selfishness, ignorance, and isolation, not an evil society. Therefore, they preach, have faith, show the hand of friendship, come together in a congenial group in which individual suffering and bafflement may be overcome in the joint search for mystical knowledge. Seichō no Ie in Japan, the House of Growth, although it claims to be not a religion but the source of "truth common to every kind of religion," fits this model quite closely, as does Christian Science.

2. *Aggressive Sects.* These are power-oriented movements. Wilson speaks of two types that partially fit this model: "The *Conversionist* sects seek to

42 Bryan Wilson, op. cit., p. 26.

alter men, and thereby to alter the world; the response is free-will optimism. The *Adventist* sects predict drastic alteration of the world, and seek to prepare for the new dispensation—a pessimistic determinism." [43] These are apt descriptions. I miss in these statements, however, and in his description of two other types, any reference to sects that seek to alter the world by direct action, sects that shade off toward political and even military protest movements, a type well illustrated by the Levellers. The range can be accounted for, in my judgment, by reference to variant as well as to dominant emphases. The Levellers were a relatively "pure" type of aggressive sect. Prophecy, not mysticism or asceticism, was their mode. Though they were not primarily alienated from the values of English life—they wanted land and political influence—they did feel alienated from its power structure; they therefore sought, through a religious movement, to attain power.

The conversionist Salvation Army and the adventist Jehovah's Witnesses, on the other hand, seek to alter the world in somewhat different ways.[44] The relatively optimistic Salvation Army leans toward Gnostic individualism. Their attack on the world is partial. And, as Wilson observes, they are likely to denominationalize quite rapidly. The more pessimistic adventist groups, however, lean toward ascetic withdrawal. The Levellers thought the world worth seizing; the Jehovah's Witnesses see it as going to hell. Their revolutionary potential is blunted, therefore, by avoidance, or what Wilson calls introversionist tendencies. They are more likely to develop into an established sect than a denomination.

E. T. Clark also speaks of pessimistic or adventist sects in a way that indicates the mixture of aggression and withdrawal. They condemn the world and have finally despaired of satisfying their needs in society.

They see no good in the world and no hope of improvement, it is rushing speedily to hell, according to the will and plan of God. The adherents of such sects magnify millenarianism and see the imminent end of the present world-order by means of a cosmic catastrophe. They have turned on the world, and they seek escape through a cataclysm which will cast down those who have been elevated, and secure to the faithful important places in a new temporal kingdom as well as eternal bliss in heaven.[45]

"They have turned on the world," *and* "they seek escape"—that is the adventist mixture. Of the conversionist groups one might say: They condemn the world, *but* by personal rectitude and faith they believe they can alter it.

Thus I see conversionist and adventist groups as aggressive-prophetic sects modified, in the first instance, by strongly individualistic acceptance tendencies, and in the second instance by ascetic withdrawal tendencies.

It is in societies confronted with major revolutionary pressures that the relatively pure type of aggressive sects are most likely to occur. Thus in

43 Op. cit., p. 26.

44 On the Salvation Army, see Roland Robertson in Bryan Wilson, op. cit., Chap. 2. For studies of the Jehovah's Witnesses, see Werner Cohn, "Jehovah's Witnesses as a Proletarian Movement," *American Scholar*, 24, 1955, pp. 281–298; William Whalen, *Armageddon Around the Corner;* and Herbert Stroup, *The Jehovah's Witness.*

45 Elmer T. Clark, *The Small Sects in America*, p. 22.

Africa in the last few decades many Christian sects have become revolutionary by redefining and politicizing their otherworldly and messianic background. In the Congo, several of these have come together in a group called *Église de Jésus-Christ sur la Terre par le Prophète Simon Kimbangu*. Even for such groups, with their quite complete Christian identity, "the words used by the prophets make it unmistakably clear that theirs is a religion of war and revolt." [46] Aggressive sects are also to be found among non-Christian and syncretist movements.[47]

Aggressive sects, in brief, are religious responses to poverty and powerlessness made by those who are relatively hopeful about chances for improving their lot in life. In Christianity, they interpret the teachings of Jesus in radical-ethical terms: His was a program and a promise of social reform. The society that treats us so badly is evil and true religion, therefore, must reorganize the social order. Such a group runs into strong opposition and, in most instances, fails. It is likely, as a result, to disappear or to be transformed into type 3. It is relatively unlikely to move toward a denomination. Again we may cite the Anabaptists as illustrative.

3. *Avoidance Sects.* If one cannot accept society, like type 1, or have hope of reforming it, like type 2, one can devalue the significance of this life, project his hopes into the supernatural world, and meanwhile reduce his problems by forming into a communion of like-minded fellows. This is a common sectarian protest in the "developed" world, where aggressive protests are more likely to be secular than religious in nature. It occurs among those who have as yet achieved little hope for improvement of their lot, such as some disprivileged minorities, and also among those who are heirs to a tradition of a radical, aggressive sectarianism that has failed to transform society. An avoidance sect faces the hard facts of life for the lower classes, as the first type does not (poverty and suffering and injustice and powerlessness are persistent); it cannot so easily be broken by failure as can the second type, for who can prove to those who believe that another life will *not* redress the ills of this world. Such a sect grows easily out of the church which, for all its failure to adjust to new problems as they emerge, has never been able to disregard the problem of evil.

This category is similar to Wilson's introversionist or pietist sect, which he characterizes as a group that places reliance on inner illumination and the development of a communty of the elect. "No evangelism is undertaken and a strong in-group morality is developed; the sect withdraws from the world, or allows its members to be active in the world only for human betterment at the behest of conscience and at the periphery of social concern." [48] The early Quakers and the various "communist" communities that appeared in the Christian world after the defeat of the left wing of the Reformation illustrate this type. In a somewhat different way it is also illustrated by the white and Negro Pentecostal groups of rural America, the "left wing of the subjectivist groups," as Clark calls them. Their avoidance responses are more symbolic than physical. They seek trances, visions,

46 Vittorio Lanternari, *The Religions of the Oppressed*, p. 17. See also Chap. 1.

47 See Georges Balandier, *Sociologie actuelle de l'Afrique noire;* and Bengt Sundkler, *Bantu Prophets of South Africa.*

48 Wilson, op. cit., p. 28.

and the "gift of tongues"—temporary escapes into a world where their standards rule. They struggle with life's problems by transforming the meaning of life, by substituting "religious status for social status," in Liston Pope's meaningful phrase. In many of these groups, concern for problems of individual morale looms larger than condemnation of an evil world which they seek to escape. Where this is true, they are properly seen as a mixture of avoidance and acceptance sects.

Relationships Among Types of Sects. Putting these three analytic types into a system, with turning points represented sharply by a triangular figure, we get the representation outlined in Figure 13–2. A circular form might more accurately indicate the shading off from one position to another, but would less well indicate the variables that underlie the system of classification.

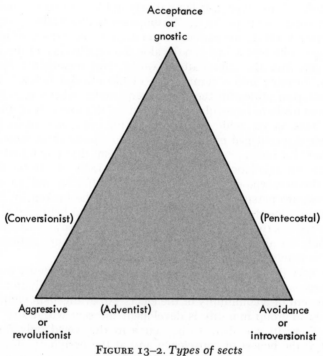

FIGURE 13–2. *Types of sects*

The three basic types of sects are abstract models, designed for purposes of comparison and contrast. Critical examination of such models is more properly directed toward the question, Are they based on analytic variables that give us maximum understanding of the range? rather than to the question, Why does not this particular group correspond closely to one of the types? Application of the model leads to placement of many groups along the side, rather than at the angles, which is to say that it leads us to pay attention to secondary as well as primary themes. Rather complicated "profiles," which indicate the proportionate use of all three themes,

Table 13–2. Comparative qualities of types of sects

Type name	Characteristic form of deprivation	Characteristic type of leadership and experience	Strategy vis-à-vis society	Principal objective	Extreme or "pure" expression	Illustrative groups
1. Acceptance	Individual morale	Mystical	Disregard or accept	Individual poise and participation	Downgrading of normal sense experience	Early Christian Science; League for Spiritual Discovery
2. Aggressive	Structural power	Prophetic	Attack	Power	Religious military movement	Münsterites; Ghost Dance
3. Avoidance	Cultural values	Ascetic	Withdraw	Achievement of values	Communist community	Hutterites; Amana Community

are as likely to be of value in comparative study of sects as the use of the three abstract types. Several aspects of our discussion of sects are summarized in Table 13–2.

The Cult

Even by combining some of the terms suggested in Table 13–2, we can classify various religious movements only with difficulty. I have not tried to introduce into the pattern one variable that becomes quite important in some circumstances, namely, the growth of alienation from the traditional religious system as well as of alienation from society. When this occurs, new or syncretist religious movements often appear. They do not appeal to the classical, the primitive, the "true" interpretation of the dominant religion, as a sect does, but claim to build *de novo*. The term *cult* is often used to refer to such new and syncretist movements in their early stages.[49] It often carries also the connotations of small size, search for a mystical experience, lack of structure, and presence of a charismatic leader. They are similar to sects, but represent a sharper break, in religious terms, from the prevailing tradition of a society. Cults are religious mutants, extreme variations on the dominant themes by means of which men struggle with their problems.

Bryan Wilson has expressed doubt about the usefulness of the concept of cult, and with good cause. Alienation from traditional religions and syncretism are matters of degree; they probably characterize most sects in some measure. After a generation a cult can claim its own tradition, as C. Eric Lincoln has observed with reference to the Black Muslims, removing even that basis for distinction. I shall not, therefore, make much use of

49 See Howard Becker, op. cit.; W. E. Mann, *Sect, Cult, and Church in Alberta;* and Geoffrey Nelson, "The Concept of Cult," *The Sociological Review,* 16, 1968, pp. 351–362.

the term. Yet it seems unwise to set it aside completely in a world where new and syncretist movements are very widespread—in Africa, Melanesia, and Japan, for example. Insofar as these represent severe disenchantment not only with the churchly embodiment of a religious tradition, but with the tradition itself, they are sectarian movements with a difference; and we need to be prepared to study the implications of that difference.

Geoffrey Nelson has given the concept of cult a searching review. He modifies the common definition primarily by suggesting that cults may, on occasion, be quite large and long-lived; and they are an important source of new religions; "all founded religions can be seen as having developed from cults." [50] To parallel the concept of "established sect" he suggests the term "permanent cult." In settings where the existing religious systems break down—in a context of anomie—a cult may develop into a new religion, a dominant rather than a marginal belief system.

This is a valuable extension of the concept of cult. It adds a necessary time dimension while noting that the course of development of a cult is conditioned by its social environment. We shall use the term cult, then, in its unqualified form, to refer to a group at the farthest extreme from the "universal church" with which we started. It is usually small, short-lived, local, and built around a charismatic leader. At this stage, cults are concerned almost wholly with problems of the individual, with little regard for questions of social change and social order. When a society is undergoing severe reorganization, however, cults may be involved in the group as well as the individual stresses that accompany drastic structural and cultural change. What was bizarre to the great majority under one set of circumstances may appeal to them under new conditions. In such a process, the cult itself is modified; structure and doctrine are added; a new religion, with its own sectarian and churchly tendencies, develops.

BIBLIOGRAPHICAL POSTSCRIPT

The following works discuss problems associated with the development of typologies of religious groups. Some of them also contain descriptions and interpretations of specific groups and movements; but the emphasis here is on explication and criticism. We shall discuss several specific groups in the next two chapters.

David Aberle, "A Note on Relative Deprivation Theory as Applied to Millenarian and Other Cult Movements," in Reader in Comparative Religion, rev. ed., W. A. Lessa and E. Z. Vogt, eds., pp. 537–541; Georges Balandier, Sociologie actuelle de l'Afrique noire; Howard Becker, Systematic Sociology, pp. 624–628; Peter Berger, "Sectarianism and Religious Sociation," American Journal of Sociology, 64, 1958, pp. 41–44; Peter Berger, "The Sociological Study of Sectarianism," Social Research, 21, 1954, pp. 467–485; G. S. Bhatt, "Brahmo Samaj, Arya Samaj, and the Church-Sect Typology," Review of Religious Research, 10, 1968, pp. 23–32; E. T. Clark, The Small Sects in America; S. D. Clark, Church and Sect in Canada; Norman Cohn, The Pursuit of the Millennium; John Coleman, "Church-Sect Typology and Organizational Precariousness," Sociological Analysis, 29, 1968, pp. 55–66; N. J. Demerath, III, and Phillip Hammond, Religion in

50 Ibid., p. 357.

Social Context, Chap. 5; Russell Dynes, "Church-Sect Typology and Socio-Economic Status," *American Sociological Review*, 20, 1955, pp. 555–560; Luther Gerlach and Virginia Hynes, "Five Factors Crucial to the Growth and Spread of a Modern Religious Movement," *Journal for the Scientific Study of Religion*, 7, 1968, pp. 23–40; W. Goddijn, "Kirche und Sekte," in *Kölner Zeitschrift für Soziologie und Sozialpsychologie*, Dietrich Goldschmidt and Joachim Matthes, eds., 6, 1962, pp. 241–252; Erich Goode, "Some Critical Observations on the Church-Sect Dimension," *Journal for the Scientific Study of Religion*, 6, 1967, pp. 69–77, followed by commentaries by N. J. Demerath, III, pp. 77–84 and by Allan Eister, pp. 85–90; Erich Goode, "Further Reflections on the Church-Sect Dimension," *Journal for the Scientific Study of Religion*, 6, 1967, pp. 270–275, followed by comments by N. J. Demerath, III, pp. 275–277; Paul Gustafson, "UO-US-PS-PO: A Restatement of Troeltsch's Church-Sect Typology," *Journal for the Scientific Study of Religion*, 6, 1967, pp. 64–68; Benton Johnson, "On Church and Sect," *American Sociological Review*, 28, 1963; Benton Johnson, "A Critical Appraisal of the Church-Sect Typology," *American Sociological Review*, 22, 1957, pp. 88–92; Vittorio Lanternari, *The Religions of the Oppressed: A Study of Modern Messianic Cults*; Lucy Mair, "Independent Religious Movements in Three Continents," *Comparative Studies in Society and History*, 1, 1959, pp. 113–136; W. E. Mann, *Sect, Cult, and Church in Alberta*; David Martin, "The Denomination," *British Journal of Sociology*, 13, 1962, pp. 1–14; Martin Marty, "Sects and Cults," *Annals of the American Academy of Political and Social Science*, 332, 1960, pp. 125–134; David Moberg, *The Church as a Social Institution*, Chap. 4; Wilhelm Mühlmann and others, *Chiliasmus und Nativismus: Studien zur Psychologie, Soziologie und historischen Kasuistik der Umsturzbewegungen*; Reinhold Niebuhr, *The Nature and Destiny of Man*, Vol. 2, pp. 169–180; John Scanzoni, "A Note on Method for the Church-Sect Typology," *Sociological Analysis*, 26, 1965, pp. 189–202; Werner Stark, *The Sociology of Religion*, 3 vols.; Yonina Talmon, "Pursuit of the Millennium: The Relation between Religious and Social Change," in Lessa and Vogt, op. cit., pp. 522–537; Glenn Vernon, *Sociology of Religion*, Chap. 9; Anthony Wallace, "Revitalization Movements," *American Anthropologist*, 58, 1956, pp. 264–281; Emilio Willems, *Followers of the New Faith. Culture Change and the Rise of Protestantism in Brazil and Chile*; Bryan Wilson, "The Migrating Sects," *British Journal of Sociology*, 18, 1967, pp. 303–317; Bryan Wilson, ed., *Patterns of Sectarianism. Organization and Ideology in Social and Religious Movements*; Bryan Wilson, *Sects and Society*.

Chapter Fourteen

RELIGION, STRATIFICATION, AND PROTEST

By the title of this chapter I mean to suggest that religion is shaped by the stratification systems of complex societies, but also that it is involved in protests against those systems. It is a tranquilizer, but also an energizer. Under some conditions it assures both the comfortable and the poor that they deserve their respective stations. But religion may also implant stirrings of doubt in the comfortable and arm the poor with a righteous anger—the latter, be it added, more commonly than the former.

From the viewpoint of classic Hinduism and Buddhism, the lowly are spinning out a fate set for themselves in an earlier life. The ancient Jews believed that a Messiah—now a Davidic king, now a superhuman savior—would rise to destroy tyrannical power and to establish the last and best kingdom, here or hereafter. The implications of these beliefs for the authority patterns of society are sharply different.

We need not be concerned here with many of the general theoretical questions concerning social stratification—whether this is a universal social phenomenon, why societies are stratified, the consequences for nonreligious aspects of a society, factors that make for mobility or rigidity in a stratification system, and the like. These are extremely important questions; but for our purposes we may take stratification as a given fact. We shall examine issues relevant to the general theory of stratification only when they involve religious patterns. This will lead us to such questions as the following: How does religious behavior vary among the different strata of a society? What are the consequences of this variation for the stratification system? Under what conditions does religion become an instrument of subgroup integration rather than societal integration, and thus become a factor in social conflict?

The relationship between religion and a stable stratification pattern is quite different from its relationship to a stratification pattern that is dynamic and changing. By helping each stratum define its status meaningfully, as part of a superempirical order (God intended it thus), religion may lend great stability even to highly inegalitarian patterns. When those patterns begin to change, however, as a result of migration, technological advance, population growth, and other secular factors that disturb the claims and expectations of the different strata, *the same religious doctrines and beliefs* can become the instruments of protest and defense.

Types of Stratification Systems. Two aspects of stratification systems that bear directly on religion require brief mention: First, such systems vary widely in the degree to which they are opened or closed; that is, in the likelihood that a person will remain in the stratum of his parents or may rise or fall into a different stratum. If the norms of the prevailing culture indicate that a person's place is determined by descent, not by his own behavior, and if stratum endogamy is strongly enforced, we have a culturally closed system. If the stratification patterns are closely related to economic, political, and educational opportunities, we have a structurally closed system. If individuals tend to accept their placement, whether it is high or low, we have a characterologically closed system. Oppositely, where behavioral criteria prevail, where there are plentiful educational, economic, and political opportunities, and where individuals regard their own placement as problematic, the stratification system is described as open.

The nouns we use to describe types of stratification systems reflect these various characteristics. In an earlier work, I have attempted to put them into the systematic framework reproduced as Table 14–1.

Table 14–1. Types of stratification systems *

	Affiliation by descent	Endogamy	Institutional support for differential treatment	Acceptance of status by lower groups
Caste system	yes	yes	yes	yes
Minority-majority system	yes	yes	no	no
Class system	no	no	no	no

* J. Milton Yinger, *A Minority Group in American Society*, p. 24. The first, second, and fourth of these criteria are used by Marvin Harris in "Caste, Class, and Minority," *Social Forces,* March, 1959, pp. 248–254.

Attempts to apply these criteria to concrete systems often result in disagreement, because each of the four is a variable. If we imagine that they range along scales from 0 to 100, and if we hypothesize that those mentioned first change least readily, we can describe many types and subtypes of stratification systems as shown in Table 14–2.

Other criteria may prove to be more decisive in distinguishing among stratification systems. And the implication here that closed systems are most likely to break down at the level of individual acceptance, whereas affiliation by descent is least likely to change, may be unwarranted or subject to exceptions. In my judgment, nevertheless, this more complex model allows us to describe societies more precisely and to take account of change more readily. India, for example, may have moved from caste system *a*

Table 14–2. Scaled types of stratification systems *

	Affiliation by descent	Endogamy	Institutional support for differential treatment	Acceptance of status by lower groups
Caste systems				
a	100	100	100	100
b	100	100	100	90
c	100	100	90	80
Minority-majority systems				
a	100	100	80	70
b	100	90	70	60
c	90	80	60	50
Class systems				
a	80	70	50	40
b	70	60	40	30
c	60	50	30	20
d	50	40	20	10

* Yinger, op. cit., p. 24.

to caste system type *c* in the last century, and perhaps to minority-majority system type *b* in some urban centers. During the seventeenth century, England may have moved from a minority-majority system (often labeled an estate system) type *a* to a minority-majority system type *c*. In each instance, however the change may be labeled, there were important religious concomitants.

Varieties of Status Inconsistency. Since Weber's definitive work, the importance of a second quality of stratification systems has been recognized. Stratification means the relatively structured (not temporary and incidental) inequalities in the distribution of prized states and objects. There are several such states and objects, however, and they do not necessarily vary together. Weber emphasized that income (control over economic goods and services), prestige (control over social honor), and power (control over the activities of other persons), although tending to cohere, may become separated. The degree of consistency or "crystallization" among these several measures of social status affects religion, politics, and perhaps even health.[1] It is an important quality of individual experience, and the average level of status consistency is a significant attribute of groups.

In recent years Weber's scheme has been modified by the addition of a perceptual variable. The objective levels of income, power, and prestige may be seen in various ways, whether one is considering other persons or himself. If one's income is going up, but he sees it as going up slowly in comparison with others, he may feel relatively deprived even in the face of

1 See Max Weber, *From Max Weber,* Hans Gerth and C. Wright Mills, eds., pp. 180–195; Gerhard Lenski, "Status Crystallization: A Non-Vertical Dimension of Social Status," *American Sociological Review,* 19, 1954, pp. 405–413; Elton Jackson, "Status Consistency and Symptoms of Stress," *American Sociological Review,* 27, 1962, pp. 469–480; N. J. Demerath, III, *Social Class in American Protestantism,* Chaps. 6 and 7; Frederick Bates and Roland Pellegrin, "Congruity and Incongruity of Status Attributes," *Social Forces,* 38, 1959, pp. 23–28.

objective improvement. The study of relative deprivation, when applied to social stratification, is one part of a larger question: How do subjective factors influence stratification systems? If one thinks of himself as middle-class, whereas others regard him as a member of the working class, he is likely to feel deprived relative to those in his presumptive class.[2]

Robert Merton has observed that the authors of The American Soldier, who made extensive use of the concept of relative deprivation, focus on deprivation more than on the full implications of the adjective relative. One can, of course, feel relatively rewarded. By bringing the concept into the framework of reference-group theory, Merton notes, the limitation to negative comparisons can be eliminated.[3]

A further extension is also needed. One can see himself as relatively deprived or relatively rewarded. But he can also be seen by others in these same ways. The two perceptions do not necessarily coincide. Indeed, it may be their disjunction that produces many of the consequences that have been observed in connection with relative deprivation, seen individually. Putting the two perspectives into one system, we get the paradigm shown in Figure 14-1.

Self-perceptions

Deprived   Equated   Rewarded

		Deprived	Equated	Rewarded
	Deprived	A	D	G
Perceptions of others	Equated	B	E	H
	Rewarded	C	F	I

FIGURE 14-1. Varieties of relative perception

I do not know of studies that explore the consequences for behavior of the various combinations of these variables, whether applied to income, power, or prestige (to return to the earlier question). However, I believe there would be general agreement on the judgment that the consequences of conjunction are quite different from the consequences of disjunction. If, for example, the members of a group feel deprived relative to others with whom they compare themselves, but they are generally regarded as being treated equally or rewarded (situations B and C), they are not only likely to see the situation as basically unjust, but also as incapable of correction. If others support them in their perception (situation A), the sense of injustice may be no less, but their belief in the possibilities of changing the situation may be greater.

2 We shall make some specific applications of the concept of relative deprivation later. Unfortunately, it has not been systematically related to studies of "subjective class placement." Perhaps the place to start in examining these two concepts is S. A. Stouffer and others, The American Soldier; and Richard Centers, The Psychology of Social Classes.

3 Robert Merton, Social Theory and Social Structure, rev. ed., Chap. 8.

There are a number of subtle interactions at work in these various patterns. Those who feel strongly that they are deprived relative to others and who see some, but not very much, support for that view from others, may be strongly motivated to deny even such support as exists. They may *need* disjunction to give them ideological clarity and to strengthen personal conviction. (Thus some American Negroes regard the civil rights movement as a "fake," any changes in opportunity as "tokenism," and any black supporters of the changes as "Uncle Toms.")

The quality of being *nouveau riche* entails not only the objective fact of recency of wealth, but various perceptions as well. A person newly rich may be seen by others as over-rewarded; he may, in fact, see himself that way (situation I). I suspect that politics, religion, and style of life are quite different in such conditions from what they are when one is seen and sees himself as justly rewarded (situation E).

Because there is no systematic body of data relating to these questions, we must seek some reasonably adequate index of the perceptual factor in stratification systems. For purposes of the next several chapters, I suggest that we put alongside the three elements suggested by Weber a fourth that is also unequally distributed, socially conditioned, and in scarce supply, namely, hope. Two groups may be equally lowly in prestige, income, and power; but if one has hope and the other does not, their religious behavior (and many other aspects of their lives) will be quite different.

I am suggesting that a person who has high hopes, even if he rated low on the other scales, has poorly crystallized status, and that his beliefs and behavior will express that fact. On the other hand, the person of relatively high income, power, and prestige, who is low in hope (he sees the world moving away from the patterns within which he has prospered), will also be affected by the lack of crystallization. When many such persons are in interaction, a social movement expressive of their common status inconsistency is likely to develop.

It would take us too far from our central concern to examine with care the various reasons given for the relationship between status discrepancy and behavior. I shall simply note that two complementary lines of argument have been developed, one emphasizing individual and the other interpersonal stresses connected with status discrepancy. In both instances, individuals are motivated to try to reduce the stress. Following Leon Festinger, one can interpret the actions of a person with poorly crystallized status as efforts to reduce cognitive dissonance. From the point of view of his place in various groups, his actions can be interpreted as efforts to reduce interpersonal and role dissonance.[4]

Gary Marx has raised questions about the supposed influence of status discrepancy by noting that consistently high-status Negroes (high in both education and occupation) are more militant than those with inconsistent status. I would suggest that the deprivation of status of the former is relatively greater than that of the latter. Having been successful educationally and occupationally, they experience the failure to receive a match-

4 See Leon Festinger, *A Theory of Cognitive Dissonance;* Everett Hughes, "Dilemmas and Contradictions of Status," *American Journal of Sociology,* 50, 1944, pp. 353–359; Edward Sampson, "Status Congruence and Cognitive Consistency," *Sociometry,* 26, 1963, pp. 146–162.

ing status as all the more unjust. By introducing a perceptual variable, some of the inconsistencies in findings about the effects of status discrepancy can be removed. Marx gives some credence to this interpretation, but comes back to what he considers "far more concrete reasons" for the greater militancy of more privileged Negroes—they have the energy, resources, morale, and self-confidence needed to challenge the oppressive system. To explain why the energy and resources should be directed in a militant way, however, requires attention to motivational factors. It is the combination that seems to me to be decisive.[5]

Of particular interest to us is the variety of ways in which motives to reduce dissonance can be expressed. Festinger has observed that one can try to reduce cognitive dissonance by attacking the system within which it is experienced, by withdrawing from the system, or by accepting its basic structure while adding emphasis to favorable elements in such a way that greater balance is obtained. (Applying this last to religion, one might hear a person say: "Although my income and education are modest, my devotion and the exclusive quality of my religious group are of greater importance.")

These are precisely the three sectarian strategies we have discussed; they can be seen as techniques for the reduction of discrepancy. I would not argue that tendencies toward sectarianism are derived entirely or even substantially from status discrepancy; but it is certainly one of several critical variables. Status placement, whether discrepant or not, is certainly of major importance. There is a wealth of evidence that sects are predominantly lower-class movements.[6] It is difficult, however, to remove the possible contributing effect of discrepancy from this evidence. Those at the very bottom seldom revolt, whether politically or religiously. Those who do revolt have experienced improvement on one or another of the status measures. If their aspirations have been raised, discrepancy in the form of relative deprivation is present.

Demerath has explored the relationship between status discrepancy and tendencies toward sectarianism in a valuable way, using data from a survey made by the National Council of Churches.[7] The sample is probably quite representative of the members of the larger Northern Protestant churches. Its weakness for the purpose in hand is that no sectarians, as that term is usually employed in the United States, are included; hence Demerath can study only sectarian tendencies among members of denominations. It may be that it is mainly those who resolve the dilemmas of discrepant status by accepting the social order (which is represented in this study by the established denominations) and emphasizing those elements in it favorable to them (as, for example, by high church attendance) who remain in the denominations. Those with sharper discrepancies, and/or those with tendencies toward attack and withdrawal as ways of handling those discrepancies, may not be found in the sample. Perhaps they are in secular protesting groups or in sects. If this qualification has merit, the relationship

5 For Marx's discussion, see his *Protest and Prejudice*, Chap. 2.

6 See Werner Stark, *The Sociology of Religion*, Vol. 2; Russell Dynes, "The Church-Sect Typology and Socio-Economic Status," *American Sociological Review*, 20, 1955, pp. 555–560; and Demerath, op. cit., Chaps. 4 and 5.

7 See Demerath, op. cit., Chaps. 6 and 7.

between status discrepancy and sectarian tendencies found by Demerath may be more significant than he suggests. When he carried his interpretation through several elaborations, the relationship was reduced to modest proportions. Had more intensely sectarian individuals been in the sample, however, it seems likely that the relationship would have been higher.[8]

RELIGION AND CLASS

Every aspect of religion can vary from class to class: beliefs, rites, aesthetic expressions of religious emotion, the structure and leadership of religious organizations, and every other phase of the process of "being religious" may be different in one class from another. One must be careful to avoid easy hypotheses to explain the details of these differences. Propositions that the beliefs of the upper classes are more rational or the rites of the underprivileged more austere may seem obvious, but the evidence is not all in their favor. Wach points out that Puritan motives may restrain the ritual of aristocratic groups and that lower classes may insist on "as lavish a service to the deity as they can possibly afford." [9] This does not demonstrate a lack of variation in religious behavior according to class, but only that the variation requires careful study, for the relationship is complicated and other lines of division may obscure its effects. Differences in needs, variations in life style and experiences, different development of facility with language and other modes of expression, variation in claims and requirements—all of which vary from class to class and among other social divisions—manifest themselves in religious behavior.

Max Weber has shown how the religious meaning of suffering and of salvation has varied. Nietzsche had developed a kind of class-determined theory of religion in his doctrine of "resentment": Religion is an expression of the repressed resentments of the powerless; it is their attempt to enchain their masters by symbolic means in face of the failures of other methods to break their control. Weber declared, however, that it is not primarily resentment, but suffering, with which religion has dealt, and goes beyond Nietzsche to show the differences in the meaning of suffering. Resentment is only one of the forms that religion may take among the deprived. And it quite fails to account for the religious values of the advantaged.

Thus on one hand there is the "theodicy of good fortune," which justifies the well-placed in their fortune by treating suffering as a sign of odiousness in the eyes of the gods and as a sign of secret guilt.

Other things being equal, classes with high social and economic privilege will scarcely be prone to evolve the idea of salvation. Rather, they assign to religion

8 We do not have a well-established way of measuring sectarian tendencies. Doubtless the results of Demerath's analysis were influenced by the way he measured sectarianism, but one cannot say in what ways. I do not find the scale he designed—based on the number of close friends in the congregation, the number of areas in which one believes his church aids him, and the extent of disapproval of ministers taking stands on public issues—to be very powerful. Dynes' scale (op. cit.) may be a better measure of fundamentalism than of sectarianism—two terms that I would not equate. One might profitably make use of the three distinctions suggested by Werner Stark: The sectarian is oriented to a glorious past or a glorious future, to an ascetic or a licentious morality, to withdrawal from or attack on society. The churchman, in each instance, would take the more "moderate" position between the polarities.

9 Joachim Wach, *Sociology of Religion*, pp. 234–235.

the primary function of legitimizing their own life pattern and situation in the world. This universal phenomenon is rooted in certain basic psychological patterns. When a man who is happy compares his position with that of one who is unhappy, he is not content with the fact of his happiness, but desires something more, the consciousness that he has earned his good fortune, in contrast to the unfortunate one who must equally have earned his misfortune. . . . What the privileged classes require of religion, if anything at all, is this psychological reassurance of legitimacy. To be sure, not every class with high privilege feels this need in the same degree.[10]

Weber's interpretation of the theodicy of good fortune is not entirely adequate. It overlooks the universal elements in unhappiness. It disregards the sense of relative deprivation that may be felt even by those in the privileged classes, for they compare themselves with those around them as well as with those who are less advantaged. And as Weber himself noted, Buddhism arose as a salvation doctrine among the privileged—as the product of reflection on ethical and religious questions. It is scarcely a proclamation of good fortune.

Yet the basic contrast is sound, for in contrast to the theodicy of good fortune we often find the glorification of suffering—even the seeking out of suffering in order to achieve salvation—on the part of the powerless. They thus seek to rescue religious victory from earthly defeat. This may take the form, as it did in ancient Judaism, of ideological resentment; ". . . the unequal distribution of mundane goods is caused by the sinfulness and the illegality of the privileged . . . sooner or later God's wrath will overtake them." [11] A similar view is a component of the Christianity of the lower classes in many contexts. Or it may, on the other hand, take the form of a theodicy of rebirth. There is no thought in Hinduism of a revolutionary change in the system of social stratification. The lower castes were most conscientious in the performance of caste duties as a prerequisite to rebirth in a higher status. Whatever their personal feelings might have been, there was no support in their religious beliefs for resentment against the higher castes.[12]

Buddhism and Hinduism are more unified so far as theodicy is concerned than Judaism and Christianity. This clearly does not mean, however, that the former are religiously undifferentiated by status levels. Sharp differences in religious duties among the castes are intrinsic to Hinduism. In Buddhism, the ways in which one seeks merit—the means to rebirth in a higher life— vary widely by class, because resources, training, and motivation vary. The more privileged may seek to approach religious truth by meditation; they may hope for merit by large gifts to a monastery. The less privileged also seek merit through gifts—a widow's mite (to view this in an ecumenical way) that represents greater sacrifice than the endowments of the wealthy. But they also express themselves in devotion, perhaps by meticulous performance of ceremonies for a deceased father, in which they are not disadvantaged.

10 Max Weber, *The Sociology of Religion*, p. 107.

11 Ibid., p. 97.

12 See Max Weber, *The Sociology of Religion*, Chap. 7; and *From Max Weber: Essays in Sociology*, Hans Gerth and C. Wright Mills, eds., Chap. 11. See also Peter Berger, *The Sacred Canopy*, Chap. 3, for instructive comments on theodicy.

The effects of class may be manifest in variations within one religious tradition or they may be revealed in the dominant themes of a total religious system. In making this point, Weber indicates that religious behavior is not a mere reflection of class, for having originated in the context of one class —and being shaped by its style of life—a religion may strongly influence persons in other classes in the societies through which it spreads. Weber thus describes the stratum of the special carriers and interpreters of the world religions:

Confucianism was the status ethic of prebendaries, of men with literary educations who were characterized by a secular rationalism. If one did not belong to this *cultured* stratum he did not count. . . .

Early Hinduism was borne by a hereditary caste of cultured literati, who, being remote from any office, functioned as a kind of ritualist and spiritual advisers for individuals and communities. . . .

Buddhism was propagated by strictly contemplative, mendicant monks, who rejected the world and, having no homes, migrated. . . .

During its first period, Islamism was a religion of world-conquering warriors, a knight order of disciplined crusaders. . . .

Since the Exile, Judaism has been the religion of a civic "pariah people. . . ."

Christianity, finally, began its course as a doctrine of itinerant artisan journeymen. During all periods of its mighty external and internal development it has been a quite specifically urban, and above all a civic, religion.[13]

Occupational and educational as well as class variables are involved in this analysis by Weber; but it serves well to illustrate the point that a religion is strongly influenced by the style of life of the stratum which is its special carrier and interpreter. If one looks upon a religion as something that has been created in all its essentials by one great founder or suddenly revealed, this analysis has little meaning. But if one sees it as a cumulative product of many persons, making their religious interpretations in a specific social and cultural environment, then the shaping influence of the values and needs of the stratum in which it develops is highly important. Once the "tone," the basic view of the nature of man and the problem of evil, is fixed in a religious system, under the selective emphases of one stratum, that tone will affect other strata who come within the religious tradition.

One must note carefully, however, that if a religion spreads from one class to others, it absorbs many elements from these new strata. Under a process of selective adaptation that builds on earlier potentialities, it is influenced by the needs and values, the style of life, of the new classes. By such a process the world religions have become multiple systems of ways for dealing with the fundamental problems of life, systems from which the different strata may select the emphases most congenial to them, at the same time sharing some common views. Thus as societies become more complicated, more highly stratified, and affected by mobility and social change, their dominant religions become loosely jointed congeries of systems of belief and practice. Although they use many common symbols and share some doctrines and rites, the classes will vary greatly in their definitions of what is evil and their conceptions of how one should deal with the problem of evil. This can be illustrated in many ways.

Louis Finkelstein interprets the differences and struggles within Judaism

13 *From Max Weber*, pp. 268–269.

in its early development, between the prophetic and pharisaic elements, as a result of the economic and cultural conflicts between the seminomadic shepherds and the settled farmers, the landless groups and the great landowners, and, in the cities, between the artisans and the nobles.[14]

It is a mistake to overlook the ways in which Judaism cuts across class and occupational lines or to ignore the influence that the religious views of one group has had on the lives of the others; but it is also necessary to see the ways in which it contains the varying needs and interpretations of different strata. An even wider range may be found among the diverse interpretations of Hinduism on different social levels, among the many denominations and sects in Buddhism, and among the variant developments of Christianity.

If, as Weber says, Christianity was first adhered to by itinerant artisan journeymen, it nevertheless became, in the course of a few centuries, the religion of peasant and nobleman, of warrior and monk, of artisan and merchant. In its very beginnings it was a complicated hybrid, building not only on Judaism, but on classic Greek humanism, and on the very different mystery cults. It drew together many different groups who were united only by their opposition to the ancient world order and their discontent with the prevailing religious attempts to deal with life's problems. It developed a conception of equality which bound them together, and yet left the differences that separated them close beneath the surface, for under the guidance of Paul, the equality that was essential to Christianity was religiously interpreted.

. . . Christianity, along with all the radical equalizing of men in the sight of God and with all the penetration of this idea in the whole life of the soul, and in all personal relations of men to one another, is yet at the same time very cautious towards any attempt to carry over this equality into the sphere of secular relationships and institutions, which have nothing to do with the real religious basis of this equality.[15]

Christianity did not, indeed could not, eliminate the status differences, with their influences on religious need and behavior. The medieval synthesis of Thomism was achieved under the favorable circumstances of a relatively stable society that had little trade and lacked a money economy. Yet even that relatively unified view was opposed by the radical individualism of mysticism, by sectarian movements, as well as by such theological protests as Nominalism.

At various times in the history of Christianity, different status groups have been drawn together in a joint effort, only to break apart when their different needs and values proved incompatible. Luther, for a few years, united several movements that were held together largely by their common opposition to the Church and the society it reinforced. Those who, like Luther himself, were primarily concerned with a reshaping of the religious view of the world, were joined by humanists, German nationalists, and peasants. Because some of these hoped to use the Lutheran movement for secular purposes, however, and because the kinds of religious formulations that could seem meaningful and satisfying varied among these

14 See Louis Finkelstein, *The Pharisees: The Sociological Background of Their Faith.*

15 Ernst Troeltsch, *The Social Teaching of the Christian Churches*, p. 75.

groups, there soon were widespread defections. The Humanists discovered that their grounds for opposition to the Church—its support of superstition and its intellectual tyranny, as they saw it—were not Luther's grounds. Many of the German nationalists were uninterested in the specifically religious problems that to Luther were central. When the political circumstances were favorable, they were easily "reconverted" by the Counter Reformation. And some of the peasants, when they found that Luther's doctrines had no reference to the land-tenure system under which they suffered, when they felt the harshness of his opposition to the means they used to redress their grievances, turned to other religious movements. It was they who were the source of that other important part of the Reformation, the radical sects, which played their role in the religious life of several societies. Those who thus left the Lutheran movement were not simply expressing secular conflicts. For many, there were religious issues involved; but differences in secular position affected the way they viewed those religious questions.

SECTARIAN PROTESTS IN CHRISTENDOM

The complicated interplay of class and religion has probably been most closely studied for the period of the Christian Reformation and the several generations of drastic change that followed upon it. I shall therefore illustrate this research by examining the situation in England in the seventeenth century. A few more general comments, however, will make the discussion more meaningful.

Drawing on their Jewish heritage, Christians of the lower classes have frequently used their faith to protest against the secular order. To put it in terms of stratification theory, their status is almost continuously lacking in "crystallization"—however low their income, power, and prestige—because they have hope that the last shall be first. By the fourth century the apocalyptic hopes of the early church were officially changed and pushed progressively further into the background as the church increased in power. "The kingdom" was of the soul. The apocalyptic tradition persisted, however, in popular religion. And when certain social conditions prevailed, it broke out in powerful movements of sectarian protest.

What must be added to messianic cultural elements to produce religious protest? Norman Cohn emphasizes the following: a surplus population, uprooted from traditional jobs and traditional kin and community ties; the lack of regular institutionalized means for expressing grievances and pressing claims; weakening of the framework of authority, both sacred and secular. "It was inevitable that many of those whose lives were condemned to hardship and insecurity should doubt whether ostentatious prelates and easy-going priests could really help them towards salvation." [16]

At the same time that traditional jobs were being lost and traditional supports broken, new possibilities have often appeared. A few persons of low status have actually been absorbed into an expanding economy; many more have *seen* the new opportunities. Thus hope has risen and the sense of relative deprivation increased. At first, the contrast with peasant society

16 Norman Cohn, *Pursuit of the Millennium*, p. 316. See pp. 314–317.

is more in the way lower-class persons regarded themselves and the possibilities around them than in their actual situation. In peasant society, as Cohn remarks, hardships are taken for granted, "part of a state of affairs which seemed to have prevailed from all eternity. Horizons were narrow. . . . In an economy which was uniformly primitive, where nobody was very rich, there was nothing to arouse new wants; certainly nothing which could stimulate men to grandiose phantasies of wealth and power." [17]

In the eleventh century, commerce, migration, population pressure, and the breakup of traditional relationships began to change the peasant patterns in many parts of Europe. New wants, hopes, problems, and opportunities began to transform the lives of those closest to the commercial and industrial centers. In terms of Table 14–2, acceptance of status as inevitable was weakened. It was no longer taken for granted that one must be poor and powerless. Institutional support for the medieval stratification pattern also began to change, because the emerging commercial-industrial economy required new kinds of workers. This change also weakened the aristocratic political structure.

What we see with particular sharpness in the chiliastic movements of medieval Christianity, especially from the fifteenth through the seventeenth centuries, is an explosive combination of cultural, structural, and character elements. We have noted how the structure of interactions and of opportunities changed. The cultural material was drawn from a long tradition: Jewish messianism; the Book of *Revelation,* that Rorschach invitation to anybody's "chosen people" dream; the Sibylline Oracles, carried along an underground current when church condemnation forced them from the surface of life; the semiapproved interpretations of Joachim of Fiore. These and other materials were ready at hand for those who sought a new life. There were many such persons, caught between the broken patterns of an old way of living and the tantalizing hopes of a new one. They were often dramatically bound together by the emotional intensity of a prophet, whose dream of grandeur was shaped by the common religious heritage. Doubtless the catalytic agent, as Cohn suggests, was often a paranoid delusion, which was acceptable to others both because it was drawn from cultural materials and also because it helped them express their own needs and anxieties. Thus character elements, of both leaders and followers, were added to the cultural and structural sources.[18]

Class and Religion in the English Civil War Period

The structural, cultural, and individual elements influencing the interactions of religion and class can be seen clearly in the development of the religious situation during the period of the English Civil War. In the

17 Ibid., p. 26.

18 See ibid., pp. 69–74, on "The psychic content of a social myth." On late medieval and early modern sects see, in addition to Cohn, George H. Williams, *The Radical Reformation;* Werner Stark, *The Sociology of Religion,* Vol. 2; Roland H. Bainton, "The Left Wing of the Reformation," *Journal of Religion,* January, 1941, pp. 124–134; Arthur C. M'Giffert, *Protestant Thought Before Kant; Preserved Smith, The Age of the Reformation;* and the several references to England that follow.

century after 1540 an industrial and commercial revolution had created powerful new classes, who found their development blocked by the Stuart government. At the same time, the revolution had enlarged the group of merchants and businessmen, had intensified the land problem of the peasants, and had created the beginnings of an urban proletariat. All these groups had reason to be unhappy with the existing political situation and discontented with a religious establishment that supported it. By the time of the death of Elizabeth, the nation was sharply divided, with the King and the Church on one side and Parliament and the Puritans (using that term in its broadest meaning) on the other. The Established Church, bound to the sovereign by statutes and oaths, was a stanch supporter of the Crown and of the landed gentry. It taught, in the Homilies, "that the King's power was from God alone; that, as it was a perilous thing to commit to subjects the judgment which prince was godly and his government good and which otherwise, as though the foot should judge the head, it was in no case lawful to resist, wicked though he might be." [19] It is clear that such a doctrine could not be accepted by the powerful new classes who opposed the feudal authority of the King. They turned away from the Church that denied their right to acquire power, and became the dominant element among the Puritans.

We are primarily concerned, however, not with the split between Church and Puritan, but with the diversity of classes, with their various religious needs and views, to be found within Puritanism itself. Religiously, the republican forces combined Presbyterians, Independents, and radical sectarians.[20] They united to carry through successfully the Civil War, but their different status positions broke them apart politically and accentuated their religious differences; ". . . the different directions in which Puritan thought developed were dependent on the economic conditions and interests of the various classes which advanced and supported the new developments." [21] As Weber frequently pointed out, it is not the founders so much as the followers of a religious movement, those who work to develop it after the first surge of enthusiasm is past, who are likely to demonstrate by their interpretations the effects of class status on religion.

The Presbyterians, the right wing of the Puritan coalition, found their chief support among the aristocrats who had joined the Parliamentary cause and among the wealthy merchants. They wanted "to limit the objectives of the revolution: to assert the effectual sovereignty not of the people but of Parliament, and to preserve at all costs the sanctity of property, whether real, personal, or political (the historic rights of the Crown and the material possessions of the Church alone excepted)." [22] At the beginning of the Civil War, the various groups under the Parliamentary banner

19 G. P. Gooch, *English Democratic Ideas in the Seventeenth Century*, p. 54.

20 The last of these should not be included within the definition of Puritan, in a strict religious sense; but they were for a time part of the Puritan coalition, as it is often defined, in a political sense. On the definition of Puritan, see Christopher Hill, *Society and Puritanism in Pre-Revolutionary England*, Chap. 1; and Charles George and Katherine George, *The Protestant Mind of the English Reformation*, pp. 397–407.

21 R. B. Schlatter, "The Problem of Historical Causation in Some Recent Studies of the English Revolution," *Journal of the History of Ideas*, June, 1943, p. 363.

22 A. S. P. Woodhouse, *Puritanism and Liberty*, p. 15.

were united in their opposition to the claims of the monarch and in their fear of Catholicism.

But when the grounds for their fears had been removed by the destruction of prelacy and they were forced to give positive expression to their convictions in a system of ecclesiastical government, they were riven by profound differences that would admit of no compromise. Whatever purely religious considerations might have been involved, the rich merchants of the City had no intentions of relaxing an ecclesiastical discipline that enabled them to control effectively the classes they wanted to exploit and to prevent the propagation of ideas they considered dangerous or subversive. The lesser gentry, the smaller merchants, the tradesmen, frightened by the avenues of oppression a system of central control opened up and aware of the drastic limitation on social criticism Presbyterianism imposed, insisted on a broader freedom than those who dominated Parliament were prepared to extend.[23]

The Independents, drawn from "the lesser gentry, the smaller merchants, the tradesmen" mentioned above, the center party of the Puritan coalition, were themselves too uncertain of their place in the new society, too mindful still of their struggle to win the rights of free religious choice and unrestricted economic activity, to agree fully with the Presbyterians. For a time, many of the sectarian protests of the English lower classes found some expression in Independency. The sectarians and the Independents agreed on the separation of Church and State and particularly on the need for complete liberty of conscience. But in the end the center group, along with the Presbyterians, moved toward a church-type accommodation to the society in which they were winning an important place.

The various sectarians, the left wing of the Puritan coalition, supported the Parliamentary group in the hope of alleviating their economic distress and powerlessness. When they discovered, however, that the leaders of the Parliamentary forces were scarcely more interested than were the Royalists in helping them to solve their economic problems, in distributing political power throughout the population, or in establishing religious liberty, they broke away from the Puritan group in both political and religious movements.

These diverse strata, although they were united in their opposition to Catholicism and had developed in common from the Reformation, could not be held together either in politics or religion. Their needs, the problems with which they struggled, were too different. They all might point to the teachings of Calvin to defend very different conclusions, for as one Puritan put it, "We can pick and choose from a Reformer what fits to the standard of our own light and reformation, and cast the other by. . . . "[24] Wide differences in doctrine, in church organization, in ethical emphasis, in style of worship, and in relationship to the state were exhibited by the various Puritan groups.

The Presbyterians gave a fundamental place to the doctrine of predestination. This inegalitarian doctrine harmonized well with their demonstrated success in this world and armed them with proof that they need not be concerned with the poor—who were obviously numbered among the

23 David W. Petegorsky, *Left-Wing Democracy in the English Civil War*, p. 61.

24 Quoted by Woodhouse, op. cit., p. 62.

damned: ". . . the restriction of salvation in the hereafter to a limited number of souls chosen out of all the rest by God alone, whatever one may choose to think of it as theology, was certainly sound political psychology." [25] Here is Weber's "theodicy of good fortune," the interpretation of suffering as a sign of guilt, of nonelection. Puritans who took the doctrine of predestination seriously, however, were not entirely convinced even by their own worldly success that they themselves were among the chosen. Accomplishments on earth were at best only a portent, not a proof. This lingering doubt may help to account for some of their rigidity of doctrine and the severity of their restrictions on worldly pleasures; for thus they sought to prove, more to themselves than to others, that they were truly elect.

To this doctrine of predestination, the lower classes raised strong religious protest. Drawing partly on the tradition of Wycliffe, but more affected by the radical and humanistic ideas of Gerrard Winstanley and others, the sectarians broke with the dominant Puritan group. Their answer to predestination was to declare the equality of all persons before God. With many persons of this group, equality had a specifically political and secular meaning, particularly during the struggles of the mid-seventeenth century. This concept was gradually transformed—although never completely—by the Quakers and other pietistic groups until it came to have largely a religious meaning.

The Puritans claimed that knowledge of God came only through the study and understanding of the Bible, thus removing the direction of religious affairs from the prelates only to put it in the hands of a literate, educated class. The sects replied by declaring that an inner spiritual inspiration was the source of religious knowledge—a source that was open to the illiterate and poor, a way that was available to any man, no matter how humble his station.[26]

Such religious differences were matched by political and economic differences. Combine the sense of election with the fear of anarchy and one has an ingredient for an authoritarian view of government. But combine the duties and disciplines of the saint with a fear of tyranny and one has an ingredient for rebellion. Both tendencies are found within Puritanism, at least partly as an expression of the class range among its members.[27]

Cromwell was able to block the political efforts of the lower classes, but he could not destroy the awareness of their problems that had been aroused by the conflicts of the Civil War period. With their hopes raised, they were no longer a relatively stable lower stratum. Their situation had been "decrystallized," despite their continuing poverty and lack of power. If political channels for expressing the psychic effects of this decrystallization were blocked, religious channels were used. Petegorsky writes:

After 1649 and 1650 that social consciousness could no longer be given direct political expression. Instead, it found its voice in the tremendous revival of

25 William Haller, *The Rise of Puritanism*, p. 169.

26 See Petegorsky, op. cit., p. 65.

27 Leo Solt, *Saints in Arms. Puritanism and Democracy in Cromwell's Army,* and Michael Walzer, *The Revolution of the Saints,* weigh the balance somewhat differently. Walzer stresses the importance of Puritanism for the development of participatory democracy, although he sees it as a frequently unintended result. Solt sees more authoritarian influences at work, but not without significant democratic effects as well.

mystical enthusiasm and millenary fervour that dates from those years. If the price of political agitation was persecution and imprisonment, it was much more convenient to shift the initiative for social change to the Lord who could risk with impunity the wrath of the dictators. And if the practical efforts of mortals had failed to achieve the desired results, surely God, in His time, would bring the eagerly awaited millennium.[28]

This is perhaps to underestimate the political and economic implications of sectarianism, even after Cromwell's victory. Winstanley propounded a radical democracy and a religious communism that attacked the existing churches and the economic-political order alike. To be sure, he did not see victory coming by force of arms, as had the Fifth Monarchy men, but by the power of an inner light bringing men to reason. Government would "wither away," as a later sectarian put it; the "despised ones of the earth" would triumph, in the words of the seventeenth-century prophet, while the rich men "weep and howl." For Christ, said Winstanley, "is the true and faithful Leveller."

True religion and undefiled is this, to make restitution of the Earth which hath been taken and held from the common people . . .[29]

And the tithing-priest stops their mouth, and tells them that "inward satisfaction of mind" was meant by the declaration "The poor shall inherit the earth." I tell you, the scripture is to be really and materially fulfilled. . . . You jeer at the name Leveller. I tell you Jesus Christ is the head Leveller.[30]

Nor was fulfillment to be long in coming; the revolution would be accomplished "ere many years wheel about." As Brailsford, who quotes this phrase, observed, Winstanley was not simply prophesying. "He had seen the mighty hurled from their seats. A king's head had fallen in Whitehall before he flung his challenge at property." [31]

But the revolution was partial at best. Cromwell continued to support religious liberty—which was probably a critical factor in determining the direction of further protests—but not the economic and political egalitarianism of the sectarians. And the Restoration even more than the rule of Cromwell made clear that the lower classes were not going to have their problems solved by the emerging new society. "The Civil War had made it certain," as Petegorsky says, "that neither an absolute king nor an absolute Church would ever again impede economic progress." That having been accomplished, the old aristocracy and the newly powerful middle classes found that they had more in common than they had supposed. Their own quarrels made them less able to oppose the demands from the lower classes that the Parliamentary government for which they fought should give them some of the promised rewards—some relief from poverty, some political influence. "The Restoration was essentially a compromise between the aristocracy and the middle classes for the exploitation of the economic opportunities an expanding society presented." [32] Anglican and right-wing Puritan alike

28 Op. cit., p. 235.
29 Quoted by Petegorsky, op. cit., p. 179.
30 Quoted by Gooch, op. cit., p. 187.
31 H. N. Brailsford, *The Levellers*, pp. 665–666.
32 Petegorsky, op. cit., pp. 240–241.

accepted the basic structure of the new social order, seeking primarily to assure individual goodness and salvation within that order. As the richest merchants and industrialists became more sharply distinguished from the lesser men of business, they felt closer to the landed gentry. By the eighteenth century, wealthy nonconformists were joining the Anglican Church. Just as their earlier class differences were matched by religious differences, so now the converging political and economic interests of the landed aristocracy and the most powerful of the new bourgeoisie were matched by converging religious inclinations.[33]

Opposed by such a united front, the sects turned further away from the hopes of men like Winstanley for immediate reform by a union of political means with religion. They turned to quiet waiting for the millennium or patient nonresistance, and to more specifically religious interpretations of life.

It is interesting to note that in the case of the English sects as in that of the German the method of non-resistance was not espoused until efforts toward a violent revolution had been found unavailing in the face of the superior power of the ruling classes, while, at the same time, the ideal of a new social order was abandoned in favor of a sectarian organization of mutual aid and brotherhood.[34]

Thus religious efforts change when attempts to solve the intrusive problems of life have been found to be inadequate. This same transformation can be seen to some degree in the development of Jewish hopes for an earthly kingdom into a conception of the kingdom of God; it is found in the "failure of nerve" of many of the Greeks after the third century B.C. and their "retreat" to the mystery cults,[35] it is important in the declining emphasis of early Christianity on the reformist hopes that at least some few had seen in it.[36] These movements vary greatly, of course, in the extent of the shift. And in none of them is the hope for solutions to the problems of this world simply given up. That is partly true, for the values of life on earth may be sharply discounted. Another aspect of the shift, however, is the adoption of religious means to replace the frustrated political, military, or economic efforts. Apocalyptic views, a literal interpretation of the belief that "he that loseth his life shall find it," and an emphasis on personal goodness and righteousness may have reference to this life, in fact, as well as to eternal salvation.

Class and Religion in America

The relationship between the stratification system and religious patterns has perhaps never been as close in the United States as it was in seventeenth-century England; but there has been and continues to be a substan-

33 See R. B. Schlatter, *The Social Ideas of Religious Leaders, 1660–1688.*

34 H. Richard Niebuhr, *The Social Sources of Denominationalism*, pp. 52–53.

35 One should note that "failure of nerve," as Gilbert Murray described it, was a Western concept with an implied value, not simply a descriptive statement. Few Buddhists, for example, would look upon a mystical religious development as a failure of nerve, but might see it rather as a courageous and intelligent response to the facts of the universe.

36 For a recent study that sees Jesus as close to the zealots of his time, see S. G. F. Brandon, *Jesus and the Zealots.*

tial connection. In the early years, status differences were correlated, to a degree, with geography, so that one could contrast the religious tendencies of the eastern part of the country with those of the frontier.

The religion of the urban, commercial East tended to take on or to retain the typical features of all bourgeois or national religion—a polity corresponding to the order and character of class organized society, an intellectual conception of the content of faith, an ethics reflecting the needs and evaluations of a stable and commercial citizenry, a sober, ritualistic type of religious expression. The religion of the West, on the other hand, accepted or produced anew many of the characistics of the faith of the disinherited, for the psychology of the frontier corresponds in many respects to the psychology of the revolutionary poor. This is especially true of the emotional character of religious experience, which seems to be required in the one case as in the other. The isolation of frontier life fostered craving for companionship, suppressed the gregarious tendency and so subjected the lonely settler to the temptations of crowd suggestions to an unusual degree.[37]

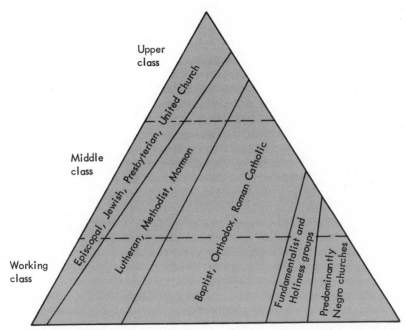

FIGURE 14–2. *Class and religion in the United States (The areas are roughly proportional to membership. The pyramidal shape may misrepresent the American class distribution which, by many criteria, approximates a diamond shape, with largest numbers in the lower-middle and upper working classes.)*

Niebuhr's statement combines the effects of several variables—degree of isolation, level of education, occupation, and so on, as well as class— thus properly alerting us to the fact that our concentration on class will not do justice to the complexity of the situation.

As the nation developed, the class-religion complex less and less closely

---

37 H. Richard Niebuhr, op. cit., p. 141.

corresponded with region. A far more important influence on that complex was the growth of the population from Africa and Europe. Lines of differentiation among white Protestants were overshadowed by the growth of separate Negro churches, of Roman Catholicism, and of Judaism. By the mid-twentieth century, these groups constituted over 50 per cent of the affiliated members (Negro churches, 10 per cent; Roman Catholics, 37 per cent; Jewish congregations, 4.5 per cent).[38]

Neither these groups nor the various Protestant denominations and sects were homogeneous by class, and they have probably become even less so. Nevertheless, some relationship to the stratification system persists. Disregarding community and regional differences and using only broad categories, we can picture the class distribution of the members of some of the largest American churches as shown in Figure 14–2, page 299.

Lower-Class Sects in the United States. I shall not undertake a full review of the interactions of religion with the stratification system in the United States, but I will examine some aspects of sectarian movements, following the line of thought developed earlier.[39] Using materials drawn primarily from England, we have seen that sects highly antagonistic to the social order appeared when certain structural and character changes were combined with a religious culture selectively interpreted. We can profitably use the seventeenth-century English situation as a model against which other situations can be set, for comparison and contrast. Many of the conditions in England during that period have become endemic around the world, but they combine in a variety of mixtures; hence the religious outcomes differ rather widely.

By the nineteenth century, the Judaic-Christian millenarian culture was "available"—credible, acceptable—to many of the urban proletariat in Europe only in attenuated form (although there are some fascinating similarities between Winstanley and Marx). In the United States, however, the rural and urbanizing lower classes were, and to a substantial degree still are, heirs of a religious culture that is both otherworldly and revolutionary. In this, they are closer to the Europe and England of the sixteenth and seventeenth centuries than of later periods.

Some of the structural changes have matched those in England, but

38 These figures should be seen as approximations of memberships of those 14 years of age or older. The data are imprecise and lacking in comparability. When self-identification rather than membership is used, these three groups drop to about 40 per cent (10, 26, and 3.2 per cent respectively), because most of the nonmembers are white Protestants. See Frank Mead, *Handbook of Denominations*, new 4th ed.; and Edwin Gausted, "America's Institutions of Faith," in *The Religious Situation: 1968*, Donald Cutler, ed., Chap. 22.

39 For a variety of observations, see David Moberg, "Social Class and the Churches," *Information Service*, June 14, 1958, pp. 6–8; N. J. Demerath, III, *Social Class in American Protestantism*; Herbert Schneider, *Religion in 20th Century America*; E. Digby Baltzell, *The Protestant Establishment*, and *An American Business Aristocracy*, Chap. 10; Glenn Vernon, *Sociology of Religion*, Chap. 19; H. P. Douglass, "Cultural Differences and Recent Religious Differences," *Christendom*, Winter, 1945, pp. 89–105; Truman B. Douglass, "Ecological Changes and the Church," *Annals of the American Academy*, 322; 1960, pp. 80–88; Erich Goode, "Social Class and Church Participation," *American Journal of Sociology*, 72, 1966, pp. 102–111. For an earlier period, H. Richard Niebuhr's *Social Sources of Denominationalism* remains a classic.

others have not. There has been for many the same uprooting from traditional jobs, the breaking of ties with small communities and kin groups. In recent years there has been the weakening framework of authority. Surplus population, which Cohn regards as particularly important, can be indexed perhaps by rates of unemployment. It has varied widely, but for groups at the lower end of the skill ladder, the sense of being part of a surplus has been a persistent experience. Means for expressing grievances and pressing claims have probably increased for the upper groups of the working class, through the growth of labor unions and political participation. But they are still rudimentary for the uneducated and unskilled, for the recent migrants to the city. It is primarily among these groups that sects form.

When a lower-class person moves from a rural area into a city, to work in mill or factory, he is confronted with a number of difficult problems of adjustment. He is forced to accept an enormous change in his style of life —in the rhythm of his work, in the nature of his associations, and in his place in a neighborhood. He is likely to be almost wholly lacking in organized social contacts, because he enters the new society at its most poorly organized level. And his sense of isolation is increased by the way in which he is looked down upon by the established urban groups.[40] This is the kind of problem with which religion might be expected to deal by saying: "You are not alone; you belong; your problems are not everlasting, or at least they have meaning in a transcendental context." But the established churches are poorly equipped to give these assurances to a lower-class migrant from a rural area. For the most part they are fully accommodated to the middle and upper classes of the city—the forms of their services of worship, the content of the preaching, the programs and leadership of the various groups in the church are all adjusted to the urban members of long standing. The lower-class sect movement in this situation, then, is an attempt to grapple with the problems faced by the migrant, a response to what Holt calls the cultural shock that comes from the shift to an urban life, an attempt to heal the distress caused by isolation and insecurity. It is not likely to be an economic protest, at least in any direct sense. The migrant may be better off financially in the city. He is almost certainly ill equipped by his earlier training to protest against his economic status. The established churches, in fact, are probably more liberal on economic issues than are the lower-class sects. The urban sect goes beyond an economic protest in its power to demonstrate the widely different personal needs and modes of expression that one finds among status levels. The religious forms that have been accommodated to one status group are felt by another to be inadequate.

Closely related to isolation as a factor in the recent rise of sects in the United States is the need for an emotional expressiveness lacking in the dignified and ritualistic services of most of the churches. Clark calls the sects "refuges of the emotionally starved." The poor "cannot afford, or do

40 See John B. Holt, "Holiness Religion: Cultural Shock and Social Reorganization," *American Sociological Review*, 5, 1940, pp. 740–747. See also W. Lawson Jones, "Some Psychological Conditions of the Development of Methodism up to 1850," *British Journal of Psychology*, November, 1951, pp. 345–354, for an interesting parallel in the British scene.

not have access to the recreations, associations, social functions, and cultural activities wherein the prosperous find outlets for their emotions." [41] More than that, the *need* for emotional release may be greater among the lower classes, because of more frustrations and the monotony of many of their jobs. Liston Pope notes, with respect to a Southern mill town, that life is monotonous and dull; production methods in the mills are largely mechanical; the worker has little opportunity for choice or control over the forces that influence his life.[42] In the small religious group, the members can set their own schedule and determine their own modes of expression.

If these are indicative of the needs that foster the growth of class-differentiated sects in American society, we may now ask: How do the sects atttempt to meet these needs? To those who feel isolated in the older churches, the new, small groups are their own, to lead and to organize as they like. (That the members may like very different things and compete for leadership is shown by the frequent splits that occur.) The sects are orthodox—according to their own standards—to the point of fanaticism. At first glance, this does not seem to be an adaptation to the problems of the religiously disinherited; but it becomes meaningful as a way of saying: "We belong to a very highly selected and exclusive association." New members are admitted only after having given evidence of a religious experience and showing that they will abide by the group's norms. There is rigid enforcement of certain standards of behavior, a kind of modern asceticism that assures the members that they deserve to belong to the exclusive group and will share the rewards it promises. Pope indicates that the sects are very quick to expel members who violate their code (for such violations tear the fabric of their solutions to life's problems): "In 1938 one Free-Will Baptist Holiness Church in Gastonia received 33 new members and expelled 24 persons, of a total membership of 88. A Church of God with 143 members has expelled 30 in the last two years; another with 95 members has expelled 40; a third with 101 members has expelled 20 in the last four years." [43] For a person to be expelled from a church in our time is a rare occurrence. The exclusiveness and insistence upon "Puritan morality" of the sect is not simply "elevating the manners they cannot well escape into moral virtues established by the will of God," as Clark describes it. It is, beyond that, the expression of the psychology of the sacrifice: We deserve religious success for our purity, in return for what we have given up. Anything or anybody who endangers that assurance must be cast out and repudiated.

Within the sect, the desires of the members for leadership, for status, for expression, for assurance that their difficult lot has some ultimate significance are all dealt with. Members can give free rein to their emotions and, as Clark says, "attribute the pleasant thrills thereof to a divine agency."

There is little direct challenge to the economic and political order within which they fare so poorly, although the "comfortable" people may be criticized for their "immorality." Most of the sects in American society today accept the basic secular institutions. Their members look for their reward

41 Clark, op. cit., p. 220.

42 Liston Pope, *Millhands and Preachers*, pp. 133–134.

43 Ibid., p. 138.

in heaven or in some apocalyptic transformation of the world. According to the dominant theology, man is depraved. Only by the second coming of Jesus will the world escape its ills. Other groups, such the Jehovah's Witnesses, emphasize the withdrawal theme more strongly: Because this is a world of sin, we must not only be indifferent to it but withdraw from it and refuse its commands over us. To put this in terms of the typology we used in the preceding chapter, American lower-class sects have avoidance as their dominant theme. They can be differentiated on the basis of secondary themes, with some pointing toward acceptance and others toward aggression.

Whatever the mixture, the sects deal with the economic problems of their members primarily by redefining them, not by offering ways in which they might be solved in terms of the world's definitions. Their solution of economic distress is a collective look to the future, beyond history. As Boisen points out, this "solution" carries certain implications: It requires coming to terms with God, as the doctrines of the sect interpret God; hence there is strong emphasis on confessions and the strict enforcement of rules. The strong realization among many sectarians that their problems will not readily be solved precludes any "easy" religious solution. Their own experience has been so hard that they would not be at all convinced by easy formulas and doctrines.

Among some sects, however, there is a tone of American individualistic optimism underlying the pessimism. The Pentecostal groups look at society less darkly than the Witnesses. Individual conversion and cleansing more than condemnation of an evil world is the characteristic message of the Salvation Army. They are but a step from Billy Graham's more denominational formulation of the same theme for a more middle-class group.

Setting aside these secondary variations for a moment, we can see a strong common element among the lower-class sects. They strive to deal with the many needs of their members in terms that harmonize with their past training, their level of education, and their experiences in life. Pope summarizes this situation well when he writes:

The sects substitute religious status for social status, a fact which may help to account for their emphasis on varying degrees of Grace. This emphasis, indeed, forms their most distinctive theological tenet. As over against the lack of religious differentiation within older denominations, the newer sects divide their members, and people in general, into several religious classifications: saved, sanctified, baptized with the Holy Ghost, baptized with water, recipient of the first, second, or third blessing and the like. What matters it, then, if a Methodist has more money but has never been baptized with the Holy Ghost? As over against segregation from the community, the newer sects affirm separation from the world; in the face of exclusion on educational, economic, and religious grounds, they affirm exclusion from their own fellowship of those who engage in mixed bathing, dancing, card playing, bobbing the hair, gambling, baseball, county fairs, drinking, and using tobacco. Because they have no jewelry to wear, they make refusal to wear jewelry, including wedding rings, a religious requirement. They transmute poverty into a symptom of Grace. Having no money, they redeem their economic status by rigid tithing of the small income they do possess, and thus far surpass members of churches of any other type or denomination in per capita contributions, despite the fact that they stand at the bottom of the economic scale.[44]

44 Ibid., pp. 137–138.

The universal human skill of making virtue of necessity is nowhere put to more extensive use.

I have indicated that American sects have seldom directly expressed an economic protest. This requires examination, however, for it does not mean that economic factors are irrelevant to their appeal. Poverty, in fact, is one of the basic causes of their growth. There was a rapid increase in such sects during the depression of the 1930's.[45] Most of the churches with which the unemployed and the poverty-stricken had been associated—for many of them were members of established denominations—had little to say about this problem. They neither pressed for secular solutions nor gave serious attention to a religious interpretation of the meaning of want. The small sects which sprang up among the poor, however, were diligently trying to give an interpretation of the economic distress of the members.

Almost none of these groups, however, gave—or give—any direct attention to the economic and political situation around them. They tend to be ascetic and introversionist. Although some are sharply critical of society, they show their criticism by partial withdrawal, as with the Jehovah's Witnesses, and by the expression of apocalyptic hopes. The Winstanleys of our time seldom use religious terms. At least among the white population (we will discuss religious movements among Negroes later) drastic protests against the social order come almost wholly from secular groups —from labor unions, political parties, and reform groups.

Why should this be so? We have noted that many of the conditions that contribute to the appearance of aggressive sects are present in the United States—economic insecurity, extensive migration to the city, disruption of accustomed interpersonal ties, and a sharp increase in relative deprivation as the full range of contrasts in a wealthy society come into view. One can also hypothesize strongly, on the basis of their written material, that the revolutionary implications of the Judaic-Christian messianic tradition are in the culture stream, available for use when supporting conditions are present. This is particularly true of the Witnesses.

Several structural conditions in the United States reduce the likelihood of an aggressive sect winning a large following. We have noted that radicalism has been secularized to an important degree in Europe; and that is partially true in America. Although I do not know how to place it precisely, the stratification system is relatively open—perhaps at about the level of class system type *b* in Table 14–2—thus allowing extensive social mobility.[46] The degree to which a stratification system is open strongly affects the nature of sectarian protests. A political democracy and an economy where workers are relatively free to organize furnish means for the expression of grievances that might otherwise be expressed religiously. The division of the working class into three separate religious structures— Catholic, Protestant, and Negro—has reduced the likelihood that they would express their grievances through a radical religious movement.

45 See A. T. Boisen, "Religion and Hard Times. A Study of the Holy Rollers," *Social Action,* March 15, 1939, pp. 8–35; and E. T. Clark, *The Small Sects in America.*

46 America is probably no more open than other urban-industrial societies today (see S. M. Lipset and Reinhard Bendix, *Social Mobility in Industrial Society*). There is a sharp contrast, however, with the early modern period which produced most of the aggressive sects.

These structural qualities are supported by some elements of the American cultural environment that also blunt the aggressiveness of sectarian movements. Whatever contrary lessons he may be taught, the sectarian is likely to learn and to be influenced by the cultural values of individualism, progressivism, and optimism. It is difficult to document this statement convincingly. Perhaps some data from the study of a sample of church members taken in California will furnish a rough index. Stark and Glock asked their respondents to state whether they believed the following statement was completely true, probably true, probably not true, or definitely not true: "A child is born into the world already guilty of sin." Agreement with such a statement is scarcely harmonious with an individualistic and optimistic view of the world. (On the other hand, disagreement does not necessarily demonstrate the presence of such a view, hence our test is quite weak.) The 255 members of sects in the sample were in the middle of the range of answers, with 46 per cent believing that the statement was completely true or probably true, compared with 4 and 11 per cent of Congregationalists and Methodists, on one hand, and with 78 and 90 per cent of Roman Catholics and Missouri Synod Lutherans on the other.[47]

How do character elements interact with these sociocultural ingredients? We have suggested that hope may increase when new opportunities for status improvement are seen, but so also may a sense of greater deprivation, relative to the life now imaginable. In the United States, the most deprived are insufficiently hopeful to be affected by this interaction. Their sectarian protest is expressed in otherworldly terms. Some of the less deprived are not inclined to view the world from a traditional religious perspective; they use politics and labor unions to press their demands. And many of the traditionally religious among the less deprived members of the working class are sufficiently hopeful that doctrines stressing individual responsibility are more attractive to them than those attacking an evil social order.

This is to say that there are two varieties of hope that may come to the religious persons among those who feel deprived: hope that society can be smashed and rebuilt in accord with one's religious values, and hope that society is open so that an individual can improve himself if he is saved. Hope, in other words, is mixed with different degrees of alienation. Alienation, in turn, is influenced by the structural and cultural elements we have discussed.

In America, the spiritual heirs of the Taborites and the Levellers are more likely to be found among the black than among the white sectarians. In the next chapter, we will see what combinations of structural, cultural, and character conditions shape religious movements among minority races and make the formation of aggressive sects more likely.

Consequences of Sectarian Movements. Having examined some of the causes of sectarianism, we can profitably inquire about its consequences, manifest and latent. Unfortunately, there is little firm evidence—a situation that encourages ideological formulations. One of two positions may be assumed, without the difficult study necessary to test it. Some middle-

---

47 Rodney Stark and Charles Glock, *American Piety: The Nature of Religious Commitment,* p. 40.

class observers who themselves would be entirely unsatisfied by sectarian religious views assume that they must be equally unrewarding to others, not realizing the differences in needs, accustomed modes of expression, and available alternatives that distinguish them from the lower-class sectarians. Others take a kind of tolerant functional view, with circular reasoning that guarantees "proof": It *must* be an effective and satisfying kind of religion, or they would not accept it. Neither of these extremes does justice to the complexity of the functional-dysfunctional situation. One can judge the "success" of a sect, of course, only in terms of certain stated objectives. If one applies a specifically religious criterion, as the sect leaders are likely to do, he asks simply: Do the members accept the doctrines and carry on the prescribed practices of the group? If they do, the movement is a success. Or one can ask a more difficult question, as the sociologist of religion is likely to do: What are the total, long-run consequences, for mental health, for economic security, and the like? Its answer would require a comparative study of two groups that were just alike in economic status, and individual tendencies and needs, one of which embraced a sectarian religious movement while the other attempted to solve its problems by other means—perhaps by economic or political action. Lacking such a study, we can only offer the informed guesses and hypotheses of the students of sect movements.

Holt observes that many of the beliefs and ethical practices of the recently urbanized "peasants" are drawn from a disintegrating agricultural tradition and may be much less adequate in the urban environment. Neighborliness, for example, has an important meaning in a fairly stable rural community; but it may have very different consequences when applied to the complicated relationships of industrial workers to an absentee management. Some sects may have a latent function for the high-status groups, because of their ability to funnel the attention and energy of the lower classes away from this world's problems onto the problems of the hereafter. Better to hate the devil than the boss—certainly from the point of view of the boss, who can sometimes be found among the financial supporters of revival services that encourage the appropriate transfer. It is not surprising, looking at the situation from the opposite side, that the boss should often believe that labor unions or others who bring him back into the focus of opposition are most certainly in the employ of the devil— however the devil may be conceived.

On the other hand, the sect may inspire hope in the migrant and encourage a type of behavior that will raise his status above his class by developing a seriousness of purpose.[48] Benton Johnson has developed this idea with reference to Holiness sects. He sees their influence as a form of anticipatory socialization through which deprived individuals acquire the perspectives and motives of the middle and upper classes.[49] Their members are frustrated and deprived; but by faith and ascetic self-denial, they can obtain eternal bliss. If they take this message to heart, the resulting discipline makes them valued workers, as Liston Pope noted. They acquire the

48 See Holt, op. cit.

49 See Benton Johnson, "Do Holiness Sects Socialize in Dominant Values?" *Social Forces*, 39, 1961, pp. 309–316.

orientation to life described by Weber as "inner-worldly asceticism," with its emphasis on individual control and achievement, moral respectability, and sobriety.

It is not enough, of course, to replace an ideological "religion is the opium of the people," with an ideological "religion is the stimulant of the people." Johnson refers, we should note, not to sects in general but specifically to Holiness and Pentecostal groups. They are close to what we have called avoidance sects, with a secondary theme of acceptance. Avoidance sects that lean toward aggression, or fully aggressive sects, are much less likely to socialize in dominant values. They emphasize the sinfulness of the world more than that of their members—an emphasis not calculated to draw them into the world. (In the next chapter, however, we will note that under some conditions, even aggressive sects serve as agents of acculturation. This is particularly true of sects among highly deprived minorities. Their need to disidentify with a social order that has treated them so badly supports aggressive sects; but they are also powerfully drawn to the values they have been denied. The tension is resolved by sharply attacking the dominant order, while accepting many of its motives and values in heavily disguised form. The religious movement may thus serve as a bridge from an old way of life over to a new one, carrying its members through a threatening anomic area.)

In observing the relationship between Holiness sects and socialization to dominant values, we must be careful to note that the causal connection is not readily established. From among the many who might join such groups, only some do. Are they perhaps the relatively more orderly and ambitious persons, who are ready for change but need acceptable sponsorship? Perhaps in the sect they find religious support for values they would like to pursue, but which they feel ambivalent about. Or perhaps they are alienated, on the conscious level, from the values of a society that has been cruel to them, while yet being subconsciously drawn to those values. Qualities that are acquired as part of the pursuit of eternal salvation will not seem to be caught in these ambivalences.

We have noted that even Freud was ready to grant that religion might be a substitute for neurosis, a substitute less destructive than its individual counterpart. This thesis has been developed more sympathetically by some observers of sectarian movements. Boisen takes a position that might be called "psychiatric functionalism" in his statement that the Holiness sects show nature's power to heal:

> They are the spontaneous attempts of the common people to deal constructively with the stresses and trials which fall with peculiar severity upon them. Their unconcern with economic and social conditions which they are powerless to change and their turning to problems for which they are directly responsible is not entirely an unwholesome reaction. . . . In any case these "holy rollers" are bringing to many distressed individuals release from the burden of guilt. They are giving them hope and courage and strength to keep going in the face of difficulties. Insofar as they succeed in doing this, their economic and social status is likely to be raised.[50]

S. D. Clark arrives at a somewhat different conclusion from his study of

50 A. T. Boisen, "Economic Distress and Religious Experience," *Psychiatry*, May, 1939, p. 194.

sectarian movements in Canada. Implicit in his statement is the thesis that some attention to the organization of society, and not just to the improvement of the status of individuals, is necessary in order to deal effectively with the needs that the sect movements express.

In the long run, perhaps, the effect of the influence of such a movement as the Salvation Army was to arrest the development of a stable urban order. People's attentions were diverted from the real problems of an industrial society; the Army following tended to be held in a state of political and economic illiteracy. The effect was particularly evident in retarding the development of working-class organizations. It may be questioned, however, whether stable secular institutions would have developed much greater strength if the Salvation Army had not emerged. Another form of fanaticism almost certainly would have grown up in place of the religious. The sort of people to whom the Army appealed in the Canadian city in the closing years of the past century were the sort of people looking for a form of social participation on the most elementary level. The task of social building required building from the bottom, and it was on the bottom that the Army built strongly and securely.[51]

A religious movement may be "functional," Clark is saying, if no question is raised regarding the nature of the social situation within which it appears. If it is just that situation, however, which is regarded as inadequate, then the religious influence must be seen in a different light; for it may retard the processes of adaptation essential in a changing society.

Dealing with a more bizarre movement, Weston LaBarre arrives at a somewhat similar interpretation. He examines the membership, the leaders, and the crosscultural precedents, of a snake-handling cult in the Southern United States. He sees snake handling as the effort of a deeply deprived and sexually repressed group to deal with the "guilty terror" embedded in their repressions. By handling the snakes, they act out their unconscious, guilt laden, but powerful sexual needs. He sees no therapy in the cult, but only a kind of bitter necessity; ". . . because of the pressures of their sadly neurotic and archaic and unhappy culture, these people have to have what satisfactions they can without any psychological self-possession, without any knowledge of who they are, and what they are like, and what they are really doing." [52] The cult may help to stabilize the system out of which it comes; but from many value perspectives—certainly LaBarre's—it would be better if the system were smashed. Here we have a clear illustration that a functional interpretation is no substitute for a value interpretation.

These differing judgments concerning the consequences of sects show the difficulty in measuring the full range. It is easy to have one's attention drawn to a particular function or dysfunction, without regard for other results. I will examine some further consequences in the next chapter, in connection with a discussion of sectarian movements among persons of minority status, and offer here only the following tentative propositions:

1. Sectarian beliefs and practices among the deprived members of a society relieve the "pain" that many people feel as a result of their highly disprivileged position.

51 S. D. Clark, *Church and Sect in Canada,* p. 424.

52 Weston LaBarre, *They Shall Take Up Serpents. Psychology of the Southern Snake-Handling Cult,* p. 175.

2. For those on the bottom of a status system, the sects are not usually dysfunctional in terms of economic and political institutions, because their adherents are not in any event equipped by training and inclination to challenge those institutions by others means. For those who are in a slightly more favorable position, however, a sectarian religion that discourages efforts to respond to deprivation by secular or religious challenges to the existing social situation may help to preserve that situation.

3. Many individual adherents are helped, by the self-disciplines that the sect encourages, to improve their own status; while at the same time the sect is irrelevant to the social and cultural causes that continue to create such disprivileged individuals.

4. The sect is inadequate, and perhaps completely irrelevant, to the basic societal problem of freedom-*and*-order, with which mankind has continually to struggle. The acceptance and avoidance sects are unable to deal with "society as the patient"; and the aggressive sects, with their inclinations toward a perfectionist view of man, are too unmindful of the difficult problem of freedom-*and*-order to make a large contribution to the reconstruction of a society. We shall see in other connections that a churchlike response, by itself, is equally inadequate to this task.

5. A sectarian challenge, by calling vivid attention to problems of adaptation and integration in the churches, and in secular institutions as well, may stimulate processes outside their own framework that are of great importance for their members. In some circumstances, the established organizations atttempt to "steal the thunder" of the sects, just as major political parties adopt the programs of influential "sectarian" third parties in the United States. At other times, the sectarian challenge leads to retrenchment and coercion, as the dominant groups seek to maintain their power. One of the important tasks for a science of religion is to specify the conditions in which these opposing interactions occur. We will examine this problem at various points in the chapters dealing with politics and social change.

Chapter Fifteen

RELIGION AND MINORITY STATUS

The religious protest movements we have discussed developed largely among persons who, although disprivileged, were culturally and racially similar to the more advantaged members of the society. New elements are added to the interaction of religion and stratification when race or culture, or both, enter into the ranking system. No sharp line can be drawn between lower-class sects and minority sects, to be sure. The bottom strata are culturally different from top strata to some degree in every society. And race is important, not for its intrinsic qualities, but because of the meaning attached to it as a status factor in many settings. It varies, therefore, in its significance for stratification systems and their religious concomitants.

Keeping these qualifications in mind, we can profitably examine some of the vast range of religious movements of the last century in which racial and cultural differences have played a part. They have been of particular importance in Africa,[1] the South Pacific and the United States, where minority-majority relations, and not simply class relations, enter the stratification picture. In Table 14–2, majority-minority systems are characterized by two ambivalences. Although status placement is determined primarily by descent, and endogamy is the rule, major institutions of the society no longer fully support the rigid assignment of persons to high or low status. In the United States, for example, the educational system and the legal-political system are substantially, although not of course fully, in opposition to claims resting solely on birth. The doors of opportunity are part way open to minority races on the basis of individual not group criteria.

---

1 To keep this chapter within manageable scope, I will not discuss the protest sects in Africa. The interested reader will find a wealth of valuable material in such works as these: Georges Balandier, *Sociologie actuelle de l'Afrique noire;* Bengt Sundkler, *Bantu Prophets in South Africa;* Vittorio Lanternari, *The Religions of the Oppressed,* Chap. 1; Wilhelm Mühlmann and others, *Chiliasmus und Nativismus,* pp. 87–140.

This institutional ambiguity has its individual counterpart. Although minority-group persons carry a load of self-doubt and even of self-hatred, they also challenge the justice and validity of their status placement, as lower caste members do not. The members of a minority regard themselves as the objects of collective discrimination. They see themselves as relatively deprived in a situation that has begun to offer them support for that perception from some majority-group members and institutional norms. That is, situations A, B, and C of Figure 14–1 mingle in stressful interaction.

These ambivalences distinguish, at least in degree, the minority situation from that of either a lower caste or a lower class. Comparison with the latter is particularly important in the modern world. Members of a minority group are not simply persons in a disprivileged status. They are *categorically* assigned to that status on the basis of prejudgments by members of the dominant group, using such criteria as national origin, race, and religion itself. Thus there is a degree of rigidity of status and often a sense of belonging to a group of similarly disprivileged persons, which are not necessarily true of a class position. Because this is not a sharp distinction, the analysis of minority status and religion must build on our earlier discussion.

We have observed that persons of disprivileged status exhibit strategies of acceptance, avoidance, and aggression in their efforts to deal with the world around them. Nowhere are the different strategies more clearly apparent than in their various religious expressions. Some religious values and practices encourage minority-group members to accept their secular situation passively; they emphasize the achievement of religious values defined in otherworldly terms. Such religious expressions often are not, strictly speaking, sects. (Acceptance sects, as we use that term, are predominantly middle class.) Although modes of worship and belief may differ widely from those of higher-status persons, they do not represent alienation from society so much as disprivilege within it. Southern Negroes in the nineteenth century (and some even today) were part of a Protestant ecclesia, in a relationship to the dominant church that was quite similar to that of the mestizo peasantry to the Catholic Church in Latin America.

Our terms are not subtle enough, however, for the full range of facts. There can be a substantial amount of disguised and deflected antagonism to the dominant social order in beliefs and practices that seem indifferent to it—what we might call an incipient sect. These tendencies do not become organizationally visible, however, until some wider view of the world is opened up for the members of the minority group. Their hopes are stirred and they begin to see the social order around them as at least partly responsible for their pain and sorrow. Some sects implicitly criticize but do not explicitly attack the dominant society, by their emphasis on withdrawal. The important thing for them is to "live right" in a pure religious communion, avoiding so far as possible an evil society that one cannot change. Other sects protest directly, on religious grounds, against an order that treats them so badly.

Variables Influencing Type of Sect. The degree to which one or another of these tendencies will predominate—they are probably never found in pure form—depends upon several variables:

1. The degree of hope the group feels about the chances for improving

their status affects the type of sect they will support. Up to a point, the more hopeful, the more likely they are to express themselves aggressively.[2] The more their aspirations have been blocked and the more overwhelming the power of the dominant group seems, the greater the likelihood that avoidance and acceptance themes will be used. The degree of hopefulness is affected by, but not precisely determined by, the actual facts of the power situation. Because of its cultural traditions, the nature of its leadership, and other variables, a group may be more optimistic about the chances for improving its situation than the facts would warrant. This may have been the case with some of the American Indian religious movements, as we shall see. Such an excess of optimism, however, is not likely to prevail for very long. The opposite kind of "misevaluation" of the situation is also possible. This "excessive resignation" in religion may be found in the same situation with *secular* movements that try to take advantage of the opportunities for improvement. This is to some degree true among American Negroes, although the situation is changing.

2. The nature of the religious and the total cultural tradition of a group influences the use of the acceptance, avoidance, and aggressive themes. A Hindu sect, for example, is far less likely to challenge the social order than is a Christian sect. The importance of the doctrines of karma and reincarnation in Hinduism make direct attacks on the social order by some reinterpretation of the Hindu tradition very difficult. Christianity, however, contains the potentialities for such attacks, even though they are usually curtailed by more dominant themes.

3. The availability of secular movements of various kinds affects and is affected by religious movements. Sometimes an aggressive secular movement seems to drain off those who, because of factors such as their cultural tradition or degree of hope, might have supported an aggressive religious sect. Occasionally the two may come together, but the difficulties minority-group members and other relatively powerless people face are so great that an optimistic religious view of the world is likely to be short-lived. If religious attack does not achieve its goals, a more pessimistic view —withdrawal or acceptance—that more accurately reflects the existing situation may replace it. Even the optimistic liberal Christianity of American middle- and upper-class Protestantism, a view that characterized the nineteenth and the first part of the twentieth century, has been sharply curtailed in its influence by more pessimistic theologies. War, tyranny, and depression tend to be problems common to powerful and powerless alike, and obscure their religious differences.

4. The degree of acculturation to the values of the dominant society also influences the nature of the religious life of a minority group. The more a group has embraced the values of the majority and the more it aspires to share those values, the less likely it is, other things being equal, to sustain a religious movement that simply accepts low status or devalues society. George E. Simpson found that in Jamaica, those among the disprivileged who were least acculturated to European values were the most likely to participate in escapist cults, while the more acculturated groups began to express some aggressive themes. Even the most aggressive cults, how-

2 When hope has mounted still higher, aggressiveness may fall. But perhaps at that point we are no longer dealing with a minority-majority situation.

ever, had a great many escapist elements—a reflection of their powerlessness. Interestingly enough, the escapism of the Ras Tafari (Haile Selassie) cult was a "this-worldly escapism," a back-to-Africa movement that represented an unwillingness to give up the hope of success in this world and yet made a very pessimistic appraisal of the chances of improvement of its members' status in Jamaica.[3] This may be a kind of halfway station between the complete projection of one's hopes into a heaven and the hopes of reforming one's own society. Among some American Negroes, there has perhaps been a trend, reflecting a similar sequence, from Marcus Garvey's "Back to Africa" movement to the Black Muslims' hope for control of a separate American region to Black Power advocacy of control of Negro communities wherever they are.

The full range of types of religious responses can be seen among American Negroes. The folk Negro of the rural South tends to accept his role as it is defined by the dominant group. His religion may be seen as an attempt to help him adjust to his station. As Negroes' aspirations have risen, however, withdrawal themes, implicit protests, and finally explicit revolutionary and reform efforts have come into their religious life. We shall explore these various types of Negro religious expressions later.

The situation among minorities that pridefully resist acculturation is somewhat different. In this circumstance, the minority is a separate social group with a separate culture, reacting against the encroachments of a dominant group. It is not a stratum within a larger society. To the degree that the members feel an intrusion and are disorganized by it, they tend to develop religious movements that aggressively oppose the dominant group. It is the *least* acculturated, the "old-timers" who are likely to lead such movements. When some of their members absorb the values and aspirations of the majority, they begin to struggle religiously with their problems as disprivileged persons more in escapist terms. We shall see how this to some degree describes the religious protests of American Indians against the white man. The difference between their situation and that of the American Negro, for example, is that the Indians had a clearly separate culture—or at least the tradition of a very recent one—whereas this is less true of Negroes, who share the dominant culture.[4] A corollary of this is that many of the Indians did not want acculturation, whereas most of the Negroes want nothing more than to be treated as Americans. With the appearance of the Black Power movement, this is less true than it was a decade ago. As we shall see, however, it is important not to judge the cur-

3 See George E. Simpson, "The Ras Tafari Movement in Jamaica: A Study of Race and Class Conflict," *Social Forces,* December, 1955, pp. 167–170.

4 This is a complicated and indeed a "touchy" subject. Negroes have made significant contributions to the total culture complex. As a "community of suffering" they have also developed many distinctive cultural elements that have only partly been absorbed into the larger culture. In my judgment these are of considerably greater importance than cultural forms from their African backgrounds. On balance, one must consider the present important—but minority—call to "come ye out from among them and be ye separate" as a sectarian protest rather than a historical judgment of the degree of cultural distinctiveness. For some comments on the cultural effects of the "community of suffering" see George E. Simpson and J. Milton Yinger, *Racial and Cultural Minorities,* 3rd ed., pp. 176–178.

rent scene by the headlines. Integrationist and separatist tendencies are both strong; but the former predominates.[5]

In sum, it is not simply the *degree* of acculturation that influences the type of religious movement, but the presence or absence of a sustaining culture of its own among the minority, and the degree of desire for acculturation. The form of the religious movement, of course—its symbols, its beliefs, its rituals—will vary widely from culture to culture.

5. The influence of leaders must be taken into account in the study of the probable type of a religious movement. We shall not discuss a theory of leadership here further than to make this brief statement: Although the kind of leader who will rise to the surface and achieve power is sharply limited by all the other variables, the exact nature of his program is not set by these influences. A leader who is inclined toward one kind of religious response may draw together the unfocused needs and tendencies of a group, which might have been pointed toward a somewhat different religious expression or toward a political or economic response, had a leader with different inclinations appeared earlier. One should not exaggerate the range of possibilities: A person who tries, for example, to develop an aggressive economic and political movement among a group whose members have very little hope and power is certain to be a voice crying in the wilderness. Yet there is a little "play" left in the limits set by the various conditions faced by a would-be leader. His tendencies and needs, then, help to determine the final outcome. One doubts very much if the organizer of a separate Negro political movement might have acquired influence just as readily as Elijah Muhammad, leader of the Black Muslims, had such a man appeared at the same time and place. The limits of history are not so tolerant. But a leader a little less inclined toward separatism or a little more interested in organized political action might have prospered equally well, had he chanced to appear.[6]

6. The character systems of followers—the whole complex of tendencies to act in various ways—must also be taken into account in trying to determine the kinds of adjustment, religious or otherwise, that will be made to the problems of life. Two persons, with equal opportunities for secular action, heirs to the same tradition, similarly acculturated, may make different adjustments because of different tendencies. One of them may, because of his early training, be particularly burdened by self-doubt, by guilt, by anxiety. Against this background, the tragedies and frustrations of life will strike him with special poignancy. The other may have been brought up under circumstances that enable him to face frustration and disappointment, his own errors and those of others, without great torment. Feeling more secure, he has a higher level of tolerance for tragedy and guilt and doubt. The first is likely to be a strong candidate for what William James has called the religion of the twice-born. The second will be drawn to a more optimistic religion or join a hopeful secular movement.

5 For data pertaining to the balance of integrationist-separatist sentiments, see The National Advisory Commission on Civil Disorders, *Supplementary Studies*, Chap. 2; and Gary Marx, *Protest and Prejudice*, pp. 21, 28, and 30.

6 "Chanced," not because he was uncaused, but because the influences that brought him to his particular inclinations can be seen as independent of the situation with which he came in contact.

Thus the nature of religion among minorities, as among others, is the result of the interplay of many forces. This complicates the task of analysis; but any attempt to understand religion as a consequence of one or two factors alone will be inadequate.

The variables we have been discussing may be summarized in the following proposition: The more a minority group does share and wants to share in the dominant culture of a society, the greater its power, the stronger its hope, the more its religious tradition encourages an emphasis on the value of life in this world, the more aggressive its leadership, the more the tendencies of the members encourage them to confront life directly, rather than inventing symbolic solutions—when these circumstances apply, the farther the religious response to the group's status will move down the road of acceptance-avoidance-aggression, and the more it will develop secular themes to supplement or to replace the religious sectarian movements.

RELIGIOUS PROTEST AND REVITALIZATION AMONG MINORITIES

The religious protests of minority groups almost always contain elements of cultural renewal and cultural distinctiveness. The religious movement serves to emphasize the very difference that the dominant group has used to downgrade the minority. But the difference is transposed from a mark of inferiority to one of equality or superiority. Lower-class movements also affirm that the last shall be first. The interpretation is more individualistic, however, with emphasis on the moral superiority of sect members rather than on their cultural distinctiveness and superiority.

The cultural contrast between minority and majority is not likely in fact to be as sharp as the protest movement interprets it to be. Indeed, one of the functions of the movement is to allow some absorption of the dominant culture by the members of the minority while still making entirely clear their opposition to the deprived status in which they are caught. These movements typically arise in times of drastic change. An old order, often filled with injustice but granting some degree of stability, is breaking down. New hopes are aroused, but obstacles are made even more visible. Units among the minority which had suffered their disprivileges separately become aware of a common fate; and some of them see the need for unifying themes. This need is heightened by personal demoralization—the loss of a sense of coherence in the moral order around them. New values and a drastic reorganization of personality are needed. Under these conditions, a religious protest may serve as a bridge by which a partially hopeful but demoralized minority can cross over into a new status. Proclaimed as a separatist movement, it may serve as the agent of integration at a new level, depending on the way in which a society responds to the mixture of hope and alienation that is its source.

These are the conditions that produce what Anthony Wallace has called a revitalization movement. He tends to emphasize its cultural element, defining it as "a deliberate, organized, conscious effort by members of a society to construct a more satisfying culture." [7] Although he refers to "members

7 Anthony Wallace, "Revitalization Movements," *American Anthropologist*, 58, 1956, p. 267.

of a society," it is clear from his discussion that he would make the same interpretation of revitalization among minorities. He sees its chief function as the reduction of cultural confusion, an effort "to bring organization into a rich but disorderly field by eliminating some of the materials (thus reducing the cultural repertoire to more manageable size) and combining what is left into a more orderly structure." [8]

Although it is implicit in his discussion, I would emphasize the conflict theme more strongly than Wallace does. Revitalization movements are efforts to wrest from a rapidly changing and anomic situation, not only a more orderly cultural structure, but also higher status. Whether the minority-group member is a Papuan overrun by European power or a recent Negro migrant to an American city, there is the same sense not only of old cultural forms smashed, but of inequities more deeply felt, while at the same time opportunities seem more tantalizingly present.

The two themes of religious protest movements—cultural renewal and status improvement—are intricately related. Minorities are often caught in a vicious circle within which the repressions they experience are reflected in their tendency toward low motivations and skills, which in turn reinforce the repressions. Through mobility and social change, their motivations, skills, and aspirations may be lifted. But how can they break away from beliefs and tendencies that derived from and tend to bind them into the old order? How, in view of their acceptance of accustomed ways and their hostilities toward those who dominate them, can they acquire those qualities that a new status requires and that new opportunities make meaningful? Certain standards and skills are needed, if the minority's status is to improve, not only because the majority requires them, but also because they are essential to the way jobs get done. Certain levels of education, responsibility, ability to defer gratification, and the like, are necessary for status improvement. But to adopt such standards, which can easily be seen as the standards of the repressive majority, may be felt as capitulation to the majority or a recognition of its superiority. Thus minorities are faced with a dilemma. Although the dilemma is perhaps not different in nature from that faced by lower classes, it is sharper. Lower-class members may consider themselves disprivileged, but they do not regard themselves as objects of discrimination—that is, of categorical disprivilege aimed at them because of their group membership. Feelings of ambivalence, therefore, are likely to be stronger among members of a minority.

Nevertheless, a powerful sect movement can reduce the sharpness of the dilemma. In the preceding chapter we noted that lower-class sects can furnish motivation to pursue desired goals even in the face of an extremely pessimistic situation. It can also reduce feelings of ambivalence toward those goals by describing them in terms of sectarian values, not as the standards of an oppressive society. These functions are even more important in minority sects. In addition, these sects reaffirm the vitality and importance of a distinctive cultural tradition, which helps to draw separate and perhaps formerly antagonistic groups together. Parts of the tradition may have to be "invented" to contribute to a unity across tribal, regional, or other lines, and to furnish guidelines for the new circumstances out of which the sect has developed. Invention is often in the form of revelation

8 Anthony Wallace, *Religion: An Anthropological View,* p. 211.

to a prophet, who proclaims the road not as something new, but as a return to the ways of the ancestors.

This generalized description should not be used to obscure the range of variation among minority-group sects. They vary in the balance between withdrawal and aggressive themes, in their attention to a glorious past or a glorious future, in their emphasis on ascetic or licentious behavior. In the brief descriptions that follow, we shall try to give due attention both to the differentiating characteristics and to the shared qualities.

THE CARGO CULTS OF MELANESIA [9]

For nearly a century the islands of Melanesia have been swept by millenarian movements by means of which the inhabitants have sought to deal with the frustration and disorganization produced by European domination.[10] Tribal societies have been seriously disrupted by a succession of culture shocks, by the labor methods of plantation and mine overseers, by racial antipathies, particularly in later decades, and by military invasion. The contrast between the values taught by missionaries and those practiced by the men who dominated the lives of the inhabitants only added to the confusion. Under these conditions, the native resident could not go back—the white man had not only disrupted his societies, but had also given him new wants and new values—nor could he go ahead, for his pay was minimal, his opportunities few, his command of the white man's ways entirely marginal. "The stage was truly set . . . for the development of independent native movements, and for the casting of social and economic aspirations in religious form." [11]

Over the years, Cargo movements have changed to some degree. At first they tended to be nativistic and revivalistic. The old order, it was affirmed, will be re-established and the invader driven from the land. In Fiji, for example, in 1877 and the years that followed a self-proclaimed prophet

9 There is an extensive literature on Cargo cults, which the reader interested in the details of belief, practice, and history will wish to consult. In this section I am drawing substantially on the following descriptions and interpretive and comparative studies: Kenelm Burridge, *Mambu: A Melanesian Millennium*; Peter Lawrence, *Road Belong Cargo*; Peter Worsley, *The Trumpet Shall Sound*; Raymond Firth, "The Theory of 'Cargo Cults': A Note on Tikopia," *Man*, 5, 1955, pp. 130–132; Lucy Mair, "Independent Religious Movements in Three Continents," *Comparative Studies in Society and History*, 1, 1959, pp. 113–136; Yonina Talmon, "Pursuit of the Millennium: The Relation between Religious Change and Social Change," *Archives Européennes de Sociologie*, 3, 1962, pp. 125–148; Wilhelm Mühlmann and others, op. cit., pp. 165–189; Vittorio Lanternari, op. cit., Chap. 5. Some of the sentences in the following paragraphs are drawn from my *Sociology Looks at Religion*, Chap. 2.

10 For some readers, the term *millenarian* may have too specifically a Christian if not a numerical connotation to make it appropriate as a general term for the movements we shall be discussing. We might shift to *chiliastic*, hoping that the Greek root is more obscure than the Latin, thus allowing a broader usage, or to *nativistic*, following Ralph Linton, or *revitalizing*, following Wallace, or *messianic*, or to a number of other possible terms. Each of the latter, however, is somewhat narrower in scope than I intend at this point. Unless specifically qualified by reference to the Book of Revelation, therefore, or to Christian messianic hopes, I shall use *millenarian* to refer to a movement that envisages a dramatic and rapid transformation of a frustrating and deprived state into a rewarding and glorious state by religious means.

11 Peter Worsley, op. cit., p. 44.

preached a "doctrine of resistance and hope." He declared that the order of things would soon be reversed, ancestors would return to the island, and independence would be restored. "Eternal life and eternal pleasures were to be the lot of the faithful. For the aged, youth would be renewed and desire would return. The shops would be jammed with calico, tinned salmon and other goods for the faithful, but unbelievers would die, or be condemned to everlasting hell-fire, or become the slaves and servants of believers." [12] The white men would be driven into the sea.

Even in this early version, there were expressions of new needs and values. As related movements spread, they became a "rudimentary form of revolutionary 'nationalism,'" as Peter Lawrence puts it, giving separate tribal groups a sense of common fate and purpose. Yet the movements were also conservative, for old values and attitudes shaped both their goals and their methods. Contact with European powers had abruptly increased the range of imagined opportunities while disrupting the established patterns of relationships. But the responses had to be built substantially out of existing cultural materials until "new men" could be formed, who were governed by different motives, skills, and values. Doubtless the need for new orientations was widely felt; but that need did not automatically transform character.

What makes the difference between an all too familiar political unrest combined with the economic disabilities of a multi-racial society, and the occurrence of a Cargo cult, is a sudden onset of moral and emotional passion concentrated to the point of action by and in the sort of man Mambu was. And the kinds of things a charismatic leader says, does, and encourages others to do, clearly reveal that the participants in a cult are striving after moral renovation. They want to put on the new man. Out of the crucible of moral regeneration they want to mould and shape for themselves and their children a new, more satisfying world. [13]

The direction and force of the cult's influence on its members were affected both by the existing cultural material and by the developing relationships with the dominant political powers. Through several decades, cults in many parts of Melanesia have developed along somewhat similar lines. In many of them, the theme of "stolen Cargo" became prominent. From the point of view of the native inhabitants of the islands, the white men in their midst were receiving vast supplies of goods by steamer and plane from unknown sources. They did not manufacture them, and they merely sent back scraps of paper. It was not difficult for the natives to believe that the goods were made by their own ancestors and stolen from them by the whites, who had control over some secret. Work was obviously not the secret. Prophets appeared to reveal the way to secure the cargoes and to re-establish native supremacy. They propounded systems of belief and ritual as ways of achieving goals that, to the prosaic eye, seemed impossible—to defeat the white man and get the mastery of his secret for obtaining vast cargoes from ships and planes.

Such millenarian movements occur when a relative harmony among the existing elements of social structure, culture, and character has been

12 Ibid., pp. 20–21.

13 Kenelm Burridge, op. cit., p. xviii.

smashed. What alternative modes of response were open to the residents of Melanesia, once their accustomed modes of life had been disrupted by European invasions? They could not simply "go back," although that was the appeal of the first versions of the Cargo cults. With their economy disrupted, their hopes raised, their contacts with other styles of life broadened, their dependence upon European goods established, any protest movement that could hold their allegiance had to help carry them over to new ground, *through anomie* to a new order.

The new order could not, however, be simply an extension of the European order. In a context of intercultural tension and against a background of political and military conflict, self-respect would not permit that, even if the partial socialization to traditional ways left some room for change. New values had to be acquired and new structures, particularly those recognizing intertribal interests, had to be built; but they could not, in a conflict situation, simply be copies of the invader's style.

The situation is thus filled with ambivalences. These are seen not only on the cultural level but on the individual level, and they help to account for the extremism characteristic of many religious protests. "The severing of old ties and the rejection of old norms demand an enormous effort and engender a deep sense of guilt, hence much of the hysteria and the aggression. Many of the antinomian manifestations are a deliberate overthrow of the accepted norms, not in order to throw overboard all morality but in order to create a new brotherhood and a new morality." [14]

These qualities characterize other minority-group religious movements to which we shall refer. Their long-run influence depends upon the secular contexts within which the sects develop. We shall reserve comment on the range of possible consequences until we have discussed several other religious protests among minority groups. Like the Cargo cults, they show the futility of separating functional interpretations from conflict interpretations, for these movements show at least the possibility that religious conflict can function to promote new forms of interaction made necessary by drastic changes in the circumstances of contact.

RELIGIOUS MOVEMENTS AMONG AMERICAN INDIANS

If the approach we have adopted to the study of religion has any validity, we would expect to find among American Indians a series of religious adjustments and movements, alongside many other types of response, resulting from the enormous disorganizing pressures to which they have been subjected. We are not here concerned with aboriginal religions [15] but with a few of the religious reactions, springing generally from a hybrid Indian-Christian situation, to white domination. The form of these religious movements was partly conditioned by the fact that Indians had a widespread myth of a culture hero who would appear to lead them to a terrestrial paradise. A large number of messianic movements have developed from this myth, growing in the context of structural change, personal deprivation, and cultural confusion. Sometimes the Indian prophets helped to bring

14 Yonina Talmon, op. cit., p. 141.

15 For a general review, see Ruth Underhill, *Red Man's Religion.*

together tribes that were normally at war with one another, allying them against their common enemy, the white intruder, and promising them that it was now the Indian's turn to conquer.

The Ghost Dance. Most dramatic and widespread of these Indian religious protests was the Ghost Dance.[16] In its development and spread, one can see religion being used in an effort to overcome personal confusion and frustration, to re-establish the validity of Indian cultures, and to oppose the overwhelming power of the white man. It spread first in the early 1870's among the tribes of the Far West, stemming from the vision of a Paiute shaman, Wodziwob. He prophesied that all the dead Indians would come back, brought to life by the dance. His own tribe did not become very excited, but his message was amplified and spread by other missionaries: Those who believed, who danced, would see their relatives in a very few years, and the white people would disappear.

"The great underlying principle of the Ghost Dance doctrine is that the time will come when the whole Indian race, living and dead, will be re-united upon a regenerated earth, to live a life of aboriginal happiness, forever free from death, disease, and misery." [17] Some tribes were unconvinced by Wodziwob or his followers. "But elsewhere the doctrine seemed better at third hand than at first hand, and it ran like a powder train." In 1871 it spread through several tribes in California, Oregon, and Nevada, receiving fresh interpretations and variations as it moved. "As it traveled, it appears that the tribes which took up the cult most hungrily were those suffering the greatest deterioration in their former ways of life, while those which were lukewarm or flatly rejected the dance were the ones who had had the least disturbance." [18]

After a few years, the Ghost Dance began to decline, for its promise of an immediate restoration of the Indian to his old place was not fulfilled. In 1890, however, another Paiute, a shaman named Wovoka, whose father had been associated with Wodziwob, received a vision that was the starting point for another wave of the dance. The nature of the vision is not entirely clear, for Wovoka proclaimed some Christian ethical views (live in peace with one another and the whites, avoid lying, stealing, and war); and yet in a letter to the Arapaho and Cheyenne tribes he repeated the idea that there would be a reunion on earth with the dead Indians, that the dance that God had given him would prevent the whites from interfering with the Indians any more. While Ghost Dance doctrine forbade war, it foresaw the annihilation of the white man.[19]

The dance spread quickly, not through the tribes that had taken it up twenty years earlier, nor among the then prosperous Navahos or the self-contained Pueblos, but across the Rockies among the Plains Indians—the

16 See James Mooney, *The Ghost-Dance and the Sioux Outbreak of 1890*; David Aberle, "The Prophet Dance and Reactions to White Contact," *Southwestern Journal of Anthropology*, 15, 1959, pp. 74–83; W. W. Howells, *The Heathens*; Bernard Barber, "Acculturation and Messianic Movements," *American Sociological Review*, October, 1941, pp. 663–669; Alexander Lesser, "Cultural Significance of the Ghost Dance," *American Anthropologist*, January–March, 1933, pp. 108–115.

17 Mooney, op. cit., p. 19.

18 Howells, op. cit., p. 270.

19 See ibid., pp. 269–273, and Mooney, op. cit., Chaps. 1 and 2.

Cheyenne and Arapaho, the Pawnee and Sioux. Here it is to be understood only against the background of white domination, cultural confusion among the Indians, the loss of the buffalo, with all that it meant for the Indian economy and way of life, and the inability to carry out the old rituals. The Ghost Dance represented a renaissance of Indian culture to the Pawnee, "the very flame of new hope to the Sioux."

Into this situation of cultural decay and gradual darkness, the Ghost Dance doctrine shown like a bright light. Indian ways were not gone, never to be recovered. Indian ways were coming back. Those who had lived before in the "golden age" were still carrying on the old ceremonies, old dances, old performances, and old games in the beyond. They were coming back; they were bringing the old ways and the buffalo. Dance, dance, dance. The white man would be destroyed by a great wind. The Indian would be left with the buffalo, with his ancestors, with his old friends and his old enemies. Cast aside the white man's ways like an old garment; put on the clothes of the Indian again. Get ready for the new day and the old times.[20]

The Ghost Dance was a last desperate attempt to re-establish the native values and to recover a sense of the worthwhileness and meaning of life, while incorporating new values from the surrounding society. Among the Sioux it led to tragedy, for it precipitated the complicated series of events that brought about the Battle of Wounded Knee where more than two hundred Indians and sixty white soldiers were killed.[21] And with them died the Dance among the Sioux.

Can we interpret this vigorous religious protest in terms of some of the variables we have been discussing? First, hope among the Indians that they could re-establish the supremacy of their way of life ran fairly high, despite the enormous defeats they had suffered. During the eighteenth and nineteenth centuries, the Plains Indians had known great prosperity and success—and this was still a living memory among them in 1890; they were proud of their cultures and not ready to accept the possibility of their extinction. This hope may seem wholly unrealistic to the outsider, but it stemmed from the Indian experience. The failures of the Ghost Dance and the continued reduction in their power soon cut away the roots of hope— and aggressive religious movements became less likely.

Second, the Ghost Dance was built out of Indian cultural materials— shamanism, a strong belief in visions and in the efficacy of the dance, with a mixture of Christian beliefs and ethical elements that had spread among the tribes. The cultural element is also shown negatively: The movement did not spread among some tribes, the Navaho for example, among whom the idea of the return of dead ancestors was entirely repugnant.

Third, effective secular protests either were lacking or had proved entirely inadequate. The Indians, to be sure, had protested militarily against the continuing intrusions into their territories and the destruction of their way of life; they had negotiated politically; but these had not stopped the white man nor re-established the old ways. The Ghost Dance can be seen as another attempt to do what war and negotiation had not done.

Fourth, the vigorous protest not only against their own deprivation and

20 Lesser, op. cit., p. 112.

21 See Mooney, op. cit., Chap. 5; and Howells, op. cit., pp. 274–278.

suffering but against the ways of the white man was a sign of low acculturation. The Indians were not fighting simply for a higher status within a
white society, but for the reaffirmation of their own cultures. Among those
who do not want a distinct cultural identity, aggressive religious movements
are more likely among the most acculturated; but when the goal is a separate culture, it is the least acculturated who support aggressive religious
—and other—movements. This does not mean that white society had made
no impact. The Ghost Dance itself, by forbidding self-mutilation, the killing
of horses, the destruction of property, and other aboriginal practices, served
as a bridge to new cultural patterns. But the nativistic conflict theme was
also prominent.

Fifth, the Ghost Dance was encouraged by some of the powerful and
irreconcilable Indian leaders. There were other types of leaders as well,
who gained power when the situation changed. But for a period the protest
theme was encouraged by aggressive religious and politico-military
leaders.

Sixth, there was probably substantial support for the Ghost Dance among
the individual members of those tribes that had experienced most severely
the pressure of white advance. We do not, however, have evidence of the
range of individual variation. Some may have been inclined toward a more
accommodative response; but in time of crisis, groups become polarized in
such a way that the impact of differences in individual tendencies is
reduced.

Mooney interpreted the Ghost Dance as one of a universal species of
religious movements that seek to recapture a lost arcadia.

The lost paradise is the world's dreamland of youth. What tribe or people has not
had its golden age, before Pandora's box was loosed, when women were nymphs
and dryads and men were gods and heroes? And when the race lies crushed and
groaning beneath an alien yoke, how natural is the dream of a redeemer, an
Arthur, who shall return from exile or awake from some long sleep to drive out
the usurper and win back for his people what they have lost. The hope becomes
a faith and the faith becomes the creed of priests and prophets, until the hero
is a god and the dream a religion, looking to some great miracle of nature for its
culmination and accomplishment. The doctrines of the Hindu avatar, the Hebrew
Messiah, the Christian millennium, and the Hesûnanin of the Indian Ghost
Dance are essentially the same, and have their origin in a hope and longing common to all humanity.[22]

The Peyote Cult. What happens, however, when hope begins to fade,
when only a few can remember a better day or can see one coming on the
basis of their own experience? Among Indians, white power and culture
intruded further and further into their lives. Avoidance and escapist and to
some degree acceptance themes came more frequently into their religious
movements. It is perhaps not to stretch things too far to compare the shift
from Diggers to Quakers in England with the shift from the Ghost Dance
to such nonaggressive movements as Peyotism and Shakerism among
American Indians. This is not to suggest that the more accommodative
movements among Indians grew out of the separatist ones, because in fact
they developed largely among different tribes. Cultural elements as well as
the nature of the relationship with white society were involved. But their

22 Mooney, op. cit., p. 1.

combination produced a variety of religious movements quite lacking in overt hostility to whites and dreams of return to a past golden age. They can be understood only against the background of the Indian situation in the United States.

Doubtless the most important of these "new religions" is the peyote cult.[23] Slotkin reported that by 1955 at least seventy-seven tribes had some Peyote members, and Aberle found that the sect was still growing in 1964. The proportion of a tribe who are members varies widely, suggesting the need for taking individual character elements into account, as well as structural and cultural factors.

The most commonly noted quality of Peyotism is the ritual use of the peyote cactus button to heighten religious experience. The effect of the drug ranges from mild euphoria to physical discomfort and anxiety, but these differences are less significant than the widely shared feeling that the stimuli surrounding one have become personally significant. Significance may relate to health, or meaning, or a sense that now one has power to deal with life. From our point of view, Peyotism is interesting as an apparently accommodative, passive response to deprivation and cultural confusion, which at the same time affirms Indian identity and self-respect. Among the Navaho, Aberle found Peyotism associated not with the absolute but with the relative level of deprivation, as measured by the severity of the loss of livestock during a period when depression and government policy brought about sharp reductions. Spindler found that Menomini members of the sect were persons without secure primary group identity. They lacked a clear image of culturally approved means to life's satisfactions and even of the nature of the goals to be pursued—they lived in anomic conditions. There was no hope of restoring aboriginal Indian ways, but only a pressing need to make two "generalized others" tolerably compatible. "Identification with Peyote literally saves the self and gives it sanctions and directives for an integration of conflicting cultural patterns." [24]

Whether the results are as uniformly favorable as Spindler suggests, we can perhaps leave open to question; but Peyotism can certainly be seen as a serious effort to build a bridge between two cultural worlds. It does not depend on what must be regarded as an impossible victory over the dominant society, which was what the Ghost Dance envisaged. It seeks instead a meaningful life for Indians as Indians in a society they can only partially control.

Its goal is not, and seems never to have been, a totally transformed social order. Rather, through moral reform, proper worship, illumination, association with

23 See J. S. Slotkin, *The Peyote Religion;* David Aberle, *The Peyote Religion Among the Navaho;* Weston LaBarre, *The Peyote Cult;* George Spindler, "Personality and Peyotism in Menomini Indian Acculturation," *Psychiatry,* 15, 1952, pp. 151–159; Bernard Barber, "A Socio-Cultural Interpretation of the Peyote Cult," *American Anthropologist,* 43, 1941, pp. 673–675; Charles Brand, "Peyotism among the Kiowa-Apache and Neighboring Tribes," *Southwestern Journal of Anthropology,* 6, 1950, pp. 212–222; Lanternari, op. cit., Chap. 2. As David Aberle notes, the use of the term *cult* with reference to Peyotism is more a matter of long usage than of technical choice. The term *sect* is more appropriate, yet not entirely accurate. To speak of a peyote religion is to minimize the Christian elements blended in it. I will use cult when drawing on material where that is the usage, but otherwise either Peyotism (which dodges the question) or sect.

24 Spindler, op. cit., p. 155.

fellow peyotists, and some reduction of the intimacy of relationships with non-peyotists, the members of the North American Church desire to create a better way of life for themselves. They further hope to extend this way to other potential believers . . . peyotism seeks a more satisfying way of life for Indian individuals in this world, in spite of the difficulties that confront Indians.[25]

Although there are significant variations in cultural content, Peyotism is similar in its bridging function to Handsome Lake's Great Message to the Iroquois, to the Bole-Maru sect in California, and the Indian Shakers in the Northwest.[26] Whether these sects will serve to carry their members over into the dominant society, having served the latent function of "socializing them to dominant values," or will stand as integrating structures, helping their members reconcile the conflicts of dual cultural membership, depends more upon the surrounding society than upon their own beliefs and actions. Continuing disprivilege will support the later tendency, whereas an improved economic and political situation in American society for the members of these groups will support the former. If there is continuing increase in contact and hope, in fact, we probably can expect a renewed form of religious protest among American Indians. It is likely to express, not the reactionary dreams of the Ghost Dance, but something closer to the reformist hopes of a modern Anabaptism. Such a development is now apparent among American Negroes, whose religious movements we can profitably examine.

RELIGIOUS MOVEMENTS AMONG AMERICAN NEGROES
Negro sectarianism is a product of the same fundamental causes as sectarianism in general, but there are some special factors that have affected it. It can be understood only in the total context of the Negro's place in American society.

In recent years there have been drastic shifts from acceptance and avoidance themes to many varieties of protest. These later forms can best be examined against a background of earlier religious expressions. With reference to its cultural content if not its functions, some attention must be paid to the persistence of at least a few African religious elements. Although there is wide disagreement concerning the extent of this persistence, this "minimum" statement would perhaps be accepted by most writers: The beliefs and rites of American Negroes, particularly of the rural and more isolated groups, contain some African elements; but the functions of these survivals are to be understood only by reference to the contemporary situations that they face. The survivals, insofar as they exist, do not explain the working of Negro sects as attempts to struggle with

25 Aberle, op. cit., p. 334.

26 See Philleo Nash, "The Place of Religious Revivalism in the Formation of the Intercultural Community on Klamath Reservation," in *Social Anthropology of North American Tribes*, Fred Eggan, ed., pp. 375–442; Fred Voget, "The American Indian in Transition: Reformation and Accommodation," *American Anthropologist*, 58, 1956, pp. 249–263; Fred Voget, "The American Indian in Transition: Reformation and Status Innovations," *American Journal of Sociology*, 62, 1957, pp. 369–378; Howells, op. cit.; and H. G. Barnett, *Indian Shakers: A Messianic Cult of the Pacific Northwest*.

life's problems; they simply help to explain the symbolic expression of those problems.[27]

Church segregation is another background factor of great importance in the development of Negro religious forms. A process of integration began in American society in the 1940's, but by 1970, most Negroes still attended segregated churches. In his report as general secretary of the National Council of Churches in 1969, R. H. Edwin Espy wrote: "Could it not be that while we celebrate the new rapprochement between Catholics, Orthodox and Protestants we may be overlooking if not looking away from the deepest, and perhaps even increasing, alienation among ourselves . . . the wide gap between black and white brothers." [28] To be sure, there are countercurrents. In large Northern cities, perhaps half of the middle-class Protestant churches are racially integrated to some slight degree; and there is substantial integration in Catholic churches. Sects, however, are seldom interracial; few churches in the South have been integrated, despite the beginnings of some support for change; and such integration as has occurred nationwide involves only a small proportion of individuals—perhaps 1 per cent of Negroes.[29]

Segregation of churches is a product of several influences—of discrimination and prejudice, of residential segregation, of a lag from earlier conditions, of a desire on the part of some Negroes for separate churches. Before the Civil War, common worship was the rule; but this was not at all a sign of equality. It was rather an attempt on the part of planters to be better able to control their slaves. At first they had opposed having Negro members in their churches, for an old unwritten law declared that a Christian could not hold a fellow believer in bondage. Most churches, however, relaxed this doctrine by the development of the comforting thought, often expressed in the history of Christianity, that equality before God had no reference to earthly status. Thus they were able to conciliate the consciences of slaveholders and win more power in the mission field. If some planters feared that Christianity would encourage the kind of revolution that shook Haiti or produce a Nat Turner-style rebellion, they were shown that the gospel, properly taught, could encourage submission and peace. Thus, says Richard Niebuhr, the union of Negro and white in churches before the Civil War was "in most instances designed to enlist the forces of religion in the task of preserving the civil relationship between masters and slaves." [30]

27 For some questions—such as the description of the history of culture contact or the degree of acculturation—the details of the surviving elements are very important and would require systematic exploration. For a range of views on the persistence of Africanisms in America, see M. J. Herskovits, *The Myth of the Negro Past,* where the importance of survivals is argued, and A. H. Fauset, *Black Gods of the Metropolis,* and E. F. Frazier, *The Negro in the United States,* where their importance is minimized.

28 *New York Times,* Jan. 22, 1969, p. 23.

29 See David Reimers, *White Protestantism and the Negro;* Mathew Ahmann, ed, *Race: Challenge to Religion;* Liston Pope, *The Kingdom Beyond Caste;* Ernest Campbell and Thomas Pettigrew, *Christianity in Racial Crisis: A Study of Little Rock's Ministry;* F. S. Loescher, *The Protestant Church and the Negro;* Dwight Culver, *Negro Segregation in the Methodist Church.*

30 H. R. Niebuhr, op. cit., pp. 252–253; see also pp. 236–263.

The appearance of more segregated churches after the Civil War has not been simply a new assertion of white discrimination. It is also to be understood in terms of the different religious needs and interests that result from the different experiences of Negroes and whites, the desire of Negroes to use religion more effectively to protest against or adjust to their status, and their desire for organizations of their own that they can control. These causes, of course, would scarcely have come into being had it not been for the prior cause of discrimination which produced these various tendencies among Negroes. Niebuhr is undoubtedly right when he states that, although Negroes have frequently taken the initiative in forming separate churches, white men have furnished the motivating force. "Their unquestioned assumption of superior privileges, their unconscious wounding of Negro self-respect, their complacent acceptance of the morality of the world as fitting for the church, have once more divided the body of Christ along the lines of social class." [31]

Types of Negro Religious Organizations and Movements

It is impossible, of course, to speak of "the" Negro church, for there is a wide variety of types. One can think of a kind of continuum ranging from the churches of the plantation South, to those of the less isolated village, to those of the lower-class urban migrant, to those of the "native" urbanite of lower-class status, and finally to the churches of the middle- and upper-class Negroes. In general, as one moves along this continuum, he finds among the members an increase in education, a larger amount of assimilation to the values of the dominant group, a greater hope in the possibilities of improvement of status, but at the same time stronger feelings of relative deprivation, more secularization of outlook, and an increase in secular alternatives for expression and for the achievement of one's goals. These all affect the tendencies, the needs, and the religious forms to be found among the various groups of Negroes.[32]

The plantation church expresses the religious needs of a group almost completely cut off from "the American dream" of equality and improvement of status. It accepts the social order as it finds it, furnishing its small and powerless congregation with the compensations of heaven. The members are given emotional release and relief from the tensions of their difficult lives by the music and shouting and dancing incorporated in the services. There is little of the asceticism and moral emphasis that begins to appear in other Negro churches as part of the effort to prove one's right to improvement of status. For this isolated group that is an improvement

31 Ibid., p. 260.

32 The discussion that follows attempts to systematize materials found in a large number of empirical studies. Among them, the following are of particular value: St. C. Drake and H. R. Cayton, *Black Metropolis;* V. E. Daniel, "Ritual and Stratification in Chicago Negro Churches," *American Sociological Review*, June, 1942, pp. 352–358; A. H. Fauset, *Black Gods of the Metropolis;* John Dollard, *Caste and Class in a Southern Town;* Charles S. Johnson, *Growing Up in the Black Belt;* Hortense Powdermaker, *After Freedom;* B. E. Mays and J. W. Nicholson, *The Negro's Church;* A. W. Davis, B. B. Gardner, and M. R. Gardner, *Deep South;* E. F. Frazier, *Negro Youth at the Crossways* and *The Negro Church in America.* See also George E. Simpson and J. Milton Yinger, *Racial and Cultural Minorities,* Chap. 18.

too unlikely to be imagined; ". . . instead of stressing self-control and bringing pressure toward impulse renunciation, they aid the individual in increasing his daily satisfaction in life by the ceremonials which relieve his guilt." [33] This kind of adjustment has become less and less common as a result both of the migration of Negroes from the plantation areas and the intrusion of urban influences into those areas.

The rural church in the nonplantation areas and in villages has taken on additional functions. The increased expectancy of recreation, in a group that is still blocked completely from any share of the recreation life of the larger community, finds somewhat more expression in the program of the church. The entrance of hope for some improvement of individual status is reflected in an increasing attention to personal conduct, an emphasis on the need for abiding by the standards of the dominant society. Greater opportunities for leadership are found in the more complicated organizational structure of the group. The otherworldly element in their doctrines is still overwhelmingly important; but an indirect note of criticism against the white man is expressed in the belief that there will be a reversal of statuses in heaven, where the last shall be first. Hortense Powdermaker makes the interesting observation that the meekness of the rural and village Negro disguises strong aggressive feelings. Humbleness is an attempt to rescue victory from defeat; suffering is only a prelude to ultimate reward; one gets power from suffering.[34]

As we shall see, the protest element in Negro religion has become much more direct in recent years, particularly among those who have experienced the explosive mixture of status improvement and continuing discrimination. But in the face of powerlessness, acceptance and avoidance themes predominate. Religion does not challenge what it cannot hope to change. During the depression of the 1930's, the Negro church in the rural South did not blame the plantation system or other economic institutions for the poverty of the tenants, but attributed it to the thriftlessness and sinfulness of individuals. In Natchez, "no preacher in either the rural or urban county was ever heard to complain in his pulpit against the plantation system. The dogma concerning economic behavior was always that the members should be hard and faithful workers." [35]

When the Negro peasant moves to the city, he acquires new problems, new aspirations, and new possibilities for the satisfaction of some of his needs. These all affect the nature of his religious life. He brings with him his rural training, of course; he is still poorly educated, still used to vivid emotional expressions in religion, still unable to formulate a critique of the society which keeps him in low status. He is also still segregated, and even more painfully aware of his inability to participate in many aspects of the life of the dominant society. The old and new influences combine to shape the nature of his religious life.

Although the city furnishes many opportunities for recreation and entertainment, they are often unavailable to the migrant, because of segregation, because they are not his accustomed modes of expression, or because

33 John Dollard, op. cit., p. 249.

34 "The Channeling of Negro Aggression by the Cultural Process," *American Journal of Sociology*, May, 1943, pp. 750–758.

35 A. W. Davis, B. B. Gardner, and M. R. Gardner, op. cit., pp. 416–417.

he cannot afford them. To some, a church continues, under these circumstances, to be a center for many aspects of life, a quasi-community center where clubs may meet, dances held, and music, plays, and visiting enjoyed. The church services themselves, with their attention to "good music" and "good speaking," are recreational events in part.

To the migrant, his religious group, which is most often a small, "storefront" sect, is a place where he tries to allay his sense of strangeness in the company of others who are similarly confused. He is taught new modes of responding to the dominant whites—a reduction in the acceptance theme, an increase in emphasis on avoidance (self-reliance and race consciousness), and some increase in open opposition.

The ecstatic services of many of the groups enable the members of the congregation to escape, for a few moments, the hardships and humiliations of life. The congeniality of the meetings of what Daniel has called the semi-demonstrative cults, "affords fellowship, personal recognition, and tension release, so consoling to the former ruralite in the urban situation.[36] There continues to be a strong supernatural emphasis in the doctrines of these groups. The deprivations of this life are interpreted as unimportant or as preludes to the rewards in heaven for those who are faithful.

The various religious organizations of lower-class, urban Negroes share many tendencies in common, but there are also important differences among them. They range from fairly standard Protestant sects to esoteric cults on the margins of the Christian tradition. The latter appeared in large numbers during the economic depression of the 1930's, offering "solutions" to the difficult problems of poverty, illness, discouragement, and discrimination. The cults shade off into organizations of charlatans, racketeers who consciously exploit human misery for gain and power. The cults are usually small, store-front groups, relatively short-lived, dominated by the leader, and often at sharp variance with the stream of Christian influence from which most of them stem.

Not all such groups remain small, however. Social conditions, a ready audience, and a charismatic leader may combine to sweep some of them into a major movement. This is true of a "Voodoo Cult" in Detroit, which is part of the background of the Black Muslims. Benyon describes its appeal to recent migrants. This esoteric cult was started about 1930 by a prophet who usually went by the name of W. D. Fard. He claimed that he had come from Mecca to teach that the black men of North America are not Negroes, but members of the lost tribe of Shebazz who had been stolen by traders from Mecca 379 years before. Fard came to restore the true language, nation, literature and religion of this lost tribe. To solve their problems, the cult followers must obey the prophet of Allah, change their names (Fard usually received ten dollars for each new name), and accept the self-disciplines and mild asceticism of the group. Most of the eight thousand persons who Benyon estimates joined the Voodoo Cult were recent migrants from the South. Shocked by the discovery that the North was not the great land of hope, disillusioned when they discovered that the whites who mistreated them worshipped the same God, caught in poverty and unemployment, crowded into slum areas, they found an appeal in this drastic redefinition

36 V. E. Daniel, op. cit., p. 358.

of their situation.[37] We shall see later that, in the more aggressive atmosphere that followed World War II, the group led by Fard merged into the Black Power movement.

Such cult tendencies are not limited to Negroes, of course. They simply experience in accentuated form many of the pressures that some white people also feel.[38] Nor are cultist movements the dominant ones among Negroes, many of whom find it uncongenial to depart so widely from the Christian heritage with which they feel closely identified. Or, on the other hand, they may be too secularized and disillusioned with churches to participate in any movement that can be identified as religious in the traditional sense.

Among those who continue to be associated with Christian churches and sects, those who are native urbanites develop somewhat different tendencies and needs, which affect their religious behavior. For most urban Negroes, of course, there remain the overwhelmingly important facts of deprivation, of frustrated hopes, of segregation. These are modified somewhat, however, and are seen in a different light. The level of education is raised; occupational and income levels are improved for some; race consciousness (a sense of a common identity and in some measure a common fate) takes on a growing importance; more of the goals of the dominant group are absorbed, so that frustrations take on an added sharpness; forms of economic and political protest are nearer at hand, making the escapist doctrines of some of the religious groups seem less attractive; secular recreation and entertainment are more readily available, partly because of improved income, partly by the growth in participation in voluntary associations. All of these developments inevitably affect the religious life of the urbanized Negro.

Despite these changes, the otherworldly emphasis remains dominant—as it does, indeed, among most churches, even those of the more prosperous whites. But moral questions receive more attention—not simply the questions of individual morality, but some that are concerned with the problems of society. With the slow improvement in their economic status, an increase in their political power, and a growing hope for a better life, urban Negroes are less willing to accept the declaration that "the meek shall inherit the earth," or the belief that "when I get to heaven, gwine put on my shoes . . . and robe . . . and crown." There is an increasing hope—and demand—that they have shoes on earth; and a religion that does not sustain and work for that hope is left behind. Whether one considers "my home is over Jordan" a deep spiritual insight and brilliant adjustive achievement or a hopeless mirage, we must all recognize that it is now being supplemented by a demand for at least a temporary cottage in Bronzeville.

The traditionally religious are *on the average* (the exceptions are important) less likely to be militant in their attitudes and actions in the civil rights movement than are those who are less closely connected with churches and sects. Among his nationwide sample of Negroes living in

37 See E. D. Benyon, "The Voodoo Cult Among Negro Migrants to Detroit," *American Journal of Sociology*, May, 1938, pp. 894–907.

38 See Charles S. Braden, "Why Are the Cults Growing," *Christian Century*, January 12, January 19, January 26, and February 2, 1944.

metropolitan areas, Gary Marx found that militancy declined from 49 per cent among those who are not at all religious to 19 per cent among the very religious.[39] It should be noted, however, that religiosity was measured by combining frequency of church attendance, orthodoxy of beliefs, and degree of importance attributed to religion into an index of religiosity. I would find it more congenial to describe this as an index of *traditional* religiosity, as may be evident in the discussion of Black Power that follows. Marx also found that members of the smaller sects were least militant, those in the predominantly Negro denominations intermediately so, and those in largely white denominations most militant. In recent years, in fact, Black Power factions have developed among Episcopalians, Lutherans, Methodists, the United Church, Catholics, and even Unitarians.[40]

This last development, which in its most extreme expression extols belief in a black Jesus with a revolutionary message, is a connecting link between the established denominations and the separatist Black Power movement. It should serve to remind us of the steady stream of protest flowing from Negro churches and religious leaders, which draws its power from a religion that ostensibly was always concerned with otherwordly bliss. Denmark Vesey and Nat Turner were preachers who drew justification for their rebellions from religion. I will leave it to a psychiatrist to develop the implications of the fact that in this generation preachers' sons (some of whom are also preachers) are numerous among the more radical protest leaders. Steady if less drastic protest, however, had already begun to develop in Northern Negro churches in the 1930's and in the Southern Negro churches in the 1950's. Religious leaders who seek to appeal to the urban population, particularly to people who have experienced some economic and educational improvement, must be "race men." They encourage support of Negro business and professional men, preaching the doctrine of the "double-duty dollar"; they encourage and often lead boycotts against firms that discriminate against black workers or customers. The 1955–56 Montgomery, Alabama, bus boycott was a prominent example of this, but it was by no means the first. It was important for projecting Martin Luther King into the forefront of Negro leaders.[41] We can use it conveniently to mark the beginning of a militant period among American Negroes. There are many religious elements in this militancy. They can best be understood, however, by seeing them in the larger context of efforts to increase Black Power.

Black Power as an Aggressive Sectarian Movement

The Black Power movement among American Negroes illustrates clearly the principle that it is among those who have experienced significant improvement in income, education, and social power that protests are most likely to occur. Once the new social patterns begin to develop, it is seldom that improvement can be sufficiently rapid or consistent to keep up with the soaring hopes. Such rewards as the old order furnished—predictability,

39 Gary Marx, *Protest and Prejudice*, p. 102.

40 See *Newsweek*, March 4, 1968, p. 90; *Cleveland Plain Dealer*, March 2, 1968, p. 14.

41 See his *Stride Toward Freedom*.

perhaps, and sacred systems that gave meaning to disprivilege—are smashed; and their place is taken, to state the situation somewhat too drastically, by relative deprivation and status decrystallization.

There is a great deal of controversy over the extent to which conditions among Negroes have improved during the last twenty-five years. Indeed, a kind of professional pessimism is characteristic of social scientists and liberals as well as black leaders. One fears to be thought insensitive to the depths of a problem if he points to gains. One proves his opposition to discrimination and his sympathy with black men by citing only the most doleful figures.[42] Tragedies that have long existed become visible against signs of improvement, and the incautious may then proclaim their discovery of the tragedy. Dependence on the news media, with their concentration on conflict, is also likely to promote a pessimistic view.

Prophetic exaggeration may have strategic and therapeutic value; or it may contribute to polarization and vicious circles. I believe one can best demonstrate his concern by careful examination of the full range of facts. Let me, therefore, state my judgment as clearly as possible: The Black Power movement has developed for several mutually influential reasons: 1) because of the gains Negroes have made in American society; 2) because of the barriers to acceleration of those gains at a pace sufficiently rapid to match rising hopes; and 3) because of the availability of cultural supports, religious and secular, for its major demands. It would take us too far from our central purpose to examine these points in detail, but each requires a brief comment.

1. Whether gains have been rapid or slow depends upon one's standard, but it is clear that in the last generation Negroes in America have sharply increased their political influence (datum: Negro registrants in the South have increased from 250,000 in 1944 to nearly 4 million in 1968); they have climbed several steps up the educational ladder (datum: in recent years, the increase in average years of schooling has been more rapid among Negroes than among whites, so that the gap as measured in this way has been nearly closed); they have improved their economic situation (datum: the average income of Negro families has risen since 1930, when it was equivalent to about 30 per cent of white family income, to about 60 per cent—but it is important to note that most of the gains came before 1953).

2. One can, of course, cite opposite items: continuing political under-representation, inferior schools (so that number of years of education is a measure of doubtful value), rates of unemployment among Negroes that are double those among whites, and income growth that has been sustained mainly by a wartime economy (greatest improvement being shown during World War II, the Korean War, and the Vietnam War). It is exactly these continuing contrasts that are seen most clearly in a context of rising expectations based in part on past gains. Robert Conot puts the issue sharply: "While liberal whites compare the Negro's present position with that of

42 The sources and consequences of this phenomenon deserve careful study. What part does it play in social change? Does it occur regularly under crisis conditions? Speaking of the winter, 1932–33, Paul Carter wrote: "For desperate intellectuals, then as now, hope for the future was a species of disloyalty." (*The Decline and Revival of the Social Gospel*, p. 163.)

30 years ago and find the gains encouraging, the Negro compares his position today with that of the whites today, and finds the gap appalling." [43] The importance of *relative* deprivation is documented by the fact that the most militant Negroes are those who are best off educationally and economically and those with highest hopes for the future. In his study of a national sample of urban Negroes, Gary Marx found the relationship between militancy and class that is expressed in Table 15–1.

Table 15–1. Class and militancy among Negroes *

	Lower class	Middle class	Upper class
Per cent militant	14	31	45
(number)	(434)	(479)	(184)

* Adapted from Gary Marx, *Protest and Prejudice*, Harper and Row, 1967, p. 63. Class is assigned by combining scores on income and education. For the items used to determine militancy, see p. 41 of Marx's volume.

The same pattern appears when we relate militancy to morale in Table 15–2.

Table 15–2. Militancy and morale *

	Low Morale 0	1	2	High Morale 3
Per cent militant	15	22	31	42
(number)	(270)	(356)	(259)	(203)

* Adapted from Gary Marx, *Protest and Prejudice*, Harper and Row, 1967, p. 87.

Those with high morale, which we can use here as an index of hope, are the most militant.

3. It is not enough, however, to know that there has been improvement in status and a corollary increase in the sense of relative deprivation. These changes in structure and in character occur in particular cultural environments. The Black Power movement in the United States, despite its hostility to many American structures and practices, draws its ideological weapons from the system it seeks to change. It draws them selectively, to be sure, as any aggressive sect does; but it does not need to go outside the religious and political traditions of the nation to find a cultural arsenal for its battles. Stokely Carmichael and Charles Hamilton see Black Power as an expression of a long-established American process:

The adoption of the concept of Black Power is one of the most legitimate and healthy developments in American politics and race relations in our time. . . . It is a call for black people in this country to unite, to recognize their heritage, to build a sense of community . . . group solidarity is necessary before a group can operate effectively from a bargaining position of strength in a pluralistic

43 Robert Conot, *Rivers of Blood, Years of Darkness*, p. 446.

society. Traditionally, each new ethnic group in this society has found the route to social and political viability through the organization of its own institutions with which to represent its needs within the larger society.[44]

Most militant movements appeal to tradition, seeking thus to reduce opposition and gain legitimacy. Reactionary, conservative, and liberal movements do the same thing, and not necessarily with greater warrant than those who appeal for the organization of Black Power. In his famous "Letter from Birmingham Jail," Martin Luther King explicitly develops the theme that civil disobedience and extremism express both Christian and American traditions, not to mention the Jewish, Greek, and other sources he drew upon. "Jesus Christ was an extremist for love, truth and goodness, and thereby rose above his environment. Perhaps the South, the nation and the world are in dire need of creative extremists." [45]

The phrase Black Power has a wide variety of meanings. The conflict element that characterizes all of its varieties shades off on one side into violence or the rhetoric of violence (violence is not a synonym for conflict), and on the other side shades off into activities that permit, or even seek, the support of the white population. Insofar as these latter activities are religious, they link the Black Power movement with protests coming from established denominations. We might think of a continuum that runs from the most antagonistic position (self-segregation; violence as a necessary strategy; belief that the existing social system must be destroyed; ideology of black domination, not just equality), to a somewhat less violence-oriented but still hostile approach (little interest in cooperation with whites; organization of blacks for focused attack on inequality by use of political, economic, and religious weapons; disdain for effort to win equality through processes of law and persuasion), to an explicit emphasis on conflict by means of nonviolent protests and the increase of black morale (civil disobedience in the Gandhi sense where needed; organized political and economic action by black people, but white cooperation sought).

This whole continuum, however, must be seen as only a segment of a larger pattern; for supporters of all varieties of Black Power can be differentiated from others in various ways. Disregarding the many complexities, we can perhaps study the range usefully by seeing it in terms of two variables: the degree to which hope and aspiration for improvement of status have been raised, and the degree to which a person is alienated from society (believes his hopes cannot be obtained within the existing social framework). These do not necessarily vary together; and the several possible combinations have quite different implications for social action. If we simply divide each variable into a high and low sector, we get the pattern shown in Figure 15–1.

Seen in this larger context, the various forms of Black Power are regarded as similar. They are the responses of those whose hopes have been raised, but who see enormous obstacles to their realization. Viewed at closer range, however, each of these influences can be further differentiated. If we examine only the lower right quadrant of Figure 15–1, we can see different forms of Black Power. Although each is related to high levels of hope and

44 Stokely Carmichael and Charles Hamilton, *Black Power*, pp. 44–45.

45 Martin Luther King, *Why We Can't Wait*, p. 89.

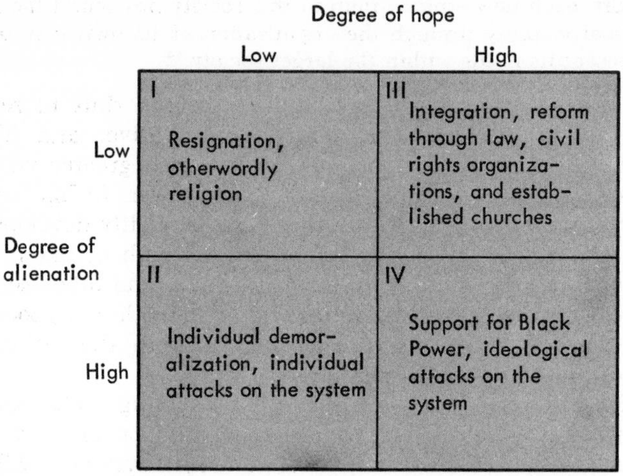

Degree of hope

	Low	High
Low	**I** Resignation, otherwordly religion	**III** Integration, reform through law, civil rights organizations, and established churches
High	**II** Individual demoralization, individual attacks on the system	**IV** Support for Black Power, ideological attacks on the system

Degree of alienation

FIGURE 15–1. *Correlates of various combinations of hope and alienation among American Negroes*

alienation, the shadings are different. If we describe them simply as "medium" or "high," we can make the distinctions in Figure 15–2, citing illustrative groups.

It is difficult to give empirical support for these informal placements. There is more evidence on the range of attitudes among Negroes than on correlations of particular combinations of attitudes with types of social protest. Thus, in 1968, *Fortune* magazine reported that 77 per cent of a sample of American Negroes were more hopeful of solving problems of discrimination than they had been a few years earlier. Only 5 per cent rejected integration as a goal.[46] In a variety of studies, including that made by *Fortune*, Martin Luther King, Roy Wilkins, and the groups they led (the Southern Christian Leadership Conference and the National Association for the Advancement of Colored People) received the support of 70 to 85 per cent of the respondents. Support for the Black Muslims and the more extreme Black Power groups is seldom as high as 15 per cent.[47]

We cannot explain the appeal of various forms of Black Power simply on the basis of differences in hope and alienation. There are other character differences as well as structural and cultural influences, which affect the availability of various forms of protest. Variation in levels of education, occupation, income, and socialization to traditional religious perspectives; degree of interaction with others of particular persuasions; opportunities furnished—or blocked—by the dominant structures—all these interact with tendencies expressive of the level of alienation and of hope to draw one person toward the Black Muslims, another to protest through traditional churches, another to a quasi-political or even a quasi-military movement.

46 *Fortune,* "Business and the Urban Crisis," January, 1968.

47 In addition to the *Fortune* study, see The National Advisory Commission on Civil Disorders, *Supplemental Study,* July, 1968, p. 21 and elsewhere; and James Conyers and William Farmer, *Black Youth in a Southern Metropolis,* Southern Regional Council, 1968.

I will refer briefly to some of the forms of Black Power, as defined above, to illustrate the range. Although reference will be primarily to groups that are generally regarded as churches, these shade off toward groups that also have religious qualities, despite their secular and even anti-religious appearance. The dedicated attention to self-discovery and justice, the sacred quality of the believing—the unquestioned truthfulness attached to the doctrines of Black Power, the sense of an exclusive brotherhood, the beatification of martyrs—these make it reasonable to say, with Nathan Wright, "Black power is fundamentally a religious concept." [48] It is, indeed, part of a long tradition, much of it religious.

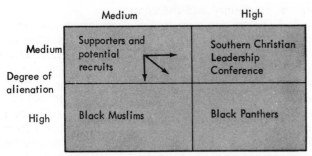

FIGURE 15–2. *Varieties of Black Power based on degrees of hope and alienation*

What is new about "Black Power" is phraseology rather than substance. Black consciousness has roots in the organization of Negro churches and mutual benefit societies in the early days of the republic, the antebellum convention movement, the Negro colonization schemes of the 19th century, DuBois' concept of Pan-Africanism, Booker T. Washington's advocacy of race pride, self-help, and racial solidarity, the Harlem Renaissance, and the Garvey movement. The decade after World War I—which saw the militant race-proud "new negro," the relatively widespread theory of retaliatory violence, and the high tide of the Negro-support-of-Negro business ideology—exhibits striking parallels with the 1960's.

Similarly, there are striking parallels between both of these periods and the late 1840's and 1850's when ideologies of self-help, racial solidarity, separatism and nationalism, and the advocacy of organized rebellion were widespread.

The theme of retaliatory violence is hardly new for American Negroes. Most racial disorders in American history until recent years, were characterized by white attacks on Negroes. But Negroes retaliated violently during Reconstruction, just after World War I, and in the last four years.[49]

It is well to be reminded of this historical continuity. The father of Malcolm X was an organizer for Marcus Garvey. Booker T. Washington does not seem so old-fashioned to black separatists as he did to their more integrationist predecessors. We should not, however, overlook new factors on the contemporary scene: the vastly greater proportion of Negroes who are

48 See "Black Power: What? Why? How?" *Social Action*, Jan., 1968, p. 24; see also Vincent Harding, "The Religion of Black Power," in *The Religious Situation: 1968*, Donald Cutler, ed., pp. 3–38.

49 *Report of the National Advisory Commission on Civil Disorders*, p. 234.

urban, whose sights have been raised and who interact intensively in densely packed communities; the great increase in levels of education and income, furnishing leadership, energy, and ambition; worldwide rebellion, with the African states particularly furnishing a stimulus to American Negroes; American affluence and its utter visibility through TV, movies, and general mobility; new machinery and tactics of violence in a society made vulnerable to the hostility of the few by its networks of interdependence.

Contemporary Negro protests, then, are part of a long tradition, not only within America, but going back to the early sectarians. They are also something new, the product of critical changes and stresses that have taken place in the last half of the twentieth century. We will understand them only if we see both the continuity and the change.

Both continuity and change are seen in the development of the Black Muslims, who have come into prominence in recent years. One of the lieutenants of W. D. Fard, whom we mentioned earlier, was a man who took the name of Elijah Muhammad. Gradually he won his way to the top of the movement. By the late 1950's, frustration over the slow pace of the civil rights movement, the mounting problems of the urban ghetto, publicity and opposition, Muhammad's own charismatic gifts, and the doctrines of the movement had combined to make the Black Muslims a nationally prominent sect. The size of the membership is not known, and estimates range from 10,000 to 200,000 or more. In various public opinion polls, support for or approval of the Black Muslims and their most important leaders, Elijah Muhammad and the late Malcolm X, has ranged around 5 per cent of the Negro respondents. It is not, therefore, a major group numerically. We should note a number of things, however, before judging its significance. Aggressive sects are seldom large. It is perhaps less important to know the size of the "hard core" than the size of the group that listens and responds. Many persons who find Muslim doctrines and style unattractive applaud its sharp challenge to a white-dominated society.[50] The Black Muslims are part of a much larger movement, with units that are variant in appeal and approach but similar in their dedication to Black Power—this heightens their influence. The effect of the Black Muslims, particularly through Malcolm X, on later expressions of Black Power has been great. His *Autobiography*, which has sold nearly a million copies, has become one of the testaments of the freedom movement. It is read, as scriptures always are, for a variety of purposes; but it is mainly his sharp challenge to "Whitey," not his more moderate Muslim views, that serve as rallying cries.

The ultimate appeal of the movement, as Eric Lincoln has put it, "is the chance to become identified with a power strong enough to overcome the domination of the white man—and perhaps even to subordinate him in turn." The aims, in the words of a Muslim minister, are "To get the white man's foot off my neck, his hand out of my pocket and his carcass off my back. To sleep in my own bed without fear, and to look straight into his cold blue eyes and call him a liar every time he parts his lips." [51]

50 See James Baldwin, *The Fire Next Time*, pp. 61–65.

51 C. Eric Lincoln, *The Black Muslims in America*, p. 27.

The manifest doctrine of the movement is built around a reconstruction of history: We are the lost nation of Islam. Our salvation rests upon the rediscovery of its tradition. All science is the product of the discoveries of twenty-four original black scientists, thousands of years ago. White men are "Yakub's devils," the creation of an evil black scientist. They were driven out of paradise into West Asia (Europe).

The sect preaches a stern ethic: Every Muslim is required to attend at least two services a week and to give generously in support of the program. He is urged to live respectably with his family, without gambling, drinking, smoking, buying on credit, or overeating. Responsible workmanship is emphasized. Separation from the white man, occupationally, educationally, residentially, as well as religiously, is preferred. This is sometimes expressed as a desire for a separate nation in the South; but with the growth in the number of mosques, schools, and businesses in the major cities of America, the rhetoric of withdrawal is heard less often.

The Black Muslims are a "revitalization movement" seeking "to construct a more satisfying culture," to use Wallace's phrase, and to discover a new self.

The lower-class Negro . . . is grateful for a mystique, especially one dignified as a religion, that rationalizes his resentment and hatred as spiritual virtues in a cosmic war of good against evil. . . . The true believer who becomes a Muslim casts off at last his old self and takes on a new identity. He changes his name, his religion, his homeland, his "natural" language, his moral and cultural values, his very purpose in living. He is no longer a Negro, so long despised by the white man that he has come almost to despise himself. Now he is a Black Man—divine, ruler of the universe, different only in degree from Allah Himself.[52]

To whom do the Black Muslims appeal? Most of their members are recent migrants into large cities, where their old accommodative ways of life have been destroyed, their aspirations have been raised, and their sense of power enhanced. Yet the painful facts of discrimination and segregation remain. They are angry at a society which has treated them so badly. By their placement in the lower left quadrant of Figure 15–2, I have suggested that their hopes have been raised quite high, although not as high as those with better jobs and education, and that their feelings of alienation from the dominant society are strong. Self-alienation is also an important element. Essien-Udom sees Elijah Muhammad's work and thought as a rather explicit attempt to reduce these forms of alienation: "He seeks to provide the Negro with a spiritual and moral context within which shaken pride and confidence may be restored and unused or abused energies directed toward an all-encompassing goal; to heal the wound of the Negro's dual membership in American society." [53]

At first glance it may seem paradoxical that a highly exclusive sect, antagonistic to whites, and dedicated to separate businesses, schools, and communities, should be seen as an effort to "heal the wound of dual

52 Ibid., pp. 48 and 108. See also E. U. Essien-Udom, *Black Nationalism: A Search for Identity in America;* and James Laue, "A Contemporary Revitalization Movement in American Race Relations: The 'Black Muslims,'" *Social Forces,* 42, 1964, pp. 315–323.

53 Essien-Udom, op. cit., p. 14.

membership." Perhaps the paradox is resolved by noting that the Muslims have shifted from the goal of individual integration to that of group integration, or, in more familiar terms, from assimilation to pluralism. The movement declares: What we have not been able to do as separate persons —win full equality and justice—we can do as a distinctive, self-respecting, well-disciplined group.

For this approach to become dominant, the extreme emphasis on separatism and hostility to whites would have to be modified. Pluralism, in fact, is not separatism but a form of integration, requiring mutual respect and involving extensive interaction. At least some of the developments among Black Muslims point in this direction. They are now much more concerned to build up their programs and businesses in the cities than to speak of a separate nation. In an interview with the *New York Times*, Minister Louis Farrakhan, Eastern representative of Muhammad, insisted that charges of Muslim anti-white racism were unfounded. He saw the doctrine rather as pro-black.[54] "The purpose was to give the poor black man pride in himself and love for himself as the first stage. The second is that he should start to build for himself—we are in the second stage now." [55]

This perhaps rationalizes the development of the sect too much, as if the stages were well planned in advance rather than evolving in response to changing circumstances. Whatever the source, however, change is occurring. It is not "from sect to church"; but from hostile, separatist sect to a more controlled, conflict-oriented and pluralistic sect. Ironically, that was the direction in which Malcolm X was moving in the last several months of his life. It was the basis for his split with the Muslims, whose racism and extreme emphasis on separatism he had come to believe were detrimental to Negro advance. On the one hand, Malcolm X began to condemn racism, whether white or black. He was encouraged in this view by a trip to Mecca and contacts with orthodox white Muslims. On the other hand, he stressed the development of separate organizations, working perhaps toward common goals, but pluralistically. When asked what white persons could do, Malcolm X replied:

> The first thing I tell them is that at least where my own particular Black Nationalist organization, the Organization of Afro-American Unity, is concerned, they can't *join* us. . . . I tell sincere white people, "Work in conjunction with us —each of us working among our own kind. . . ." Working separately, the sincere white people and sincere black people actually will be working together.[56]

Although they seem to be moving in that direction, the Black Muslims have not yet come to this position; nor have those who most often appeal to the memory of Malcolm X—the most militant wing of the Black Power movement. They are a secularized and politicized version of the Black

54 This is not entirely true, certainly, of the earlier work of the Muslims. A drama written and staged by the Muslims in many parts of the country carries the lines: "I charge the white man with being the greatest liar on earth! I charge the white man with being the greatest drunkard on earth. . . . I charge the white man with being the greatest gambler on earth. I charge the white man, ladies and gentlemen of the jury, with being the greatest peace-breaker on earth. I charge the white man with being the greatest adulterer on earth. . . ." Quoted by C. Eric Lincoln, op. cit., pp. 3–4.

55 *New York Times*, Thomas A. Johnson reporting, Jan. 13, 1969, p. 26.

56 *The Autobiography of Malcolm X*, pp. 376–377.

Muslims, who appeal to a more educated, sophisticated and, despite appearances, a more hopeful group. They find ample warrant in the life and writings of Malcolm X for their strategy of violence. Those who call for the pulling down of American society or for black supremacy if necessary to win justice are not inclined toward pluralistic tolerance. I have suggested that they are not only highly alienated, but also very hopeful. They are hopeful not only in the sense that they believe they can win (they speak of the vulnerability of modern cities to disruption by a small group), but in the more important sense that they think the battle worthwhile, that the values obtained by smashing society—the power, the wealth, the control over one's life chances that presumably would accrue—are significant. In this they express their thorough absorption by society, as compared with those who hold to otherworldly goals.

We stretch our definition to its utmost limits if we include the more extreme Black Power positions under the label of religion. When violence is not only accepted as a bitter necessity by a movement but exalted as a purifying force, it is not easily seen as a road to salvation. Yet I think we will not see the full implications of black radicalism if we fail to see even in its most violent forms the ultimate commitment and ultimate concern that mark its religious qualities. Contemporary heirs of the Judaic-Christian tradition are aware of the prophetic "Woe be unto you" or "I come not to bring peace but a sword"; but they relate them to ancient struggles against a distant empire. The sixteenth-century Peasants' Revolt may seem a little closer, and the words of one of its more extreme advocates, Thomas Müntzer, are no less severe than those of today's revolutionaries:

"Dearly beloved brethren, don't put up any shallow pretence that God's might will do it without your laying on with the sword, otherwise your sword might rust in its scabbard. . . ." Priests, monks, and godless rulers must all perish; and the preacher insists: "The sword is necessary to exterminate them." [57]

Contemporary phraseology and justification are different, but violence is still acclaimed as a religious process.[58] Jean-Paul Sartre writes: "Fanon . . . shows clearly that this irrepressible violence is neither sound nor fury, nor the resurrection of savage instincts, nor even the effect of resentment: it is man recreating himself." [59]

For a revolutionary movement, violence serves some of the same functions that severe asceticism, stern membership standards, and "chosen people" separatism serve in a less drastic way for an aggressive sect. Violence cuts the participant off irrevocably from dominant society, helping to guarantee his loyalty and utter dedication to the movement, for he has no other place to go.[60] It may be an effort also to control ambivalence: If I hate them enough to be ready to attack them or even to kill them, I clearly do not share any of their values, accept their appraisal of me, or

57 Quoted by Norman Cohn, *The Pursuit of the Millennium*, p. 256.

58 This is a descriptive not a valuative statement. To say that violence may be associated with religious feelings and processes is not to say that it is good.

59 In the Preface to Frantz Fanon's *The Wretched of the Earth*, p. 21.

60 See Fanon, op. cit., pp. 63–64.

recognize that somehow we share the burdens of the human condition. Extremists spend a great deal of emotional energy in repressing that second self, who might endanger a dearly bought dedication to a new and difficult doctrine of salvation.

Against the words of Müntzer or of Fanon, the words of most Black-Power advocates in the United States seem somewhat less extreme. Stokely Carmichael, perhaps the most prominent of these, has taken a range of positions. The most extreme calls for guerrilla warfare, and predictions of overt and organized revolution have been expressed when he was in Cuba or Africa. In *Black Power,* he and Charles Hamilton take a stand closer to American political radicalism. The book is conflict oriented, but it speaks a language of political struggle and, as we have noted, of pluralism. The tone is well expressed by a quotation its authors use from Frederick Douglass:

> Those who profess to favor freedom yet deprecate agitation, are men who want crops without plowing up the ground; they want rain without thunder and lightning. They want the ocean without the awful roar of its many waters. . . . Power concedes nothing without demand. It never did and it never will. Find out just what any people will quietly submit to and you have found out the exact measure of injustice and wrong which will be imposed upon them, and these will continue till they are resisted with either words or blow, or with both. The limits of tyrants are prescribed by the endurance of those whom they oppress.[61]

It is important to note that Carmichael has little by way of an organizational base. This is also true of Rap Brown, Eldridge Cleaver, Harry Edwards, and other currently visible black radicals. They are denounced by black liberals [62] and largely ignored by the masses. Writing in 1969, in fact, one must underscore the general lack of an organizational base for the expression of Negro protests as one of the important—and perhaps catastrophic—aspects of the current scene. Malcolm X might have been able to transform the Black Muslim sect into a more indigenous movement, less bound by a rigid ideology, more adaptable to changing circumstances. (As I have indicated, some of this transformation is taking place; but it has not proceeded very far.) Martin Luther King had by far the largest charismatic appeal of any Negro in the 1960's. His Southern Christian Leadership Conference in the twelve years of his leadership (1956–1968) was developing into an aggressive sect with a national base. It was being radicalized in a context of growing impatience and in competition with more extreme Black Power advocates; so that King was beginning to advocate not simply nonviolent resistance but civil disobedience to disrupt society and obtain more black control of ghettoes.[63] He continued, however, to emphasize nonviolence, cooperation with whites in civil rights movements, and integration. It remains to be seen whether without King's leadership, the Southern Christian Leadership Conference will maintain this direction and continue to be influential.

61 Quoted by Stokely Carmichael and Charles Hamilton in *Black Power,* p. x.

62 See the *New York Times,* July 30, 1967, p. 54 and Nov. 5, 1967, p. 35 for statements by Whitney Young, Jr., and Kenneth Clark.

63 Compare *Stride Toward Freedom,* 1958, with *Why We Can't Wait,* 1963, and *The Trumpet of Conscience,* 1968.

I believe it is not mere sentimentalism to suggest that Malcolm X and Martin Luther King, who were assassinated in 1965 aand 1968, respectively, were the men most likely to lead major protest sects—the former appealing to the more alienated and conflict-oriented, the latter to the more hopeful and integrationist-minded, but both drawing on the same large pool of America's deeply frustrated, angry, and action-minded black population. Faced by great obstacles, these people find meaningful only the *sanctified* knowledge, not subject to constant refutation, that their burdens will be lifted. Lacking a faith that develops a controlled and focused anger along with discipline, they are likely to be drawn into random and nihilistic acts of protest that cannot re-form but only destroy, or into bitter self-destroying resignation. If this interpretation is correct, a critical question for America in the years just ahead is this: Will an aggressive sect emerge, with power from charismatic leadership and organization, to help carry through the destruction of racism and the rebuilding of broken spirits, while preserving the larger sense of community? The answer depends not so much on the appearance of a prophet—there are probably several candidates around—as on the total context. Continued deprivation, modified by "all deliberate speed," seems unlikely to support such a bridging sect, able to help carry America over into a new pattern of relationships. Random protest, increasing alienation, and quasi-military action seem more likely. Sharp improvements in the conditions of life for America's black population, however, would support such a sect, which in turn would promote those improvements. Even then it will be an aggressive sect, pressing hard against the social order, more pluralistic than integrationist in emphasis, for the memory of inequality and injustice will be vivid for decades to come even if the most rapid imaginable speed is applied to reducing them.

The Consequences of Religious Trends Among Minorities

Most of the comments we made in the preceding chapter with regard to the consequences of lower-class sects apply also to minorities; but a few additional observations may serve to summarize our discussion of the relationship between sectarianism and stratification.

There are sharply contrasting judgments concerning the effects of the avoidance sects characteristic of the most deprived rural and urban groups. Fauset writes:

It *must* come [italics mine] as a great relief as well as release to such people to enter into the spirit of a group like one of the holiness cults, with its offer of assurance through grace and sanctification, and the knowledge that they will be aided not only in their efforts to support their customary burdens, but that in addition they will be equipped to measure arms with the white man, something they scarcely dreamed of doing previous to their advent into the North.[64]

On the other hand, Sperry points out:

Way back in the 1830's Harriet Martineau noted the advertisements in the New Orleans papers of the sales of occasional lots of "pious negroes" as being an especially good bargain. They would give no trouble here and now. The modern

64 Op. cit., p. 81.

radical Negro agitator regards his pious brothers as one of his liabilities; they are an obstacle to the full and final freedom of the race.[65]

These two supposed results of Negro religion—making a terribly difficult status bearable at the same time that it makes it more likely—are not mutually exclusive; in fact, the second may flow from the first. Whether they are functional or dysfunctional depends, of course, on the value premises from which one starts. To one who wants to keep the Negro in subservience, the second is functional and therefore the first is also, if it helps to assure the second. I put it in this way to emphasize again that functional analysis is no substitute for value analysis. To a person, white or black, who opposes racial discrimination, the reinforcement of low status by religious beliefs and practices is a dysfunction; and the effect of making a difficult status bearable, although desirable by itself, may also be tied to a chain of dysfunction.

One must be cautious, however, about assuming such consequences too quickly, on the basis of manifest characteristics of a sect. An otherworldly sect may plant seeds of hope which, when the situation changes somewhat, blossom quite rapidly. It is particularly important that the doctrine of a minority sect not be read only on the literal level. There may be deflected and disguised aggression in an accommodative sect; and a doctrine of aggression may serve to hide a program of accommodation. Aberle emphasizes this latter distinction with reference to the Ghost Dance. Its oppositional aim was partly contradicted by accommodative actions.[66] I would add that its oppositional aim partly *made possible* an accommodative program by defining the latter as an element of an independent, self-assertive Indian movement, which was not the product of the white man's power.

The part-whole and part-part question in functional analysis must be asked not only in connection with different consequences for minority and majority groups, but also with respect to subdivisions of a minority group. A Negro minister, for example, may find his various needs for leadership, for financial support from influential white persons, and the like, well served by a segregated church and the beliefs that support it. These are almost certain to be latent functions, not mentioned in any ideology by which he defends the segregated pattern. Members of his congregation may have some of their important desires frustrated by this same pattern. Needless to say, some Negro ministers set the highest value on Christian brotherhood and the elimination of discrimination; for them, both the latent and manifest consequences of segregated churches may be undersirable. Those Negroes who are most seriously disprivileged may be well served by religious beliefs and practices that help them to bear a status that in any event they are powerless to change, while those who live in a situation where there is some chance for improvement of status may be poorly served by the same beliefs and practices.

This last point raises again the question of functional alternatives. There are many ways in which men respond to the difficult problems they face. Not only are there various kinds of religious expressions, but these, seen

65 Willard L. Sperry, *Religion in America*, pp. 195–196. This is given contemporary support by the research of Gary Marx cited above.

66 See David Aberle, op. cit., p. 341.

together, are only one of a number of possible reactions. Individuals may respond by utter personal demoralization, a loss of any will to act or even to live. This has happened to some American Indians and to members of other societies overwhelmed by a powerful invading group. Mental illness may be interpreted as a form of adjustment or escape from problems that are too difficult for the individual to face on a realistic basis. Any attempt to judge a religious movement must surely ask: For what other way of struggling with life's problems is this an alternative? An American police chief has stated: "I see a remarkable parallel between the Black Muslims and the Nazis, as a matter of fact. The Muslims preach a fanatical religion based on hatred, just as Hitler did." [67] Aside from his rather gross parallel, he might have wondered for what activities this fanaticism is a substitute. Would members of the Muslims be gentle, self-respecting, law-abiding, white-man-loving, responsible workers were it not for the influence of the sect? Or does the group deal with persons filled with anger, self-doubt, and hatred; is it faced with the difficult task of remoralization? Aggressive sects doubtless create some hostility. But more importantly, they express it, give it a symbolic interpretation, and under some circumstances use it to carry the group over into a new life, a life that is beginning to open for them yet is blocked by enormous barriers of self and structure. We might describe the more positive aspects of the Muslims in terms used by W. E. H. Stanner to describe the Cargo Cults. They are "a redemptive act of faith by which what is realized as pragmatically difficult or impossible, of attainment, is seen under charismatic leadership as becoming possible by the grace of the spirits or ancestors." [68] This suggests what I have called the bridging function.

The bridge must be anchored, however, on both sides. The responses of the majority group are critical in determining the long-run consequences of an aggressive sect. Repression and disregard of the conditions from which it springs escalate the conflict, with hostility spilling over into violence. Under other circumstances, the sect may be seen as a sign of needed changes. Churches may take over some of the message; political and economic changes may moderate the problems from which the sect has sprung. If more effective economic and political means for seeking immediate values become available, the protest element in religion abates.

To put the sequences of change in an oversimple formula: When an aggressive sect meets escalating resistance and repression, it first redoubles its attack on society. It thereby loses its more moderate members and alienates groups with which it had worked in coalition earlier. With hope diminished, fewer persons are attracted to its promise of decisive victory. Withdrawal sects, with otherworldly goals or with visions of the Kingdom of God being present in pure and isolated communities, take its place. This was the sequence of events for the left wing of the Protestant Reformation. We see some elements of it in America today with respect to Black Power. Liberal Negro leaders are divided in their attitudes, but many are condemning it. The great majority of black persons are opposed to its most hostile forms. The black-white coalition that has been involved in the civil

67 *Cleveland Press*, Sept. 2, 1963, p. A-4.

68 Quoted by Mair, op. cit., p. 118.

rights movement is seriously strained by it. Insofar as this trend continues, the radical wing of the Black Power movement will become increasingly hostile and increasingly isolated. Its religious doctrine that the immediate, violent, and drastic revision of the social order is the way to salvation will attract fewer adherents. Repression and self-segregation will increase.

When an aggressive sect operates in a context where the grave problems which are its source are sharply reduced, however, a different sequence of events follows. The sect itself becomes more moderate. It does not take such intense resocialization and remoralization to work within a society that sustains one's hope. Efforts to win secular improvement are shifted into political and economic channels. So long as barriers to such improvement are so high that the very grounds of self-respect are threatened, questions of income, housing, political participation, and the like, are religious questions—they involve ultimate issues. One attempts to deal with them by applying his most sacred beliefs and rites, not by secular bargaining. But when the ground of one's being is not thus threatened, he can "afford" to transfer these issues into the secular sphere.

There are evidences of such shifts in the United States, alongside contrary evidences of mounting hostility and repression. The election of Negroes to high public office, for example, is as much a sign of hope on the part of the electorate as a cause for hope. When such election comes from a black-white coalition, it is a sign that tendencies toward repression are outweighed by readiness to change. Black Power as a holy crusade cannot survive such successes, hence its spokesmen are quick to condemn them as tokenism.

It is not at all clear whether the deprivation-aggression-repression-withdrawal cycle or the deprivation-aggression-modification-participation cycle is dominant in the United States today. Both are likely to be operative for years to come. I write this at a time when escalation cycles are common throughout the world, leading me to the feeling that mankind has not suffered enough yet to know how to prevent mundane questions from evolving into religious questions—sacralized by conflict. But there are indications to the contrary, at least with respect to minority-majority relations within societies. If these develop, Black Power as a hostile and aggressive sect will be moderated into an established sect, critical of but not wholly alienated from society, working alongside political and economic movements with more specific, more negotiable goals.

Among minority groups, however, there are persons still too lacking in hope to be attracted to sectarian protest. For many, a withdrawal theme is most congenial. We know too little to predict with confidence which of the various responses will be chosen by a particular individual or group, and we are not certain which ones are objectively possible, granted all the forces at work in a specific situation. It is unwise to complain that an escapist religion rigidifies the status pattern, if the only other adjustments available to individuals are utter demoralization and mental illness. But it is equally unwise to say that religion helps a group to bear the enormous burdens of low status, if that very religion obscures real possibilities of other kinds of action that might reduce those burdens. It is unwise to regret that an aggressive sect converts mundane issues into religious questions, incapable of rational examination, if society furnishes few secular means for the resolution of those issues. A severe religion may be the only way to save the selves of those who have escaped serfdom, have had their hopes mightily raised, only to run into insuperable barriers. Yet it is unwise to applaud an aggressive sect that polarizes a society and converts the pursuit of its goals into a sacred battle—when it has quite effective secular means and many potential allies to help in their attainment.

In my judgment, there is a *tendency* for the religious movements of minority groups to be functional in the general sense (seeking the satisfaction of the maximum possible needs of the individuals and group). That is, they slowly and partially demonstrate an adjustment to the actual limiting conditions and possibilities of life. It is in the *lag*, however, the slowness to respond to changes in the conditions and possibilities, that critics of religion (friendly or otherwise) are likely to find their most useful point of departure and the analyst of religion some of his most difficult problems.

Chapter Sixteen

RELIGION AND ECONOMICS

The central problems of economics, as a science, are the determination of the way in which value is ascribed to goods and services, the analysis of how a society distributes its income, and the study of the organizations and the processes through which the various scarce resources are combined to produce the desired values. This last shades off into the study of technology, to which, strictly speaking, the problem of the scarcity of the resources is irrelevant. A plant manager asks a technological question when he considers how he can produce a given object; he asks an economic question when he wonders whether it is worthwhile for him to produce that object (instead of using labor, materials, plant in alternative ways). Although economic and technological questions can be clearly distinguished, they mutually affect each other in important ways: The costs of the various resources are among the factors that determine a technological decision on *how* to produce; and the available technical processes of production are among the factors determining an economic decision on *whether* to produce.

Religion is involved both in the strictly economic and in the technological questions. We shall be primarily concerned with the former, which has through the course of history become the more significant relationship, but will deal briefly first with the latter problem.

RELIGION AND TECHNOLOGY

It would be an oversimplification to state, without qualification, that the more primitive the technology and the more precarious and uncertain the results from one's efforts to obtain food and other goods, the more religion is used to bolster man's efforts. Yet the correlation is undoubtedly high. Religion is widely used as one of the techniques by which success in the hunt, productivity of the garden, or protection for the flocks is sought in primitive societies. Some writers describe the desire to reinforce a desperately inadequate technology as one of the complex of forces that lie at the very origin of religion. Radin writes:

To understand the beginnings of religion we must try to visualize as accurately as we can the conditions under which man lived at the dawn of civilization. Manifestly he lived in a variable and essentially inimical physical environment and possessed a most inadequate technological preparation for defending himself against this environment. . . . His methods of food production were of the simplest kind—the gathering of grubs and berries and the most elementary type of fishing and hunting. He had no fixed dwellings, living in caves or natural shelters. No economic security could have existed, and we cannot go far wrong in assuming that, where economic security does not exist, emotional insecurity and its correlates, the sense of powerlessness and the feeling of insignificance, are bound to develop.[1]

Out of this context, says Radin, came the beliefs and rites of primitive religion.

Whether or not the inadequacy of the technical resources of man was involved in the origin of religion, it certainly was involved in many of its expressions. It is not surprising to find in societies whose very survival depended upon the annual rains that their most sacred beliefs and most devout rites were appeals for rain—as among the Zuni, the Lovedu, or the aboriginal Australians. Religious rites shade off toward magical practices, following the distinction we developed in Chapter Four; and those more individual, more immediate, and more practical activities that we call magic are also closely related to technology.

In a society where agricultural production has been vastly improved, where storage granaries and rapid transportation have virtually eliminated the technological if not the economic base of starvation, rain-making becomes, not a matter of religiomagical ceremony, but of airplanes "seeding" silver iodide in the sky. Even in societies that have achieved a great deal of technical efficiency, however, food production is sometimes threatened by drought. The welfare of a region and the livelihood, if not the survival, of thousands of families may be endangered. Religious beliefs (that the drought is punishment for evil or a test of faith) and practices (prayers that the drought may be broken) may then return as marginal, if not basic, activities in connection with food production.

The relationship between technology and religion is a complicated one requiring attention to several qualifications: Some societies with fairly proficient techniques of production nevertheless have developed an intricate connection between their technology and religion; some religious beliefs and practices that are clearly antithetical to efficient production are devoutly defended anyway, because they are religiously right; and many of the observances to assure productivity are more nearly magical than religious. These qualifications, which we will keep in mind as we discuss and illustrate the connections between religion and technology, should prevent us from making any easy technological explanation of religion. They do not, however, eliminate the fact of a broad pattern of relationship.

1 Paul Radin, *Primitive Religion: Its Nature and Origin*, pp. 6–7.

Societies with pantheistic religions generally are well supplied with gods and goddesses who are the patrons of crafts, protectors of flocks, or guarantors of fertility. Ceremonial detail is interwoven with technical acts; sacrifices and petitions to the deities are considered essential for success; holy days and festivals are devoted to praise of the protecting deities. Concerning the Zuni, Benedict writes:

If they are asked the purpose of any religious observance, they have a ready answer. It is for rain. This is of course a more or less conventional answer. But it reflects a deep-seated Zuni attitude. Fertility is above all else the blessing within the bestowal of the gods, and in the desert country of the Zuni plateau, rain is the prime requisite for the growth of crops. The retreats of the priests, the dances of the masked gods, even many of the activities of the medicine societies are judged by whether or not there has been rain. To "bless with water" is the synonym of all blessing. Thus, in the prayers, the fixed epithet the gods apply in blessing to the rooms in Zuni to which they come, is "water-filled," their ladders are "water-ladders," and the scalp taken in warfare is the "water-filled covering." The dead, too, come back in rain clouds, bringing the universal blessing. People say to the children when the summer afternoon rain clouds come up the sky, "Your grandfathers are coming," and the reference is not to the individual dead relatives, but applies impersonally to all forebears. The masked gods also are the rain and when they dance they constrain their own being—rain—to descend upon the people. The priests, again, in their retreat before their altars sit motionless and withdrawn for eight days, summoning the rain. . . . Rain, however, is only one of the aspects of fertility for which prayers are constantly made in Zuni. Increase in gardens and increase in the tribe are thought of together.[2]

Malinowski found, among the Trobriand Islanders, an interesting contrast that points up the way in which magical practice supplements technological activity, particularly in societies that live a precarious existence. In the situation he describes, more than in the case of the Zuni, the beliefs and rites that are connected with technology incline toward magic rather than toward religion. The reference is to a specific goal more than to general social welfare. The practices are not thought to be ends in themselves, but means to ends. But as we have seen, one cannot readily assign the complexes of belief and ritual simply to magic or to religion. Malinowski found that two closely related tribes approached their common task of fishing quite differently. One tribe, which fished largely in protected inland waters and lagoons where there was little danger and little chance of failure, carried on their work quite matter-of-factly. There was no room for precautionary rituals aimed at protecting the men and insuring a good catch. The other tribe fished in the open sea, where the catch was much less certain and the hazards far greater. Around their work they had developed an elaborate system of rites, in an effort to placate the unknown forces that constantly threatened their success and to rid themselves of the sense of insecurity.[3]

Such practices are not, as Malinowski makes abundantly clear, simply a mistaken or crude kind of technology, a kind of "primitive science," rooted in complete lack of knowledge of the real causes of events. Primitive man

2 Ruth Benedict, *Patterns of Culture*, pp. 58–59.

3 See Bronislaw Malinowski, *Argonauts of the Western Pacific*.

follows his technology as far as it will take him—and he often manifests an extensive understanding of the technical facts. But he knows also that no matter how carefully he does his work he may, for reasons beyond his control and usually beyond his comprehension, fail to get a good catch or harvest a good crop. It is at this point that he grasps for the assurance of magical and religious practices.[4]

In some societies, the relationship between religion and technology is exceedingly close even though they have developed a fairly abundant and stable source of food. This is true, for example, of the Todas of South India, whose economy is built around dairying activities. A large share of the work in caring for the cattle is carried on in accordance with the prescribed ceremonial forms by dairymen-priests.[5] These are not desperate attempts to bolster a shaky technology by supernatural means, for the Todas have a fairly adequate and secure food supply. Some may assume that the intricate connection between religion and technology demonstrates the survival of beliefs and rites that originated in more difficult times; but this assumption requires more careful proof than the data now permit. It is possible, in fact, that the relationship was the other way around: the religiously prescribed value assigned to cattle and to their care may have helped to bolster the economy. Or the relationship may have been interactive.

This qualification suggests the further comment that religious requirements may be clearly opposed to the efficient production and use of economic goods. They may be recognized as such, and defended on religious grounds, or they may be held to be subtle aids to technology. The actual effects would be, under such circumstances, latent dysfunctions. Taboos on the consumption of certain foods—ritualistic restriction on the use of totem animals to certain periods of the years, for example—may sometimes help to protect a food supply; but at other times, taboos permanently remove an available food from human use. Religiously protected animals, in fact, may be substantial consumers of scarce food. Ceremonial restrictions on techniques of production may prevent the development of efficient processes. The observance of holy days and festivals or the carrying out of the requirements of mourning rituals may prevent work for significant periods of time. These are in part strictly economic influences on production because they determine how the members of a society shall use scarce goods or scarce time; but they are in part also technological influences, for they affect the work processes themselves.

On the other hand, religious observance may increase productivity. As Goode says, "the very cooperation expected by ritual conformity may actually increase efficiency at the time." Religious demands for particular care of gardens or animals may increase the supply of food. Craftsmen may be religiously motivated to develop a higher skill in their work. These are primarily technological effects. It is more likely, however, that the religious encouragement to production will be economic rather than technological. It is not so likely to affect the actual techniques of work as it is to influence the use of time and material. Yang notes that in China, "the

4 See Malinowski's paper "Magic, Science, and Religion," in *Science, Religion and Reality*, Joseph Needham, ed., pp. 30–32.

5 W. H. R. Rivers, *The Todas*.

cults of the agricultural gods formed a part of the peasants' age-old struggle against the hazards of nature, serving as the rallying points for community consciousness and collective action in the face of common crises." [6]

Religious requirements may motivate the members of a society to productive activity rather than to some alternate use of time, just as they may have the opposite effect. Thrift may be religiously obligatory. "In order to please the gods one must save or acquire enough food or wealth for the payments, gifts, or offerings needed." [7] Weber has argued, as we shall see later, that the religious prescriptions of Calvinism have strongly influenced the productivity of capitalist societies. The relationship is perhaps more complicated than he made it out to be, but, carefully stated, his thesis is a clear demonstration of the significance of religion for technological and economic matters. In a similar vein, Robert Bellah writes: "This then is the nubbin of Confucian economic policy, in its ideal expression: encourage production and discourage consumption." [8]

Whether one concludes that religion basically contributes to or interferes with technological efficiency, it is a mistake to assume that the members of a society, in following the religious norms, think of themselves simply as using an efficient process to increase production. The technological relevance of religion is distinctly secondary to the basic problems of group integration and individual salvation. There are *implications* for technology in religious belief and action, but seldom direct concern. The relationship is well analyzed by Goode, in *Religion Among the Primitives*, particularly in his discussion of the Manus, a society that stresses the importance of shrewd economic calculation. Their religious life centers around a personal deity, Sir Ghost; but the Manus do not regard their deities simply as powerful forces who can bring them food, prestige, health, and so on, if they are properly manipulated. Such a secular and rational attitude would deny the religious relationship.

Goode notes the strongly rationalistic element in the economic system of the Manus, the readiness to exploit even one's kin. This might lead one to expect a "contractual" element in their religious lives—a belief that worship and sacrifice would be repaid by personal success. To some degree this is true. But more than a contractual relationship, the connection between the Manus and their Sir Ghosts is a covenant that has important community implications. The personal deities give aid, but they insist upon various economic obligations—the careful use of resources, allocating one's wealth farsightedly and generously, and energetic production.

Although he is interested in the full range of consequences, Roy Rappaport, in his study of the Tsembaga of New Guinea, also shows convincingly how religion influences technological and economic processes. The relationship is demonstrated particularly by the ways in which ritual governs the size of pig herds and the distribution of pork. Religious ritual moves through a cycle related to intertribal hostilities and the rise and fall in the size of the herds. Disregarding the relationship to warfare, which in fact is closely tied to the whole process, we can see the ritual connection with

6 C. K. Yang, *Religion in Chinese Society*, p. 69.

7 See William J. Goode, *Religion Among the Primitives*, pp. 135–137.

8 *Tokugawa Religion*, p. 109.

technology and economics as one which prevents the herds from getting too small or too large, defines rights over disputed land, and governs the distribution of a scarce and valuable food. Because sacred ideas are involved, the likelihood of short-run and purely individual decisions is reduced in favor of long-run community decisions. And ritual helps to balance out or reconcile the series of partly conflicting requirements by making them part of the total system. Altogether "the regulatory function of ritual among the Tsembaga and other Maring helps to maintain an undegraded environment, limits fighting to frequencies that do not endanger the existence of the regional population, adapts man-land ratios, facilitates trade, distributes local surpluses of pig in the form of pork throughout the regional population, and assures people of high-quality protein when they most need it." [9]

Thus religion, struggling with the fundamental problems of human existence, inevitably reaches out to affect technology, as it affects all other aspects of life, in the effort to solve these problems. It is in turn affected by the technological facts and requirements of society. The nature of this interaction varies widely. The fact that religious "solutions" are largely symbolic means that a wide range of possibilities may be tried. There are only a certain number of ways to plant and care for a garden that will yield a crop. But there are infinite possibilities for variations in religious rituals that are calculated to assure a good harvest. The religious influence on technology is particularly likely to be strong in those societies that have least successfully solved the problems of production, because it is in just such societies that the individual and group functions of religion are persistently affected by low productivity. If a religious system is to carry out these functions, it must deal with the problems (low productivity, individual anxiety, more illness and death, and so on) that derive from inadequate technology. And so it tries.

By the same token, the level of technology affects religion by influencing the kinds of problems that will be regarded as ultimate. If the food supply is precarious—not occasionally but endemically—its protection is an ultimate concern. Men will not leave such protection to an unreliable or patently insufficient technology, however much they may exploit their technological resources to the full, but will bring into play their most sacred beliefs and practices. First-fruits are offered to the gods; taboos are imposed; the full moral resources of the community are marshaled.

In technically efficient societies, other problems are more likely to press in on religion for solution. Technology tends to be secularized; and the effects of the level of technology on religion are less direct. It is sometimes observed that efficiency in the production of goods makes a society materialistic. The "spiritual" East, for example, may be contrasted with the "materialistic" West. If this means a greater interest in the West than in the East in whatever goods are available or imaginable I think the contrast is subject to serious doubt. If it means that the pursuit of goods is less secularized, more hedged about by religious and magical practices, in some societies than in others, there can be little question about its truth. As Weber put it: "The unrestricted lust for gain of the Asiatics in large and in

9 Roy Rappaport, *Pigs for the Ancestors: Ritual in the Ecology of a New Guinea People,* p. 224.

small is notoriously unequalled in the rest of the world. However, it is precisely a 'drive for gain' pursued with every possible means including universal magic." [10]

There are doubtless many indirect effects of developed technology on religion. High-speed printing makes religious works widely available and probably increases the role of laymen in religious process and evolution. Scientific medicine reduces or at least changes the focus of attention in the arts of religious healing. Techniques of rapid transportation and communication bring adherents of different faiths into extensive contact, making both religious conflict and ecumenism more possible. [10a]

RELIGION AND THE DISTRIBUTION OF WEALTH

In the preceding discussion, some aspects of the relationship of religion to economic questions were raised, particularly those associated with production, because of their inevitably close association with technology. We have noted that the ways in which scarce time, skill, and resources are used are often affected by religiously motivated decisions. The frequency of holidays and the activities associated with them can influence both the amount and types of production. The structure of work groups and situations may be influenced by religion. Thus the study of a Hindu caste, or a medieval manor, or some labor unions reveals that economic questions concerning the production of goods and services are conditioned by religious values.

A second economic question—how to describe the way in which comparative values are ascribed to the products of society—is also influenced, at least to a small degree, by religious considerations. Some goods and services are worth more—have a higher economic value—because they have a religious value, and others are worth less because religion places a negative value upon them. A primitive man may invest a great deal of time and skill—an economic decision—in carving the appropriate symbols or designs on a sacred drum, because they contribute to its religious efficacy. Were it not for their religious meaning, he would not value them so highly and would be unwilling to spend so much for them. Similarly, a church may invest a great deal of money in a stained-glass window, because of the meaning it has for the members. Thus religion affects the demand side of the familiar supply-demand equation. On the other hand, it may influence the supply side, if the values it upholds encourage or discourage the production of various goods and services.

These are rather specific economic problems, and we shall not, therefore, give them further attention. It is in the influences on the distribution of wealth and income that religion has its most significant economic effects on society, culture, and personality. Hence the sociologist of religion must explore this question carefully.

Wealth and Income of the Churches. Religious activity everywhere receives a certain share—often a fairly large share—of the wealth of a

10 *The Religion of India,* p. 337.

10a For a thoughtful discussion of some of the effects of technology, see Robert A. Nisbet, "The Impact of Technology on Ethical Decision-Making," in *Religion and Social Conflict,* Robert Lee and Martin Marty, eds., pp. 9–23.

society. Even those groups that live on the edge of subsistence devote part of their substance to the maintenance of holy places, sacrifices, ceremonial feasts, sacred objects, and the like. Indeed, if there is any correlation between the amount of wealth of a society and the proportion of its wealth that is spent for religion, it may be an inverse one: the poorer the society or group, the higher the proportion of its wealth that is devoted to religious activity.

Part of this expenditure, in societies where religious specialists have appeared, is used to support the priestly class. This adds a new dimension to the question of the economic significance of religion, especially where there is no clear-cut determination by the religious values themselves of the appropriate share of the income that should go to the religious professionals. The traditions may encourage mendicancy, as with the early Buddhists or some Christian monastics. But more commonly the religious norms encourage, or at least permit, the priestly group to strive for a larger share of the wealth. The religious views may then combine with secular ambitions among the clergy, who in most instances have secular as well as religious interests, to bring them substantial incomes. As mediators if not as dispensers of salvation, they are often in a commanding position. If their religious authority is combined, by a churchly decision, with the power of secular authorities, they may dominate or share in the ruling of the society and even acquire substantial wealth.

Some will say at this point: This is not a description of the economic power of religion, but of the transformation of religion into a secular quest, under religious guise. Perhaps so. But it is precisely in the possibilities of such transformation, in the frequency with which religious institutions take on secular power, that many of the implications of religion for society reside. Sometimes it is the religious professionals themselves who gain wealth and power; sometimes it is a secular group that acquires religious sponsorship for its claims to hold, or to win, wealth and power; often it is both.

Analysis of the conditions under which these various possibilities occur is an important task. The following variables seem to be involved, and we shall have them in mind as we discuss some of the evidence relating to religion and the distribution of wealth.

1. *The Degree of Secularization.* Where most of the questions of life have a religious aspect, the importance of religion for economics is likely to be large, and the priestly class likely to be well supported. Where many important questions—as, for example, health and technology—are thought of primarily in secular terms, as in the United States today, the economic influence of religion is reduced.

2. *The Nature of the Religious Traditions and Organizations.* Religions in which ethical questions are least important, those in which the means to salvation are most thoroughly institutionalized, most under the domination of one ecclesiastical group, and least under the control of the individual believer, are those that aid the acquisition of power by the professional religious leaders.

3. *The Nature of Power Distribution in the Secular Aspects of Society.* When economic and political power are highly concentrated in the hands of a small ruling group, the higher clergy are likely to occupy positions of

influence and to share generously in the income of a society. In such circumstances, churchly compromise with "the world" is carried to great lengths; the rulers and their practices are upheld and defended with a minimum of criticism. This is partly because the dilemma of religious leaders which we have discussed is particularly sharp in authoritarian societies; and it is partly because the secular gains for the clergy, if they will support the ruling group, are large in such societies. In democratic situations, where power is diffused, the dominant group is less willing to share influence and income with religious leaders if they will sanctify their dominant position. Powerful secular groups have little to gain thereby, because the lower strata of society have other means—political action, labor unions, etc.—of making their claims in any event. It is of little value to block one hole in a sieve, of little value to inhibit the lower classes' claims to a greater share of life's goods under religious auspices if they are going to have other auspices anyway. Moreover, the lower classes, in a democratic society, are less likely to accept a religious system that has accommodated itself thoroughly to the dominant groups, because they have other means of working for their goals.

These three variables are closely interrelated. Their combined effect can be to influence strongly the wealth of the churches and the income of the clergy. In the United States, for example, religious professionals are not, on the average, well paid. Their income is below that of industrial workers. Pastors of middle- and upper-class congregations are paid above the average; but their incomes are usually below those of their parishioners.[11] Each of the variables contributes to this result: Many questions that formerly had a strong religious aspect have been substantially secularized; there is an emphasis on religious toleration and the right of an individual to be his own religious interpreter—the opposite of a monopoly on the means of salvation; and secular power is quite extensively diffused.

When such a situation is compared with that of medieval Europe, the importance of the three factors in affecting the wealth of the church and the income of the clergy is well shown. In medieval times, the interpretation of medical, agricultural, astronomical, and other kinds of events was far less secularized. The Roman Catholic Church, organized into an elaborate hierarchy with a monopoly over sacraments and using a language unknown to the mass of people, dominated the religious scene. Individual initiative in religious matters, the expression of the belief that the layman could have dealings directly with God, without the need for the intercession of the Church, were heretical acts, justifying severe punishment. Finally, the secular setting was one in which power was highly concentrated in the hands of the hereditary nobility. In these circumstances, the churches and the clergy commanded a great deal of wealth. It was very unequally dis-

11 There is, of course, a wide range in ministerial salaries, from the few dollars a week earned by the store-front pastor, who often has a second job, to the $40,000 salaries of a few suburban clergymen, to even higher incomes for a small number whose writing and lecturing fees add substantially to their salaries. The exact figures change too rapidly with the price level to be of much value. In 1967, the National Council of Churches estimated the median salary of Protestant ministers to be just under $7,000 per year. Catholic priests may have lower cash incomes but be better off financially because they are furnished a rectory, where they eat and sleep, and have no family obligations. See the *New York Times*, Feb. 18, 1968, pp. 1 and 66.

tributed, to be sure; the majority of priests were far from affluent; but the total wealth, especially in land, was great. Preserved Smith writes:

The wealth of the church was enormous, though exaggerated by those contemporaries who estimated it at one-third of the total real estate of Western Europe. In addition to revenue from her own land, the church collected tithes and taxes . . . the clergy paid dues to the curia . . . the priests recouped themselves by charging high fees for their ministrations. At a time when the Christian ideal was one of "apostolic poverty" the riches of the clergy were often felt as a scandal to the pious.[12]

This is not a Christian situation only; nor did it end with the Middle Ages. In some areas, Buddhist and Hindu property holdings are large and at least a few priests and monks have high incomes.[13] In Catholic countries, the Church has retained substantial landed wealth; in other countries it did so until twentieth-century revolutionary movements seized and redistributed church lands. The Vatican today has large financial interests in corporations in many parts of the world.[14] Churches in the West German Republic are supported by a state-collected income tax amounting to 800 million dollars in 1968.[15] Although the Church of England has a declining membership, and even more rapidly declining participation, it has substantial inherited wealth from which perhaps half its income is derived.

On an absolute, if not on a relative basis, the wealth and income of American churches is enormous. Martin Larson has estimated the real-estate wealth of churches in the United States at 79.5 billion dollars, and the value of tax exemption at 1.6 billion dollars annually.[16] Total church income is between 6 billion and 8 billion dollars annually.[17] Although this is less than 1 per cent of national income, the way in which it is spent has a significant impact on the economy. In recent years, tax exemption and the uses of church income have become matters of sharp criticism from at least a few Americans.[18] Because taxes *not* collected from churches are made up elsewhere, constitutional questions about tax exemption are raised. Are nonmembers being taxed to support churches indirectly? Does tax exemption represent governmental support of religion? Those who believe it does not, cite the public functions of churches, matching those of such other tax-exempt organizations as hospitals and schools. These functions are pre-

12 *The Age of the Reformation*, pp. 21–22.

13 For some data on the Hindu situation, see J. D. M. Derrett, "The Reform of Hindu Religious Endowments," in *South Asian Politics and Religion*, D. E. Smith, ed., Chap. 14.

14 See Nino LoBello, *The Vatican Empire*.

15 Although church attendance in Germany is low, 95 per cent of the population claim membership in Catholic or Protestant churches and thus are subject to the tax. The money is used for many activities besides the support of churches—for hospitals, orphanages, homes for the aged, and so on. See *Newsweek*, Jan. 6, 1969, p. 38.

16 Martin Larson, *Church Wealth and Business Income*, cited by Alfred Balk, *The Religion Business*, pp. 8 and 36.

17 See D. B. Robertson, *Should Churches Be Taxed?*, pp. 155–156. Chap. 7 of this work is a useful commentary on the unreliability of data regarding church income.

18 In adition to the works already cited, see James Pike, "Tax Organized Religion," *Playboy*, April, 1967; Guild of St. Ives, "A Report on Churches and Taxation," in *The Religious Situation: 1968*, Donald Cutler, ed., pp. 931–952; and the "Commentary" by Jack Mendelsohn that follows, pp. 952–960.

sumed to be wholly outside the commercial or business economy, to be "non-profit." Even if this argument is accepted for some purposes, it does not necessarily apply to some of the publishing activities, housing projects, and recreational facilities of churches; and it is even more questionable whether it applies to the income from the billions of dollars of investment by church pension funds and other assets in purely secular commercial and industrial companies.

Bishop Pike did not argue in favor of taxation of church income primarily on constitutional grounds. He believed such a change would compel the church to reassess its priorities, promote ecumenism, and break the tendency to associate the church with real property. Others wonder whether a poorer church would necessarily move along these lines. It might instead curtail its program and become more conservative.

Another line of criticism of church financial matters relates to the form of its expenditures rather than to the sources of its income. A National Committee on Tithing in Investment urges churches, as well as unions, foundations, colleges, and individuals, to spend a portion of their income on integrated housing. Other groups and individuals have sought to persuade churches to withhold investment funds from companies with discriminatory hiring policies, with investments in South Africa, with large military contracts, and the like. This is a double-edged sword, however, unless one can persuade only those churches that share his values to act. The Reverend John Reedy asks: "What does the liberal who backs Project Equality say to someone else who thinks that Catholic hospitals should boycott pharmaceutical firms that manufacture birth control pills?" His question is not intended to discourage church economic action, however, for he goes on to say: "We must find some way of responsibly confronting the fact that when churches don't recognize their economic power, they simply reenforce the status quo." [19]

Religious Influences on Income Distribution and Economic Values Among Laymen

In the analysis of the influence of religion and religious institutions on the distribution of wealth it is not the effects upon churches themselves or upon the priestly class that have received most attention or are most important. In modern societies, at least, church properties represent a fairly small part of the economy and religious professionals a small proportion of the population. The use of religion to hold or to acquire a greater share of the wealth by *secular* classes and groups, from all levels of society, is the more fundamental phenomenon. The analysis of the factors affecting the income of professional religious leaders can be brought within this larger question, for it is the nature of their association with the secular groups that is largely responsible for their income position. In our further discussion of religion and the distribution of wealth, therefore, we shall deal with these two aspects together.

Description of the use of religion by secular groups to hold or acquire scarce values is very closely related to the topic of religion and social stratifi-

19 Quoted by Jack Mendelsohn, op. cit., p. 957.

cation, with which we dealt in the preceding two chapters. Our concern here, however, is not so much with the variations in beliefs, rites, and religious-group structure among social strata and the several reasons for these variations. It is more with the processes of interaction by means of which religion is used to justify specifically economic claims. This will require that we explore, more fully than we have up to now, the various aspects of the churches of the middle and upper classes, as we have already studied the sects of the lower classes. The sects have seldom, at least for long, made direct economic claims on the basis of religion. The actual facts of the situation have too persistently frustrated their desire to improve their status through appeals to religion for them to retain much hope of success. Their religious expressions, therefore, have been more inclined to redefine the meaning of their economic status (poverty is a sign of virtue; this life is scarcely significant in any case) than to attack it. The consequences of their religious beliefs for economic matters have been more indirect than direct, latent rather than manifest functions. This is true whether those consequences have been to make their status more rigid, by reducing the motivation toward change, or to make it less rigid, by encouraging frugality and industry.

It is otherwise with the middle and upper classes. They face many serious difficulties, to be sure, but their economic hopes have been substantially rewarded, not frustrated. Their task is not to adjust to poverty and powerlessness, but to feel justified in their good fortune. This too can be a difficult problem, particularly among those who share a religious tradition that embodies a large measure of the insights and responses of persons who have been dealing with ill-fortune. This is true of all major religions. They are substantially the products of suffering, of a sense of evil, of unhappiness, often as these problems have been developed in the minds of people peculiarly sensitive to them. The well-to-do share these religions because they are brought up in societies where they prevail, but more importantly because they too, in the last analysis, face the problems of suffering and evil, even if in somewhat different ways. So they embrace religions that help them struggle with these difficulties. But they do not suffer from poverty. Can they get religious sponsorship for this *lack* of suffering? They succeed in doing so in the churches; but this cannot be done without transforming them, to a greater or lesser degree, into secular institutions, thereby reducing their ability to help other classes, and, in the long run, weakening their ability to deal with the particularly religious problems of the dominant classes themselves.

American Protestantism and the Distribution of Income. As an illustration of the interactions between church doctrines and economic values, I will refer briefly to the ways upper- and middle-class American Protestant churches have dealt with the prosperity of their members in a society that is by no means lacking in economic tension and poverty. These churches trace their origins to the Reformation—and of course beyond—but they have also been significantly affected by their immediate surroundings. If Luther, Calvin, and Wesley sought, each in his own way, to bring the life of the world under religious control, this was scarcely the preoccupation of most of their followers. Through the generations, the reformers' doctrines were gradually reshaped, more to support than to restrain the claims of their adherents. These groups, having won their way to great influence in many nations, had lost a great deal of the sense of tragedy and depravity and of God's saving grace that the reformers never escaped. Luther's keen awareness of the evil of life, Calvin's concern lest the glory of God be obscured by self-glorification, even Wesley's more middle-class conception of the "stewardship of wealth," with its implications of radical sharing, were highly incompatible with the self-confident and optimistic view of the world of the successful commercial and industrial groups. An examination of the religious perspectives of some of the heirs to the Reformation can shed a great deal of light on the relationship of economic forces and religion.

In the United States, by the latter half of the nineteenth century, there was scarcely a doubt in the established Protestant churches that the "Gilded Age" was solving most of man's problems, that the economic theories of the middle and upper classes were religiously valid—and that those who opposed the prevailing distribution of power and wealth, therefore, were anti-Christian. Adam Smith (at least the Smith of the *Wealth of Nations,* if not of the *Theory of Moral Sentiments*) became a church father. During the 1880's, students of ethics in American colleges were familiar with D. S. Gregory's *Christian Ethics,* wherein it was argued:

By the proper use of wealth man may greatly elevate and extend his moral work. It is therefore his duty to seek to secure wealth for this high end, and to make a diligent use of what the Moral Governor may bestow upon him for the same end. . . . The Moral Governor has placed the power of acquisitiveness in man for a good and noble purpose.[20]

And a few years later, Bishop Lawrence of Massachusetts declared:

In the long run, it is only to the man of morality that wealth comes. We believe in the harmony of God's universe. We know that it is only by working along His laws natural and spiritual that we can work with efficiency. . . . Godliness is in league with riches. . . . Material prosperity is helping to make the national character sweeter, more joyous, more unselfish, more Christlike. That is my answer to the question as to the relation of material prosperity to morality.[21]

Workingmen did not always appreciate the harmony in God's universe, nor agree that godliness was in league with riches. By the 1870's they were expressing their discontents in mass meetings, in strikes, and sometimes in violence. They found little support for their protests among the churchmen. During the strikes of 1877, the *Christian Union* wrote: "What a sorry set of ignoramuses they must be who imagine that they are fighting for the rights of labor in combining together to prevent other men from working for low wages because, forsooth, they are discontented with them." And the *Congregationalist* called for drastic measures:

Bring on then the troops—the armed police—in over-whelming numbers. Bring out the Gatling guns. Let there be no fooling with blank cartridges. But let the mob know, everywhere, that for it to stand one moment after it has been ordered by proper authorities to disperse, will be to be shot down in its tracks. . . . A little of the vigor of the first Napoleon is the thing we now need. Compromise would simply sow the wind for "future whirlwind-reaping." [22]

20 Quoted by Walter G. Muelder, *Religion and Economic Responsibility,* p. 69.

21 Quoted in ibid., p. 70.

22 Quoted by Henry F. May, *Protestant Churches and Industrial America,* p. 93.

Henry Ward Beecher, who had achieved considerable wealth as a preacher and writer, and liked to display that wealth, denounced the strikers for not bearing their poverty more nobly:

It is said that a dollar a day is not enough for a wife and five or six children. No, not if the man smokes or drinks beer. It is not enough if they are to live as he would be glad to have them live. It is not enough to enable them to live as perhaps they would have a right to live in prosperous times. But is not a dollar a day enough to buy bread with? Water costs nothing; and a man who cannot live on bread is not fit to live. What is the use of civilization that simply makes men incompetent to live under the conditions which exist. . . .[23]

A few years later, when Governor Altgeld of Illinois pardoned two of the men convicted after the Haymarket riot, Lyman Abbott denounced him from the pulpit as "the crowned hero and worshipped deity of the anarchists of the northwest." And the *Congregationalist* rejoiced that the governor had been hung in effigy "by the indignant citizens of Illinois." [24]

The significance of this attitude toward economic conflicts among the religious leaders can be understood only in the context of the changes that were taking place in society. Increases in commerce, industrial specialization, the development of larger and larger factories with their costly machine tools and equipment, rapid urbanization—these and other changes were forcing the reorganization of the lives of ever-increasing numbers of people. The relatively self-sufficient and independent farmer and handicraftsman lost control of the tools with which they worked and the skills that had given them some independence. In large numbers they were becoming unskilled and semiskilled factory workers. The whole society became vastly more interdependent, creating moral problems that had been unknown to stable, agricultural societies.

Along with the technical changes, there was a great increase in the power of the owners, financiers, and managers of the industrial and commercial enterprises. Like many dominant groups in the first upsurge of their power, they had little sense of *noblesse oblige;* they were impatient of any restraints on their demands. The kinds of civilizing checks and countervailing powers that develop in a democratic society had not yet had time to gather much strength, with the result that power tended to become more concentrated in the hands of the new elite. Between 1860 and 1890, national wealth in the United States increased by almost 500 per cent, but the increase was not universally shared. In the decade of the 1870's, real wages, which had always been at the subsistence level, declined from an average of four hundred dollars to three hundred dollars. "The American industrial revolution, in the process of creating wealth such as the world had never seen or dreamed of, produced also a sullen proletariat resentful of the poverty it had obtained as its share of the bounty. . . ." [25] Labor unions began to gain strength, some of them under the leadership of émigré German socialists. Their strikes were bitter and harshly suppressed. Between

23 *Christian Union*, August 1, 1877, p. 93; quoted in May, op. cit., pp. 93–94.

24 See Arthur E. Holt, "Organized Religion as a Pressure Group," *Annals of the American Academy of Political and Social Science*, May, 1935, pp. 47–48.

25 C. H. Hopkins, *The Rise of the Social Gospel in American Protestantism, 1865–1915*, pp. 79–80.

1881 and 1894 there were fourteen thousand strikes and lockouts in the United States, involving 4 million workers. Many of these conflicts have achieved notoriety as a thinly veiled industrial war.

This is the setting in which church support of the dominant groups, the praise of wealth, the vigorous protests against strikes must be understood. It is not surprising that many workmen lost interest in the religion of these churches, and turned either to secular movements or to religious groups of their own. Terence Powderly, head of the Knights of Labor, made the statement that if the Sermon on the Mount were preached without reference to its author, the preacher would be warned not to repeat such utopian ravings, and "the fashionable pews would be emptied." Samuel Gompers wrote in 1898: "My associates have come to look upon the church and the ministry as the apologists and defenders of the wrong committed against the interest of the people. . . ." [26]

Gradually, as we shall see, some concern for the problems of an industrial society began to appear in American churches; but the large majority continued to accept the values and to support the claims of the middle and upper classes, seeking only to "Christianize" those claims. This was implicit in the very definition of a church. Liston Pope, in his careful study of the churches in a mill town in the South, describes the way in which the ministers and churches responded to sharp economic conflict in these words:

To sum up, for emphasis, in statements too sharply put: in the cultural crisis of 1929 Gastonia ministers revealed that their economic ethicways were products of the economic system in which they lived, with no serious modification by any transcendent economic or religious standard. They were willing to allow the power of religious institutions to be used against those who challenged this economic system, and themselves assisted in such use. At no important point did they stand in opposition to the prevailing economic arrangements or to drastic methods employed for their preservation. In no significant respect was their role productive of change in economic life. By and large, they contributed unqualified and effective sanction to their economic culture, insofar as their words and deeds make it possible to judge.[27]

At about the time described by Liston Pope, Episcopal Bishop Charles Williams of Detroit made a similar observation: " 'In the weightier matters of social justice,' said the bishop, 'there are only two Christians in Detroit, and they are both Jews.' " [28]

Value positions with regard to the situation we have been describing range all the way from thankfulness that the majority of churches have stood for the right (and Right) to condemnation because they have been mere agents of the powerful classes. Either extreme is liable to obscure objective analysis of the two basic reasons for the transformation of the religious formulations of the Protestant innovators into institutional supports for the middle and upper classes. These are the two reasons we have discussed in our definition of "church." From the point of view of the laymen, only if the church supported the main outlines of the society in which

26 Ibid., p. 85.

27 See Liston Pope, *Millhands and Preachers*, pp. 330–331.

28 Quoted by Reinhold Niebuhr, *Man's Nature and His Communities*, p. 18.

they were dominant would they give it allegiance. Religion was only one of their interests, and probably for most of them not the most powerful one. If the beliefs and practices of the churches had obstructed their search for power, made no place for their new occupations, denied their claims to authority, they would not have accepted those beliefs and practices to turn their backs on the society in which success—as they defined it—was being won. They would, rather, have turned their backs on the church and looked for other religious sponsorship.

Religious leaders felt some of these same influences, but their support of the churchlike decision is to be explained, insofar as they were primarily interested in religion, by the second reason for religious differentiation: the dilemma of religious leaders. For them to have denied the claims to power and income of the dominant groups would have been to give up the effort to "Christianize" those groups. It is unlikely that they would have persuaded many of the laymen of the middle and upper classes, who were usually characterized by a less than urgent religious concern, to abdicate their positions of authority. The clergy chose rather (it was hardly a conscious decision, of course) to accept and defend the social structure. This had important implications for their religion, setting limits within which it must develop: For example, they had inevitably to continue to emphasize eternal salvation, rather than the elimination of problems on earth, for the latter might have required an examination of the secular institutions that their congregations thoroughly supported. For the same reasons, they were inevitably led, in ethical questions, to a concern for personal good conduct —generosity, honesty, neighborliness—rather than to an exploration of the ethical questions implicit in the social structure itself. The limits imposed on the directions which churchlike religious institutions can take are reflected in the remark by Walter Rauschenbusch that

the older brethren told us that the true function of the ministry was not to "serve tables," but to save the immortal souls of men. One told me that these were "mere questions of mine and thine," and had nothing to do with the Gospel. A young missionary going to Africa to an early death implored me almost with tears to dismiss these social questions and give myself to "Christian work." [29]

Some American churchmen carried accommodation to the dominant groups to such great lengths that it became not simply an acceptance, but a positive acclamation of support. In *The Man Nobody Knows*, Bruce Barton made Jesus into an astute businessman (The Man Whom Nobody but Bruce Barton Knows, as someone has retitled it). This is more than a modern variation of the eighteenth-century *Navigation Spiritualized* or *The Religious Weaver*, for these earlier attempts to formulate the religious problems of an occupation were less concerned to give religious sanction to an occupation than to restrain its excessive secular interests.

We have not been describing the full range of facts concerning the values and actions of established American Protestantism. There is also a reform element that reaches back many generations, as we shall see in the next section. And the kind of complacency toward social problems if not an active support for a conservative view, which characterized the churches has probably declined, not only among the activists, but more generally

29 Walter Rauschenbusch, *Christianizing the Social Order*, p. 92.

among laymen and clergy. Nevertheless churchlike accommodation is still a dominant fact. The suburbanization of a large proportion of America's middle- and upper-class population both reflects and reinforces conservative views. In the last fifty years, thousands of churches have left the city for the suburbs, following their parishioners, and leaving major sections of cities "unchurched." (Various sects, underground movements and quasi-religious groups have filled the vacuum.) The majority of respectable churches are probably no more concerned with urban blight and ghetto formation than the churches of the latter nineteenth century were concerned with the working conditions and incomes of industrial laborers. The crises of recent years, in fact, may have produced some reaction *against* church involvement in social issues. In Chapter Two we noted that between 1957 and 1968 there was a drop from 47 per cent to 40 per cent of Americans who thought that churches ought to express their views on social and political questions. Without a denominational and class breakdown of the data, we cannot compare higher with lower status groups, hence this may not indicate a falling-off of social action views among the more affluent. Catholics were less inclined to support the expression of views than Protestants (35 per cent against 42 per cent) and older persons less than younger. Because readiness to agree that churches should express their views represents a modest degree of social involvement, we cannot regard religious activism, whatever its distribution through various denominations, as very widespread.

Opposition to social and political stands by the churches is not synonymous, we should emphasize, with indifference to the critical problems faced by society. If American churchmen accepted the main outlines of the social structure through the period of rapid industrialization, most of them did not give up the effort to impose religious restraints on the secular activities of powerful people. They were concerned with suffering and injustice; but, as churchmen, they were inclined to deal with these problems by an appeal to "character," rather than by attempts to change institutional patterns. This approach is shown by the highly popular novel of Charles M. Sheldon, *In His Steps* (1898), a book that sold 23 million copies in English editions, was translated into twenty-one other languages, and made into a movie. In the story, a "dusty, worn, shabby-looking young man" arose in church one morning and told his story of privation and suffering, and then collapsed in the aisle. A few days later he died. Moved by this story, and with the encouragement of the minister, fifty members of the congregation—including an heiress, a college president, a railroad executive, a newspaper editor, and a merchant—resolved never to do anything without first asking themselves the question, "What would Jesus do?" Needless to say, their lives underwent an abrupt change. By means of this novel, millions of people found to their satisfaction that the alleviation of suffering required only the personal conversion of persons in high places. "Moral Rearmament" was anticipated.

Social Factors in the Rise of the "Social Gospel"
Accommodation to a society dominated by the middle and upper classes and appeals to personal morality do not tell the whole story of the rela-

tionship between Protestant churches and the secular powers in the United States. They are not so closely tied to class interests as the discussion heretofore might seem to indicate. Even though it is true that an important latent function of the churches has been to legitimatize the power situation, their primary direct concern has been with the human problems that are at the heart of religion.

Moreover, a small minority within the churches has criticized and sought to reorganize some aspects of the social structure. They have assumed that Christianity had direct relevance for society. Although their criticisms of secular institutions share some things in common with sects, these religious leaders are not sectarians, for they work within the framework of the churches. An oversimplified economic interpretation of religious movements finds it difficult to explain these developments within the established churches.

I shall define the "social gospel" as religiously based efforts, emanating from churches, to change major secular practices and institutions. The attempt is based on the belief, as Paul Carter puts it, "that social good and evil is collective in nature . . . , not simply a sum total of the good and evil of individuals. . . . [Therefore] men are obliged to act directly upon the social order and work for its reconstruction, as part of their religious responsibility to their fellow men." [30] Sociologically, the task is to account for the appearance of sharp criticisms of the social order from religious organizations that are presumably accommodated to that order. There is ample precedent for the social gospel in the gospel itself, of course, and in the succession of attacks on the established order by prophets and sectarian movements. But these are a constant resource, whereas social criticism from the churches rises and falls, and hence must be accounted for on other grounds.

Before turning to an examination of the causes of this "unchurchlike" behavior in the churches and the reasons for its cyclical qualities, let us describe briefly some of its manifestations in American Protestantism. Before the Civil War changes were taking place in Protestant churches that helped to make later manifestations of the social gospel possible. There were also important elements of social criticism. It is a mistake, as Timothy Smith points out, to regard revivalism as purely a quest for personal holiness. It was accompanied by significant changes in church organization and doctrine—the priority of ethics over dogma. the perfectionism of man combined with millennial hopes rather than Calvinistic predestinarianism, interdenominational cooperation, and the importance of lay leadership.[31] Associated with these changes that grew partly out of revivalism was an emphasis on service and reform. Charles G. Finney's evangelical slogan was "saved for service." Excessive attention to the emotionalism and the emphasis on personal salvation of mid-nineteenth century revivalism has obscured its connection with the peace movement, prison reform, women's rights, and particularly the abolition of slavery. We must note, to be sure, that the abolition movement was strong only in that part of the country

30 Paul Carter, *The Decline and Revival of the Social Gospel*, p. 5.

31 See Timothy Smith, *Revivalism and Social Reform in Mid-Nineteenth Century America*. See also H. Richard Niebuhr, *The Kingdom of God in America*.

where owning groups had already given up slavery. Most of the churchmen of the South made a vigorous scriptural defense of slavery. Yet the abolitionists pressed the secular leaders into more active roles than they might otherwise have taken.

A quite different source of the social gospel movement—which however converged with revivalism in some of its interests—was transcendentalism, an offshoot of the Unitarian movement. It was somewhat hospitable to socialism. Along with some Episcopalians, the transcendentalists had close ties with England and Europe, and were influenced by an environment that was creating Christian Socialism in the Church of England, the liberal writings of Kingsley and Maurice, and social Catholicism on the Continent.

The crisis of the Civil War, however, and the pressures toward accommodation and normalcy after the conflicts of the reconstruction period, smothered the mid-century expressions of the social gospel. Not until the 1880's did it begin to reappear, and not until the turn of the century did it arouse significant attention. We shall not here try to trace in detail its development in courses in "social ethics" in many seminaries; in the writing and preaching of several nationally famous religious leaders; in the formation of social-service boards or commissions in most of the large denominations; in the declaration of social creeds that indicated the interest of the churches in the problems of the industrial worker; in the organization in 1908 of the Federal Council of Churches of Christ in America (now the National Council); in the ecumenical movement, which has, as one of its aspects, a concern for the way in which class divisions and economic conflict divide "the church"; and, most recently, in the growing concern for problems of the city and particularly for the way in which Negroes are segregated, economically, educationally, and religiously.[32]

This has not been a steady interest. The social gospel of the Rauschenbusch era, during the early years of the twentieth century, grew out of the dislocation of rapid industrialization. It was almost stopped by the First World War, but reappeared in the early 1920's in the form of resistance to the isolationist trend and support for the efforts of industrial workers to win better working conditions and the right to organize. The Interchurch Report on the steel strike of 1919 helped significantly to focus opposition to the twelve-hour work day and other problems of industrial workers.[33]

Two factors in the middle and late 1920's, however, pushed the social gospel into the background again, showing how sensitive it is to its social context. Isolationism, prosperity, and appeals to "normalcy" obscured its message; and the struggle surrounding the prohibition of alcohol divided its ranks. This latter factor was particularly important. For decades, the temperance movement had been part of reform efforts; [34] but when it became

32 In addition to the works of Carter, Hopkins, and May, already cited, see Charles Stelzle, *The Church and Labor;* Federal Council of Churches of Christ in America, *The Social Ideals of the Churches;* Donald Meyer, *The Protestant Search for Political Realism, 1919–1941;* Robert Miller, *American Protestantism and Social Issues, 1919–1939;* E. D. Baltzell, *The Protestant Establishment,* Chap. 7.

33 See Carter, op. cit., pp. 20–22.

34 "Thus in 1872 the Prohibition Party came out for the direct election of Senators, the abolition of the electoral college, and woman suffrage; in 1876 it called for 'the separation of the money of Government from all banking institutions,' thirty-seven years be-

the focus of attention, as it did for many church people, new lines of alliance were formed.[35] Prohibitionist sentiments were strongest in the rural areas and small towns of the Middle West and South, where interest in the rights of industrial workers, international organization, civil liberties, and racial harmony was weakest. Those who were interested in these latter causes but were more concerned to preserve the Eighteenth Amendment found themselves with allies who had little interest in or were antagonistic to the social gospel.

With the coming of the great depression (and the repeal of the Eighteenth Amendment), the pendulum swung again. Not only was there strong support for the New Deal among churchmen, but some took a much more radical position. The Theological Discussion Group in New York, in which Reinhold Niebuhr, Henry Van Dusen, Paul Tillich, Wilhelm Pauck, Richard Niebuhr, and Robert Calhoun were among the central figures, were leading spokesmen for radical programs, even as they developed theological ideas—of which neo-orthodoxy was most prominent—with quite different implications. In his influential book *Moral Man and Immoral Society*, Reinhold Niebuhr argued that groups could not be expected to work against their own interests; that privileged classes, therefore, inevitably oppose change; and that in a time when major reorganization is clearly needed, the interests of the proletariat are most likely to correspond to requisite changes.

Niebuhr's socialism brought him into alliance with another branch of radical Christianity for whom pacifism was a central theme (one which Niebuhr himself at first shared). But like the coalition of the 1920's this one was highly unstable. It was split apart by the rise of Hitler. We will discuss pacifism in a later chapter, and need say here only that pacifist radicals—persons for whom opposition to war was the primary issue— were driven to seek allies among the isolationist and conservative groups (never did politics make stranger bedfellows); meanwhile the neo-orthodox radicals, confirmed in their judgment of the sinfulness of man by the rise of Nazism and Fascism, found themselves in alliance with superpatriots and what today we would call the military-industrial complex. (There were, of course, many other groups in the alliance.)

For nearly a decade, then (c. 1937–1945), the social gospel was divided and quite ineffective, very much as was liberal political action in the United States during that period. For a few years after the close of the Second World War there was a renaissance, with a rise in concern for reconciliation, reconstruction, and the establishment of an international order. There followed, however, the same kind of retrenchment that America had experienced in the 1920's. Senator Joseph McCarthy caricatured what many Americans half believed—and thus he paralyzed them. Religious individuals and organizations who were inclined toward social gospel activities, many of them carry-overs from the 1930's and not well attuned to the burgeoning but as yet invisible problems of the 1950's, were

---

fore the Federal Reserve Act was passed; and in the Roosevelt-Wilson era its platforms endorsed a variety of other social changes, including employers' liability legislation and the abolition of child labor, which specifically identified this as a party of the American left." (Ibid., pp. 32–33)

35 See ibid., Chap. 3, for a careful development of this theme.

attacked from within the church and from without.[36] Less concerned Protestants moved happily to the suburbs by the millions, carrying their churches with them, assuming that they had left behind the problems of the cities.

But that was not the final swing of the pendulum.[37] The nation recovered from the shattering doubts of the McCarthy period; the tensions of the Cold War relaxed somewhat; what appeared to be the apathy of the 1950's (produced perhaps by cross-pressures, as apathy often is) gave way to growing concern; the Supreme Court nudged us a bit; dozens of new nations appeared, as empires fell apart; increased communication, travel, economic interdependence, and the universal plight brought by "the Bomb" created an ecumenical fact—the whole inhabited earth was one—that had only to be recognized; and the black man strode into the streets declaring he was invisible no more. In such a context, the social gospel has been rejuvenated.[38] It is not possible to say whether, overall, the social gospel is as strong as or stronger than it was in earlier periods. Clearly the interest in racial justice, the problems of the inner city, ecumenism, and the problems of war (at least, of the Vietnam War) has risen significantly among churchmen in the 1960's. On each issue, however, we are talking about a minority, and probably a small minority, of active participants in programs of amelioration. Continued segregation and comfortable unconcern over the overwhelming problems of the city still characterize most middle- and upper-class churches.[39] Appeals to law and order are attractive to many more of them than are calls for a radical reform of unjust social arrangements. Bafflement, acceptance of the nation-state system, and the ideological splits in the world prevent most people from maintaining persistent interest in efforts toward international conciliation. Even a minority movement, however, is significant and requires explanation. Let us return, there-

36 See the Epilogue in Meyer, op. cit.

37 "Final" in the context of this book. One hesitates to put a period on the description of such a series for fear the next swing of the pendulum will knock him over before he can get the manuscript in the mail.

38 See, for example, George Younger, *The Church and Urban Renewal;* Gibson Winter, *The Suburban Captivity of the Churches, especially* Chaps. 6 and 7; A. Dudley Ward, *The Social Creed of the Methodist Church,* rev. ed.; Harvey Cox, *On* NOT *Leaving It to the Snake,* Chap. 12; Mathew Ahmann, ed., *Race: Challenge to Religion;* John C. Bennett, *Christian Ethics and Social Policy;* John A. Hutchinson, ed., *Christian Faith and Social Action;* Walter Mueldor, op. cit.; J. Richard Spann, ed., *The Church and Social Responsibility;* Reinhold Niebuhr, *Christian Realism and Political Problems;* Six Ecumenical Surveys, a document prepared for the Second Assembly of the World Council of Churches, 1954; a six-volume series on "Christian Ethics and Economic Life" prepared for the National Council of Churches, 1953; an interpretation and commentary on these volumes by Marquis Childs and Douglas Cater, *Ethics in a Business Society;* and frequent articles in such journals as *Christianity and Crisis* and *Christian Century.* Social-action implications of ecumenism are referred to frequently in Robert M. Brown, *The Ecumenical Revolution.* There is perhaps no contemporary match for Rauschenbusch's work on a theology for the social gospel; but there are valuable observations in Paul Van Buren, *The Secular Meaning of the Gospel;* and Harvey Cox, *The Secular City.*

39 One item: The head of the New York City Mission Society reported that major Protestant denominations gave in 1967 a total of only $15,750 for work in Bedford-Stuyvesant—a major ghetto—despite expressions of interest and support for programs there. See the *New York Times,* May 25, 1968, p. 38.

fore, to the questions we raised at the beginning of this section and ask: Why the alternation in emphasis on the social gospel? And what are the conditions which bring about such activities within the context of the religious organizations of higher status groups?

Conditions That Influence the Social Gospel. Swings from social activism to relative quietism among churchmen are the product of several forces. They do not indicate, in my judgment, variation in religious interest nearly so much as they indicate variation in the ways that interest is expressed. A critical social problem grows in intensity and visibility; secular as well as religious movements arise to deal with it; new policies and structures are hammered out. Gradually the perspectives of "social Christianity" (in the illustration we have used) are absorbed into the whole body of the church, secular structures are developed for dealing with the problem, and to some degree it is solved (child labor is sharply reduced, labor organizations become an accepted part of the industrial world, the twelve-hour work day is eliminated—to cite a few earlier illustrations). This is one aspect of the "social gospel cycle."

There are other aspects, however. Opposition to the social gospel mounts in connection with the less tractable, more controversial issues. Interest in such issues is neither absorbed into the churches nor expressed in secular structures; it is attacked as heretical and seditious. This development occurs when the issue in question is related to a growing crisis that must be faced by society. Thus social welfare legislation may recede as a social gospel question because of the relative success of religious and secular forces. Pacifism, however, fades out because of their failures—and the mounting criticism of such a social gospel position when international relations are polarized.

This aspect of the cycle is closely connected with another to which we have already alluded: If a serious problem becomes even worse, despite religious and secular efforts (not worse, necessarily, in an absolute sense, but in relation to changing perceptions), social gospel coalitions may fall apart. Allies become opponents as they find themselves in disagreement over priorities. We have noted that this happened to the progressive-temperance and the radical-pacifist coalitions. There are serious strains now in the "racial equality-ecumenism-opposition to war" coalition, which is the social gospel of our time. If the crises continue to grow, if there is not some greater measure of success, this phase of the social gospel may fade out, not because it has succeeded sufficiently to be absorbed, but because the problems with which it deals are so intractable and disagreements over strategy and priorities so severe that necessary cooperation and mutual support are lost.

These comments on the social gospel cycle deal with only one part of the larger question: How can we account, sociologically, for the very fact of such criticism of society from within churches that are, in the main, accommodated to that society? The answer is necessarily complex, involving attention to the diverse elements in the culture of a religion, to the structure of interactions at a given time, and to the individual propensities and life conditions of various laymen and churchmen. The cultural roots of the social gospel we have been discussing are found in the very nature of the synthesis of Christianity, which, as we have seen, is capable of being interpreted in ways that make of it a program of reform. But the prophetic element in Christianity is a constant resource. Why is it almost overlooked in some situations although it is emphasized in others?

Few will deny that the social gospel represents, in American Protestant churches,[40] an extensive growth of interest in the institutional problems of modern industrial society. How is this growth to be explained? Is it an intrinsic religious development, a reaffirmation of some of the ethical concerns of "primitive" Christianity that has been stimulated by the new problems created by urbanization? Is it the manifestation of the religious force of a few leaders—modern prophets—who are peculiarly sensitive to the revolutionary implications of Christianity? Is it a religious protest from churchmen (and to some degree religiously inclined intellectuals, students, and others) who are experiencing various subtle forms of relative deprivation and status inconsistency? Is it simply churchlike recognition of the new forces abroad in the world, of changes already partly accomplished by secular and sectarian pressures, to which the churches have had to give some recognition or relinquish completely their claim and hope for a universal brotherhood?

Although all four of these factors, and others too, are doubtless involved, in my judgment the last has been most important in getting the "social Christianity" movement under way. The other factors then began to give it force and direction. Churchmen, whose strategic situation is not unlike that of politicians, understand the advice of Sir Robert Peel: "If you see a move coming . . . *head* it." American religious leaders did not succeed in heading the movements to improve the working conditions and income of the lower classes, to reduce child labor, or to eliminate racial discrimination; but some of them, when they saw important secular movements struggling with these problems, at least jogged up to the head of the column to give the leaders "moral support." A few actively participated in the campaigns.

That the social gospel was, and is, primarily a churchlike accommodation to new forces, and not a demonstration that churches easily transcended the class lines that limit their appeal and their sphere of action, is indicated by the following facts: 1) The problems that social Christianity became seriously aware of only in the late nineteenth century had been long in existence. 2) Secular movements—political agitation, labor unions, associations for the advancement of colored people—preceded any extensive religious protests by about a generation. 3) Some business leaders, politicians, editors, and scholars were discovering, from a secular point of view, that in a mass-production economy, the interests and power of the middle and upper classes were *not* injured by such things as higher wages, social security, and the abandonment of discrimination in hiring policy. 4) Extensive concern with social questions has continued to characterize the work of only a minority of churchmen; and these have been more largely represented in seminaries, religious publications, "institutional" downtown churches with predominantly lower-class congregations (being, therefore,

40 Although we are using Protestantism as our illustrative case study, equally instructive material is to be found in the story of American Catholicism. Because of its closer tie to the lower classes in the United States, however, the Catholic Church has had a different pattern of development of social gospel themes.

largely sectarian), among college chaplains and ministers,[41] and on various boards and agencies that are somewhat separated, as national organizations, from continuous contact with most laymen, than they have been found in local pulpits, where any deviations from "respectable" religious views would be readily apparent to the middle- and upper-class congregations.

The social gospel is substantially, although not completely, a clerical movement, as contrasted with sects, where the support of laymen is much more critical. American Protestant churchmen are often more liberal than their congregations.[42] Clergymen have been at the forefront of the civil rights movement; [43] the inner-city church movement is a product of seminarians and ministers.

A liberal is likely to see these facts as fairly obvious—as the natural result of careful professional study of and concern for the Christian message in a changing society. No doubt this is part of the explanation; but it is not wholly adequate. I believe it is important to note that seminary-trained clergymen, who contribute most of the participants in social gospel movements, suffer from endemic status inconsistency. They are often in rather close contact with middle- and upper-class families; their educational levels are high (seminary faculties seem inclined to underscore their status inconsistency, however, by granting their students baccalaureate degrees after three years of graduate study); they are granted various symbols of high social honor (although in a "business civilization" their professional interests are deemed slightly precious, if not irrelevant, by many influential persons). Their social power, however, is relatively low; and their incomes are well below those of other professionals with equivalent training. In the seminaries, they have been trained to the full range of interpretations of Christianity, with the prophetic element perhaps getting unusual stress from professors who share some of the same pattern of status inconsistency.

In oversimple terms, then, the social gospel is a church response to prolonged institutional crisis, led by persons whose training has made them particularly sensitive to the radical implications of Christianity and whose personal experience of status inconsistency encourages them in the belief that the social order is out of joint.

To analyze the social gospel in this way is not to dismiss it as meaning-

41 See Phillip Hammond, *The Campus Clergyman;* and Phillip Hammond and Robert Mitchell, "Segmentation of Radicalism—The Case of the Protestant Campus Minister," *American Journal of Sociology,* 71, 1965, pp. 133–143. Hammond and Mitchell develop the interesting thesis that the institution of the campus ministry allows denominations to make use of their radicals (to attract students, to hold their critical members—whose criticisms need to be heard—and the like) and yet to segment them, to partially isolate them. This interpretation may also be applicable to others who support the social gospel movement.

42 See Charles Glock, Benjamin Ringer, and Earl Babbie, *To Comfort and to Challenge,* pp. 120–125; Gerhard Lenski, *The Religious Factor,* pp. 300–318.

43 Almost every denomination has taken a strong public stand in favor of full equality for black men. On the local level, however, clergymen are less able to escape the dilemma of the churches in those areas where there is strong resistance to desegregation among the laymen. For a valuable study of the effects of this dilemma, see Ernest Campbell and Thomas Pettigrew, *Christians in Racial Crisis. A Study of Little Rock's Ministry.*

less. Even though their own class identity and outlook and the dilemma that they face may force churchmen to support class-oriented religious practices, there can scarcely be any doubt that those who give serious thought to their religious situation must and do resist this tendency. Such serious thought may be stimulated, however, only by crisis, and the direction of the "solutions" that emerge from that thought will be strongly affected by the whole secular context. Industrial conflict, depression, war, and the bitter fruits of prejudice have dealt a severe blow to the complacency and easy optimism about society that characterized most American churches a few decades ago. It is not so easy to be certain, with Russell Conwell, that there are "Acres of Diamonds" all around us. For decades, churchmen had been relatively indifferent to the way in which the unrestrained pursuit of wealth can destroy religious interest, as they themselves defined it. But repeated crises forced them to re-examine that problem, to consider whether or not Wesley was right when he declared that "if I leave behind me £10, . . . I bear witness against me that I lived and died a thief and a robber." Few American churchmen have agreed with Wesley, but some of them have begun, at least, to consider the problems of modern society and to reframe their religious responses to that society.

The religiously thoughtful person, facing the difficulties of our time, can say, with Walter Rauschenbusch, there must be something wrong with a society that can manifest such un-Christian tensions; or he can say, with Karl Barth, that we have not comprehended the depth of the tragedy of earthly existence, that we have been wrong in giving ourselves to the hope that the evil in man can be reduced by human organizations instead of by a transcendental gift of grace from God; or he can, with Reinhold Niebuhr, maintain both of these positions, in a kind of uneasy coexistence. But a church that talks of human brotherhood and of a Christ who knows no rich or poor, in whom there is "no East or West," must say some of these things, or in some other way deal with the intrusive crises of our time, if it is to express the full range of its tradition. When we look back at the history of the social gospel it is obvious that a complacent middle-class church was not going to be able to attract workingmen who felt the brunt of industrial crisis nor could it hold the allegiance of those members of the dominant classes who felt the confusions and tragedies of the day in acute form. Religious leaders could see many workers looking for some "profane salvation," or leaving their churches for more satisfactory religious expressions; they could also see that the workingman was winning a measure of economic and political power. In these circumstances, more and more churchmen "discovered" that strikes, when properly qualified, were sometimes justified, that hours of labor should be shortened, that child labor was a menace, rather than a brace, to character. This was not the triumph of a radical Christianity, forcing society to justice, but the emergence of new forces to which the churches had to adjust—as they had adjusted to the rising commercial classes of the seventeenth century—if they were not to lose what influence they still maintained over a large group of people and give up their cherished belief in a universally valid Christianity.

On the basis of his careful study of the evidence, May writes:

In 1876 Protestantism presented a massive, almost unbroken front in its defense of the social status quo. Two decades later social criticism had penetrated deeply into each major church. Some of the most prominent Protestant leaders were calling for social reform; Christian radicals, not unheard, were demanding complete reorganization of society. The immediate cause of this important change lay neither in theological innovation nor in the world "climate of opinion" but in the resistless intrusion of social crisis, and particularly in a series of large-scale, violent labor conflicts. For a generation slums and depressions, farmer protests and labor parties had been pictured by church theorists as necessary, incidental flaws in the inevitable improvement of society. The events of 1877, of 1886, and of 1892–94 were, however, impossible to ignore and difficult to explain away. Optimistic theory had to be reconsidered in the light of burning freight cars. Spokesmen of religion were forced, like editors and professors, to answer the question why, in the home of Christian progress, desperate men were refusing well-meant advice, defying authority, organizing and battling with the determination of despair.[44]

If it took two decades after the beginning of serious industrial conflict—expressive of the problems faced by workers in a new industrial society—before American churchmen began to give more than passing attention to the issue, it was four or five decades after the first stirrings of the civil rights movement before a significant number of churchmen began to struggle with the problems faced by black Americans. The National Association for the Advancement of Colored People was founded in 1909 and the Urban League in 1910 (with some ministerial support, to be sure); heavy migration to cities began during the First World War; the depression of the 1930's bore particularly heavily on Negroes. Throughout this period, however, white churches remained basically segregated and substantially unconcerned. In the 1940's, church condemnation of discrimination and segregation became much more common. By the later years of the decade, and increasingly in the 1950's and 1960's, words were backed by actions—inner-city parishes, participation in "freedom rides" and "sit-ins," integration of more churches and a few ministerial staffs, active work in the planning and execution of the 1963 March on Washington which culminated in Martin Luther King's famous speech: "I have a dream." It is only a small minority of white churchmen who have this dream—or who have waked from it and attempted to make it a reality. But the movement to win justice for the black man is a significant part of the social gospel today, brought forcefully to the attention of churchmen by the crisis in race relations.

To say that it was primarily the great secular problems and crises that caused some churches and religious leaders to re-examine their views of society is not to say that the process and results of this re-examination are merely symptomatic. Once set in motion, they became part of the causal stream that brought about various responses to these problems. When a Methodist bishop supports unionism, it is more difficult to dismiss it as an ungodly attack on democracy and freedom. When the National Council of Churches publishes an interracial news service and works for racial equality, it becomes more difficult to defend segregation and discrimination on religious grounds. One may consider these developments, as Veblen might say, "salutary or the reverse," but he cannot in either case dismiss them simply as effects.

It must be taken as axiomatic that churches would not lead the move-

44 May, op. cit., p. 91.

ment for integration and racial justice in a society that is highly segregated and contains a great deal of institutionalized discrimination. A few churchmen with sectarian inclinations become involved at early stages; but the churches themselves are too closely tied to the institutions of society to break away from them. It is only when major structural changes are well under way, when disprivileged groups have begun to challenge their status sharply, and a few "poorly accommodated" persons within the churches have entered the movement that the way is opened for direct and active participation by the churches themselves.

This should be read and judged as an analytic rather than a critical statement. People who start from a theological definition of the church will find it inappropriate; from their perspective, one does not see the church as one institution among many, bound into a larger social system with fairly effective homeostatic processes. For scientific purposes, however, that is a useful point of departure. When the homeostatic processes are weakened by major pressures on some parts of the system, when for a time there are "openings" for change, the churches have opportunities for effective action. With the civil rights movement strongly under way, for example, churches can affect its pace, its goals, and the qualities of the transition period.

In assessing the influence of the social gospel, it would be a mistake to forget the limitations imposed on a church by its very nature, or to forget the dilemma of religious leaders. Christianity, by any strict definition, is a minority movement. To disregard this limitation is to misunderstand the nature of its influence in the social movements of the twentieth century. If the last few decades have witnessed a somewhat strengthened effort on the part of churchmen to bring the whole society into one religious framework, they have not seen—and ensuing decades will not see—the majority of churchmen supporting a society in which the claims of all groups are held to be equally valid. The church cannot change basic secular institutions, and it will sponsor modification of them only when important groups have already moved in that direction.

Nevertheless, it can have an indirect influence on the distribution of economic and political power. If the appeal to Christian motivation does not change the class situation, it can at least soften some of the harshness of the conflicts in that situation. It can help to maintain some sense, among all classes, of a common identity. This is vital, for history shows that the inevitable processes of change are made most brutal and violent when classes are most sharply divided. When the groups within a society feel no sense of common destiny, when even their religious life sets different aspirations and beliefs, the mutual adjustments that human life demands are made far more difficult. For a church, as we have defined it, to help to integrate a complex modern society is a supremely difficult task; but there has been some reaching out toward this goal, which the student of religion, as well as the practitioner, cannot afford to disregard.

Chapter Seventeen

RELIGION AND ECONOMIC DEVELOPMENT

In our earlier discussion of the relationship between religion and economic processes we have assumed that major economic structures have remained relatively stable. At various points in history, however, there are sharp discontinuities in the economizing processes by which value is determined, scarce resources distributed, and economic activities organized. Feudal estates, governmental monopolies and charters, and guild restrictions give way, in face of expanding commercial and industrial opportunities, to relatively open competition among numerous units of production, operating in a money economy. Or, in recent decades, small units of production and distribution are substantially replaced by very large ones; and, in some societies, by an economic plan under governmental auspices.

It is inconceivable that such major changes in the economy could proceed without having powerful effects on religion. They drastically reorganize the relations of men to one another—the productive relations, as Marx called them; they alter the distribution of income, power, and prestige; they put received systems of value under severe strain; they open up new avenues of hope and aspiration. If the economic changes are accompanied by increased productivity, some problems may be alleviated; but during the periods of rapid transition, chaos also grows. The three forms of chaos we have discussed at various points—the threats of meaninglessness, of unbearable suffering, of injustice—all tend to increase, in the perceptions of men if not by some absolute standard, when stable economic patterns are broken up. Religious developments reflect this changed context.

Except for those who regard religion as an entirely autonomous sphere, the impact of major changes in its environment are readily granted. But arguments that reverse the pattern of influence are more controversial. Can a new religious perspective enter a stable or slowly changing economic setting, and decisively affect the speed and direction of change? Specifically, in the theme of this chapter, do religious differences help to account for variation in economic development? In a brilliant and provocative series of monographs, Max Weber answered Yes. His answer, however, has not proved universally acceptable, and must be carefully reviewed. In the last analysis, his question may be more important than his answer.

After a brief examination of some background information from the Protestant Reformation, we will study Weber's thesis; and then we will follow applications of it in the contemporary world, in technologically advanced societies and in technologically developing societies. Our aim will be to show the need for systematic study of the interactions of structural, cultural, and character influences. The processes by which these influences move from one relatively homeostatic system to another—one or another of them having "wobbled" too much for the homeostatic process of the existing system to handle—are of great significance to the student of human behavior. In this discussion, as in many previous sections, we shall be anticipating problems connected with the study of religion and social change, which will be the more directed object of our attention in later chapters.

SOME ECONOMIC ASPECTS OF THE REFORMATION

There is no doubt that the Protestant Reformation correlated with the development of new economic patterns, most particularly with the rapid increase in importance of the bourgeoisie. From activities that were marginal to landlord-peasant relationships, the commercial and industrial work of the new middle classes became the central economic activities in some societies. Parallel with this development was the appearance and spread of Protestantism. We shall not be concerned with a description of all phases of this religious movement, but only with the way in which it was involved, as cause and/or effect, in the gradual development of power among the middle classes.[1] There are several possible explanations of the significance of the Reformation in the rise of the middle classes: 1) It may be claimed that the Reformation, particularly its Calvinist phase, was primarily an invention of the new classes to justify their new vocations and claims to power. 2) Oppositely, it may be declared that the Reformation was a strictly religious movement, with no implications for the economic situation of the time. 3) It may be held that it was substantially religious in its origins, but that the ways in which it dealt with the problems of evil and salvation were peculiarly influential in shaping motivational and ethical approaches to economic questions. 4) Finally, it may be argued that the Reformation was a complex movement with many different possibilities within it, that it was a product of developments intrinsic to religious thought, of continuity

[1] Among the large number of studies of the Reformation, the following works are particularly helpful in the analysis of its economic and political significance: H. B. Workman, *The Dawn of the Reformation;* T. N. Lindsay, *A History of the Reformation;* Preserved Smith, *The Age of the Reformation;* G. G. Coulton, *Five Centuries of Religion,* Vol. 3; A. C. McGiffert, *Protestant Thought Before Kant;* Ernst Troeltsch, *The Social Teaching of the Christian Churches,* Vol. 2; Max Weber, *The Protestant Ethic and the Spirit of Capitalism;* R. H. Tawney, *Religion and the Rise of Capitalism;* Wilhelm Pauck, *The Heritage of the Reformation.* Several paragraphs in this chapter have been taken from the writer's *Religion in the Struggle for Power.*

with the medieval church, and of the problems of the emerging new society; and that from this complexity, different groups with different economic needs, selected and shaped beliefs and practices that were meaningful to them.

The first two of these explanations seem to the writer to be clearly inadequate. The latter two offer far better possibilities for a valid theory, particularly if they are combined in such a way as to emphasize the *interaction* of the economic requirements of the new classes and the religious requirements of the new movements. We shall approach the subject primarily from the perspective of the fourth statement, but with the addition of some aspects of the third. The *origins* of a religious movement cannot be explained simply in terms of the economic and other needs of the groups who may later embrace it, although it is in part a product of economic and other secular problems. In the beginning, it intrudes into an economic situation with some force of its own, setting the direction of economic change to some degree, even though through the course of the years and generations the religious movement will itself be reshaped by various classes in ways that support their various claims and needs.

It is no accident that the Reformation occurred during a period of political upheaval and economic change. It was, in fact, one of several developments—and by no means the first—that protested against the religious, political, and economic situation of the late medieval and early modern periods. Territorial and national churches, designed to buttress the emerging nations against the claims of the papacy, are part of the history of England, France, Germany, and elsewhere. Several sect movements—Cathars, Waldenses, Lollards, Hussites—preceded Luther and to some degree prepared the ground for the Reformation. Peasant uprisings expressed discontent; a secular literature, such as the work of Marsiglio of Padua, called for the dominance of the State, with the Church's powers limited to religious functions. The Conciliar Movement sought to reduce the power of the papacy and to decentralize the authority of the Church. Such developments as these expressed the widespread discontent with the religious and secular patterns of the time.

Part of the protest against the Church was secular. The ecclesiastical system was not simply a religious organization but a government, controlling vast lands and collecting large sums of money. The history of the papacy itself up to the Reformation had been a story of increasing secularization.

At Rome the popes came to occupy the position of princes of one of the Italian states, and were elected, like the doges of Venice, by a small oligarchy. Within seventy years the families of Borgia, Piccolomini, Rovere, and Medici were each represented by more than one pontiff, and a majority of the others were nearly related by blood or marriage to one of these great stocks. The cardinals were appointed from the pontiff's sons or nephews, and the numerous other offices in their patronage, save as they were sold, were distributed to personal or political friends.[2]

The political murders organized by Sixtus IV (1471–1484), the bribes paid by Innocent VIII for his election, the intrigues associated with Alex-

2 Preserved Smith, op. cit., pp. 15–16.

ander VI and his son Cesare Borgia and his daughter Lucrezia all testify to the secularization of the papacy.

The significance of this development is increased by the fact that through the course of centuries the participation of laymen in the affairs of the Church had been sharply curtailed. Salvation was available only through the ministrations of the priests. And this monopolization of the means of salvation was used as an instrument of political power and a source of extensive wealth. Income from land holdings, tithes, and taxes, was great. In addition, many Church offices were filled by sale, and dues were often levied on the first year's income from an ecclesiastical appointment. These charges were passed on to the constituents of the parish. It is easy to suppose that such practices weakened the "faith" both of those who were becoming more and more involved in the expanding commercial economy and of the more traditionally religious peasants and artisans. As Smith says, "The common man's conscience was wounded by the smart in his purse."

The sale of indulgences was another rich source of revenue which became more and more an ordinary means of raising money for the ecclesiastical powers.

How thoroughly commercialized the business of selling grace and remission of the penalties of sin had become is shown by the fact that the agents of the pope were often bankers who organized the sales on purely business lines in return for a percentage of the net receipts plus the indirect profits accruing to those who handle large sums. Of the net receipts the financiers usually got about ten per cent; an equal amount was given to the emperor or other civil ruler for permitting the pardoners to enter his territory, commissions were also paid to the local bishop and clergy, and of course the pedlars of the pardons received a proportion of the profits in order to stimulate their zeal. On the average from thirty to forty-five per cent of the gross receipts were turned into the Roman treasury.[3]

Thus the territories were drained of vast resources. It is not difficult to see in this situation the seeds of revolt. Two classes shared a common grievance against the Church: "the lower class, earlier in the field, struggling for existence, and the middle class, struggling for power."[4]

It would be a mistake, of course, to suppose that the Reformation was simply an economic and political revolt disguised in religious symbols. Concomitant with the secularization of the ecclesiastical structure and its position as a secular power was the decline of its ability to satisfy the religious needs of many people. A religion that "integrates" society only on the basis of the relationships of an agrarian and feudal system can only help to "disintegrate" a society that is coming more and more to involve urban, commercial, and industrial groups; for this societal function of religion can be carried out only if these new groups are given a place in the social order and if the new problems that urban life brings with it are given attention. A religion that deals fairly successfully with the personal needs of an illiterate peasantry and a self-confident nobility may find that its system of beliefs, rites, and church structure is quite inadequate for a more mobile and secularized urban proletariat.

It is from this last group that candidates for the various sects of the

3 Ibid, p. 24.

4 E. S. Bates, *American Faith,* p. 26.

left wing of the Reformation were drawn, as we have seen. Such a religion would have appeared equally unsatisfactory for commercial classes who had been affected by a Renaissance, by the intellectual climate that produced a Petrarch, a Boccaccio, an Erasmus, and by a growing spirit of individualism, as well as by their need to be convinced that their new occupations were legitimate. The ecclesiastical institutions that preceded the Reformation were also unsatisfactory to those priests and monks and others whose primary concern continued to be with religion. In 1372 the monasteries of the Rhineland entered into a compact to resist the levy of Gregory XI, who was demanding a tithe of their revenues. They wrote:

In consequence . . . of the exactions with which the Papal Court burdens the clergy, the Apostolic See has fallen into such contempt that the Catholic faith in these parts seems to be seriously imperilled. The laity speak slightingly of the Church, because, departing from the custom of former days, she hardly ever sends forth preachers or reformers, but rather ostentatious men, cunning, selfish and greedy. Things have come to such a pass that few are Christians more than in name.[5]

Societal Factors in Lutheranism. The prophets and the reformers themselves cannot be understood outside their particular secular context, but it is their concern for the inadequacies of the medieval Church as a religious institution that represents the center of the Reformation as they developed it. Their work was then embraced, and changed, by many groups who saw in it possibilities for solutions of their own secular and religious problems. Luther's propositions had relevance immediately for several of these problems, particularly for those of the groups who were rising to power. Their secular interests were related to the emergence of independent states, freed from the domination of Rome. Germany had had, even before Luther, a long history of opposition to the dominance of the pope. The economic interests of individuals on almost every level of society would be affected by a reduction in papal authority. We need not undertake an analysis of the complexities of Luther's thought except to point out ways in which the doctrines that he emphasized are relevant to the topic of this chapter.

Perhaps most significant in this regard is the emphasis he gave to the doctrine that salvation comes, not by works, but from faith only. Not the acceptance of proper sacraments, but faith is the mark of the Christian. This was a revolutionary challenge to the Church. If avenues of salvation were no longer to be controlled by the priest, the Church itself was endangered. In this, Luther followed Wycliffe, who worked for a priestless church; but it was the German reformer who established independent parishes, with laymen involved in the selection and, if necessary, the deposition of their vicars. In his later years, to be sure, Luther came to disagree with Wycliffe and Huss and other more complete Protestants in seeing the Church as an indispensable means of salvation—not because, as with the Catholics, it dispenses grace, but because it teaches the gospel.

In this we see the second significant element of Luther's protest—the shift from the claim that religious truth was revealed in Church doctrines and traditions and the interpretations of the hierarchy, to the declaration that the Bible was the fountain of truth. Luther supported this declaration

5 Quoted by H. B. Workman, op. cit., Vol. I, pp. 36–37.

by his translation of the Bible. Because this made its study available to the layman, religious thought and interpretation were, to a still larger degree, democratized and individualized.

As one aspect of his protest against the selling of indulgences, Luther accepted the doctrine of predestination, a belief that supported his attack on the Church as the mediator of salvation and harmonized with his conception of justification by faith alone. We shall be concerned later with the way in which predestinarianism may have influenced the behavior of the middle classes. It can affect individuals in very different ways, so that it is important to discover why one person or group interprets it one way, while others interpret it differently. To an intensively religious person, it may permit the development of a disinterestedness in his own needs, a selflessness in charity—for if one is already saved, his concern for others need not disguise a deeper concern for himself. "No one can give himself in self-forgetful love to the service of his neighbor so long as he is anxious and troubled about his own fate." [6] The effects of the doctrine of predestination, however, may be different with others. It may encourage a passive resignation—for why should one try to change a situation, or even to act, when one's lot is determined even before he is born? This is likely to be the reaction of those who, because of the discouraging outlook of their lives, are already inclined toward resignation. On the other hand, there may be those who are encouraged for other reasons (expanding economic opportunity, for example) to act vigorously, who will be persuaded by predestinarianism to act even more energetically in order to convince themselves and others that they are of the elect. Just as the same wind can blow two boats in opposite directions, so one doctrine can influence people who are already inclined in different ways to respond quite differently. Thus a predestinarianism that was given a place of importance by Luther (and even more emphasis by Calvin) had one meaning for the religious leaders and different (latent) consequences for the various groups that accepted it.

The beliefs and activities of Luther that we have discussed had implicit within them forces that supported the rising urban and commercial society. Luther's influence, however, was more negative than positive in this regard; it helped to clear the ground, but it did not build a modern edifice. Luther contributed to the destruction of the hold of the papacy, supported the development of nation-states, and gave some support to individualism. Yet Luther was no modern. The emphasis on lay religion, the attacks on ecclesiastical monopoly that he made in his famous early essays, *Address to the Christian Nobility of the German Nation* and *Concerning Christian Liberty*, gave way in his later years to a new emphasis on the church system, with purity (rigidity) of doctrine, supported and dominated by the state. As Milton expressed it later on, "New presbyter was but old priest writ large." Luther could scarcely have written in his later years what he said in his *Address to the Christian Nobility:* "It is not my intention here to judge John Huss's belief and to defend his errors, although my understanding has not been able to find any error in him. . . ." Huss's sectarianism and his attacks on the secular order were in sharp contrast to developed Lutheranism.

Luther's enormous respect for authority and the growth of a church-type

6 A. C. McGiffert, op. cit., p. 37.

organization well accommodated to the powerful classes destroyed the appeal that his attack on the papacy and his emphasis on personal religious experience had originally had for many members of the lower classes. "Luther accepted the social hierarchy, with its principles of status and subordination, though he knocked away the ecclesiastical rungs in the ladder." [7] He repudiated the radical implications of sectarian Christianity, which called for good works and not faith alone. "Divine grace is only obscured by human effort."

The way in which Lutheranism developed and changed, even within the lifetime and in the writings of the founder, make it impossible to accept without qualification the thesis that in its early years, the influence of a religious movement is primarily the result of its own internally developed religious ideas, relatively uninfluenced by the secular situation. This is the position taken by Weber and Troeltsch with respect to Calvinism, as we shall see. It needs to be qualified by the recognition (a) that even the origin of religious ideas is affected by the whole circle of social forces by which the religious thinker and leader is surrounded, (b) that his own development will be subtly affected by the secular and religious interests of the people (the audience) to whom he tries to appeal, and (c) that the audience will select and emphasize those aspects of the religious innovator that serve their particular needs and correspond with their interests. These are qualifications of the thesis—rather severe ones, to be sure—but they do not refute it. The religious material is not completely malleable. Having accepted a religious system, perhaps because it seemed to harmonize with their needs, a group is influenced by that religion's inner compulsions.

The composition of the group that supported Luther gradually changed. The intellectuals who were with him at Worms later found him to be quite medieval, an opponent of learning who became more and more narrowly dogmatic. Restless peasants and radical urban groups were told by Luther to accept their lot and obey the authorities: "There ought to be no serfs because Christ has set us all free. What then is that? This means that Christian freedom would be quite carnal—did not Abraham and other patriarchs and prophets also have bondmen?" Luther was opposed to the whole economic development of his age; he attacked large-scale commerce and opposed usury even more vigorously than the Catholic Church of his time. He described as his ideal society, a traditionally stratified rural society with a natural rather than a money economy and with personal, face-to-face economic dealings:

I do not see many good manners that have ever come into a land through commerce . . . without doubt the greatest misfortune of the Germans is buying on usury. . . . The system has not been in force for more than one hundred years, and has already brought poverty, misery, and destruction on almost all princes, foundations, cities, nobles, and heirs. If it continues for another hundred years Germany will be left without a farthing, and we shall be reduced to eating one another. . . . All I know is that it were much more godly to encourage agriculture and lessen commerce; and they do the best who, according to the Scriptures, till the ground to get their living. . . .[8]

7 Tawney, op. cit., p. 93.

8 *Address to the Christian Nobility.*

To understand Luther's position with respect to trade, however, one must remember that the economic setting in which he lived was far from modern. There were only the beginnings of capitalism, and these did more to disrupt the "natural economy" than to bring wealth to most people. Production was for a small market, money was unimportant in the traditional rural economy, commerce and finance were incidents rather than central elements in the economic system.[9] The restless competition for gain which was beginning to appear upset the stability of the existing order and left confusion, while its possible achievements within a new order could not yet be seen. Luther sought, therefore, to solidify the old order against the disorganizing effects of the new developments.

With the loss of many of the intellectuals and the sectarians, and its low appeal to commercial middle classes, "official Lutheranism became an established church, predominantly an aristocratic and middle-class party of vested interest and privilege."[10] The individualism, the challenges to authority, the opposition to an established church that were found in early Lutheranism were destroyed or sharply curtailed; the quietism, the support to nationalism, the support to the aristocracy of a semifeudal society were emphasized. It became an instrument of power for a basically conservative ruling group, justifying their power at the same time that it sought to moralize and restrain it. Gradually it adapted itself to the commercial and industrial classes who came more and more into prominence. It succeeded only poorly in incorporating doctrines that appealed to the lower classes, particularly of the cities. Hence the force of the Anabaptist movement in Germany (and in part perhaps even of the secular protests that sprang from German soil centuries later).

These results cannot be regarded as the inevitable consequences of Lutheranism. A different pattern evolved in the Scandinavian countries. As we turn to the study of the interaction of Calvinism and emerging capitalism, it is particularly important to stress that major religious movements have a wide range of possibilities within them. How they develop is partly determined by the opportunities and obstacles that are found in various settings.

THE PROTESTANT ETHIC AND THE SPIRIT OF CAPITALISM

Calvin was strongly influenced by the Lutheran movement. He appeared in a different situation, however, and from the start gave emphasis to different religious concepts. Gradually his teachings, and more particularly those of his followers, came to harmonize more and more with the requirements of the new commercial and industrial groups. How did this development take place?

The relationship between "the Protestant ethic and the spirit of capitalism" has undoubtedly received more intensive examination than any other question in the sociology of religion. Since 1904 when Max Weber published his famous essay, dozens of scholars have studied the problem, only to

9 See R. H. Tawney, "Religious Thought on Social and Economic Questions in the Sixteenth and Seventeenth Centuries. III. The Social Ethics of Puritanism," *Journal of Political Economy,* 1923, p. 805.

10 Smith, op. cit., p. 100.

arrive at very diverse conclusions.[11] Some have taken Weber's thesis—that Protestantism, particularly its Calvinist phase, was *one important factor* in the development of the spirit of capitalism—and, disregarding his qualifications, used it to "prove" the primary force of religion in secular affairs. Others contend that religious change was only symbolic of more basic changes in the economic and political situation, that the rise of Calvinism simply indicates that new classes develop new religious tendencies harmonious with their interests and needs. Some hold that religious factors were important in the development of capitalism, but that Weber should have given greater attention to Catholicism or Judaism. And many have given some support to Weber's thesis, but believe that he was insufficiently alert to the *selective* development of Calvinism through many generations, as a result of its constant interaction with the many forces involved in the emergence of the modern world.

I will develop this last position, emphasizing the ways in which religion and society interact. In terms of the topic of this chapter, one might state the proposition in this way: The emergence of a society in which business and industrial interests are becoming progressively more important will strongly influence the *churches* of that society in the direction of doctrines, rituals, and organizational patterns satisfying and acceptable to the newly powerful groups. Oppositely, the religious organizations of the society, partly as a result of their own "inner development" at the hands of religious specialists, will affect and set limits to the types of developments possible in economic matters.

New religious ideas may be proclaimed, but they will develop and spread only if structural changes create a favorable context and weaken the hold of traditional religious expressions. They will have an impact on the economic and political systems only if they help to shape a new man, with different motives and values. Before developing this argument further, let us examine Weber's thesis in greater detail.

A glance at occupational statistics, Weber remarks in the opening sentence of his first chapter, reveals that in countries with both Protestant and Catholic citizens, the business leaders, owners of capital, technically and commercially trained persons, and skilled workers are "overwhelmingly Protestant." This can scarcely be explained as a search for independence from a restrictive Catholicism, for at the time control by the Catholic Church was "scarcely perceptible in practice," while the regulation of conduct imposed by Calvinism "was infinitely burdensome and earnestly enforced." How then is the relationship between Calvinism and economic success to be accounted for? Not, it should be emphasized, by denying eco-

---

11 In addition to Weber's *The Protestant Ethic and the Spirit of Capitalism*, a partial list of the books that deal with this question includes R. H. Tawney, *Religion and the Rise of Capitalism*; H. M. Robertson, *Aspects of the Rise of Economic Individualism*; Talcott Parsons, *Structure of Social Action*; Werner Sombart, *The Jews and Modern Capitalism*; Amintore Fanfani, *Catholicism, Protestantism, and Capitalism*; Ernst Troeltsch, *The Social Teaching of the Christian Churches*; H. R. Niebuhr, *The Social Sources of Denominationalism*; Albert Hyma, *Christianity, Capitalism and Communism*; J. Milton Yinger, *Religion in the Struggle for Power*; Reinhard Bendix, *Max Weber. An Intellectual Portrait*; Kurt Samuelsson, *Religion and Economic Action*; S. N. Eisenstadt, ed., *The Protestant Ethic and Modernization*; R. W. Green, *Protestantism and Capitalism. The Weber Thesis and Its Critics*.

nomic influences. Weber noted that many of the most highly developed areas with rich resources became Protestant. He had no desire to deny economic influences; ". . . we have no intention whatever of maintaining such a foolish and doctrinaire thesis as that the spirit of capitalism . . . could only have arisen as the result of certain effects of the Reformation, or even that capitalism as an economic system is a creation of the Reformation." [12] Weber describes the peculiar spirit of economic enterprise among early Protestants, however, as being a critical factor in economic growth. That spirit is disciplined, rational, and highly ascetic. These qualities are a product, as Weber saw it, of Calvin's religious approach—the desire not to be simply a "vessel of the Holy Spirit," which was characteristic of Luther's mysticism, but "the tool of the divine will." ". . . Since Calvin viewed all pure feelings and emotions, no matter how exalted they might seem to be, with suspicion, faith had to be proved by its objective results in order to provide a firm foundation for the *certitudo salutis*." [13]

Good works were useless as means for attaining salvation, but they were regarded as "indispensable as a sign of election," as a way of freeing one's self from the fear of damnation. "In practice this means that God helps those who help themselves."

Christian asceticism . . . now . . . strode into the market-place of life, slammed the door of the monastery behind it, and undertook to penetrate just that daily routine of life with its methodicalness, to fashion it into a life in the world, but neither of nor for this world. . . . This worldly Protestant asceticism . . . acted powerfully against the spontaneous enjoyment of possessions; it restricted consumption, especially of luxuries. On the other hand, it had the psychological effect of freeing acquisition of goods from the inhibitions of traditionalistic ethics. It broke the bonds of the impulse to acquisition in that it not only legalized it, but (in the sense discussed) looked upon it as directly willed by God.[14]

Three basic questions arise in connection with Weber's thesis: How valid is his description of Protestant "this-worldly asceticism"? How adequate is his theoretical interpretation of the meaning of the relationship between Protestantism and capitalism? [15] What use can be made of his argument to interpret the interaction of religion and economic behavior in other settings? Each of these requires some comment.

The Range of Protestant Asceticism

The stern, activist, rationalistic asceticism that Weber describes was an important, if not the only, expression of early Protestantism. He was well

12 Weber, op. cit., p. 91.

13 Ibid., p. 114.

14 Ibid., pp. 154, 170–171.

15 Such critics as H. M. Robertson, op. cit., and Kurt Samuelsson, op. cit., refuse to meet Weber on his own ground. They stress economic elements in the rise of capitalism which Weber, although not without occasional slips, was ready to grant. Unless one sees human values and motives purely as reflexes of the economic system, however, one needs to ask further how they also influence economic processes. This Robertson and Samuelsson fail to do. My criticism of Weber on this score, as will be indicated below, does not rest on the fact that he focused attention on values and motives; but because he failed to see these in the context of larger systems, he gave them a primacy which no one of a series of *interacting* forces can have.

aware of other expressions, but believed they were less significant for an explanation of the appearance of the peculiar spirit of modern capitalism.[16] His failure to explore fully the relationship of other forms of Protestantism to emerging capitalism, and his matching failure to give sufficient attention to the evolution of Calvinism itself, led him, in my judgment, to overlook processes of interaction and selection that were of great importance for the problem he studied. It is essential to study not only what Calvin taught, but what happened to Calvinism. What characterized Calvinism in Geneva in the sixteenth century was not identical with its expressions in England in the seventeenth century nor with the form it took in New England in the eighteenth. What characterized the writing of leading clergymen and prophets was not necessarily descriptive of the beliefs of the average layman whose economic behavior Weber sought to explain.

When Troeltsch writes: "I would rate still higher the difference which Weber emphasizes between Calvin and Calvinism . . . ,"[17] he is putting the case mildly, for Weber gives it too little attention. As Troeltsch rightly points out, there are contradictory currents in every mass movement. This is scarcely less true of Calvinism than of the primitive church. The Geneva movement was at the same time traditional and radical, collectivistic and individualistic; it contained a sober prudence and a divine recklessness. "Primitive Calvinism is the daughter of Lutheranism." It emphasized obedience to the word of God revealed in the Bible, and stressed its connection with the primitive church. Like Lutheranism, it accepted secular culture and the idea of a calling which was the fulfilling of one's place in the divine scheme. It identified the Decalogue and law of nature. In other regards, however, primitive Calvinism had distinctive features. It had a strong element of individualism. For Luther, happpiness because of the assurance of the forgiveness of sin was the important thing; but expression of the glory of God was central with Calvin; therefore, let there be activity. As we have seen, Calvinism also emphasized predestination: pure, unmerited grace as an expression of God's absolute will. And this grace fell only to the few. Luther, who had held to this doctrine in the early days, never wholly abandoned it; but under the pressure of conditions he was forced to adopt a creed that taught that grace was revocable, and able to be won and rewon by humility and faith.

Now it is of the utmost importance to discover what influences selected the teachings of Calvin that were to survive, what teachings were reinterpreted, and what new doctrines added, as well as to understand the original setting that may have influenced the nature of this religious development.

The doctrine of predestination, for instance, underwent a rather important change and development. With Calvin himself, the elect were God's invisible church. For ordinary men, however, the *recognizability* of the state of grace was of supreme importance; all men did not have Calvin's self-assurance—they wanted a visible sign of salvation. There were also institutional reasons for wanting to know who the elect were. Who were to take and administer the sacraments? For the laymen it came about, therefore, that self-assurance was the chief proof of divine grace. How could God's favor better be demonstrated to businessmen than by success in this world's activities? Worldly achievement and good works came to

16 See Weber, op. cit., especially pp. 128–154.
17 *The Social Teaching of the Christian Churches*, p. 894n.

be, not the technical means of winning salvation, as in Catholicism, but the best way to get rid of the fear of damnation. We get, therefore, in place of the humble sinners to whom Luther promises grace, a group of self-confident saints. It is not difficult to see, as Weber shows us, how this kind of doctrine leads to enterprise.

It is of great importance to ask at this point, however: Why did this particular solution to the problem of salvation—a solution that is not necessarily the logical development of original Calvinism—appear, in contrast to the Lutheran and Catholic solutions of the same problem? Why is it that among the various tendencies within Calvinism, those that were favorable to the rising economic system were "sorted out" so to speak, and emphasized to the minimization of other tendencies that were just as important in early Calvinism? Why did not the quietistic tendencies to which predestination can just as logically lead, prevail rather than its stimulating effects? This may be explained in terms of the origin of Calvinism and its setting. What could be more convincing to a businessman, who also was seriously interested in his eternal salvation, than the theory that worldy success was a sign of God's favor? (Just as vast numbers of the poor had been taught for centuries, and continued to be taught by Calvin, Baxter, and other churchmen, that their salvation was the better because of their worldly "failure.") It was not inevitable in the logic of the idea nor in Calvin's use of it that the doctrine of predestination should become a stimulus to worldly success.

The earlier teachings in Geneva had put severe restrictions on the businessman. Calvin and the church in general preached unceasingly against unjust moneylenders and avarice. The Council of Geneva, who were businessmen, heard the ministers on thrift and simplicity, sent their children to catechism, and supported the church. On business matters, however, they were obdurate. They were glad to invoke the sanction of religion for traits that their secular activity found valuable—honesty, industry, sobriety, as well as the dynamic interpretation of predestination. But, as Richard Niebuhr points out, the less useful virtues of solidarity, sympathy, and fraternity were ignored. The ministers did not capitulate to the businessmen; but those who emphasized elements in the all-embracing Calvinist doctrine that were in tune with the times secured an audience and prospered. Calvin himself, unlike Luther, was a man of affairs. His movement was an urban movement. Although he preached against the dangers of riches and commerce, he started with the assumption that they were an acceptable part of the Christian order. ". . . The Geneva situation helped determine Calvin's political, social, and economic ideal." [18]

Calvin himself shared the Lutheran view of the value of work, emphasizing its moral qualities, the need for moderation in wealth, and even the value of poverty in fostering Christian virtues. By preaching rigorous self-denial and condemning greed and profit, Calvin, especially in his early years, restricted trade and sponsored disdain of this world almost as rigidly as did Luther. In the *Institutes* he writes:

With whatever kind of tribulation we may be afflicted, we should always keep this end in view, to habituate ourselves to a contempt of the present life that we may thereby be excited to meditation on that which is to come. . . . There is no

18 Ibid., p. 625.

medium between these two extremes, either the earth must become vile in our estimation, or it must retain our immoderate love. Wherefore if we have any concern about eternity, we must use our most diligent efforts to extricate ourselves from these fetters. . . . But believers should accustom themselves to such a contempt of the present life, as may not generate either hatred of life, or ingratitude towards God. For this life, though it is replete with innumerable miseries, is yet deservedly reckoned among the Divine blessings which must not be despised. . . . It should be the object of believers, therefore, in judging of this mortal life that, understanding it to be of itself nothing but misery, they may apply themselves wholly with increasing cheerfulness and readiness to meditate on the future and eternal life. When we come to this comparison, then indeed the former will be not only securely neglected, but in competition with the latter altogether despised and abhorred. For if heaven is our country, what is the earth but a place of exile? If the departure out of the world is an entrance into life, what is the world but a sepulchre? What is a continuance in it but an absorption in death? If deliverance from the body is an introduction into genuine liberty, what is the body but a prison? If to enjoy the presence of God is the summit of felicity, is it not misery to be destitute of it? But till we escape out of the world "we are absent from the Lord." Therefore, if the terrestrial life be compared with the celestial, it should undoubtedly be despised and accounted of no value.[19]

How far this is from a call to vigorous worldly activity to prove one's divine election! And surely if it is claimed, as Weber does, that it was not the intention of the reformers, but the unconscious and quite unexpected effects of their teachings that were crucial in producing the capitalistic spirit, then it is quite meaningless to say that the religious ethic "caused" the spirit, for in truth it was the interpretation given to the ethic that is associated with the spirit. The important question, therefore, becomes: Why was the original meaning of Calvinism interpreted in the way it was, rather than in other possible and equally logical ways?

This can be accounted for in terms of a process of churchly adaptation to its environment. Because that environment itself was changing, however, there was a "rolling adaptation" of new religious, economic, and political structures to one another. This is well shown in the work of Richard Baxter, whom Weber cites frequently. Baxter stands midway in the process of transition from early to late Calvinism; ". . . he was constantly wavering between the two opposing camps of Puritanism on the one hand and its deadly enemy at that time, 'Independency,' on the other. His very influence was to some degree based upon his blowing neither too hot nor too cold to displease any, and even in Anglo-Catholic circles he was read and enjoyed." [20] Baxter, who was a man of great practical experience, is an excellent example of the way churchmen attempt to moralize from within a social order. He did not want to alienate an important group who had taken to a life of trade, with or without the church's permission, for England had already gone far toward capitalism, but neither did he give up the task of trying to control their behavior. He stressed the dangers of trade and wealth, but did not condemn them. Baxter allowed lending upon pledges, pawns, and mortgages for security, provided that the loans were not made against something necessary to a poor man's livelihood. And a mortgage

19 *Institutes*, Vol. I, pp. 639–642.

20 T. C. Hall, *The Religious Background of American Culture*, p. 217.

might be taken if the pledge is "among merchants and rich men." Taking of interest is also lawful when the borrower has profited by the use of the money; it is unlawful when it violates justice and charity. The two great principles of justice in trade Baxter held to be love of one's neighbor and self-denial. "When the tempter draweth you to think only of your own commodity and gain, remember how much more you will lose by sin, than your gain can any way amount to." [21] One gets the impression in reading his "directions for the rich" that Baxter is preaching to a group who are already, willy-nilly, involved in a life of business and wealth: He seeks only to enfold that group within the Christian doctrine.

To the poor he counsels patience, eyes on the next world, contentment with one's status, and lack of covetousness. There the traditional element in his preaching looms large, and is a long way from giving the dynamic impetus to the capitalistic spirit that Weber held was in *the* Protestant ethic.

We are like runners in a race, and heaven or hell will be our end; and therefore woe to us, if by looking aside, or turning back, or stopping, or trifling about these matters, or burdening ourselves with worldly trash, we should lose the race, and lose our souls. O sirs, what greater matters than poverty or riches have we to mind! Can these souls that must shortly be in heaven or hell, have time to bestow any serious thought upon these impertinencies? . . . "Stedfastly believe that, ordinarily, riches are far more dangerous to the soul than poverty, and a greater hindrance to men's salvation." Believe experience; how few of the rich and rulers of the earth are holy, heavenly, self-denying, mortified men? Believe your Saviour, "How hardly shall they that have riches enter into the kingdom of God! For it is easier for a camel to go through a needle's eye than for a rich man to enter into the kingdom of God. And they that heard it said, who then can be saved? And he said, The things which are impossible with men, are possible with God." So that you see the difficulty is so great of saving such as are rich that to men it is a thing impossible, but to God's omnipotency only it is possible. . . . Also you will be tempted to be coveting after more; satan maketh poverty a snare to draw many needy creatures, to greater covetousness than many of the rich are guilty of; none thirst more eagerly after more; and yet their poverty blindeth them, so that they cannot see that they are covetous, or else excuse it as a justifiable thing. They think that they desire no more but necessaries, and that it is not covetousness; if they desire not superfluities. But do you not covet more than God allotteth you? And are you not discontent with his allowance? And doth not he know best what is necessary for you, and what superfluous? What then is covetousness, if this be not? [22]

This is scarcely a call for ascetic rational pursuit of gain. Baxter is a direct descendant of medieval doctrine. "The Christian avoids sin rather than loss." He modifies his teachings only enough—and that rather reluctantly—to bring the businessmen within the fold of the church, for only then may it have a claim upon their conduct. Baxter's work may be somewhat contradictory and ambiguous, although of the utmost sincerity; but what effective "political" action is not?

The whole history of the spread of Calvinism teaches us to beware of facile generalizations regarding its influence, for it could evolve in many directions. Its rigorous asceticism could be a tonic to those who stood to

21 Richard Baxter, *A Christian Directory,* Vol. VI, p. 287.

22 Ibid., Vol. IV, pp. 379–384.

gain by vigorous activity. But the doctrine of the depravity of the flesh, taken emotionally, could lead to a deadening of earthly activity. This was manifest in some aspects of Pietism, which emphasized the aspect of asceticism that meant withdrawal from the world, in contrast to the activist tendencies in Calvinism in general. Weber himself noted that "the doctrine of predestination could lead to fatalism if, contrary to the predominant tendencies of rational Calvinism, it were made the object of emotional contemplation." [23]

One may note too, alongside the main emphasis of Calvinism, a kind of Christian socialism, which taught that goods ought to be inexpensive, interest rates low (Calvin held that 2.5 per cent was high enough), and regard for others the dominant ethic. Weber wrote: ". . . the desire to separate the elect from the world could, with a strong emotional intensity, lead to a sort of monastic community life of half-communistic character, as the history of Pietism, even within the Reformed Church, has shown again and again." [24] This is one of the sources of Christian socialism today; but it did not (and one may perhaps say it does not) receive much attention because it was moving against contemporary developments. When one understands "the social sources of denominationalism," he is surprised neither at the infrequency of this interpretation of Calvinism nor at its occasional appearance.

A Field Interpretation of the Relationship of Protestantism to Capitalism

In our brief discussion of the range and development of Protestant asceticism, we have already indicated the lines of possible modifications of Weber's theory. By consciously choosing to explore only one side of the interaction between Calvinism and capitalism,[25] he ran the risk of seeming to disregard the ways in which the former was shaped and interpreted to harmonize with the inclinations and interests of its adherents, even while it shaped their motivations toward and definitions of proper economic behavior. There was, in his own later phrase, an "elective affinity" between certain interpretations of the complex doctrines of Calvin and the secular concerns of his middle-class followers. To the reformer, the purpose of the universe was to glorify God; man possesses reason in order that he may more fittingly glorify God. This doctrine might as readily lead to mysticism or to an ascetic denial of the importance of this world as to vigorous pursuit of a worldly calling. Thus Calvinism did not directly create the spirit of capitalism. The needs and tendencies of capitalists and would-be capitalists were involved in a process that selected from various possibilities those elements in Calvinism that gave meaning, purpose, and justification to their lives. Once those possibilities were chosen, however, they imposed on their adherents certain limitations and obligations.

23 *The Protestant Ethic,* p. 131.

24 Ibid., p. 131.

25 That he continually refers to the need for tracing the influence from the other direction also is ignored by his critics. ("But it would also further be necessary to investigate how Protestant Asceticism was in turn influenced in its development and its character by the totality of social conditions, especially economic." Weber, op. cit., p. 183.) That he tends to overlook his own qualification is sometimes forgotten by his followers.

Perhaps the situation can be clarified by seeing it in terms of a general theory of change. For expository purposes, we will start with a model of a "balanced" society in which the structure of interactions is reinforced and justified by the existing culture and by socialization procedures that lead to character structures harmonious with the ongoing system. There is, of course, in any imaginable society, some "wobble" in each of the three elements of the system. Some individuals are "poorly socialized"; new cultural elements are invented or imported; the usual patterns of interaction are upset by unusual economic, demographic, or political events—a drought, the plague, or invasion from the outside. In some periods, such irregularities are corrected by various homeostatic processes. Variations are sealed off so that they cannot spread; individual deviants are resocialized or isolated; new cultural forms are censored; the possible disruptive effects of drought on accepted patterns of interaction are minimized by systems of sharing, by religiously supported interpretations, and the like.

Under other conditions, however, the wobbles in one or more of the elements of a system are too severe for the homeostatic processes to handle. They intensify rather than being dampened. We might be wise to leave open the possibility that any one of the elements can be the starting point of such a sequence. A "great man" theory of history says in effect that one decisive individual can crash into a system with such impact that its stabilizing mechanisms are upset: cultural and structural changes are set in motion. Weber said that a new cultural force—Calvinism—hit certain slowly industrializing societies with such strength that realignments both of character and of social structure resulted. There is always enough variability in each part of the system that a good case can be made for an argument that a major sequence of change began with a particular variation. To know what will happen to those beginnings, however, demands knowledge of the total system.

In the matter of Protestantism and capitalism, the most decisive first breaks in the relatively stable medieval system began, in my judgment, in the social structure. By the twelfth century, the growth of commercial cities had changed patterns of interaction in important ways. Crosscultural contact was further increased by trade, by the Crusades, by the European discovery of the Americas, and in symbolic form by the development of printing. To cite such illustrations of new patterns of interaction, however, is at once to imply the likelihood of character and cultural changes. Peasants drawn or driven to the cities expressed new needs and desires; the motives and values of their earlier lives were inadequate for their contemporary situations. Merchants, warriors, crusaders, or explorers returning to their home communities, and all the others who traveled with them symbolically, had acquired new inclinations. Wobble in the social structure had been sufficiently strong to upset relatively stable socialization processes. "Acceptable" levels of character variation (those that were capable of being handled by established homeostatic processes) were exceeded. Individual and group deviation increased. Anomie, "the absence of structured complementarity," as Talcott Parsons calls it, grew. Individuals did not know what they could count on from their associates.

Such conditions are experienced as stressful; and many efforts to reduce the stress are set in motion. There are efforts to re-establish the old social order and to inhibit character variation by the repression of deviation. Most important under conditions of extensive structural and character change, however, is cultural inventiveness. New definitions of the way life should be organized, of appropriate human relationships, of ultimate meaning are proposed. Perhaps they come most often from those who have experienced the stress in a peculiarly intensive way. These new values and norms start out as character variations, expressive of one person's or a few individuals' efforts to achieve a new personal balance. Many of them get no farther than the individual.[26] But some prove meaningful to large numbers who share a stressful condition, who define the anomie around them in similar terms, and who find the new cultural forms—in the area of our concern, religious ideas—meaningful.

Following this general conception of the processes of change, one comes to Calvinism last, not first, in the structural-character-cultural sequence. It is not for that reason any less important. My theoretical statement is not so sharply at variance with Weber's thesis as a quick reading might indicate. I am trying to place the sequence he described into a larger system by observing that Calvinism could have the effects it had only because major structural and character changes preceding it had already overwhelmed the homeostatic processes of medieval society, leaving the field open for new cultural syntheses more in harmony with existing interactions and opportunities. In this sense, we note that once again religion serves a bridging function, helping to carry people over into a new world by furnishing ultimate definitions and procedures relevant to that world. Because this requires the building of new men as well as new structures, only a force capable of commanding ultimate allegiance can accomplish the task.

To continue the rather inelegant cybernetic language: Character was wobbling wildly because of basic changes in human interaction; religion helped to re-establish stability by defining which of several sharply contrasting values and motives were appropriate and giving them ultimate sanction. Anomie meant wobble in interpersonal relationships, for there was lack of agreement on the norms governing interaction. Calvinism proclaimed the normative in terms which, as they evolved, were credible to those experiencing a new world against the background of their traditional training.

In terms too simple (because we disregard the evolutionary process of selection by which many forms that are offered fail to survive) we might chart the sequence of events as in Figure 17–1.

This is a generalized scheme, implying, by the pattern of arrows, that major social reorganization can begin at many different points, but that it develops only if an original impulse is reinforced from other points (that is, if it proves strong enough to break through the homeostatic processes of the system). I am inclined to see the shift to modern capitalism coming from internal and external structural changes in the first instance; these modify

26 Sponsorship by a charismatic religious leader, Weber argued, was often the process by which new values became socially important. "In order that a manner of life so well adapted to the peculiarities of capitalism could be selected at all, i.e., should come to dominate others, it had to originate somewhere, and not in isolated individuals alone, but as a way of life common to whole groups of men. This origin is what really needs explanation." (Weber, op. cit., p. 55.) Would it not be more accurate to say: This origin, plus its evolution, plus its selection are what need explanation?

character in a stressful direction; persons particularly sensitive to that stress design religious and secular systems to deal with incoherence and anxiety; some of these systems reach audiences attuned to their messages. Once significant changes in the system, and not simply homeostatic adjustment of that system, are under way, influences flow from each point to the others.

Various interpretations of the relationship between Protestantism and capitalism cut into this sequence of events at different points and describe different portions of the full range. Weber's explanation, in schematic terms, was this: Calvinism, the result of the inner dialectic of religious thought, was accepted by a number of people as a powerful new way of dealing with life religiously. (It may have appealed particularly to those who were in rapidly changing and favorable economic and political circumstances.) It forcefully restructured the motives and values of its adherents. Their economic behavior, which in any event was inclined toward the new commercial and industrial opportunities, was given an intensity, an ascetic quality, a rationality that transformed it from the simple pursuit of money into a dedicated, religiously motivated calling.

David McClelland adds a few links to this chain. Protestantism so restructured personal relationships, particularly within the family, that training for independency and mastery was greatly strengthened. Such training is associated with strong achievement needs. These needs, coming from a religious context, lent the spirit to modern capitalism that is described by Weber: "It seems reasonable enough to interpret Weber's argument for the connection between Protestantism and the rise of capitalism in terms of a revolution in the family leading to more sons with high need for achievement." [27] More indirectly, the Reformation helped to dissolve traditionalism, thus freeing men for newly possible forms of economic activity that medieval economic ethics had curtailed.

McClelland's research is illustrative of a line of questioning, growing out of Weber's work, that is concerned with the transformative capacities of different religions. "By transformative capacity is meant the capacity to legitimize, in religious or ideological terms, the development of new motivations, activities, and institutions which were not encompassed by their original impulses and views." [28] This capacity in Protestantism grows, Eisenstadt notes, from the combination of this-worldliness and transcendentalism, the emphasis on individual activism and responsibility, and the direct relationship of the individual to the sacred. These capacities do not necessarily become associated with particular economic results. Paradoxically, they were least likely to be effective where Protestantism was more thoroughly established, as in South Africa, where "their more totalistic and therefore restrictive impulses became dominant." [29]

27 David McClelland, *The Achieving Society*, p. 49. There is now a large literature dealing with the sources of achievement motive, taking the subject beyond our interest in its religious dimension. See, e.g., David McClelland, and others, *The Achievement Motive;* Bernard Rosen and R. G. D'Andrade, "The Psychosocial Origins of Achievement Motivation," *Sociometry*, 22, 1959, pp. 185–218.

28 S. N. Eisenstadt, op. cit., p. 10.

29 Ibid., p. 15; see Jan Loubser, "Calvinism, Equality, and Inclusion: The Case of Afrikaner Calvinism," in ibid., Chap. 18.

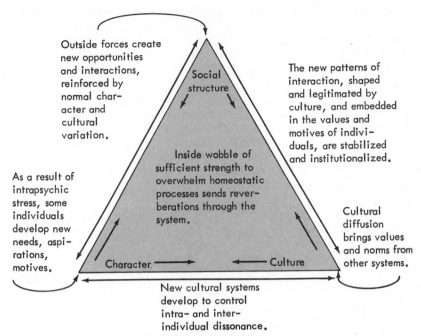

Outside forces create
new opportunities
and interactions,
reinforced by
normal char-
acter and
cultural
variation.

Social
structure

The new patterns of
interaction, shaped
and legitimated by
culture, and embedded
in the values and
motives of indivi-
duals, are stabilized
and institutionalized.

Inside wobble of
sufficient strength to
overwhelm homeostatic
processes sends rever-
berations through the
system.

As a result of
intrapsychic
stress, some
individuals
develop new
needs, aspi-
rations,
motives.

Cultural
diffusion
brings values
and norms from
other systems.

Character   Culture

New cultural systems
develop to control
intra- and inter-
individual dissonance.

FIGURE 17–1. *A field interpretation of social change*

This emphasizes once again that the effects of one factor in a system depend upon the other factors with which it is interacting.[30] Where Protestants were among the "secondary elites," in Eisenstadt's term, they exhibited the individualistic and activistic qualities much more strongly. In a related idea, Richard Means suggests that minority status for Protestants may have been associated with their energetic founding of universities (being blocked from the established ones), their interest in science, and thus indirectly with their contributions to the emergence of modern industrial society.[31] These ideas are close to Weber's emphasis on the importance of sectarian control and communion as sources of asceticism and devotion to one's work.[32]

Herbert Lüthy calls attention, in a valuable comparative analysis, to the

30 The importance of interaction is also emphasized by Herman Israel, "Some Religious Factors in the Emergence of Industrial Society in England," *American Sociological Review*, 31, 1966, pp. 589–599.

31 Richard Means, "Protestantism and Economic Institutions: Auxiliary Theories to Weber's Protestant Ethic," *Social Forces*, 44, 1966, pp. 372–381. The other theories suggested by Means are useful extensions of the Weber tradition. Put briefly they are: Protestant emphasis on the Bible as the Word leads to literacy, which leads to book-keeping, science, and so on; doctrines of transcendence and of man's sinfulness are readily associated with attitudes of liberty and distrust of the state, which lead to a stress on individualism and laissez-faire. The fourth "auxiliary theory" that Means suggests is also noted by Weber, but more particularly by Troeltsch. We have already referred to it: Protestantism can be a source of anticapitalist humanitarianism and socialism. Emphasis on brotherhood leads to the idea that salvation can come from giving aid, which leads to humanitarianism, public welfare, and private welfare.

32 See *From Max Weber*, pp. 302–322.

importance of structural factors in determining the effect of cultural innovation. It may be, he suggests, that Protestantism seemed to stimulate economic activity more than in fact it did only because it did not stand in the way of ongoing forces, while the Catholic Counter Reformation blocked those forces.

In the period of the Reformation all the bases of the modern world—capital, wealth, the highest technological and artistic level of development, global power, world trade—all these were almost exclusively present in countries that were and remained Catholic. Italy was the uncontested center of material and intellectual culture. Spain and Portugal enjoyed the monopoly of colonizing and exploiting both the Indies, the most important field of enterprise and the greatest source of wealth in the opening years of the modern age.[33]

That is, I believe, to overstate the case; but it may be a useful exaggeration to call attention to a neglected problem: ". . . as if the sudden breaking of an ascendant curve of development [in Catholic countries] did not constitute a far greater problem than its continuance [in Protestant countries]." [34]

The Counter Reformation, heresy trials, the Inquisition, and the expulsion of Jews took Catholic countries out of the stream of development. Despite the pre-eminence of Italian commerce and banking, of Spanish and Portuguese explorations, within a century after the beginnings of the Counter Reformation, "all this was petrifaction and decay." Calvinism, on the other hand, carried nations where its influence was strong into the stream of development partly because of its political failures; it "thereby remained almost free of political-opportunistic considerations and princely usurpations, and so allowed the revolutionary impulse to religious reform to flower free and uncontaminated." [35] Eisenstadt expresses the same idea: "Protestantism produced an impetus toward modernity only after this initial socio-religious impulse failed." [36] The observed results, then, were not simply a product of Protestantism as a cultural system.

RELIGIOUS VALUES AND ECONOMIC BEHAVIOR IN SEVERAL SETTINGS
We come now to the third question arising from Weber's thesis concerning Protestantism and capitalism. How far can it be used in other contexts? Does his statement have general properties that can be applied to religious economic interactions outside Europe and America and beyond the sixteenth- to eighteenth-century period with which he dealt? In a time of deep interest in economic development, the stimulating or inhibiting qualities of religion have again become subjects of investigation.

Weber's Comparative Studies
The place to begin is with Weber's own comparative work. His analysis of the impact of Protestantism on the spirit of capitalism was part of a series

33 Herbert Lüthy, in Eisenstadt, op. cit., p. 96.

34 Ibid.

35 Ibid., pp. 102–103.

36 S. N. Eisenstadt, "Transformation of Social, Political, and Cultural Orders in Modernization," *American Sociological Review*, 30, 1965, p. 671.

of monographs in which he explored the significance of religion for economic matters. In studies of Confucianism and Taoism, Hinduism and Buddhism, and Ancient Judaism, he sought to discover the ways in which religious ideas blocked or encouraged the appearance of rational business enterprise.[37] In each case, he took account of the political, economic, and other social forces at work, thus sketching a broader picture than in his essay on Protestantism, in which he described only one side of the causal chain.

Weber found that Confucianism, for example, contained a great deal of the rationalism characteristic of Western business ethics; it was quite definitely utilitarian; it had a positive evaluation of wealth. Despite all this, however, Confucianism was limited by a fundamental traditionalism. The ideal of the Confucian gentleman was a static idea—the assimilation of the established body of literary culture as expressed in the classics. Tradition was not only accepted but sanctified. Moreover, the specialization of Western bureaucratic structure was thoroughly opposed in the classical education of the Confucian gentleman, who was to become a well-rounded harmonious work of art.

There were also more specifically religious contrasts:

Completely absent in Confucian ethic was any tension between nature and deity, between ethical demand and human shortcoming, consciousness of sin and need for salvation, conduct on earth and compensation in the beyond, religious duty and sociopolitical reality. Hence, there was no leverage for influencing conduct through inner forces freed of tradition and convention.[38]

The Western ethic rests on universalism and on far-reaching mutual confidence even among strangers. Confucianism, on the contrary, was primarily concerned with a "particularistic" structure of relationships built around the kinship system. Finally, the basic metaphysical foundation of Confucianism, says Weber, the concept of Tao, the principle of Order, is in contrast to the evolutionism, the idea of development in Judaic-Christian thought.

As an interpretation of the relationship between religious influences and economic affairs, this essay raises several fundamental problems. Why is it that China continued to be bound by Confucian traditionalism, while Europe was gradually freed from the equally or more restrictive influence of Christian traditionalism? If one answers, as Weber does, that Christianity was reinterpreted by the Protestant "prophecy," the question immediately arises: Why did the prophets appear in Europe? Why did Confucianism not have a Reformation? The natural congeniality of Christianity for prophecy is probably a legitimate part of the explanation. (The cause of this congeniality can be disregarded for Weber's immediate problem, although it is of the utmost importance for other questions in the sociology of religion.) That conditions in sixteenth-century Europe were ripe, however, for all kinds of prophecy is proved by the series of revolutions—commer-

37 See *Gesammelte Aufsätze zur Religionssoziologie*. Most of this series has now appeared in English translation. In addition to *The Protestant Ethic*, see *Ancient Judaism*, *The Religion of India*, *The Religion of China*, *The Sociology of Religion*, and *From Max Weber*.

38 *The Religion of China*, pp. 235–236.

cial, legal, political—that were going on. This limits Weber's conception of the immanence of the religious developments.[39]

Several of the forces discussed by Weber have one kind of influence in a particular context, but a quite different influence in another context. They cannot be used, therefore, as direct explanations of events; they are only one element in a compound. Recent events have shown, for example, that particularistic relationships built around kinship can be a powerful stimulus to economic activity and success *under conditions of rapidly expanding economic opportunity.* In some situations, it has been precisely the Chinese and Japanese family particularity that has promoted their economic success.

Nor is it intrinsic to the Confucian lack of tension between nature and deity as compared with the Calvinist sense of sin, that the former should lead to traditionalism and the latter to a driving, inner-worldly search for salvation. The self-confidence associated with the former can promote enterprise; the tension associated with the latter can, under some conditions, promote otherworldiness.

Classic Hinduism, to refer briefly to one other of Weber's comparative studies, much more decisively inhibits economic innovation than does Confucianism. Traditionalism of the artisan and other workers was "heightened to the extreme" by the doctrine of dharma—the duty associated with particular positions in society. Numerous taboos inhibited the use of resources. (Today a rapid increase in cattle population places a burden on economic modernization as does the increase in human population.) Most importantly, the karma doctrine—with its promise of rebirth at a higher level if one's caste duties are faithfully performed—gave every believer a strong interest in maintaining the system. There were in addition, of course, nonreligious factors preventing economic growth; ". . . frequent conquests, the instability of the political order, ruthless fiscal extortion, diverted energies and wealth from productive purposes." [40]

Even in India, however, the situation was not unambiguous. Weber wrote: "A ritual law in which every change of occupation, every change in work technique, may result in ritual degradation is certainly not capable of giving birth to economic and technical revolutions from within itself, or even of facilitating the first germination of capitalism in its midst." [41] Yet he also noted that "the law of caste has proved just as elastic in the face of the necessities of the concentration of labor in workshops as it did in the face of a need for concentration of labor and service in the noble household." [42] Without wanting to quarrel with Weber's basic thesis, perhaps we ought to note several qualifications. Viewing India as a whole, he might have given more attention to the inner-worldly asceticism of the Jains,

---

39 It is important to remember, moreover, that there were prophets and sectarian protest movements in China. These wobbles in the system, however, did not spread. They were not accentuated by other changes. See C. K. Yang, *Religion in Chinese Society,* Chap. 9.

40 Stanislav Andreski in Eisenstadt, op. cit., p. 62.

41 *The Religion of India,* p. 112.

42 Ibid., p. 111.

Lingāyats, and other sects.[43] The fatalism characteristic of Hindu doctrine, proves, on examination, to be a multifaceted belief, capable of development in different directions under varying conditions.[44] The drive for caste mobility, as contrasted with individual mobility, may have powerful economic effects.[45] And it is at least imaginable that the doctrines of karma and dharma themselves might, under conditions of expanding opportunity, become associated with energetic activity, just as belief in predestination can sometimes do so, despite its quietistic implications. Prediction from knowledge of doctrines alone, without regard to the situations within which they are expressed and believed, is always hazardous.

One additional qualification applies to a problem of interpretation of Weber's essay series, seen as a whole. To demonstrate that a religious ethic can *restrict* the appearance of a new economic form and to claim that a religious ethic can *precipitate* a new economic form are two different things. All of Weber's essays, except *The Protestant Ethic*, seek to show how the appearance of capitalism was greatly restricted by a religious system. Few will deny, except in points of detail, the thoroughness of his demonstration. The most rabid historical materialist is the one who insists that "religion is the opiate of the people"—an admission that it has a telling effect on their behavior. A religion once established (and whatever the cause of its own doctrine) certainly becomes in its turn a cause of succeeding events. It is one of the homeostatic processes whereby instabilities in a social system are corrected. But in *The Protestant Ethic*, Weber argues precisely that the congeniality of Calvinism for capitalism preceded the major development of capitalism and was greatly responsible for its peculiar spirit. Moreover, he held that this Calvinistic doctrine emerged—although not entirely—out of a religious dialectic, and became conjoined with emerging capitalism only by a "historical accident." That this claim is on an entirely different level from that of the others he makes is immediately apparent. We have suggested that such a claim takes insufficient account of the selective development of religious movements, of the "elective affinity" that Weber himself is alert to in other connections. We can explore this problem by an examination of some more recent manifestations of the interconnections of religion and economics.

Recent Studies of Religion and Economic Behavior in the United States

Whatever role Protestantism may have had in the appearance of capitalism, does it contribute to the economic success of its adherents in a highly developed economy? [46] When all other factors are controlled, can it be said

43 See the excellent review of *The Religion of India* by Milton Singer, *American Anthropologist*, 63, 1961, pp. 143–151; see also Robert E. Kennedy, Jr., "The Protestant Ethic and the Parsis," *American Journal of Sociology*, 68, 1962, pp. 11–20.

44 See Joseph Elder, "Religious Beliefs and Political Attitudes," in *South Asian Politics and Religion*, D. E. Smith, ed., Chap. 12.

45 See M. N. Srinivas, *Caste in Modern India*.

46 For a variety of views, see for example, Norval Glenn and Ruth Hyland, "Religious Preference and Worldly Success: Some Evidence from National Surveys," *American Sociological Review*, 32, 1967, pp. 73–85; Albert Mayer and Harry Sharp, "Religious

with reference specifically to the United States that the values and motives of Protestants are different from Catholics in ways that influence occupational choice, educational achievement, economic initiative, and ascetic disciplines? [47] It is difficult to control for the numerous variables that might obscure the relationship of religion and economic behavior; and most studies have been only partially successful in isolating that relationship for examination. Race, national origin, recency of migration to the United States or into a city, class of parents, available opportunities, and reference groups—such factors as these must be taken into account before we can assume that observed relationships between religion and economic behavior are not spurious.[48] In comparing levels of aspiration and attainment, it is important to measure not only the absolute levels but the distance traveled or reached. To say that one boy aspires to a college degree and a professional job while another aspires to a high school diploma and a craftsman's job is to indicate very little if the former comes from a professional family while the latter is the son of a semiskilled migrant from a depressed rural area.[49] Because such relative measures are seldom used, we must use the available material with caution.

In terms of objective measures of economic success, there has been a significant shift during the last generation: Catholics have moved from a position clearly below that of white Protestants to one of equality or slight advantage. This is the dominant conclusion to be drawn from the several studies reviewed by Glenn and Hyland. Differences in income, educational

---

Preference and Worldly Success," *American Sociological Review*, 27, 1962, pp. 218–227; Andrew Greeley, *Religion and Career: A Study of College Graduates;* Andrew Greeley, "The Protestant Ethic: Time for a Moratorium," *Sociological Analysis*, 25, 1964, pp. 20–33; Helmut Wagner, "The Protestant Ethic: A Mid-Twentieth Century View," *Sociological Analysis*, 25, 1964, pp. 34–40; Bernice Goldstein and Robert Eichhorn, "The Changing Protestant Ethic: Rural Patterns in Health, Work and Leisure," *American Sociological Review*, 26, 1961, pp. 557–565; Gerhard Lenski, *The Religious Factor;* Joseph Veroff, Sheila Feld, and Gerald Gurin, "Achievement Motivation and Religious Background," *American Sociological Review*, 27, 1962, pp. 205–217; Bernard Rosen, "Race, Ethnicity, and the Achievement Syndrome," *American Sociological Review*, 24, 1959, pp. 47–60; David McClelland, op. cit.; Raymond Mack, Raymond Murphy, and Seymour Yellin, "The Protestant Ethic, Level of Aspiration, and Social Mobility: An Empirical Test," *American Sociological Review*, 21, 1956, pp. 295–300.

47 I shall comment only on the Protestant-Catholic comparison. It is clear that Jews have attained higher levels of education and income than Protestants. In recent years, Americans of Chinese and Japanese descent—some of whom are Buddhists, others Catholic or Protestant, with a fairly large proportion indicating no religious identification—have also shown a great deal of educational and occupational initiative. These cases indicate that Protestantism at most is only one of a series of sources of the characteristics necessary for economic success.

48 From studies of education we have learned that the school and community settings and the available reference groups must be taken into account before variations in aspiration and attainment as presumed qualities of individuals can be measured. From a large literature I will mention only a few items: Theodore Kemper, "Reference Groups, Socialization, and Achievement," *American Sociological Review*, 33, 1968, pp. 31–45; William Sewell and Vimal Shah, "Socioeconomic Status, Intelligence, and the Attainment of Higher Education," *Sociology of Education*, 40, 1967, pp. 1–23; James S. Coleman and others, *Equality of Educational Opportunity.*

49 See John Porter, "The Future of Upward Mobility," *American Sociological Review*, 33, 1968, pp. 5–19.

level, and occupational prestige are now small. Protestants over 30 seem somewhat more likely to have entered college and to have graduated; but younger respondents (aged 20–24) to a series of national polls taken since 1960 show a different pattern: A larger proportion of Catholics had finished high school than Protestants (80 as against 73 per cent) and had entered college (33 as against 29 per cent). Of those who had started college, however, a larger proportion of Protestants than Catholics had finished (40 as against 36 per cent).[50] Because more Protestants come from the South, from rural areas and small towns, direct comparisons are inadequate. When residents of non-Southern metropolitan areas are compared, Catholic-Protestant differences are small, with the latter being slightly advantaged in the proportions on the highest income, educational, and occupational prestige levels.

Disregarding various differences in the distribution profiles, which for some purposes would be important, we can say that insofar as occupational, educational, and income data measure an ethic of hard work and economic achievement, differences between white American Protestants and Catholics are minimal.

A second line of investigation has studied levels of achievement motivation and values, rather than objective measures of income, occupation, and education. Interviews and thematic apperception tests have been used to compare various groups, including persons of different religious identity, on their economic attitudes and motivations. Several studies using respondents primarily from the northeastern part of the United States and from Detroit have found that Protestants are more achievement-motivated and have a more positive orientation toward work than do Catholics.[51] Lenski saw the difference as a sharp one: "In view of the social heritage of contemporary Catholicism, it seems unlikely that in the foreseeable future any devoutly Catholic state will become a leading industrial nation—one in the forefront of economic development and progress." [52]

A national sample, however, found higher achievement scores among Catholic than Protestant men, with Jewish men, as in most other studies, higher than either.[53] When this finding was specified by age and income, some interesting variations appeared: It was the younger, lower-income Catholics with larger families who were most likely to have high achievement scores; high-income Catholics had lower scores. There was smaller variation among Protestants, with a slight tendency for higher-income persons to have higher scores, except in the youngest age group. Veroff, Feld, and Gurin suggest that "Catholic men's achievement motivation is aroused by the specific pressures of economic hardship," whereas, among Protestants, such motivation is more likely to be the product of child-training

50 Glenn and Hyland, op. cit. This item is qualified by the fact that in this age group, not all who would finish college had yet done so. The studies cited by Glenn and Hyland can profitably be compared with the summaries of international research by Seymour Lipset and Reinhard Bendix. They found that rates of social mobility no longer correlated with religious affiliation. See *Social Mobility in Industrial Society*, pp. 49–54.

51 See the works of Lenski, McClelland, and Rosen, cited earlier.

52 Op. cit., p. 349.

53 Veroff, Feld and Gurin, op. cit., pp. 205–217.

methods that encourage independence.[54] A desire for achievement, at least as measured by thematic apperception tests, can apparently derive from a variety of sources—from the character effects of child training, from supportive cultural values, and from the opportunities and pressures of the social structure.[55]

How can we interpret these various findings? It is necessary first of all to note a major methodological problem: Most of the studies cited use membership or simply self-identification as an indication of Protestantism or Catholicism. However, because the aim is usually to measure a chain of relationship that involves religiously derived values, individual motives, and economic behavior, such generalized group identification is inadequate. To say that a person calls himself a Protestant is scarcely to determine the degree to which certain presumed Protestant values motivate his behavior. Averages can be quite deceiving in this kind of situation. Suppose it is the "least Catholic" Catholics and the "most Protestant" Protestants who have certain views or manifest certain behaviors? Average scores of the groups might be identical, yet the implications of religious identity for the views and behavior in question would be in sharp contrast.

Lenski is well aware of this problem and gives valuable information in trying to solve it. He found that among Protestants, children of devout working-class or farm parents rose to middle-class positions in larger proportion than did the children of less devout parents (51 as against 31 per cent). Among Catholics, however, the opposite relationship prevails: 31 per cent of the children of devout working-class and farm families had become middle class; whereas 39 per cent of the less devout had done so.[56] We cannot draw a firm conclusion from these data, because measures of parental devoutness are used as an index of children's values and motives. The more devout may have been on somewhat higher educational and status levels in the case of Protestants and, in the case of Catholics, on somewhat lower educational and status levels, thus furnishing differential support for the mobility of the children. Lenski has more direct measures of individual attitudes, however, and these reveal the same pattern. Active Protestants, whether middle class or working class, are more likely to agree with items "consonant with the spirit of capitalism," than are marginal Protestants; the relationship among Catholics is the reverse. The differences, it should be noted, are small; and they do not appear on all of the items. They are not found in connection with aspirations for economic advancement nor, among men, in the distribution of positive attitudes toward work.[57] The differential effect of Protestant and Catholic values on economic attitudes in an American metropolis in mid-twentieth century, then, is small, yet not entirely absent.

There are several other considerations, however, that require brief mention before the contemporary situation can be adequately understood. The convergence of Catholic and Protestant attitudes, economic behavior, and

54 See ibid.; see also Daniel Miller and Guy Swanson, *The Changing American Parent.*

55 See Bernard Rosen, "The Achievement Syndrome," *American Sociological Review,* 21, 1956, pp. 203–211.

56 Lenski, op. cit., pp. 115–118.

57 Ibid., pp. 118–123.

status, insofar as it has occurred, does not necessarily show that the influence of religion has declined. It may show that in some measure Catholics have been "Protestantized" and Protestants have been influenced by Catholics (who now number about one-quarter of the population), and both have been Americanized. Lenski's finding that third- and fourth-generation Catholics differ more widely from Protestants than do more recent migrants casts doubt on this; but it may be a result of ethnic differences by generation. Perhaps more likely than any of these is Weber's view that the pursuit of wealth is now quite secularized in the West, so that its correlations with any religious tendencies or identities are low.

In connection with our discussion of the effects of early Calvinism, we noted that its status as a minority religious movement probably influenced economic values and motivations in ways similar to its doctrines. This "minority-group effect" operates on Catholics in the United States, increasing their economic and political activism. It no longer influences "main line Protestants," however, as it did in many settings where their ancestors lived. The strongest influence of the Protestant ethic in the United States today is probably in the sects, where members think of themselves as a small, select minority, a saving remnant. There we are most likely to find values that approach Weber's description of "inner-worldly asceticism." Their economic ethic is much closer to laissez-faire individualism than is that of the more prosperous denominations. It is among such groups as the Seventh Day Adventists, Jehovah's Witnesses, Salvation Army, and Mormons, diverse as they are in many ways, that the specifically religious stimulus to economic activity is now most likely to be found.[58]

Religion and Development in the Twentieth Century

Since the end of World War II the desire for rapid economic development has become virtually universal among nations (although it is not shared as a goal by all persons within them). A few nations have moved from the level of traditional economies, with relatively low and fixed incomes, into the ranks of nations that have attained high incomes and self-sustaining patterns of economic growth. Many more, however, have not made this transition, despite their strenuous efforts to do so. What accounts for the variation? There are obviously many material factors: the economic base from which they start, available resources, outside aid, the share of the economy used by the military, and the like. There are also political factors that influence the way resources are allocated and citizens motivated. But beyond these is the continuing importance of "the Weber problem." Are there certain kinds of religious systems which, through the ways they define ethical obligations and the road to salvation—and thereby influence the values and motives of their adherents—promote economic activity and growth? Are there other religious systems that inhibit such activity and growth even though one might expect rapid development on the basis of purely material factors? If religious forces do seem to be involved, can certain structural and cultural conditions be identified which produce

58 We might well add the Black Muslims, even though their Protestantism has been set aside for a new religious identity.

economically activist religious movements; or are they mutants, charismatic accidents that may or may not hit at a time ready for them?

These are extremely complicated questions that raise once again the whole debate concerning the influence of the Protestant ethic. We are clearly not talking simply about Protestantism, unless it is assumed to be "one of a kind" without which rapid economic growth is impossible. In various ways and to varying degrees the experience of Japan, the Soviet Union, Israel, Puerto Rico, and other societies disproves such an assumption. It is the more general question that requires study: Can the world's traditional religions lend support, under certain conditions, to economic development? Do new religions or drastic reformations of old religions appear, under some conditions, with the power to make new men—producing value and character realignments that correspond with existing or possible structural changes?

Under some conditions I think it might be argued that communism is the Calvinism of the secular. I will not undertake to explicate this complicated relationship, however, but will confine my discussion to a brief examination of the influence of more traditional religions on the process of economic development.[59] Viewed historically, the religions of societies that are composed primarily of small farmers, peasants, and villagers, and characterized by low levels of social and physical mobility, have fostered traditionalism in economics. This is simply to say that religion has reflected and affected conditions of stability, low economic opportunity, and few sources of innovation. Viewed functionally, a religion that stimulated economic enterprise, encouraged capital savings, and supported independence and achievement training is quite unimaginable. It would have contradicted the life conditions of the people so sharply as to be beyond belief. This does not mean, however, that residents of such a society have no desire for economic goods and services or are unmotivated to acquire them. It means that they work within the framework of opportunities as they see them and along lines set by values adjusted to those opportunities.

The Burmese villager, for example, seems quite improvident by Western standards. A large share of any surplus he can wring from a basic subsistence he spends on religion—alms to the monks, gold leaf for the pagoda spires, elaborate ceremonies. Saving for capital investment is not only lacking but is religiously proscribed. Seen in context, however, these practices are neither indications of lack of interest in material well-being nor signs of improvidence. "Given *their* behavioral environment, religious spending is more efficacious for the satisfaction of material desires than economic savings." [60] Granted the small amount he could save, the political instability of his environment, and the lack of economic opportunities, he

59 There are numerous studies in which religion is examined as an inhibitory or contributory factor in development. See, for example, Robert Bellah, *Tokugawa Religion;* Robert Bellah, ed., *Religion and Progress in Modern Asia;* Eisenstadt, op. cit., Pt. III; Kalman Silvert, ed., *Churches and States. The Religious Institution and Modernization;* Henri Desroche, "Religion et développement. La thème de leurs rapports réciproques et ses variations," *Archives de Sociologie des Religions,* 12, 1961, pp. 3–34; E. B. Ayal, "Value Systems and Economic Development in Japan and Thailand," *Journal of Social Issues,* 19, 1963, pp. 35–51.

60 Melford Spiro, "Buddhism and Economic Action in Burma," *American Anthropologist,* 68, 1966, pp. 1165–1166.

could hope for little security or gain by the practice of economically oriented asceticism. Viewing the world through his religious training, he sees the chance to win merit through charity and thus speed his escape from the cycle of rebirths. If he at the same time wins prestige from his fellows and enjoyment from the ceremonies, these are bonuses.[61] Spiro makes the interesting point that such religiously motivated action has some of the qualities of the sternest asceticism, for it shows training in the ability to defer gratification, even to a later existence.[62]

This description can be matched in many parts of the world among persons with widely varying religious training. Catholic peasants in South America, Moslem *abangan* (with their strong mixtures of other religions) in the villages of Java, lower strata in India assiduously performing their caste duties, all divide their scarce resources between present enjoyment and activities to promote religiously defined salvation.

In some societies, these cultural forms have been matched by such stabilities of structure and of character that few changes have occurred through several centuries. Homeostatic processes have dampened the possible disturbing effects of "poorly socialized" individuals whose values and motives did not fit the system, of new cultural forms, perhaps imported from outside, and of structural disturbances in the shape either of unusual stress or unusual opportunities. But that day has gone, perhaps for good. The twentieth century has seen such stable systems overwhelmed by reverberations that they could not handle. In almost every part of the world, individuals are interacting in ways and with types of people quite unknown to their earlier experience. Values from drastically different systems become widely known and often forcefully propagated. In a context of rapid change, socialization patterns are obstructed and generation gaps widen, so that values and motives congruent with traditional norms and structures no longer characterize a population. In my judgment, these shocks to what seem in retrospect to have been relatively stable systems are now endemic. They will not stop until the whole world is brought within a new balance of structure, culture, and character. And, of course, that may never be achieved. Our species may not be capable of handling changes of such depth and frequency while trying to build a system that has some relationship to the realities of the world situation: instant communication, vastly increased actual and potential productivity, rapidly growing population, and incredible powers of destruction.

At the present time, however, efforts to attain a new balance are being made primarily on the societal level. New systems of value are inevitably involved. If traditional religious systems capable of adaptation are not available, new faiths are invented—communism, nationalism, or a mixture

61 There are functional similarities here to the generosity patterns reported by William Whyte in *Street Corner Society*. To save for college or a major economic purpose seemed, on the one hand, futile to the members of highly disprivileged groups. On the other hand, generosity won them group support and prestige. Similar processes, but on the level of magic, are found in the appeal of "the numbers game." Impoverished slum-dwellers will "throw away" their last dime or quarter by putting it on a number, in the remote hope of winning a large return from the gambler. Their arithmetic may be poor, but it has to be judged in a context where the hopeless process of saving is set against the exciting possibility of miraculous return.

62 See Melford Spiro, op. cit., pp. 1163–1173.

of the two being most common in our time. I am concerned here, however, with the traditional religions. Can they play, are they playing a part in the making of new men and new societies? The answer is a complex one.

We must note first of all that pressures toward drastic revision of a structure-culture-character system may strike a small part of a population long before they affect the majority. Those who are most mobile, literate, and aware of changes—often the urban middle and upper classes—will see new opportunities, become aware of new values, and develop new motivations while the majority are still highly traditionalist. Some of the elite seek to revise their received religion, in the hope of maintaining some continuity in the face of change. Others see the traditional faith as being hopelessly outmoded. Religious professionals seek to preserve the sacred order not only because change is likely to weaken their position, but also because the majority of the population still live in the world that it sanctified. Thus it was not out of sheer rigidity that the Catholic Church tabooed usury (the lending and borrowing of money at interest) until the middle of the nineteenth century. Even down to that time the great majority of her members were peasants whose entire lives were spent almost outside the money economy. They borrowed money only in emergencies. To charge interest then was truly to hit a man when he was down. (Meanwhile, a growing list of exceptions were granted for that part of the urban population that used money to *make* money.)

How, then, shall Buddhism or Hinduism or any other religion deal with the wide variety of situations faced by its adherents? Slow change will appear to the intellectuals to be rigidity and to the peasants, revolution. Each of the major religions is complex and capable of a variety of interpretations. Despite a predominant otherworldliness, all of them have conceptions of the good society that can serve as a basis for criticism of a rigid and unjust social order. Given time, those aspects consonant with new social realities can be emphasized. But there may not be time, particularly for those religious systems which have been stabilized for centuries around life in quite isolated villages. We see various efforts at reform, sectarian movements, and conversion to new faiths, alongside traditionalism; but structural change may be too rapid for the evolution of value systems.

Societies that import major structural changes from outside face more difficult problems of cultural and character realignment than do those within which the changes first evolved. In a biological analogy that probably overstates the case, the evolution of new tissues disrupts an organism less than the transplanting of tissue from another organism. There are serious problems of allergic response and rejection in the latter case. Compatibility cannot be assumed; it has to be studied. Weber saw Germany as an illustration of the effects of the importation of industrialization into a system that had not undergone structural revision—neither in its political, family, and educational systems, nor in the motives of individuals. Rather than a new homeostatic balance, there was persistent and violent disruption. Some observers believe that Germany is still characterized by these inconsistencies.

Incongruities are characteristic of all modern societies, so we are speaking here of matters of more or less. Japan may share many elements of the German situation. It is not that religion stood in the way of modernization.

As in Germany, the religious values and accompanying motives were at least amenable and probably actively supportive of orderly, responsible, highly skilled work and of the ability to defer gratification that is necessary for education and training.[63] These did not come in, however, on a wave that also brought individualism and opposition to domination. They could be harnessed, therefore, by traditional authorities.

Looking at economic growth as our sole criterion, we are inclined to consider Japan as a rather unambiguous success story. But to Japanese intellectuals who feel as acutely as Weber did the failure of modern Japan to carry through certain critical structural transformations which are associated with modern society, the evaluation of Japan's modern history is much more problematic.[64]

We may be faced here with a serious dilemma: Modernization accomplished with relatively minor readjustments of traditional value systems and character structures is easier to carry through; but it brings about a society that is both available to an aggressive elite and vulnerable to authoritarian patterns (Germany, Japan). Modernization that cannot be accomplished without major reconstruction of the sacred systems and major reorganization of personalities is first of all delayed and then brought in by a violent quasi-religion (the Soviet Union, China). Is there a possible way to avoid the horns of this dilemma? There is, I believe, a small chance. Modernization accompanied by drastic sectarian protests and reform movements *within* the sacred systems may be able to accomplish the structural transformations lacking in the first case and to avoid the anomie-totalitarian cycle of the second.

If there is any validity in this analysis, we should observe sectarian and religious reform movements in the developing world with great care, whether we regard them as agents of modernization or simply as indices that the process will be accomplished without major catastrophe. I cannot here review such movements, but will simply indicate a few signs that they are neither abundant nor entirely lacking. It is important to recognize that modernization is not synonymous with westernization; [65] yet there are limits to cultural variability. Certain characteristics are essential and others are highly supportive, whatever the cultural framework within which they are expressed. The skill level of the population must be raised; a greater openness to new experience, tolerance of differences, and readiness for mobility are requisite. Although one cannot speak with confidence on this question, it seems likely that greater appreciation for this life and a decline in otherworldliness are not only a consequence of modernization, but also a requirement for it. A need for autonomy, a sense of independence, which E. E. Hagen believes necessary for innovative behavior, and the psychic mobility, the ability to empathize with persons in other situations, which Daniel Lerner emphasizes, may also be important sources of modernization as well as products of it.

63 See Robert Bellah, *Tokugawa Religion.*

64 Bellah in Eisenstadt, op. cit., p. 248.

65 Nor do I assume that modernization is necessarily a fortunate development. From the point of view of my values, and I suppose the values of many others, it is at least open to question whether the gains have exceeded the losses. But however one evaluates the process, it seems inevitable that industrialization and urbanization will increase.

Several of these qualities are involved in Bellah's description of modernization in cybernetic terms, as the capacity of a social system to receive and process information and to act appropriately on it. "Progress thus involves not merely learning but also learning capacity, an increasing ability to 'learn to learn.' This kind of learning capacity includes the 'capacity for deep rearrangements of inner structure, and thus for the development of radically new functions.'" [66]

In some settings, the extreme otherworldliness of Buddhism is being modified by greater attention to problems of this world and the emphasis on a hierarchy of religious participants is being changed in favor of greater attention to laymen. In Ceylon, "Modern reformers encourage everyone to strive for religious virtuosity in this life itself." [67] Ames believes that events in Ceylon are close parallels to developments during the Christian Reformation: There has been an increase in participation by laymen and growth of this-worldly interests. Nirvana is not regarded by the reformers as hundreds of rebirths away. "One may work for salvation 'here and now' even while pursuing an ordinary family life." There is a stronger orientation to achievement; ". . . members of the new intelligentsia point out that [the Buddha] was an individual who attained Enlightenment through hard and very human striving. The Buddha is seen by them as a person to be emulated more than adored." And there is "a protest against the excessive ritualism and idolatry of the traditional monks and unsophisticated villagers. The Buddhist way for all people is held to be the simple and rational path of meditation . . ." [68] Where conditions support emphasis on these qualities of Buddhism, it can maintain its influence among urban and industrialized people. It should be noted that these developments are not regarded as changes in belief by Buddhists themselves, but as particular expressions of fundamental Buddhism.

Compared with Buddhism, Islam is more legalistic and prescriptive. Whether or not Muhammad said "all innovation is the work of the devil," his followers in many contexts have acted that way. ". . . The traditional or classical Islamic concept of law and its role in society . . . constitutes a most formidable obstacle to progress." [69] Yet the Islamic tradition has proved to be capable of many interpretations, so that groups in many settings who for reasons of education, mobility, occupation, or other characteristics, are inclined toward secular change have been able to find and take

66 *Religion and Progress in Modern Asia*, pp. 169–170.

67 Michael Ames, "Ideological and Social Change in Ceylon," in Eisenstadt, op. cit., p. 272.

68 Ibid, p. 278. Ediriweera Sarachandra, it should be noted, gives greater emphasis to the hold of traditionalism. See his "Traditional Values and the Modernization of a Buddhist Society: The Case of Ceylon," in *Religion and Progress in Modern Asia*, pp. 109–123. In his study of Buddhism in Burma, Manning Nash takes a middle position, which is an interesting comparison with Ceylon. He predicts "that remote Nibbana will come to be replaced by more proximate religious states of salvation, and that a more austere and puritanical element will come to mark Burmese Buddhism." But he goes on to say that "it does take more, and a different sort of, incentive to get a Buddhist into economic activity in Burma, as against say a Muslim, or a Chinese Confucian, or even a Sikh or Hindu." See *The Golden Road to Modernity. Village Life in Contemporary Burma*, p. 165.

69 Noel Coulson in *Religion and Progress in Modern Asia*, Robert Bellah, ed., p. 74.

part in religious modernization as well.[70] If there are as yet few positive religious supports for rational, this-worldly asceticism in Islam, one may say, as Allan Eister does of Pakistan, that "Islam, in the ways it is practiced among our respondents, appears to offer no fixed or impenetrable bar to more rapid development in the villages. And for the country as a whole there appears to be a very considerable capacity to absorb continuing change in the direction of modernity." [71].

Clifford Geertz sees strong support for economic development among the Muslim traders, the *santri*, in the cities of Indonesia. This group shows fewer mixtures of Hinduism or animism than other parts of the Indonesian population. Values of rationality and asceticism are readily drawn from the several interpretations of Islamic law. The *santri* have quite readily modified their religious schools to teach secular subjects as well.[72]

We have quoted Lenski's judgment that no devoutly Catholic nation is likely to move to the forefront of industrial development. Predominantly Catholic Western European nations are highly industrialized, but one could scarcely call them devout. (It is instructive to recall, however, during a period of rapid development in Italy, that her earlier lack of development was often accounted for by value barriers.) The situation in Latin America may be better for studying the interplay of religion and development; yet even there, Catholicism in everything but a formal sense is a minority movement. "In many countries, less than 20 per cent of the population is made up of practicing Catholics. The literate minorities who actually participate in society are often violently anticlerical—that is, hostile to the personnel and institutions of the Church, though not necessarily to the Catholic faith." [73] It is by no means assured, Pike goes on to say, that religious influences will play a significant part in the process of change under way in Latin America.

Whatever the formal adherence of South Americans to the Church, Catholicism has been of powerful influence in shaping the culture in the direction of particularistic, ascriptive, and diffuse values. Historical experience had downgraded universalism and economic activism.

. . . Spain and Portugal, prior to colonizing the Americas, had been engaged for eight centuries in conflict with the Moors, resulting in the glorification of the roles of soldier and priest, and in the denigration of commercial and banking activities, often in the hands of Jews and Moslems. Iberian values and institutions were transferred to the American continent.[74]

It is important to recognize the range of Catholicism, however, even within one country, particularly where several orders or several national

70 See Leonard Binder, *Religion and Politics in Pakistan*, Chap. 2. On some of the problems as well as the possibilities of modernization in Islam see Clifford Geertz, "Modernization in a Muslim Society," in Bellah, op. cit.; and Robert Bellah, "Religious Aspects of Modernization in Turkey and Japan," *American Journal of Sociology*, 64, 1958, pp. 1–5.

71 "Perspective on the Functions of Religion in a Developing Country: Islam in Pakistan," *Journal for the Scientific Study of Religion*, 3, 1964, p. 237.

72 See Clifford Geertz, *The Religion of Java*.

73 Frederick Pike in *Religion, Revolution, and Reform: New Forces for Change in Latin America*, William D'Antonio and Frederick Pike, eds., p. 5.

74 Seymour Lipset, *Revolution and Counterrevolution*, p. 70.

churches are represented. There may be a sharp split between a European-(largely Spanish-) oriented priesthood in a Latin American country and the indigenous priests. The latter are more likely to be liberal, closer to the peasantry, more sympathetic with worker movements. Different religious orders compete with one another for influence, for support from the cardinal, thus opening up the possibility that one will be more responsive to change than others.

Latin America is now experiencing the revolutionary force of an urbanizing peasantry—the "surplus" population that so often breaks away from tradition. Their expectations have been raised, but their opportunities lag. Because of a long history of Church support for colonial oligarchies, the present ruling groups are anticlerical. They find it easy to oppose any reform efforts that come from the Church as "political meddling." Nevertheless some small signs of change are apparent: distribution of some ecclesiastical lands to peasants, calls by a few priests for greater liberty and equality of income, modernization of Church-supported schools, and the organization of reform-oriented Christian Democratic political parties.[75] It remains to be seen whether these tendencies will grow stronger and whether they will have that impact on the values and motives of the population that is so essential an ingredient for modernization.

Alongside these changes of Catholicism, one sees a growing Protestantism in Latin America. It still involves only a small minority of the population—scarcely 5 per cent—but it has expanded rapidly among the working classes of the rapidly industrializing cities. We see the familiar complex of factors: a recently urbanized population cut off from accustomed supports in village and family; a dramatic rise in aspirations; a sense of helplessness in dealing with a society that on one hand is governed by traditional privileges and pre-industrial institutions, but on the other is faced by growing anomie. In this context, Pentecostal sects particularly have begun to win converts. They challenge the very structure of the old order; they emphasize individualism; they encourage personal conduct patterned after the model of developed countries. "Protestantism thus seems to perform an adaptive function with regard to a series of highly disruptive changes which cannot otherwise be controlled or averted. And it seems capable of performing that function because it is change itself—a new, although certainly not the only available, resource for the solution of new problems."[76]

The Pentecostal sects in Latin America, as elsewhere, are predominantly otherworldly in doctrine. Their effect on economic development, if there is such an effect, will be indirect, transmitted by the ways in which they reorganize the values and motives of their adherents in relation to the society around them, while helping them deal with the stresses imposed by that society. How these values and motives will be translated into behavior de-

75 See ibid.; and John J. Johnson, ed., *Continuity and Change in Latin America.*

76 Emilio Willems, *Followers of the New Faith: Culture Change and the Rise of Protestantism in Brazil and Chile,* p. 256; see also his papers in D'Antonio and Pike, op. cit., Chap. 5, and "Validation of Authority in Pentecostal Sects of Chile and Brazil," *Journal for the Scientific Study of Religion,* 6, 1967, pp. 253–258. For comparative studies of Protestantism among Latin American populations, see Bryan Roberts, "Protestant Groups and Coping with Urban Life in Guatemala City," *American Journal of Sociology,* 73, 1968, pp. 753–767; and Anne Parsons, "The Pentecostal Immigrants," *Journal for the Scientific Study of Religion,* 4, 1965, pp. 183–197.

pends upon the structure of opportunities, with the latent qualities of inner-worldly asceticism, individualism, and economic activism becoming manifest only in situations where an expanding economy gives them reinforcement and meaning.[77]

These brief references to religious change in societies where traditional faiths have been closely tied to slowly changing, isolated, peasant conditions may indicate that the process of religious involvement, as one factor out of several in the process of modernization, is not a thing of the past. The evidences of religious involvement, however, are few. The effort to make new men and new societies in our time, as I have indicated, has come primarily from revolutionary quasi-religions. Unless there is great acceleration in the rate of change in the world religions, this seems likely to be the case in the future in most parts of the technologically developing world.

[77] This situational interpretation is emphasized by Bryan Roberts, op. cit.

Chapter Eighteen

RELIGION AND POLITICS

Many of the principles discussed in the chapters on social stratification and economics are applicable to the study of the relationships between religion and politics. We have referred to political processes and institutions at several points; however, they now become the focus of our attention. Though we shall be looking at some of the same facts, new questions arise when religio-political patterns are made the central interest.

Because many of the values for which men strive—power, prestige, income—are in scarce supply, every society is faced with disruptive tensions. If everyone were permitted to pursue these values by means of his own choosing, an organized society would be impossible. In every society, therefore, certain means (which differ widely from society to society) are approved as ways of maintaining or securing scarce values. Political institutions are the norms that designate how the ultimate coercive power—even to the extreme of the administration of death—shall be used, and by whom, to enforce the approved ways of achieving life's values.

The existence of a political system—and it will be explicit only in the more complex societies—does not solve the problem of order; it does not guarantee that the approved means for achieving scarce values will be employed. If the norms are not substantially self-enforcing, as a result of the socialization of the members of the society, the level of coercion has to be very high, with an increase in disruptive tensions. Moreover, the political authorities themselves, those who have the culturally established right to use coercive power, may violate the approved means to their own advantage. These influences are particularly important in the modern world, where continuous shifts in the claims and aspirations of many persons and groups affect not only the allocation of political power but the degree of acceptance of the legitimacy of the political systems themselves.

TYPES OF RELATIONSHIP BETWEEN RELIGION AND POLITICS

Religion may become involved in this political problem in many different ways:

1. Religious beliefs and practices may help to create socialized individuals who are substantially ready to abide by the norms of the society; and by its system of rewards and punishments, religion may inhibit the violations of those who have been inadequately socialized. The religious system may also help to set and enforce the limits on the use of coercive power by those who possess it. And by emphasizing common values, religion may reduce the sharpness of the tensions that result from the pursuit of scarce values. Although these relationships between religion and politics are present even in mobile and complex societies, they are seen in their purest form in stable, sacred societies. On this level, religious community and political community are virtually identical. These patterns are what one usually has in mind when he refers to "the integrative function of religion."

2. In societies where social differentiation and social change are important, other modes of relationship between religion and politics appear, supplementing and often contradicting the integrative relationship. On the one hand, the political authorities may become so powerful that, rather than having their use of coercive means limited and governed by religious values, they may succeed in transforming the religious institutions precisely into another instrument of coercion. To the degree that this happens (and nowhere is this tendency carried to its logical extreme, both because the rulers are themselves limited by the instrument they employ and because the less powerful members of a society would not long accept a religion that was *merely* a political agent), religious beliefs and practices become simply one manifestation of the political situation, and their control one phase of the basic political problem: preventing authorities from using their power to their own advantage. This development implies a change in the religious tradition and organization, a *selective* application of its doctrines, rites, and structures, emphasizing those that enhance the power of the rulers, and denying or obscuring those that might restrain it.

3. On the other hand, there may develop a sharp tension between religion and the political system. The founders and developers of the world religions, struggling with the problems of evil and suffering, have propounded "radical" solutions that make no reference to political boundaries. They may devalue, or even oppose, political institutions and the claims for the allegiance of individuals that are made by the state. The religious requirements may even contradict political requirements.

The key task of the sociology of religion in its examination of religion and politics is to discover the conditions under which these various relationships occur and their consequences for society. One pattern is seldom found in "pure" form, of course, so the task is complicated by the need to study various combinations, to analyze the effects of the interaction between a religion of world brotherhood, with its suprapolitical claims, and a political order in which the authorities are trying to forge religion into another instrument of power.

Identity of Religious-Group and Political-Group Membership. The first mode of relationship—religion as a factor in the integration of society—relatively uncomplicated by the other two modes is most likely to occur in isolated, preliterate societies, especially where religious specialists have not yet appeared to an important degree. The boundaries of the tribe or society and the boundaries of the religious system are identical. The gods of the group guarantee or represent its values; they fight its opponents. The beliefs and rites of the group express the sharing of a common fate.[1] No religious system has been "invented," in such settings, that could challenge the validity of the group's norms or give them a merely relative position, for this requires that individuals be given some point of reference outside the tribe from which to see and judge its standards. With fewer religious specialists present, there has been less development of a separate religious structure, a center of power that might compete with the political structures. And the political authorities, without such a system to manipulate, are themselves fully circumscribed in their views by the beliefs of their own society. Thus they are unlikely to be able to use the religious patterns to reinforce their own power beyond the limits of the established norms.

In primitive societies it is impossible to draw sharp distinctions among the institutional patterns of religion, kinship, economics, government, and education. They are part of a closely articulated social whole. This does not mean that the members of "sacred" societies make no distinction between religious acts and other acts, nor that members of "secular" societies clearly differentiate religion from the rest of life. The contrast is not so sharp. Even in highly secularized societies, as we shall see, a sense of common purpose between religion and politics, particularly in times of crisis, is by no means lacking. This is vastly more true, however, in relatively stable and isolated situations, even where a universalistic religious creed is accepted. As Robertson Smith writes:

The Spanish peasants who insult the Madonna of the neighbouring village, and come to blows over the merits of rival local saints, still do homage to the same antique conception of religion which in Egypt animated the feuds of Ombos and Tentyra, and made hatred for each other's gods the formula that summed up all the local jealousies of the two towns.[2]

This tendency toward an identity of religious communion and civil community is clearly shown in the early history of Israel. Separation of church and state was, of course, utterly inconceivable. To change nationality was to change religion. Smith expresses it well:

When David in the bitterness of his heart complains of those who "have driven him out from connection with the heritage of Jehovah," he represents them as saying to him, "Go, serve other gods." In driving him to seek refuge in another land and another nationality, they compel him to change his religion, for a man's religion is part of his political connection. "Thy sister," says Naomi to Ruth, "is gone back unto her people and unto her gods"; and Ruth replies, "Thy people shall be my people, and thy God my God": the change of nationality involves a change of cult.[3]

1 This does not mean that religious beliefs and rites are free of the tensions and conflicts which characterize all human societies. Indeed, those tensions and conflicts often find religious expression; but in such a way that they are less likely to escalate, to produce a permanent split in the social structure. See, for example, John Middleton, *Lugbara Religion;* and Godfrey Lienhardt, *Divinity and Experience.*

2 W. Robertson Smith, *Lectures on the Religion of the Semites,* p. 32.

3 Ibid., p. 36.

The Use of Religion by Political Powers. The relationship between religion and politics becomes more complicated in societies that are more highly stratified and have developed religious specialists. This is often accompanied by some culture contact and social change—and the opportunity, therefore, for some groups to see that their values are not universally shared.[4] This loosens the hold of the social norms; it raises the possibility that some members of the society will acquire an instrumental attitude toward religion—seeing in it an instrument of power—an attitude that is unlikely so long as religion is seen and experienced only within the confines of one stable society. The ruling class is now able to see in religion a means of preserving order—an order that places them at the apex. It is probably seldom that they simply cynically manipulate a religious system. They too believe in it—in fact, they find it very easy to believe in a religion that helps to preserve the social patterns that reward them so richly; and they are therefore likely to be zealous.[5]

"In all societies studied here," Eisenstadt writes in his important comparative work, "the rulers attempted to portray themselves and the political systems they established as the bearers of special cultural symbols and missions." [6] They founded and promoted academies, schools, and religious institutions; and they sought to control, and sometimes to repress, independent institutions. In a contemporary illustration, President Nguyen Van Thieu of South Vietnam has ordered authorities to arrest Buddhist monks and Catholic priests who make "political sermons" to "inflame the people." "Monks and priests are free to go to their pagodas and churches to conduct ceremonies and pray. But if they deliver political sermons to stir up the people, the province chiefs should arrest them and then report to me." [7]

The religious groups, however, were not without power; they fought to preserve autonomy and to win some control within the political order, sometimes against severe odds. In a recent paper, Vatro Murvar has observed that "in contrast to the peculiarly fluctuating Western relationship of religious and political powers, continuously in conflict with each other, the Russian religious structures consistently follow the more common pattern of monistic unity and are characterized by total subordination to the political system." [8] He describes the rather rapid accommodation of the Russian Orthodox Church to the Soviet regime. Yet in the same paper he reports that "at least 117 to 125 bishops were kept in prison more or less

4 The contrast among values may take place within a society, in the form of distinct religious traditions. Under some conditions, this heightens the tension between religion and politics, as we shall see.

5 Explicit political use of religion can be illustrated in almost every tradition. See, for example, C. K. Yang, *Religion in Chinese Society*, Chap. 5; Melford Spiro, *Burmese Supernaturalism*, pp. 131–138; Donald E. Smith, *Religion and Politics in Burma*, Chap. 1; S. N. Eisenstadt, *The Political Systems of Empires;* Reuben Levy, *The Social Structure of Islam*, Chap. 7; Preserved Smith, *The Age of the Reformation;* Ray Abrams, *Preachers Present Arms.*

6 Op. cit., p. 141.

7 *Honolulu Advertiser*, Feb. 2, 1969, p. 1.

8 "Russian Religious Structures. A Study in Persistent Church Subservience," *Journal for the Scientific Study of Religion,* 7, 1968, p. 1.

permanently." [9] The use of religion by political powers, it seems fair to say, is not without some opposition, even under highly autocratic conditions.[10]

It is difficult to distinguish between a situation in which religion reinforces a stable social order and one in which religion is used by those who possess political power to their own advantage, in violation of the norms of that order. Most outsiders might agree that the Russian Orthodox Church of 1915 was not simply "integrating" Russian society, but was clearly an instrument of power in the hands of the aristocracy. Or it might perhaps be shown that the fairly explicit and organized effort to revive Shintoism in Japan in the nineteenth century was rooted in the desire of the ruling classes to increase their power and to oppose or control the tradition-breaking effects of industrialization. Can one be so certain, however, of the relationship between religion and the political authority in Ancient Egypt? There is a grave danger that one will claim that religion is simply another coercive force used by the ruling class when he is referring to a social order that he does not like, and will hold that it is "integrative of social order" in referring to a social system of which he approves or about which he is indifferent. An objective solution of this problem is impossible so long as "order" and "integration" are implicitly assumed to be normal and good. Perhaps we can reduce this hazard if we remind ourselves again that a social order may be evil, from the perspective of a given value. We also get an important clue to the distinction between the integrative and the political function of religion by observing the *selective* development of the religious system. If those elements that might challenge the power of the ruling group are denied or even forcibly suppressed (as in the case of many Christian sectarian movements), there is a clear sign of the political use of religion. Kai Erikson has shown that the antinomian controversy in the Massachusetts Bay Colony, though couched in the language of religion, was basically a political struggle. The elders could fight Anne Hutchinson and her supporters more effectively, and probably more earnestly, on doctrinal than on organizational and political grounds.[11]

Religious Challenges to Political Authority. The third type of relationship between religion and politics has its beginning in the appearance of religious specialists, although other factors must be added before it can develop fully. When religious life is simply part of the daily activity of laymen, it will not be separated from the economic, political, and other questions with which they are concerned. The kinds of solutions to life's great problems that religion will develop in such circumstances will be tied closely to the rest of the culture of the society. Ritual may be fairly elaborate, but theology and religious-group structure will be far simpler. Even where the management of the religious system moves away from the whole group

9 Ibid., p. 11.

10 On the whole, German churches accommodated themselves to Hitler. It should be noted, of course, that for a number of years, secular powers did so too, as shown in the Munich Agreement. For discussions of the responses of churches to Hitler, see Guenther Lewy, *The Catholic Church and Nazi Germany;* Gordon Zahn, *German Catholics in Hitler's Wars;* Franklin Littel, "The Protestant Churches and Totalitarianism (Germany, 1933–1945)," in *Totalitarianism,* Carl Friedrich, ed., pp. 109–116.

11 See Kai Erikson, *Wayward Puritans,* pp. 71–107. The struggle against the Quakers twenty years later also had strong political elements. (pp. 107–136.)

into the hands of the chief or ruler, the conception of a universal religion is still impossible. The political structure and the religious structure are identical; their conceptions are mutually harmonious. The political manipulation of religion to enhance the power of the rulers may come in at this point, although this is unlikely until culture contact has pointed up the variations that exist in social norms among societies—including the norms of religion. Nonspecialists practicing a received religion or a priest-king ruling over a stable society will not develop a conception of religion that reaches beyond the boundaries of that society, however, because they cannot conceive of a view that is not tied completely to the social system.

Whenever specialists appear, however, new forces are set in motion. Even if these specialists are functionaries of the ruler, their organization will begin to take on some measure of autonomy, for they will be the experts in managing the approved rites, the authorities in matters of dogma. Because they give full time to religion, they can develop more elaborate systems to deal with the problems with which religion is concerned. The stage is set for personal struggles for power between religious and political leaders, for clashes in principle, for conflicts between the ecclesiastical and political organizations. These struggles may be entirely political, involving only disagreements over the use or distribution of secular power. But they may represent the appearance of religious ideas that are not harmonious with the secular institutions, that contradict their claims or values. This marks the appearance of a new stage in the relationship of religion to society. Religion seems to transcend society.

How is this development to be explained? Some writers believe that the appearance of great religious leaders cannot be explained simply in terms of their own societies and their cultures, that, indeed, an objective interpretation of their appearance is impossible. Joachim Wach wrote:

Now we must concentrate our attention on one of the most significant phenomena in religion and one that has repeated itself often enough to have tremendous historical importance—the emergence of a *new faith* prepared for by the protest against the rejection of the traditional cult. The change affects all fields of expression of religious experience—theology, cult, and organization. . . . It is generally agreed that the emergence of a great new religious faith is one of the inexplicable mysteries which have accompanied the ascent of man and bears the most convincing testimony to the contingency and spontaneity of his spiritual history. We have reviewed the origin of the great founded religions from this point of view and have stressed the fact that no prior preparation and path-breaking could alone explain the emergence of the new inspiration and its effect.[12]

This is the kind of question about which debate is likely to be particularly fruitless, because of differences in basic assumptions. The scientist cannot afford to be dogmatic, for he certainly cannot show empirically that Professor Wach was in error. He can only say: *If my assumptions are correct,* or, *to the degree that they are correct,* the emergence of a great new faith is not "one of the inexplicable mysteries," but the product of certain interacting forces. And he must try to go as far as he can from that starting point, unsatisfactory as it will be to those who prefer a different starting

12 Joachim Wach, *Sociology of Religion,* p. 307.

point. For the scientist to give up his fundamental premises when confronted by the enormously difficult questions pertaining to the appearance of the world religions or in face of the sacred attitudes that surround contemporary faiths, is only to become a poor theologian. Better than this, in the writer's judgment, is to be consistent in one's interpretation, however unimportant a science of religion may be considered by some to be.

From this point of view, then, we shall hold that the development of religions that seem to transcend the social systems from which they come is the work of creative religious leaders, struggling with the problems with which religion is basically concerned. Social change and culture contact have made them discontented with the traditional solutions. They propound or invent partially new interpretations of suffering and roads to salvation. The believer is likely to give his primary attention to the "new" elements, whereas the objective student must also point out the continuity with tradition and the borrowing. Arnold Toynbee lists eighty-seven correspondences between the story of Jesus' life and the accounts of various Hellenic "saviors." The discoveries of the Dead Sea Scrolls support the idea that there was substantial continuity between Christianity and earlier religious developments. Yet the founders of the universalist religions must also be recognized as important turning points in religious development. They appear in settings where the social systems have been peculiarly unable to fill the needs with which religion deals. Suffering—not simply physical deprivation—has been acute, and the religious imagination leaps the bounds of the society that has caused that suffering. It refuses to accept the answer that the pains of earthly existence within a society seem to require.[13] The world religions, moreover, have appeared at world cross-roads, at points where the limitations not simply of a society, but of society itself, might be observed and felt. Such a setting also accounts for the blending of diverse elements and for the inventiveness that so frequently springs from culture contact. One who follows such a train of thought is not among those who "generally agree" that the founded religions are inexplicable mysteries.

What are the implications of universalist religions for politics? These religions create tensions with the political order; they encourage loyalties that are larger than the tribe or nation. A unified God for the entire world, particularly a God of love, brings a demand for brotherliness that may sharply contradict the requirements of citizenship. As Weber pointed out, the ultimate appeal of a political group is to force; it is concerned with power, and "reasons of state" may require action that is repugnant to or meaningless to religion:

The state's absolute end is to safeguard (or to change) the external and internal distribution of power; ultimately, this end must seem meaningless to any universalist religion of salvation. This fact has held and still holds, even more so, for foreign policy. It is absolutely essential for every political association to appeal to the naked violence of coercive means in the face of outsiders as well as in the face of internal enemies. It is only this very appeal to violence that constitutes a political association in our terminology. The state is an association that

13 There was a strong quality of world rejection in the universalistic religions, particularly in their earliest forms. See Robert Bellah, "Religious Evolution," *American Sociological Review*, 29, 1964, pp. 358–374.

claims the monopoly of the legitimate use of violence, and cannot be defined in any other manner.

The Sermon on the Mount says "resist no evil." In opposition, the state asserts: "You *shall* help right to triumph by the use of *force,* otherwise you too may be responsible for injustice." [14]

Such a conflict could not occur between a tribal religion and the political processes of that tribe. A religion that is confined to one stable society is an instrument in the pursuit of its individual and group values and a compensation for the failure to achieve them; but it is never a repudiation of those values. The universal religions, however, represent a certain amount of disillusionment. The absolute level of suffering has probably not been greater in the settings where they developed than that experienced by many other groups, but it was an experience of suffering in the context of greater aspirations. The growing complexity of culture and the increased intercultural contact encouraged dreams of change and accomplishment. Frustration and disappointment took on an added poignancy in the setting of the tribal conflicts and religious confusion of the Arabian peoples, or in face of the repeated denials of the Jewish hope for national independence and greatness, or as a result of the rigidity of an orthodox Hinduism that led to the Buddha's "sectarian" protest. Only an enormously vivid and radical religious formula could seem to yield satisfaction in such situations as these. Particularly among those in whom the religious interest was strongest, but also to some degree among their followers, the quest for earthly success and the hope for alleviation of suffering through secular processes seemed vain.

This conflict between the universal religions and "the world" is only one tendency among several, of course, and it is constantly obscured and modified by the other modes of relationship we have discussed. It achieves a fairly full institutional embodiment only in sects that, by definition, are relatively powerless minority movements. Yet the conflict is there, even in the churches, which are accommodated to society and its political institutions but never fully in agreement with them. In the last analysis, a universalist religion, consistently carried through, *must* conflict at various points with the political activity of a society, which is concerned for only a segment of mankind and makes its ultimate appeal to force. In some circumstances, the conflict may be very rudimentary, almost lost in the shaping of the religious institutions into political instruments, but unless the religious system around which those institutions have been built is completely destroyed, an implicit conflict will still remain. Indeed, as the world grows smaller and more interdependent, it would seem that *only* a universalist religion can offer a road to salvation that will be meaningful to those who recognize this interdependence.

Weber has brilliantly described how politics may enter into direct competition with religion at decisive points, particularly in the requirements of modern war for "an unconditionally devoted and sacrificial community among the combatants," a community that is nationwide, not a universal brotherhood.

Moreover, war does something to the warrior which, in its concrete meaning, is unique: it makes him experience a consecrated meaning of death which is

14 Max Weber, *From Max Weber,* H. H. Gerth and C. W. Mills, eds., p. 334.

characteristic only of death in war. . . . Death on the field of battle differs from death that is only man's common lot. . . . As the values of culture increasingly unfold and are sublimated to immeasurable heights, such ordinary death marks an end where only a beginning seems to make sense. Death on the field of battle differs from this merely unavoidable dying in that in war, and in this massiveness *only* in war, the individual can *believe* that he knows he is dying "for" something. The why and the wherefore of his facing death can, as a rule, be so indubitable to him that the problem of the "meaning" of death does not even occur to him. . . .

This location of death within a series of meaningful and consecrated events ultimately lies at the base of all endeavors to support the autonomous dignity of the polity resting on force. Yet the way in which death can be conceived as meaningful in such endeavors points in directions that differ radically from the direction in which the theodicy of death in a religion of brotherliness may point. The brotherliness of a group of men bound together in war must appear devalued in such brotherly religions. It must be seen as a mere reflection of the technically sophisticated brutality of the struggle. And the inner-worldly consecration of death in war must appear as a glorification of fratricide.[15]

That the churches of the world religions frequently support the national interpretation of death does not contradict Weber's point, but it does show the limits of its application. The universalist theme is often driven into the background by social integration and political themes, in the relationship between religion and nations. What kinds of responses can religion make to these tensions with politics? The nature and the degree of the conflict that Weber described will vary with the religious tradition and with the structure of power in society. The responses are affected by the same influences. The religious institutions may themselves employ violence to establish the supremacy of their claims over what they consider to be merely political claims. This is not uncommon, particularly in the history of Christianity and Islam. This is one of the two "solutions" that Weber holds are consistent with the universalist views of the world religions in their dealings with the counter claims of politics. He calls them puritanism and mysticism. "Puritanism, with its particularism of grace and vocational asceticism, believes in the fixed and revealed commandments of a God who is otherwise quite incomprehensible. It interprets God's will to mean that these commandments should be imposed upon the creatural world by the means of this world, namely violence—for the world is subject to violence and ethical barbarism." [16] It is not difficult to see how such a response, even if it starts out primarily as a religious protest against limiting secular claims, might readily be transformed into a secular and political movement itself, thinly disguised as a universalist religion.

On the other hand, the mystic's "solution" to the conflict between the claims of religion and politics is an extreme antipolitical attitude: Resist not evil, Turn the other cheek. "It withdraws from the pragma of violence which no political action can escape." [17] This entails as many risks for an ethic of brotherliness as does puritanism, for in disregarding the hard tasks of politics, it does not eliminate them. Only a few are privileged or con-

15 Weber, op. cit., pp. 335–336.

16 Ibid., p. 336.

17 Ibid.

demned—as you wish—to become mystics, while the rest of mankind continues to pursue scarce values. So long as that is true, the political problem of order remains, and a religious response that forgets this leaves the solution to other forces.

Neither puritanism or mysticism, then, escapes the dilemma of religion, which is rooted in the fact that religion is only one of man's interests and the predominant one for only a few. The universalist religions have brought a new factor into the interaction of politics and religion, but they have not transformed that interaction; the two earlier modes of relationship continue to prevail.

FACTORS INFLUENCING RELIGIO-POLITICAL RELATIONSHIPS

We shall be concerned primarily with examination of religion and politics in those societies characterized by complex governmental systems and by highly institutionalized religions with universalist traditions. These patterns of church-state relationship, which we can conveniently call them, will be the object of our attention in the next chapter. They will be better understood, however, if they are seen in context with a wider range of patterns. I will try to suggest that context by brief discussions of three general conditions, involving important theoretical problems, which influence the relationships of religion and politics: the interaction of the three modes we have noted; competition between religious and political action; and types of relationship, from pluralistic to segmental, between religious structures and other elements in the social structure.

Interaction of the Three Modes of Relationship of Religion and Politics

We have emphasized that older relationships between the religious and political orders do not disappear when newer ones are added. A "layered" pattern is more likely to develop, with several religious traditions interacting with the political situation in different ways. Figure 18–1 may suggest the possible relationships.

In most societies today, all three levels of interaction can be found, although in widely differing mixtures. From the point of view of this chapter, the second pattern is most interesting—the competitive use of religion in political controversy. It is almost always qualified, however, by pressures toward a civil religion, designed to unify the nation, and a universalist religion, which criticizes the political processes from a supranational perspective.

The nature of the mixture of these various forms of relationship cannot be accounted for simply by reference to the values of the religions involved. Knowledge of both the stratification system and the history of the society is essential. An almost miscellaneous listing of situations in which Catholicism has influenced politics, for example, reveals the Church as a source of internal unity, as a symbol of internal struggle, as a focus of opposition in nation-building, and as an instrument of supranational cohesion: To the Irish, the Catholic Church is a symbol of their long struggle against the British; hence many identify strongly with it. In South Vietnam, the Catholic population tend to be those who were in relatively favored positions

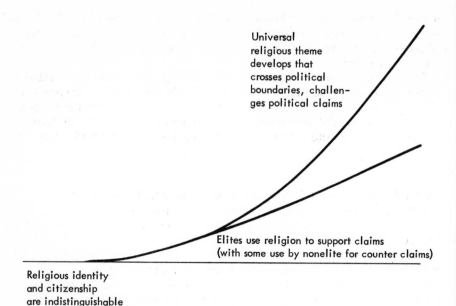

Universal religious theme develops that crosses political boundaries, challenges political claims

Elites use religion to support claims (with some use by nonelite for counter claims)

Religious identity and citizenship are indistinguishable

Time ⟶

FIGURE 18–1. *Modes of relationship between religion and politics*

during the French era; many are refugees from North Vietnam; their status and probably their beliefs have made them intensely anticommunist. Because the experience and the interests of the Buddhists in Vietnam tend to be different, the election of more than half of the senators by Catholic-bloc voters (representing 10 per cent of the population) in the 1967 election is a source of continuing political controversy. In the Philippines, the early nationalist movement was anticlerical, in protest against the favored position of the Spanish clergy.[18] While the Hapsburgs, through several generations, ruled the Austro-Hungarian Empire, they used the Catholic Church as a symbol of unity, because they were unable, as were the more homogeneous Western states, to use a common nationhood for this purpose.[19] These situations affected the relationships between religion and politics differently. That is not to say that the values and polity of the Catholic Church were not involved, but to emphasize the way in which they were affected by particular settings.

To reverse our perspective, we can examine elements of value and polity that influence the relationships between religion and politics. Donald E. Smith has specified a number of them for Asian religions:

1. *Theory of history.* Great concern with the course of history tends to increase a religion's involvement in politics.

2. *Attitude toward other religions.* Attitudes of intolerance reinforce the tendency to use the political process for communal advantage.

18 See Fred von der Mehden, *Religion and Nationalism in Southeast Asia.*

19 See Dennison Rusinow, in *Churches and States: The Religious Institution and Modernization,* Kalman Silvert, ed., Chap. 4.

3. *Capacity for ecclesiastical organization.* The more highly organized a religion, the greater its involvement in politics.

4. *Political and religious functions.* Tradition of fusion of these two functions tends to increase a religion's involvement in politics.

5. *Tendency to regulate society.* The stronger this tendency, the greater the area of conflict between religious authority and the state.[20]

In Asia, the sharpest contrast on the basis of these criteria is between Islam and Buddhism, with Hinduism in between, closer to the latter than to the former. To Buddhism, history is not ultimately significant (although in practice it is often taken seriously); to Islam, history is decisive and this world is of primary importance. Buddhism is highly tolerant of other religions; Islam tends to be intolerant. Neither has a complex ecclesiastical organization, although the Sangha, the Buddhist monastic order, may be well organized, and the Ulama, doctors of law, in Islam can be mobilized to action. Buddhist monks renounce the world; but from Muhammad onward, temporal and spiritual authority have been merged in Islam. There is no attempt in Buddhism to regulate society, whereas in Islam, the law is detailed and full.[21]

These are general descriptions, of course, and disregard variation in space and time. In recent years, one could not readily say that in most Buddhist lands, "the most important thing that the individual can do is to extricate himself from history." [22] (And, oppositely, otherworldly sects are not unknown in Islam.) Under some conditions, Buddhist tolerance gives way to political activity and pressure. In Ceylon, for example, the Sinhalese Buddhist majority, inferior in economic power and education, has used the state to strengthen a politically oriented communalism by which they have sought, since the mid-1950's, to improve their situation.[23] Such variations from the "typical" pattern of relationship between religion and society emphasize the need for taking account of the structural setting. They do not, however, argue for disregard of variation in the religious cultures involved.

Competition Between Religious and Political Action

It has often been observed that religion and politics compete, under some conditions, as modes of adaptation. Sven Rydenfelt has shown that two counties in Northern Sweden, although similarly disadvantaged economically, have different patterns of religion and politics. In one, the Communist vote was 2 per cent, the vote for the Liberal Party, associated with religious radicalism, was 30 per cent. In the other he found a contrasting pattern: a 21 per cent vote for the Communist Party and 9 per cent for the Liberal Party.[24] H. Richard Niebuhr has attributed the relative absence of sectarian protest movements in Western industrial societies during the last

20 Donald Smith, *South Asian Politics and Religion,* p. 19.

21 Ibid., Chap. 1.

22 Ibid., p. 10.

23 See A. Jeyaratnam Wilson and C. D. S. Siriwardane, ibid., Chaps. 23 and 24. See also E. Sarkisyanz, *Buddhist Backgrounds of the Burmese Revolution.*

24 Cited by Seymour Lipset, *Political Man,* pp. 488–489.

several generations to the availability of radical political programs.[25] In some contexts, potential members for political protest movements may abound in religious organizations and vice versa. "Leon Trotsky was so aware of the similarity of revolutionary Marxism to sectarianism that in the late 1890's he successfully recruited the first working-class members of the South Russian Worker's Union among adherents to religious sects." [26]

Deprivation As a Source of Religious and Political Action. To interpret these patterns, we need to explore the conditions that support a religious, and those that support a political, expression of protest. If we assume that some forms of deprivation predispose the members of a group to protest or to adopt some other adaptation-seeking activity, how can we predict the nature of that activity? Lipset notes that deprivation does not automatically lead to support for political parties with programs of social change. "Three conditions facilitate such a response: effective channels of communication, low belief in the possibilities of individual social mobility, and the absence of traditionalist ties to a conservative party." [27] One can extend this idea by suggesting that the strength of channels of communication from religious movements and the presence or absence of ties to political parties may influence the likelihood of a religious expression of discontent. The dominant response, of course may be neither religious nor political. Thus we might chart possible results of deprivation as in Figure 18–2.

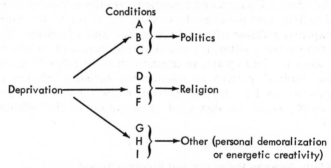

FIGURE 18–2. *Deprivation, politics, and religion*

In general terms, the conditions can be specified on structural, cultural, and character levels as in Figure 18–3, so that conditions approximating those in the lefthand column are likely to lead to political action; those approximating the righthand column are likely to lead to religious action.[28]

Many mixed situations, of course, can be described. A person close to the religious end of the scale on the character dimension may find himself

25 *The Social Sources of Denominationalism.*

26 Rodney Stark, "Class, Radicalism, and Religious Involvement in Great Britain," *American Sociological Review*, 29, 1964, p. 701.

27 Op. cit., p. 248.

28 "In France, for example, ecological studies which contrast degree of religious practice with Communist strength show that the Communists are most successful in regions in which the 'anticlerical' wave had previously suppressed much of the traditional fidelity to Catholicism." Seymour Lipset, *The First New Nation*, p. 530.

Political action likely		Religious action likely
A. Extensive channels of communication to strong party system. Extensive contact with politically oriented reference groups, etc.	Structure ├─────────────┤	D. Extensive channels of communication to strong religious organizations. Extensive contact with religiously oriented reference groups, etc.
B. Values of the surrounding culture and subculture expressed primarily in political terms.	Culture ├─────────────┤	E. Values of the surrounding culture and subculture expressed primarily in religious terms.
C. Individual has been social- ized to secular views. Other character tend- encies also predispose to political action.	Character ├─────────────┤	F. Individual has been social- ized to religious views. Other character tend- encies also predispose to religious action.

FIGURE 18–3. *Conditions supporting a religious or political response*

surrounded by political values and interacting with politically oriented persons. If one or the other pull is much stronger, it may win out; or the individual may feel so cross-pressured that he withdraws. If both political and religious influences are strong, a person may support a religiously toned political movement or a politically toned religious movement; or he may be active in both religion and politics, simultaneously or succession- ally.

The union of religious and political motives is probably an unstable one, since the road to power and the road to salvation seldom seem to run parallel courses. In a remarkable account of the Protestant social move- ment in Germany and Austria in the late nineteenth century, Paul Göhre describes the efforts of the evangelisch-soziale Kongress to integrate the Christian-Socialist party and the Protestant labor associations (*evangelische Arbeitervereine*). The Congress saw itself in contrast with both the purely secular Social Democrats and the purely religious leaders of the Protestant church. It could not, however, encompass for long its own internal divisions, between an older, more conservative approach and a younger, more pro- letarian approach, and between those who wanted the movement to pro- mote a social-ethical trend within the churches and those who supported a social-political trend aimed at establishing a genuine party.[29]

It can be hypothesized, to return to our paradigm, that persons who fit none of these situations, who lack resources, either political or religious, on the structural, cultural, and character levels, are likely to respond to deprivation in more individualistic terms. Whether their responses will be creative or destructive will depend on the resources they have available.

This outline of the problem may take us a certain way in determining who will struggle with deprivation in religious, political, or other terms. It leaves a major question unexamined, however. What will be the *direc-*

29 Paul Göhre, *Die evangelisch-soziale Bewegung* (*ihre Geschichte und ihre Ziele*).

tion of his protest? Will he be politically left, right, or center? Will he support a religious movement that attacks, ignores, or withdraws from the world around it?

We can begin to answer these questions by noting that deprivation can take many forms. There is a large literature developing the concept of *relative* deprivation. It is not so much the absolute levels of income, power, and prestige, for example, that influence the political and religious behavior of an individual or the policies of a group as it is their levels when compared with significant reference individuals and groups. It can be argued that the addition of the concept of "relative" to studies of deprivation is almost a redundancy, since virtually everything can be stated in relative terms. We cannot even know whether we are rich or poor, powerful or powerless, prestigeful or disdained without a standard of comparison. We use our memories or our hopes, the Joneses or the national median.

Research on relative deprivation is valuable, not because it underlines this relativity, but because it is beginning to specify the structure of comparisons: Who is deprived of what, in comparison with what standards, and with what results? It is often social change—a shift in the relative balance of various values—that makes a comparison visible. When it becomes visible, its salience for religious and political action increases.

In an earlier chapter we noted that a special form of relative deprivation has received a great deal of attention and has led to controversial interpretations. I refer to the absence of status consistency or status crystallization. If one measures himself and is measured by several scales—income, education, occupational prestige, ethnicity—the possibility arises that outcomes for the several scales will be different. Thus one may be high educationally, but medium or low in income and ethnic rating; or high in income though low in education and prestige. Measures of the consequences of the various mixtures have not been consistent. Problems of definition, of determining breaks in the various scales, of taking account of the effects of the context have proved to be severe. In addition, little attention has been paid to the character variable. It seems likely that the effects of various forms of status inconsistency vary, depending upon the ways in which they are perceived by the individuals involved, how important they rate the various measures, and with whom they compare themselves. Thus a high education-low income combination may have one consequence for the person who ranks intellectual values highly, relates most fully to other highly educated persons, and is relatively uninterested in making money. It may have another consequence for a person with the same combination of education and income who brings different character tendencies to bear.[30]

Since the research on status inconsistency has not explored its possible consequences for religious behavior, I simply mention here some hypotheses regarding the probable effects of deprivation. We would expect on theoretical grounds, but cannot support empirically, that those who felt culturally

30 Fred Silberstein and Melvin Seeman found that a character variable—attitudes toward mobility—was essential to the interpretation of the relationship between mobility experience and prejudice. See "Social Mobility and Prejudice," *American Journal of Sociology*, Nov., 1959, pp. 258–264.

deprived, who, for example, sensed they had "insufficient" prestige because of their low educational or occupational rank, would tend toward a conservative religious perspective. A person with low power—as measured perhaps by income—but a higher ranking according to prevailing cultural values would be structurally deprived; he would tend toward a liberal or an "aggressive sectarian" type of religion. One who felt deprived of self-confidence, poise, mental or physical health, and other qualities as a person —what in our terms can best be called a sense of character deprivation— would tend toward middle-of-the-road movements that accepted, but tended to disregard, the social order.

Charles Glock has developed ideas along this line with the suggestion that five types of deprivation can be distinguished and related to various forms of religious movement.[31] He refers to economic, social, organismic, ethical, and psychic forms of deprivation. These can, I believe, be reduced to three without doing an injustice to his argument, for he sees one of his categories, psychic deprivation, as being "primarily a consequence of severe and unresolved social deprivation," and also "somewhat akin to ethical deprivation." [32] To approach the empirical range, we doubtless need a statement of the several possible dominant-variant combinations. (There would be six logical possibilities if we started with three dominant types of deprivation.) Using only three types, however, based on the "primary" or dominant form of deprivation, we can associate them with oppositional social movements (whether religious or political) in the case of structural or economic deprivation, with conservative movements in the case of cultural (social) deprivation, and with various forms of "ritualism" involving acceptance of the social order in the case of character deprivation.[33]

It should not be forgotten that these are analytic categories. At best they indicate primary types of adaptation to the specified conditions. Actual religious or political movements are likely to derive their "energy" from all three sources of deprivation, so that the task for the preparation of a more adequate typology is to chart the common empirical mixtures on the basis of careful measurements. It is not difficult to contrast the more extreme cases. The radical left, and its religious equivalent, the aggressive sect, is made up of those who see their hope for a new society frustrated, and they see no way, within the system, of attaining it. The radical right and its religious equivalent, the withdrawal sect, is made up of those who see their vision of the good life disappearing, and they see no way of restoring it within the system. Since both require drastic changes of structure or of the dominant trends, they are alike in strategy. They deny the legitimacy

31 "The Role of Deprivation in the Origin and Evolution of Religious Groups," in *Religion and Social Conflict*, Robert Lee and Martin Marty, eds., pp. 24–36. He does not, however, deal with status inconsistency as an element in deprivation.

32 Ibid., pp. 28–29.

33 Use of "ritualism" in this context may suggest some parallel—and I think correctly —with Robert Merton's discussion of types of response to anomie. See his *Social Theory and Social Structure*, rev. ed., Chap. 4. There are also valuable parallels in Melvin Seeman's paper, "On the Meaning of Alienation," *American Sociological Review*, 24, 1959, pp. 783–791, which I will not at this time attempt to develop. When we achieve some consistency in our concepts dealing with deprivation, alienation, and anomie, they will become more powerful instruments of analysis.

of the prevailing structure, refuse to accept compromise, and promote polarizing strategies.

When several forms of deprivation pile up, the tendency toward deviation becomes powerful. In the United States today, for example: 1) There are strong forces weakening the structures of white supremacy. 2) Fundamentalist religion, Protestant and Catholic, is severely challenged. 3) Those trained to believe in a laissez-faire type of economy (small business, family farms, and individual initiative) see the rapid growth of a managerial economy, with large bureaucracies and universalistic hiring practices, and an ever-present government. 4) Simple virtues of hard work and categorical moral views no longer seem adequate in a complex, specialized, computerized, rapidly changing society. 5) The more old-fashioned military men, who have found their intellectual exhilaration in studying competing strategies for the battle of Gettysburg, find decision-making farmed out to the Rand Corporation or other "think tanks"—or to "Rand types" within the Pentagon. 6) East European immigrants and refugees, seeking satisfying positions in a new society, see the societies in which they held some status dominated by a radical program that has little room for their values or their kinds of skills; they become specialists in warning their new land about the first signs of presumably similar developments.

This somewhat random list contains several forms of structural and cultural deprivation, but the emphasis is on the latter: A wide range of values is being threatened for those in certain social locations in American society. Some will be peculiarly sensitive to the value shifts in three or four of the areas mentioned above. They are prime candidates for fundamentalist movements, whether religious or political.[34] Not all who experience such threats, however, are equally ready to support such movements. There are a few small-town, high-school-graduate, Southern businessmen, lifelong members of the Southern Baptist Church, who preferred Nixon or Humphrey to Wallace in 1968. Character variables must be brought into the analysis. Special circumstances have led them to internalize values that are uncommon among their fellows. And variation in the degree of self-acceptance, authoritarianism, and other tendencies qualifies the effects of cultural deprivation.

When we examine the deprivations of those who make radical religious or political responses, we see that they are more structural than cultural. These people know the kind of world they want; indeed, they see slow movement toward it. But their aspirations for change have been sharply raised by visions of what might be; and, frustrated by the reversals, the rigidities, and the retardation, they are burdened with a great feeling of powerlessness. Many of those who are making radical responses in the United States, for example, possess the skills necessary for success; they support the slowly emerging new set of values; but rather than being content with the trends, they are deeply unhappy at the speed of change. (Some, in an effort to overcome their own ambivalences—they do not *wholeheartedly* approve of the directions of change, or they actually believe change is proceeding as fast as possible, but do not want to seem unduly satisfied among their fellows—even misperceive the direction of the change.) Thus we see

34 I shall make some reference to this topic in the next chapter.

again that revolution, whether religious or political, is not typically carried through by the most deprived, but by those for whom the trends of history have opened up new visions of possible worlds. Their problem is not norm-lessness but a sense of powerlessness. As they view contemporary American society, they see a civil rights movement that crawls; they see religious changes that are minimal, even though headed in the right direction according to their values; they see the fruits of economic productivity being unevenly distributed and expended for trivial rather than basic goods; they see the possibilities of a world order continually smashed, despite occasional small accomplishments, by nationally sovereign decisions to use violence to achieve parochial goals; they see their parents—from a generation that opened up the possibilities of a new world—moving toward it with great hesitation. In short, they see the Establishment, in the government, the university, the church, the family, the corporation. And the radical left has designed strategies they believe will overcome their powerlessness in face of this Establishment. Their critics, friendly and unfriendly, see not so much a designed strategy as a frustrated cry, springing from a failure to recognize the agonizingly difficult problems in overhauling a social system. There is perhaps something of both in the new left, in the Black Power movement, in the student revolt, and in the religious protests against racism, war, and received theology.

In connection with this brief description of the extremes, we should note again, referring back to Figure 18–3, that variation in structural, cultural, and character conditions may incline one person toward a political, another toward a religious response. Other persons may have contact with values and groups that lead them to support both, either simultaneously or at different times. It is important to note that other persons, equally deprived, equally "ready" for various forms of social action, may have contact with neither, and thus be led to individual or small-group responses of an attack, withdrawal, or acceptance variety. In this sense, it is not so much that religious and political movements are functional alternatives for each other as that together they are alternatives to individual responses.

RELIGIOUS PLURALISM, RELIGIOUS SEGMENTATION, AND THE RELATIONS OF POLITICS AND RELIGION

In our discussion of religion and politics so far, we have disregarded the fact that many societies have a variety of religious traditions. Under some conditions, this is a central influence on the interaction of politics and religion. The significance of religious differentiation for politics varies with the extent to which it corresponds, or fails to correspond, with other forms of differentiation. Three possibilities can be described as models, for purposes of comparison.

1. Religious differences may match rather closely those based on class, as well as ethnic or linguistic group and region, thus reinforcing the stratification system.

2. Religious differences may cut across class lines, but match ethnic, linguistic, regional, or other lines, creating parallel columns in the social structure.

3. Religious differences may vary independently of other major lines of differentiation. Each religion is found on every class level and among various ethnic groups.

Thinking in terms of three religions (A, B, C), three classes (I, II, III), and three ethnic-linguistic groups (1, 2, 3), we can chart the types as show in Figure 18–4.

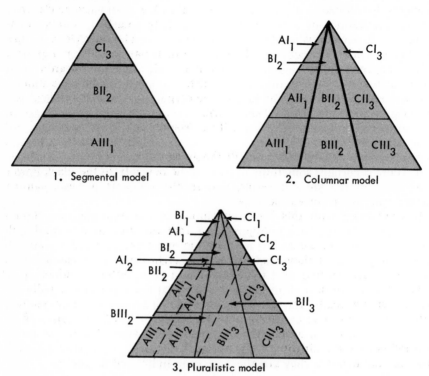

FIGURE 18–4. *Models of social structures using religion, class, and ethnicity*

No society is likely to fit one of these models precisely, but perhaps they illustrate in graphic form the meaning of "cross-cutting" memberships. In the first, which is approximated in Ceylon or Yugoslavia, religious differences are reinforced by class and ethnic-linguistic differences. Conditions that strengthen feelings of national identity prevent such internal divisions from dominating interaction in the society. Conditions that strengthen the salience of religious, linguistic, and ethnic identities, however, split the society severely. Within the political process, they support the formation of "parties of integration," as Lipset calls them, which are held together by so many shared interests and symbols that political compromise with other groups is made difficult. "The necessary rules of democratic politics assume that conversion both ways, into and out of a party, is possible and proper, and parties which hope to gain a majority by democratic methods must ultimately give up their integrationist emphasis."[35] It seems unlikely that

35 Lipset, op. cit., p. 87.

parties will give up their integration emphasis so long as they represent a group bound together by many significant shared identities. Such parties may become irrelevant, however, as cross-cutting memberships grow in importance.

I have suggested that Yugoslavia approximates the first model, yet she has not developed parties of integration except remotely. This should alert us to the fact that the models of social structure we are describing are not directly causal. Other items of history and present situation must be taken into account. The common struggle for survival during World War II, the power of a charismatic leader, the widely shared opposition to Russian dominance, and the tight control over the political process by the central Yugoslavian government have, for a quarter of a century, prevented the reinforcing differences of religion, language, and economic position from splitting the nation. It may be fair to say that traditional religious differences, in any case, are of relatively small importance in face of a widely shared political religion that is less decisively split.

This should lead us to note that reinforcing divisions may, in some circumstances, actually contribute to a democratic political process. This is based on two assumptions: that the integrated groups may serve as training grounds for political skills and staging grounds for the organization of interests, and that overarching identities with the nation compete with and modify the religious-ethnic-class identity. Kornhauser has noted that the nonconformist sects in England proved to be a source of pluralistic strength:

It was in the village chapels of the 18th and 19th centuries that many local leaders of working-class organizations learned to think for themselves, as well as to conduct public meetings and administer finances. Wherever nonconformity was strong, labor unions and cooperatives were strong; in fact, the trade unions have been aptly called the present-day descendants of the earlier nonconformist congregations.[36]

The second model describes a society in which all religious groups are represented, in approximately equal ratios, on each class level; but they are differentiated by ethnicity and language as well as by faith; hence the "columnar" lines of demarcation in the society are sharp. Holland is close to this model, Canada somewhat less so because of greater economic differentiation across religious lines. This columnar structure, in its pure form, insulates individuals from all but formal contacts with those of other religions. Moberg writes, in connection with the Netherlands:

A person may spend his entire life with very few contacts with persons and influences outside of his own "column." He may be born in a confessional hospital and educated through the trade school or university level in confessional schools. His employment will be found with someone of his own religious affiliation. . . . His civic and social organizations and activities are likely to be organized along denominational lines, even if they center primarily around gymnastics, bird-watching, music bands, or teetotalism. . . . His isolation from persons of other religious faiths is likely to be broken only in certain community celebrations, business contacts, and other occasional life experiences unless he deviates from the position of faithfulness decreed by his church.[37]

36 William Kornhauser, *The Politics of Mass Society*, p. 138, quoting Ebenstein.

37 David Moberg, "Social Differentiation in the Netherlands," *Social Forces*, 39, 1961, p. 333.

Where such conditions prevail, a religiously supported dogmatism may be introduced into the political process, political compromise is made difficult, and the society faces a major split if the unifying forces are weakened. We have noted in Chapter Twelve, however, that these consequences are at a minimum in Holland, despite its columnar structure. Such a pattern is only one element among many that determine social processes; its influences can be offset by other elements, as Lijphart has shown for Holland.[38] As with any abstract proposition, therefore, we must note that the consequences of the columnar pattern, as contrasted with the segmented or pluralistic pattern, will be visible only when "other things are equal."

The third model represents a situation in which religiously homogeneous subsocieties are not possible because of the heterogeneity of class, ethnic identity, region, occupation, and the like within each religious group, and the sharing of these various characteristics across religious lines. The United States has been moving in this direction from a somewhat more "columnar" structure several decades ago. It is no longer true that to be fundamentalist Protestant is almost automatically to be small-town or rural, Southern or Middle Western, lower- or lower-middle class, and of "Anglo-Saxon" heritage. One must now include—although not in proportionate numbers—oil millionaires and Puerto Rican migrants, industrial workers in Northern cities, and even a few college-trained students of the social sciences (Billy Graham majored in anthropology). It needs less to be pointed out that to be Roman Catholic in the United States does not automatically imply "urban worker of recent European origin." It may mean Mexican-American peasant or Boston aristocrat, Minnesota intellectual or Chicago pragmatist.

These statements are not meant to indicate that the United States is close to model 3. The evidence does not allow one to speak with confidence on this matter. Doubtless one can say that the United States is somewhere between models 2 and 3 and moving toward 3; but the precise location and the speed of movement are matters of conjecture. Linguistic, occupational, regional, and educational differences among religious groups are declining. Private associations, residence, friendship patterns, however, are still substantially influenced by religious identity. Intermarriage, at least between Catholic and Protestant, is common; yet many intermarried couples—probably the majority—are pulled into one or the other orbit of friendship and private associations, thus renewing, even if at a different level of intensity, the religious community as a factor in their life organization.[39]

To make clear that the three types we have been describing are instruments of measurement and comparison, and not empirical descriptions, it may be wise to locate them on a scale, emphasizing that societies may fall at any point along the scale and may move from one point to another. The

38 See Arend Lijphart, *The Politics of Accommodation.*

39 For a variety of references on these points, see Charles Anderson, "Religious Communality among Academics," *Journal for the Scientific Study of Religion,* 7, 1968, pp. 87–96; Charles Anderson, "Religious Communality among White Protestants, Catholics, and Mormons," *Social Forces,* 46, 1968, pp. 501–508; Milton Gordon, *Assimilation in American Life;* Will Herberg, *Protestant-Catholic-Jew;* Gerhard Lenski, *The Religious Factor.*

two ends represent different forms of solidarity (mechanical and organic, to use Durkheim's terms). To indicate their similarity, yet difference, I have drawn the scale in Figure 18–5 as a not-quite-closed circle, with the three models located on the circumference. The placement of societies along the range should be seen as a preliminary estimate.

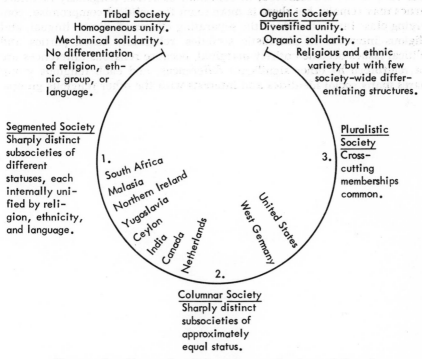

FIGURE 18–5. *Types of societies in terms of unity and diversity*

All three lines of differentiation we have used—religion, language, and ethnicity—may not always be involved; or some may divide a society only partially. In South Africa, for example, most of the black inhabitants as well as most of the white are nominally Christians. Increasingly, however, they are members of separate sects. Language separation is also partial. Yet altogether South Africa is quite close to the segmental model. It is difficult to identify societies that are close to pluralism, as I have defined it. Where religion, language, and ethnicity all differentiate a population, a columnar structure may be obtained, with approximate equality for the various subsocieties, but infrequent cross-cutting memberships. Language separation is probably the critical variable. When that begins to break down, either by extensive bilinguality or by the appearance of a common tongue, pluralism becomes possible. In the United States, where language separation is quite unimportant, Jewish-Gentile relations are fairly close to the columnar model; but those between Catholics and Protestants have become more pluralistic. Politically, as we shall see in the next chapter, this means that Jews vote Democratic in a much higher ratio than one would expect on class grounds, while the pattern of Democratic "over-voting" by Catholics has declined.

In sum, the religio-political interaction is affected by the degree to which religion, as a line of division in society, is reinforced by class, ethnic, and lingual lines. Where they all converge, in segmented societies, the basis is laid for a religiously oriented party system or political process. When the class differences are removed, in columnar societies, religiously identified parties may remain, but there is more room for political compromise; con-verging class interests reduce the separating effects of ethnic, lingual, and religious interests. In pluralistic societies, religiously based parties and political issues become entirely marginal, because religious differences are not reinforced by other significant differences, and each religious group shares many social identities and interests with the other religious groups.

Chapter Nineteen

CHURCH AND STATE IN COMPLEX SOCIETIES

In this chapter we move from the level of general principles involved in the relationships of religion and politics to more specific considerations. Several of the principles will be employed in a discussion of various aspects of the relationship between church and state, or more precisely between religion and citizenship. They are revealed particularly sharply by the study of the responses of churches and individuals to war, to which we will devote the next chapter.

Varieties of Relationship Between Church and State

Modern nations are characterized by contrasting types of relationship between church and state—products of their different histories and different social structures.[1] Patterns in the contemporary Christian world cannot be understood without reference to the early experience of Jews and the first centuries of development of the church. The frustrating political history of the Jews had made painfully clear to them that the political com-

1 On Christendom, see Heinrich Geffken, *Church and State*, for a basic historical treatment; Luigi Sturzo, *Church and State* is a scholarly Catholic work; Anson Phelps Stokes, *Church and State in the United States* and Leo Pfeffer, *Church, State and Freedom* are valuable works with emphasis on the United States; Mark D. Howe, *The Garden and the Wilderness. Religion and Government in American Constitutional History* is a useful constitutional study; William D'Antonio and Frederick Pike, eds., *Religion, Revolution, and Reform*, and Lloyd Mecham, *Church and State in Latin America* describe the South American picture. For comparative works, see Gabriel Almond and James Coleman, *The Politics of Developing Areas*; Leonard Binder, *Religion and Politics in Pakistan*, Jerrold Schecter, *The New Faces of Buddha: Buddhism and Political Power in Southeast Asia*; Donald E. Smith, *South Asian Politics and Religion*; Fred von der Mehden, *Religion and Nationalism in Southeast Asia*; Kalman Silvert, ed., *Churches and States: The Religious Institution and Modernization.*

munities into which they were forced were not the religious community of their hopes. Despite the intricate union of religion and citizenship in their early history, "church" and "state" came to mean clearly separate facts. There was no danger that the Jews would mistake the Assyrian or Babylonian empires, or later the Roman Empire, which held political power over them, for their own religious community.

It is in such contexts that universalist, nonparochial religious concepts develop. This was, of course, a major element in the early period of Christianity. After Constantine, however, the Christian Church was directly involved in the political situation. As a small and persecuted sect, the Christian community had opposed emperor worship, but it had been more indifferent than hostile to the state. As a church, however, becoming more and more involved in secular affairs, it could be neither hostile nor indifferent; yet it was confronted with the tensions that are inevitably generated between a universalist religion and the requirements of politics. It sought to resolve this difficulty by balancing two statements from Scripture: "The powers that be are ordained by God," but if those powers require action that is contrary to religious belief, "We must obey God rather than man." This gradually developed into the doctrine, closely akin to the thinking of the Stoics, of "relative natural law": The state, along with other secular institutions, is part of the natural law; it is inevitable and God-ordained. Yet it embodies the weaknesses of men, the cloudiness of reason that resulted from the "fall," and hence is only relative. As the church developed in power and wealth, it became more and more highly identified with the secular institutions, and thus less and less able to assert that they were relative. For the most part it was only in some of the monasteries that the relative quality of the state was stressed; and even there, it was largely by implication.

With the church so closely identified with the Roman Empire, it was inevitable that when the empire began to break up, so would the church, first in the great schism that divided the East and West, reflecting the growth of Byzantine power, and later in Western Europe, with the growth of nationalism in that area. These conflicts were not primarily an expression of the tension between a universalist religion and national political leaders who sought to use religion for political purposes: they were conflicts between rival political structures. The medieval church, accommodated to, and indeed a part of, the political and economic system of the empire, opposed the rising power of the national kings and princes. But church and empire could not stand against the growing national consciousness in those areas favored by linguistic and cultural unity and a certain geographical identity; nor could they defeat the growing power of commerce (which required an end to localism in matters of money, tariffs, commercial law, and economic self-sufficiency).

I shall not develop further the complicated story of the relationship between religion and citizenship in pre-Reformation Europe, although one can discover in that story a great deal of information of value to the sociology of religion. We turn rather to the modern scene, because the development of distinctly secular states and of religious institutions that are partially separate, if not actually independent, from the state has created a situation that points up in a clear way the various modes of relationship between church and state.

The presence of a monotheistic, universalist religion that stresses allegiance to God above all other loyalties does not resolve the problems of church and state; it does not establish a clear-cut hierarchy of values. Conflicting demands and competing values lead to many different patterns of relationship. To declare that one should "render unto Caesar the things that are Caesar's and unto God the things that are God's" is only to pose the question. The nature of the reconciliation will vary widely, depending on the location of political power, the culturally valued road to salvation, the structure of the ecclesiastical organization, the needs of the individuals involved, and the distribution of economic power. In my judgment, the actual separation of church and state—or, to put it in another way, the effective presence of a universalist element in religion which is capable, at times, of challenging, modifying, or denying the claims of politics—is possible only where power is diffused. Those forces that give to "the average man" some measure of economic freedom, political instruments for expressing his individual judgment, unhampered sources of information on which to base his opinions, and the like, create a setting in which religious challenges to the secular power structure are most likely to occur. Where these are lacking, church and state are not likely to be effectively separate, whatever the formal institutional structures may be. The ecclesiastical structure may be the dominant one, or, more commonly, the political authorities will dominate the church; but in either case church and state will not be separate. Put in sociological terms, this is to say that the relationships between religion and politics are embedded in a whole social structure and will vary with variations in that structure.

There can be a great variety of connections between church and state, even among those situations that exhibit formal union. Does the state nominate important church officials and otherwise influence clerical recruitment and training; does it control religious publications, and sharply limit the freedom of nonofficial churches (Spain)? Or does it accept simply a broadly defined "established church," granting it a great deal of autonomy, and allowing freedom of action to other churches (Great Britain)? These reflect wide differences in the total social structure, and in their turn they affect the societal developments in different ways.

Anson Phelps Stokes has given us a useful summary of the types of relation between church and state in Christian societies. Among the early patterns attempted, he distinguishes: 1) imperial domination (subordination and often persecution of the church until 313 A.D.); 2) church-state alliance (St. Augustine, *De Civitate Dei*); 3) ecclesiastical domination (Gregory the Great, 540–604); 4) the ecclesiastical state or theocracy (the papal states, and later, Calvin's Geneva). Among the modern solutions attempted, Stokes distinguishes: 1) the Erastian plan (in which the state determined the policy of the church and virtually controlled its conduct, as in Czarist Russia); 2) the state-church plan (in which the official church is given much autonomy and other sects are allowed freedom, as in Great Britain); 3) the jurisdictional plan (equal status for several confessions, all supervised by the state, which was the pattern of the Peace of

Westphalia); 4) the separation plan (this may be benevolent, as in the United States, or hostile, as in Mexico in the first decades after the revolution).[2]

The task of the sociology of religion is to try to discover the conditions under which these various patterns of relationship between church and state develop. We have noted above some of the variables involved, along with the suggestion that the range from most to least autonomy for religious organizations was very strongly dependent upon the degree of diffusion of power. It should be made clear that the autonomy to which we refer is the independent power to challenge the state—its war pattern, its demands on the citizen, its influence on the distribution of economic values, and the like. Freedom to preach a universalism that has only otherworldly significance may be found—and even encouraged—in situations where secular power is highly concentrated. Even here, the secular authorities may be ambivalent, for the line between otherworldly and this-worldly influence is not clear.

Religious values and structures as well as the secular situation affect the nature of the relationship between church and state. The sharp separation of the duties of Brahmans and Kshatriyas in Hinduism lays the basis for separation of church and state and for the rise of a secular leadership. The lack of an ecclesiastical structure among the Brahmans also supports this development. Their influence being that of individual priests, they have not generally been in a position to challenge secular authority. Thus it has been relatively easy to establish a secular state in India.[3]

In theory, Buddhism equally supports the separation of church and state. Buddhist monks have rejected this world as of little consequence. They are not bound together by a complex institutional structure through which their shared concerns and interests can be expressed. For the most part, therefore, politicians can use religious themes and the feelings of religious identity of their constituencies, in Buddhist as in Hindu areas, without fear of organized ecclesiastical power. In practice, however, the situation is not so simple, for Buddhism is found in many different contexts, and in some it has been the focal point of political movements. When a predominantly Buddhist nation confronts a non-Buddhist imperial power, as in the case of Burma, the nationalist movement may be built in part around a religious identity; and religious factors may persist into the period after freedom has been won, qualifying the expected separation of church and state.[4] Or when a predominantly Buddhist element within a nation finds itself, or believes itself, to be at an economic and political disadvantage, as in Ceylon, their fight for economic and political power may be organized around religious themes. If religious differences are paralleled by ethnic and lingual

2 See Stokes, op. cit., pp. 37–49. Perhaps it should be noted that communism, as a civil religion, is generally controlled by an "Erastian plan." Yet in every communist society there are ideological quarrels, and in some there is a partially independent communist movement that criticizes the state for its doctrinal impurities.

3 See Myron Weiner, "The Politics of South Asia," in *The Politics of the Developing Areas*, Gabriel Almond and James S. Coleman, eds., pp. 153–246.

4 See Winston King, *A Thousand Lives Away: Buddhism in Contemporary Burma*; Donald Smith, *Religion and Politics in Burma*; Michael Mendelson, "Buddhism, and the Burmese Establishment," *Archives de sociologie des religions*, 9, 1964, pp. 85–95.

differences a communal conflict quite uncharacteristic of Buddhist doctrine may develop.

Of the major religions, Islam most nearly supports the identity of church and state. In the traditional view, no line can be drawn between religious and secular affairs.[5] Even contemporary states have an explicitly Islamic character, as shown by the Islamic Republic of Pakistan (the title adopted by the first amendment to its current constitution in 1964). The President must be a Muslim, and the Advisory Council is obliged to review all laws, "existing as well as future, with the object of bringing them into 'conformity with the Holy Qur'an and the Sunnah.' "[6]

In practice, this picture is complicated by nationalism, secularism, and sectarianism. Religious interests and concerns to some degree compete with those based on national and economic development. There are non-Muslim minorities in many "Islamic" states. And different strata express themselves religiously, as well as in other ways, by variation in their interpretations of the faith. As a result of these influences, one only begins his analysis when he speaks of the theoretical union of religious and political identity in Islam. In fact, Islamic law has undergone extensive development and reinterpretation.[7] The very union of political and religious ideology has meant that protest movements have usually taken the form of sectarianism in Muslim lands, creating diversity in the interpretations of doctrines.[8] The "social sources of denominationalism" are shown in Islam as elsewhere, so that persons differently related to the course of contemporary events express their religious ideas and feelings differently. Leonard Binder describes the traditionalist, the modernist, and the fundamentalist views in Islam.[9] Politicians attempting to manage a diverse and modernizing state, yet one in which the traditional doctrine of the unity of religion with society is ardently defended not only by the Ulama but by the "common man," are encouraged to see in that traditional doctrine the support they need for governmental policies—i.e., they modernize it. In this they are supported by many businessmen and professionals. Thus Pakistan, for all of its appearance as an Islamic state, guarantees freedom of religion and equality before the law for all citizens. Binder notes that some citizens criticize the traditional view, not because it has failed to modernize, but because it has drifted away from the fundamental Islamic teachings as they understand them. From somewhat different perspectives, many rather traditional middle-class Muslims and some students have taken this fundamentalist view. They call for revitalization. In addition, Binder points out that a few highly westernized persons in Pakistan take a rather thorough-

5 See Reuben Levy, *The Social Structure of Islam;* and W. Montgomery Watt, *Islam and the Integration of Society.*

6 Freeland Abbott, in *South Asian Politics and Religion,* Donald Smith, ed., p. 352.

7 See Noel J. Coulson, "The Concept of Progress and Islamic Law," in *Religion and Progress in Modern Asia,* Robert Bellah, ed., pp. 74–92.

8 See Dankwart A. Rustow, "The Politics of the Near East," in Almond and Coleman, op. cit., pp. 369–454; Allan Eister, "Perspectives on the Functions of Religion in a Developing Country: Islam in Pakistan," *Journal for the Scientific Study of Religion,* 3, 1964, pp. 227–238; Emile Marmorstein, "Religious Opposition to Nationalism in the Middle East," *International Affairs,* July, 1952, pp. 344–359.

9. Op. cit.

going secular position with regard to Islam. They regard it as largely irrelevant to the development of a modern state.

CHURCH AND STATE IN THE UNITED STATES

In the United States, all three of the modes of relationship between religion and politics that we have discussed can be found in complicated interaction. Although the society is highly secularized, religious values are an important part of the value core that holds it together as a society, giving it the minimum consensus necessary to a common life. Bates declares that the roots of democracy

are to be found in the attempted revival of primitive Christianity by the radical lower-class sects of the Protestant Reformation, those peasants and yeomen who were our own ancestors, and who initiated the Reformation and eventually carried out its basic principles—especially in America—to conclusions undreamt of in the beginning. . . . Democracy was envisaged in religious terms long before it assumed a political terminology.[10]

Bates doubtless overstates the case. Both the French and American revolutions were carried on without, and to a strong degree against, the churches. Many of the leaders were inspired by the rationalism of the Enlightenment. Important secular forces were involved in the whole process of the development of democratic societies. There is widespread agreement, however, on the less specific claim that Christianity furnishes many of the "first premises" by which Americans make their value decisions. Whether this is objectively true or not—it would seem to the writer to be substantially true—is perhaps less important for our purposes than that it is widely accepted as true, and is acted upon and used in societal interaction. An editorial in *Fortune* illustrates the situation well.

As the leading democracy of the world, therefore, the United States is perforce the leading practical exponent of Christianity. The U. S. is not Christian in any formal religious sense; its churches are not full on Sundays and its citizens transgress the precepts freely. But it is Christian in the sense of absorption, the basic teachings of Christianity are in its blood stream. . . . Christian idealism is manifest in the culture and habits of the people, in the arguments that orators and politicians use to gain their ends; in the popular ideas of good taste, which control advertising, movies, radio, and all forms of public opinion; in the laws, the manners, and the standards of our people.[11]

To the careful student of American mass media of communication, of American manners and morals, this too must seem to be an overstatement; but its very use indicates the kind of *final* appeal on value questions that is likely to be used. The Supreme Court has given it an official sanction by declaring (in 1892 and at other times) that the United States is a Christian nation, in the broad sense that Christian principles underlie its laws and values. It has only partially revised these positions in recent decisions that sharply separate church and state; for these decisions dealt with questions of direct government involvement, not with the informal support for religion that is extensive in American governmental policies.

10 E. S. Bates, *American Faith*, p. 9; see also Ralph Barton Perry, *Puritanism and Democracy.*

11 *Fortune*, January, 1940, p. 26.

Civil Religion in America. It is a mistake to overemphasize the specifically Christian element in American religiosity. From the first days of the republic, as Robert Bellah has shown convincingly, national leaders have used religious themes. Washington proclaimed in his first inaugural address that "the propitious smiles of Heaven can never be expected on a nation that disregards the eternal rules of order and right which Heaven itself has ordained." Jefferson drew a parallel between the flight of the Israelites from Egypt and the flight of the colonists from Europe to America, as he appealed for "the favor of that Being in whose hands we are." [12] Such themes come down to the present day as testimony to the religious tone continuously heard in American public life. There is little, however, that is related to specific doctrines.

Though much is selectively derived from Christianity, this religion is clearly not itself Christianity. . . . neither Washington nor Adams nor Jefferson mentions Christ in his inaugural address; nor do any of the subsequent presidents, although not one of them fails to mention God. The God of the civil religion is not only rather "unitarian," he is also on the austere side, much more related to order, law, and right than to salvation and love.[13]

The civil religion is made manifest in times of crisis. Sidney Verba interprets the individual religious acts and feelings at the time of President Kennedy's assassination, and the public mourning rituals in essentially Durkheimian terms: "The assassination crisis is important here because it is probably the nearest equivalent in a large modern nation-state to the kind of intense mutual rededication ceremony that is possible in a smaller and simpler society." [14] Perhaps crisis is now sufficiently endemic that we can use the same explanation for the prayer services introduced in the White House by President Nixon. During the first several months they were led by Protestant clergymen; but a service in the State Department before his inaugural was led by Catholic, Jewish, and Protestant clergymen.

This, of course, is not a new departure. Most American presidents have called upon God for support. Congress has added the words "under God" to the pledge of allegiance to the flag and has had an interdenominational room for prayer and meditation built in the Capitol.

If there has been any modification of civil religion in America in recent years, it has not been in the direction of a lessening of the generalized religious quality of public life, and certainly not in the direction of making it more specifically Christian. Rather, it has been a tendency to emphasize more fully the pluralistic nature of the American religious situation. In a sense, the distinctive traditions—the Catholic, Protestant, Jewish, and to a lesser degree the Buddhist, the humanist, and others—have been made

12 Robert Bellah, "Civil Religion in America," *Daedalus*, 96, 1967, pp. 7–8.

13 Ibid., p. 7. There is something of Rousseau in this. He developed the idea of a nondoctrinal, rather rationalistic civil religion in his *Social Contract*. Comte and Durkheim follow the same theme.

14 Sidney Verba in *The Kennedy Assassination and the American Public*, Bradley Greenberg and Edwin Parker, eds., p. 354. For a general study of the symbolic penetration of religious and national themes, see W. Lloyd Warner, *The Family of God: A Symbolic Study of Christian Life in America*.

more visible, while at the same time their common legitimacy in and their shared concern for American society have been emphasized.[15]

The degree to which America's "civil religion" is a nationalist religion, an "American Shinto," working against the universalism of the traditions on which it is based, is a matter of dispute. As we shall see in our discussion of the churches and war, it is not difficult to find evidence of a parochial use of religion for nationalistic purposes, in the United States as elsewhere. Bellah argues, however, that it is difficult to use the words of Jefferson or Lincoln for narrow goals. The defenders of slavery or contemporary supporters of the far right are more likely to oppose and try to change the overarching religious themes than they are to exploit them. Bellah recognizes that on international issues the civil religion may more readily be pulled away from universalistic themes; but he notes that even on such issues, America's religious tradition furnishes support for the nonconformists. "I would remind my countrymen," Thoreau wrote, "that they are men first, and Americans at a late and convenient hour." [16] Bellah explicitly rejects the idea that the civil religion is a least common denominator of the major traditional faiths: it is rather an expression of those faiths interpreted in the light of American historical experience.[17] Whitney, on the other hand, emphasizes the continuing tension between civil religion and the "transcivil" traditional religions which, to cite one element of the tension, "persist in cultic activities that clearly assert an opposition to any state claims upon their people's absolute loyalty." [18]

Both of these interpretations seem plausible. We are scarcely able, however, to weigh with any confidence the extent to which the American setting has nationalized the civil religion and the extent to which religious forces have universalized American nationalism; although the former seems to be the stronger influence.

Political Use of Religion. The kind of blending of religious and national values characteristic of the civil religion is difficult to distinguish from the use of religion for less fully shared purposes, in the name, to be sure, of universal values. On this second level, we find the widespread use of religious values and symbols to try to win various kinds of political struggles. Thus we have such groups as the Christian Front and Spiritual Mobilization on the right and the Fellowship of Christian Socialists on the left, each of which claims a religious mandate for various political policies. The roster of lobbyists in Washington who work for churches and other religious organizations is an extensive one.[19] The Roman Catholic Church has had offices in Washington for nearly half a century; and most of the Protestant agencies have maintained offices there since World War II. There is no threat, of course, of religious domination; for the church agencies, even if they were unified in their positions and interests, are not a powerful influence. "Moreover, the attempts of religious groups to influence government

15 See particularly Will Herberg, *Protestant-Catholic-Jew.*

16 Quoted by Bellah, op. cit., p. 18.

17 See Bellah in *The Religious Situation: 1968*, Donald Cutler, ed., p. 389.

18 John R. Whitney in ibid., p. 379.

19 See Luke E. Ebersole, *Church Lobbying in the Nation's Capitol;* Ralph L. Roy, *Apostles of Discord.*

are usually based on utilitarian and broadly ethical considerations, rather than on strictly sectarian and theological grounds." [20]

Political candidates and parties not infrequently encourage the belief that their election will strengthen religious values. And in international affairs many Americans find it difficult to distinguish between a political struggle and a religious crusade. This is not to suggest, be it noted, that in these various political conflicts, no religious issues are involved, nor that all claims are equally to be accepted, or denied. It is only to note that mutually contradictory claims—each made in the name of the same religious tradition—can scarcely all be valid. America well illustrates the principle that in a heterogeneous society religious symbols will be used by competing interests to support their various demands and values.

THE SEPARATION OF CHURCH AND STATE IN THE UNITED STATES

It is the third mode of relationship between religion and politics, however, that is usually thought to be most expressive of the American pattern. Relatively few societies have developed so distinctly the formal principle of "the separation of church and state" as has the United States. The scientist is concerned to ask: Under what conditions does this principle develop? Do the informal patterns of relationship between the two institutions reinforce or modify the principle of separation? Does it mean also the separation of religion and citizenship? What are the conditions under which this mode of relationship is changed? What are its consequences?

The original constitutional statement is an expression of the combined influence of several forces working in American society in the late eighteenth century. Leanings toward an Established Church—and they were not entirely lacking among Puritans and Episcopalians—were blocked, because there could have been no agreement on a single church. This was probably not the major factor, however. There was, as part of the total struggle for liberty, widespread opposition to any Establishment. Even among the Calvinist clergy, there had begun what might be called the "Americanization" of their theology. This process became much more explicit in the development of Unitarianism in the nineteenth century, but it was already implicit in the writing of the liberal group of pre-Revolutionary ministers. As Sperry says:

The laymen of Massachusetts who went to the second Continental Congress and the Constitutional Convention, first to declare American Independence and then to fashion the Constitution, were of the liberal rather than the conservative party, theologically. They would have no interest in trying to foist the passing theocracy of an earlier time upon the country as a whole. If the Episcopal Church in Virginia was weakened by the exodus of its loyal clergy, the Puritan Church in New England was weakened by theological controversies within its own borders.[21]

A further influence in the development of the principle of the separation of church and state has sometimes been overlooked in the context of recent discussions that have emphasized America's religious background. Anti-

20 Luke Ebersole, "Religion and Politics," *Annals of the American Academy of Political and Social Science*, 332, 1960, p. 104.
21 Willard L. Sperry, *Religion in America*, p. 52.

clericalism and rationalism were vigorous at the time the Constitution was written. Sperry's judicious words well express their influence:

the prevalence of enlightened deistic ideas among educated classes was in part responsible for the studied silences of the document as to the existence of God, and its unwillingness to commit itself, even in the most general terms, to any Christian ideas. One can only say that, given the prior history of colonial times and the subsequent record, the framers of the Constitution must be credited with religious understatement, rather than with overstatement. There had been and there was to be more religion in American life than the Constitution would seem to suggest. But it is probably true that the deliberate silences of the document upon the whole matter, and its understatements were the price which had then to be paid for a vindication of the principles of toleration and liberty in matters religious.[22]

Modifications of the Principle of Separation of Church and State

That the Constitution understates the mutual influence of religion and government in the United States can be shown by a simple listing of some of the ways in which they affect each other: church interest and influence in marriage and divorce laws and in birth control legislation; the concern of many church groups with "social legislation," governing areas such as child labor and social security; the interest of some churches with processes in the courts and prisons; government chaplaincies and religious services in the armed forces; required oaths; blasphemy laws; Sunday observance laws; government observance of special religious days and occasions; concern of the churches over the Bill of Rights, which includes religious freedom and involves the problem of censorship; church interest in radio and television, the protection of religion in programming and the granting of time to religious groups, in part by legal requirements; exemption of church property from taxation.[23]

Only a very few persons in the United States contend that such mutual influences as these represent violations of the constitutional principle of the separation of church and state.

The great majority of presumably religious Americans allowed these encroachments on the strict "neutrality" of the state to accumulate with relatively little concern or with ineffective opposition. There were always minor complaints arising from the introduction of religious materials in the public schools: Jews protested at being taught Christmas carols, Catholics protested against the use of the King James version of the Bible, atheists protested against the use of prayers in legislatures and the presence of sectarian religious workers and teachers on state university campuses.[24]

Since Schneider wrote this, some of the issues to which he referred have become controversial, as we shall see. There has been, in fact, a steady stream of issues, some of them still open questions, some of them now involved in public policy. They can be illustrated by drawing from a long list given by Stroup:

22 Ibid., p. 58.

23 See Stokes, op. cit., Vol. III, Chap. 20.

24 H. W. Schneider, *Religion in 20th Century America*, pp. 31–32.

Should church-related hospitals accept federal subsidies? . . . Should church-related agencies accept governmental surplus food for distribution abroad? . . . Should laws . . . which require that adoptive placement of children be only in homes of the same religious faith as that of the parents of the children be continued? . . . Should clergymen and nuns, when qualified, be permitted to teach in the public schools while wearing distinctive religious garb? . . . Should school credit for courses in religion, wherever held, be given? [25]

The present legal and constitutional situation (as interpreted by the Supreme Court) reflects the shifting balance among many forces, with their various positions on the question of the relationship of church to state. Just as there are few who openly avow and work for the complete separation of religion and government, so there are few who support a formal union, an Establishment. In between, however, is a wide range of opinion indicative of the heterogeneity of American society. There are those who want government support and encouragement for religious values, but who oppose any direct government support for churches as organizations, even if they are all treated alike. This distinction is often a difficult one to draw. Virtually no one in this group, for example, opposes the tax-exempt status of churches; [26] many of them support "released time" from schools for religious education.[27] There are relatively few objections to the maintenance of a chaplain corps by the armed forces, although the American Jewish Congress has called for its abolition.[28] Most Americans would probably agree with Theodore Leskes that the army, as a surrogate society, service in which is compulsory, is obliged to make available to men all the services of civilian life from which they have been cut off, including a religious life.[29]

In the religiously heterogeneous situation of the United States, however, enthusiastic support for government encouragements to religion is hindered, not only by the belief in the separation of church and state, but also, especially for the dominant Protestant groups, by the realization that government encouragement is likely to yield a *comparative* advantage to "minority" religious organizations, particularly Catholicism and the Protestant sects, precisely because it puts them all on an equal level. This realization is made the clearer by the more vigorous use often made of such government encouragement as released time from schools by the "minority" churches.

The Roman Catholic bishops of the United States have shown more concern over secularism and indifference to religion in government than over any weakening of constitutional separation. They have suggested the formula, "the cooperation of church and state," and call for government support not only of religious values but also of churches, so long as all preferential treatment is avoided. They claim—as do the defenders of each

25 Herbert Stroup, *Church and State in Confrontation*, pp. 9–11.

26 There are a few exceptions. See the references in footnotes 16–18, Chap. 16.

27 Several recent books affirm this position. In addition to the cited works of Pfeffer and Stokes, see C. H. Moehlman, *The Wall of Separation Between Church and State* and J. H. Nichols, *Democracy and the Churches.*

28 The *New York Times*, May 18, 1968, p. 10.

29 Cited by Milton Himmelfarb, "Church and State: How High a Wall," *Commentary*, July, 1966.

of the other positions—constitutional support for their interpretation. It is a monopolistic Establishment that is prohibited, in their judgment, not government support of the work of the churches.

We feel deep conviction that for the sake of both good citizenship and religion there should be a reaffirmation of our original American tradition of free cooperation between government and religious bodies—cooperation involving no special privilege to any group and no restriction on the religious liberty of any citizen. We solemnly disclaim any intent or desire to alter this prudent and fair American policy of government in dealing with the delicate problems that have their source in the divided religious allegiance of our citizens. . . .

We stand ready to cooperate in fairness and charity with all who believe in God and are devoted to freedom under God to avert the impending danger of a judicial "establishment of secularism" that would ban God from public life. For secularism is threatening the religious foundations of our national life and preparing the way for the advent of the omnipotent state.[30]

Thus a diversified society, with a somewhat ambiguous constitutional principle, exhibits a wide range of opinions concerning the proper relationship between church and state. There is an almost equally wide range of action. In my judgment, there has been a trend in the direction of what might be called—to change the phrase of the Catholic bishops slightly—"the cooperation of churches and state." In a period of crisis, particularly from 1917 until the early 1920's and from 1940 until the present time, one of the aspects of the search for unity and consensus in American society has been a stress on religion and the religious foundations of the nation— all in the context of much reaffirmation of the principle of the separation of church and state. Decisions by the Supreme Court have registered this hesitant trend. In *Everson versus Board of Education*, 1947, the Court allowed transportation expenses out of public funds to be given to parochial schools because, and to the extent that, these schools met the state's secular education needs. In 1948, in the *McCollum* case, the Supreme Court invalidated a state statute permitting the release of children from public-school time to take religious instruction on the school premises. But in the *Zorach* case, in 1952, a New York City law allowing released time away from the school was upheld. The Court held that no absolute separation of church and state is required by the Constitution. It is required only that there be no interference with the free exercise of religion and that there be no Establishment. The many ways in which the state does indeed deal with religion were noted in the decision.[31]

In this ambiguous situation, it is not easy to see the dominant trends. Two related principles seem to have guided the most recent legal and judicial actions with regard to religion in the United States: First, a desire to strengthen religious pluralism, to make certain that separation of church and state did not imply the creation of conditions in which freedom of religious choice was made difficult or impossible; and second, a recognition that application of the "separation" formula often involved the society in dilemmas of choice. The intricacies of the relationship between church and state may be shown by some examination of these two principles.

30 From the manifesto of the American Roman Catholic Bishops, November 20, 1948; see *The National Catholic Almanac*, 1949, pp. 86–91.

31 See Pfeffer, op. cit. and Fred Kritsky, ed., *The Politics of Religion in America.*

In recent years, the Supreme Court has held that Seventh Day Adventists must be exempted from provisions of unemployment-compensation laws that require willingness to accept Saturday work. Social security laws have been modified to exempt members of religious groups opposed to insurance from compulsory taxation. "These are examples of what Justice Harlan called the 'many areas in which the pervasive activities of the State justify some special provision for religion to prevent it from being submerged in an all-embracing secularism.' " [32] Separation, as defined by such actions, is not synonymous with indifference, whatever the consequences; it is defined as neutrality in creating conditions within which diverse religious perspectives may be maintained.[33] Difficulty in defining this neutrality is shown by the fact that in 1969, in contrast to the decisions just cited, a U.S. District Court judge denied citizenship to two Jehovah's Witnesses because their faith prevented them from voting, undertaking jury duty, or serving in the armed forces.

Religion and the Schools. Recent decisions on public support for private schools and religion in public schools further illustrate the development of the principle of pluralism, as well as a recognition of the dilemmas involved in applying the principle of separation of church and state. In 1962, a major Supreme Court decision in the *Engels* case seemed to underline a strict interpretation of the doctrine of separation. The New York State Board of Regents had directed each teacher to open the school day with this prayer in class: "Almighty God, we acknowledge our dependence upon Thee, and we beg Thy blessings upon us, our parents, our teachers and our country." Saying the prayer was to be optional for the pupils. In a six-to-one decision, the Court ruled that the practice was inconsistent with the establishment clause of the First Amendment. A year later, in the *Schempp* case, the Court ruled that a Pennsylvania statute requiring the reading of at least ten verses from the Bible at the opening of each school day in each school, even though parents could request exemption for their children, was unconstitutional. In each case, the argument of the Court emphasized that the aim was not to enforce secularism, but to insure freedom of religion. "The very purpose of a Bill of Rights was to withdraw certain subjects from the vicissitudes of political controversy, to place them beyond the reach of majorities. . . . One's right to . . . freedom of worship . . . and other fundamental rights may not be submitted to vote, they depend on the outcome of no elections." [34]

These decisions aroused a great deal of opposition; a number of amendments to overturn them were designed. (It should be noticed that widespread and in some instances rather open violation of these rulings exists, particularly in the South.) In the last analysis, however, the Supreme Court's interpretation has been supported by a combination of views: some want to keep the schools utterly secular; some want to see religion intro-

32 Wilbur Katz and Harold Sutherland, "Religious Pluralism and the Supreme Court," *Daedalus*, 96, 1967, p. 187.

33 See Wilbur Katz, *Religion and American Constitutions.*

34 Justice Jackson, quoted in *Religion in the Public Schools,* Commission on Religion in the Public Schools, American Association of School Administrators, pp. 24–25. See also, Richard Dierenfeld, *Religion in American Public Schools;* and Katz and Sutherland, op. cit.

duced as a topic of study and analysis, but not as worship—a point emphasized by the Court; and some want to prevent the development of a "least-common-denominator" form of religion, a position well expressed in the statement that "the threat is not the secularization of our schools but the secularization of our religion."

Although the *Engels* and *Schempp* decisions reaffirmed the separation of church and state, they scarcely ended the controversy. In the long run, sharper conflict seems likely to be attached to the question of federal aid to parochial schools than to the question of religious practices in public schools. The former question is more persistent because it raises a sharper dilemma: Shall we maintain utter separation even if it means poorer education for many children and an unequal burden for some families? [35] A generation ago, the lines were fairly clearly drawn. On the minority side were those, mainly Catholic, who said that parochial schools rendered important secular teaching services to society; they relieved the public of tax burdens. Freedom of religion meant little if a double financial burden greatly reduced the ability of a religious community to teach its children in matters deemed essential to the faith. On the majority side—as measured by the fact that most public decisions supported their views—were those who believed that support for private schools was clear violation of the Constitution. The small public contributions in the form of bus transportation for parochial-school children was opposed on principle. Holders of this new point were also concerned that tax support for private schools was bound to injure the public school system.

This Protestant position, however, has not been without ambivalences. Although opposition to direct financial aid to parochial schools has been general, support for nondenominational religious training in the schools is also strong. This has been stated by the General Board of the National Council of Churches, for example, in these words: "It is expected that they (the public schools) shall teach that religion is an essential aspect of our national heritage and culture, that this nation subsists under the governance of God and that our moral and ethical values rest upon religious grounds and sanctions." [36]

By 1965, the balance on the question of financial aid from government had shifted, when support for teaching personnel was written into the Elementary and Secondary Education Act. ". . . At present about $150-million in Federal anti-poverty funds and school aid is spent annually on programs run by church-related institutions, and additional tax funds go to the construction of buildings on religious campuses." [37] In 1968 the Supreme Court upheld a New York law that requires public schools to "lend" textbooks to pupils in private and parochial schools,[38] a provision now added to contributions in the form of bus transportation and free lunches.

35 The same problem attaches to other federal programs, such as the "war on poverty." For a generally critical survey of trends in government support to church-sponsored programs see American Civil Liberties Union, *The Church-State Problem Has Been Handed to You.*

36 Quoted by Dierenfeld, op. cit., p. 3.

37 *New York Times*, June 16, 1968, p. E-13.

38 Ibid.

These are aids, the Court argued, to students, not to religious institutions. Justice Black, who wrote the 1947 decision supporting the use of public funds for bus transportation, however, dissented from this view, along with Justices Douglas and Fortas. "To transport children to school, give them lunch or provide fire and police protection is entirely different from the use of tax funds to buy books for children in religious schools. . . . Books . . . are the heart of any school." [39]

A majority (six) of the justices, however, did not agree. Nor has Congress, which has appropriated substantial funds for private schools in recent education bills. How can we account for the shift? Several trends in American society have helped to throw the balance, however slightly, on the side of support for parochial schools:

    1. Catholics have grown in political and economic power.

    2. The rapidly increasing costs of their parochial school system—among other reasons, because more and more salaried lay teachers are needed to compensate for the insufficiency of teachers from the various orders—has increased the importance of the issue for Catholics.

    3. The number of Jewish, and to a lesser degree Protestant, schools has increased. If this has not brought active support for programs of public aid, it has at least brought some recognition of the problems Catholics have been facing.

    4. The greatly increased costs of public schools have made some persons aware of the extent to which parochial schools have relieved school districts of tax burdens.

    5. The Catholic Church has to some degree been "Americanized" and— if Catholic readers will forgive me—"Protestantized." It has become, and is recognized, as more open, less monolithic, more influenced by laymen. Opposition based partly on stereotype and partly on perceived differences has therefore been sharply reduced.

The increase in governmental aid to church-related schools does not mean that the controversy has been eliminated or that the dilemma has been resolved. In the same session in which they upheld the New York statute requiring public schools to lend textbooks to pupils in private schools, the justices of the Supreme Court, by an eight-to-one margin also ruled, reversing a long-standing judgment, that taxpayers had a right to challenge in the courts any laws that they believed provided federal support for religious schools. Thus the ambiguity remains. Catholic spokesmen have acclaimed the increase in public support designed to give children "quality education regardless of school of attendance." But most of the Protestant and liberal organizations continue to oppose the practice. Yet some have changed their minds. Himmelfarb wonders if separation has not become a rigid dogma, unmindful of the genuine problems of Catholic parents. Many Protestants and Jews who can afford it send their children to private schools, or move to suburbs where they can supervise school quality; but they resist Catholics' efforts to achieve something of the same result. With Walter Lippmann, Himmelfarb argues that education has a more urgent claim on the country than the maintenance of a strict separation rule, that a strong pluralism is more essential than a rigid interpretation of the First Amendment. "What if excluding a church or a church-related institution in this or that neigh-

39 Ibid.

borhood weakens the effort to help the poor raise themselves out of poverty?" [40]

These are civilized questions, but perhaps not complicated enough. What if public support for parochial schools so weakens the public schools that *others* of the poor cannot raise themselves out of poverty? What if the few steps the United States has taken in support of private schools are extended until we approach the situation of the Netherlands, where the public schools have faded, and the separate schools help to maintain not so much a pluralistic as a columnar type of social structure?

However one views this dilemma, it seems likely, from the perspective of the student of society, that any further changes in the program of support for private schools depend upon the whole national context: Will differences between Catholic and non-Catholic continue to be modified? Will the civil rights movement move into a stage where major improvements in the public schools are accomplished; and will parochial schools take a more active role in the civil rights movement? Will an extended released-time program be developed, encouraging church leaders to emphasize religious training for all of their children for part of the time, rather than general training for some of their children throughout the school day? [41] Will economic and residential patterns continue to support communal aspects of religious identity at the present level, or will these aspects change —*decline* seems the more likely word—in favor of a more strictly associational identity?

These questions are meant simply to suggest that the "church-state problem"—seen here in connection with education—can be understood only in the context of the total society.

Effects of the American Pattern of Relationship Between Church and State

From the point of view of the central problem of this chapter, these developments raise the question: What are the influences of the principle of separation and its modification on the three modes of relationship between religion and politics? One can speak here only in a most tentative way; but our perspective permits us to offer some hypotheses.

Consider first the effects of the emphasis on the separation of church and state. This can scarcely be said to promote an integrating system of values rooted in religion—the first mode of relationship—but it at least prevents the aggravation of differences. A high level of coercion, not integration, would be the result of a politically sponsored religious unity in a religiously heterogeneous society. The political manipulation of religion—the second mode of relationship—is made less likely by the separation of church and state. In a religiously diverse society, where each church has equal political rights, one can scarcely make unambiguous claims that his own political views are religiously sustained. Equally powerful religious claims for different political views can be offered. That is the reason that those who seek to prove that their political program has God's blessing must first try to prove

40 Himmelfarb, op. cit.

41 This is seen as a basis for compromise between opponents and supporters of federal aid in George R. LaNoue, *Public Funds for Parochial Schools.*

that their religious views are the truly American ones—an established religious ideology, at least, if not an Established Church.

The development of religious institutions free to, and capable of, effective criticism of the established political pattern—the mode of relationship we have called universalism—is in some ways encouraged and in some ways blocked by the separation of church and state. The central thesis of Stokes, Pfeffer, and others is that separation (without antagonism) has fostered the growth of freedom in the United States and has increased the influence of religion on many aspects of American society, as contrasted with a state-church situation. Separation is supported because it allows greater freedom to both the churches and the state. Where the religious leaders lack direct political influence, they also escape direct political domination, are freer to criticize political processes and the structure of power, and are less invaded by political demands. The state, in turn, is given greater flexibility when it is not tied to an ecclesiastical structure.

The evidence does not, however, wholly support this view. Freedom from the structures of power raises the question of powerlessness. "The dilemma of the churches" is clear at this point, for to claim separation from the state is to reduce one's ability to influence the decisions of the state; institutional union, however, raises the likelihood that a church that seems to have a voice in political decisions is only serving as an echo of decisions actually made on political grounds. There is no easy way to avoid this dilemma in the search for an anchorage for an effectively autonomous religious influence in politics. Even the concepts of a monotheistic and universalistic religion run the risk of political irrelevancy if they are tied to a thoroughgoing separation of church and state, and run the opposite risk of being twisted to the purposes of the nation-state (in the name of universalism) if the institutional connection is a close one.

How to be simultaneously in politics (thus to influence it) and beyond politics (thus to challenge it) is an ancient problem among the world religions. Islam has tended strongly toward the former pole (although some mystical sectarian movements challenge this position), and has thus frequently served only to reinforce the political power of the ruling classes of Islamic societies. Buddhism has tended toward the latter pole, although not without exceptions, particularly in recent decades, and thus has often been irrelevant to political problems—a position that is equally likely to reinforce the power of the ruling groups. The situation in Christianity has been more complicated. There has been a more explicit recognition of the dilemma, stemming in an important degree from the Judaic background of Christianity. It has been formulated in a skilled way in such concepts as St. Thomas's "relative natural law." Recognition of a dilemma is not synonymous, however, with its resolution. The history of Christian societies is filled with illustrations of religious movements that have (always with qualifications) "joined the state" in "Islamic" fashion (Spain today, for example), and of other movements that have disregarded the problems of politics in "Buddhist" fashion. (It is sociologically interesting that this latter approach is most commonly found among the extremely disprivileged members of a society whose status makes such a pessimistic view of this world congenial.)

To avoid both horns of the dilemma requires not so much skilled maneuvering by religious leaders (though this is not unimportant) as a favorable sociocultural context. In the broadest terms we have defined this context as one of diffused power, based on relatively autonomous economic, political, educational, technical, and other social structures.

It is perhaps the recognition of this dilemma that has been partly responsible for the recent reduction in the sharpness of separation of churches and state in the United States. There is, of course, no question of a formal connection; but as we have seen, political leaders have been more likely to use the language of religion, and religious organizations in recent decades have become much more concerned with "social action." They have sought to influence political decisions by organized effort, by carefully worked out pronouncements from national councils, and by lobbying. How has this modification of the sharper separation of church and state that characterized the earlier period of American development affected the balance of the three modes of relationship with which we are concerned?

Religious concern for political decisions can promote the value integration of a society only to the degree that diverse religious groups emphasize common values. If they enter the political arena in competition with each other, creedal differences will be emphasized and the tensions of the society increased. Integration is scarcely served when religious leaders become concerned with political and economic questions, only to take sharply diverse views.

We will cite some evidences for diversity later. Probably more significant, however, at least on the national level where political action by churches tends to be focused, is the extent of agreement. There is substantial value agreement in the views of large numbers of religious spokesmen on the requisites of a just and good society. Witness the convergence of views, and to some degree the active cooperation, among the National Catholic Welfare Conference, the Central Conference of American Rabbis, and the Protestant National Council of Churches.[42] Their cumulative influence is to underline a dominant, if not a universally shared, value core. They represent an adaptation of a religiously heterogeneous society that is seeking to maintain at least a minimum value consensus. There is no evidence that universal agreement on this value core is necessary—or even, from some perspectives, desirable—for the continuation of a changing modern society; but if the conception of society we have adopted is correct, some strong central tendency is required. The *balance* of contemporary religious developments in the United States would seem to be contributing to the maintenance of this central core of values.

It should be noted, however, that in a society of diverse religious connections, the reinforcements of ritual and the supports of dogma are "not available," for they accentuate the differences within the society, not its unity. It is partly for this reason that symbols of nation, rather than of creed, are most expressive of the unity of a modern, complex society. Or a less nationalistic civil religion may carry something of the universalist tradition in a way that can reduce differences.

The second mode of relationship between religion and politics—the use of religious symbols for the political purposes of part of the society—has probably been increased by the reduction of the sharpness of separation of

42 See Stokes, op. cit., Vol. III, pp. 3–32.

church and state in the United States. Political claims in the name of religion are given more credence in a situation in which the two spheres are thought to be mutually significant.

To understand the effects of this reduction in sharpness of separation of church and state upon the third mode of relationship—a universalist religious emphasis capable of imposing restraints on the state—we must refer again to the dilemma of the churches. When prominent church leaders, denominational boards, and interdenominational conferences give more vigorous attention to questions of racial, or labor, or international relations, seeking to influence and guide the government, they reduce the likelihood of powerlessness; at the same time, however, they run the risk both of mistaking their various parochial views with universal judgments and of a reduction in the full flexibility of action. "The state" will listen to "the church" only if there is agreement on certain basic premises—and it is often precisely these premises that a universal perspective might bring most sharply under criticism. At a time when instruments of destruction of incalculable power have shattered the adequacy of existing political structures, when we know that a few hydrogen bombs can kill tens of millions of human beings, one might expect a universalist religion to offer dramatic and persistent challenges to the secular structures that divide the world. But one finds little of this on the local level, in the writer's judgment. Tolerance of the widespread use of violence by governments is very widespread. It is made sharply visible against the background of great *intolerance* for intranational violence and protests which, in my judgment, are partly a product of governments' claims and use of violence in international affairs.

Even in the National Council of Churches and the World Council of Churches, as they have sought to influence the course of action in international relations in the last decade, one senses a tendency to proclaim their approval of peace and disarmament, but some reticence in relating their concerns directly to the existing patterns and the basic premises of governmental policy. From various value perspectives this may be looked upon as a happy or an unhappy development; but it indicates the dilemma of the churches, which must seek influence in a world that has many powers and many values besides their own.

Effects of Religion on Political Behavior in the United States. Setting aside these comments on the effects of American patterns upon the various modes of relationship between religion and politics, we can turn to some of the empirical work that studies this relationship. It can readily be established that there is a statistical correlation between religious-group membership and political behavior in many countries. In the United States, white Protestants are more likely to be Republicans, and Catholics and Jews are more likely to be Democrats than one would predict from their respective ratios in the population. The size of the correlation varies from election to election, and it has fallen in recent years, especially for the Catholic group; nevertheless, the relationship remains. What does it mean? Is it a spurious correlation, merely reflecting class differences? Does it reflect ethnic identity and the effects of a minority-majority situation? Or do religious values enter directly into the relationship, influencing political behavior in ways that deflect class- and interest-based politics?

The evidence seems to show that each of these questions can be answered affirmatively. It would be foolish to take the simple correlations as signs of a direct influence of religion on political behavior; but it would equally be a mistake to disregard the ways in which religious values affect political choice. Studies made in Erie County, 1940, Elmira, 1948, and the Detroit area, 1957–58, all show that the relationship between party preference or voting behavior and church identity remains after controls have been made for class.[43] Lenski found, for example, that the Republican preference of middle-class white Protestants in Detroit was 54 per cent; that of white Catholics was 30 per cent. Among the working class, the Republican preferences for Protestant and Catholic fell to 30 and 13 per cent, respectively, showing that class as well as religious group was involved.[44]

If class standing cannot explain all of the variation in political preference among religious groups, can some of it be accounted for by minority status? Many authors have interpreted the support that Jews give to liberal political programs as a result of the fact that their economic achievements have not been accompanied by equivalent status victories.[45] The identification of Catholics with the Democratic Party began at a time when a large proportion of them were immigrants suffering some measure of discrimination. "In cities with large Catholic populations the Democratic party early became an agency of Catholic social participation, protest, and power. Once established, party allegiance tended to be transmitted within the group and from generation to generation." [46] As minority status has receded, so has the close identification of Catholics with the Democratic party. There is some tendency currently, in fact, for the tables to be turned, as a somewhat shaky status among the majority is bolstered by a shift to the Republican party, and in some instances to right-wing political movements, even among those for whom union membership, traditional party identification, and "bread-and-butter issues" are supportive of allegiance to the Democratic party.

It is difficult to isolate, out of the complex of class, ethnic, and other factors with which it is connected, a specifically religious influence on political behavior. Value elements of religious perspectives however, seem clearly to play a part. Wilson and Banfield, in a study of twenty referenda held in seven American cities between 1956 and 1963, found that many of the groups most likely to profit from the increased medical, educational, and recreational services—and least likely to be taxed heavily to support them—voted in highest proportion against them.[47] These were the Catholic ethnic groups. Upper-income white Protestants and Jews voted for the bond

43 See, for example, Paul Lazarsfeld, Bernard Berelson, and Hazel Gaudet, The People's Choice; Bernard Berelson, Paul Lazarsfeld, and William McPhee, Voting; Oscar Glantz, "Protestant and Catholic Voting Behavior in a Metropolitan Area," Public Opinion Quarterly, 23, 1959, pp. 73–82; Luke Ebersole, "Religion and Politics," Annals of the American Academy of Political and Social Science, 332, 1960, pp. 101–111; and Gerhard Lenski, The Religious Factor.

44 Lenski, op. cit., p. 125. It should be noted that a simple two-class analysis leaves room for error. If many of the Protestants are upper-middle-class, whereas many of the Catholics are lower-middle-class, for example, the effects of religion are obscured.

45 Ibid., p. 141; and Lawrence Fuchs, The Political Behavior of American Jews.

46 Ebersole, "Religion and Politics," op. cit., p. 108.

47 James Q. Wilson and Edward C. Banfield, "Public Regardingness as a Value Premise in Voting Behavior," American Political Science Review, 58, 1964, pp. 876–887.

issues, even though they would profit least and be taxed most. Only low-income Negroes seemed to vote as one might predict from a purely rational self-interest perspective. How account for this contrast? Wilson and Banfield conclude that the Protestant and Jewish subcultures teach a more public-regarding ethic than does the Catholic. The contrast between the Judaic and Catholic belief systems has been spelled out in detail by Parenti.[48] He argues that Jewish liberalism is related closely to three facts: There is little tension between faith and intellect in Judaism; the spiritual leader is an expert in interpreting and applying the law, not an ascetic or otherworldly person. "In modern times, Judaism has been less an otherworldly theology and formulated creed than a system of practices, observances, and moral commitments." [49] An important part of the moral code, in fact, was a commitment to work for justice. And third, Judaism does not teach ascetic renunciation as the road to salvation, but life affirmation, partly in the form of programs to increase well-being on this earth.

Catholic beliefs, Parenti argues, contrast rather sharply: There is an emphasis on unchanging truth and sacred dogma, on lay obedience to hierarchical teachings rather than on investigation, which can support a strain of anti-intellectualism.[50] Catholicism emphasizes a theology of personal salvation more than one of social reform. And by its emphasis on man's inherent propensity for sin it encourages a form of asceticism that supports doctrines of individual responsibility rather than social reform.

Each of these generalizations requires qualification. At the least, the distinction that Parenti draws between fundamentalist and liberal Protestantism is required also with reference to Catholicism. Strong currents of change are moving through the Catholic Church; laymen are growing in influence; differences in educational level and class position between Catholics and Protestants have declined sharply and probably have disappeared entirely. This is not to deny the validity of the contrast that Parenti draws, however, but to emphasize the need for contemporary empirical support. In a sample taken on the West Coast, Glock and Stark found that Catholics agreed with fundamentalist Protestants on many issues, but that on some they were closer to members of the liberal Protestant denominations. For example, their responses to the statements that "men cannot help doing evil" and that "doing good for others" is "absolutely necessary" for salvation were very similar to the responses given to the same statements by the members of liberal Protestant denominations.[51]

In a series of papers, Benton Johnson has advanced the study of the influence of religious values on political behavior, class factors being controlled, by noting the need for distinguishing between liberal and fundamentalist Protestant groups, even among those generally associated with the "ascetic" tradition. In samples drawn from a city in the Northwest and another in the South, he found that those who frequently attended the liberal churches, whether they were white-collar or blue-collar, were *less*

48 Michael Parenti, "Political Values and Religious Cultures: Jews, Catholics, and Protestants," *Journal for the Scientific Study of Religion*, 6, 1967, pp. 259–269.

49 Ibid., p. 262.

50 See Thomas F. O'Dea, *American Catholic Dilemma*.

51 Charles Glock and Rodney Stark, *Religion and Society in Tension*, pp. 99 and 106.

likely to vote Republican than those who attended seldom; while those who attended the fundamentalist churches frequently were *more* likely to vote Republican than those who attended seldom.[52] He cannot, from the evidence in hand, tell whether it is the values they hold, the messages they hear, and the group support they receive that produces this relationship or whether it is a consequence of selectivity. Johnson gives major weight, however, to a causal interpretation: "It is our contention that socializing influences in the form of politically relevant values emanating from the two major factions of Ascetic Protestantism are largely responsible for the findings. . . ."[53]

This is a plausible interpretation. A partial replication of Johnson's work in a different region of the country, it should be noted, obtained different results. Donald Anderson did not find the same relationship between church attendance and political preference among the liberal Protestants in a sample drawn from an Illinois county.[54] Those who attended frequently, in fact, were more likely to have a Republican preference than those who seldom attended. Among fundamentalist Protestants, Anderson's findings did support Johnson's; but this means simply that Anderson found *all* classes of frequent church attenders to be more Republican. Unfortunately, the Illinois study is not a precise replication of the Northwest and Southern studies. In particular, Anderson classified Baptists among the liberals, as Johnson did not, because the branch represented in his sample was associated with the National Council of Churches. Since denominational data are not given, one cannot measure the extent to which this influenced the result. Anderson classified churches as liberal by their denominational affiliation rather than by the views of the pastor, as Johnson had done. Various difficulties of interpretation arise also from the fact that in both studies, all variables were treated as dichotomies. Such crude categories, with the possibility that in one sample the mean is near the top of the category while in the other it is near the bottom, leave all interpretations problematic. The preponderance of the evidence, however, gives tentative support to the view that religious values have influenced political preference.

Empirical study of the relationships between religion and political behavior is often hampered by serious methodological questions. There are problems of definition and measurement. Is religion simply an attribute, to be measured by church membership or self-identification with a religious tradition; or it is a variable—or even a series of variables—requiring that individuals be located in multivariate "space" before the implications of their

52 Benton Johnson, "Ascetic Protestantism and Political Preference," *Public Opinion Quarterly*, 26, 1962, pp. 35–46; "Ascetic Protestantism and Political Preference in the Deep South," *American Journal of Sociology*, 69, 1964, pp. 359–366. Two studies of clergymen by Johnson yielded similar results: "Theology and Party Preference among Protestant Clergymen," *American Sociological Review*, 31, 1966, pp. 200–208; and "Theology and the Position of Pastors on Public Issues," *American Sociological Review*, 32, 1967, pp. 433–442.

53 Benton Johnson, "Ascetic Protestantism and Political Preference," pp. 44–45.

54 Donald N. Anderson, "Ascetic Protestantism and Political Preference," *Review of Religious Research*, 7, 1966, pp. 167–171. See also Benton Johnson and Richard White, "Protestantism, Political Preference, and the Nature of Religious Influence: Comment on Anderson's Paper," *Review of Religious Research*, 9, 1967, pp. 28–35.

religion for behavior can be studied? Assuming an adequate definition, we are faced with the need for introducing sufficient controls, so that any observed differences can confidently be accounted for by the religio-political interaction. Interpretations of the relationship between fundamentalist religion and right-wing politics, for example, are made difficult by the task of controlling for the effects of education, income, regional subculture other than religion, and other variables. Since interaction effects are likely to be important, moreover, it is not enough to try to isolate a "purely religious" element. One must seek to discover its influence (or its response) in the various clusters of variables within which it is embedded.

We will be wise to keep these methodological problems in mind as we examine studies of the relationship between religion and extremist politics. There are several partially competing, partially complementary hypotheses: fundamentalist or conservative religion supports right-wing politics; religion and politics are interchangeable responses, not likely to be found together, to deprivation; relative deprivation is more powerful as an explanatory variable than absolute deprivation.

On a descriptive level, one can find evidence in many societies of a relationship between conservative religious views and reactionary politics. Most of those who have supported the right wing in France in the twentieth century—the *déclassé* nobility, some of the military, many of the *petite bourgeoisie,* and some of the peasantry—have held a conservative, clerical view of "the good society" in which the Church would be a prominent source of order and authority.[55] Protestants, Jews, and secularists are seen as the source of a republican society that has destroyed the traditional status of these groups.

The union of reactionary politics and conservative religion seems at first glance to be quite different in South Africa, for the Africaners are not fighting to reverse a lost revolution. They have won political power. Yet, seen in the light of their history and the contemporary economic situation, the status of the Dutch-descended South Africans has interesting similarities with that of the supporters of Action Française. The Dutch settled the Cape area before the British, but were driven out. They moved inland into what proved to be gold and diamond territory, but the British took it over, eventually by war. Despite their political dominance, the Dutch-descended South Africans are less influential economically, less at home in an urban, industrial society, than are those of British and Jewish descent. To speak of religious support for apartheid requires that we see it in this larger context. In my judgment, it is less useful to see this support as an intrinsic expression of Dutch Calvinist theology and polity than as another indication that men use their religion to struggle for control, at whatever level their situations permit.[56]

In the United States today it is frequently affirmed that religious fundamentalism is associated with right-wing politics, opposition to civil rights, and chauvinism in international relations. Because it can also be shown,

55 See Edward R. Tannenbaum, *The Action Française: Die-Hard Reactionaries in Twentieth-Century France.*

56 On South Africa see, for example, G. W. Carter, *The Politics of Inequality;* Norman Phillips, *The Tragedy of Apartheid;* Edwin Munger, *Africaner and African Nationalism;* Pierre van den Berghe, *South Africa: A Study in Conflict.*

however, that religion is associated with liberal politics, and even on occasion with radicalism, it is essential here, as in the cases of France and South Africa, that we study carefully the system of which religion forms a part.

When in 1962 the Supreme Court of the United States ruled that a prayer prescribed by the New York State Board of Regents for all public schools was unconstitutional, several Senators, all of them from the South, proposed bills to nullify the decision. Their arguments were often to the effect that " 'the twisted thinking' of Court members 'fits beautifully with the Communist Master Plan.' " [57] Among many conservatively inclined citizens, nonreligious or antireligious beliefs and actions are synonymous with un-American activity: church and state may be separate, but religion and citizenship are identical. When asked to define a "Communist," some say that it is a person who is against religion or one who teaches things contrary to the Bible. Thus political and national conflicts become identified with religious controversies. Samuel Stouffer wrote: "It has perhaps not been adequately appreciated that a considerable element in the opposition to a free market in ideas in America is religious in origin." [58] Numerous studies have established a correlation between fundamentalism in religion and right-wing politics.[59]

The meaning of the correlation, however, is not self-evident. Some of the studies fall into the "ecological error," by failing to show that particular individuals in a region high in fundamentalism are the same individuals who are high in rightist sentiments. Simply to show, for example, that rightist movements are strong in the American "Bible Belt" is not enough. Detailed study of the doctrines of fundamentalist groups is more likely to reveal a generalized opposition to politics and tendencies toward withdrawal than an espousal of reactionary policies.[60] Measurement of religious beliefs is often neglected in favor of data on church membership or church attendance. If the several dimensions of religiosity relate differently to political belief and action, we need to study them separately.[61]

There is need to describe much more fully than has yet been done in research on the relationships of religion and politics, the exact nature of the link between fundamentalism and right-wing politics. The causal sequence often implied, if not sharply formulated, is as follows: A child receives training in a fundamentalist religion by parental choice, not his own; he learns certain religious values, opinions, and tendencies as a result of that training; when these are applied to politics, they naturally support right-wing positions. This formula is far too simple. We need information

57 Betty E. Chmaj, "Paranoid Politics. The Radical Right and the South," *Atlantic Monthly*, November, 1962, p. 93.

58 Stouffer, *Communists, Conformity, and Civil Liberties*.

59 See, for example. Brooks Walker, *The Christian Fright Peddlers*; Robert Rosenstone, ed., *Protest From the Right*; Gary Maranell, "An Examination of Some Religious and Political Attitude Correlates of Bigotry," *Social Forces*, 45, 1967, pp. 356–363; Ralph Roy, op. cit.; Arnold Forster and B. R. Epstein, *Danger on the Right*; Harry Overstreet and B. Overstreet, *The Strange Tactics of Extremism*; Daniel Bell, ed., *The Radical Right*.

60 Howard Elinson, "The Implications of Pentecostal Religion for Intellectualism, Politics, and Race Relations," *American Journal of Sociology*, 70, 1965, pp. 403–415.

61 Frederick Whitam, "Subdimensions of Religiosity and Race Prejudice," *Review of Religious Research*, 3, 1962, pp. 166–174.

on such questions as the following: Are fundamentalist beliefs sometimes the result of individual selection, not family influence, so that the reasons for the selection rather than the nature of the training are the prior, causal variable? In this case, we would not have:

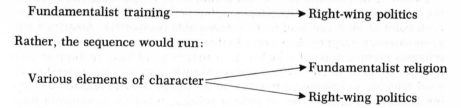

Fundamentalist training ⟶ Right-wing politics

Rather, the sequence would run:

Various elements of character ⟶ Fundamentalist religion
⟶ Right-wing politics

Such information would help us to establish the time sequence, but would be insufficient to determine the nature of the relationship. We need also to ask: Among those with fundamentalist training, what proportion support right-wing politics? All? Some? A few? If only some, then we need to know what differences in their experience—perhaps in the structure of the opportunities that surrounded them or the group support for various interpretations—pulled them in one direction while others took a different road. The pattern might be as follows:

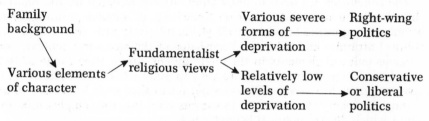

Family background ⟶ Various elements of character ⟶ Fundamentalist religious views ⟶ Various severe forms of deprivation ⟶ Right-wing politics
⟶ Relatively low levels of deprivation ⟶ Conservative or liberal politics

One can formulate other and more complicated sequences, but this may illustrate the need for going well beyond simple correlations. The correlation we are discussing may be high simply because most of those trained to fundamentalism happen also to be persons who were faced by many serious deprivations.

Such methodological considerations do not lead me to the view that fundamentalist religion is unrelated to support for right-wing politics. They do, however, require careful specification of the relationship. Fundamentalist religion does not "cause" reactionary politics any more than hydrogen "causes" sugar, regardless of the availability of carbon and oxygen. It may, if present in the right amounts along with the other necessary elements in the right amounts, and under particular conditions, be part of a compound. But in different situations, other compounds are formed.

Shifting briefly to a macroscopic view of the effects of religion on political behavior in the United States, we can ask whether high religiosity strengthens or weakens the democratic political process. At least since Tocqueville, America has been seen as more religious than Europe; and more democratic as a result.[62] Other observers take the opposite point of view. Berger remarks that on American campuses, "the religious organizations are all too often the gathering place for the most conformist, the most

62 Seymour Lipset, *Political Man*, pp. 39–40.

anti-intellectual, the most prejudiced segments of the student population. And the view of society we find among our clergy and clericalized laymen is all too often a collection plate for every delusion to be found in the market." [63]

I know of no evidence that would permit us to weigh these two contrasting influences in any definitive fashion; but perhaps a fuller specification of each point of view can lead us to a reasonable perspective. America's religious situation supports democracy in these ways: Because there are several religious groups, none of which is in a majority, all have to support civil liberties to some degree. The various religious groups have proved to be good vehicles for bringing interests into the political arena and for developing leaders. As alternatives to radical politics, religious movements have kept the political system from serious, perhaps destructive, pressures. Many basic religious values directly support a democratic polity.

On the other hand, there is some evidence that the most "religious" people, at least as measured on various traditional scales, are often the most intolerant.[64] Religious conflict has sometimes been disruptive, most visibly on the national, but perhaps most seriously on the local level. Some religious values are antidemocratic, as regards free speech, full rights for "unbelievers," and rigidity toward other systems of such a nature that the conduct of American foreign affairs may be made inflexible.[65]

The conclusion we need to draw from current research on the relationship of religion and politics is clear: Knowledge of religious training, membership, or expressed belief by itself yields relatively little power to predict political attitudes and behavior. Knowledge of the structural context, nonreligious cultural elements in the environment, and a wide range of individual tendencies is needed before we can state what the implications of given religious forces are. This does not mean that such forces are unimportant. It means that they enter in various ways into the complex mixtures out of which diverse political behavior is born.

63 Peter Berger, *The Noise of Solemn Assemblies*, p. 14.

64 Problems of measurement on this question, however, are severe. There is some danger that liberally inclined researchers have designed scales that make those who see the world through fundamentalist glasses into rigid-minded, angry, and even quasi-paranoiac individuals. They are angry and rigid *in the contemporary setting*. They are angry at a society in which their values, their power to control their own lives, and their status are threatened. More recently, liberals and radicals have become angry and not a little rigid *in certain settings*. It is instructive to compare the measurement processes and the conclusions of T. W. Adorno and others, *The Authoritarian Personality*, with those of Milton Rokeach, *The Open and Closed Mind*. Rokeach has sought to design a "dogmatism scale" independent of right or left inclinations. He found dogmatism on both left and right. "If we had only the F and ethnocentrism means to go on, we would be tempted to conclude that the Catholic groups are relatively high in authoritarianism and prejudice, while the nonbelievers and Communists are relatively low." (Ibid., p. 117; see Chap. 6 of this work.) Unfortunately, Rokeach also deals with correlations, and not with situationally expressed tendencies. Although based on a limited sample, a useful effort to isolate a purely religious element and to study its relationship to prejudice is the study of Bernard Spilka and James Reynolds, "Religion and Prejudice: A Factor Analytic Study," *Review of Religious Research*, 6, 1965, pp. 163–168.

65 For some data on attitudes toward international affairs, classified by religious identity, see Alfred Hero, "The American Public and the U.N.," *Journal of Conflict Resolution*, 10, 1966, pp. 467–468.

Chapter Twenty

RELIGION AND WAR

The relationships between religion and citizenship in the modern world are revealed in their sharpest forms under conditions of warfare. However long the values and interests of the state and of religion may flow parallel to each other, there comes a point at which they move in different and even opposite directions. The final concern of the state is with self-preservation, whatever the means; the final concern of religion is with salvation, whatever the costs. These may not contradict one another in some circumstances; but under other conditions, a choice must be made between irreconcilable values and requirements. In examining this issue, we will give primary attention to situations in which a universal religion confronts the problem of war, with its inevitable divisive impact; for it is in such situations that the full complexity of the relationship is found. We can indicate the other patterns briefly.

In those situations where religious membership and social membership are identical, war is scarcely a problem. If the society is at war, the gods give their support; religion is used unambiguously to sustain the society's claim; ritual and prayer and sacrifice are devoted to the cause of victory. The enemies of Jehovah, in the earliest days, were simply the enemies of Israel; Asshur gave strength in battle to Assyria; the Guardian Spirit of a Dakota Indian was at his side in battle. Thus religion was used to weld the society together and to give the individual courage, in order to bring victory and to help the adherents to face the risks and sacrifices of war.

Where a growing social complexity has produced a differentiation between the political and religious structures—with the possibility of clashes of policy and competition for power, and the greater likelihood of differences in interest among the members of the society—the relationship between religion and war is not so unambiguous. There is still no question of war as such being a problem, for religious views are still society-bound, but there are questions of when and where and how war should be employed, based on differences of interest and value. In these circumstances, a religious ideology may be manipulated by those in power to support a war that is given only reluctant backing or even opposed by large segments of society.

The modern Japanese situation illustrates this mode of relationship, although not without complicating aspects. The West tended to look upon Japan before and during the Second World War as a nation of wholly dedicated belligerents. But this was scarcely an accurate picture. "Only the common people," said a Japanese writer in 1939, "know the bitterness of war." The ruling group exploited the powerful symbols of National Shinto to tie the nation together in unified support of its war program. According to the ideology of Shinto, "The sacred quality of the divine emperor attaches to a Japanese war. All the wars of Japan are holy wars since they are under the supreme command of an emperor who can do nothing wrong." [1] Shinto made the Japanese state not merely a secular power, but a sacred church as well, "founded on the arrogation that in the last analysis the validity of its decisions was superhuman or supernatural." [2] Although this shares some elements with a simple tribal religion lending support to the nation in its external conflicts, the situation is actually far more complicated than that. It is a great mistake to think of the ceremonies and ideologies of National Shinto as one would think of the religious war dances and beliefs of a small, relatively homogeneous, tribal society. A nation of 80 million people, with its diverse classes and interests, its various hopes, its widely different outlooks on the world, indeed, its variety of religions, developed only by great effort the degree of unity necessary for modern war. The explicit *revival* of Shinto in the last third of the nineteenth century, in the face of a strong Buddhist and some Christian influence—with their theoretical opposition to war—is the clearest sign of the manipulative aspect that is the basic element in the second mode of relationship between religion and government.

It is not sufficient, however, to speak only of Shinto in Japan in relation to war, for religions of brotherhood are a significant part of the religious scene. In Japan, as in other societies where religions with a universalist emphasis are predominant, war itself has become a problem, for it clearly represents a sharp split in the universal brotherhood of man, which these religions support. But if war is a problem, so is defeat and the possibility of the nation being dominated by another nation. In no case, therefore, do we find the churches of such societies dwelling solely on the universal theme, opposing war, and refusing to cooperate with the government.

A powerful nationalistic movement and concentrated economic power sharply limit the range of religious action. ". . . Japanese Buddhism and Confucianism, in yielding to and supporting the morality of nation and emperor as primary in the hierarchy of values, depart markedly from the interpretation in the other Buddhist nations and in Chinese Confucianism." [3] Although the terminology is not often used with reference to Chris-

1 D. C. Holtom, *Modern Japan and Shinto Nationalism,* p. 54; see also Robert O. Ballou, *Shinto, the Unconquered Enemy.*

2 Holtom, op. cit., p. 176.

3 Robert Bobilin, in *The Religious Situation: 1968,* Donald R. Cutler, ed., p. 463. See also Hajime Nakamura, *The Ways of Thinking of Eastern Peoples.*

tian societies, the following statement might readily be transposed to refer to Germany, England, or the United States: ". . . the Japanese case seems to be an illustration of the assimilation of the 'great tradition' of classical Buddhism to the 'little tradition' of popular religion as it syncretized with Japanese culture." [4] Christian churches in Japan, in fact, were scarcely different. In supporting the war against China, the Japanese National Christian Council wrote: "With tears in our hearts we have raised aloft the whips of love." [5]

The themes of "tribal unity," the manipulation of religion by partial interests, and universalism mingle in complicated interaction. The task of the sociology of "religion and war" is to try to discover the conditions under which various balances among these themes occur.

RESPONSES OF CHRISTIAN CHURCHES IN THE WEST TO WAR
Some reference to the response of Christian churches to war will be of value in helping to find these conditions. During the early centuries when Christianity was a small and persecuted sect, pacifism was its dominant theme. This is not surprising, for the sect had neither the responsibilities nor the coercive possibilities of power. By the time of St. Augustine, however, Christianity had become a powerful secular as well as religious force. The pacifist position was gradually given up as the Church became involved in problems of coercion and conflict. St. Augustine drew on an accumulating doctrine of justification for Christian participation in war to formulate what is still the essential pattern of the Catholic, and to a substantial degree the Lutheran and Anglican, doctrine of war: the Church can give its support to a war only if the cause of one side is manifestly just and only if it is fought without vindictiveness, a kind of reluctant participation in a "just and mournful war."

Through the centuries, St. Augustine's doctrine of the "just war" has been elaborated in various ways, but the essential ideal remains: The evils of war must be weighed against the evils that may occur if injustice prevails. To oppose war may not be to oppose violence; it may only be to permit those who are willing to use unjust violence to succeed. The moral dilemma is recognized, but a way out is seen in the strict requirements that the cause of one side be just, that the "innocent" shall not suffer, that violence shall be directed only toward military personnel and targets.

Each of these requirements, of course, is difficult to establish. Who is to determine which side is just, and by what criteria? Who are the innocent and who are the guilty? The vocabulary of praise and blame for the tragedies of the human condition seems to some to be anachronistic. How, under modern conditions of warfare, can the violence be focused on military personnel and targets; even if it be accepted that such a course can be justified because it leads to a speedier reduction of violence?

Thus the dilemma that the "just war" doctrine seeks to resolve continues to press in on man. Efforts to reduce its sharpness or to evade its implications fall along a scale, ranging from the position that the threat of destruc-

4 Bobilin, op. cit., p. 491.

5 Charles W. Iglehart, *A Century of Protestant Christianity in Japan*, quoted by Bobilin, op. cit.

tion or oppression of one's own group is so serious that other values must be set aside, to the position that the threat of destruction of the proscription against killing is so great that all war must be opposed. Thus on the one side there remains the crusade—at first a holy cause fought under the authority of the church, but of late a national cause fought with the blessing of the church—and on the other pacifism, found largely in the sects.[6] The following scale points may help to define the range:

Crusade; "holy war"	"Just war"	"Reluctant and mournful war"	Opposition to "this war"	Non-violent resistance; vocational pacifism	Non-resistance; refusal to register; withdrawal
---✗---------	✗---------	✗---------	✗---------	✗---------	✗----

Except for those at the extreme ends of the range, the dilemma involved in the policies toward violence is scarcely hidden. Those who give "reluctant and mournful" support to a war, for example, may reduce their cognitive and moral dissonance by overt recognition of their own fallibility, by emphasizing the need for speedy reconciliation, by declaring the mixed quality of every moral decision. These demurs may, indeed, reduce the sharpness of the dilemma they face. In the last analysis, however, the dilemma is still there; and it will remain there as a major problem for religions of brotherhood so long as the use of organized violence to obtain goals is part of the human scene.

The depth of the problem is indicated by the rapid changes that often occur in the attitudes of religious spokesmen. When a crisis occurs, the relatively smooth scale we have described begins to break down; there is a strong tendency toward polarization. Sometimes within a few months, the dominant attitude can shift from sharp condemnation of war, mixed with pacifism, to vigorous support of a government in the prosecution of a war. The sociological meaning of "church" as a religious institution thoroughly integrated with a society, as well as the concept of the dilemma of the churches, can help us to interpret this shift. It is inconceivable that a church —by its very definition—should fail to support a nation in a major war. Church leaders could scarcely hope to be effective in a society if they turned away completely from the basic struggle in which that society was engaged. They accept the reality of much that is inevitable,[7] so far as their own power is concerned, in order—it is their hope—to be able to exert a qualified influence. This does not necessarily mean that they have relinquished the universalist theme of their religion, although it may signify that. It may demonstrate only the recognition of the dilemma that they face and the difficulty in gaining perspective. Viewing from a distance, one can see the enormous practical task that the religious people in a nation face in trying to define a "just war," constrained as they are by the situation they are in.

6 See Roland Bainton, *Christian Attitudes Toward War and Peace.*

7 I do not imply here the inevitability of war as an institution, but only that it is and has been part of the fixed environment so far as churches are concerned.

The degree to which war will be supported by churches only as part of the "relative natural law"—that is, the degree to which war will continue to be criticized for its destruction of universality at the same time that it is being supported—varies greatly, even in the course of a few years. American churches during World War I, for example, were strongly inclined, with few exceptions, to give the war unqualified support.[8] During World War II, however, there was much more restraint, a more frequent expression of America's responsibilities in the sequence of events that led to the war, and a stronger insistence that victory be used as an opportunity for promoting world brotherhood. Early in 1942, for example, the editors of *Christianity and Crisis* stated their aims for the year to be: (1) to recognize responsibilities as citizens of a belligerent nation; (2) to "resist tyranny and help to establish justice without hatred or bitterness. This can only be done if we avoid self-righteousness . . ."; (3) to develop the resources of the church for service to both civilians and men in the armed forces; (4) to keep the consciousness of the universal church alive; (5) to deal at length with the problems of postwar reconstruction.[9] Here is certainly a modern version of St. Augustine's just and mournful war, by men who had insisted that America should join the war several months before hostilities actually began, but who continued to stress its dangers and weaknesses as an instrument of justice. Shortly after Pearl Harbor, the executive committee of the Federal Council of Churches, while condemning "the calculated treachery of recent aggressions," also pointed to America's involvement in the events that led up to the conflict, emphasized the separate tasks of the church, as distinct from the government, during wartime, declared that "the church must be in the vanguard of preparation for a just and durable peace," and underlined the universalist theme:

As members of the world-wide church which transcends all difference of race and nation, we have obligations which reach beyond our own country. We must preserve at all costs the world-wide Christian fellowship without which no free world order of justice and peace can be achieved.[10]

To point to such data is not to prove that the churches *effectively* promoted a universalist program in the midst of war. This is not to disparage their efforts, but to point to the serious question of power. It would be difficult to uphold the proposition that in the decades after the Second World War there was a smaller harvest of bitterness, a less divided world than after the First World War. This does not prove the ineffectiveness of the efforts of the churches to promote universalism, of course, for the second war was much more divisive and destructive than the first: the world might be even more divided were it not for religious efforts. It does, however, warn us not to mistake church pronouncements for effective political action. It is well to remember several things in this connection: probably only a minority of churchmen took part in these actions; a great many secular groups (not without religious motivation in part) were also con-

8 See Ray Abrams, *Preachers Present Arms*; Anson P. Stokes, *Church and State in the United States*, Vol. III, Chap. 21; J. Milton Yinger, *Religion in the Struggle for Power*, Chap. 5.

9 *Christianity and Crisis*, January 12, 1942, pp. 1–2.

10 *Christian Century*, January 14, 1942, p. 60.

cerned with problems of peace and international justice; a verbal bow to a universal ideology is a very common accompaniment of war in the modern world (even National Shinto declared that Japanese victory would bring "the whole world under one roof")—such a bow is perhaps a necessity to relieve the sense of guilt of peoples to whom war has become a social problem; and the churches found it easier to agree on aims than on procedures, without which the aims must remain unfulfilled.

Yet even conferences and declarations show that a religion with a universal ethic may, in some circumstances, resist many of the pressures that would make it simply a symbolic arm of a government in conflict.

The Churches and War in the Atomic Age

What is surely the sharpest discontinuity in the history of warfare occurred with the development of fission and fusion bombs. There has been no such discontinuity in the development of religious attitudes toward war. In fact, there has been relatively little discussion among churchmen of the significance of our new capacity for violence—probably less than among nuclear scientists and less than one might suppose was minimally called for. Such discussion as there has been tends to emphasize the need for bringing the principle of a "just war" up to date. These works show that war is still "thinkable" to many religious spokesmen, as it is to Herman Kahn,[11] and clearly, of course, to governments.

How are the paucity of examinations and the "just war" positions to be accounted for? Perhaps the very enormity of the holocaust that would result from an atomic and hydrogen-bomb war, rather than prompting churchmen to intense efforts to state and implement the universalist idea, has partially paralyzed their efforts—as it has the efforts of many who are not identified with the churches. Perhaps the severity of the crisis and the threat, in the conditions obtaining today, intensifies the sense of identity with the nation, producing a polarization that is characteristic of conditions in wartime. Maybe the quantum leap in the destructiveness of modern weapons has not changed the nature of the dilemma that the churches face, but has only lifted it to a new level of intensity.

In my judgment, all three of these things are true: The absence of continuous, widespread, and intensive re-examination of the problem on war on the part of churchmen is impressive. (It is difficult to give a quantitative measure to this observation. There have been, of course, dozens of books, scores of conferences, hundreds of articles. Others may see these as signs of major attention to the problem. Seen against the enormity of the issue, however, they impress me by their scarcity.) What is equally impressive is that those examinations that have been made reveal the continuing dilemma.

11 For a variety of points of view, see Herman Kahn, *On Thermonuclear War;* Edward Reed, ed., *Pacem in Terris;* Thomas Murray, *Nuclear Policy for War and Peace;* John Bennett, ed., *Nuclear Weapons and the Conflict of Conscience;* Paul Ramsey, *War and the Christian Conscience;* William Nagle, ed., *Morality and Modern Warfare;* James Douglass, *The Non-Violent Cross. A Theology of Revolution and Peace;* Robert Tucker, *Just War and Vatican Council II: A Critique;* Edward Long, *War and Conscience in America.*

Pope John XXIII's encyclical, *Pacem in Terris*, 1963, illustrates the dilemma more by implication than directly.[12] These parts of the encyclical that bear on international relations are a fervent plea for international order, for disarmament, for the banning of all nuclear weapons, for a shift from reliance on equality of arms to mutual trust. Because these propositions were stated with great clarity, they were widely acclaimed by non-Catholics as well as Catholics. Pope John emphasized that a system of order based on independent nations was a "structural defect" that prevented the solution of international problems, however high the spirit of good will. At the same time, the encyclical makes clear that nations *are* heavily armed and that mutual trust does *not* govern their relations. John's plea is urgent precisely because its basic concerns are *not* the dominant ones operating among nations. Thus the dilemma remains.

Interpretations of *Pacem in Terris* varied widely. Almost everybody applauded the appeal for trust and the fervent hope for peace; but some saw the document as utopian, whereas others emphasized its realism. Paul-Henri Spaak wrote: "Peaceful coexistence is therefore a necessity, a reality before which we must bow. . . . First and foremost, we must renounce war—unrestrictedly. We must not accept the differentiation that may be drawn between 'just' and 'unjust' wars." [13] James Douglass wrote of "the non-violent power of *Pacem in Terris*." [14] Paul Tillich did not agree: "I think the absolute ruling-out of any war is ideologically impossible, because there are situations in which the right to resist might lead first . . . to rebellion and then to revolution and then to war. Ruling out any form of resistance would give to those who violate the principle of personality the security of not having to be bothered any longer about what they are doing." [15] Tillich re-emphasized the need for distinctions regarding the use of force and believed that the encyclical was weak in failing to discuss the use of coercion in the just exercise of power. He "distinguished between Utopian hopes of a world ruled by peace, justice, and love, which must await the end of history, and more realistic hopes for a world community capable of avoiding self-destruction." [16]

Some saw *Pacem in Terris* as a decisive shift in church doctrine because it turned away from the "just war" concept; others saw no such change. "For many years the issue of 'the just war' remained uncertain. . . . *Pacem in Terris* has made it absolutely clear that the just war is ruled out." "Pope John did not throw out all wars. For some time many people have had the attitude that they are not against wars for 'justice.' . . . I do not see anything in the encyclical that disagrees with that." [17] We should never underestimate our capacity to read into a document what we expect or hope to find. Running that risk for myself, I would judge that the absence in the encyclical of any reference to war as a legitimate instrument of national

12 For the text, see *The Papal Encyclicals in Their Historical Context*, Anne Fremantle, ed., pp. 393–424.

13 In Reed, op. cit., p. 50.

14 Op. cit., Chap. 4.

15 In Reed, op. cit., p. 123.

16 Reed in ibid., p. xix.

17 Stanley Sheinbaum and Herman Kahn, in ibid., pp. 121 and 123.

policy gives support to those who interpret it as a repudiation of war in the atomic age.

This position, however, was not supported by the Vatican Council, which developed a modified version of the "just war" doctrine. "As long as the danger of war remains and there is no competent and sufficiently powerful authority at the international level, governments cannot be denied the right to legitimate defense once every means of peaceful settlement has been exhausted." [18] There is explicit condemnation of indiscriminate destruction of cities or entire areas, but no direct reference to the principle of noncombatant immunity. The Council defines "just war" narrowly, particularly by its limitation to acts of self-defense and by its emphasis on the need for exploring every possible peaceful means before resorting to force. Pope John's ringing condemnation of war, however, could scarcely be the product of 2,300 men from many nations preparing a document all could share.[19]

Protestant and Orthodox concern over atomic war also reflects the dilemma. A study document, "Christians and the Prevention of War in an Atomic Age—A Theological Discussion," issued by the Division of Studies of the World Council of Churches, declares that Christians must never consent to the use of nuclear weapons in war and "must oppose all policies which give evidence of leading to all-out war." Yet the authors also accept nuclear armament. "A first requirement is for a discipline which is capable of possessing nuclear weapons and the means of their delivery, but of never using them in all-out warfare." [20] This seems to avoid the dilemma; but Bennett notes that reliance on American power of deterrence has obscured questions that emerge in a world where nuclear capabilities are more widely shared: ". . . so long as we assumed that the possession of the nuclear bombs would prevent their use, we could avoid the hardest questions. Now we must face the ultimate ethical issue involved in their use." [21]

When he faces that issue, Bennett comes back to the dilemma of power:

One side of this dilemma is the implacability of the adversary and the threat that at least by blackmail his power may be extended unless he finds himself limited by an unyielding force. But the other side of the dilemma can only be spelled out in terms of the human consequences of nuclear war, even of the nuclear arms race itself, and this cannot be done without raising the question of the degree of destruction a nuclear war might cause us to inflict on human beings in another nation.[22]

Those who see the contemporary situation in this way tend to accept the doctrine of "just war," but undertake to specify sharply the conditions under which war is thinkable. As moral propositions, the limits are defined very narrowly, so that war is hedged about with numerous restrictions. Ramsey sees it as a single, clearly defined, limited exception to the pro-

18 Second Vatican Council, *Pastoral Constitution on the Church in the Modern World, December 7, 1965.* For the statement on war, see Part II, Chap. V.

19 Robert Tucker's discussion of the Vatican Council's efforts to deal with the dilemma of the churches is a valuable and thoughtful commentary. See op. cit., pp. 7–50.

20 Quoted by Ramsey, op. cit., p. 96.

21 Bennett, op. cit., p. 96.

22 Ibid., p. 10.

scription against killing: ". . . Christian conscience took the form of allowing any killing at all of men for whom Christ died only because military personnel were judged to stand at the point where there converged many multilateral relations of a Christian to his neighbors. Out of neighbor-regarding love for all one's fellowmen, preferential decision among one's neighbors may and can and must be made." [23] Bennett has noted that discussion of atomic war has been grossly quantitative, without regard to the quality of life that might survive. He emphasizes his opposition to attacks on centers of population even in the most "just" cause; he notes that an arms race, even without war, may dull our moral sense and transform the quality of national life, as the military-industrial complex gains in power. Yet he too finally accepts a "just war" position, although with even greater hesitation than does Ramsey.

Such thoughtful examinations of the moral dilemmas of warfare are leagues removed from the remarks of the American major who said of a Vietnamese village his men had just shattered: "We had to destroy it in order to save it." It should also be said, however, that the massive constraints that religious leaders may impose on any support they are willing to give to war tend to fade away in the heat of actual battle. Well before the atomic bombs were dropped on Japan, saturation bombing in Europe and Asia had sharply violated many limits of "just war" doctrine. There were few protests from churchmen. A nuclear war may begin with the use of a few tactical, battlefield weapons. It may grow into a battle where enormously more destructive weapons are used, inevitably bringing death to hundreds of thousands of noncombatants and "innocents." And the doctrines of the "just war" will be shattered along with the people. To the cynical, this sequence of events, which has been repeated over and over again in human history, is a sign that the whole effort to set limits for religiously acceptable warfare is a charade, that in the last analysis, military necessity and military decision-makers take over. To the sympathetic, the effort to set limits to war is a wise recognition of the dilemma faced by the religiously motivated; it constrains the mighty, while buying a little time for the creation of a world in which the mighty do not use violence for their purposes. The use of this time is perhaps the weakest aspect of the work of the "just war" thinkers.

In my judgment, even the most sophisticated attempts to rethink the doctrines of a "just war" for the present time have failed to confront the new conditions. Little has been said that goes beyond the sixteenth- and seventeenth-century work of Francisco de Vitoria and Hugo Grotius. In particular, there are few examinations, of the moral implications, on the one hand, of internal and guerrilla warfare, and on the other, of the presence—or absence—of international forces. It is not my purpose, nor am I qualified, to try to compensate for these omissions. I point to them only as further indications of the way in which the thought of churchmen, even including many of the most sensitive, is governed by the sociopolitical context of their times. Were this not the case, those re-examining the doctrines of "just war" might be asking: How do we apply the principles related to innocents and noncombatants and the requirement that war be declared by a legitimate public authority to guerrilla warfare? Can one deny to black

23 Ramsey, op. cit., p. 305.

South Africans, for example, the right to revolt against their own entrapment? They are as capable of cruelty, self-righteousness, and unnecessary violence as are their oppressors; but they are down, and they are being held down. Oppressed people in many places are beginning to develop a theory of the role of violence in social change.[24] It appeals to their anger. Does it equally appeal to the intellectual and moral examination of religious thinkers?

Internal war has become a major moral and political issue of our time, as it has been of other times.[25] To those who are convinced that the existing order is riddled with injustice, conspiracy may become righteous.[26] By what criteria shall they know when a rebellion is just? Is the burden of proof always on those who attack the prevailing order? To the Elizabethans, whether seen through Shakespeare or history, the problem was how to conspire nobly. In our time the issue may be how to protest injustice without precipitating and supporting an escalation of violence that destroys all proportion and consumes the very values one wishes to enlarge.

A second major reassessment is needed in connection with the control and use of violence on an international basis. There is no lack of support for the United Nations and other international agencies. There has been a succession of statements from popes and from the World Council of Churches, for example. I am raising a further question here: Must any statement of "just war" doctrine now be made in international terms? Is it possible any longer, even if it once were, for one nation to see the cause of justice and to seek to carry it out? Although the place of military force was not examined by Pope John, the internationalization of the system of order was the clearest message of *Pacem in Terris*. Perhaps at last we need to go beyond Grotius, to add one word to his first principle: War must be declared by the legitimate *international* public authority. This will not, of course, bring the millennium. But it may be a necessary minimum step to approximate the conditions of justice laid down as essential to a "just war."

Sects and War

The least ambiguous assertion of a universalist ethic in the face of the divisions of war (but not necessarily, therefore, the most powerful) is found in sectarian pacifism. Here is direct opposition to the policies of government. This is always the position of a minority; but the size even of the minority varies widely from situation to situation. During peacetime, pacifism may have substantial support, even in the churches; but in wartime, the conflicting loyalties and the dilemmas of influence persuade all but a small number to change their positions. This was especially true during World War I.[27] During World War II, however, there were many more

24 See Frantz Fanon, *Wretched of the Earth.*

25 See Harry Eckstein, ed., *Internal War;* Richard Hartigan, "Urban Riots, Guerrilla Wars, and 'Just War' Ethics," in *The Religious Situation: 1968,* Donald Cutler, ed., pp. 443–460.

26 Although the traditional religious vocabulary is lacking, America's current radicals share many qualities with England's seventeenth-century Puritans. See Michael Walzer, *The Revolution of the Saints,* Chap. 8.

27 See Abrams, op. cit. For a variety of documents on history and types of pacifism in the United States, see Joseph Conlin, ed., *American Anti-War Movements;* and Lillian Schlissel, ed., *Conscience in America. A Documentary History of Conscientious Objection in America, 1757–1967.*

pacifist churchmen, just as there was more insistence, on the part of churchmen who supported the war, on a continuous pursuit of "just war" aims. The pacifists included a number of this country's most prominent ministers. The most common position among them can perhaps be summarized in these words: The church does not obstruct the work of the government, but it has a different task—to reduce hate, to plan continuously for peace, to defend civil liberties, to improve race relations, to carry on all those tasks that can minimize the division of the world and keep alive the sense of community necessary for the postwar world. The Vietnam War has aroused strong opposition among churchmen, as among others, but it is not clear how much of this is pacifist in the sense of principled opposition to the war pattern.

Although there is pacifism in the churches, showing the inaccuracy of any scheme of classification, it is found in largest proportions in the sects. Here again, the number of actual opponents of war was greater during World War II than during World War I. This follows the trend toward more restrained judgments among secular and church leaders that we have already remarked and doubtless also reflects a more favorable legal situation. Perhaps the most accurate index of the extent of pacifism is the number of conscientious objectors. (We need not here explore various distinctions that are sometimes drawn between pacifism and conscientious objection.) The data are by no means accurate—it seems likely, in fact, that there was a persistent effort on the part of Selective Service officials to minimize the number who claimed exemption from military service on conscientious grounds—but a very careful appraisal by Sibley and Jacob arrives at the number 100,000 as the total number of conscientious objectors in the United States between 1940 and 1947.[28] Of this total number, about 12,000 were assigned to "Civilian Public Service" camps and more than 6,000 were sentenced to prison for refusal, at various points, to accept the draft. A large proportion of these most vigorous objectors came from sectarian religious groups. Over 60 per cent were members of the three "historic peace churches" (Mennonites, Brethren, and Quakers) and the Jehovah's Witnesses.

These groups exhibit a wide range in types of opposition to the claims of the state in war. The opposition of many of the Jehovah's Witnesses has expressed itself not only in unwillingness to participate in war, but in a much more complete withdrawal from the "world of sin." Many of them refused to register in the draft; for this and other reasons, some 5,000 Witnesses served time in prison. Mennonites tended toward nonresistance, as contrasted with nonviolent resistance; whereas many Quakers shared Gandhi's idea of *satyagraha*—an active struggle for peace, using nonviolent means. (In Gandhi's case, of course, this meant the actual pursuit of political power, the use of boycott, civil disobedience, and other vigorous measures of protest, so long as they were nonviolent.) Somewhat different from this, although still far removed from the sectarian withdrawal of the Jehovah's Witnesses, is the concept of "vocational Christian pacifism." This describes a role very similar to that of the pacifist churchmen we

28 See Mulford Sibley and Philip Jacob, *Conscription of Conscience*, pp. 83–84. This is probably less than half the ratio found in Great Britain, whose legal pattern was more tolerant of the conscientious objector. There were four times as many objectors in Great Britain during World War II as in World War I. See ibid., pp. 2–7.

have described above. Pacifists are thought of as a small minority whose task it is to keep before the majority, who are caught in the midst of a conflict, a different picture of how the world may be ordered. This concept is well expressed by Elton Trueblood:

The pacifist who keeps alive this different conception is contributing to the future welfare of his people by providing a balance to the extremes of hatred which arise, and by holding aloft the principles of ultimate peace which might otherwise be forgotten. He is keeping a humble fire burning, to light the new fires which must burn again after the storm is over. If he understands his position rightly he accords his government the same courtesies which he expects. That is, the government grants him a measure of recognition of his conscientious objection and he, in turn, does not try to embarrass the government. It is for this reason that some of the recognized leaders of English Quakerdom have refused to sign a petition asking the government to sue for peace now.[29]

Members of withdrawal sects contend that this involves so much compromise that the fundamental condemnation of war is lost. Others have called it a return to monasticism—where a small group maintained the religious principles in relatively pure form and lived them vicariously for the whole society. From the point of view of the sociology of religion, it would seem to be an attempt to reduce the sharpness of the dilemma of religious influence by criticizing the pattern of war but not withdrawing from the problems of the society. Active attention to those problems has taken not only the familiar form of relief and rehabilitation, but more recently the pattern of an attempt to keep open the channels of informal communication among diplomats. This has been done, for example, by maintenance of Quaker House beside the United Nations buildings in New York, where representatives of all nations may meet in informal conversations, and by sponsorship of informal seminars for diplomats in Europe.[30]

Just as some churchmen have avoided the sharp reduction in influence that comes from accepting completely the aims and methods of the secular society, so some sectarians have won a measure of influence by avoiding the extremes of "withdrawal."

Governmental Responses to Pacifism. Laws and governmental actions relating to pacifism vary widely in space and time. In the United States, although the definition and the rights of conscientious objectors have been rather narrowly interpreted, they have gradually been extended. An earlier requirement that the claimant to the status of conscientious objection must be a member of one of the historic "peace churches" was abandoned several decades ago. In 1963 the Supreme Court ruled, in the *Seeger* case, that sincere religious conviction, not necessarily belief in God, was the critical test. When Congress rewrote the draft law in 1967, they substituted "by reason of religious training and belief" for the "Supreme Being" clause. Even this phrase, however, was ruled unconstitutional by a federal judge, in 1969, because it discriminated against agnostics, atheists, and others who are motivated by "profound moral beliefs" opposed to war.

In recent months there has been growing attention to an additional modi-

29 Elton Trueblood, "Vocational Christian Pacifism," *Christianity and Crisis*, November 3, 1941, pp. 2–5.

30 See Elmore Jackson, *Meeting of Minds.*

fication, urged by some, opposed by others: Should conscientious objection to particular wars be allowed? Several American national denominations have said *Yes*, including the United Presbyterian Church in the U.S.A., the Council for Christian Social Action of the United Church of Christ, the Lutheran Church in America, and the Roman Catholic bishops. Many seminary students, particularly in the interdenominational Protestant seminaries, have taken this stand. And in 1968 the World Council of Churches declared "that the legal right of the individual to refrain from participation in 'particular wars' on grounds of conscience must be regarded now as essential to the protection of fundamental human rights." [31]

The proposal that one has the right, in the name of individual conscience, to determine which wars he shall support is much more controversial than the more absolutistic definition of conscientious objection. The former is inherently political, for selective objection involves rejection of a specific act of the state, whereas the latter can be seen as the affirmation of a general religious principle.

Some of those who oppose legitimating selective objection see in it the possibility of a "haven for draft dodgers." More sympathetic critics wonder how the principle can be embodied in a realistic law that is capable of reasonably precise interpretation.

Those who support extension of the rights of conscientious objection to include opposition to particular wars see little chance that it would be used purely to escape service. Some form of alternative service would continue to be required; various forms of social pressure limit the number who seek C.O. status; if the nation's survival were at stake, C.O. claimants would be few; and in the last analysis, Congress could change the provision. On the other hand, they argue that such a provision might strengthen the diversity of views that a modern society needs, furnishing a restraint on those in power; it would support the development of individual conscience and sense of responsibility. In some ways, it would simply extend the doctrine of the "just war," which has developed as a kind of selective objection for religious leaders. In a more contemporary vein, the right to oppose particular wars is seen by some as a responsibility similar to that propounded in the Nuremberg trials and the prosecution of Japanese war criminals after World War II: One cannot claim innocence, according to the principles underlying these trials, simply because he was following orders. Against this background, and in the context of intense disagreements over the morality of the war in Vietnam, it is scarcely surprising that the principle of selective objection has received growing support.

The Field Sources of Pacifism. Under what conditions is conscientious objection to war likely to occur? We tend to take support for war for granted: national loyalty, governmental pressures and powers, individual fears and hostilities are variously combined to account for the fact that in most situations the majority of a population support their nation at war. To account for the minority who do not, requires us to examine the cultural, structural, and character conditions in a given setting. Once again I will

31 See Edward B. Fiske, in the *New York Times*, July 17, 1968, pp. 1 and 10; see also his articles of February 5, 1967, p. E-5 and March 3, 1968, pp. 1 and 78. A discussion of the issues is also found in *Civil Liberties*, April, 1967, pp. 3–5, by Nanette Dembitz and David Carliner.

argue that these three conditions are multiplicative. Unless there is some support for conscientious objection on each of these three levels it will not occur.

On the cultural level, the doctrines and values of the world's religions vary in the support they give to pacifism.[32] Hinduism and Buddhism support what might be called a pacifism of withdrawal—a downgrading of affairs of state.[33] But that is an incomplete picture. The duty of the Kshatriya caste is to fight and rule; yet out of Hinduism can also come the practice of *satyagraha*, an active challenge to the way of violence, as was demonstrated by Gandhi and Bhave. Under some conditions, an active, politically oriented pacifism also develops in Buddhism. Bobilin traces evidences of this throughout the twentieth century in Japan, with an increase after World War II. The movements have been small; but one should note that, particularly before 1945, the setting was highly uncongenial to pacifism.[34]

It is difficult to compare Judaism with other universalistic religions, because for most of its history it has been associated with a minority status in society; thus the purely cultural themes are obscured. The strong emphasis on the development of a moral community, however, gives support to Weber's interpretation that Judaism "never in theory rejected the state and its coercion." [35] Yet its strong emphasis on brotherhood gives some support to pacifist values. Attention to the development of a moral community is decisively the case in Islam. It is the least world-rejecting of the major religions. The use of force for divine and moral purposes is accepted on principle.[36] Even in Islam, however, the ethic of brotherhood furnishes values on which objection to the use of violence may be built, as is shown in some of the developments of Sufism and the Shi'ite sect. The situation in Christianity is perhaps the most complex, with values that are supportive of withdrawal pacifism and politically-oriented pacifism existing alongside the dominant nonpacifist "Puritan" strain, as Weber identifies it, concerned with the establishment of God's kingdom on earth.

Since each of the religions we have referred to has, at least in some measure, diverse values relating to pacifism and war, the structural conditions in a given situation must be examined to see which of the values are likely to be promoted and which inhibited. We have not been able to avoid reference to structure, in fact, in our examination of the cultural level. Politically oriented pacifism develops in Japanese Buddhism, for example, not only because it contains these value possibilities, but also because of the Japanese defeat in World War II. When examining the structural support, we ask: With whom is one interacting, in what context? That nuclear pacifism has developed more strongly in Great Britain than in the United States cannot readily be accounted for by differences in their religious values. Their situations do vary significantly, however, because the United States

32 See David Martin. *Pacifism. An Historical and Sociological Study.*

33 See Donald Smith, ed., *South Asian Politics and Religion.*

34 See Bobilin, op. cit.

35 *The Sociology of Religion,* p. 228.

36 See Wilfred C. Smith, *Pakistan as an Islamic State.*

possesses major nuclear capability whereas Britain does not. Pacifism prospers best among those who possess little advantage in coercion.[37]

The network of communication and interaction is also an important structural determinant of the level of opposition to war. Putney and Middleton found, in a study of students in sixteen colleges and universities, that the best informed, and those most involved in politics, were most likely to find nuclear war both credible and acceptable. This surprised the authors, so they undertook further study to identify the sources of information of the best informed. They proved to be standard newspapers, journals of opinion, and radio and TV broadcasts. These sources, they noted, tended to present nuclear war as "a possible and plausible national policy." When groups were tested before and after reading material that informed them about nuclear weapons but also showed concern for the problem of war, both their knowledge and their degree of pacifism increased.[38] This study demonstrates clearly that the structure of interaction is a critical factor in determining the level of pacifism.

Character tendencies must also be taken into account. Granted a religious tradition in which values supportive of pacifism are available; granted a structure in which pacifist ideas circulate; one must still note that only some of those experiencing this situation will become pacifists. Tendencies most predisposing to pacifism have not been well identified; but two, I believe, are of major importance. Those who have been most powerfully socialized to the values of brotherhood and nonviolence and those who, for whatever psychodynamic reasons, are anti-establishment, anti-authoritarian (sometimes, it must be inferred, in a rather authoritarian manner), are those who will respond most readily to the pacifist possibilities in their cultural and structural situation. Neither of these tendencies by itself will support the choice of a minority and usually unpopular view. When combined in a supportive context, however, they may do so.

Pacifism is most likely to occur, then, when cultural, structural, and character supports are all present. If we are not yet able to measure these supports with any precision, we can at least imagine the scales along which they might fall, and put them together into a system, as shown in Figure 20–1.

There is no difficulty in interpreting profiles A and B. The former may be descriptive of an elite member of an Arab society, for example, the latter of a student in a British or American Protestant seminary. Interpretation of profiles C and D, however, is more problematic, not only because we have no precise way to locate individuals along the range, but also because the threshold level, the multiplicative product of the three "scores," required to produce pacifist behavior can only be surmised. But I believe this way of viewing the problem can help us to understand the complex varieties of possibilities.

Profile C might be descriptive of a person brought up in a community rich in pacifist values and supportive groups, but who, as a result of the accidents of his socialization, places high priority on conformity to the

37 See Bennett, op. cit., pp. 9 and 97.

38 Snell Putney and Russell Middleton, "Some Factors Associated with Student Acceptance or Rejection of War," *American Sociological Review*, 27, 1962, pp. 655–667.

larger society or on success. Profile D might refer to a fairly typically trained member of the American middle class who, for reasons peculiar to his biography, has been led to place the injunction against killing in top priority among his values. Whether this will lead to overt pacifism or not will depend in part on possible changes on the structural level. If his values lead him to seek—and if he finds—group support for pacifism, he may be carried over the threshold. This is to say, we need to keep a time dimension in mind while examining the system suggested above. It is a cybernetic model, with various feedback processes from one level to another, with consequent changes through time.

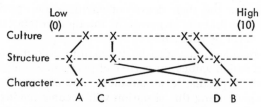

FIGURE 20–1. *Sources of pacifism*

Political Domination of the Universalist Theme

Any account of religion and war would be inadequate that did not give fuller attention than we have up to now to the frequency with which a universalist religious doctrine has been twisted to national and class purposes. Time and distance make it seem clear that universalist claims for a "holy war" are often disguises for limited aims. We are likely to be more myopic in judging situations the closer they are to us in time and space.[39] An adequate sociology of religion must specify variables so precisely that trained observers on both sides of a conflict would agree on the degree to which the belligerents were using the symbols of a universalist religion to justify limited goals and the degree to which religion was concerned with the genuine problems of humanity. It need scarcely be noted that such agreement is now very unlikely, at least for the analysis of any conflict contemporary with the observers. When a Japanese Buddhist writes that, "Japan is a lover of peace, so even if she goes to war, it is always a war for peace," [40] Americans have no difficulty in recognizing this as inaccurate. Presumably Japanese observers were equally persuaded that any claims by American churchmen that victory for the United States in World War II was vital for the cause of world brotherhood were not accurate. It was clear, outside Germany, in 1917, that *Gott mit uns* was pretension; but it was probably equally clear inside Germany that there were many inaccuracies in the statement by the Federal Council of Churches of Christ in

39 Erich Fromm challenges our myopia when he asks: "Is there really as much difference as we think between the Aztec human sacrifices to their gods and the modern human sacrifices to the idols of nationalism and the sovereign state?" (*You Shall Be as Gods*, p. 48.)

40 Quoted by Holtom, op. cit., pp. 149–150.

America that America was fighting "to vindicate the principles of righteousness."

This is not to imply that all these claims are equally valid (or invalid)—the writer cannot so easily escape his own myopia—but only to suggest that their relative validity can be determined only by a careful specification of "criteria of universality." The following criteria seem to be useful in distinguishing between the fact and the pretense of claims to a universal emphasis made by religious leaders and churches during war; or, to put it more accurately, to determine the *degree* of accuracy of the claims, for it is doubtless always a continuum:

1. The degree to which the *full range* of the religious ideology is emphasized. When a Japanese Christian stresses the contribution made by Christianity to the code of *Bushido*—the way of the warrior—through its emphasis on self-sacrifice, loyalty, courage, discipline,[41] but pays little regard to the different elements in the Christian ideology ("resist not evil," "all men are brothers"), we have an example of the distortion of a universalist religion for limited aims.

2. The degree to which a conflict is described in "all or none" terms. If religious spokesmen describe the enemy as absolute beasts, if there is no recognition of the interactional sources and the mutual involvement of nations in the generation of conflicts, no appreciation of one's own errors, then claims to universality are likely to be invalid. This is based on the premise that the causes of conflict are reciprocal and cumulative—that the Smoot-Hawley tariff had something to do with Japanese foreign policy after 1930—and are not simply the evil of one side alone.

3. The degree to which churches—even though giving basic support to a government during war—continue to criticize specific acts and policies of the government as incompatible with universalist aims. An age of "total war" presents especially sharp problems of this kind. Saturation bombing, unconditional surrender, massive retaliation, and anticipatory defense are concepts that raise important questions for the world religions. Problems of civil liberties, the rights of conscientious objectors, the treatment of enemy captives, responsibilities for refugees, and the like are likely to be seen in military terms by a nation at war. Do the churches continue to insist on a broader interpretation?

4. The degree to which churches take direct part in military and supporting activities, as contrasted with emphasis on separate (even though complementary) tasks. The ability to emphasize universalist goals is obscured if the churches do not maintain a sharp sense of organizational separation from the state. (This, incidentally, is compatible with the status of Established Church.) When churches sell war bonds or recruit soldiers from the pulpit (as some American churches did during World War I), as contrasted with giving care to bombed-out civilians or giving attention to the problems of war-boom communities (tasks which are equally important for a nation at war), the likelihood that they will maintain a universalist perspective is reduced.

5. The degree to which the churches carry on action that continues to emphasize their conception of universality. This is closely related to the

41 See Arimichi Ebisawa, "The Relation Between the Ethics of *Bushido* and Christianity," *Cultural Nippon*, December, 1939, p. 27.

previous criterion. Verbal reaffirmation of world brotherhood by itself is as often related to limited actions as it is to actions with a universal concern. Virtually every national participant in war in the modern world, in fact, contends that it is fighting for a cause of world significance. Churches, for their part, validate this claim only by actions that have more than national import.

These criteria have scarcely been put to an adequate test. The most that can be said for them is that the writer has found them useful in trying to answer the question: How can one measure the degree to which the world religions have maintained a universal perspective in the face of the limiting pressures upon a nation at war? Their validation requires that other persons, preferably with very different value stands, apply them to the same data that we have referred to in this chapter, and arrive at similar conclusions.

THE SOCIOCULTURAL CONTEXT OF UNIVERSALISM

Even were the usefulness of these criteria established, we would not have an answer to the more basic question: What are the conditions under which universalism will be most strongly affirmed? The criteria we have listed are an index of measurement, but only indirectly a statement of causes. At various points in this chapter we have referred to causal factors. It may be well now to try to draw them together.

1. We have suggested, in the first place, that a universal religion will be invented only in a particular sociocultural context. There must be extensive social differentiation, religious specialists, culture contact, and a long period of frustration of major needs and aspirations. The culture must be one in which the values encourage religious struggles with these problems, as contrasted with (or in addition to) economic, political, military, and other struggles with them. There is a need for individuals peculiarly sensitive to these influences and qualified, by personal makeup, to deal with them in religious terms. Frequently one individual will stand out in this regard (Buddha, Jesus, Muhammad); but this is not necessarily the case, as the development of Judaism shows. Moreover, it is important not to disregard the cumulative development that led up to the advent of "the founder," so clearly shown in the case of Christianity and Islam. We know too little about the situation in India preceding Buddha to judge the cumulative element in his case. Nor should we forget the influence of followers, as well as predecessors in "creating" a founder. St. Paul, St. Augustine, and Luther, for example, each shaped Christianity in vital ways.

2. The sociocultural factors in the origin of universalism in religion must be distinguished from the factors that are involved in its influence in particular situations. It has been our thesis that the effective presence of a universalist theme, challenging and contradicting limited political claims, varies most significantly with the degree of the diffusion of power. Where secular power is most heavily concentrated, the universal theme is most completely obscured.

3. Sectarian movements emphasizing a universal theme will be most common in a society where major groups feel frustrated in their basic hopes and thus feel no real stake in the society to which they belong. Drawing on

their religious tradition, they criticize that society in the name of universal values. At first glance, this may seem to be a contradiction of the previous point, for certainly frustration and secular powerlessness will be most common in societies where power is not diffused. We need to refer again to the various types of sects to eliminate this apparent contradiction. Sects in situations where power is least diffused, where hope and aspirations for this world are lowest, will tend to be of the withdrawal variety. Their universalism is otherworldly. Only in situations where hopes for improvement on earth loom large, where the disinherited, though weak, are not indeed powerless, do we find sects aggressively working for a universalism relevant to this world.

4. Universalism will vary with the immediate historical context. Situations differ in the amount of international communication, the degree of awareness of the lives and problems of persons in other nations, races, or classes, and particularly in the degree of actual interdependence. All of these have increased in the modern world, so that thoughtful religious people are continuously confronted with problems that existing political structures are incompetent to handle, or may be handling in ways contradictory to the theme of universalism. Another aspect of the immediate historical situation concerns the swings in emphasis in a complicated religious tradition. If one part of that tradition is given predominant attention, a movement to emphasize other parts is likely to appear—sponsored both by religious specialists, who professionally seek to encompass the whole tradition, and by those laymen who find their own needs and values unsatisfied by the existing balance of emphases. This may account for the stronger awareness of universal values in American churches during World War II than during World War I: there was a revulsion away from the enormous enthusiasm for unqualified support of government policy that many churches had shown.

5. The patterns of group relationship are not of primary significance, yet they play some part in affecting the degree of universalism. An Established Church, for example, may demonstrate a great deal of autonomy, while churches sharply separate from the state in the formal sense may be subservient to its commands or incapable of influencing its policies. Whatever the formal relationship, the pattern of church-state connection that allows independent judgments and actions and at the same time encourages religious groups to be concerned with problems of politics—in the broadest sense—is most likely to promote the universalist emphasis.

6. Finally, we may mention leadership. Weber's concept of charisma—leadership that is a specifically revolutionary new force in human affairs—is scarcely adequate until it too has been explained. Religious leadership, whether charismatic or of a more prosaic variety, must be referred, by the sociologist of religion, to its sociocultural setting. On the most general level, this means that certain contexts help both to create persons with certain tendencies and to draw them into positions of influence. The leaders, in turn, act back upon that situation and take their part in the stream of influences at work.

These several variables, and doubtless the many others that might be added, interacting together, shape the degree to which the universalist theme in a religion will be emphasized or obscured.

Chapter Twenty-one

SOCIAL CHANGE AND RELIGIOUS CHANGE

Theories of social change are abundant. Evolutionary, dialectical, cyclical explanations, biological analogies of the birth and death of civilizations, descriptions of timeless and trendless fluctuations, one-factor emphases on technology, geography, and theology—these are among the sweeping yet often exciting interpretations of changes in human institutions and behavior.

If we lack anything approaching a generally accepted theory, it is mainly because of the great complexity of the problem. It is partly, however, out of failure to break the problem down into component parts, while describing them in such a way that their relationships can be examined. The result has been wide disagreement over the very definition of social change. In the hope of making the problem somewhat more manageable, I will offer a general definition of social change, before turning to its religious aspects, and then specify the elements of which it is composed.[1]

Social change is the process of movement of a social system from one relatively homeostatic structural-cultural-character balance toward another. Shifts in the structure of interaction are not social change unless they are sufficiently powerful and prolonged to cause modifications in the culture and in individuals' motivations and values. New designs in the "blueprints for action" are another element in the compound; but such cultural changes should not be confused with the social changes of which they are a part. Shifts in individual motives, needs, and tendencies are less likely to be confused with social change than are structural and cultural shifts. They are, nevertheless, part of the total. Social change, as I am

1 I shall not try to suggest the vast literature on social change. For a few valuable leads, see E. E. Hagen, *On the Theory of Social Change;* Daniel Lerner, *The Passing of Traditional Society;* David McClelland, *The Achieving Society;* Wilbert Moore, *Order and Change;* Amitai Etzioni and Eva Etzioni, eds., *Social Change;* George Zollschan and Walter Hirsch, eds., *Explorations in Social Change.*

using the term, occurs only when there has been realignment in all parts of the system.

There is no implication in this description that societies move continuously from situations of relative balance, through periods of disruption, into new situations of balance. New forces may enter a system at such a rate that the realignment process cannot proceed rapidly enough. Mankind may have entered a time when structural-cultural-character elements are continuously out of phase. We do not know the consequences of such endemic social change; but we will be wise, I believe, not to judge those consequences against a presumed normal model of stability. My picture of homeostatic balance is an analytic concept to be used as a point of reference, against which various forms of movement can be seen and compared; it is not a description of the normal or desirable social order. Even traditional societies are not the static, culturally homogeneous social systems they are sometimes taken to be.[2]

From my point of view it is a mistake to assume, *a priori*, that change must begin with one part of the system, with other elements simply reflecting, by their changes, the altered circumstances around them. The sequence of events in any system is a matter for empirical investigation. And however a process gets started, social change results only when all parts of the system are modified through various feedback processes.

It is clear that any adequate theory of society must be a theory of change, and not simply a theory of homeostatic processes. In other words, it must be a theory of how societies evolve into different forms—or fail to—and not only one of how they operate. Yet social systems are tough. They can sustain quite a lot of "wobble" in some of their parts without being overwhelmed. American race relations, for example, have undergone a great deal of structural change. Patterns of interaction between black and white have been significantly modified as the Negro population has moved into the cities, dispersed through the nation, entered new occupations, and shifted to integrated schools. Cultural patterns, however, and the tendencies and motives of individuals, have changed less drastically. An older order is still "justified" by widely shared norms and still defended by individuals who are socialized to those norms, although not without changes in each instance. This is to suggest, in terms of our problem, that extensive religious change is not the inevitable consequence of modifications in the setting; nor does prior religious change inevitably initiate major shifts elsewhere.

Referring again to the "Weber problem," we might describe it, in the briefest terms relevant to this chapter, in the following way: Culture change led to character change led to structural change. Any weakness of his interpretation is not the result of the thesis that culture change carried out by a charismatic leader could be a good place to begin. It was, rather, his insufficient development of an answer to the question: Why did the homeostatic processes of the existing north European societies not swallow up or correct the wobble in the religious system? Perhaps it was because urbanization, migration, the "discoveries," the growth of commerce, and

2 See Joseph Gusfield, "Tradition and Modernity: Misplaced Polarities in the Study of Social Change," *American Journal of Sociology*, 72, 1967, pp. 351–362.

the like, had put too great a stress on the character and structural systems themselves, so that they were vulnerable or receptive to the cultural innovations coming from a religious movement.

Religious development, to be sure, is not simply a matter of culture, of revision of its normative dimension. It also involves structural shifts and the growth of new individual motives and values. Changes in the size and homogeneity of the congregational unit, the rise or decline of participation by laymen, redefinition of hierarchical patterns, and the extent of congregational isolation from or involvement with the surrounding community are among the important structural shifts, and they can occur in conjunction with, or to some degree independently of, cultural shifts. The cultural changes in religion—the redefinition of shared sacred beliefs and rites— have an impact outside the specifically religious sphere, moreover, only if they help to create new men, whose needs, values, and motives redirect their energies.

In recent years, several important theories of social change have given serious attention to this character level. Daniel Lerner holds that modernization can occur only when substantial numbers of "mobile personalities" have appeared—persons capable of identification with different perspectives, of empathy. David McClelland, following Weber, sees the need for a strong achievement motive, a desire to test oneself and to succeed. E. E. Hagen has put emphasis on the capacity for innovation, for rearranging experience and seeing it in a different light.[3] Although these men stress different structural sources (Lerner, the growth of cities, literacy, mass media, and political participation; McClelland, training for independence and achievement in the family; Hagen, marginality), none takes the qualities of character they describe as entirely independent variables. They are intervening variables, which catch up the force of changes in the environment, transmitting and augmenting them as they evolve. A critical force in determining the nature of that transmittal and augmentation is the quality of the ultimate value system—whether it be a traditional religion, a reformation, or a secular quasi-religion—that is available to them.[4]

Despite their differences, the approaches of Lerner, McClelland, and Hagen may share in common a Western orientation that is not entirely adequate for other parts of the world. The sequence of events in societies that invent their own new structures may be different from the sequence in societies where many new patterns are imported. The invention and development of an industrial-commercial society may require drastic cultural and character changes. The structure of power, however, may be more critical in understanding which societies will undergo rapid development in a world where industrial models are already available. Thus an explanation adequate for the English-American sequence may be quite inadequate for the Japanese or Russian sequence.

3 The works of Lerner, McClelland and Hagen are cited in footnote 1.

4 See Philip Rieff, *The Triumph of the Therapeutic*, especially Chap. 8, for a thoughtful discussion of the role of religious change in reworking the "control" and "release" processes of culture. Cultural revolution occurs when the releasing symbolisms are more powerful than the controlling ones. Aggression, destructive attack on the social order grows, as in our time, until new and acceptable symbols of faith arise that are of sufficient power to reintroduce controls.

This is definitely not to say, however, that cultural elements and their character counterparts are unimportant in the change processes of Japan and the Soviet Union. I mean to say only that the timing of change patterns can vary. There is little doubt that the Confucian and Shinto values combined in Japan to support development. Emphasis on loyalty, obedience, frugality, and hard work could readily be transposed into support for modernization by an elite dedicated to that goal.[5] Even filial piety could be given a commercial dimension, with firms being built around family groups, using family symbolism in relationship to their workers, and developing a pattern of lifelong identification with the same company. Thus existing elements of culture and character supported changes that were initiated in the social structure. Those elements had been insufficient by themselves to set the process of modernization in motion.

The Soviet situation is somewhat different, sharing elements of both the English and the Japanese sequence. Communism as a quasi-religion had begun something of the culture-character reorganization that characterized Protestantism. This had touched only a small minority of the population, however. Major structural shifts were the decisive point of change. The elite, rather than being propelled to the front as representative new men, sought precisely to make new men and new cultural supports for the structures they were building.

The human costs of these different sequences of change may vary widely.[6] Structural changes that occur as a result of decisions by an elite, and to an important degree over cultural and character resistance, can lead into a new social system only if new values can be legitimized and the population socialized to accept them.[7] The chain of generations must be broken; sons must be set against fathers; and those elements of the traditional faith, with its supporting structures, that stand in the way of change must be obliterated. Qualities of inquisition, witch-hunting, and ideological rigidity become associated with the process.

Under other conditions, structural changes may not involve explicit efforts to institutionalize a new faith and build a new man. For reasons growing out of its traditional culture and its history, India, for example, has sought reform, not cultural revolution. It has used various elements of English institutions, to be sure, but for that very reason the government has not sought to impose a new system of values. This contrasts rather sharply with the situation in China. There the leaders have made vigorous efforts to shape cultural supports and to resocialize individuals in ways that reinforce the structural changes. We have before us a fascinating, if inexact, experiment. It may help to answer the questions: Is a choice of strategies available to nations in a world where aspirations have risen

5 See Robert Bellah, *Tokugawa Religion.*

6 See Richard Lowenthal, "Government in the Developing Countries: Its Functions and Its Forms," in *Democracy in a Changing World,* Henry Ehrmann, ed., pp. 177–210.

7 Edward Shils argues for a rather specifically Weberian interpretation of this transformation: "It is indispensable that men and women in underdeveloped societies come to feel and believe that a 'spark of the divine,' or some other manifestation of what is sacred in human life, dwells as much in those who live outside the circle of authority as it does in those who live within it." See "The Concentration and Dispersion of Charisma: Their Bearing on Economic Policy in Underdeveloped Countries," *World Politics,* 11, 1958, p. 19.

rapidly? What is the balance of gains and costs, seen against specified values, of the various strategies?

Variety of Relationships Between Religious Change and Social Change. In coming to the analysis of the mutual influence of religious change and social change, we approach what may well be the central problem of the scientific study of religion. We have dealt with this problem in almost every chapter, in connection with particular questions,[8] but it now requires more direct and explicit examination. It can serve, in fact, as a useful summary of the many principles we have used throughout this book.

There are several logically possible relationships between religious and social change: 1) There is no connection between the two; they flow along separate channels. 2) Religious change reflects changes in its environment. 3) Religion is a barrier to change, whether as "the opiate of the people" or as the conserver of tested values. 4) Religion initiates change. 5) Religion is part of an interdependent system. At a given moment it may best be regarded as a dependent variable, the result of other developments, but it feeds back into the system that produced it, modifying that system in various ways. At another moment it may best be regarded as the starting point for the analysis of a sequence of events. It may be an important part of the explanation of social change in one setting and inconsequential in another. Various conditions, which we must try to identify, maximize the influence of religion whereas others minimize its influence. The degree of autonomy in the religious sphere is the critical factor in determining the level of its influence; but sources of that autonomy must also be studied. We have suggested some of those sources in the discussion of religion and politics and will keep them in mind during this examination of social change.

Although I will not try to keep the discussion of religion as a dependent variable sharply distinct from the discussion of its independent influence —this would require a high level of abstraction—we can profitably give primary attention to one and then the other relationship.

RELIGIOUS CHANGE AS THE RESULT OF SOCIAL CHANGE

No clearer indication of the functional interdependence of religion with society can be found than the changes that religions undergo when their social settings change. Only those who hold that religions, in all their complexity, are the products of one flash of inspiration or revelation are likely to deny that religious systems develop and grow in various directions because of changes in the society in which they are found. Virtually all theologians and church historians today will readily grant that beliefs, rites, and religious group structure are affected by social changes, although many of them would contend that the *fundamental* elements in their faith (and perhaps in other world religions, if not in all religions) have their own intrinsic origin and quality, which is not subject to modification by society.

Social Change and the Development of Early Judaism

The gradual transformation of Judaism from a tribal religion, infused with magic, with a god of "hosts" (battles) who insists on the total destruction

8 See especially Figure 17–1 and the discussion relative to it.

of the Canaanites, into a monotheistic, universalist religion, with a god of justice and love, is a process that can best be understood by studying it in the context of the social forces affecting the Jewish people.[9] Before the changes accomplished by the prophets, through the course of several generations, the religion of Yahweh had contained the common beliefs that suffering was the result of sin and that sacrifice could win atonement. In the face of acute and prolonged suffering, however, these beliefs are likely to be unsatisfying; they are patently "false"; they do not "work." A new conception of God begins to emerge. Sacrifice has clearly not atoned for sin. What then does God require? That one put away evil and walk justly. "I hate, I despise your feasts. . . . But let judgment roll down as waters, and righteousness as a mighty stream." God has been transformed from an anthropomorphic being, delighting in gifts and homage, into a spirit; "and they who worship him must worship him in spirit and in truth." This was the prevailing message of the early prophets who transformed Yahweh worship, with its burnt-offerings and sacrifices and its tribal limitations, into a monotheistic religion that emphasized repentance.

Yet the suffering continued. Living at the crossroads of empires, the Jews were overrun by powerful neighbors, they were carried into captivity, and their hopes for power and success were destroyed. One could say that this was punishment for evil, that Israel had not put away its evil ways, that the cities were corrupt, and that faith had been placed in false gods. Or one could give the prolonged suffering a new meaning and find a place for it in God's scheme of things, a place that would remove the religious beliefs from the constant doubt that is felt when a faith is considered to be more or less directly a way of solving life's immediate problems. The later Jewish prophets did both of these things. They continued to call for righteousness and justice, but they began to declare that suffering had a meaning and a value of its own. Israel became the suffering servant, "despised, and rejected of men, a man of sorrows and acquainted with grief." The Jewish victory was to be a spiritual victory; God had chosen them to bring righteousness to the world.

Growing social differentiation within Israel, as well as external attacks, influenced the development of Judaism. The clear-cut monotheism of Amos appeared in the context of sharp protests against the great contrast of wealth and poverty that he found in the cities. These religious inventions were not, of course, the inevitable products of the social changes experienced by the Jewish people. There were other possible "solutions" to their difficulties: They might have concluded that their continued suffering proved the inferiority of their god and deserted him for the gods of Babylon, as some doubtless did. They might have met their difficulties with a renewed nationalism; and despite the continued frustration of their national ambitions, this theme was never completely obliterated. Many religious interpretations of the meaning of life were doubtless tried, but most were to be found unsatisfying in the face of the persistent difficulties that overwhelmed them. An explanation of the development of Judaism must

9 See W. Robertson Smith, *Lectures on the Religion of the Semites;* L. T. Hobhouse, *Morals in Evolution;* Louis Finkelstein, *The Pharisees: The Sociological Background of Their Faith;* Max Weber, *Ancient Judaism;* Louis Wallis, *Sociological Study of the Bible;* Homer W. Smith, *Man and His Gods.*

leave full room for the role of the religious innovator. Yet the social situation set definite limits to the kind of religious development that could be adequate for individuals and the group. It is interesting that the combination of emphasis on individual righteousness, eschatological hope, faith in ultimate vindication, and a belief that they must keep the true faith alive for others—all important in Judaism—are central in the religious movements of many contemporary Christians who suffer most: the sects of minority groups and lower classes. Many of these elements appear, in fact, in other religions, among those who have had to face deprivation and continuous suffering. As Hobhouse says, in commenting on the development of Judaism: ". . . by a very different road and with much difference of implied meaning, we are reaching the Buddhist doctrine of renunciation and humility—those cardinal points of spiritualized religion." [10]

Early Christianity and Social Change

Developments in Christianity, even during its earliest years, can scarcely be understood without relating them to the Jewish background that we have discussed briefly, and to the social situation in which it appeared. The picture of a religion, founded in all of its complexity by Jesus, with the whole range of its teachings embodied in a sacred and changeless literature, has been supplanted—not least of all by Biblical scholars and church historians—by the story of a religious synthesis from many societies. Christianity was strongly influenced by the setting in which it developed; it changed and adapted itself to the different situations with which it was confronted. The Sermon on the Mount, the very epitome of the ethical teachings of Jesus, is almost certainly a collective product, evolved through a number of years in response to a growing consensus among early Christian leaders.[11]

Historical research has shown that many of the elements of Christianity that were long thought by its adherents to be unique were common ideas, practices, and myths in the ancient world. Some of its doctrines and practices were added, during the course of several generations, as it developed from a small Jewish cult into a dominant religion. Resurrected gods had been worshiped in many societies for several centuries before the appearance of Christianity. The doctrine of virgin birth was familiar to pagans; and it is significant that the doctrine was not used by Paul nor by Mark, author of the earliest Gospel, who said nothing about the early years of Jesus' life. A kind of eucharistic meal was found in many pagan cults. And belief in miraculous powers was virtually universal in the ancient world.

Jesus turned water into wine, as did Dionysus on January sixth of every year; and multiplied loaves of bread as did Elisha. He walked on water like Orion, Poseidon's son. He raised men from the dead, as did Elijah and Elisha—this feat had once been so common that Aristophanes in *The Frogs* (ca. 405 B.C.) made Dionysus say of Hermes and Hermes's father, that performing resurrections was a family profession.[12]

10 Hobhouse, op. cit., p. 495.

11 See W. D. Davies, *The Setting of the Sermon on the Mount*.

12 Homer Smith, op. cit., p. 202.

That there is no mention of Jesus' miraculous powers in Paul's Epistles gives support to Smith's contention that the miraculous elements were added to Christianity in an effort to convert the pagans and to convince the Jews that Jesus was the true Messiah.

Many of the Christian holy days were blended with celebrations of ancient origin. The death and resurrection of Attis, the god of vegetation, had been celebrated in Rome on March 24th and 25th, the spring equinox being the appropriate time for his revival. It seems certain that the official dates for the commemoration of the death and resurrection of Christ were assimilated into this established custom; and the nativity of Christ was placed at the winter solstice in December—the date that was widely celebrated as the birth date of the sun.

There is little doubt that Christianity drew from ancient mystery cults, from Greek philosophy (especially Stoicism), as well as from Judaism. The discoveries of the Dead Sea Scrolls tend to give support to this conception of the pre-Christian existence of many Christian ideas. There is much scholarly work yet to be done before the full significance of the Scrolls can be ascertained. It is now generally accepted, if not proved, that they are authentic documents of a Jewish sect—perhaps the Essenes—dated about 100 B.C.. Insofar as they are Biblical texts, they tend to confirm the authenticity of other texts. The new documents among the Scrolls present a picture of a sect that in many ways is similar to the earliest Christian groups.

The controversies surrounding the Dead Sea Scrolls have gone beyond those of scholarship and have become partly matters of faith. It is interesting to inquire why this latest indication of the ways in which Christianity was embedded in the situation of the ancient world should arouse debate. Biblical criticism is many centuries old; even its modern approaches date back two hundred years. It may be that the existence of many actual documents brings a sharper challenge to the conceptions of revelation and the uniqueness of Jesus than earlier studies did. The Scrolls have also received wider publicity than did earlier research, thus seeming to pose a greater threat to those who look upon Jesus as a starting point. This conception of a starting point is certainly a central thesis in Pauline Christianity, which lies at the foundation of most branches of Christian interpretation today. It is conceivable that the fact that nowhere in the Bible are the Essenes mentioned, despite their similarity to Christians, is an indication of the effort to establish the uniqueness of Jesus.[13]

Even the most liberal interpretation of the Scrolls does not establish a historical connection between Jesus and the Essenes. These documents do, however, add weight to the accumulating evidence that in the very building of Christianity, elements were assimilated from many sources, that it changed and developed as it reached out to many different cultures. Without this process, it could not have appealed to the Roman masses and to their rulers and to the barbarians of Northern Europe. "This Christian

13 See Millar Burrows, *The Dead Sea Scrolls;* Frank M. Cross, Jr., *The Ancient Library of Qumran;* Theodore Gaster, *The Dead Sea Scriptures;* Edmund Wilson, *The Scrolls from the Dead Sea;* John M. Allegro, "The Untold Story of the Dead Sea Scrolls," *Harper's*, 233, 1966, pp. 46–54; W. D. Davies, op. cit., pp. 208–256; A. Powell Davies, *The Meaning of the Dead Sea Scrolls.*

synthesis was marvelously inclusive; everything in the Roman world seems to have found a place, from Greek rationalism and humanism to the ideas and ideals of Egyptian and Babylonian priests, already old before the Greeks discovered Greece." [14] And as the experiences, values, and problems of its adherents have changed, Christianity has continued to change, continued to absorb new elements.

Christianity, of course, is not in the least unique in this process of absorption. Every major religion has actively incorporated or marginally used the beliefs and practices of the local, pagan, and folk religions with which they have come in contact.[15]

Not all aspects of a religious system are changed with equal speed or ease, but the process of development can be seen in every phase of religious life, from forms of worship and aesthetic symbolism, to group organization and polity, to theology and doctrine. A religion will not long hold the allegiance of a group of people who have acquired—as a result of nonreligious causes—new aesthetic tastes, new intellectual perspectives, new occupational interests, new moral conceptions—unless that religion adjusts to those changes. *Semper idem*, the motto of the Catholic Church, is a valid claim only in a stable society, as the history of the Church itself shows, for Catholicism has proved marvelously adaptable to changing circumstance. Always the same—except that it drops its defense of medieval cosmology, after decades of opposition to the astronomers; it reverses its opposition to trade unions, in environments where Catholic workers are finding unions helpful; it supports the integration of church and state, except in the United States and other countries where such a doctrine is frowned upon; it opposes usury, except when the development of a commercial and industrial economy changes the significance of lending money at interest. These changes often come slowly and painfully, both because of institutional rigidity and because a change favorable to or supported by some members of a complex organization may be injurious to other members. The changes are cited, not to show the inconsistency of the Catholic Church, but to illustrate how a religious organization, seeking to be effective in a changed situation, adapts itself. Protestantism has undoubtedly changed even more. One need only mention the decline of the doctrine of predestination, the assimilation of the idea of evolution, the qualified acceptance of divorce, to suggest the variety of changes.

Perhaps the most obvious changes in religion occur in the process of adjustment to major intellectual developments. The Randalls point out how strongly Christianity has been affected in this way:

On three separate occasions Christianity was confronted by imposing bodies of belief, great systems of carefully worked out and articulated ideas. Each time able thinkers arose to fit the Christian faith into those bodies of science. The simple gospel of the early Christians met the great Platonic philosophy of the Hellenistic age. The outcome was not disintegration; it was the formulation of Christian theology by the Alexandrian Fathers of the Church, Clement and Origen and Athanasius, and the marvelously rich system of Augustine. The crude and primitive religious life of the early Middle Ages was confronted by the scientific

14 See J. H. Randall and J. H. Randall, Jr., *Religion and the Modern World*, pp. 16–17.

15 See, for example, Max Weber, *The Religion of India*, especially Chapter 9; Clifford Geertz, *The Religion of Java*; and Winston King, *A Thousand Lives Away*.

thought of Aristotle. The result was not the abandonment of faith; it was the intellectual synthesis of the Scholastics, now hailed as orthodoxy by the Catholic Church. Profoundly shaken by the humanism of the Renaissance and the mysticism of the Reformation, Christianity was brought face to face with the negative rationalism of 17th century physics. The culmination of a long struggle was, intellectually, the religious philosophies of the idealistic movement, and practically, the mass revivals of the early 19th century. Need we imagine that the fourth great set of scientific ideas, the biological and social sciences of the last two generations, will destroy man's faith at last because it throws such a flood of light upon it? [16]

If our conception of religion is correct, the answer to the question in the previous sentence is No; but the content of faith will continue to change. And this change will not proceed only until some vital center is reached; it will continue indefinitely. Proponents of a faith are likely to contend that changes in their religion have taken place only in the "outer layers," that the inner core remains unmodified. Every religious system certainly contains a group of fundamental beliefs and rites that are highly resistant to modification. In face of basic changes in society, however, even these may be revised so drastically that the old is scarcely visible beneath the new. Then controversies are likely to arise between those who claim that anyone who accepts the new doctrines or practices has deserted the faith and those who contend that the new formulations are necessary and logical developments. Those who embrace the new religious elements will be those who have experienced the changes in society in the most complete way. If they modify the old faith, rather than accepting a new one, they will do so gradually, through reinterpretations, through the discovery that beliefs which formerly were accepted as literally true are simply symbolic representations.

RELIGIOUS CHANGES IN THE UNITED STATES

This brief statement of a perspective and the illustrative references to early Judaism and the founding period of Christianity may serve to introduce the problem of the relation between social change and religious change in more recent times. The topic has special relevance for the modern world, in which changes are so dramatically rapid. In a day of strong nationalistic aspirations, Buddhism develops a more vigorous concern for political struggles, or it loses ground to secular and religious competitors.[17] As India becomes more industrialized and in more extensive contact with the West, her religious views show some increase in this-worldly emphasis.[18] When Europe began to feel the impact of growing trade, more extensive culture contact, urbanization, growth of knowledge, nationalism, and the many other aspects of "the modern world," her religious life inevitably changed.

16 Randall and Randall, op. cit., pp. 14–15.

17 See Wing-tsit Chan, *Religious Trends in Modern China*; C. S. Braden, *War, Communism and World Religions*; D. C. Holtom, *Modern Japan and Shinto Nationalism*; Donald E. Smith, ed., *South Asian Politics and Religion*.

18 See Hajime Nakamura, "The Changing Value of Man in Modern India," in *Symbols and Values*, Conference on Science, Philosophy and Religion, 1954, pp. 701–731.

The Protestant Reformation is one dramatic indication of this relationship; but the change was not so abrupt as we sometimes suppose. There was a great deal of continuity with the past (St. Augustine would not have felt uncomfortable with most of the ideas of Luther or Calvin); and religious change in the post-Reformation period continued unabated.

When Puritanism, one of the complex religious movements that were developed in England, was brought to America, it was drastically modified. Rites, theology, and church polity that had developed in thirteenth-century Italy, sixteenth-century Germany and Geneva, and seventeenth-century England (to oversimplify the case) were not likely to go unmodified in eighteenth-century America. The stern doctrine of election, the tightly controlled church system of Puritanism, the emphasis on man's sinfulness, from which he can be rescued only by the grace of God—such patterns as these were not likely to be congenial to many people in the New World. It was not difficult to accept the Cromwellian idea of a Holy Commonwealth, but its meaning was drastically changed. The earliest religious writers in America, the heirs of the right wing of European Protestantism, accepted most of the traditional Puritan framework. By the middle of the eighteenth century, however, and particularly by the time independence was won, important religious leaders had reshaped that tradition in significant ways. "The expectation of a Holy Commonwealth to be brought into being on these shores by an act of God was restated as a vote of political confidence in the average man and his corporate ability to achieve a democratic Utopia." [19] Or, as Laski wrote:

by the time of Jonathan Edwards the sense of this world as a vale of tears and the acceptance of the doctrines of grace and election were speedily losing ground before the conviction, so evident in the rise of innumerable socialist communities and in the Emersonian doctrine of self-reliance, that man saves himself by his own effort and that he accomplishes his salvation in the world of here and now. [20]

There is little doubt that "God himself became republican" in America, particularly in the religion of the middle and upper classes and in the thinking of most of our writers. Certainly Emerson's "doctrine of self-reliance" is closer to this aspect of America than is "saved by God's election." There is a danger here, however, as there so often is when one judges past events by the thoughts of well-known people, that the less articulate members of a society will be forgotten. Much of the traditional theology survived in the religious life of the lower classes especially. The otherworldliness, the strong conviction of the sinfulness of man, the reliance on God's help were by no means eliminated. They were mingled, to be sure, with ideas of individual responsibility, of equality before God (as opposed to predestination), and with conceptions of church polity that emphasized the role of laymen and freedom of religious choice. Thus both fundamentalism and liberalism are to be found in the American environment, sharing together some of the influences of that environment, but demonstrating also different religious backgrounds and needs.

What are some of the sociocultural factors involved in these trends in the direction of the "Americanization of Christianity"? Perhaps most im-

19 Willard L. Sperry, *Religion in America*, p. 250.

20 Harold J. Laski, *The American Democracy*, p. 729.

portant was the fact that in a land where status assignments were not rigid, where new land and new economic opportunities were extensive, where population was sparse, it was easy to develop a theory—nourished by many facts—that men could shape their own destiny. A pessimistic theology was not likely to survive in a situation where so much hope and optimism prevailed (always remembering the strong qualifications on this statement when one refers to the large number for whom hope continued to be distant). A doctrine of predestination was scarcely likely to be congenial to people who saw all around them a social mobility unprecedented in European societies.

A Calvinist theory of the church found equally poor soil. Many of the migrants to America, particularly outside New England and Virginia, were from the lower classes. In Europe they had been in closer touch with Anabaptist movements or other phases of the left wing of the Reformation than with Puritanism. Thus a concept of a free church, with strong lay influence, emphasizing religion as an intensely personal matter was already important for them. This was strengthened by pioneering conditions, which cut them off from most connections with ecclesiastical organizations. Puritanism itself contained an inner contradiction that continually challenged ecclesiastical structure—inner religion, purity of doctrine, and direct contact with God were held in high esteem. It has frequently been stated that the highly disciplined and restrained services of early Puritanism were entirely inadequate to the emotional needs and patterns of expression of the isolated, poorly educated people on the frontier. This is a plausible hypothesis, but the personality processes involved have scarcely been adequately described.

We have described some of the factors that created the constitutional guarantees of religious freedom and the separation of church and state in the United States. The competition among church organizations and, more importantly, the opposition to ecclesiastical authority as part of the larger struggle for freedom were important in creating the American pattern of religious organization. One of the most significant consequences of this situation was the ease with which new religious groups could be formed, reflecting large or small variations in religious interpretation, social circumstance, or personal need—a kind of free enterprise in religion to match the pattern in business (for we should not forget the matching ideology of "separation of business and state" and the matching modifications of the last half century). This pattern of diversity was encouraged by the heterogeneity of the immigrant groups, regional differences, industrialization, and the general fact of the speed of social changes.[21]

To speak in terms of a broad generalization, the religious situation in the United States in the nineteenth century can be described as an extension of the trends we have outlined. Among the middle and upper classes an

21 On the early American religious situation, see Thomas C. Hall, *The Religious Background of American Culture;* H. R. Niebuhr, *The Social Sources of Denominationalism;* Winfred E. Garrison, "Social and Cultural Factors in Our Divisions," *Ecumenical Review,* October, 1952, pp. 43–51; Sperry, op. cit.; Kai Erikson, *Wayward Puritans;* Winthrop Hudson, *Religion in America;* John M. Mecklin, *The Story of American Dissent;* and the several works of W. W. Sweet, including *The American Churches. An Interpretation* and *The Story of Religion in America.*

optimistic view of human possibilities and a strong emphasis on self-reliance were matched by theological liberalism and religious individualism. The society around them was to their liking, so there was little need for a social gospel, and their own careers were filled with success and hope, so theirs was largely the religion of the "once-born." A contemporary critic is likely to declare that their theology was superficial, insufficiently aware of the tragedy and evil in life, too naively reliant on human enterprise. The liberal school of American religious thinkers, for their part, was likely to dismiss orthodox theology for its pessimism, its dark picture of human nature, its irrelevance to a democratic society. The sociologist of religion is interested in the way these various interpretations have been affected by the social and cultural forces around them.

The nineteenth century was not without its fundamentalism of course. It lingered in the larger denominations, particularly those which, like the Baptists and Methodists, had won many of their adherents from the lower classes. And it was the predominant doctrine of the sects. There was a lively sense of evil and sin in the camp meeting and the revival and in the fervent services of the sects. The second coming was a firm belief, mingled in a complex way with otherworldliness—a messianic hope for the dramatic improvement of this world by God's intervention alongside doctrines that devalued this world, as a kind of second line of defense.

New religious groups continued to appear, encouraged by immigration, migration to the West, urbanization, and other forces. There was little tendency to modify the separation of church and state or the separation of religion and economics that characterized a situation in which individual salvation was so strongly emphasized.

American Religious Trends in the Twentieth Century
After the Civil War, and particularly by the beginning of the twentieth century, the social and cultural environment of American religious movements changed with great speed. Theology, church organization, patterns of worship, and conceptions of the right relationship of religion to government and economic problems have all shown some of the marks of that change. We have already discussed several aspects of this process, for example, the development of the social gospel as one manifestation of religious response to new problems of the industrial age and developments in the concept of separation of church and state. Those movements are clear illustrations of the way in which social changes precipitate religious changes, which in turn influence the environment out of which they came. Other religious changes that we shall discuss also clearly reveal the impact of the social situation.

Is Religion Prospering or Disappearing? Both the revival and the sharp decline of religion have been confidently proclaimed in the last several decades. In most instances, the reference has been to churches and traditional religious activities, in an effort to discover whether there has been a return to religion or an increase of secularism. From my point of view the question has been wrongly put. Men everywhere have ultimate concerns. In all times these are the subject of sacred beliefs, beyond the reach of continuous disconfirmation, and of ritual, "a way of renewing contact with ultimate things," as Edward Shils has defined it. We will be better students of the human situation in my judgment if we ask, not whether, but how people are religious, as a result of what circumstances, and with what consequences.

In this section, I shall examine some general aspects of the American religious scene, with some attention given specifically to Protestantism. In the following sections, Catholicism and Judaism will be the focus of attention.

We are well supplied with data regarding church attendance, church membership, and readiness to respond positively or negatively to certain traditional religious beliefs. Even these data are often seriously lacking in comparability and validity; [22] but their greater weakness is a bias toward fundamentalist definitions of religious belief and a reliance on church indicators as adequate measures of religious involvement.

During the 1950's it was widely observed that America was experiencing a return to religion. Membership figures of churches climbed to 60 per cent or more of the adult population (although it had been almost that high earlier in the century); [23] attendance at church on any given Sunday was between 40 and 50 per cent, if one does not question the accuracy of responses given to public opinion pollers; [24] billions of dollars were spent annually for church buildings and programs; many religious books appeared on bestseller lists; mass-circulation magazines published numerous articles about religion; political leaders affirmed the national religious heritage. During this period, Paul Hutchinson wrote:

there are so many prayer meetings for the mighty along the Potomac that the subject is beginning to attract derisive comment . . . conspicuous devotion is by no means confined to official circles. In the Southwest Conference they start football games with prayer; I happened to be in Dallas when the selection of a bathing beauty queen was begun under the same evangelical auspices.[25]

The American Institute of Public Opinion reported that 97 per cent of Americans identify themselves with one of the major religious groups.[26] Eighty per cent of adult Americans say they believe the Bible to be the "revealed word of God."

Many of the indicators of more recent years reveal a situation similar to that of the 1950's. Growth in membership and attendance may not have quite kept up with the growth of population in the 1960's, but support for church programs remained high and traditional beliefs have not been sharply altered. The Gallup Poll, in an international comparison, reported significant shifts in Europe over a twenty year period, but little change in

22 For valuable discussions of problems associated with reports of church membership and attendance, see N. J. Demerath, III, *Indicators of Social Change*, Eleanor Sheldon and Wilbert Moore, eds., pp. 352–369; Seymour Lipset, *The First New Nation*, Chap. Four; Winthrop Hudson, "Are Churches Really Booming?" *Christian Century*, 72, 1955, pp. 1494–1496; and B. G. Mulvaney, "Catholic Population Revealed in Catholic Baptisms," *American Ecclesiastical Review*, 133, 1955, pp. 183–193.

23 See Michael Argyle, *Religious Behavior*, p. 28.

24 But see ibid., and Demerath, op. cit., for indications that one ought to apply a discount.

25 *Life*, April 11, 1955, p. 138.

26 Public Opinion News Service, March 20, 1955.

the United States. Belief in life after death, for example, went up in the United States, between 1948 and 1968, from 68 to 73 per cent. It fell off rather drastically in the European countries sampled (for example, from 58 to 35 per cent in France; from 49 to 38 per cent in Britain). Ninety-eight per cent of the American respondents indicated their belief in God. Percentages in the other countries ranged from 96 in Greece to 60 in Sweden.[27]

These findings, however, should be seen alongside indications that Americans believe that religion is on the decline. For several years now, the Gallup Poll has asked a random sample of the American population: "At the present time, do you think religion as a whole is increasing its influence on American life, or losing its influence?" Between 1957 and 1968 there was a sharp reversal (see Table 21–1).

Table 21–1. Opinions regarding the influence of religion in America [28]

	1957	1962	1968
Influence increasing	69	45	18
Influence decreasing	14	31	67
No difference or no opinion	17	24	15

With reference to the 1968 figures, churchgoers were only a little less likely to see religious influence decreasing than nonchurchgoers (62 to 70 per cent). As in 1957, younger persons were more likely to see a declining influence than older persons, but the rate of change was about the same for all age groups, from 20 to 77 per cent for those 21–29, from 13 to 68 per cent for those 30–49, and from 10 to 62 per cent for those 50 years of age or older.

Such a sharp reversal is extremely rare in public opinion polling; it presents difficult problems of interpretation. Without further data, one can only guess about the combination of influences that produced this result, but I think the following statements are probably true: There was a high point of what one might call "verbal traditional religiosity" in the 1950's, hence the contrast is sharper than it might be if measures for the 1930's or 1940's were available. Opinions about the influence of religion are not an index of the individuals' own religious views. This means that among the 67 per cent who, in 1968, believed that religious influence was declining were some who were unhappy about their own appraisal, others who were neutral, and still others who were happy about it. They agreed only on the observation that religious influence was declining, affected in common by serious public disorders, a flood of accounts of a presumed "sexual revolution," and a rather widespread feeling that the nation was faced by a series of problems almost too large for the institutions of order to handle.

27 The New York Times, December 26, 1968, p. 21. When the question was put to an American sample in a very decisive way ("I know God really exists and I have no doubt about it") the percentage agreeing fell to 79 per cent among Protestants and 85 per cent among Catholics. See Rodney Stark and Charles Glock, American Piety, p. 30.

28 Adapted from the New York Times, May 5, 1968, p. 38.

We have no barometer readings of anomie or of individuals' feelings concerning the level of anomie around them; but I would regard this Gallup Poll question as a good equivalent. Its specific value as a measure of religious opinion perhaps cannot be judged until we have matching questions with regard to the family, government, and other agencies of socialization and control. I would guess that in 1968 the American people would have judged that all of these were losing influence, even if from different bases and at different rates.

An additional factor producing the belief that religion was losing its influence may be a kind of catching up of opinions with some of the realities of the 1940–1960 return to religion (to give it a set of arbitary dates). A number of observers had warned that the indexes used to measure the return were superficial. The Bible may be acclaimed as the revealed word of God, but if 53 per cent of those who thus acclaim it cannot name even one of the first four books of the New Testament, the significance of their views is small. "Every aspect of contemporary religious life reflects this paradox—pervasive secularism amid mounting religiosity, 'the strengthening of the religious structure in spite of increasing secularization.'" [29] The return to religion can be understood only by noting the simultaneous secularization of the church. What one returns to is an institution that makes few creedal demands. It has been so secularized that to join many middle-class churches is not sharply different from joining Kiwanis. As Robin Williams has pointed out, Americans are not irreligious, but there has been a withdrawal of "affect," of pervasive emotional involvement with traditional religions. Religious organizations are unusually separate from other structures. There is a tendency to think that religion is good because it is useful for *other* major values, thus reversing the means-end relationship in which religion is thought to be the ultimate value. This is related to the fact that many of the key values of American society are not couched in religious terms, but in secular, and particularly in national, terms.[30] The very tolerance of Americans in religious matters is an indication that their key values, the first premises from which they start, are not found in their traditional religious patterns.

It is the American Way of Life that supplies American society with an "overarching sense of unity" amid conflict. It is the American Way of Life about which Americans are admittedly and unashamedly "intolerant." It is the American Way of Life that provides the framework in terms of which the crucial values of American existence are couched. By every realistic criterion the American Way of Life is the operative faith of the American people.[31]

As Herberg well realized, this was to overstate the case in 1955. It has become even more of an overstatement. For many members of ethnic-immigrant churches, for some Lutheran and Reformed groups, for some sections of Catholicism, for sects of the disinherited, for a large share of the black population, for many theologians, whether fundamentalist or radical, for religious liberals, for students in protest against a range of establishments, the "operative faith" could scarcely be limited to the sys-

29 Will Herberg, *Protestant-Catholic-Jew*, p. 14.

30 See Robin Williams, *American Society*, Chap. 9.

31 Herberg, op. cit., p. 88.

tem of values, beliefs, and practices that can be identified with the American way of life. Much of American religion today is outside the churches; it is "invisible" to those who look only for traditional expressions.[32]

Moreover, "Americanism" as a civil religion, as we noted earlier, has many religious roots. It is a relatively creedless and formless national church that obscures differences while furnishing a common value frame. In this sense, it is an emergent religious movement in a society of heterogeneous religious traditions and of pervasive secularism.

It would be a serious mistake, in any attempt to appraise the strength of religion in America, to overlook the strong continuity in the religious views of the middle strata. Theologians may move in dialectic fashion from Schleiermacher to Barth and Niebuhr to Tillich and Bonhoeffer. They are sensitive to world events and world intellectual currents. But the average layman is concerned with a religion that speaks to his immediate individual problems and harmonizes with his deep-rooted attitudes.[33] In the mid-1950's I wrote, with reference to neo-orthodoxy, of my strong impression that the emphasis on the evil in man, the insistence on his incapacity to deal alone with a history inevitably filled with tragedy, had not really persuaded the respectable and successful members of the congregations in which these doctrines were being preached. The laymen were deeply disturbed by the enormous difficulties of the time; they were at least ready to listen to this "new" theology; their easy confidence in an inevitable progress had been shattered. But their belief in individualism was too deep-seated, the habit of asking secular questions about the problems they face too well established, their own relative success—despite the world's problems—too real to them in terms of the values they place high, to permit them to accept the neo-orthodox view wholeheartedly.

Despite mounting crises, this continues to characterize the religious thought of many Americans. Confronted with a chaotic world, faced by individual problems of anxiety and guilt, many contemporary Americans, particularly in the middle classes, are likely to turn to a religious version of "how to win friends and influence people" or to a psychotherapy clothed in religious terms that promises solutions that seem to be within their grasp. Few are inclined to embrace a difficult theology that contradicts much of what they have been taught about the power and perfectability of man. The "power of positive thinking" is a religion for those who are successful, or are climbing, but still find themselves somehow anxious and unhappy. It was difficult enough in an earlier day to keep up with the Joneses— but now everybody has become Jones. Thus the need for reassurance is strong.

If neo-orthodoxy was somewhat remote from the thinking of laymen in an earlier period, the radical theology of the day seems only slightly less remote,[34] if one judges by the continuing indications of quite fundamen-

32 See Thomas Luckmann, *The Invisible Religion.*

33 One source of documentation of these views is a content analysis of popular inspirational religious literature. See Louis Schneider and Sanford Dornbusch, *Popular Religion: Inspirational Books in America.*

34 I will discuss these theological positions in the next chapter.

talist and orthodox views in the American population. For sheer volume of published material, frequency of church attendance, and ratio of income given for religious programs, it is the more conservative religious groups and individuals who are in the lead. Differences in participation and support are not, in my judgment, drawn primarily along class lines. Those who are highly participant are drawn from working-class Jehovah's Witnesses, for example, lower-middle-class participants in Billy Graham's crusades, and upper-middle-class suburbanites who are attracted to Norman Vincent Peale's gospel. What they share in common is an emphasis on the need for individual regeneration and strength, however differently that need may be expressed. Among some, this takes the form of an emphasis on ortherworldliness, fundamentalism in doctrine, and revivalism in form. This represents a strong continuity in the Christian tradition and in American experience. From the Great Awakening, to the Western Revival in the early part of the nineteenth century, to Dwight L. Moody, to Billy Sunday, to Billy Graham is a path that involves many turnings but no basic change in direction. Yet revivalism also demonstrates the influence of changes in the social setting. There are obvious differences in the types of worship—compare a frontier camp meeting with an elaborate revival meeting in the Hollywood Bowl. The impact of radio and television has been felt among the fundamentalist groups, as it has among other religious organizations. Billy Graham's non-parish-church form of worship, for all its appearance of unstructured spontaneity, is a carefully planned program, influenced, in style and technology by the TV and movie spectaculars to which his congregation has become accustomed. Like earlier revivalism, it appeals to the broad middle strata of the American population, not to the sectarian.[35] It shades off by fairly small steps to the religion of the conservative members of the upper middle and upper classes, of suburban parishes, and, in many instances, of the White House.

All of this is not to suggest that there has been no change in religious belief and practice in recent years. There is a new breed of religious activists, as Harvey Cox calls them; there are "underground churches," representing what some have called a "rebellious ecumenism" of small, private, nondoctrinal groups. A " 'Christian Left' Makes the Scene," a *New York Times* headline tells us, trying to remake Christianity into a faith that appeals to a radicalized student group while keeping its Christian identity. The effort is well caught up in one student's remark: "God is not dead. He simply needs a new name—or maybe no name." [36] God needs no name and the church needs no structure for those who would carry religion into the streets, the factories, the ghettoes, and the plantations. This is the new version of the "institutional church," which at an earlier time brought many activities—recreation, nursery schools, discussion groups, therapy sessions —into the church. The radical ministry of the day carries religion out of

35 This has been documented by Frederick L. Whitam, "Revivalism as Institutionalized Behavior: An Analysis of the Social Base of a Billy Graham Crusade," unpublished Ms., 1967. For comparative material see William G. McLoughlin, Jr., *Modern Revivalism*.

36 The *New York Times*, Dec. 31, 1967, p. 44.

the church into the civil rights march, the picket line, the rent strike.[37] The Black Power movement too, as I have suggested earlier, has many religious qualities.

There is, then, a radical religious element in America, but it is not numerically strong. It picks up the long tradition of religious protest and expresses it in contemporary terms. Some observers see this as a sign of the weakening of Christianity. Rodney Stark and Charles Glock write: "As sociologists, we find it difficult to imagine a Christian church without Jesus Christ as Divine Saviour, without a God conceived of in personal terms, without the promise of eternal life." [38] I should suppose that as sociologists they are obliged to study empirically what Christians are saying and doing, not designate standards of orthodoxy. Today's "heresies" seem no more extreme than those of St. Thomas and Luther, measured against the orthodoxies of their day. Thomas's opponents accused him of heresy; through years of struggle they proclaimed that they found it difficult to imagine a Christian doctrine that did not separate truth and faith absolutely, whereas Thomas sought a great synthesis. Those who fought Luther found it difficult to imagine that faith alone, without regard for the sacraments of the church, could bring salvation. Scientists, I expect, will be wise to observe these and contemporary disagreements among Christians as important indicators of the range of views in large and complex religious movements, and to seek to discover what are their social sources and consequences.

There are numerous other religious changes that we might mention in an attempt to assess religious trends in America. Some of them we have discussed in other connections. The ecumenical movement, for example, has grown in strength. It is not clear, however, whether this represents "the huddling together of Christians into an ecumenical movement," as Herbert Schneider put it, or a sign of resurgence. Older denominations, even of the most congregational variety, are experiencing the bureaucratization so common to the secular institutions around them.[39] On the other hand, highly unbureaucratic, spontaneous, and unorthodox groups express the desire to reformulate both doctrines and institutional structures.

Stability and Change in American Catholicism. Because many of the evidences we have used in discussing these various trends have been drawn from studies of Protestantism, we need to examine contemporary Catholicism and Judaism to get a fuller picture of the religious situation in America. We have noted that in the last generation, Catholics in America have dispersed, in approximately proportionate numbers, through the occupational and educational structure. They have intermarried with Protestants in large numbers, so that many families have a mixed religious identity and many more have one member who has been converted from Protestantism to Catholicism or vice versa. (Data regarding the number of conversions, whether through marriage or otherwise, are highly unreliable. The Public

37 For a variety of discussions of these activities, see Ross W. Sanderson, *The Church Serves the Changing City;* H. P. Douglass and Edmund de S. Brunner, *The Protestant Church as a Social Institution;* Leon Howell, "The Delta Ministry," *Christianity and Crisis,* 26, 1966, pp. 189–192; Harvey Cox, op. cit., Chap. 12.

38 Stark and Glock, op. cit., p. 210.

39 This is well documented by Paul Harrison in *Authority and Power in the Free Church Tradition: A Social Case Study of the American Baptist Convention.*

Opinion News Service estimated in the mid-1950's that about 1.4 million people had moved each way. Conversions as a result of intermarriage since then have probably doubled that number; and there are other shifts less easily identified. Perhaps we would not be far wrong if we suggested that 3 or 4 million Catholics were raised as Protestants and 3 or 4 million Protestants were raised as Catholics. How many of these have that intensity of belief associated with the convert and how many are purely formal transfers of persons already marginal is a subject for conjecture.)

The consequence of these trends and others has been a sharp decline, in the last two decades, of Catholic separation and interfaith conflict. In various ways, although not in all, Catholics have been "Americanized," or as Wakin and Scheuer put it "de-Romanized." [40] This trend has been supported by international changes, dramatically represented by the Second Vatican Council, which also indicates some slight de-Romanization of the Church.

The reduction of Catholic exclusiveness and a tendency toward stereotypy on the part of some Protestants has been quite recent and quite rapid. In 1954, on the eve of the assembly of the World Council of Churches in Evanston, Samuel Cardinal Stritch, Archbishop of Chicago, warned Catholics that they could not join persons of other faiths in religious assemblies, because theirs is "the one and only church of Christ." The Vatican Council, however, recognized authentic Christianity outside the Church; interfaith cooperation on the local and national levels has now become fairly common.

Many American Protestants have regarded the Catholic Church as somehow alien and undemocratic. It is unclear where "alien" begins and ends in this land of immigrants, but there is no question that Catholic organizational structure, like that of many other churches, is hierarchical. It has also been influenced, however, by its environment. A generalized ideological interpretation is likely to miss the changes and variations. Some Americans believe they can predict the day-by-day policy of the Kremlin by reading the *Communist Manifesto*. Paul Blanshard in some of his work, and other writers too, have given something of this same impression in their analyses of American Catholicism. In a chapter entitled "The Catholic Plan for America," Blanshard made it appear that were the Catholic Church to become dominant in the United States, it would scarcely differ in its program from the present situation in Spain or Portugal.[41] It may be, as Robert Brown suggests, that Blanshard's view of Catholicism is only a detailed formulation of a view quite widely held, at least until the last few years, by Protestants. Brown quotes a 1962 statement from a book published by the Presbyterian and Reformed Publishing Company: "In order to see clearly what Roman Catholicism really is we must see it as it was during the Middle Ages, or as it has continued to be in certain countries such as Spain, Portugal, Italy, France, Southern Ireland and Latin America. . . . [There] we see the true fruits of the system in the lives of the people, with

40 Edward Wakin and Joseph Scheuer, *The De-Romanization of the American Catholic Church.*

41 See Paul Blanshard, *American Freedom and Catholic Power.* More recently, Blanshard has modified his position; in a book on Vatican II he takes a stand that on the whole is favorable to the Council. See *Paul Blanshard on Vatican II.*

all of their poverty, ignorance, superstition and low moral standards." [42] Or, as it was put in a flyer appealing for funds for "Protestants and Other Americans United for Separation of Church and State": "Every day that America sleeps, the closer we come to being dominated by the rulers of one religion."

Rather than assuming that some particular expressions of Catholicism are its "true fruits," the scientist must study the full range and inquire about the way in which the setting of the Church affects its program and doctrine.

There can be no doubt that the long European experience of the Catholic Church and its elaborate international organization, which holds the national churches in a common framework, have created tendencies that resist the Americanization of the Catholic Church in the United States. These influences were, until mid-twentieth century, accentuated by the recency of much of the immigration of Catholics to this country. At the time of the Revolution, they constituted only 1 per cent of the population. Even the large Irish migration of the mid-nineteenth century was far exceeded by the Italian and Polish migrations of the late nineteenth and early twentieth centuries. The emphasis laid from the beginning of the United States upon religious freedom and equality may have retarded the Americanization of the religions of the immigrants. Some pressure has been brought on them to change "their foreign ways" in most areas of life, but because of freedom of religion, this has been least apparent in the religious field. This point must not be weighed too heavily, however, because it can also be argued that, under some conditions, the *lack* of pressure is most conducive to rapid assimilation.

It would be a mistake to argue on sociological grounds that the Catholic Church in the United States will soon become "simply another denomination." [43] The weight of its ideology and the organization of its hierarchy on an international basis argue against this. Those who defend the thesis that Catholicism is out of harmony with the traditional American pattern of cooperation and mutual tolerance among denominations, the separation of church and state, the supremacy of public schools, and the like are not lacking in evidence. Occasionally an influential Catholic will indicate that he believes the present separation of church and state, with all denominations treated equally, is not an ideal arrangement, but a necessary *modus vivendi* under the present circumstances.[44]

This is not the whole story, however. Indeed the whole thesis of this book —that religions are embedded in the societies of which they are a part— would be seriously weakened if there were not evidences of the Americanization of Catholicism. The Catholic Church is a large and complex organization, with a wide range of opinions within it, making it possible to prove by careful selection of material that many different trends are the "essential" Catholic position.

42 Quoted by Robert M. Brown, *The Ecumenical Revolution*, p. 6.

43 John F. Kennedy's campaign for the Presidency, however, can be read, insofar as it dealt with his Catholicism, as an effort to interpret the Catholic Church in that way. See Lawrence Fuchs, *John F. Kennedy and American Catholicism*.

44 See Blanshard, *American Freedom and Catholic Power*, p. 49.

A useful hypothesis is that as one moves from the top hierarchy to the parish priest to the laymen, other things being equal, one finds a progressively larger American element in the phenomenon of "being Catholic."[45] One would expect this on the basis of training, organizational connections, roles, and values. (This broad generalization is qualified, of course, by the variety of perspectives on each level.) As Catholics become increasingly "old American," as a larger proportion of the priesthood and hierarchy are native born, as the American branch of the Church grows in influence in the international organization, as its members are spread throughout the class and occupational structure of the United States in a pattern matching that of the majority—thus sharing secular values, roles, and organizations—in short, as Catholicism gets more deeply involved in American culture and society, we can expect extensive changes. These changes have already been carried quite far, of course.[46]

This does not mean that distinctive Catholic patterns and organization will become scarce. In an earlier chapter we have noted that America tends to be pluralistic or even columnar in structure. Will Herberg has developed the thesis that Catholicism, and Judaism, although they are strongly affected by the American environment, are nevertheless maintaining their distinctive patterns. We have not a single but a triple melting pot, somewhat separate subcultures among Protestants, Catholics, and Jews, with one of which the vast majority of the population identifies. This is not a sign, however, that Catholicism has been unaffected by the American situation. Indeed, it is a manifestation of the American pattern of religious freedom, of a pervasive secularization that makes it less important what one's religious identity is than to have an underlying shared belief in "the American way." It also represents a need, in a heterogeneous and very mobile society, to find one's identity, to find a group to which he can indubitably belong, to establish his own "brand name." The effect of these forces is to preserve and perhaps to strengthen the separate identity of Catholicism in the very midst of a situation where that identity is less important. The American creed has become the operative and shared religion of the nation to a substantial degree.[47]

Herberg may underestimate the forces that blur the line between Catholics and Protestants (at least a third of Catholics marry persons who were raised as Protestants); and his thesis, unless carefully stated, tends to underestimate the variation within each of the major traditions as well as the pressures upon it from the outside to change. In the Catholic case, these are best illustrated by the Second Vatican Council, 1962–1965.

At first it appeared that the Council might not only offer progressive resolutions—which it did in abundance—but so reorganize the Vatican bureaucracy that decision-making would be placed on a broader base. This

45 From given value stands this can be a happy or an unhappy fact. It is related to the increase in independence among laymen, which can take the form, for example, of readiness on the part of only 21 per cent of American Catholics to be morally bound by their priests' instructions to integrate their neighborhoods. See *Newsweek*, March 26, 1967, p. 69. In other matters laymen are likely to be more liberal than their priests.

46 See Anson Phelps Stokes, *Church and State in the United States*, Vol. III, pp. 480–483.

47 See Will Herberg, *Protestant-Catholic-Jew*, especially Chaps. 2 and 3.

was not done. Although preservation of centralized power in the Vatican is often attributed to the shift, during the period of the Council, from Pope John to Pope Paul, it is perhaps equally well seen as simply another instance of the tendency of those in power to hold on to it.

Many liberal decisions were made by the Council: The Index of Prohibited Books was abolished; non-Catholics were recognized as authentic Christians; local languages were permitted for parts of the mass; ecumenism was promoted. Altogether, however, the *aggiornamento*, the bringing of the Church up to date, was not accomplished. Many observers, including some Catholics, believe that the impulse toward change expressed so strongly by Pope John in planning the Council has been severely constrained by Pope Paul in carrying through its recommendations and continuing its general spirit.[48] There was official recognition at the Vatican Council that there were many ways of being Catholic. This collides, however, with the fact that in an era of radio and television, pronouncements from the Vatican suddenly have a worldwide currency and directness they have never had before. Where it was easier, at an earlier time, to blur them and adapt them to local conditions, they now are starkly visible. This has meant, on the one hand, sharper protests from priests and laymen than the Church has experienced in a long time; and on the other, it has meant, under Pope Paul, strong reaffirmation of papal supremacy. In 1968 he cautioned against a "passion for change," declared again the tenet of papal infallability, and, in what has been the most controversial of his decisions, issued an encyclical renewing Catholic prohibition on all "artificial" means of birth control.

This last was no more interesting to the student of the Church than were the responses. Roman Catholic bishops in the United States backed the Pope's decision, but also declared that Catholic couples who in good conscience use birth control need not feel cut off from the Church and its sacraments. Eighty-seven Catholic theologians, most of them priests, declared that the encyclical was not binding, and that couples could responsibly decide for themselves.[49] Many laymen had been doing so, in fact, well before the encyclical. In a 1967 poll, *Newsweek* reported that 60 per cent of Catholic couples under 35 years of age had used contraceptive techniques unacceptable to the Church, and that 70 per cent of all respondents wanted the ban to be lifted.[50] When a cardinal punished several priests for opposing the birth control encyclical, groups of laymen accused him of harsh and un-Christian behavior; others left a church service when a message from the cardinal was read.

48 For a variety of views see F. E. Cartus, "The Vatican Council Ends. Reform on Borrowed Time?" *Harper's*, 231, 1965, pp. 100–114; Rocco Caporale, "The Dynamics of Hierocracy: Processes of Continuity-in-Change of the Roman Catholic System During Vatican II," *Sociological Analysis*, 28, 1967, pp. 59–68; Michael Novak, *Belief and Unbelief*; Thomas O'Dea, *The Catholic Crisis*; Jeremiah Newman, *Change and the Catholic Church*; François Houtart, "Critical Decisions and Institutional Tensions in a Religious Institution: The Case of Vatican II," *Review of Religious Research*, 9, 1968, pp. 131–146.

49 See *The New York Times*, July 31, 1968, pp. 1 and 16.

50 *Newsweek*, March 20, 1967, pp. 70–75. For an interesting account of the subtle modifications of thinking about birth control in one influential Catholic journal (*America*), see Carl Reiterman, "Birth Control and Catholics," *Journal for the Scientific Study of Religion*, 4, 1965, pp. 213–233.

Such actions by laymen are among the most significant developments in contemporary Catholicism. In 1967, the 2,900 delegates to the Third World Congress of the Lay Apostolate demonstrated not only that they took more progressive views than the Pope, bishops, and priests, but also that they were not inclined to keep their views hidden. The resolutions they passed —asking for liberalization of the ban on contraceptives, for an authoritative condemnation of racial discrimination, for contributions from developed countries of 1 per cent of their gross national product for aid to developing countries, and others—are perhaps not as significant sociologically as the resolution that asked for a structured, democratic role for laymen in the decision-making process of the Church.[51]

Elements of this change are beginning to appear, but in a setting that is filled with contradictions and stresses. For example, Hans Küng has called for participation by laymen in the selection of the pope; the Universities of Notre Dame and St. Louis have shifted control to boards of trustees made up predominantly of laymen, including some non-Catholics; small, underground, "free" churches have appeared in many cities—expressive of opposition to the paternalistic and conservative qualities of the established Church. At the same time, Catholic University has banned Hans Küng and three other speakers, all of whom were theological experts at the Vatican Council, from its campus. The Pontiff has called the idea of regular, democratic participation of laymen in church decision-making an absurdity.

Pressure to continue the process of change begun by the Council has been widespread, and has included open dissenting actions against papal decisions. "These have included renunciation of vows by many hundreds of priests and by two Latin-American bishops; publication, despite Vatican disapproval, of a Dutch catechism challenging many points of orthodox doctrine, and demands from French and Latin-American clergy that the church renounce pomp and power and become again the 'church of the poor.' "[52] In the face of such actions, Pope Paul has declared that the Church is the victim of "a practically schismatic ferment," and has accused the dissident clerics of "crucifying" the Church.[53]

It is difficult to weigh the balance of these contrasting elements; one can, however, predict continuing stress. To put it symbolically: Nuns who have marched on the picket line for civil rights are not likely to be content with modest changes in habit and modes of address. The impressive capacity of the Catholic Church to adapt to changes in its environment is now being put to its severest test, for it has become, almost everywhere, a minority movement (even in those lands where, formally, Catholics are in the majority). The issue is well stated by Michael Novak:

It seems that the bishops, particularly those of the United States, have hardly grasped the extent to which not only the Middle Ages but also the modern age is at an end; a new, technical, secular, urban, pluralistic age has begun. Language appropriate for an agricultural society no longer conveys meaning; even the word "father" means something different for the human spirit after Freud,

51 See the *New York Times*, Oct. 22, 1967, p. 6-E.

52 The *New York Times*, April 4, 1969, p. 1.

53 Ibid.

not to mention what it means in "broken" homes or in those millions of families whose lives center not on parents but on teenagers.[54]

In face of the drastic reorganization of lives in the contemporary world, I believe it can confidently be stated: Either the Catholic Church (and other churches as well, of course) in America and elsewhere will undertake extensive revision, a full *aggiornamento*, or its influence will seriously decline.

Stability and Change in American Judaism. Study of the degree to which there has been an Americanization of Judaism, or, as a more general problem, the degree to which Judaism is shaped by its social context, raises questions that parallel those we have noted with reference to Catholicism. Here too is the pull of opposite forces. On one side is the long, self-conscious history of Jews as a distinct people, with a vital religious and cultural tradition; there is the renewed sense of a common weal and a common fate brought about by prejudice, by persecution, by the re-establishment of Israel; there is the relative recency of migration of most Jews to the United States. On the other side is the speed with which many Jews have penetrated to the middle and upper strata of American society, thus giving them a strong sense of identity with that society; there is freedom of religion, public education, and the relative absence of barriers to economic and political activity; there is the increase in congregational church polity, with strong influence from the laymen; there are the different national origins, which impose some barriers to a sense of common Jewishness.

Under the influence of these various forces, Judaism has changed in the United States, yet it has retained its identity. Using an oversimple formula, but one that is basically correct, one can say that Reform Judaism represents the predominance of the pressures toward change, a continuation of the trend toward assimilation to a modern, urban society that was begun in Germany, France, and elsewhere. Orthodoxy represents the predominance of the forces of conservation, an island of security and familiarity for the more recent immigrants. It is also the denomination likely to be chosen by those who want to emphasize the full range of their Jewish identity, in its religious, cultural, and ethnic elements. Conservative Judaism is an attempt to mediate between these two forces—to preserve all that is basic to Judaism in the thought of its supporters, yet to encourage beliefs and practices in harmony with the American environment. The very title of a book by Marshall Sklare captures this idea, *Conservative Judaism: An American Religious Movement.* He describes the changes and the continuity. "Since Conservatism is a response to the process of embourgeoisement, it is the change to the *style of life* and worship characteristic of the new peer group which has been the chief concern. This holds true because ideologies and philosophical orientations change more slowly than less basic matters such as manners, dress, and aesthetic sensibilities." [55]

A sociological study of American Judaism can profitably make use of the concepts of "the social sources of denominationalism," and "the dilemma

54 Michael Novak, "American Catholicism after the Council," *Commentary*, August, 1965, p. 53.

55 Marshall Sklare, *Conservative Judaism: An American Religious Movement*, p. 118.

of the churches"—a dilemma that requires changes if a religious organization is to survive or have influence in a new environment. Changes in Judaism did not begin in the United States, of course. Reform Judaism, for example, might first be thought of in terms of the "Europeanization" of Jews. It was a movement of those who were most successful in winning a place in Western European societies and who wanted to insure full cultural, economic, and political participation. Yet they wanted also to maintain their historical connection with Judaism. To work for both of these ends required drastic modification of Orthodox views and practices, many of which had lost their meaning to persons fully assimilated to Western societies. Judaism was no longer considered to be a national religion; it was not a complete way of life, with cultural and political implications, but a universalist religion.

At first, Reform Judaism in the United States continued the trends that had developed in Germany. But the new environment created even stronger pressures toward change. The lack of any history of political or economic disability, the freedom of religion, the expanding economic situation, and other forces all tended to dissolve the sense of being members in a unique religious community. As Handlin says: "The new views compelled the Jews radically to revise their own conceptions of themselves and of the nature of their culture." [56] Some Jewish leaders felt that unless it made drastic changes to adjust to the new environment, Judaism would disappear in the United States. Building on the doctrinal and theological developments of the German Reform movement, American Jews in mid-nineteenth century began a rapid change in synagogue procedures and forms of worship.

there was a call for more decorum, for the revisions of the liturgy to permit shorter and more intelligible services, for the replacement of "German and Slavonic dialects" by English, for family pews to eliminate the segregation of women, for sermons in the American style, for mixed choirs and organs. Later, demands for the "simplification" of kashrut (dietary) and Sabbath prohibitions were heard.[57]

These changes had been extensively adopted when the immigration of Eastern European Jews began in large numbers. Of the 2 million Jews who entered the United States between 1870 and 1914, more than 60 per cent were from Russia. For the most part, they had lived in Orthodox Jewish communities; they had suffered serious political and economic disprivilege and violent persecution. Having little sense of identity with the Russian state and society, they felt a vital connection with the shtetl, the self-contained Jewish community, with the conception of a Jewish homeland, and with Judaism as a total way of life. It is not surprising that the Jews in the United States, many of whom were "Old American," should have received the new flood of immigration with mixed feelings. There was a sense of common religious allegiance, yet also the fear of being "Russified" and of losing the gains of a century. Religious perspectives themselves varied widely, of course—the Reform Jew being as close to liberal Protestantism, perhaps, as to Orthodox Judaism. Thus by 1880, American Jews had entered

56 Oscar Handlin, Adventures in Freedom, p. 73.

57 Herberg, op. cit., p. 189.

upon a period of change, and indeed of internal conflict, that was to last for two generations.

We shall not undertake to tell the complicated story of the changes and the tensions of this period.[58] The most significant new development, for our concern, was the appearance of Conservative Judaism. Sociologically speaking, this movement accomplished for the large number of Eastern European migrants, particularly those of the second and third generations in the United States, what the Reform movement had done for the earlier migrants from Western Europe: it formed a link between the total Jewish culture of the past and the requirements and possibilities of the American present. It did not duplicate Reform Judaism in the size and direction of its changes for several reasons: America's tradition of freedom of religion required that it "give up" fewer of its distinctive patterns; the greatly increased size of the Jewish population encouraged the maintenance of some of the older forms, because contact with non-Jews was often limited; the lively memories of persecution were not readily dismissed; the continuing immigration of Orthodox Jews from Europe renewed the established ways; support for a Zionist cause—not for themselves, but for European coreligionists—helped to sustain a strong sense of identity with Judaism as they had known it; and finally, the new eruptions of anti-Semitism, from the Dreyfus affair to the ghastly genocide of Hitler's New Order, revitalized the meaning of Judaism as a religious response to the tragedies of life.[59]

Despite such forces as these, which retarded the Americanization of Judaism, powerful influences have been at work on the other side to shape the religious beliefs and practices of American Jews. As they were absorbed into the secular structure of American society, it was inevitable that their religious needs, the kinds of doctrine, ritual, and church organization that would appeal to them, would change. The impacts of public, secular schools, job diversification, status improvement, political freedom and participation, and increasing contact with the members of other religious groups have modified Judaism in many ways. In the Conservative branch, there is still a strong tie to traditional Jewish beliefs. Forms of worship and of congregational polity have been more likely to change than systems of belief. The total effect, however, of location in a society so different from those in which Orthodox Judaism developed has been to produce major transformations in the course of two generations. Sklare states clearly a functional interpretation of these changes:

The greatest contribution of the German Reform movement may be said to be its function as the provider of a cushion for the disintegrative effects of emancipation. It helped to indicate a *modus vivendi* between assimilation and a no-longer acceptable Orthodoxy. In the same tradition, American Conservatism has cushioned the effects of the dissolution of Judaism as an integrated and highly traditional sacred system. It too has offered a *modus vivendi* for the alienated. True, its public has been different from that of German-Jewish Reform, and the condi-

58 See the works of Handlin, Herberg, and Sklare cited earlier; see also, Stuart Rosenberg, *The Search for Jewish Identity in America;* Rufus Learsi, *The Jews in America;* and Joseph Zeitlin, *Disciples of the Wise: The Religious and Social Opinions of American Rabbis.*

59 For a discussion of anti-Semitism, see George E. Simpson and J. Milton Yinger, *Racial and Cultural Minorities,* Chaps. 9 and 10.

tions under which it has developed have also been radically different. Thus, while both movements have taken divergent paths, they do express the same need. In summary, the signal contribution of Conservatism would seem to be that of offering an acceptable pattern of adjustment to the American environment for many East-European-derived Jews.[60]

This is perhaps to assume the functionalist position, in a narrow sense, too quickly. That Conservatism has actually served to produce some desired balance between an over-rapid deculturization, with attendant personal confusion, and an over-slow assimilation, with attendant alienation, is a proposition that seems to have a great deal of merit. Its full validation, however, must await more comparative research into all the consequences for those who adopted different patterns of adaptation to the American scene. The need is for comparative study, not only of the functions and dysfunctions of membership in the various branches of Judaism, but also of the other religious decisions and secular alternatives that some Jews have selected.

A sociological study of American Judaism cannot stop with the brief examination of the Orthodox-Conservative-Reform pattern. Recent developments, let us arbitrarily say since 1940, have set other forces in motion that are strongly affecting Judaism. Broadly speaking, we may say that there has been a renewal of interest in religion and a blurring of the lines of distinction among the three denominations of American Jews. Orthodoxy continues to change; but perhaps more surprisingly, there is some return to traditional patterns among the Reform groups. This expresses in part the general return to religion that we have discussed. Many of the forces affecting a neo-orthodoxy in Christianity were also influential among Jews, and there has been less of a swing away from that position in Judaism than in Christianity in recent years.

There are, however, some additional factors: The tragedies of the Hitlerian period undoubtedly gave vitality and a sense of common identity to all branches of Judaism. Economic distinctions have been reduced, so that the picture—always an over-simplified one—of the German employer and the Russian employee is less and less accurate. Residential migration into mixed suburbs, where one's Jewishness cannot be taken for granted, where one's children are more likely to ask, "What is a Jew?" has led many to rethink their religious origins. During the several decades of reduced immigration, the association of Jewishness with foreignness and with the "strange" ways of unmodified Orthodoxy has been greatly diminished. And the rise of Israel with its promise and its problems has furnished a vivid picture of a shared tradition.

The results of these forces on Judaism can be understood only in terms of the American environment, which discourages many aspects of ethnic-group survival, but which permits religious differentiation. Those who would like to see a continuation of Jewish identity, therefore, are led more and more to emphasize its strictly religious meaning.[61] Yet the religious aspects of Jewishness are probably less salient for most American Jews

60 Sklare, op. cit., p. 249.

61 See Nathan Glazer, "The Jewish Revival in America," *Commentary*, December, 1955, pp. 493–499 and January, 1956, pp. 17–24.

than are the ethnic and general cultural aspects. At least in this generation, the lines among Catholic, Protestant, and Jew remain sharp, despite the reduction in secular differences among the constituent groups, and despite the secularity of most Jews, many Protestants, and some Catholics. This may well express the tensions of a society in which we seek to "escape from freedom" by embracing a partially traditional system of answers; it may be a manifestation of "the lonely crowd," in which we seek a feeling of identity by relating ourselves more closely with an established group; and these may be possible because close identity with a religious group does not alienate us from the total society to which we give our basic allegiance. If this argument is valid, then the renewal of interest in Judaism and the reduction of differences among its various denominations are not signs of the slowing down of the Americanization of Jews. They are, indeed, the signs of how deeply involved Jews are in the total pattern of American society.[62]

In recent years a number of studies have sought to measure and discuss the balance between pluralism and assimilation, as the issue is often stated. There is some disagreement over the facts, and substantially more disagreement over the important values involved.[63] The predominant view is that the communal element has remained strong among American Jews. Rates of intermarriage are low (perhaps one fourth of the rate among Catholics, for example); friendship circles are predominantly Jewish; affiliation with synagogues has significantly increased in the last twenty years; and enrollment in Jewish schools or in after-school programs of instruction in Judaism has gone up.[64]

62 See Herbert J. Gans, "American Jewry: Present and Future," *Commentary*, May, 1956, pp. 422–430; and "The Future of American Jewry," *Commentary*, June, 1956, pp. 555–563.

63 See, for example, Nathan Glazer, *American Judaism*; Milton Gordon, *Assimilation in American Life*; Judith Kramer and Seymour Leventman, *Children of the Gilded Ghetto*; C. Bezalel Sherman, *The Jew Within American Society: A Study of Ethnic Individuality*; Erich Rosenthal, "Acculturation Without Assimilation? The Jewish Community of Chicago, Illinois," *American Journal of Sociology*, 66, 1960, pp. 275–288; Amitai Etzioni, "The Ghetto—a Re-evaluation," *Social Forces*, March, 1959, pp. 255–262; Marshall Sklare, "Assimilation and the Sociologists," *Commentary*, May, 1965, pp. 63–67; Richard Rubenstein, "Homeland and Holocaust: Issues in the Jewish Religious Situation," in *The Religious Situation: 1968*, Donald Cutler, ed., pp. 39–64, and the commentaries that follow by Milton Himmelfarb, Zalman Schachter, Arthur Cohen, and Irving Greenberg, pp. 64–111; Benjamin Ringer, *The Edge of Friendliness: A Study of Jewish-Gentile Relations*; Marshall Sklare and Joseph Greenblum, *Jewish Identity on the Suburban Frontier: A Study of Group Survival in the Open Society*; Stephen Steinberg, "The Anatomy of Jewish Identification: A Historical and Theoretical View," *Review of Religious Research*, 7, 1965, pp. 1–8; Rosenberg, op. cit.; Will Herberg, op. cit.; Gerhard Lenski, *The Religious Factor*; Peter Rose, "Small-Town Jews and Their Neighbors in the United States," *Jewish Journal of Sociology*, 3, 1961, pp. 174–191; Marshall Sklare, ed., *The Jews*.

64 For data on intermarriage see United States Bureau of the Census, "Religion Reported by the Civilian Population of the United States: March, 1957," *Current Population Reports*, Series P-20, No. 79, 1958; but this material must be interpreted carefully, as I have tried to suggest in "A Research Note on Interfaith Marriage Statistics," *Journal for the Scientific Study of Religion*, 7, 1968, pp. 97–103. See also Erich Rosenthal, "Studies in Jewish Intermarriage in the United States," *American Jewish Yearbook*, 64, 1963, pp. 3–53. Many of the references in the preceding footnote contain useful information on communalism among Jews. Most of the studies pertain to specific

Are these conditions likely to continue? Efforts to interpret the impact of the surrounding society on a religious group are often lacking in time perspective. Thus Louis Wirth, in his valuable study of *The Ghetto*, tended to project conditions of the 1920's into the future and to foresee, therefore, extensive assimilation. In recent years the pendulum has swung the other way. The Nazi-Israel-suburbanization syndrome, to put it too simply, has powerfully affected the sense of identity with Judaism. Pride in a tradition of great strength has been reinforced. Continued anti-Semitism, particularly in the Soviet Union but in some small measure also in the United States, keeps historical memories alive. These have led to an emphasis on the pluralistic distinctiveness of Jews. Some of these forces, however, may lose strength and others tend to offset them. The full impact of occupational, educational, and residential integration of Jews and Gentiles—now a substantial fact in America—has yet to be felt. It is not clear how much the highly secularized version of Judaism, which is the predominant version, can serve as a focal point of pluralistic identification. Rosenberg puts the issue sharply: "For the Jewish secular ideology to thrive in America, it cannot take refuge under the mythical banner of 'cultural pluralism' while its own partisans actually remain monocultural—little more than Anglicized, middle-class conformists whose secular 'Jewish culture' consists of raising funds or offering encouragement in support of 'Jewish culture' in Israel." [65]

Sometimes the desire to emphasize the strength of pluralism among Jews leads to rather unusual interpretations. Sklare and Greenblum, for example, note that few Jews consider themselves Orthodox, so that marriage to an Orthodox Jew should be unattractive, in their phrase, "to say the least." "Nevertheless, a Gentile with no interest in organized religion is considered no more preferable than an Orthodox Jew: the Jew is selected by 43 per cent, and the Gentile by 44 per cent." [66] By the same logic, ought not one to note that no Jews consider themselves Gentiles, so that marriage to a Gentile should be unattractive, "to say the least"? Yet, to continue the paraphrase, an Orthodox Jew is considered no more preferable than a Gentile with no interest in organized religion. I am inclined to interpret the Sklare and Greenblum data as a sign of rather weak pluralistic identity, not, as they imply, of its strength.

It also seems possible that the long-run influence of Israel on American Judaism will be different from the short-run influence. Undoubtedly the founding of a Jewish state and its struggles to survive have increased the sense of ethnic if not of religious identity of many American Jews. During the 1967 Arab-Israeli war, "Jews throughout the world manifested an unprecedented emotional and practical involvement in the fate of Israel. Jewish leaders universally report that the response was of far greater intensity

---

communities, however, and present various problems of sampling (persons who no longer identify themselves as Jews and marginal Jews tend to be under-represented). In light of these problems, I have not cited precise data but have been content with the broad generalizations that seem supported by the evidence.

65 Op cit., p. 101.

66 Op. cit., p. 315.

than they could have anticipated before the event." [67] For a people who nearly three millennia ago moved from a tribal to a universal religion—not, of course, without continuous struggle and continuous setbacks—contemporary Israel stands as a decisive religious fact. If an important source of one's Jewishness is identification with a nation-state that is caught up in all the military problems of the contemporary world, where the citizenry is a trained militia and the military leader a hero, the tribal-universalist tension in Judaism is once again increased. Jewishness may be supported while Judaism suffers.[68]

More significantly, the internal situation is modifying Judaism in the United States. Sklare and Greenblum note that in "Lakeville," Judaism is becoming a thing of the synagogue not of the home. Some home rituals survive, but they are rather severely restricted by several conditions. They are most likely to be retained when 1) they are capable of redefinition in modern terms; 2) they do not demand social isolation or adoption of a unique style of life; 3) they accord with the religious culture of the larger community, providing a Jewish alternative when such a need is felt; 4) they are centered on the child; 5) when performance of the ritual is annual or infrequent.[69]

Consistent with these is the list of things Lakeville Jews believe essential to being a good Jew and the things that make no difference or should be avoided. I will cite in Table 21–2 from the long list given by Sklare and

Table 21–2. Behavior deemed essential and behavior deemed inessential by "Lakeville" Jews *

	Per cent
Essential to do	
Lead an ethical and moral life	93
Accept his being a Jew and not try to hide it	85
Support all humanitarian causes	67
Promote civic betterment and improvement in the community	67
Gain respect of Christian neighbors	59
Help the underprivileged improve their lot	58
Makes no difference or essential not to do	
Give Jewish candidates for political office preference	93
Promote the use of Yiddish	93
Have mostly Jewish friends	89
Observe the dietary laws	88
Support Zionism	68
Attend weekly services	50

* Adapted from Marshall Sklare and Joseph Greenblum, *Jewish Identity on the Suburban Frontier: A Study of Group Survival in the Open Society,* New York: Basic, 1967, p. 322.

67 Rubenstein, op. cit., p. 44.

68 These are, of course, highly problematic statements. Although they are meant to be simply descriptive of possible religious effects of Israel's military situation, some may read them as evaluations of Israel's policies. Were I to make an evaluative statement on the situation, however, it would be something to this effect: I lament the hawkishness of Israel almost as much as I lament the hawkishness of the Arabs. But most of all I lament the inadequacy of human hearts and heads—in this instance, particularly of those resident in Moscow and Washington.

69 Sklare and Greenblum, op. cit., p. 57.

Greenblum only those that were selected, either positively or negatively, by 50 per cent or more of the respondents.

Few of the items in the "essential" list are distinctive to Judaism. The items that make no difference or are essential to avoid are those qualities that would set Jews apart. These items summarize well the current balance between assimilation and pluralism—continuing identity with a group that becomes less and less distinctive. Judaism in America has been powerfully influenced by its environment; but it has also powerfully influenced that environment and adapted itself to it. Further developments depend upon its own inner processes and on the current of events in the country and in the world.

Chapter Twenty-two

RELIGIOUS CHANGE AND SOCIAL CHANGE:
Patterns of Interaction

Most of our attention in Chapter Twenty-one was devoted to particular historical situations, in an effort to show their influence on religious developments. We shift now to a more macroscopic view, with our attention focused on a general statement of the relationships of religious change to social change. This will require that we pay more attention to religion as the initiator, and not simply the reflector, of change. From a different perspective, religion can be studied as a conserver of values, or, in a different tone, as a barrier to change. (It is indicative of the lack of objective study in this area that we have no neutral vocabulary to subsume these two value perspectives.) Seen in this way, religion is not a thoroughly independent variable but is part of a causal complex. The cause-effect, independent-dependent dichotomies are in most instances quite inadequate for the sciences of human institutions and behavior. Concepts of interaction and "levels of causation" are, under most conditions, more appropriate. When one speaks of religion as a barrier to change, for example, he implies an instrumental quality. It is being *used*, and is therefore regarded as causal only on a low level. This is less obvious in the thinking of many who regard religion favorably as the conserver of the best. In their thinking it is likely to be taken as a "given," to be regarded as an independent variable, or at the least to be placed at a high level of causation—more effective than affected by the cycles of interaction.

THE INTERACTION OF IDEAS AND SOCIAL ACTION
In its broadest terms, the problem of the influence of values and concepts is clearly not limited to the sociology of religion, but is basic to the whole

of social science and philosophy. What is the role of ideas in history? One's answer to the question put in this way is more likely to take the form of a methodological proposition or a philosophical assumption than of an empirically demonstrated relationship. This does not mean that the answers are wholly arbitrary, from the point of view of science, for some methodological propositions are far more fruitful of research and theory than others, and some philosophical assumptions are more harmonious with the scientific perspective than others. We have proceeded on the basis of interaction and functional interdependence, repudiating the idea that science must look for *the* cause, or the prime cause, whether it be thought to reside in ideas or in material conditions.

One might sketch the range of possible views concerning the place of ideas, and arbitrarily locate certain important thinkers, along a continuum in the following way:

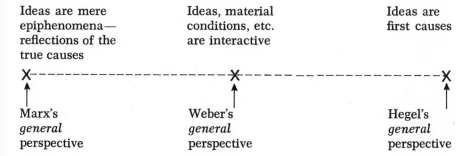

Ideas are mere epiphenomena— reflections of the true causes	Ideas, material conditions, etc. are interactive	Ideas are first causes
Marx's *general* perspective	Weber's *general* perspective	Hegel's *general* perspective

In our view no general perspective is adequate, because the situations that require interpretation do not exist "in general." An adequate scientific perspective will seek out the conditions under which the interaction of the several forces approaches one or the other end of the continuum. Each situation, then, will be interpreted according to the degree to which these various conditions are present. And for some purposes it is scientifically legitimate to concentrate on one phase of an interacting situation, taking some force or forces as "givens," provided that one does not forget that in his abstraction he cannot explain the whole sequence of events.

An instrumental approach to ideas and values refers, not to their content, but to their function. There are wide differences, however, in the ways in which this approach to ideas may be developed. These ways vary greatly in the amount of immanence assigned to ideas. Marx and Nietzsche, for example, in very different ways, see ideas as manifestations of interests. The former interpreted ideas in terms of their functions in the struggles among classes, the latter primarily in terms of their psychological function for individuals.[1] It had been observed long before Marx and Nietzsche, of course, that ideas are a function of interests. One need only mention the names of Machiavelli, Bacon, and Hume to illustrate this point. Only at a time of intensive culture contact and great change, however, could this observation become a central concern. In the twentieth century, the relationship of ideas and of the life of consciousness to the total self and its social

[1] See Max Weber, *From Max Weber*, introduction by Hans Gerth and C. Wright Mills, pp. 61–62.

roles has been even more thoroughly explored in the work of Freud, Mannheim, and others. Gradually, the observations are going beyond the unmasking of the pretensions of one's opponents or "exposing" the thought of strange and inferior people, to include systematic and empirical study. This development required a social theory of self and an explicit formulation of the concepts of society and culture. Out of these developments we are getting a sociology and psychology of knowledge that is of great importance to the sociology of religion.[2]

There is a tendency on the part of Marx and Nietzsche to treat all ideas in the same manner, to assume that they all have the same relationship to interests and to action. The kind of distinction that Parsons draws between "existential ideas" (the description and analysis of things as they exist, or are thought to exist) and "normative ideas" (conceptions about the way things ought to be) is essential to the study of the relationship between ideas and action.[3] This distinction is rooted deep in the history of this problem; but for all that, it has not been effectively used, even by Mannheim, who has contributed so much to the sociological study of thought.[4]

One class of existential ideas, those based on empirical study, verifiable by others, clearly has a measure of autonomy and of initiatory power. The mathematical and physical study that led to $E=MC^2$ can clearly be understood as an important cause of later events, whatever its own origins may be. Only a *faithful* materialist will find it meaningful to claim that nevertheless, in the last analysis, these ideas can be explained as an effect of the conditions out of which they came. This kind of reductionism to some supposed ultimate starting point is meaningless to science. It is more pertinent to observe with Parsons that

The very processes of technological change to which many of our "materialists" assign so fundamental a role are in part a function of knowledge, i.e., of ideas, in exactly the same sense in which economic processes are. And there, far more than in the narrowly economic realm, knowledge has become a variable which we think of as to a high degree autonomous.[5]

More important for our purposes is the question of the degree of autonomy in normative ideas and in a second class of existential ideas, those propositions about nature or existence that are unverifiable, which are posed in such a way that scientific criteria are inapplicable. Parsons warns against the "positivistic bias" that assumes that these latter propositions could be tested, if our evidence were adequate, by scientific methods. They are *non*scientific, rather than *un*scientific; in Pareto's phrase, they "surpass experience." Belief in the doctrine of reincarnation or a concept of predestination can scarcely be shown to be true or false by empirical research. Are such ideas, in the first instance, merely a reflection of the material situation,

2 See Robert Merton, *Social Theory and Social Structure*, rev. ed., Chaps. 12 and 13; and Peter Berger and Thomas Luckmann, *The Social Construction of Reality: A Treatise in the Sociology of Knowledge*.

3 Talcott Parsons, "The Role of Ideas in Social Action," *Essays in Sociological Theory Pure and Applied*, pp. 151–165.

4 See Karl Mannheim, *Ideology and Utopia* and *Essays on the Sociology of Knowledge*.

5 Parsons, op. cit., p. 155.

becoming, once they are established, a barrier to social change? Or do they enter actively into the process of social change?

Even Marx, and more particularly Engels, recognized that there was some autonomy in the idea sphere, particularly in the field of natural science, but also to some degree in the normative sphere and among the nonempirical, existential ideas of Parsons' classification. Engels pointed out that when professional lawyers appeared, for example, an independent source of ideas was created, for they began to elaborate a system, built around such values as justice, that sought consistency in itself; ". . . in order to achieve this, the faithful reflection of economic conditions is more and more infringed upon." [6] This internal development is true also of religious and philosophical ideas.

To indicate that ideas may originate out of the internal elaborations of a religious system is not to claim, however, that they enter directly into the processes of social action and social change. To Marx and Engels, only those ideas that had relevance to the struggles of classes and parties would survive or enter effectively into social interaction. Thus ideas are more instruments than causes, in their view. This anticipates a concept developed more fully by Weber, especially in his phrase "elective affinity." Having admitted some degree of autonomy to the origin of ideas, however, Weber does not then deny their continuing influence by his use of this concept. He goes on to stress the mutual modifiability of ideas and interests, the possibility of tensions between them. Ideas are not completely plastic, to be selected and molded according to individual need and desire or according to group interests. Once developed and accepted, they make demands of their own.

Gerth and Mills well express Weber's conception of the origin of ideas, when they write:

For Weber, there is hardly ever a close connection between the interests or the social origin of the speaker or of his following with the content of the idea during its inception. The ancient Hebrew prophets, the leaders of the Reformation, or the revolutionary vanguard of modern class movements were not necessarily recruited from the strata which in due course became the prime bearers of their respective ideas. Only during the process of routinization do the followers "elect" those features of the idea with which they have an "affinity," a "point of coincidence" or "convergence." [7]

In their next statement Gerth and Mills may exaggerate the degree to which Weber moves back toward a Marxian position. This is an exaggeration, however, which is invited by Weber's own development of the concept of elective affinity. They write:

in time, ideas are discredited in the face of history unless they point in the direction of conduct that various interests promote. Ideas, selected and reinterpreted from the original doctrine, do gain an affinity with the interests of certain members of special strata; if they do not gain such an affinity, they are abandoned. Thus by distinguishing the phases of the personal and charismatic origin of ideas and their routinization and social impact, Weber is able to take into account a number of complications, which are reflected in changing shades of meaning.

6 Engels, quoted by Robert K. Merton, op. cit., p. 468.

7 *From Max Weber*, pp. 62–63.

Both the ideas and their publics are seen as independent; by a selective process elements in both find their affinity.[8]

The last sentence seems to describe most accurately Weber's thought, for it indicates the *continuing* place that he gives to ideas in social interaction. Thus Calvinism had important elements of immanent religious development within it, in Weber's view; these were shaped and selected by the emerging capitalist classes; but they in turn were shaped by it—by its concept of salvation and its ethical requirements, for example.

The concept of interaction basic to Weber's view is perhaps better formulated by others. Otto Hintze, for example, expressed it well:

All human action arises from a common source, in political as well as in religious life. Everywhere the first impulse to social action is given as a rule by real interests, i.e., by political and economic interests. But ideal interests lend wings to these real interests, give them a spiritual meaning, and serve to justify them. . . . Interests without such "spiritual wings" are lame; but on the other hand, ideas can win out in history only if and insofar as they are associated with real interests.[9]

The concept of an immanent quality about ideas does not imply that they are spontaneous generations, that do not themselves require explanation. Why are men interested in religious ideas in the first place? To Weber, the driving force was a "religious interest," but he was not content to posit this as an "explanation," after the fashion of the "four wishes" or "six basic interests" that were fashionable in early sociology. (Such curiosity-stoppers are no more useful than are "instincts" in scientific explanations.) He made some effort to account for this interest in the nature of individual and social life. "A typical example is the interest in salvation, an interest which has in turn a complex derivation from, among other things, certain stresses and strains to which individuals are sometimes subjected in social situations where frustration of the worldly ends seems inevitable and founded in the nature of things." [10] This is, of course, no final explanation, but using it as a starting point, the key question, from the point of view of the problem with which we are dealing, becomes: Do different conceptions of salvation have different consequences for human action?

Weber, as we have seen, answered *Yes* to this question. His whole series of studies that sought to discover the relationship between economic developments and religious beliefs led to the conclusion that different conceptions of salvation strongly influenced economic behavior. The doctrine of transmigration, for example, makes any effort to seek salvation by intensive worldly effort meaningless, whereas a doctrine of "calling," in the Calvinist sense, encourages one to seek salvation by vigorous activity. At least belief in transmigration is likely to dampen effort under conditions of severe economic hardship. I do not agree with Weber that this is the inevitable result of the doctrine, however, whatever the conditions may be. It seems at least as likely that the doctrine of karma might stimulate energetic activity under conditions where this-worldly gains are visible and

8 Ibid., p. 63.

9 Otto Hintze, quoted by Reinhard Bendix in *Max Weber. An Intellectual Portrait*, p. 69.

10 Parsons, op. cit., p. 159.

imaginable, as that the doctrine of predestination would do so. One's actions are relevant, after all, in the transmigration process; they are not relevant to predestinarianism, strictly interpreted. The influence of ideas must be examined contextually.

In an earlier chapter we noted that it was one thing to declare that a religious belief blocked economic development and other changes, as do the doctrines of karma and transmigration under many conditions, and another thing to hold that a belief motivated one to economic activity, as Weber held that the doctrine of the "elect" and the idea of a "calling" did. Virtually no one will disagree with the former position. Here is religion as the conserver or the barrier. The latter must be explored in light of Weber's own conception of elective affinity. There are many shades of meaning that may be given to election or predestination, with widely different implications for action. A doctrine of a calling can be associated with quiet acceptance of one's status and traditional activity; predestination can lead to quietism. Until one describes more fully than did Weber the process whereby they developed into supports for energetic worldly endeavor, claims for the autonomy of religious ideas, growing out of their own "inner dialectic," are not entirely supported.

All but the most ardent defenders of religion agree that it is more likely to be a conserver of old values than a creator of new ones. Religious values and requirements compete, in the lives of most men, with other powerful interests and claims. He who seeks, through religion, to change individuals or society must recognize and respond to that fact. As an institution that is adjusted to the secular claims and requirements of a society, the church is a recognition of these powerful competing interests. The churches of a society represent the values, the needs, and the interest of the people who are involved in them. As Arthur Swift has said, one cannot expect them to be ahead of themselves.

The conservation of values and social patterns by religion may be considered a happy or an unhappy fact. To the ruler of an Islamic society, it may seem only obvious that the religious reinforcement of the patterns of that society—including the legitimacy of his own authority—is a good thing. To those who oppose his rule as the leader of government, it may seem to be an unhappy fact that to attack the caliphate is to demand religious reform. In fact, they may be far less able to oppose him, both because they share the religious ideology that legitimates his rule, and because, even if they do not, if the majority of the society *do*, the caliph can still maintain support by appeal to religious sanctions.

This is not to say that religion prevents change, but that it may be used in an attempt to prevent change. The final result may be only to slow down changes that are being promoted by powerful developments in society, thus helping to guarantee that the changes, when they do occur, will be more drastic and accompanied by more violence. The experience of Czarist Russia well illustrates this situation. If the pressures toward change are not powerful, the religious sanctions for the existing order (along with the other sanctions available) may be adequate to prevent change for long periods. This has been substantially the case in many of the Islamic countries through the last several generations; but one would be rash to predict that the present rulers of these Moslem societies can continue to control change, in part by the appeal to religious symbols. They may only insure that more rapid change, when it does come, will be explosive and extreme.

If this interpretation of the place of religious ideas in a causal complex is valid, it would seem that Weber—and most other writers—paid too little attention to the conditions under which charismatic ideas will appear, their routinization will be rapid or slow, and the shaping and interpretation of ideas to put them into the service of individual or group interests will be extensive or slight. Religion cannot be understood simply as a force that blocks or retards change—whether for good or ill. The extent of its independent influence as compared with the extent to which it simply expresses other influences can be measured only when we give up the attempt to arrive at a *general* formula. At several points we have referred to some of the specific variables that influence the relationship between religion and social change. Only by more careful attention to such variables in scientific research can we hope to specify with more precision the place of religion in social change.

RELIGIOUS EVOLUTION

The extent of possible autonomy in the religious sphere and the concerns that loom as ultimate to a people are conditioned by the nature of the society being studied. This leads us to ask whether in religion, as in other social structures and processes, there are discernible evolutionary sequences. An evolutionary perspective strongly influenced the thought of many nineteenth-century students of religion. As we have noted earlier, however, the first applications of evolutionary theory to religion tended to be rigid and ethnocentric. A simple formula of stages imposed a time order on evidences from the past, regardless of how difficult it was to determine the origin of beliefs and practices and the periods during which they prevailed. The formula was also used for value-laden predictions of the future of religion.

In reaction against these weaknesses, most social scientists dismissed evolutionary theory, for a period of several decades, not simply as inadequate but as erroneous. Only in recent years have new efforts been made to discover whether or not social changes, when studied comparatively, are random in direction, or cyclical, or evolutionary, or precede by some other pattern. Renewed interest in evolution has inevitably influenced studies of religion; but they are being developed with full awareness of the ideological quality of earlier evolutionary theory and with a resolve not to duplicate its rigidities. In a seminal paper, Robert Bellah has proposed three levels on which religious evolution proceeds and noted the cautions necessary in their investigation:

First and most central is the evolution of religious symbol systems which are described as moving from "compact" to "differentiated." In close conjunction with this evolution religious collectivities become more differentiated from other social structures and there is an increasing consciousness of the self as a religious subject. Five ideal typical stages of development are posited but it is recognized that these stages are not inevitable, that there is a wide variety of types within each stage, and that actual cases present many important features which cannot be neatly characterized in terms of any one stage.[11]

11 Robert Bellah, "Religious Evolution," *American Sociological Review*, 29, 1964, p. 358. I shall draw extensively on this paper in the next several paragraphs. See also Anthony Wallace, *Religion: An Anthropological View*, pp. 255–264.

Bellah then describes primitive, archaic, historic, early modern, and modern "ideal typical" stages through which religion tends to move. Much more work still needs to be done to isolate the conditions that determine this sequence, but the following seem likely to be involved: degree to which survival of the group is precarious (level of technological resources); degree of internal social differentiation; range of contact across tribal or societal lines; presence of religious specialists and in particular of a religious elite; development of writing; level of knowledge concerning the formation of self and social process.

I will note only briefly the ways in which Bellah and others have drawn the connections between life conditions and religious expressions, with reference to the way the latter evolve with the former. The development of religious symbolization among primitive men represents a way of interpreting and handling suffering. Among prereligious men, suffering could only be endured. But with the "imaging of the grounds of suffering in a particular power," as Lienhardt says of the Dinka, they "can grasp its nature intellectually in a way which satisfied them, and thus to some extent transcend and dominate it in this act of knowledge." [12] Religion is an evolutionary advance because it takes men past the passive endurance of suffering to a situation in which they can, in some measure, "transcend and dominate" it.

Archaic religion begins to appear when societies become more socially differentiated. Its characteristic quality is the emergence of a cult "in which the distinction between men as subjects and gods as objects is much more definite than in primitive religion." [13] This distinction requires the greater development of means of communication with the gods. It is in this context that worship and sacrifice, communication systems *par excellence*, appear.[14]

Historic religions, the third of Bellah's stages, emerged in many parts of the literate world in the first millennium B.C. They were characterized by world rejection—something unknown to the primitive—and by universalism, although each of these themes was qualified by the continuation of earlier elements. Another realm of reality was exalted; this world was rejected—perhaps most vividly by Buddha's image "that the world is a burning house and man's urgent need is to escape from it." Religious action in the historic religions is action designed to attain salvation from the horrors of this world.

Primitive man can only accept the world in its manifold givenness. Archaic man can through sacrifice fulfill his religious obligations and attain peace with the gods. But the historic religions promise man for the first time that he can understand the fundamental structure of reality and through salvation participate actively in it. The opportunity is far greater than before but so is the risk of failure.[15]

Religious specialists and a religious elite emerge more fully within the structures of the historic religions. The universalistic ideology and the par-

---

12 Godfrey Lienhardt, *Divinity and Experience*, quoted by Bellah, op. cit., p. 361.

13 Ibid., p. 365.

14 See Henri Hubert and Marcel Mauss, *Sacrifice: Its Nature and Function.*

15 Bellah, op. cit., p. 367.

tially autonomous position of religious leaders increased the possibility of conflict between them and secular rulers. Under these conditions there was a greater likelihood, although still perhaps a small one, that religiously motivated reform and revolutionary movements would influence the course of social change. The potential for change was not greater because religious leaders themselves developed interests in particular forms for mediating salvation, however much these might vary among the various traditions. The early modern stage, the fourth in Bellah's discussion, emerged when this monopoly of the means to salvation was broken and the possibility of salvation's being attained by worldly activity appeared. This is best represented by the Protestant Reformation. "What the Reformation did was in principle, with the usual reservations and mortgages to the past, to break through the whole mediated system of salvation and declare salvation potentially available to any man no matter what his station or calling might be." [16]

The modern stage, which Bellah traces from Kant, through Schleiermacher, to Bultmann, Bonhoeffer, and Tillich, and beyond, opens up the possibility of a continuously self-revising religious system—not only on the structural, but also on the cultural and character levels. This poses for man the possibilities both of greater disorder and of greater creativity. "In the modern phase knowledge of the laws of the formation of the self, as well as much more about the structure of the world, has opened up almost unlimited new directions of exploration and development." [17] Many observers, to be sure, look upon this "almost unlimited" exploration, some of the theological aspects of which we shall discuss later, as a sign of the grave weakening if not of the death of religion. An evolutionary perspective leads us, however, to see the unfolding of new religious forms as the conditions of life are drastically revised, but not the disappearance of ultimate questions and of shared modes for dealing with them.[18]

Types of Religious Leaders
We have suggested that religious evolution is strongly influenced by changes in the major conditions of human life, but that religion in turn affects the nature of responses to those conditions. These interactions are clearly shown in the study of religious leaders, a topic we have dealt with heretofore only marginally.

We will not examine the wide range of general interpretations of the influence of leaders. To some, they are the prime movers of history; to others, leaders are only the symbolic manifestations of social forces. An analytic view requires that we not attempt to arrive at any such general proposition. The task is to specify the conditions that affect the degree of leadership influence; or, to put the matter somewhat differently, the need

16 Ibid., p. 369.

17 Ibid., p. 374.

18 For perceptive discussions of contemporary forms of religion, see Talcott Parsons, in *Sociological Theory, Values, and Sociocultural Change. Essays in Honor of Pitirim A. Sorokin,* Edward Tiryakian, ed., pp. 33–70; and Thomas Luckmann, *The Invisible Religion. The Problem of Religion in Modern Society.*

is to describe types of leaders, indicating the kinds of situations in which they appear and the variations in their influence.

There are many typologies of religious leaders, most of them primarily descriptive. They indicate different patterns of relationship between leaders and the religious organizations and followers with which they are connected, on the basis of various principles of classification. Some systems of classification are primarily interested in patterns of authority in a religious system as a whole; others are concerned with types of leaders on the local or congregational level.

The first variety is well illustrated by Joachim Wach's list of nine types of religious authority: founder, reformer, prophet, seer, magician, diviner, saint, priest, and "religiosus" (a plain man who lives a highly religious life). Wach's careful definitions of these types help in the systematic ordering of the wide variety of leaders to be found in a complex religious pattern. To some degree—although he is less helpful here—he explores the social factors involved in the appearance of these types of authority, and the nature of their influence.[19]

Classifications concerned with the local religious group are perhaps more likely to describe types of functions than types of leaders. The functions may all be performed by one man, or there may be some division of labor. Drawing on a typology worked out by the "University Seminar in the Professions in Modern Society" at Columbia University, Sklare describes eight functions of contemporary church leaders: priest (conductor of public worship), preacher, cleric (a functionary of the state, empowered to perform certain ceremonies), rector (administrator of an organization), pastor (counsellor), father (head of a congregation in a psychological sense), parson (representative of the church to the community), and rabbi (teacher and interpreter of religious doctrines). Sklare's specific interest is in the way that forces in the American environment have modified the traditional rabbi role, adding to it several functions that are more familiar to Christian priests and ministers.[20] The typology is also useful, however, for more general questions concerning the functions of religious leaders. The study of changes in emphasis, of additions to and subtractions from the functions of ministers, is an important guide to the interaction of religion and society.

Other typologies of religious leaders are directly concerned with the question of social change. This problem is implicit in the distinction between the prophet and the priest, which has been widely and somewhat carelessly used. The former, whose own origin is often left unexplained, is thought of as a dramatic new force, challenging the existing patterns and, if successful, changing the lives of his followers by the impact of his message or example. The latter is part of a functioning system, one who carries out established patterns (often with the implication that they have become outmoded) without influencing them. Max Weber has sought to bring the

19 See Joachim Wach, *Sociology of Religion*, pp. 331–383.

20 See Marshall Sklare, *Conservative Judaism*, pp. 177–180. See also Elaine Cumming and Charles Harrington, "Clergyman as Counselor," *The American Journal of Sociology*, 69, 1963, pp. 234–243; David Moberg, *The Church as a Social Institution*, Chap. 18; Joseph Fichter, "The Religious Professional," *Review of Religious Research*, 1, 1960, pp. 89–101; and Glenn Vernon, *Sociology of Religion*, Chap. 10.

concept of prophet-priest into the framework of a sociological analysis by more careful definition of terms and by exploration of the social contexts with which leaders interact. A prophet, in his terms, is a religious manifestation of charismatic leadership. "The term 'charisma' will be applied to a certain quality of an individual personality by virtue of which he is set apart from ordinary men and treated as endowed with supernatural, superhuman, or at least specifically exceptional powers or qualities." [21] The charisma is validated only by the free acceptance of it by those subject to the leader's influence, such recognition being a sign of personal devotion and trust, rather than of traditional patterns or institutional power.

In Weber's view, charismatic leadership brings a new force onto the scene:

The genuine prophet, like the genuine military leader and every true leader in this sense, preaches, creates, or demands *new* obligations. . . . Charismatic authority is thus specifically outside the realm of everyday routine and the profane sphere. In this respect, it is sharply opposed both to rational, and particularly bureaucratic, authority, and to traditional authority. . . . Within the sphere of its claims, charismatic authority repudiates the past, and is in this sense a specifically revolutionary force. . . . Pure charisma is specifically foreign to economic considerations. . . . In traditionally stereotyped periods, charisma is the greatest revolutionary force. The equally revolutionary force of "reason" works from without by altering the situations of action. . . . Charisma, on the other hand, may involve a subjective or internal reorientation born out of suffering, conflicts, or enthusiasm. It may then result in a radical alteration of the central system of attitudes and directions of action with a completely new orientation of all attitudes toward the different problems and structures of the "world." [22]

As a proposition concerning the influence of religious leaders on social change, Weber's concept of charisma raises two difficult questions. What is the context out of which charismatic leaders come? (Even a "specifically revolutionary force" has to be explained.) And what happens to their demands for new obligations? Who follows them, for how long, and in what ways are they modified? Weber furnishes a much more satisfactory answer to the second than to the first question. He relied heavily on the statement that men are very differently qualified for religious experience, a fact that "stands at the beginning of the history of religion." To state such a fact is to make clear the need for social-psychological and cultural study to explain it. The degree to which charisma is a "revolutionary force" can be meaningfully interpreted only when its own origins are more thoroughly explored. Although Weber seems insufficiently aware of this problem, he did not disregard it entirely. In *Ancient Judaism*, for example, he writes: "The prophecy of doom can largely be traced to the psychic dispositions of the prophets, as conditioned by constitution and experience. It is no less certain that it was indeed the historical fate of Israel, which provided this prophecy

21 Max Weber, *The Theory of Social and Economic Organization*, p. 358. See also Edward Shils, "Charisma, Order, and Status," *American Sociological Review*, 30, 1965, pp. 199–213. Shils shows that the concept of charisma can appropriately be applied to a wider range of phenomena than suggested by Weber.

22 Weber, *The Theory of Social and Economic Organization*, pp. 361–363. See also Weber's, *The Sociology of Religion*, Chaps. 4 and 5.

with its position in the religious development." [23] Weber's awareness of the societal and cultural factors involved in conditioning charisma is shown by the distinction he draws between exemplary and emissary prophecy. In his view, the former leads toward a contemplative and perhaps even an apathetic response to the world, close to that of the mystic, whereas the latter addresses its demands precisely to the world. Whether a religious virtuoso will be an exemplary or an emissary prophet is strongly affected by the religious tradition and the social stratum from which he springs.[24]

Weber seemed to be insufficiently aware, however, of the possible institutional sources of prophecy. Peter Berger shows that Weber made an excessively sharp distinction between the supposedly individualistic prophets and the highly institutionalized priests of ancient Israel. On the basis of the research of Sigmund Mowinckel and others, Berger emphasizes that prophetic inspiration, far from being independent of and in opposition to the established religious organization, "was part and parcel of Israelite worship." [25] It would equally be a mistake today to draw a sharp line between the priests, as agents of institutionalized religion, and prophets, as possessors of charisma who burst into history on a wholly individualistic and unpredictable basis. Some of today's prophets in matters of social justice, civil rights, and urban reconstruction, for example, work from within the church. Sometimes they are "segmented," as Hammond and Mitchell have suggested in connection with the campus ministers,[26] but they are used, not expelled. I expect that the Israelite establishment also sought to keep its prophets under control; but this is quite different from seeing them as thoroughly oppositional.

This is not the whole story, of course. Some prophets are expelled and martyred; others work entirely apart from the institutionalized church. It should be noted that in contemporary America many men are leaving the parish ministry, and in some of the liberal seminaries only a minority of the students are interested in a regular parish career. The role of the prophet, I think it is fair to say, is an uncertain one within any established institutional order. We need to avoid glib dichotomies in studying religious leadership, but we need also to be prepared to make necessary distinctions.

Berger observes that the institutional source of prophecy in Israel, though it qualifies Weber's interpretation in various ways, supports his main idea even more strongly than does a thoroughly individualistic view of prophecy. It indicates the autonomy of religious ideas flowing with the force to make some change in society from within religious institutions. "Charisma may, indeed, be characteristic of socially marginal individuals; coming into a society in the role of strangers, perhaps even legitimating their authority by virtue of this strangeness. But charisma may also be a trait of individ-

23 Weber, *Ancient Judaism*, p. 307.

24 See *From Max Weber*, pp. 285–290.

25 Peter Berger, "Charisma and Religious Innovation: The Social Location of Israelite Prophecy," *American Sociological Review*, 28, 1963, pp. 940–950.

26 Phillip Hammond and Robert Mitchell, "Segmentation of Radicalism—The Case of the Protestant Campus Minister," *American Journal of Sociology*, 71, 1965, pp. 133–143.

uals located at the center of the institutional fabric in question, a power of 'radicalization' from within rather than of challenge from without." [27]

Thus the sources of charisma itself require examination. This is not to deny, however, that once set in motion, prophetic leadership may well "result in a radical alteration of the central system of attitudes and directions of action." Surely one may define Vinoba Bhave as a prophet. The new demands that he is making in India today are based on the old Hindu ideal of *tapas* (renunciation); but the precise nature of the demands is new. He has persuaded Indian landlords, at last report, to give more than 4 million acres to landless peasants. Here is a religiously generated motivation and goal effecting an important social change. Jayaprakash Narayan, a prominent socialist, has joined Bhave's campaign. Despite his doubts, he observes: "There are only two ways—Vinoba's or Mao Tse-tung's." [28] (Perhaps it should be remarked that Bhave is much more nearly an emissary than an exemplary prophet, in Weber's terms, which indicates the need to avoid identifying one or the other type specifically with various world religions.)

It is at the beginning of his challenge, Weber believes, that a prophetic leader is most influential. Gradually, there is a cooling off of the ardor which he had generated and an institutionalization of his followers. As his message spreads through a group, the diverse interests and needs of the members act upon it—selecting, interpreting, forgetting. "Indeed, in its pure form charismatic authority may be said to exist only in the process of originating." [29] Rather quickly, the process of "routinization of charisma" begins.[30] Those for whom the prophet's demands have an "elective affinity" continue to follow him, but in the process, his specifically religious thought is assimilated to their economic, political, and social, as well as their religious, needs. In such a situation, he is a "cause" of the developments and changes only in a very limited sense. Indeed, many unintended consequences may flow from the interpretations that his followers place upon his teachings. It is unlikely that Calvin wholly anticipated all the results that were related to his emphasis on "this-worldly asceticism."

In sum, a religious leader is part of a complicated causal nexus. He cannot be understood without knowledge of his social and cultural environment, including information on culture contact and borrowing. His impact is intricately related to the needs and tendencies of the people who come in contact with him. Some who hear him will be unaffected and those who do respond will respond each in his own way. For the explanation of certain problems—the abstraction of a limited piece of time and circumstance that the scientist may wish to explain—the religious leader may profitably be regarded as a cause, as a starting point for some sequence of interaction. For another problem, he must be seen as a product of other forces, an effect, a carrier of influence but not its source. There is little warrant in science for a more general conception.

Some Contemporary Theological Changes. A valuable way to examine

27 Berger, op. cit., p. 949.

28 The *New York Times,* Dec. 23, 1968, p. 10.

29 Weber, *The Theory of Social and Economic Organization*, p. 364.

30 See ibid., pp. 363–386.

the interactions of religious leadership and social context is to study the work of professional religious thinkers, the theologians. Insofar as they try to make religious sense out of the human condition of a given generation, they must deal with the stressful changes that people are experiencing by trying to give those changes some kind of an ultimate interpretation. In doing so, they show the way in which their own thought is affected by their time and place even while they help to influence the responses of those around them to the exigencies of that time and place.

By way of illustration, we will comment on some of the developments in American theology. During the last several decades there have been a number of significant shifts (although this should not lead us to overlook the continuity or slow change in the religious thought of laymen and per-haps of most clergymen). Late nineteenth- and early twentieth-century American theology was affected not only by its generally optimistic and democratic environment, but also by the strong currents of theological liberalism coming particularly out of Germany. Church history and Biblical studies, along with more specifically theological work, were opening re-ceived ideas to a flood of new thought on the sources of Christianity and the relationships of the church to its environment. These led, as in the case of Friedrich Schleiermacher, toward a "natural" religion, with an emphasis on individual experience, on reason, and on ethics, with little attention paid to supernatural views.

World War I dealt liberal theology in Europe a shattering blow. Karl Barth's neo-orthodoxy seemed to a growing number of German Protestants to speak more precisely to the human condition. Hitler's rise to power in-creased this feeling. As Peter Berger remarks: "A good case can be made for correlating this gain with the developing struggle between Nazism and the segment of German Protestantism known as the 'Confessing Church.' In this struggle Barthian neo-orthodoxy took on the character of a resistance ideology." [31]

By the middle 1930's, some American theologians, particularly those who were in touch with the German situation, were developing neo-ortho-dox views. Reinhold Niebuhr rapidly became and remained the most influ-ential of these.[32] Prolonged depression and World War II gave support to their interpretation of the human situation. One cannot speak with confi-dence concerning the strength of the influence of neo-orthodoxy, especially the degree to which it affected laymen. One is probably correct in stating, however, that among seminary-trained Protestant clergy in the twenty or so years following 1935 neo-orthodoxy was the most influential theological development in America.[33]

Neo-orthodoxy is a complex movement with many shades of meaning, which we need not explore for our purposes. It is not simply a reassertion of fundamentalism, although it shares some of its views. (And in some of

31 Peter Berger, *The Sacred Canopy*, p. 161.

32 See particularly his *The Nature and Destiny of Man*.

33 Thomas Hamilton gives some empirical support to this. In a sample of sermons pub-lished in the *Christian Century Pulpit*, from 1929 to 1940, he found a decline in the optimistic and social gospel emphasis from 95 per cent to 36 per cent; and an increase in pessimistic sermons, emphasizing the sinfulness of man and the need for faith, from 5 per cent to 64 per cent. *Public Opinion Quarterly*, Summer, 1942, pp. 280–283.

its less intellectually inclined exponents the distinction is not easy to draw. As the doctrines move from Broadway to Main Street they are reshaped by the different setting. Clergymen who had never lived happily with "modernism" and liberalism, enthusiastically accepted the "new" trends, happy about their intellectual respectability and brilliant sponsors, but unmindful of the new thinking they involved.) Neo-orthodoxy is an attempt to develop a theology for a democratic and urban situation, alert to the impact of "the social gospel and concerned with political problems," yet seeking to re-emphasize what it considers to be the insights of history and theology —the incapacity of man to grapple alone with evil and tragedy, the tendency he has of mistaking his partially successful efforts for fundamental solutions.

Neo-orthodoxy calls for responsible political and social action in the context of full recognition of how easy it is for man to fail. Critics of this view—indeed, some who have felt quite close to it—are likely to contend that this is a basically unstable union of two ideas. Walter Horton, for example, though "affirming the profundity of the orthodox insight, nevertheless simultaneously insisted that orthodoxy had not known how to control its insight: '. . . it laid such stress upon sin in general, as a universal human condition, that it failed to grapple realistically with the cause of particular sins.' " [34] The renewed emphasis on a pessimistic picture of man is often quite unaccompanied by interest in political and social questions. Catholic critics are likely to hold that insofar as "neo"-orthodoxy has relevance, it is little different from Thomist orthodoxy—an affirmation of the need to work with the "relative" values of this world, while remaining fully aware of their relativity (the evil they contain as human products) from the perspective of religious absolutes. The proponents of neo-orthodoxy might be expected to reply to the first criticism that the two ideas, far from being in unstable alliance, are an essentially correct view of the human situation (or perhaps that the instability derives from a failure to grasp the total system); and to the other they might reply that the Thomist system, in its attempt to organize the whole of life, fell constantly into the errors of confusing the relative with the absolute and of an excessive pessimism concerning politics.

We have noted that the immediate sources of the emphases of neo-orthodoxy are the tragedies and crises of our time—depression, war, tyranny— that have so clearly revealed the enormous obstacles in the way of the realization of the liberal dreams of modern man. (There is no one-to-one relationship between tragedy and the strength of new-orthodoxy, however. In a different total situation, as we shall see, continuing tragedy can lead to existentialism and "religious atheism.")

Another source of change in theological emphasis was the internal development of religious thought. Liberal theology, which neo-orthodoxy put on the defensive, although by no means eliminated, is an unsatisfying view of man's lot to those who are particularly sensitive to the succession of tragedies and conflicts of modern life. Liberalism, of course, has many diverse elements within it. The various perspectives perhaps stem in common from the opposition to fatalism, to extreme otherworldliness, to literal

34 Quoted by Donald Meyer, *The Protestant Search for Political Realism, 1919–1941,* p. 246. Meyer cites a similar statement by John Bennett.

interpretations of the Bible. To many intellectuals, these were impressive protests. But in a day of repeated catastrophes liberalism seemed less impressive, because of its lack of concern with the whole range of human life—its darker aspects as well as the more hopeful ones.[35] To many theologians, the liberal tendencies in religion that placed man and his welfare in the forefront of concern ran the risk of making man himself the object of worship. In less theological terms, this is to increase the danger, as opponents saw it, of parochialism—of putting one's faith in the partial, the temporary, the customs and the forms of a time and place. This, of course, is the perennial problem of all religion.

There were also secular intellectual sources for neo-orthodoxy. Its disillusionment with man, its pessimism with regard to the claims of inevitable progress in democratic societies, were anticipated and accompanied by developments in science, literature, and criticism. The theologians write—as they would readily agree—in a context in which biological science, from Darwin to Freud and after, has emphasized man's hostile potentialities. "If not Adam, then the ape and the tiger live on in us, to say nothing, as Bishop Creighton used to add, of that much more intractable animal, the donkey." [36] Kierkegaard, Nietzsche, and Kafka, each in his own way, helped to set the tone for later theological developments. Social science has stressed, indeed perhaps exaggerated, the place of violence and conflict within and between societies. The realism and naturalism of William Dean Howells, Frank Norris, Theodore Dreiser, and Sinclair Lewis; the muckraking of Lincoln Steffens and others; the repudiation of an unqualified acceptance of American economic, political, and cultural life by such writers as Henry Adams and Ludwig Lewisohn—all of these represent a degree of pessimism and disillusionment that are also part of the situation in which neo-orthodoxy developed.

By 1960, and perhaps earlier, neo-orthodoxy had lost its place as the preeminent theology of American Protestantism—or more exactly, of its intellectual and academic expressions. A more radical and "secular" theology, strongly influenced by neo-orthodoxy to be sure but quite distinct from it, is now prominent in many seminaries and among younger ministers. Once again, European thought and experience have influenced the direction of American thinking, along with developments inside the country. Secular existentialism, particularly the writing of Albert Camus and Jean-Paul Sartre, and some of the Theater of the Absurd, have had a powerful effect on many of the younger theologians. Despite their explicit atheism, or indeed perhaps because of it, Camus and Sartre are seen as speaking directly to the central issue of our time—the recovery of a sense of personhood, of purpose, of responsibility, of "becoming a saint without God." In Sartre's term, "existence precedes essence"; each man must be made aware of what he is, of his responsibility to himself and to all men. This awareness has

35 To avoid misunderstanding, perhaps the author may be permitted to say that were he to attempt an amateur theology, he would be inclined toward religious naturalism and liberalism. There is no logical incompatibility between central concern with problems of this life and faith in rational efforts on the one hand and full recognition of the "evil" in man, the enormity of the problem, on the other. See J. Milton Yinger, *Religion in the Struggle for Power*, footnote 43, pp. 232–234.

36 Sperry, op. cit., p. 254.

been made extremely difficult in a mechanical, overpowering age that has lost its God without finding in his place some new source of coherence. God is rejected, not because he commands our obedience and allegiance, but because he is the unjust bystander, as in Camus' *The Plague*, at the bedside of a dying child, allowing the innocent to suffer.

Some elements of contemporary theater can be read as efforts to shock us into a search for a new basis for dealing with human anguish.

In expressing the tragic sense of loss at the disappearance of ultimate certainties the Theatre of the Absurd, by a strange paradox, is also a symptom of what probably comes nearest to being a genuine religious quest in our age: an effort, however timed and tentative, to sing, to laugh, to weep—and to growl—if not in praise of God (whose name, in Adamov's phrase, has for so long been degraded by usage that it has lost its meaning), at least in search of a dimension of the Ineffable; an effort to make man aware of the ultimate realities of his condition, to instill in him again the lost sense of cosmic wonder and primeval anguish, to shock him out of an existence that has become trite, mechanical, complacent, and deprived of the dignity that comes of awareness.[37]

References to the ineffable and wonder are less appropriate, perhaps, for Camus and Sartre. In their work one sees a tough-minded search for ground on which modern man, in full use of his intellect, can stand, affirming his existence, yet remaining fully aware of the tragedies that engulf him. In this they share much with Freud; but they go beyond Freud's search for individual integrity, with both id and superego under firm control. They see not only individuals suffering but mankind suffering and they respond with a sense of compassion. Their atheism is no barrier to many religious thinkers who see them as allies against the complacent and the cruel. "Those few who are serious about their atheism or their belief require one another, for the battle against the hucksters, who daily increase and multiply, striving to possess the earth, is desperate. In the churches as in the buildings of our cities, there are countless petty men for whom persons are not ends but means: fodder for organizations, functions of society, useful citizens, faithful followers." [38]

Out of what we can call this "existential context" theological work was inevitably changed. It is convenient to mark that change with Bonhoeffer, even though developments through a century or more already indicated the direction that his thought would take. His work is filled with paradox and ambiguity, of statements that "God is teaching us that we must live as men who can get along very well without him," but the major direction is toward a radical theology, as indicated by this excerpt from one of his letters:

I expect you remember Bultmann's essay on the "demythologizing" of the New Testament? My view of it today would be, not that he went "too far," as most people thought, but that he did not go far enough. It is not only the "mythological" concepts, such as miracle, ascension, and so on (which are not in principle separable from the concepts of God, faith, etc.), but "religious" concepts generally, which are problematic. You cannot, as Bultmann supposes, separate God and miracle, but you must be able to interpret and proclaim *both* in a "non-

37 Martin Esslin, *The Theatre of the Absurd*, reprinted in *Religion and Contemporary Western Culture*, Edward Cell, ed., p. 168.

38 Michael Novak, "Christianity: Renewed or Slowly Abandoned?" *Daedalus*, 96, 1967, p. 261.

religious" sense. Bultmann's approach is fundamentally still a liberal one (i.e., abridging the gospel), whereas I am trying to think theologically.[39]

In the United States and Europe Paul Tillich has stood as the major bridge, spanning theological and secular thought from neo-orthodoxy to existentialism to radicalism. He sought to make theology relevant to the situation of men in an urban, mobile, depersonalizing world. Rather than the optimistic naturalism one finds in Schleiermacher, however, Tillich declared that man must find "The Courage to Be" even in a deeply dismaying and crushing time, and at a moment when the religious symbols of the past have lost their meaning.[40]

The work of Bultmann, Bonhoeffer, and Tillich reached "the man in the street," or in the pew, only indirectly, despite their importance to religious professionals. It was not until Bishop John Robinson wrote *Honest to God*, in 1963, that the sharp theological controversies of the day began to be read by a wide audience. This book has sold hundreds of thousands of copies in both England and America. Its message, stated here too simply, is that God is a quality within us, not a being "out there." Or to put it in Tillich's terms, for Robinson's book was strongly influenced by Tillich, God is the "ground of our being," not an outside force.

Tillich's work was highly abstract and somewhat guarded, for he was aware of a great continuity. Even Robinson's call for a shift from a transcendent to an immanent image of God drew on a substantial tradition. The break with orthodoxy and neo-orthodoxy is much more explicit in the recent "God is dead" theology. In 1959, Peter Berger wrote: "In many ways American religion still lives under an *ancien régime*, in what may well be intellectually the least modern of Western countries. Atheists are even rarer among us than Communists. If history has any lessons, however, we may expect an end to this state of innocence." [41] Berger was quite correct. Nietzsche's proclamation was reissued in a series of lively volumes in the United States during the 1960's. The "God is dead" theologians varied among themselves; they were sharply criticized; and it is not clear how widely they were listened to outside intellectual circles. But they expressed in unmistakable terms the radical theology that had been developing over several decades.[42]

These scattered references to certain new elements in contemporary theology (leaving aside the slowly evolving orthodoxies of the majority) lead us to ask: What are its sources? How does one account for the rather

39 Dietrich Bonhoeffer, *Letters and Papers from Prison*, p. 156.

40 *Systematic Theology*, 3 vols., is his main theological work. See also *The Courage to Be* and *The Shaking of the Foundations*.

41 In the *Christian Century*, April 8, 1959. His two essays in this and the April 15, 1959 issues, pp. 417–418 and 450–452, entitled "Camus, Bonhöffer, and the World Coming of Age," are valuable commentaries on the issues with which we are here concerned.

42 See Gabriel Vahanian, *The Death of God*; Thomas Altizer and William Hamilton, *Radical Theology and the Death of God*. These shade off toward works that are more directly concerned with problems of the relevance of religious thinking for the contemporary secular world. See, for example, Harvey Cox, *The Secular City*; and Paul Van Buren, *The Secular Meaning of the Gospel*. See also David Edwards, ed., *The Honest to God Debate*; Daniel Callahan, ed., *The Secular City Debate*; and Peter Berger, "A Sociological View of the Secularization of Theology," *Journal for the Scientific Study of Religion*, 6, 1967, pp. 3–16.

abrupt shift from neo-orthodoxy to radicalism? It is not difficult to note a series of proximate causes. Langdon Gilkey has specified a number of important influences: The continuing triumphs of science have encouraged the view that religious truth is symbolic; nineteenth-century emphasis on historical relativity has reduced the hold of absolute views; emphasis on this-worldly values in the surrounding society supports a shift in theology from concern for salvation to one for "authentic existence"; a shift in ethics from stress on personal holiness to love of neighbor—drawing on the tradition of the radical sectarians of the sixteenth and seventeenth centuries, on humanism, the Enlightenment, and Kant—underlines the view that each person should be treated as an end, not a means.[43]

Harvey Cox suggests that "the new breed" of American clergymen, those who are directly involved in the political and social struggles of the day, are in some ways not new at all. They are expressing what Richard Niebuhr identifies as the most persistent theme in American theology: the ideal of establishing the Kingdom of God on earth. "Those who see in the New Breed a mere outburst of secular activism reveal a lack of familiarity with the history of religion in America. The Kingdom of God, which in the neo-orthodox period had become an 'impossible possibility,' has become once again something for which to work." [44]

Somewhat in contrast, Michael Novak suggests that Protestant theology has been drastically affected by the discovery that it no longer lives in a rural and Protestant world, but in one that is "urban, utilitarian, and secular." Catholic political pragmatists, Negro moral heroes, and Jewish leaders in the arts and the intellectual world have all come on stage. "The cultural hegemony of the white Anglo-Saxon Protestant has been shattered; he must now take seriously interpretations of human life other than his own. Thus only now, a century later, is he experiencing Nietzsche's perception that God is dead, only now is he facing the accumulated secularization of daily life in America." [45]

What we have, in sum, are many serious religious efforts to relate theology both to the crises and to the key elements of contemporary life. Theological thought, seen sociologically, is a sensitive index to the ways in which social change and religious change interact. Religious thought is powerfully influenced by a changing social context. But the resulting forms of religious restatement help to redefine the values of society in its contemporary circumstances and help to shape the motives and goals of individuals who are facing new opportunities and new threats.

RELIGION INITIATES CHANGE

We have stressed the continuous interaction of religious change and social change. Are there, however, some circumstances when it is appropriate to emphasize religion's independent role? Almost all that we can say on this subject has been said in other parts of this book. It remains only to make a

43 See Langdon Gilkey, "Social and Intellectual Sources of Contemporary Protestant Theology in America," *Daedalus*, 96, 1967, pp. 69–98.

44 Harvey Cox, *On Not Leaving It to the Snake*, p. 139.

45 Michael Novak, op. cit., p. 249.

brief summary statement. The whole weight of the evidence of contemporary behavioral science makes it appear certain that the life of the mind is shaped by individual needs and interests and by social roles and group structures. Religious beliefs, from this perspective, cannot be seen as intrusive forces from outside; they spring from human life and are shaped by its imperatives. It is equally clear, however, that ideas and beliefs enter into life. They organize experience and influence that *selective* response to the environment that characterizes human behavior. Perception is affected by what one believes is there, by what one has been taught to see and hear, by what one wants to perceive, by the groups within which one perceives. There is no reason to suppose that religious beliefs, religiously defined needs, and religious groups fall outside this rule; they shape our perception of the world. Motivation is equally influenced by what one believes and by one's group identities. Machine operators may work slowly or show a high rate of absenteeism, if they define a situation as unjust or dull or of only marginal interest to them. The norms of the groups to which they belong will strongly influence their levels of achievement and aspiration. If the work situation corresponds with their sense of justice, if they feel involved in its planning, if their group encourages vigorous activity, production levels will rise and absenteeism fall.

Again, there is no reason to suppose that the influence of religious beliefs and religious groups falls outside this social psychology and sociology of motivation. One of the main efforts of this study has been to show that an adequate science of religion must be brought into the framework of a general theory of human behavior. Religious beliefs and group patterns may contribute to a slowdown of effort, to "absenteeism from this world," or to vigorous activity and intensive efforts to change the world.

To try to change the world, of course, is not synonymous with changing it, although effort is an essential ingredient. And even the origin of the beliefs and groups that lead to the desire to try has to be explained. We have tried to show that it is related to the individual, social, and cultural facts of a given situation. Once started, religious ideas and structures are continuously involved in the interactions of human life. For example, a Mormon community in the days of the charismatic leadership of Joseph Smith was different and continues to be today. The course of its development is shaped, in part, by religiously defined patterns.

There are also unintended effects that flow from religious influence. It is not clear how much religion is appropriately considered, in such a situation, to be the cause of events it brings about. At the very least, a distinction is needed between those consequences that are sought after and those that are unintended and perhaps even unwanted. This distinction is well illustrated in missionary activity. The result sought, in most instances, is the conversion of those among whom a missionary works, a change in values, beliefs, and religious practices on the part of those whom he reaches.[46] He may or may not succeed in this (and if he does, he is likely

46 This is not the place to evaluate missionary activity. Opinions range from the belief that all missionary effort is religious imperialism and organized ethnocentrism to the belief that it represents one of the highest expressions of brotherliness on an international basis. Since the work of missionaries varies so widely and its consequences are so diverse, I do not find any such general opinion to be of much value. Most people, it

to achieve a hybrid form of the religion he serves); but he almost certainly will influence those who hear him in other ways, particularly if he is a representative of a technically more advanced society. Mission activity, if it is the work of more than a few scattered individuals, is likely to disrupt the prevailing power arrangements, disturb kinship patterns, affect the stratification system, and set new political processes in motion. In cybernetic terms, it increases the wobble in various parts of the old order beyond the capacity of the homeostatic processes to handle. This is particularly likely to be true of missionary work in small, preliterate societies.[47]

Whether this is a happy or unhappy fact will depend upon one's evaluation of the aboriginal society, the extent of turmoil during the period of transition, and the way in which the changed society is incorporated into the larger structures to which it becomes related as a result of these contacts. Because the latter two issues are much more likely to be in the hands of military or government officials than of missionaries, religious activity from abroad is often more successful in breaking down an old order than in building up a new one. Putting it in over-cynical terms: Having failed to civilize their own societies, judging by the policies and actions of those societies in dealing with the mission areas, missionaries are able only to contribute to the disruption of others. This, of course, is to overlook their medical, agricultural, and educational contributions; and it is also to overlook the increased options opened up for the local inhabitants by the presence and teaching of the missionaries—political options, as they come to see themselves in intertribal terms, educational options, and economic options. After the coming of the missionaries the local inhabitants cannot go back to their former life style, but there may be more choices available to them than there would be if only the trader, the plantation overseer, and the soldier had brought them into the larger world.

Larger, heterogeneous civilizations, already characterized by a world religion, are much more likely to soften the impact of an outside religion. Converts, who are derived mainly from the lower strata, see their transfer of faith as a way of escaping their lowly status. New paths of education and employment may be opened to them; but unless there is a major religious shift by the elite, the convert group becomes another enclave in an already heterogeneous society. The enclave may prove to be quite powerful, as Christian, Buddhist, Hindu, and Muslim groups have been in many societies; but it does not break up the social order.

This brief reference to missionary activity is designed only to suggest its

appears to me, are inclined to be missionaries for the beliefs and values they hold most deeply. Many of those who are opposed to traditional missionary work are inclined to be quite stern, if not downright inquisitional, in the propagation of their own faith—whether they believe in communism, or Radio Free Europe, or are university students eager to establish a new way of doing things. I know many students who have sought to persuade Southern white people to give up their "pagan" ways in race relations. None of them has thought of himself as a missionary. Perhaps those who achieve this self-definition will be led to ask more subtle and valuable questions about the place of value propagation in a divided world.

47 For comments on missions, see Elliott Skinner, "Christianity and Islam among the Mossi," *American Anthropologist,* 60, 1958, pp. 1102–1119; Raymond Hopkins, "Christianity and Sociopolitical Change in Sub-Saharan Africa," *Social Forces,* 44, 1966, pp. 555–562.

importance to the scientific study of religion and to the general study of societies and social change. Mission work is a valuable test case for examination of the questions: What is the role of ideas, of cultural innovation, in change? What is the relationship of deprivation to susceptibility to a new movement? When elements from one system are grafted on to another, while leaving intact many aspects of the first system, is there "tissue rejection"? Does missionary activity get a start only if the system it encounters is already seriously unstable; or can it get a start on the basis of the normal tensions characteristic of any society? In a sweeping answer, which merely suggests the lines inquiry might follow: Only a total system analysis, based on the recognition of the interdependence of structural, cultural, and character elements, can take the full complexity of the situation into account.[48]

Let us observe once again that the force of religion may be chained to economically or politically defined goals, to the injury or defeat of the religiously defined goals—the quest for human brotherhood in the "universal religions," for example. And it may be well to repeat that such initiatory or causal influence as religion has is not intrinsically good or bad. If communism shares many of the characteristics of a religion, its power to initiate social change is seen to be very unfortunate by contemporary Americans. The dedication of a kamikaze pilot, inspired by the ceremonies and beliefs of National Shinto, was not looked upon with equal enthusiasm by all whose lives he changed. The influence of some parts of the Calvinist ethic is not regarded in the same light by a psychoanalyst and a fundamentalist minister.

Apart from these value questions—which are, of course, of enormous importance—what may one say about the initiatory power of religion, not in any primary sense, but in the sense of one of the levels of causation? Our argument can perhaps be summarized in this statement: Religious influence on the course of social change will be greatest when the strategic decisions of religious individuals are made with clearest recognition of "the dilemma of the churches," when prophetic or charismatic leadership is most abundant, when religious institutions are most effectively autonomous from the secular institutions of power. Strategy, prophecy, and autonomy are highly interactive, of course. And they too require explanation by the sociology of religion—an explanation that we have attempted in part, at various points in our discussion. Moreover, these influences apply almost wholly to universal religions, not to tribal or societal religions, for in situations of which the latter are a part, it is almost meaningless to isolate a specifically religious influence on social change.

The observation that the influence of religion varies is rooted deep in the thought and action of "the average man" and in the more sophisticated ideas of philosophers and theologians. The task of science is not only to test the validity of this general observation, but more particularly to discover the conditions that underlie the variations. Bergson's interesting philosophical ideas contribute little to a science of religion when he asserts —even if he demonstrates its truth—that a fresh religious impulse may break into society with revolutionary force. Under what influences does

48 For some valuable comments on the scientific study of mission activity, see David Heise, "Prefatory Findings in the Sociology of Missions," *Journal for the Scientific Study of Religion,* 6, 1967, pp. 49–63.

this occur and in what situations does the institutionalization of the "creative impulse" proceed? Troeltsch poses a key problem for science but is less concerned to solve it, when he describes a great antinomy running through Christianity—a quiescent "aesthetic-ritualistic piety" and an "ethical-prophetic piety." Science must try to discover in whom the one and the other will predominate. MacMurray states what is in effect a hypothesis in the sociology of religion, when he writes: ". . . the main evidence that Christianity is a real creative force in history is the pressure and the struggle to realize, by reform and revolution, a society based on the principles of freedom and equality." [49] But his evidences are largely propositions of faith. Niebuhr recognizes the variations in religious influence:

Traditional and institutional religion . . . tend to impart the aura of the absolute to the existing order of things. . . . Religion in its quintessential character is devotion to the absolute and a yearning after value and truth which transcends the partial, the relative and the historical. Since the absolute must always be symbolized in terms of the relative it leads naturally to the absolutizing of the relative, so that devotion to God comes to mean loyalty to "holy Russia" or obedience to the Jewish law, or acceptance of the prejudices of western civilization, or conformity to puritan moral standards or maintenance of a capitalistic civilization. Yet religion is never exhausted in these corruptions. [50]

A scientific study would avoid the adjectives, for what is one man's quintessence is another's corruption. And it would ask: What are the circumstances that cause religion to accept the existing order or to "transcend the partial"?

CONCLUSION

The relentless search for causes, for conditions, for variables may seem to many to "take the heart out of religion." One can argue that if religion can be undermined by analysis, so be it. But it is possible that growing knowledge of the nature of religion can only add to its contribution to the quality of man's adjustment to the universe of which he is a part. The author subscribes to the latter view. This, to be sure, is an affirmation and not a statement of fact. One is scarcely able to prove it. Some exploration of the reasoning and feeling behind it, however, may help in the understanding of its meaning. Thus we come back to a question raised in the first pages of this volume in the hope that we can now examine it more fruitfully. These last paragraphs are not "the scientific study of religion"; they are estimates and projections and affirmations. But they express what the author believes to be judgments that flow naturally from the study of religion and society.

Effects of the Scientific Study of Religion. The initial impact of scientific studies on religions may be different from the long-run effects. "A little learning is a dangerous thing," to be sure, but ignorance may be even more dangerous. What are some of the immediate effects of the scientific study of religion? It makes a naive, simple, unquestioning belief in some changeless religious view less likely. The emphasis on functions, the attention to religious institutions, with their involvement in all aspects of the secular

49 John MacMurray, *The Clue to History*, p. 69.

50 Reinhold Niebuhr, *Reflections on the End of an Era*, pp. 183–184.

society, the development of a comparative view of many religions—these require that one pull back from his faith to see it at a distance. For many people, religion is accepted without thought, by habit or perhaps by fear; they believe many aspects of it that in fact contradict other conceptions that they accept. Such contradictions are less likely to be noticed if religion is not studied. Scientific examination may "weaken the faith" of persons thus inclined.

Science inevitably takes a naturalistic view of religion. This is a necessary *assumption*, not a demonstrated truth, from which all science proceeds. Religion is in man; it is to be understood by the analysis of his needs, tendencies, and potentialities. The scientist presses forward from this starting point as far as his evidence will carry him. Insofar as sociology has any effect on religious starting points, it will probably be to encourage naturalism. This will not be because it has proved its "ultimate validity"—an impossibility—but because the capacity of human beings for compartmentalized thinking is limited. There is a tendency, however slowly it may develop, for a person to accept harmonious premises. For those who identify religion with supernatural views of the world, it must appear that scientific analysis may weaken religion.

Those who define religion functionally do not regard the loss of belief in specific items of a traditional faith or the increased likelihood of naturalistic premises as forces that weaken religion. Moreover, there are other influences set in motion by serious scientific study that may, in the long run, strengthen religion and help to renew it in the modern world:

First, scientific study has revealed the great significance of religion for individuals and for groups, leading to the conclusion that religion is a permanent, necessary, and inevitable part of human life. Man is "incurably religious." If a well-integrated and acceptable system of beliefs and practices is not available, he invents one, joins a movement, follows a leader. The implication to be drawn from scientific study is not simply that religion is important in human affairs, but also that the *kind* of religion is vital. Simply to believe is not enough. We shall come back to this question.

Second, the distinction we have drawn between the changing content and the basic functions of religion may help to create a situation in which a religion adjusted to the contemporary world, and therefore more effective in it, can more readily develop. If one identifies religion with a system of established beliefs and rites, he opposes a developmental approach. But failure to change can only alienate from religion the people whose whole life situation is undergoing rapid transformation. They may become indifferent to or reject completely a religion that contains a great many insights into human life—insights won through centuries of tragedy and struggle— only to embrace a protoreligion whose road to salvation may seem shorter but whose detours have been quite uncharted. The anthropologist or sociologist, by noting that religion is a product of societies, by his attention to its cultural sources, by his examination of social change and culture lags, may help to facilitate the process whereby a religion adequate to this dynamic situation may be strengthened.

Third, a scientific study of religion can make an important contribution to the understanding of the relationship of religion to morality. In Chapter Three we have suggested that there are many types of relationship between them. Not all of these are equally appropriate—in terms of the achievement of stated values—to a changing, heterogeneous society. In a "sacred" society, the tradition-building process has time to embody guide lines to action that have relatively foreseeable consequences. One does not need to be a philosopher and a scientist to "know" the consequences of his actions —these can be embedded in moral rules that emerge out of the repetitions of human experience. This is not true of a rapidly changing social situation. Today it is far more difficult to be moral, because the results of our actions are far more difficult to predict. Our behavior now affects persons far removed from us in time and space. The vast interdependence of the world means that we affect strangers as often as friends. The decisions of the rulers of China affect a farm boy in Iowa; the actions of the American Congress influence the trends in Egypt. A few moral formulas he learned as a child cannot adequately guide the contemporary man; there is no easy way out of the difficult task of trying to discover the probable consequences of various actions. *How* does one love his neighbor today? Do we continue to press the building of a large stockpile of atomic and hydrogen bombs? Do we bring German troops into a Euro-American defense system? These are new problems. If one thinks of a changeless religious system embodying a moral code that is adequate to the needs of men today, he can only hinder the search for answers to such questions. Scientific study that explores the interdependence of religion and society points to the conclusion that our type of society needs a highly flexible, undogmatic religion, and one that is dedicated to the free study of society, if religion is to contribute to the solution of our major moral problems.

What Religious Perspective for the Modern World? Not all kinds of religion fit equally well into the complex framework of contemporary societies. Some men have gloried in the opposition of their faith to reason. Their faith was something fixed and final. This, in a diverse and changing world, is a guarantee of conflict, for systems of faith continually meet and sharply conflict; and man's changing situation constantly requires new religious thought. This does not mean that a great deal cannot be drawn from the religious efforts of those who have preceded us; but each generation must struggle with its own religious situation. In the words of Wilhelm Pauck (though we would not attribute to him the implications carried here): "The church must always be reformed."

If some men have gloried in the opposition of faith and reason, others require the use of reason to the fullest extent in a constant search for truth, in order that faith may not prove ephemeral. "Faith is the substance of things hoped for," the projection of a society's most fundamental aspirations outward in time and into areas where science is inapplicable—the realm of ideals and value-choices. That the author of the Book of Hebrews should complete his sentence by stating that faith is "the evidence of things not seen" is an indication of the deep antinomy running through Christianity. If faith is "evidence" it can lead to sharp conflicts with reason and can result in doctrinal rigidity.[51] These are religious tendencies, in the writer's judgment, that make extremely difficult the religious quest of modern societies.

No effective "return to religion" can be of a thirteenth- or sixteenth- or

51 See J. H. Randall and J. H. Randall, Jr., *Religion and the Modern World*, Chap. 11.

even an early twentieth-century variety. Churches continue to receive strong support, at least in the United States, but that support seems relatively superficial. The true situation is more accurately marked by Kierkegaard's call, echoed by many contemporary theologians and church leaders: Where are the Christians in Christendom? Their scarcity is partly to be accounted for by the weakness of the continuing reformation, and the failure to develop a religion whose symbols and problems are meaningful to men today. The result is that a great deal of the operating faith resides in political ideologies and national creeds. These creeds are not complete departures from the religious traditions to which they are related, of course, but they give weight to the limited and parochial views of those religions—at a time when the universalism of man has been transformed from an exciting vision to a vital necessity.

If scientific analysis tends to lead one to the conclusion that a religious system is necessary for human life, it also suggests that an effective religion must be fully sensitive to the training, the perspectives, the problems, the total life situation of the contemporary generation. Concern for this question led John Stuart Mill to suggest the need for *lack* of agreement in religious matters, to prevent the growth of hierarchical institutions that might block the necessary changes in a dynamic society. There is a part truth in this observation. It is sensitive to the dangers of rigidity and is aware of the diversity of religious needs. But it fails to recognize that if the explicit religious patterns lack a unifying theme, this theme will get support in some other social pattern—often one more limited and rigid than the religion it replaced.

Mankind has come to a great turning. By his own hand he has built the structure of a unified world, for we are all tied together, whether for weal or woe, by the economic, political, military, and communication facts of our time. We have not yet, however, developed a cultural system to match this structure nor socialization procedures to develop persons who are truly at home in it.

It is at these points that religion will play, or fail to play, a significant role. It seems unlikely that the major existing religions, as embodied in their established institutions, will have a vital part in the reorganization of man's religious life in ways that will deal with the situation we are in. This is simply to say that churches will act like churches. The new "over-beliefs," the new rituals, the new religious structures will come from sectarian protests against the established churches, from religious innovation springing from contemporary soil, from syntheses of some of the quasi-religions that have developed in the modern world. Or they will fail to come, and the world will be shattered.

Only the rudiments of a genuine universalism lie before us. The "world" religions have found it possible, partly because of their supernaturalism, to live comfortably with a great deal of injustice, suffering, and ignorance. But the urban world is being de-supernaturalized (not secularized—for man has always been both secular and religious). Injustice is bearable if this world is written off as a temporary and unimportant vale of tears; it becomes an ultimate concern to those who are concerned only with this existence. And so it is with pain and ignorance. We have noted earlier that major (although in my judgment seriously inadequate) quasi-religions have developed, in a desacralized world, around each of these concerns, most importantly in Marxism, Freudianism, and Positivism. Indeed, there are powerful efforts to bring them together, if not self-consciously as religious movements, at least as individual ideologies and philosophical systems. The work of many secular thinkers is well seen as a parallel effort to that of the theologians and innovating religious leaders we have discussed. Four men, despite their great differences, can represent these efforts: Jean-Paul Sartre, Albert Camus, Herbert Marcuse, and Erich Fromm. I do not find them equally appealing—or equally understandable. None has asked the religious questions explicitly: By what beliefs, rites, and institutional arrangements can we increase the likelihood that justice "will roll down like waters and righteousness like an overflowing stream"? *And* how shall we deal with the fact that we are bound to fail, that human justice is partial? How shall we minimize human suffering? *And*, having only partially succeeded, how can we make sense of the suffering that remains? How can we employ man's intellectual powers to the full to read the meaning and the possibilities of the universe? *And* what shall we *believe* when our comprehension runs out?

The writers I have mentioned deal with important segments of these questions. Marcuse possesses and generates the anger that may be necessary to break through established forms; he is sensitive to the questions, but his thinking is more negative than creative despite his "sectarian" Utopianism. His work is reminiscent of Rousseau—more the harbinger of revolution to come than architect of a new society. Fromm is most explicitly prophetic in the religious sense; yet he seems, especially in his later writings, somewhat blitheful about the ease with which we can achieve "sanity" in our institutional and individual lives. Sartre and Camus faced the dreadfully dark mid-twentieth century and managed to see a ray of light, but only a ray. It may be that profound pessimism is the necessary realistic base for a religion for contemporary man. The more optimistic ideologies of Marcuse and Fromm, for all their sharp criticism of the institutional orders, may hide the dreadful malaise of the human situation. A modern religion, like those of old, must face despair yet not turn away.

Despite their differences, the men mentioned, and the several others who might be added (Julian Huxley, Pierre Teilhard de Chardin, and in an earlier style, John Dewey, for example) come together in their shared concern for the weight of injustice, suffering, and ignorance. None seems an apt candidate as the founder of a religion; but they indicate to me, along with some current theological work and the activism of some religious leaders, that the conditions are ripe for substantial rebuilding. These may be minor prophets of a naturalistic faith that is emerging out of the realities of a highly interdependent world, desacralized and ailing.

Many elements of contemporary youth movements also seem to me, despite their nihilistic and anomic qualities, to express a profound search for sacred ideas and qualities. They are sensitive to the fact that new ultimate questions press in on man, in this first era of full interdependence, demanding our most dedicated attention. If the youth today have not developed a glorious religion we should not be surprised nor dismayed. Not surprised, for the task is inherently, supremely difficult; not dismayed, for many of them are at least searching, which is the first necessary step.

The twentieth century has been and continues to be a powerfully religious age—but its religions are partial and divisive. We are not lacking in world-encompassing values, but there are few structures through which they can be expressed and few procedures through which individuals can be trained to accept them at the deepest levels. We have failed, as Julian Huxley says, to ritualize our behavior effectively "in relation to the radically new psychosocial situations of today. This applies to all three aspects of successful ritualization—its communicatory, its conflict-reducing, and its positive-bonding functions." [52] We have not learned how to move skillfully from one sacred system to another.

We are fully aware of the great difficulties in a continuing reformation. The task is similar to that of rebuilding Grand Central Station while keeping the trains running. One must avoid waiting so long that the building collapses, yet build so skillfully that traffic may continue. In religious matters, for fear of "stopping traffic" many people resist the building process; others, dismayed at the shakiness of the ancient structure, try to halt all traffic until a new structure can be built. (This cannot be done; the customers buy a ticket on some other road to salvation.) Beyond some contribution to the intrinsic tasks of science, one may hope that this difficult struggle with the analysis of religion may suggest some reconciliation between those who are dedicated to keeping the trains running and those who are convinced that the structure must be rebuilt. If the present writer is inclined to emphasize the latter, it is only out of conviction that the need for continuous rebuilding is more likely to be forgotten than the need for the leap of faith.

52 In *The Religious Situation: 1968*, Donald Cutler, ed., p. 708.

BIBLIOGRAPHY

AARONSON, BERNARD S. "Mystic and Schizophreniform States and the Experience of Depth." *Journal for the Scientific Study of Religion*, 6 (Fall 1967), 246–252.

ABBOTT, WALTER, ed. *Documents of Vatican II.* New York: Herder and Herder, 1966.

ABEL, THEODORE. *Systematic Sociology in Germany.* New York: Columbia University Press, 1929.

ABELL, AARON I. *The Urban Impact on American Protestantism, 1865–1900.* Cambridge, Mass.: Harvard University Press, 1943.

ABERLE, DAVID F. *The Peyote Religion Among the Navaho.* Chicago, Ill.: Aldine Publishing Company, 1966.

———. "The Prophet Dance and Reactions to White Contact." *Southwestern Journal of Anthropology*, 15 (1959), 74–83.

———. COHEN, A., A. DAVIS, M. LEVY, and F. SUTTON. "The Functional Prerequisites of Society." *Ethics*, 60 (1950), 100–111.

ABRAMS, RAY H. *Preachers Present Arms.* Philadelphia, Pa.: Round Table Press, 1933.

———, ed. "Organized Religion in the United States." *Annals of the American Academy of Political and Social Science*, 256 (March 1948).

ACADEMY OF RELIGION AND MENTAL HEALTH. *Research in Religion and Health* (Proceedings of the Fifth Academy Symposium, 1961). New York: Fordham University Press, 1963.

AHLSTROM, SYDNEY E. "The Levels of Religious Revival." *Confluence*, 4 (April 1955), 32–43.

———. "Theology and the Present-Day Revival." *Annals of the American Academy*, 332 (November 1960), 20–36.

AHMANN, MATHEW, ed. *Race: Challenge to Religion.* Chicago, Ill.: Henry Regnery Company, 1963.

ALEXANDER, W. W. *Racial Segregation in the American Protestant Church.* New York: Friendship Press, 1946.

ALLAND, ALEXANDER, JR. " 'Possession' in a Revivalistic Negro Church." *Journal for the Scientific Study of Religion*, I (Spring 1962), 204–213.

ALLEN, PHILIP J. "Growth of Strata in Early Organizational Development." *American Journal of Sociology*, 68 (July 1962), 34–46.

ALLEN, RUSSELL O., and BERNARD SPILKA. "Committed and Consensual Religion: A Specification of Religion-Prejudice Relationships." *Journal for the Scientific Study of Religion*, 6 (Fall 1967), 191–206.

ALLPORT, GORDON W. *The Individual and His Religion.* New York : The Macmillan Company, 1950.

——. *Personality and Social Encounter.* Boston, Mass.: The Beacon Press, 1960.

——, JAMES M. GILLESPIE, and JACQUELINE YOUNG. "The Religion of the Post-War College Student." *The Journal of Psychology* (January 1948), 3–33.

ALMOND, GABRIEL A. *The Appeals of Communism.* Princeton, N.J.: Princeton University Press, 1954.

——, and JAMES S. COLEMAN, eds. *The Politics of the Developing Areas.* Princeton, N.J.: Princeton University Press, 1960.

ALPERT, HARRY. *Emile Durkheim and His Sociology.* New York: Columbia University Press, 1939.

ALTIZER, THOMAS J. J., and WILLIAM HAMILTON. *Radical Theology and the Death of God.* Indianapolis, Ind.: The Bobbs-Merrill Co., Inc., 1966.

AMERICAN CIVIL LIBERTIES UNION. *The Church-State Problem Has Been Handed to You.* New York: American Civil Liberties Union, 1967.

——. *Conscience and the War. A Report on the Treatment of Conscientious Objectors in World War II.* New York: American Civil Liberties Union, September, 1943.

AMERICAN FRIENDS SERVICE COMMITTEE. *The Experience of the American Friends Service Committee in Civilian Public Service.* Philadelphia: American Friends Service Committee, 1945.

American Jewish Yearbook, 1965. Morris Fine, and Milton Himmelfarb, eds. Philadelphia: Jewish Publication Society of America, 1965.

AMES, MICHAEL. "An Outline of Recent Social and Religious Changes in Ceylon." *Human Organization,* 22 (1963), 45–53.

ANDERSON, CHARLES H. "Religious Communality among Academics." *Journal for the Scientific Study of Religion,* 7 (Spring 1968), 87–96.

——. "Religious Communality among White Protestants, Catholics, and Mormons." *Social Forces,* 46 (June 1968), 501–508.

ANDERSON, DONALD N. "Ascetic Protestantism and Political Preference." *Review of Religious Research,* 7 (Spring 1966), 167–171.

ARBOUSSE-BASTIDE, PAUL. "Auguste Comte et la sociologie religieuse." *Archives de Sociologie des Religions,* 22 (Juillet-Décembre 1966), 3–57.

ARGYLE, MICHAEL. *Religious Behaviour.* London: Routledge and Kegan Paul, 1958.

BABBIE, EARL R. "The Third Civilization. An Examination of Sokagakkai." *Review of Religious Research,* 7 (Winter 1966), 101–121.

BAILEY, KENNETH K. *Southern White Protestantism in the Twentieth Century.* New York: Harper and Row, Publishers, Inc., 1964.

BAINTON, ROLAND H. *Christian Attitudes Toward War and Peace.* Nashville, Tenn.: Abingdon Press, 1960.

——. "The Churches Shift on War." *Religion in Life* (Summer 1943), 323–335.

——. "The Left Wing of the Reformation." *Journal of Religion* (January 1941), 124–134.

——. "The Sectarian Theory of the Church." *Christendom* (Summer 1946), 382–387.

BALANDIER, GEORGES. *Sociologie actuelle de l'Afrique noire.* Paris: Presses Universitaires de France, 1955.

BALK, ALFRED. *The Religion Business.* Richmond, Va.: John Knox, Press, 1968.

BALLOU, ROBERT O. *Shinto, The Unconquered Enemy.* New York: The Viking Press, Inc., 1945.

BALTZELL, E. DIGBY. *An American Business Aristocracy.* New York: Collier Books, 1962.

——. *The Protestant Establishment. Aristocracy and Caste in America.* New York: Random House, Inc., 1964.

BANTON, MICHAEL, ed. *Anthropological Approaches to the Study of Religion*. New York: Frederick A. Praeger, Inc., 1966.

BARBER, BERNARD. "Acculturation and Messianic Movements." *American Sociological Review*, 6 (October 1941), 663–669.

———. "A Socio-Cultural Interpretation of the Peyote Cult." *American Anthropologist*, 43 (October–December 1941), 673–675.

BARNES, HARRY E. *The Twilight of Christianity*. New York: Richard R. Smith, Inc., 1931.

———, ed. *An Introduction to the History of Sociology*. Chicago, Ill.: University of Chicago Press, 1948.

———, and HOWARD BECKER. *Social Thought from Lore to Science*. 2 vols. Boston, Mass.: D. C. Heath & Company, 1938.

———, and F. B. BECKER, eds. *Contemporary Social Theory*. New York: Appleton-Century-Crofts, Inc., 1940.

BARNETT, HOMER G. *Indian Shakers. A Messianic Cult of the Pacific Northwest*. Carbondale, Ill.: Southern Illinois University Press, 1957.

BARNETT, JAMES H. "The Easter Festival—A Study in Cultural Change." *American Sociological Review*, 14 (February 1949), 62–70.

BARON, SALO W. "Impact of Wars on Religion." *Political Science Quarterly* (December 1952), 534–572.

———. *Modern Nationalism and Religion*. New York: Harper and Row, Publishers, Inc., 1947.

———. *A Social and Religious History of the Jews*. Second edition, revised and enlarged. New York: Columbia University Press, 1952.

———, and JOSEPH L. BLAU. *Judaism, Postbiblical and Talmudic Period*. New York: The Liberal Arts Press, 1954.

BATES, ERNEST S. *American Faith*. New York: W. W. Norton & Company, Inc., 1940.

BAUMER, FRANKLIN L. *Religion and the Rise of Scepticism*. New York: Harcourt, Brace & World, Inc., 1960.

BAXTER, RICHARD. *Practical Works*. 23 vols. Edited by William Orme. London: James Duncan, 1830.

BEA, AUGUSTIN CARDINAL. *The Church and the Jewish People*. New York: Harper and Row, Publishers, Inc., 1966.

BECKER, CARL. *The Heavenly City of the Eighteenth Century Philosophers*. New Haven, Conn.: Yale University Press, 1932.

BECKER, HOWARD. "Supreme Values and the Sociologist." *American Sociological Review*, 6 (April 1941), 155–172.

———. *Systematic Sociology*, on the basis of the *Beziehungslehre* and *Gebilderlehre* of Leopold von Wiese. New York: John Wiley & Sons, Inc., 1932.

———. *Through Values to Social Interpretation*. Durham, N.C.: Duke University Press, 1950.

BELLAH, ROBERT N. "Civil Religion in America." *Daedalus*, 96 (Winter 1967), 1–21.

———. "Reflections on the Protestant Ethic Analogy in Asia." *Journal of Social Issues*, 19 (1963), 52–60.

———, ed. *Religion and Progress in Modern Asia*. New York: The Free Press, 1965.

———. "Religious Aspects of Modernization in Turkey and Japan." *American Journal of Sociology*, 64 (July 1958), 1–5.

———, "Religious Evolution." *American Sociological Review*, 29 (June 1964), 358–374.

———. *Tokugawa Religion*. New York: The Free Press, 1957.

BENDIX, REINHARD. *Max Weber: An Intellectual Portrait*. Garden City, N.Y.: Doubleday & Company, Inc., 1960.

BENEDICT, RUTH. *The Concept of the Guardian Spirit in Native North America.* American Anthropological Association, Memoir No. 29, 1923.
———. *Patterns of Culture.* Boston, Mass.: Houghton Mifflin Company, 1934. Reprinted by Penguin Books, 1946.
BENNETT, JOHN C., ed. *Nuclear Weapons and the Conflict of Conscience.* New York: Charles Scribner's Sons, 1962.
———. *Christian Ethics and Social Policy.* New York: Charles Scribner's Sons, 1946.
———, HOWARD R. BOWEN, WILLIAM A. BROWN, JR., and G. BROMLEY OXNAM. *Christian Values and Economic Life.* New York: Harper and Row, Publishers, Inc., 1954.
BENNINGSEN, ALEXANDRE and CHANTAL LEMERCIER-QUELQUEJAY. *Islam in the Soviet Union.* New York: Frederick A. Praeger, Inc., 1967.
BENNION, LOWELL L. *Max Weber's Methodology.* Paris: Les Presses Modernes, 1933.
BENSON, P. H. *Religion in Contemporary Culture.* New York: Harper and Row, Publishers, Inc., 1960.
BENYON, ERDMANN D. "The Voodoo Cult Among Negro Migrants to Detroit." *American Journal of Sociology,* 43 (May 1938), 894–907.
BERGER, PETER L. "Charisma and Religious Innovation: The Social Location of Israelite Prophecy." *American Sociological Review,* 28 (December 1963), 940–950.
———. *The Noise of Solemn Assemblies.* Garden City, N.Y.: Doubleday & Company, Inc., 1961.
———. *The Precarious Vision.* Garden City, N.Y.: Doubleday & Company, Inc., 1961.
———. *The Sacred Canopy: Elements of a Sociological Theory of Religion.* Garden City, N.Y.: Doubleday & Company, Inc., 1967.
———. "A Sociological View of the Secularization of Theology." *Journal for the Scientific Study of Religion,* 6 (Spring 1967), 3–16.
———. "The Sociological Study of Sectarianism." *Social Research,* 21 (1954), 467–485.
———, and THOMAS LUCKMANN. *The Social Construction of Reality: A Treatise in the Sociology of Knowledge.* Garden City, N.Y.: Doubleday & Company, Inc., 1966.
BERGSON, HENRI. *The Two Sources of Morality and Religion.* Translated by R. Ashley Audra and Cloudesley Brereton, with the assistance of W. Horsfall Carter. New York: Holt, Rinehart & Winston, Inc., 1935.
BERKOWITZ, MORRIS I., and EDMUND J. JOHNSON. *Social Scientific Studies of Religion. A Bibliography.* Pittsburgh, Pa.: University of Pittsburgh Press, 1967.
BERNARD, L. L. *Social Control in Its Sociological Aspects.* New York: The Macmillan Company, 1939.
———. "The Sociological Interpretation of Religion." *The Journal of Religion* (January 1938), 1–18.
BERTON, PIERRE. *The Comfortable Pew.* Philadelphia, Pa.: J. B. Lippincott Company, 1965.
BESANCENEY, PAUL H. "On Reporting Rates of Intermarriage." *The American Journal of Sociology,* 70 (May 1965), 717–721.
BHATT, G. S. "Brahmo Samaj, Arya Samaj, and the Church-Sect Typology." *Review of Religious Research,* 10 (Fall 1968), 23–32.
BIDNEY, DAVID. "The Ethnology of Religion and the Problem of Human Evolution." *American Anthropologist,* 56 (February 1954), 1–18.
BINDER, LEONARD, *Religion and Politics in Pakistan.* Berkeley, Calif.: University of California Press, 1963.

BIRNBAUM, NORMAN. "Conflicting Interpretations of the Rise of Capitalism: Marx and Weber." *British Journal of Sociology* (June 1953), 125–141.

——, and GERTRUDE LENZER. *Sociology and Religion. A Book of Readings.* Englewood Cliffs, N.J.: Prentice-Hall, Inc., 1969.

BLACK, MAX, ed. *The Social Theories of Talcott Parsons.* Englewood Cliffs, N.J.: Prentice-Hall, Inc., 1961.

BLANSHARD, PAUL. *American Freedom and Catholic Power*, rev. ed. Boston, Mass.: The Beacon Press, 1958.

——. *Communism, Democracy, and Catholic Power.* Boston, Mass.: The Beacon Press, 1951.

——. *God and Man in Washington.* Boston, Mass.: The Beacon Press, 1960.

——. *Paul Blanshard on Vatican II.* Boston, Mass.: The Beacon Press, 1966.

BOAS, FRANZ, ed. *General Anthropology.* Boston, Mass.: D. C. Heath & Company, 1938.

BOCK, E. WILBUR. "Symbols in Conflict: Official versus Folk Religion." *Journal for the Scientific Study of Religion*, 5 (Spring 1966), 204–212.

BOISEN, ANTON T. "Economic Distress and Religious Experience." *Psychiatry* (May 1939), 185–194.

——. *The Exploration of the Inner World. A Study of Mental Disorder and Religious Experience.* New York: Harper and Row, Publishers, Inc., 1936.

——. "Religion and Hard Times. A Study of the Holy Rollers." *Social Action* (March 15, 1939), 8–35.

BONHOEFFER, DIETRICH. *Letters and Papers from Prison*, third ed. Edited by Eberhard Bethge. London: SCM Press, 1967.

——. *The Way to Freedom.* New York: Harper and Row, Publishers, Inc., 1967.

BORHEK, J. T. "Role-Orientations and Organizational Stability." *Human Organization*, 24 (Winter 1965), 332–338.

BOULARD, FERNAND. *An Introduction to Religious Sociology, Pioneer Work in France.* Translated by M. J. Jackson. London: Darton, Longman and Todd, 1960.

BRADEN, CHARLES S. *Christian Science Today: Power, Policy, Practice.* Dallas, Texas: Southern Methodist University Press, 1958.

——. *The Rise and Development of New Thought.* Dallas, Texas: Southern Methodist University Press, 1963.

——. *These Also Believe. A Study of Modern American Cults and Minority Religious Movements.* New York: The Macmillan Company, 1949.

——. *War, Communism, and World Religions.* New York: Harper and Row, Publishers, Inc., 1953.

——. "Why Are the Cults Growing?" *Christian Century* (January 12, 1944), 45–47; (January 19, 1944), 78–80; (January 26, 1944), 108–110; (February 2, 1944), 137–140.

BRADEN, WILLIAM. *The Private Sea: LSD and the Search for God.* New York: Quadrangle Books, 1967.

BRAILSFORD, H. N. *The Levellers and the English Revolution.* Edited and prepared for publication by Christopher Hill. London: The Cresset Press, 1961.

BRANDON, S. G. F. *Jesus and the Zealots.* New York: Charles Scribner's Sons, 1968.

BRANT, CHARLES. "Peyotism Among the Kiowa-Apache and Neighboring Tribes." *Southwestern Journal of Anthropology*, 6 (1950), 212–222.

BREASTED, JAMES H. *The Dawn of Conscience.* New York: Charles Scribner's Sons, 1933.

——. *Development of Religion and Thought in Ancient Egypt.* New York: Charles Scribner's Sons, 1912.

BREDEMEIER, HARRY C. "The Methodology of Functionalism." *American Sociological Review*, 20 (April 1955), 173–180.

BRESSLER, MARVIN, and CHARLES J. WESTOFF. "Catholic Education, Economic Values, and Achievement." *The American Journal of Sociology*, 69 (November 1963), 225–233.

BREWER, EARL D. C. "Sect and Church in Methodism." *Social Forces*, 30 (May 1952), 400–408.

BRIDSTON, KEITH R., and DWIGHT W. CULVER, eds. *The Making of Ministers: Essays on Clergy Training Today.* Minneapolis, Minn.: Augsburg Publishing House, 1964.

BROCK, TIMOTHY C. "Implications of Conversion and Magnitude of Cognitive Dissonance." *Journal for the Scientific Study of Religion*, 1 (Spring 1962), 198–203.

BROTHERS, JOAN, ed. *Readings in the Sociology of Religion.* London: Pergamon Press, 1967.

BROWN, DANIEL G. and WARNER L. LOWE. "Religious Beliefs and Personality Characteristics of College Students." *Journal of Social Psychology* (February 1951), 103–129.

BROWN, L. B. "The Structure of Religious Belief." *Journal for the Scientific Study of Religion*, 5 (Spring 1966), 259–272.

BROWN, WILLIAM MCAFEE. *The Ecumenical Revolution.* Garden City, N.Y.: Doubleday & Company, Inc., 1967.

BRUNNER, HEINRICH E. *Christianity and Civilization*, 2 vols. New York: Charles Scribner's Sons, 1948 and 1949.

BRYCE, JAMES. *The American Commonwealth*, new ed. New York: The Macmillan Company, 1917.

BUBER, MARTIN. *I and Thou*, second ed. Trans. by Ronald G. Smith. New York: Charles Scribner's Sons, 1958.

BUCK, PETER H. *Anthropology and Religion.* New Haven, Conn.: Yale University Press, 1939.

BUCKLEY, WALTER, ed. *Modern Systems Research for the Behavioral Scientists.* Chicago: Aldine Publishing Co., 1968.

———. *Sociology and Modern Systems Theory.* Englewood Cliffs, N.J.: Prentice-Hall, Inc., 1967.

BULTMANN, RUDOLF. *Jesus Christ and Mythology.* New York: Charles Scribner's Sons, 1958.

BURCHARD, WALDO W. "Role Conflicts of Military Chaplains." *American Sociological Review*, 19 (October 1954), 528–535.

BURCHINAL, LEE G. and LOREN E. CHANCELLOR. "Proportions of Catholics, Urbanism, and Mixed-Catholic Marriage Rates Among Iowa Counties." *Social Problems*, 9 (Spring 1962), 359–365.

———. "Survival Rates Among Religiously Homogamous and Interreligious Marriages." *Social Forces*, 41 (May 1963), 353–362.

BURR, NELSON, R. *A Critical Bibliography of Religion in America.* Vol. 4 of the Princeton Studies in American Civilization. Princeton, N.J.: Princeton University Press, 1961.

BURRIDGE, KENELM. *Mambu: A Melanesian Millennium.* London: Methuen and Co., Ltd., 1960.

BURROWS, MILLAR. *The Dead Sea Scrolls.* New York: The Viking Press, Inc., 1955.

CAHNMAN, WERNER J., ed. *Intermarriage and Jewish Life: A Symposium.* New York: The Herzl Press, 1963.

CALLAHAN, DANIEL. "The Quest for Social Relevance." *Daedalus*, 96 (Winter 1967), 151–179.

———, ed. *The Secular City Debate.* New York: The Macmillan Company, 1966.

CALVIN, JOHN. *Institutes of the Christian Religion*, 2 vols. Trans. by John Allen.

Sixth American ed. Revised and corrected. Philadelphia, Pa.: Presbyterian Board of Publication, 1921.

CAMPBELL, ERNST Q. and T. F. PETTIGREW. *Christians in Racial Crisis. A Study of Little Rock's Ministry.* Washington, D.C.: Public Affairs Press, 1959.

CAMPBELL, JOSEPH. *The Masks of God,* 3 vols. New York: The Viking Press, Inc., 1959–1964.

CAMUS, ALBERT. *The Collected Fiction of Albert Camus.* London: Hamish Hamilton, 1960.

———. *The Myth of Sisyphus and Other Essays.* Trans. by Justin O'Brien. New York: Alfred Knopf, Inc., 1955.

CANTRIL, HADLEY. *The Psychology of Social Movements.* New York: John Wiley & Sons, Inc., 1941.

CAPORALE, ROCCO. "The Dynamics of Hierocracy: Processes of Continuity-in-Change of the Roman Catholic System During Vatican II." *Sociological Analysis,* 28 (Summer 1967), 59–68.

CARMICHAEL, STOKELY and CHARLES V. HAMILTON. *Black Power.* New York: Vintage Books, 1967.

CARRIER, HERVÉ. "La Religion des Étudiants Américains." *Archives de Sociologie des Religion,* 12 (1961), 89–102.

———. *The Sociology of Religious Belonging.* New York: Herder and Herder, 1965.

———, and EMILLE PIN. *Sociologie du Christianisme. Bibliographie Internationale.* In French and English. Rome: Presses de l'Université Grégorienne, 1964.

CARTER, PAUL ALLEN. *The Decline and Revival of the Social Gospel: Social and Political Liberalism in American Protestant Churches, 1920–1940.* Ithaca, N.Y.: Cornell University Press, 1956.

CATTELL, R. B. "The Principal Culture Patterns Discoverable in the Syntal Dimensions of Existing Nations." *Journal of Social Psychology,* 32 (1950), 215–253.

CATTON, WILLIAM R., JR. *From Animistic to Naturalistic Sociology.* New York: McGraw-Hill Book Company, Inc., 1966.

———. "What Kind of People Does a Religious Cult Attract?" *American Sociological Review,* 22 (October 1957), 561–566.

CELL, EDWARD, ed. *Religion and Contemporary Western Culture.* Nashville, Tenn.: Abingdon Press, 1967.

CHAN, WING-TSIT. *Religious Trends in Modern China.* New York: Columbia University Press, 1953.

CHILDS, MARQUIS W. and DOUGLASS CATER. *Ethics in a Business Society.* New York: Mentor Books, 1954.

CHMAJ, BETTY E. "Paranoid Politics. The Radical Right and the South." *Atlantic Monthly,* 210 (November 1962), 91–97.

CLARK, ELMER T. "Non-Theological Factors in Church Diversity." *Ecumenical Review* (July 1951), 347–356.

———. *The Small Sects in America.* Revised and enlarged ed. New York: Abindon-Cokesbury Press, 1949.

CLARK, S. D. *Church and Sect in Canada.* Toronto, Ont.: University of Toronto Press, 1948.

CLARK, WALTER H. *The Oxford Group. Its History and Significance.* New York: Bookman Associates, 1951.

———. *The Psychology of Religion.* New York: The Macmillan Company, 1958.

COGLEY, JOHN. *Religion in a Secular Age. The Search for Final Meaning.* New York: Frederick A. Praeger, Inc., 1968.

COHN, NORMAN. *The Pursuit of the Millennium,* 2nd ed. New York: Harper and Row, Publishers, Inc., 1961.

COHN, WERNER. "Is Religion Universal? Problems of Definition." *Journal for the Scientific Study of Religion,* 2 (Fall 1962), 25–33.

COHN, WERNER. "Jehovah's Witnesses as a Proletarian Movement." *The American Scholar,* 24 (Summer 1955), 281–298.

——. "What Is Religion? An Analysis for Cross-Cultural Comparisons." *Journal of Christian Education,* 7 (November 1964), 116–138.

COLEMAN, JAMES S. "Social Cleavage and Religious Conflict." *Journal of Social Issues,* 12 (1956), 44–56.

COLEMAN, JOHN A. "Church-Sect Typology and Organizational Precariousness." *Sociological Analysis,* 29 (Summer 1968), 55–66.

COMMISSION ON RELIGION IN THE PUBLIC SCHOOLS. *Religion in the Public Schools.* Washington, D.C.: American Association of School Administrators, 1964.

COMPTON, JOHN J. "Some Contributions of the History of Science to Self-Clarity in Religion." *Journal for the Scientific Study of Religion,* 3 (Spring 1964), 147–157.

COMTE, AUGUSTE. *System of Positive Polity. Instituting the Religion of Humanity,* 4 vols. New York: Burt Franklin, Research and Source Works Series, 1966.

CONLIN, JOSEPH R., ed. *American Anti-War Movements.* Beverly Hills, Calif.: The Glencoe Press, 1968.

CORNFORD, Francis M. *From Religion to Philosophy.* New York: Longmans, Green & Company, 1912.

COSER, LEWIS A. *Continuities in the Study of Social Conflict.* New York: The Free Press, 1967.

——. *The Functions of Social Conflict.* New York: The Free Press, 1954.

COULTON, G. G. *Five Centuries of Religion,* 4 vols. Cambridge, England: Cambridge University Press, 1923–1936.

COX, HARVEY. *On NOT Leaving It to the Snake.* New York: The Macmillan Company, 1967.

——. "The 'New Breed' in American Churches: Sources of Social Activism in American Religion." *Daedalus,* 96 (Winter 1967), 135–150.

——. *The Secular City.* New York: The Macmillan Company, 1965.

——. "Sociology of Religion in a Post-Religious Era." *The Christian Scholar,* 48 (Spring 1965), 9–26.

CRAGG, G. R. "Disunities Created by Differing Patterns of Church Life." *Ecumenical Review* (April 1952), 276–281.

CROOG, SYDNEY H. and JAMES E. TEELE. "Religious Identity and Church Attendance of Sons of Religious Intermarriages." *American Sociological Review,* 32 (February 1967), 93–103.

CROSS, FRANK MOORE, JR. *The Ancient Library of Qumran and Modern Biblical Studies,* rev. ed. Garden City, N.Y.: Doubleday & Company, Inc., 1961.

CROSSMAN, RICHARD, ed. *The God That Failed.* New York: Harper and Row, Publishers, Inc., 1949.

CROW, PAUL A. *The Ecumenical Movement in Bibliographic Outline.* New York: National Council of Churches, 1965.

CULVER, DWIGHT W. *Negro Segregation in the Methodist Church.* New Haven, Conn.: Yale University Press, 1953.

CUMMING, ELAINE and CHARLES HARRINGTON. "Clergyman as Counselor." *The American Journal of Sociology,* 69 (November 1963), 234–243.

CURTI, MERLE. *Peace or War, The American Struggle, 1636–1936.* New York: W. W. Norton & Company, Inc., 1936.

CURTISS, JOHN S. *Church and State in Russia, The Last Years of the Empire, 1900–1917.* New York: Columbia University Press, 1940.

——. *The Russian Church and the Soviet State, 1917–1950.* Boston, Mass.: Little, Brown and Company, 1953.

CUTLER, DONALD R., ed. *The Religious Situation: 1968.* Boston, Mass.: Beacon Press, 1968.

Daedalus. "Religion in America." 96 (Winter 1967), Whole Issue.

DAHRENDORF, RALF. *Class and Class Conflict in Industrial Society.* Stanford, Calif.: Stanford University Press, 1959.

———. *Essays in the Theory of Society.* Stanford, Calif.: Stanford University Press, 1968.

———. *Gesellschaft und Freiheit.* Munich: R. Piper and Co., 1961.

———. "Out of Utopia: Toward a Reorientation of Sociological Analysis." *American Journal of Sociology,* 64 (September 1958), 115–127.

DANIEL, VATTEL E. "Ritual and Stratification in Chicago Negro Churches." *American Sociological Review,* 7 (June 1942), 352–361.

D'ANTONIO, WILLIAM V. and FREDERICK B. PIKE, eds. *Religion, Revolution, and Reform: New Forces for Change in Latin America.* New York: Frederick A. Praeger, Inc., 1964.

DANZIG, DAVID. "The Radical Right and the Rise of the Fundamentalist Minority." *Commentary* (April 1962), 291–298.

DATOR, JAMES ALLEN. "The Sōka Gakkai: A Socio-Political Interpretation." *Contemporary Religions in Japan,* 6 (September 1965), 205–242.

DAVIES, A. POWELL. *The Meaning of the Dead Sea Scrolls.* New York: The New American Library, 1956.

DAVIES, W. D. *The Setting of the Sermon on the Mount.* Cambridge, England: Cambridge University Press, 1964.

DAVIS, ALLISON W., B. B. GARDNER, and M. R. GARDNER. *Deep South.* Chicago, Ill.: University of Chicago Press, 1941.

DAVIS, KINGSLEY. *Human Society.* New York: The Macmillan Company, 1949.

———. "The Myth of Functional Analysis as a Special Method in Sociology and Anthropology." *American Sociological Review,* 24 (December 1959), 752–772.

DEMERATH, N. J., III. *Social Class in American Protestantism.* Chicago, Ill.: Rand McNally & Company, 1965.

———. "Synecdoche and Structural-Functionalism." *Social Forces,* 44 (March 1966), 390–401.

———, and PHILLIP E. HAMMOND. *Religion in Social Context.* New York: Random House, Inc., 1969.

DEMERATH, N. J., III, and RICHARD A. PETERSON, eds. *System, Change, and Conflict.* New York: The Free Press, 1967.

DEMERATH, N. J., III, and VICTOR THIESSEN. "On Spitting Against the Wind: Organizational Precariousness and American Irreligion." *The American Journal of Sociology,* 71 (May 1966), 674–687.

DESROCHE, HENRI. *Marxisme et Religions.* Paris: Presses Universitaires de France, 1962.

———. "Religion et développement. Le thème de leurs rapports réciproques et ses variations." *Archives de Sociologie des Religion* (1961), 3–34.

———. *Socialismes et Sociologie religieuse.* (Textes de Friedrich Engels traduits et présentés avec le concours de G. Dunstheimer et M. L. Letendre.) Paris: Éditions Cujas, 1965.

———. "Sociologie religieuse et sociologie fonctionnelle." *Archives de Sociologie des Religions,* 23 (January–June 1967), 3–17.

DEWEY, JOHN A. *A Common Faith.* New Haven, Conn.: Yale University Press, 1934.

———. *Intelligence in the Modern World.* Ed. by Joseph Ratner. New York: The Modern Library, 1939.

———, and JAMES H. TUFTS. *Ethics.* New York: Holt, Rinehart & Winston, Inc., 1908.

DIAMONT, ALFRED. *Austrian Catholics and the First Republic.* Princeton, N.J.: Princeton University Press, 1960.

DIERENFIELD, RICHARD B. *Religion in American Public Schools.* Washington, D.C.: Public Affairs Press, 1962.

DILLINGHAM, HARRY C. "Protestant Religion and Social Status." *The American Journal of Sociology,* 70 (January 1965), 416–422.

DITTES, JAMES E. "Secular Religion: Dilemma of Churches and Researchers." *Review of Religious Research,* 10 (Winter 1969), 65–81.

DOLLARD, JOHN. *Caste and Class in a Southern Town.* New Haven, Conn.: Yale University Press, 1937.

DOUGLASS, H. PAUL. *The Church in the Changing City.* New York: Harper and Row, Publishers, Inc., 1927.

———. "Cultural Differences and Recent Religious Divisions." *Christendom* (Winter 1945), 89–105.

———. *The Springfield Church Survey.* New York: George H. Doran Co., 1926.

———, and EDMUND DE S. BRUNNER. *The Protestant Church as a Social Institution.* New York: Harper and Row, Publishers, Inc., 1935.

DOUGLASS, JAMES W. *The Non-Violent Cross. A Theology of Revolution and Peace.* New York: The Macmillan Company, 1968.

DOUGLASS, TRUMAN B. "Ecological Changes and the Church." *Annals of the American Academy,* 332 (November 1960), 80–88.

DRAKE, ST. CLAIR, and HORACE R. CAYTON. *Black Metropolis.* New York: Harcourt, Brace & World, Inc., 1945.

DREGER, RALPH M. "Some Personality Correlates of Religious Attitudes as Determined by Projective Techniques." *Psychological Monographs,* **66** (1952).

DUCASSE, C. J. *A Philosophical Scrutiny of Religion.* New York: The Ronald Press Company, 1953.

DUNLAP, KNIGHT. *Religion. Its Functions in Human Life.* New York: McGraw-Hill Book Company, Inc., 1946.

DURKHEIM, EMILE. *The Division of Labor in Society.* Trans. by George Simpson. New York: The Free Press, 1947.

———. *The Elementary Forms of the Religious Life.* Trans. by Joseph W. Swain. New York: The Free Press, 1947.

———. *Moral Education. A Study in the Theory and Application of the Sociology of Education.* Everett K. Wilson, ed. Trans. by Everett K. Wilson and Herman Schnurer. New York: The Free Press, 1961.

———. *The Rules of Sociological Method,* 8th ed. Chicago, Ill.: University of Chicago Press, 1938.

———. *Sociology and Philosophy.* Trans. by D. F. Pocock. New York: The Free Press, 1953.

DURNBAUGH, DONALD F. *The Believers' Church. The History and Character of Radical Protestantism.* New York: The Macmillan Company, 1968.

DYNES, RUSSELL R. "Church-Sect Typology and Socio-Economic Status." *American Sociological Review,* 20 (October 1955), 555–560.

———. "The Consequences of Sectarianism for Social Participation." *Social Forces,* 35 (May 1957), 331–334.

EATON, JOSEPH W. and ROBERT J. WEIL. *Culture and Mental Disorders.* New York: The Free Press, 1955.

EBERSOLE, LUKE E. *Church Lobbying in the Nation's Capitol.* New York: The Macmillan Company, 1951.

———. "Religion and Politics." *Annals of the American Academy,* 332 (November 1960), 101–111.

ECKARDT, A. ROY. *The Surge of Piety in America. An Appraisal.* New York: Association Press, 1958.

EDDY, MARY BAKER G. *Science and Health With Key to the Scriptures,* 19th ed., revised, Boston, Mass.: Published by the Author, 1886.

EDEL, ABRAHAM. *Ethical Judgment. The Use of Science in Ethics.* New York: The Free Press, 1955.

EDWARDS, DAVID L., ed. *The Honest to God Debate.* London: SCM Press, 1963.

EHRMANN, HENRY W., ed. *Democracy in a Changing Society.* New York: Frederick A. Praeger, Inc., 1964.

EISENSTADT, S. N. *The Political Systems of Empires.* New York: The Free Press, 1963.

——, ed. *The Protestant Ethic and Modernization. A Comparative View.* New York: Basic Books, Inc., 1968.

——. "Transformation of Social, Political, and Cultural Orders in Modernization." *American Sociological Review,* 30 (October 1965), 659–673.

EISTER, ALLAN W. *Drawing Room Conversion: A Sociological Account of the Oxford Group Movement.* Durham, N.C.: Duke University Press, 1950.

——. "Perspective on the Functions of Religion in a Developing Country: Islam in Pakistan." *Journal for the Scientific Study of Religion,* 3 (Spring 1964), 227–238.

——. "Religious Institutions in Complex Societies: Difficulties in the Theoretic Specification of Functions." *American Sociological Review,* 22 (August 1957), 387–391.

ELIADE, MIRCEA. *Cosmos and History.* Trans. by Willard R. Trask. New York: Harper and Row, Publishers, Inc., 1959.

——. *The Sacred and the Profane.* Trans. by Willard R. Trask. New York: Harcourt, Brace & World, Inc., 1959.

——. *Shamanism. Archaic Techniques of Ecstasy.* Trans. by Willard R. Trask. New York: Bollingen Foundation, 1964.

——, and JOSEPH KITAGAWA, eds. *The History of Religions. Essays in Methodology.* Chicago, Ill.: University of Chicago Press, 1959.

ELINSON, HOWARD. "The Implications of Pentecostal Religion for Intellectualism, Politics, and Race Relations." *The American Journal of Sociology,* 70 (January 1965), 403–415.

ELLSWORTH, CLAYTON S. "The American Churches and the Mexican War." *American Historical Review* (January 1940), 301–326.

ENGLAND, R. W. "Some Aspects of Christian Science as Reflected in Letters of Testimony." *American Journal of Sociology,* 59 (March 1954), 448–453.

ENNIS, PHILIP H. "Ecstasy and Everyday Life." *Journal for the Scientific Study of Religion,* 6 (Spring 1967), 40–48.

ERASMUS, CHARLES J. "Obviating the Functions of Functionalism." *Social Forces,* 45 (March 1967), 319–328.

ERIKSON, ERIK H. *Young Man Luther. A Study in Psychoanalysis and History.* New York: W. W. Norton and Co., 1958.

ERIKSON, KAI T. *Wayward Puritans: A Study in the Sociology of Deviance.* New York: John Wiley & Sons, Inc., 1966.

ERNST, MORRIS L. and DAVID LOTH. *Report on the American Communist.* New York: Holt, Rinehart & Winston, Inc., 1952.

ERSKINE, HAZEL G. "The Polls: Personal Religion." *Public Opinion Quarterly,* 29 (Spring 1965), 145–157.

ESSIEN-UDOM, E. U. *Black Nationalism. A Search for Identity in America.* Chicago, Ill.: University of Chicago Press, 1962.

ETZIONI, AMITAI. "The Ghetto—A Re-Evaluation." *Social Forces,* 37 (March 1959), 255–262.

——, and EVA ETZIONI, eds. *Social Change. Sources, Patterns, and Consequences.* New York: Basic Books, 1964.

EVANS-PRITCHARD, E. E. *Nuer Religion.* Oxford: Oxford University Press, 1956.

——. *Theories of Primitive Religion.* Oxford: The Clarendon Press, 1965.

——. *Witchcraft, Oracles, and Magic Among the Azande.* Oxford: The Clarendon Press, 1937.

EVERS, HANS-DIETER. "The Buddhist Sangha in Ceylon and Thailand." *Sociologus*, 18 (1968), 20–35.

FACKENHEIM, EMIL L. "On the Self-Exposure of Faith to the Modern-Secular World: Philosophical Reflections in the Light of Jewish Experience." *Daedalus*, 96 (Winter 1967), 193–219.

FALLDING, HAROLD. "A Proposal for the Empirical Study of Values." *American Sociological Review*, 30 (April 1965), 223–233.

FANFANI, AMINTORE. *Catholicism, Protestantism, and Capitalism*. London: Sheed and Ward, 1935.

FANON, FRANTZ. *The Wretched of the Earth*. (Preface by Jean-Paul Sartre.) New York: Grove Press, 1963.

FAULKNER, JOSEPH E. and GORDON F. DEJONG. "Religiosity in 5-D: An Empirical Analysis." *Social Forces*, 45 (December 1966), 246–254.

FAUSET, ARTHUR H. *Black Gods of the Metropolis*. Vol. 3 of publications of Philadelphia Anthropological Society. Philadelphia, Pa.: University of Pennsylvania Press, 1944.

FEDERAL COUNCIL OF CHURCHES OF CHRIST IN AMERICA. "The Malvern Conference Report—Official Version." *Information Service* (May 31, 1941).

——. *A Message from the National Study Conference on the Churches and a Just and Durable Peace*, March 3–5, 1942.

——. *Report of the First Meeting* (Philadelphia, 1908). New York: Fleming H. Revell Company, 1909.

FENN, RICHARD K. "The Death of God: An Analysis of Ideological Crisis." *Review of Religious Research*, 9 (Spring 1968), 171–181.

FESTINGER, LEON. *A Theory of Cognitive Dissonance*. Evanston, Ill.: Row, Peterson, & Company, 1957.

——, and RIECKEN, HENRY. *When Prophecy Fails*. Minneapolis, Minn.: University of Minnesota Press, 1956.

FETTER, GEORGE C. "A Comparative Study of Attitudes of Christian and of Moslem Lebanese Villagers." *Journal for the Scientific Study of Religion*, 4 (Fall 1964), 48–59.

FEUER, LEWIS S., and MERVYN W. PERRINE. "Religion in a Northern Vermont Town: A Cross-Century Comparative Study." *Journal for the Scientific Study of Religion*, 5 (Fall 1966), 367–382.

FEUERBACH, LUDWIG. *The Essence of Christianity*. Trans. by George Eliot. New York: Harper and Row, Publishers, Inc., 1957.

FICHTER, JOSEPH H. *Dynamics of a City Church*. Chicago, Ill.: University of Chicago Press, 1951.

——. "The Marginal Catholic: An Institutional Approach." *Social Forces* (December 1953), 167–173.

——. *Parochial School: A Sociological Study*. Notre Dame, Ind.: University of Notre Dame Press, 1958.

——. *Priest and People*. New York: Sheed & Ward, Inc., 1965.

——. *Social Relations in the Urban Parish*. Chicago, Ill.: University of Chicago Press, 1954.

FINKELSTEIN, LOUIS. *The Jews, Their History, Culture, and Religion*, 2 vols. New York: Harper and Row, Publishers, Inc., 1949.

——. *The Pharisees: The Sociological Background of Their Faith*, 2 vols. Philadelphia, Pa.: The Jewish Publication Society of America, 1938.

FIRTH, RAYMOND. *The Fate of the Soul*. Cambridge, England: Cambridge University Press, 1955.

——. "The Theory of 'Cargo Cults'; a Note on Tikopia." *Man*, 5 (1955), 130–132.

——. *The Work of the Gods in Tikopia*, 2 vols. London: London School of Economics and Political Science, Monographs on Social Anthropology, Nos. 1 and 2, 1940.

FLETCHER, JOSEPH. *Situation Ethics.* Philadelphia, Pa.: Westminster Press, 1966.

FLETCHER, WILLIAM C. *A Study in Survival: The Church in Russia, 1927–1943.* New York: The Macmillan Company, 1965.

FORD, THOMAS R. "Status, Residence, and Fundamentalist Religious Beliefs in the Southern Appalachians." *Social Forces,* 39 (October 1960), 41–49.

FORTES, MEYER. *Oedipus and Job in West African Religion.* Cambridge: Cambridge University Press, 1959.

FORTUNE, R. F. "Manus Religion." *Memoirs of the American Philosophical Society,* 3 (1935).

FRANCIS, E. K. "The Russian Mennonites: From Religion to Ethnic Group." *American Journal of Sociology,* 54 (September 1948), 101–107.

FRANK, JEROME D. *Persuasion and Healing.* Baltimore, Md.: Johns Hopkins Press, 1961.

FRANKFORT, HENRI. *Ancient Egyptian Religion.* New York: Columbia University Press, 1948.

FRAZER, JAMES G. *The Golden Bough.* New York: The Macmillan Company, 1922.

FRAZIER, E. FRANKLIN. *The Negro Church in America.* New York: Schocken Books, Inc., 1963.

———. *Negro Youth at the Crossways.* Washington, D.C.: American Council on Education, 1940.

FREEMAN, SUSAN TAX. "Religious Aspects of the Social Organization of a Castilian Village." *American Anthropologist,* 70 (February 1968), 34–49.

FREMANTLE, ANNE, ed. *The Papal Encyclicals in Their Historical Context.* New York: The New American Library of World Literature, 1963.

FREUD, SIGMUND. *Civilization and Its Discontents.* Trans. by Joan Riviere. New York: Jonathan Cape and Harrison Smith, 1930.

———. *The Future of an Illusion.* Trans. by W. D. Robson-Scott. New York: Horace Liveright and The Institute of Psycho-Analysis, 1928.

———. *Moses and Monotheism.* Trans. by Katherine Jones. New York: Vintage Books, 1955.

———. *Totem and Taboo.* Trans. by A. A. Brill. New York: Moffat, Yard & Co., 1918.

FRIEDRICH, CARL J., ed. *Totalitarianism.* Cambridge, Mass.: Harvard University Press, 1954.

FRIESS, HORACE L., ed. "Religion and Health." *Review of Religion* (May 1946, March 1949), whole issues.

FROMM, ERICH. *Escape from Freedom.* New York: Holt, Rinehart & Winston, Inc., 1941.

———. *Man for Himself.* New York: Holt, Rinehart & Winston, Inc., 1947.

———. *Psychoanalysis and Religion.* New Haven, Conn.: Yale University Press, 1950.

———. *You Shall Be As Gods: A Radical Interpretation of the Old Testament and Its Tradition.* New York: Holt, Rinehart & Winston, Inc., 1966.

FUCHS, LAWRENCE H. *John F. Kennedy and American Catholicism.* New York: Meredith Press, 1967.

FÜRSTENBERG, FRIEDRICH, ed. *Religionssoziologie.* "Soziologische Texte," Vol. 19. Neuwied am Rhein and Berlin: Hermann Luchterhand Verlag, 1964.

FUKUYAMA, YOSHIO. "The Major Dimensions of Church Membership." *Review of Religious Research,* 2 (Spring 1961), 154–161.

GALLAGHER, BUELL G. *Color and Conscience: The Irrepressible Conflict.* New York: Harper and Row, Publishers, Inc., 1946.

GANS, HERBERT J. "American Jewry: Present and Future." *Commentary,* 21 (May 1956), 422–430.

———. "The Future of American Jewry." *Commentary* (June 1956), 555–563.

GARAUDY, ROGER, and QUENTIN LAUER. *A Christian-Communist Dialogue.* New York: Doubleday, 1969.

GARRISON, WINFRED E. "Characteristics of American Organized Religion." *Annals of the American Academy of Political and Social Science* (March 1948), 14–24.
———. "Social and Cultural Factors in Our Divisions." *Ecumenical Review* (October 1952), 43–51.
GASTER, THEODORE. *The Dead Sea Scriptures.* Garden City, N.Y.: Doubleday & Company, Inc., 1956.
GEERTZ, CLIFFORD. *The Religion of Java.* New York: The Free Press, 1960.
———. "Ritual and Social Change: A Javanese Example." *American Anthropologist,* 59 (1957), 23–54.
GEFFCKEN, HEINRICH. *Church and State,* 2 vols. London: Longmans, Green & Co., 1877.
GEORGE, CHARLES H. and KATHERINE GEORGE. *The Protestant Mind of the English Reformation, 1570–1640.* Princeton, N.J.: Princeton University Press, 1961.
GERLACH, LUTHER P. and VIRGINIA H. HINE. "Five Factors Crucial to the Growth and Spread of a Modern Religious Movement." *Journal for the Scientific Study of Religion,* 7 (Spring 1968), 23–40.
GERTH, HANS H. and C. WRIGHT MILLS. *Character and Social Structure.* New York: Harcourt, Brace & World, Inc., 1953.
GIBB, H. A. R. *Modern Trends in Islam.* Chicago, Ill.: University of Chicago Press, 1947.
GILKEY, LANGDON. "Social and Intellectual Sources of Contemporary Protestant Theology in America." *Daedalus,* 96 (Winter 1967), 69–98.
GILLILAND, A. R. "Changes in Religious Beliefs of College Students." *Journal of Social Psychology* (February 1953), 113–116.
GLADDEN, WASHINGTON. *Applied Christianity,* 6th ed. Boston, Mass.: Houghton Mifflin Company, 1886.
GLAZER, NATHAN. *American Judaism.* Chicago, Ill.: University of Chicago Press, 1957.
———. "The Jewish Revival in America." *Commentary,* 20 (December 1955), 493–499; (January 1956), 17–24.
———. "Negroes and Jews: The New Challenge to Pluralism." *Commentary,* 38 (December 1964), 29–34.
GLENN, NORVAL D., and RUTH HYLAND. "Religious Preference and Worldly Success: Some Evidence from National Surveys." *American Sociological Review,* 32 (February 1967), 73–85.
GLOCK, CHARLES Y. "The Sociology of Religion," in *Sociology Today,* Robert Merton, Leonard Broom, and Leonard Cottrell, eds. New York: Basic Books, 1959, 153–177.
———, BENJAMIN B. RINGER, and EARL R. BABBIE. *To Comfort and to Challenge.* Berkeley, Calif.: University of California Press, 1967.
GLOCK, CHARLES Y., and RODNEY STARK. *Christian Beliefs and Anti-Semitism.* New York: Harper and Row, Publishers, Inc., 1966.
———. *Religion and Society in Tension.* Chicago, Ill.: Rand McNally & Company, 1965.
GLUCKMAN, MAX. *Custom and Conflict in Africa.* New York: The Free Press, 1956.
GÖHRE, PAUL. *Die evangelisch-soziale Bewegung (ihre Geschichte und ihre Ziele).* Leipzig: Fr. Wilh. Grunow, 1896.
GOLDENWEISER, ALEXANDER. *Anthropology. An Introduction to Primitive Culture.* New York: Appleton-Century-Crofts, Inc., 1937.
GOLDSCHMIDT, DIETRICH. "Religionssoziologie in der Bundesrepublik Deutschland." *Archives de Sociologie des Religions,* 8 (1959), 53–70.
———, FRANZ GREINER, and HELMUT SCHELSKY, eds. *Soziologie der Kirchengemeinde.* Stuttgart: Ferdinand Enke Verlag, 1960.
GOLDSCHMIDT, DIETRICH, and JOACHIM MATTHES, eds. "Probleme der Religionsso-

ziologie." *Kölner Zeitschrift für Soziologie und sozialpsychologie, Sonderheft* 6 (1962).

GOLDSCHMIDT, WALTER. *Comparative Functionalism. An Essay in Anthropological Theory.* Berkeley, Calif.: University of California Press, 1966.

GOLDSEN, ROSE K., MORRIS ROSENBERG, ROBIN M. WILLIAMS, JR., and EDWARD A. SUCHMAN. *What College Students Think.* Princeton, N.J.: D. Van Nostrand Company, Inc., 1960.

GOLDSTEIN, BERNICE, and ROBERT L. EICHHORN. "The Changing Protestant Ethic: Rural Patterns in Health, Work, and Leisure." *American Sociological Review,* 26 (August 1961), 557–565.

GOOCH, G. P. *English Democratic Ideas in the Seventeenth Century.* Second ed., with supplementary notes and appendices by H. J. Laski. Cambridge: Cambridge University Press, 1927.

GOODE, ERICH. "Further Reflections on the Church-Sect Dimension." *Journal for the Scientific Study of Religion,* 6 (Fall 1967), 270–275. (A comment follows by N. J. Demerath, III, 275–279.)

———. "Social Class and Church Participation." *The American Journal of Sociology,* 72 (July 1966), 102–111.

———. "Some Critical Observations on the Church-Sect Dimension." *Journal for the Scientific Study of Religion,* 6 (Spring 1967), 69–77. (Comments follow by N. J. Demerath, III, and Allan W. Eister, 77–90.)

GOODE, WILLIAM J. *Religion Among the Primitives.* New York: The Free Press, 1951.

GOODENOUGH, ERWIN RAMSDELL. *The Psychology of Religious Experiences.* New York: Basic Books, 1965.

GOODY, JACK. "Religion and Ritual: The Definitial Problem." *British Journal of Sociology,* 12 (1961), 142–164.

GORDON, ALBERT I. *The Nature of Conversion.* Boston, Mass.: The Beacon Press, 1967.

GORDON, MILTON M. *Assimilation in American Life.* New York: Oxford University Press, 1964.

GORLOW, LEON, and HAROLD E. SCHROEDER. "Motives for Participating in the Religious Experience." *Journal for the Scientific Study of Religion,* 7 (Fall 1968), 241–251.

GOULDNER, ALVIN W. "Anti-Minotaur: The Myth of a Value-Free Sociology," *Social Problems,* 9 (Winter 1962), 199–213.

———. "Reciprocity and Autonomy in Functional Theory." *Symposium on Sociological Theory.* Llewellyn Gross, ed. Evanston, Ill.: Row, Peterson & Company, 1959, 241–270.

GRAFTON, THOMAS H. "Religious Origins and Sociological Theory." *American Sociological Review,* 10 (December 1945), 726–739.

GRANET, MARCEL. *Chinese Civilization.* Trans. by Kathleen Innes and Mabel Brailsford. London: Routledge and Kegan Paul, 1950.

GREELEY, ANDREW M. (with the assistance of William Van Cleve and Grace Ann Carroll). *The Changing Catholic College.* Chicago, Ill.: Aldine Publishing Co., 1967.

———. "Influence of the 'Religious Factor' on Career Plans and Occupational Values of College Graduates." *The American Journal of Sociology,* 68 (May 1963), 658–671.

———. "A Note on the Origins of Religious Differences." *Journal for the Scientific Study of Religion,* 3 (Fall 1963), 21–31.

———. "The Protestant Ethic: Time for a Moratorium." *Sociological Analysis,* 25 (Spring 1964), 20–33.

———. *Religion and Career: A Study of College Graduates.* New York: Sheed & Ward, Inc., 1963.

GREELEY, ANDREW M. "The Religious Behavior of Graduate Students." *Journal for the Scientific Study of Religion*, 5 (1965), 34–40.

——, and PETER H. ROSSI. *The Education of Catholic Americans*. Chicago, Ill.: Aldine Publishing Co., 1966.

GREEN, ROBERT W., ed. *Protestantism and Capitalism: The Weber Thesis and Its Critics*. Boston, Mass.: D. C. Heath & Company, 1959.

GREENBERG, BRADLEY S., and EDWIN B. PARKER, eds. *The Kennedy Assassination and the American Public*. Stanford, Calif.: Stanford University Press, 1965.

GREENSLADE, S. L. *Schism in the Early Church*. New York: Harper and Row, Publishers, Inc., 1953.

GREGOR, JAMES A. "Political Science and the Uses of Functional Analysis." *American Political Science Review*, 62 (June 1968), 425–439.

GROUP FOR THE ADVANCEMENT OF PSYCHIATRY. *Psychiatry and Religion: Some Steps Toward Mutual Understanding and Usefulness*. New York: Group for the Advancement of Psychiatry, 1960.

GRUNEBAUM, G. E. VON. "Studies in Islamic Cultural History." Comparative Studies of Cultures and Civilizations, No. 2. Robert Redfield and Milton Singer, eds. *American Anthropologist* (April 1954).

GUNTRIP, HENRY. *Psychotherapy and Religion*. New York: Harper and Row, Publishers, Inc., 1957.

GUSTAFSON, JAMES M. "The Clergy in the United States." *Daedalus*, 92 (1963), 724–744.

——. *Treasure in Earthen Vessels. The Church As a Human Community*. New York: Harper and Row, Publishers, Inc., 1961.

GUSTAFSON, PAUL. "UO-US-PS-PO: A Restatement of Troeltsch's Church-Sect Typology." *Journal for the Scientific Study of Religion*, 6 (Spring 1967), 64–68.

HAGEN, EVERETT E. *On the Theory of Social Change*. Homewood, Ill.: The Dorsey Press, 1962.

HAGER, DON J., CHARLES Y. GLOCK, and ISIDOR CHEIN, eds. "Religious Conflict in the United States." *Journal of Social Issues*, 12, No. 3 (1956), Whole Issue.

HAGOPIAN, ELAINE C. "Islam and Society-Formation in Morocco Past and Present." *Journal for the Scientific Study of Religion*, 3 (Fall 1963), 70–80.

HALL, THOMAS C. *The Religious Background of American Culture*. Boston, Mass.: Little, Brown, and Company, 1930.

HALLER, WILLIAM. *The Rise of Puritanism*. New York: Columbia University Press, 1938.

HAMILTON, THOMAS. "Social Optimism and Pessimism in American Protestantism." *Public Opinion Quarterly* (Summer 1942), 280–283.

HAMILTON, WILLIAM, and THOMAS J. J. ALTIZER. *Radical Theology and the Death of God*. Indianapolis, Ind.: The Bobbs-Merrill Co., Inc., 1966.

HAMMOND, J. L., and BARBARA HAMMOND. *The Town Labourer, 1760–1832. The New Civilisation*. New York: Longmans, Green & Company, 1928.

HAMMOND, PHILLIP E. *The Campus Clergyman*. New York: Basic Books, 1966.

——. "The Migrating Sect: An Illustration from Early Norwegian Immigration." *Social Forces*, 41 (March 1963), 275–283.

——. "Religion and the 'Informing' of Culture." *Journal for the Scientific Study of Religion*, 3 (Fall 1963), 97–105.

——, and ROBERT E. MITCHELL. "Segmentation of Radicalism—The Case of the Protestant Campus Minister." *American Journal of Sociology*, 71 (September 1965), 133–143.

HANDLIN, OSCAR. *Adventures in Freedom: Three Hundred Years of Jewish Life in America*. New York: McGraw-Hill Book Company, Inc., 1954.

HARRISON, JANE E. *Themis. A Study of the Social Origins of Greek Religion*. Cambridge, England: Cambridge University Press, 1912.

HARRISON, PAUL M. *Authority and Power in the Free Church Tradition: A Social Case Study of the American Baptist Convention.* Princeton, N.J.: Princeton University Press, 1959.

——. "Church and Laity Among Protestants." *Annals of the American Academy,* 332 (November 1960), 37–49.

HAVENS, JOSEPH. "The Changing Climate of Research on the College Student and His Religion." *Journal for the Scientific Study of Religion,* 3 (Fall 1963), 52–69.

——. "Memo on the Religious Implications of the Consciousness-Changing Drugs." *Journal for the Scientific Study of Religion,* 3 (Spring 1964), 216–226.

——. "The Participant's versus the Observer's Frame of Reference in the Psychological Study of Religion." *Journal for the Scientific Study of Religion,* 1 (October 1961), 79–87.

HAYES, CARLTON J. H. *Nationalism: A Religion.* New York: The Macmillan Company, 1960.

HEER, DAVID M. "The Trend of Interfaith Marriages in Canada: 1922–1957." *American Sociological Review,* 27 (April 1962), 245–250.

HEIMANN, BETTY. *Facets of Indian Thought.* New York: Schocken Books, 1964.

HEISE, DAVID R. "Prefatory Findings in the Sociology of Missions." *Journal for the Scientific Study of Religion,* 6 (Spring 1967), 49–63.

HEISS, JEROLD. "Premarital Characteristics of the Religiously Intermarried in an Urban Area." *American Sociological Review,* 25 (February 1960), 47–55.

HEMPEL, CARL G. "The Logic of Functional Analysis." *Symposium on Sociological Theory.* Llewellyn Gross, ed. Evanston, Ill.: Row, Peterson & Company, 1959, 271–310.

HERBERG, WILL. *Protestant-Catholic-Jew. An Essay in American Religious Sociology.* Garden City, N.Y.: Doubleday & Company, Inc., 1955.

——. "Religion in a Secularized Society." *Review of Religious Research,* 3 (Spring 1962), 145–158; and 4 (Fall 1962), 33–45.

HERO, ALFRED O., JR. "The American Public and the U.N." *The Journal of Conflict Resolution,* 10 (December 1966), 436–477.

HERSKOVITS, MELVILLE J. *Man and His Works.* New York: Alfred A. Knopf, Inc., 1951.

HIGHET, JOHN. "Scottish Religious Adherence." *British Journal of Sociology* (June 1953), 142–159.

HILL, CHRISTOPHER. *Society and Puritanism in Pre-Revolutionary England.* New York: Schocken Books, 1964.

HILTNER, SEWARD. "Freud for the Pastor." *Pastoral Psychology,* 5 (January 1955), 41–57.

HIMMELFARB, MILTON. "Church and State: How High a Wall." *Commentary* (July 1966). (A Commentary Report.)

HIRIYANNA, MYSORE. *The Essentials of Indian Philosophy.* London: George Allen & Unwin, Ltd., 1949.

HOBHOUSE, LEONARD T. *Morals in Evolution,* 6th ed. New York: Holt, Rinehart & Winston, Inc., 1929.

HOFFER, ERIC. *The True Believer.* New York: Harper and Row, Publishers, Inc., 1951.

HOLLOWAY, VERNON H. "Power Politics and the Christian Conscience." *Social Action* (February 1950), 5–35.

HOLT, ARTHUR E. "Organized Religion as a Pressure Group." *Annals of the American Academy of Political and Social Science* (May 1935), 42–49.

HOLT, JOHN B. "Holiness Religion: Cultural Shock and Social Reorganization." *American Sociological Review,* 5 (October 1940), 740–747.

HOLT, ROBERT T. and JOHN E. TURNER. *The Political Basis of Economic Develop-*

ment. An Exploration in Comparative Political Analysis. Princeton, N.J.: D. Van Nostrand Company, Inc., 1966.

HOLTOM, D. C. *Modern Japan and Shinto Nationalism.* Chicago, Ill.: University of Chicago Press, 1947.

HOMANS, GEORGE C. "Bringing Men Back In." *American Sociological Review,* 29 (December 1964), 809–815.

———. *The Human Group.* New York: Harcourt, Brace & World, Inc., 1950.

HOOK, SIDNEY. "The New Failure of Nerve." *Partisan Review* (January–February 1943), 2–23.

HOPKINS, CHARLES H. *The Rise of the Social Gospel in American Protestantism, 1865–1915.* New Haven, Conn.: Yale University Press, 1940.

HOPKINS, RAYMOND F. "Christianity and Sociopolitical Change in Sub-Saharan Africa." *Social Forces,* 44 (June 1966), 555–562.

HORI, ICHIRO. *Folk Religion in Japan. Continuity and Change.* Ed. by Joseph M. Kitagawa and Alan L. Miller. Chicago, Ill.: University of Chicago Press, 1968.

HORTON, ROBIN. "A Definition of Religion, and Its Uses." *Journal of the Royal Anthropological Institute,* 90, Pt. 2 (July–December 1960), 201–226.

HOUGH, JOSEPH C., JR. *Black Power and White Protestants: A Christian Response to the New Negro Pluralism.* New York: Oxford University Press, 1968.

HOULT, THOMAS. *The Sociology of Religion.* New York: Holt, Rinehart & Winston, Inc., 1958.

HOUTART, FRANÇOIS. "Les effets du changement social sur la religion catholique en Amérique latine." *Archives de Sociologie des Religions,* 12 (1961), 63–73.

———. "Critical Decisions and Institutional Tensions in a Religious Institution: The Case of Vatican II." *Review of Religion Research,* 9 (Spring 1968), 131–146.

HOWARD, PETER. *The World Rebuilt. The True Story of Frank Buchman and the Achievements of Moral Re-Armament.* New York: Duell, Sloan and Pearce, 1951.

HOWE, MARK DEWOLFE. *The Garden and the Wilderness. Religion and Government in American Constitutional History.* Chicago, Ill.: University of Chicago Press, 1965.

HOWELL, LEON. "The Delta Ministry." *Christianity and Crisis,* 26 (1966), 189–192.

HOWELLS, WILLIAM W. *The Heathens, Primitive Man and His Religions.* Garden City, N.Y.: Doubleday & Company, Inc., 1948.

HSU, FRANCIS L. K. *Americans and Chinese: Two Ways of Life.* New York: Abelard-Schuman, Ltd., 1953.

———. *Clan, Caste, and Club.* Princeton, N.J.: D. Van Nostrand Company, Inc., 1963.

HUBERT, HENRI, and MARCEL MAUSS. *Sacrifice: Its Nature and Function.* Trans. by W. D. Halls. Chicago, Ill.: University of Chicago Press, 1964.

HUDSON, WINTHROP S. "Are Churches Really Booming?" *Christian Century,* 72 (1955), 1494–1496.

———. "Puritanism and the Spirit of Capitalism." *Church History* (March 1949), 3–17.

———. *Religion in America.* New York: Charles Scribner's Sons, 1965.

HUGHES, H. STUART. *Conscience and Society: The Reorientation of European Thought, 1890–1930.* New York: Alfred A. Knopf, Inc., 1958.

HUNT, RICHARD A. "The Interpretation of the Religious Scale of the Allport-Vernon-Lindzey Study of Values." *Journal for the Scientific Study of Religion,* 7 (Spring 1968), 65–77.

HUNT, ROLFE LANIER. "Religion and Education." *Annals of the American Academy,* 332 (November 1960), 89–100.

HUNTER, GUY. *South-East Asia—Race, Culture, and Nation.* New York: Oxford University Press, 1966.

HUTCHISON, JOHN A., ed. *Christian Faith and Social Action.* New York: Charles Scribner's Sons, 1953.

HUTCHINSON, PAUL. "Have We a 'New' Religion?" *Life* (April 1955), 138–158.

HUXLEY, ALDOUS. *Doors of Perception and Heaven and Hell.* New York: Harper and Row, Publishers, Inc., 1954.

HUXLEY, JULIAN S. *Man Stands Alone.* New York: Harper and Row, Publishers, Inc., 1941.

———. *Religion Without Revelation.* New York: Mentor Books, 1958.

HYMA, ALBERT. *Christianity, Capitalism and Communism.* Ann Arbor, Mich.: Published by the author, 1937.

ISRAEL, HERMAN. "A Religious Basis for Solidarity in Industrial Society." *Social Forces,* 45 (September 1966), 84–95.

———. "Some Religious Factors in the Emergence of Industrial Society in England." *American Sociological Review,* 31 (October 1966), 589–599.

JACKSON, ELMORE. *Meeting of Minds.* New York: McGraw-Hill Book Company, Inc., 1952.

JACKSON, MICHAEL. "An Account of Religious Sociology in France." *The Sociological Review,* 7 (December 1959), 197–212.

JAMES, E. O. *Myth and Ritual in the Ancient Near East: An Archaeological and Documentary Study.* New York: Frederick A. Praeger, Inc., 1958.

———. *The Nature and Function of Priesthood: A Comparative and Anthropological Study.* New York: Vanguard Press, Inc., 1955.

JAMES, WILLIAM. *The Varieties of Religious Experience.* New York: The Modern Library. Originally published by Longmans, Green & Co., 1902.

JITODAI, TED T. "Migrant Status and Church Attendance." *Social Forces,* 43 (1964), 241–248.

JOHNSON, BENTON. "A Critical Appraisal of the Church-Sect Typology." *American Sociological Review,* 22 (February 1957), 88–92.

———. "Ascetic Protestantism and Political Preference." *Public Opinion Quarterly,* 26 (Spring 1962), 35–46.

———. "Ascetic Protestantism and Political Preference in the Deep South." *American Journal of Sociology,* 69 (January 1964), 359–366.

———. "Do Holiness Sects Socialize in Dominant Values?" *Social Forces,* 39 (May 1961), 309–316.

———. "On Church and Sect." *American Sociological Review,* 28 (August 1963). 539–549.

———. "Theology and Party Preference Among Protestant Clergymen." *American Sociological Review,* 31 (April 1966), 200–208.

———. "Theology and the Position of Pastors on Public Issues." *American Sociological Review,* 32 (June 1967), 433–442.

———, and RICHARD H. WHITE. "Protestantism, Political Preference, and the Nature of Religious Influence: Comment on Anderson's Paper." *Review of Religious Research,* 9 (Fall 1967), 28–35.

JOHNSON, CHARLES S. *Growing Up in the Black Belt.* Washington, D.C.: American Council on Education, 1941.

JONASSEN, CHRISTEN T. "The Protestant Ethic and the Spirit of Capitalism in Norway." *American Sociological Review,* 12 (December 1947), 676–686.

JONES, W. LAWSON. "Some Psychological Conditions of the Development of Methodism Up to 1850." *British Journal of .Psychology* (November 1951), 345–354.

JUNG, CARL G. *Modern Man in Search of a Soul.* Trans. by W. S. Dell and C. F. Boynes. New York: Harcourt, Brace & World, Inc., 1933.

———. *Psychology and Religion.* New Haven, Conn.: Yale University Press, 1938.

KANE, JOHN J. "Church and Laity Among Catholics." *Annals of the American Academy,* 332 (November 1960), 50–59.

KATZ, WILBUR G. *Religion and American Constitutions.* Evanston, Ill.: Northwestern University Press, 1964.

———, and HAROLD P. SOUTHERLAND. "Religious Pluralism and the Supreme Court." *Daedalus,* 96 (Winter 1967), 180–192.

KAUFMANN, WALTER A. *Nietzsche: Philosopher, Psychologist, Antichrist.* Princeton, N.J.: Princeton University Press, 1950.

KEENE, JAMES J. "Baha'i World Faith: Redefinition of Religion." *Journal for the Scientific Study of Religion,* 6 (Fall 1967), 221–235.

———. "Religious Behavior and Neuroticism, Spontaneity, and Worldmindedness." *Sociometry,* 30 (June 1967), 137–157.

KENNEDY, JOHN G. "Mushahara: A Nubian Concept of Supernatural Danger and the Theory of Taboo." *American Anthropologist,* 69 (December 1967), 685–702.

KENNEDY, ROBERT E., JR. "The Protestant Ethic and the Parsis." *American Journal of Sociology,* 68 (July 1962), 11–20.

KIDD, BENJAMIN. *Social Evolution.* New York: G. P. Putnam's Sons, 1920.

KIERKEGAARD, SÖREN. *Fear and Trembling* and *The Sickness Unto Death.* Trans. with intro. and notes by Walter Lowrie. Garden City, N.Y.: Doubleday & Company, Inc., 1954.

KIEV, ARI, ed. *Magic, Faith, and Healing. Studies in Primitive Psychiatry Today.* New York: The Free Press, 1964.

KING, IRVING. *The Development of Religion. A Study in Anthropology and Social Psychology.* New York: The Macmillan Company, 1910.

KING, LARRY L. "Bob Jones University: The Buckle on the Bible Belt." *Harper's,* 232 (June 1966), 51–57.

KING, MARTIN LUTHER, JR. *Stride Toward Freedom: The Montgomery Story.* New York: Harper and Row, Publishers, Inc., 1958.

———. *The Trumpet of Conscience.* New York: Harper and Row, Publishers, Inc., 1968.

———. *Why We Can't Wait.* New York: Harper and Row, Publishers, Inc., 1963.

KING, MORTON. "Measuring the Religious Variable: Nine Proposed Dimensions." *Journal for the Scientific Study of Religion,* 6 (Fall 1967), 173–190.

KING, WINSTON L. *Introduction to Religion.* New York: Harper and Row, Publishers, Inc., 1954.

———. *A Thousand Lives Away: Buddhism in Contemporary Burma.* Cambridge, Mass.: Harvard University Press, 1964.

KIRKPATRICK, CLIFFORD. *Religion in Human Affairs.* New York: John Wiley & Sons, Inc., 1929.

KITAGAWA, JOSEPH M. *Religion in Japanese History.* New York: Columbia University Press, 1966.

KLAUSNER, SAMUEL Z. "Images of Man: An Empirical Inquiry." *Journal for the Scientific Study of Religion,* 1 (October 1961), 61–73.

———. *Psychiatry and Religion.* New York: The Free Press, 1964.

———. "The Social Psychology of Courage." *Review of Religious Research,* 3 (1961), 63–72.

KLOETZLI, WALTER. *The Church and the Urban Challenge.* Philadelphia, Pa.: Muhlenberg Press, 1961.

KLOHR, OLAF, ed. *Religion und Atheism Heute. Ergebnisse und Aufgaben Marxistischer Religionssoziologie.* Berlin: VEB Deutsches Verlag der Wissenschaft, 1966.

KLUCKHOHN, CLYDE. *Navaho Witchcraft. Papers of the Peabody Museum of American Archaeology and Ethnology,* Harvard University, 22 (1944).

KLUCKHOHN, FLORENCE, and F. L. STRODTBECK. *Variations in Value-Orientations.* New York: Harper and Row, Publishers, Inc., 1961.

KNAPP, ROBERT H., and H. B. GOODRICH. *Origins of American Scientists.* Chicago, Ill.: University of Chicago Press, 1952.

KNUDTEN, RICHARD D., ed. *The Sociology of Religion. An Anthology.* New York: Appleton-Century-Crofts, 1967.

KOESTLER, ARTHUR. *The Age of Longing.* New York: The Macmillan Company, 1951.

———. *The Yogi and the Commissar.* New York: The Macmillan Company, 1946.

KOLARZ, WALTER. *Religion in the Soviet Union.* New York: St. Martin's Press, Inc., 1962.

KOLB, WILLIAM L. "Values, Postivism, and the Functional Theory of Religion: The Growth of a Moral Dilemma." *Social Forces,* 31 (May 1953), 305–311.

KRAMER, JUDITH R., and SEYMOUR LEVENTMAN. *Children of the Gilded Ghetto.* New Haven, Conn.: Yale University Press, 1961.

KRIKORIAN, YERVANT H., ed. *Naturalism and the Human Spirit.* New York: Columbia University Press, 1944.

KRINSKY, FRED, ed. *The Politics of Religion in America.* Beverly Hills, Calif.: The Glencoe Press, 1968.

KROEBER, A. L. *Anthropology.* New ed., revised. New York: Harcourt, Brace & World, Inc., 1948.

KUEHNELT-LEDDIHN, ERIK VON. "How Catholic are American Catholics?" *Catholic World,* 203 (April 1966), 42–47.

LABARRE, WESTON. *The Peyote Cult. Yale University Publication in Anthropology,* No. 19 (1938).

———. "Primitive Psychotherapy in Native American Cultures: Peyotism and Confession." *The Journal of Abnormal and Social Psychology,* 42 (July 1947), 294–309.

———. *They Shall Take Up Serpents: Psychology of the Southern Snake-Handling Cult.* Minneapolis, Minn.: University of Minnesota Press, 1962.

LADD, JOHN. *The Structure of a Moral Code.* Cambridge, Mass.: Harvard University Press, 1957.

LAMBERT, RICHARD D., issue ed. "Religion in American Society." *Annals of the American Academy of Political and Social Science,* 332 (November 1960), Whole Issue.

LANDIS, BENSON Y. "A Guide to the Literature on Statistics of Religious Affiliation with Reference to Related Social Studies." *Journal of the American Statistical Association,* 54 (June 1959), 335–357.

LANG, ANDREW. *Magic and Religion.* London: Longmans, Green & Co., 1901.

———. *The Making of Religion.* London: Longmans, Green & Co., 1898.

LANGER, SUZANNE K. *Philosophy in a New Key. A Study in the Symbolism of Reason, Rite, and Art,* 3rd ed. Cambridge, Mass.: Harvard University Press, 1957.

LANOUE, GEORGE R. *Public Funds for Parochial Schools?* New York: National Council of the Churches of Christ in the U.S.A., 1963.

LANTERNARI, VITTORIO. *The Religions of the Oppressed. A Study of Modern Messianic Cults.* Trans. by Lisa Sergio. New York: Alfred A. Knopf. Inc., 1963.

LASKI, HAROLD J. *The American Democracy.* New York: The Viking Press, Inc., 1948.

LASKI, MARGHANITA. *Ecstasy. A Study of Some Secular and Religious Experiences.* Bloomington, Ind.: Indiana University Press, 1961.

LATOURETTE, KENNETH S. *A History of Christianity.* New York: Harper and Row, Publishers, Inc., 1953.

LATREILLE, ANDRÉ, and ANDRÉ SIEGFRIED. *Les Forces Religieuses et la Vie Politique.* Paris: Librairie Armand Colin, 1951.

LAUE, JAMES H. "A Contemporary Revitalization Movement in American Race Relations: The 'Black Muslims'." *Social Forces,* 42 (March 1964), 315–323.

LAUMANN, EDWARD O. "The Social Structure of Religious and Ethnoreligious Groups in a Metropolitan Community." *American Sociological Review,* 34 (April 1969), 182–193.

LAWRENCE, PETER. *Road Belong Cargo.* Manchester: Manchester University Press, 1964.

LAZERWITZ, BERNARD. "A Comparison of Major United States Religious Groups." *Journal of the American Statistical Association,* 56 (September 1961), 568–579.

———. "Membership in Voluntary Associations and Frequency of Church Attendance." *Journal for the Scientific Study of Religion,* 2 (Fall 1962), 74–84.

———. "Some Factors Associated with Variation in Church Attendance." *Social Forces,* 39 (May 1961), 301–309.

———, and LOUIS ROWITZ. "The Three-Generations Hypothesis." *The American Journal of Sociology,* 69 (March 1964), 529–538.

LEARSI, RUFUS. *The Jews in America.* Cleveland: The World Publishing Co., 1954.

LEARY, TIMOTHY. *High Priest.* New York: New American Library, 1968.

LEBRA, WILLIAM. *Okinawan Religion.* Honolulu, Hawaii: University of Hawaii Press, 1966.

LEBRAS, GABRIEL. *Études de Sociologie Religieuse,* 2 vols. Paris: Presses Universitaires de France, 1955.

LEE, DOROTHY D. *Religious Perspectives in College Teaching in Anthropology.* New Haven, Conn.: The Edward W. Hazen Foundation.

LEE, JAMES M. *Catholic Education in the Western World.* Notre Dame, Ind.: University of Notre Dame Press, 1967.

LEE, J. OSCAR. "Religion among Ethnic and Racial Minorities." *Annals of the American Academy,* 332 (November 1960), 112–124.

LEE, ROBERT. *The Social Sources of Church Unity. An Interpretation of Unitive Movements in American Protestantism.* Nashville, Tenn.: Abingdon Press, 1960.

———, and MARTIN E. MARTY, eds. *Religion and Social Conflict.* New York: Oxford University Press, 1964.

LEEMING, BERNARD. *The Vatican Council and Christian Unity.* New York: Harper and Row, Publishers, Inc., 1966.

LENIN, V. I. *Religion.* New York: International Publishers, 1933.

LENSKI, GERHARD. *Power and Privilege: A Theory of Social Stratification.* New York: McGraw-Hill Book Company, Inc., 1966.

———. "Religion's Impact on Secular Institutions." *Review of Religious Research,* 4 (Fall 1962), 1–16.

———. *The Religious Factor. A Sociological Study of Religion's Impact on Politics, Economics, and Family Life.* Garden City, N.Y.: Doubleday & Company, Inc., 1961.

———. "Social Correlates of Religious Interest." *American Sociological Review,* 18 (October 1953), 533–544.

LEO XIII, POPE. *The Great Encyclical Letters of Pope Leo XIII,* 2nd ed. New York: Benziger Brothers, Inc., 1903.

LESLIE, CHARLES, ed. *Anthropology of Folk Religion.* New York: Vintage Books, 1960.

LESSA, WILLIAM A., and EVON Z. VOGT, eds. *Reader in Comparative Religion: An Anthropological Approach,* 2nd ed. New York: Harper and Row, Publishers, Inc., 1965.

LESSER, ALEXANDER. "Cultural Significance of the Ghost Dance." *American Anthropologist,* 35 (January–March 1933), 108–115.

LEUBA, JAMES H. *The Belief in God and Immortality*, 2nd ed. Chicago, Ill.: Open Court Publishing Company, 1921.
———. *The Psychology of Religious Mysticism*, 2nd ed. London: Routledge and Kegan Paul, Ltd., 1929.
———. *The Reformation of the Churches*. Boston, Mass.: The Beacon Press, 1950.
LEVI, WERNER. "Religion and Political Development: A Theoretical Analysis." *Bucknell Review*, 15 (1967), 70–95.
LEVY, MARION J., JR. *The Structure of Society*. Princeton, N.J.: Princeton University Press, 1952.
LEVY, REUBEN. *The Social Structure of Islam*. Cambridge: Cambridge University Press, 1957.
LEWIS, JOHN, KARL POLANYI, and DONALD K. KITCHIN, eds. *Christianity and the Social Revolution*. London: Victor Gollancz, Ltd., 1935.
LEWY, GUENTER. *The Catholic Church and Nazi Germany*. New York: McGraw-Hill Book Company, Inc., 1964.
LIEBMAN, JOSHUA L. *Peace of Mind*. New York: Simon and Schuster, Inc., 1946.
LIENHARDT, GODFREY. *Divinity and Experience*. London: Oxford University Press, 1961.
LIJPHART, AREND. *The Politics of Accommodation. Pluralism and Democracy in the Netherlands*. Berkeley, Calif.: University of California Press, 1968.
LINCOLN, C. ERIC. *The Black Muslims in America*. Boston, Mass.: The Beacon Press, 1961.
LINDSAY, THOMAS N. *A History of the Reformation*, 2 vols. New York: Charles Scribner's Sons, 1928.
LINTON, RALPH. "Nativistic Movements." *American Anthropologist*, 45 (April–June 1943), 230–240.
LIPSET, SEYMOUR M. *The First New Nation. The United States in Historical and Comparative Perspective*. New York: Basic Books, Inc., 1963.
———. *Revolution and Counterrevolution: Change and Persistence in Social Structures*. New York: Basic Books, 1968.
LIPSITZ, LEWIS. "If, as Verba Says, the State Functions as a Religion, What Are We to Do Then to Save Our Souls?" *American Political Science Review*, 62 (June 1968), 527–535.
LIU, WILLIAM T. "The Marginal Catholics in the South. A Revision of Concepts." *American Journal of Sociology*, 65 (January 1960), 383–390.
LO BELLO, NINO. *The Vatican Empire*. New York: Trident Press, 1968.
LOCKWOOD, DAVID. "Some Remarks on the 'Social System'." *British Journal of Sociology*, 7 (June 1956), 134–146.
LOESCHER, F. S. *The Protestant Church and the Negro*. New York: Association Press, 1948.
LOFLAND, JOHN. *Doomsday Cult*. Englewood Cliffs, N.J.: Prentice-Hall, Inc., 1966.
———, and RODNEY STARK. "Becoming a World-Saver: A Theory of Conversion to a Deviant Perspective." *American Sociological Review*, 30 (December 1965), 862–875.
LONG, EDWARD L. *War and Conscience in America*. Philadelphia, Pa.: Westminster Press, 1968.
LOOS, A. WILLIAM, ed. *Religious Faith and World Culture*. Englewood Cliffs, N.J.: Prentice-Hall, Inc., 1951.
LOWENTHAL, LEO, and NORBERT GUTERMAN. *Prophets of Deceit. A Study in the Techniques of the American Agitator*. New York: Harper and Row, Publishers, Inc., 1949.
LOWIE, ROBERT H. *Primitive Religion*. New York: Boni & Liveright, 1924.
LUCKMANN, THOMAS. *The Invisible Religion*. New York: The Macmillan Company, 1967.

LUTHER, MARTIN. *Luther's Primary Works.* Ed. by Henry Wace and C. A. Buckhein. London, 1896.

MACARTHUR, KATHLEEN W. *The Economic Ethics of John Wesley.* New York: The Abingdon Press, 1936.

McFARLAND, H. NEILL. *The Rush Hour of the Gods. A Study of New Religious Movements in Japan.* New York: The Macmillan Company, 1967.

McGIFFERT, ARTHUR C. *Martin Luther. The Man and His Work.* New York: Appleton-Century-Crofts, 1910.

MACIVER, R. M. *Social Causation.* Boston, Mass.: Ginn and Company, 1942.

———, and CHARLES H. PAGE. *Society. An Introductory Analysis.* New York: Holt, Rinehart & Winston, Inc., 1949.

MACK, RAYMOND W., RAYMOND J. MURPHY, and SEYMOUR YELLIN. "The Protestant Ethic, Level of Aspiration, and Social Mobility: An Empirical Test." *American Sociological Review,* 21 (June 1956), 295–300.

MACK, RAYMOND W., and RICHARD C. SNYDER. "The Analysis of Social Conflict—Toward an Over-view and Synthesis." *Journal of Conflict Resolution,* 1 (June 1957), 212–248.

McKINNEY, JOHN C. *Constructive Typology and Social Theory.* New York: Appleton-Century-Crofts, 1966.

MACKINSON, JAMES. *Calvin and the Reformation.* London: Longmans, Green & Co., 1936.

McLOUGHLIN, WILLIAM G. "Is There a Third Force in Christendom?" *Daedalus,* 96 (Winter 1967), 43–68.

———. *Modern Revivalism.* New York: The Ronald Press Company, 1959.

MacMURRAY, JOHN. *The Clue to History.* London: SCM Press, 1938.

———. *Creative Society. A Study of the Relation of Christianity to Communism.* New York: Association Press, 1936.

McNAMARA, ROBERT J. "Catholics and Academia." *Review of Religious Research,* 8 (Winter 1967), 81–95.

MAIR, LUCY P. "Independent Religious Movements in Three Continents." *Comparative Studies in Society and History,* 1 (January 1959), 113–136.

MALINOWSKI, BRONISLAW. *Argonauts of the Western Pacific.* London: Routledge and Kegan Paul, 1932.

———. *Coral Gardens and Their Magic,* 2 vols. London: George Allen and Unwin, Ltd., 1935.

———. *The Foundation of Faith and Morals.* London: Oxford University Press, 1936.

———. "Magic, Science, and Religion." *Science, Religion and Reality,* Joseph Needham, ed. New York: The Macmillan Company, 1925, 18–94.

———. *A Scientific Theory of Culture and Other Essays.* Chapel Hill, N.C.: The Univ. of North Carolina Press, 1944.

MANN, W. E. *Sect, Cult, and Church in Alberta.* Toronto, Ont.: University of Toronto Press, 1955.

MANNHEIM, KARL. *Diagnosis of Our Time.* London: Routledge and Kegan Paul, 1943.

———. *Essays on the Sociology of Knowledge.* Ed. by Paul Kecskemeti. New York: Oxford University Press, 1952.

———. *Freedom, Power, and Democratic Planning.* New York: Oxford University Press, 1950.

———. *Ideology and Utopia.* Trans. by Louis Wirth and Edward Shils. New York: Harcourt, Brace & World, Inc., 1936.

MAQUET, JACQUES J. *The Sociology of Knowledge.* Boston, Mass.: The Beacon Press, 1951.

MARANELL, GARY M. "An Examination of Some Religious and Political Attitude Correlates of Bigotry." *Social Forces,* 45 (March 1967), 356–363.

MARCUSE, HERBERT. *Eros and Civilization. A Philosophical Inquiry into Freud.* Boston, Mass.: The Beacon Press, 1966.

———. *Negations: Essays in Critical Theory.* Boston, Mass.: The Beacon Press, 1968.

———. *One Dimensional Man. Studies in the Ideology of Advanced Industrial Society.* Boston, Mass.: The Beacon Press, 1964.

MARETT, R. R. *The Threshold of Religion,* 2nd ed. London: Methuen & Co., Ltd., 1914.

———. *Faith, Hope and Charity in Primitive Religion.* Oxford: The Clarendon Press, 1932.

MARITAIN, JACQUES. *True Humanism.* Trans. by M. R. Adamson. London: Geoffrey Bles: The Centenary Press, 1938.

MARMORSTEIN, EMILE. "Religious Opposition to Nationalism in the Middle East." *International Affairs* (July 1952), 344–359.

MARRIOTT, McKIM. "Village India. Studies in the Little Community." *American Anthropologist,* 57 (June 1955), 53–77.

MARSH, ROBERT M. *Comparative Sociology.* New York: Harcourt, Brace and World, Inc., 1967.

MARTIN, DAVID A. "The Denomination." *British Journal of Sociology,* 13 (March 1962), 1–14.

———. *Pacifism. An Historical and Sociological Study.* London: Routledge and Kegan Paul, 1965.

———. *A Sociology of English Religion.* London: SCM Press, 1967.

MARTINDALE, DON, ed. *Functionalism in the Social Sciences. American Academy of Political and Social Sciences, Monograph* No. 5 (February 1965).

———. *The Nature and Types of Sociological Theory.* Boston, Mass.: Houghton Mifflin Company, 1960.

MARTY, MARTIN E. *The New Shape of American Religion.* New York: Harper and Row, Publishers, Inc., 1959.

———. "Sects and Cults." *Annals of the American Academy,* 332 (November 1960), 125–134.

———. "The Spirit's Holy Errand: The Search for a Spiritual Style in Secular America." *Daedalus,* 96 (Winter 1967), 99–115.

———. *Varieties of Unbelief.* New York: Holt, Rinehart and Winston, Inc., 1964.

MARX, GARY T. *Protest and Prejudice.* New York: Harper and Row, 1967.

———. "Religion: Opiate or Inspiration of Civil Rights Militancy Among Negroes?" *American Sociological Review,* 32 (February 1967), 64–72.

MARK, KARL and FRIEDRICH ENGELS. *Communist Manifesto.* Chicago, Ill.: Charles H. Kerr & Company, 1940.

———. *The German Ideology.* New York: International Publishers, 1939.

MASLOW, ABRAHAM H. *Religions, Values, and Peak-Experiences.* Columbus, Ohio: Ohio State University Press, 1964.

MATHER, RICHARD. "The Conflict of Buddhism with Native Chinese Ideologies." *The Review of Religion* (November 1955), 27–37.

MAY, HENRY F. *Protestant Churches and Industrial America.* New York: Harper and Row, Publishers, Inc., 1949.

MAY, ROLLO, ed. *Existence: A New Dimension in Psychiatry and Psychology.* New York: Basic Books, 1958.

MAYER, ALBERT J., and HARRY SHARP. "Religious Preference and Worldly Success." *American Sociological Review,* 27 (April 1962), 218–227.

MAYS, BENJAMIN E., and JOSEPH W. NICHOLSON. *The Negro's Church.* New York: Institute of Social and Religious Research, 1933.

MEAD, FRANK S. *Handbook of Denominations in the United States,* new 4th ed. New York: Abingdon Press, 1965.

MEANS, RICHARD L. "Protestantism and Economic Institutions: Auxiliary Theories to Weber's Protestant Ethic." *Social Forces*, 44 (March 1966), 372–381.

MECHAM, J. Lloyd. *Church and State in Latin America*, rev. ed. Chapel Hill: University of North Carolina Press, 1966.

MECKLIN, JOHN M. *The Story of American Dissent*. New York: Harcourt, Brace & World, Inc., 1934.

MEISSNER, W. W. *Annotated Bibliography in Religion and Psychology*. New York: The Academy of Religion and Mental Health, 1961.

MENDELSON, MICHAEL E. "Buddhism and the Burmese Establishment." *Archives de sociologie des religions*, 9 (January 1964), 85–95.

MENSCHING, GUSTAV. *Soziologie der Religion*. Bonn: Ludwig Rohrscheid Verlag, 1947.

MERTON, ROBERT K. *Social Theory and Social Structure*, rev. and enlarged ed. London: Collier-Macmillan, Ltd., 1957.

METRAUX, ALFRED. *Voodoo in Haiti*. New York: Oxford University Press, 1959.

MEYER, DONALD B. *The Protestant Search for Political Realism, 1919–1941*. Berkeley, Calif.: University of California Press, 1960.

MICKLEM, NATHANIEL. *National Socialism and the Roman Catholic Church*. London: Oxford University Press, 1939.

MIDDLETON, JOHN, ed. *Gods and Rituals. Readings in Religious Beliefs and Practices*. Garden City, N.Y.: The Natural History Press, 1967.

———. *Lugbara Religion. Ritual and Authority Among an East African People*. London: Oxford University Press, 1960.

———, ed. *Magic, Witchcraft, and Curing*. Garden City, N.Y.: The Natural History Press, 1967.

MIDDLETON, RUSSELL, and SNELL PUTNEY. "Religion, Normative Standards, and Behavior." *Sociometry*, 25 (June 1962), 141–152.

MILLER, ROBERT M. *American Protestantism and Social Issues, 1919–1939*. Chapel Hill, N.C.: University of North Carolina Press, 1958.

MILLER, WILLIAM L. "Piety Along the Potomac." *The Reporter* (August 1954), 25–28.

———. "Some Negative Thinking About Norman Vincent Peale." *The Reporter* (January 1955), 19–24.

MILLS, C. WRIGHT. *The Sociological Imagination*. New York: Grove Press, 1961.

MISIAK, HENRY. "Psychosomatic Medicine and Religion." *Catholic World* (February 1953), 342–345.

MITCHELL, ROBERT EDWARD. "Polity, Church Attractiveness, and Ministers' Careers: An Eight-Denomination Study of Interchurch Mobility." *Journal for the Scientific Study of Religion*, 5 (Spring 1966), 241–258.

MIYAKAWA, T. SCOTT. *Protestants and Pioneers. Individualism and Conformity on the American Frontier*. Chicago, Ill.: University of Chicago Press, 1964.

MOBERG, DAVID O. *The Church as a Social Institution. The Sociology of American Religion*. Englewood Cliffs, N.J.: Prentice-Hall, Inc., 1962.

———. "Social Class and the Churches." *Information Service*, 37 (June 1958), 6–8.

———. "Social Differentiation in the Netherlands." *Social Forces*, 39 (May 1961), 333–337.

MOEHLMAN, CONRAD H. *The Wall of Separation Between Church and State*. Boston, Mass.: The Beacon Press, 1951.

MOL, J. J. "Churches and Immigrants. A Sociological Study of the Mutual Effect of Religion and Emigrant Adjustment." *Research Group for European Migration Problems Bulletin*, 9, Supp. 5 (May 1961), whole issue.

MOLLEGEN, A. T. "A Christian View of Psychoanalysis." *Journal of Pastoral Care*, 6 (1952), 1–14.

MONOGHAN, ROBERT R. "Three Faces of the True Believer. Motivations for Attending a Fundamentalist Church." *Journal for the Scientific Study of Religion*, 6 (Fall 1967), 236–245.

MOONEY, JAMES. *The Ghost-Dance Religion and the Sioux Outbreak of 1890.* Abridged, with an Intro. by Anthony F. C. Wallace. Chicago, Ill.: University of Chicago Press, 1965.

MOORE, WILBERT E. *Order and Change: Essays in Comparative Sociology.* New York: John Wiley & Sons, Inc., 1967.

MORGAN, KENNETH W., ed. *The Religion of the Hindus.* New York: The Ronald Press Company, 1953.

MORIOKA, KIYOMI, and WILLIAM H. NEWELL. *The Sociology of Japanese Religion.* International Studies in Sociology and Social Anthropology, 6. Leiden: E. J. Brill, 1968.

MORRIS, CHARLES. *Varieties of Human Value.* Chicago, Ill.: University of Chicago Press, 1956.

MUELDER, WALTER G. *Methodism and Society in the Twentieth Century.* New York: Abingdon Press, 1961.

———. "From Sect to Church." *Christendom* (Autumn 1945), 450–462.

———. *Religion and Economic Responsibility.* New York: Charles Scribner's Sons, 1953.

MÜHLMANN, WILHELM E., and others. *Chiliasmus und Nativismus: Studien zur Psychologie, Soziologie und historischen Kasuistik der Umsturzbewegungen.* Berlin: Dietrich Reimer Verlag, 1961.

MULVANEY, B. G. "Catholic Population Revealed in Catholic Baptisms." *American Ecclesiastical Review*, 133 (1955), 183–193.

MURRAY, GILBERT. *Five Stages of Greek Religion*, 2nd ed. New York: Columbia University Press, 1925.

MURRAY, THOMAS E. *Nuclear Policy for War and Peace.* Cleveland, Ohio: The World Publishing Co., 1960.

MURVAR, VATRO. "Russian Religious Structures. A Study in Persistent Church Subservience." *Journal for the Scientific Study of Religion*, 7 (Spring 1968), 1–22.

MYERS, GEORGE C. "Patterns of Church Distribution and Movement." *Social Forces*, 40 (May 1962), 354–363.

MYRDAL, GUNNAR. *Asian Drama. An Inquiry into the Poverty of Nations*, 3 vols. New York: Random House, Inc., 1968.

NADEL, S. F. *Nupe Religion.* London: Routledge and Kegan Paul, 1954.

———. *The Theory of Social Structure.* New York: The Free Press, 1957.

———. "Two Nuba Religions: An Essay in Comparison." *American Anthropologist*, 57 (August 1955), 661–679.

NAGEL, ERNEST. *Logic Without Metaphysics*, New York: The Free Press, 1956.

———. *The Structure of Science.* New York: Harcourt, Brace & World, Inc., 1961.

NAGLE, WILLIAM J., ed. *Morality and Modern Warfare.* Baltimore, Md.: Helicon Press, 1960.

NASH, MANNING. *The Golden Road to Modernity. Village Life in Contemporary Burma.* New York: John Wiley and Sons, Inc., 1965.

NASH, PHILLEO. "The Place of Religious Revivalism in the Formation of the Intercultural Community on Klamath Reservation." *Social Anthropology of North American Tribes.* Fred Eggan, ed. Chicago, Ill.: University of Chicago Press, 1937.

NEEDHAM, JOSEPH, ed. *Science, Religion and Reality.* New York: The Macmillan Company, 1925.

NELSON, LOWRY. *The Mormon Village.* Salt Lake City, Utah: University of Utah Press, 1952.

NEUWIEN, REGINALD A., ed. *Catholic Schools in Action.* Notre Dame, Ind.: University of Notre Dame Press, 1966.

NEWMAN, JEREMIAH. *Change and the Catholic Church.* Baltimore, Md.: Helicon Press, 1965.

NICHOLS, JAMES H. *Democracy and the Churches.* Philadelphia, Pa.: Westminster Press, 1951.

NIEBUHR, H. RICHARD. *Christ and Culture.* New York: Harper and Row, Publishers, Inc., 1951.

———. *The Kingdom of God in America.* Chicago, Ill.: Willett, Clark & Company, 1937.

———. *The Social Sources of Denominationalism.* New York: Holt, Rinehart & Winston, Inc., 1929. Reprinted by The Shoestring Press, 1954.

NIEBUHR, REINHOLD. *Christianity and Power Politics.* New York: Charles Scribner's Sons, 1940.

———. "Co-Existence or Total War?" *Christian Century* (August 1954), 971–973.

———. *Man's Nature and His Communities.* New York: Charles Scribner's Sons, 1965.

———. *Moral Man and Immoral Society.* New York: Charles Scribner's Sons, 1932.

———. *The Nature and Destiny of Man,* 1 vol. ed. New York: Charles Scribner's Sons, 1946.

———. *Reflections on the End of an Era.* New York: Charles Scribner's Sons, 1934.

———. *The Self and the Dramas of History.* New York: Charles Scribner's Sons, 1955.

———. *Why the Christian Church Is Not Pacifist.* London: SCM Press, 1940.

NORBECK, EDWARD. "African Rituals of Conflict." *American Anthropologist,* **65** (1963), 1254–1279.

———. *Religion in Primitive Society.* New York: Harper and Row, Publishers, Inc., 1961.

NORTHWOOD, LAURENCE K. "Ecological and Attitudinal Factors in Church Desegregation." *Social Problems,* 6 (Fall 1958), 150–163.

NOTTINGHAM, ELIZABETH K. *Methodism and the Frontier. Indiana Proving Ground.* New York: Columbia University Press, 1941.

———. *Religion and Society.* Garden City, N.Y.: Doubleday & Company, Inc., 1954.

NOVAK, MICHAEL. "American Catholicism After the Council." *Commentary,* **40** (August 1965), 50–58.

———. *Belief and Unbelief.* New York: The Macmillan Company, 1965.

———. "Christianity: Renewed or Slowly Abandoned?" *Daedalus,* **96** (Winter 1967), 237–266.

NUESSE, C. J., and THOMAS J. HARTE, eds. *The Sociology of the Parish.* Milwaukee, Wis.: The Bruce Publishing Company, 1951.

O'DEA, THOMAS F. *American Catholic Dilemma: An Inquiry into the Intellectual Life.* New York: Sheed & Ward, Inc., 1958.

———. *The Catholic Crisis.* Boston, Mass.: The Beacon Press, 1967.

———. *The Mormons.* Chicago, Ill.: University of Chicago Press, 1957.

———. *The Sociology of Religion.* Englewood Cliffs, N.J.: Prentice-Hall, Inc., 1966.

Official Catholic Directory. Thomas B. Kennedy, ed. New York: P. J. Kenedy & Sons, 1968.

OTTO, RUDOLF. *The Idea of the Holy,* rev. ed. Trans. by John W. Harvey. London: Oxford University Press, 1923.

OUTLER, ALBERT C. *Psychotherapy and the Christian Message.* New York: Harper and Row, Publishers, Inc., 1954.

OVERSTREET, HARRY, and BONARO OVERSTREET. *The Strange Tactics of Extremism.* New York: W. W. Norton & Company, Inc., 1964.

PARENTI, MICHAEL. "Political Values and Religious Cultures: Jews, Catholics, and Protestants." *Journal for the Scientific Study of Religion*, 6 (Fall 1967), 259–269.

PARKER, EVERETT C., DAVID W. BARRY, and DALLAS W. SMYTHE. *The Television-Radio Audience and Religion.* New York: Harper and Row, Publishers, Inc., 1955.

PARRINDER, E. GEOFFREY. *African Traditional Religion.* London: Hutchinson & Co., Ltd., 1954.

PARSONS, ANNE. "The Pentecostal Immigrants: A Study of an Ethnic Central City Church." *Journal for the Scientific Study of Religion*, 4 (Spring 1965), 183–197.

PARSONS, TALCOTT. *Essays in Sociological Theory Pure and Applied.* New York: The Free Press, 1949.

——. "H. M. Robertson on Max Weber and His School." *Journal of Political Economy* (October 1935), 688–696.

——. *Religious Perspectives of College Teaching in Sociology and Social Psychology.* New Haven, Conn.: The Edward W. Hazen Foundation.

——. *The Social System.* New York: The Free Press, 1951.

——. *Structure and Process in Modern Societies.* New York: The Free Press, 1960.

——. *Structure of Social Action.* New York: McGraw-Hill Book Company, Inc., 1937.

——, ROBERT F. BALES, and EDWARD A. SHILS. *Working Papers in the Theory of Action.* New York: The Free Press, 1953.

PARSONS, TALCOTT, and EDWARD A. SHILS, eds. *Toward a General Theory of Action.* Cambridge, Mass.: Harvard University Press, 1951.

——, KASPAR D. NAEGELE, and JESSE R. PITTS, eds. *Theories of Society: Foundations of Modern Sociological Theory.* New York: The Free Press, 1961.

PARSONS, TALCOTT, and NEAL J. SMELSER. *Economy and Society. A Study in the Integration of Economic and Social Theory.* New York: The Free Press, 1956.

PAUCK, WILHELM. *The Heritage of the Reformation*, rev. and enlarged ed. New York: The Free Press, 1961.

PEALE, NORMAN VINCENT. *Enthusiasm Makes the Difference.* Englewood Cliffs, N.J.: Prentice-Hall, Inc., 1967.

——. *A Guide to Confident Living.* Englewood Cliffs, N.J.: Prentice-Hall, Inc., 1948.

PERRY, RALPH B. *Puritanism and Democracy.* New York: Vanguard Press, Inc., 1944.

The Persecution of the Catholic Church in the Third Reich. Facts and documents trans. from the German. London: Burns, Oates & Washburn, Ltd., 1940.

PETEGORSKY, DAVID W. *Left-Wing Democracy in the English Civil War. A Study of the Social Philosophy of Gerrard Winstanley.* London: Victor Gollancz, Ltd., 1940.

PETERS, VICTOR. *All Things Common: The Hutterite Way of Life.* Minneapolis, Minn.: University of Minnesota Press, 1965.

PETERSON, WILLIAM. "Religious Statistics in the United States." *Journal for the Scientific Study of Religion*, 1 (Spring 1962), 165–178.

PFAUTZ, HAROLD W. "Christian Science: A Case Study of the Social Psychological Aspect of Secularization." *Social Forces*, 34 (March 1956), 246–251.

——. "The Sociology of Secularization: Religious Groups." *American Journal of Sociology*, 61 (September 1955), 121–128.

PFEFFER, LEO. *Church, State, and Freedom*, rev. ed. Boston, Mass.: The Beacon Press, 1967.

PFUETZE, PAUL E. *The Social Self*. New York: Bookman Associates, 1954.

PHOTIADIS, JOHN D., and JEANNE BIGGAR. "Religiosity, Education, and Ethnic Distance." *American Journal of Sociology*, 69 (May 1962), 666–672.

PHOTIADIS, JOHN D., and ARTHUR L. JOHNSON. "Orthodoxy, Church Participation, and Authoritarianism." *The American Journal of Sociology*, 69 (November 1963), 244–248.

PIKE, JAMES A., with DIANE KENNEDY. *The Other Side: An Account of My Experiences with Psychic Phenomena*. Garden City, N.Y.: Doubleday & Company, Inc., 1968.

PIKE, ROYSTON. *Jehovah's Witnesses*. New York: Philosophical Library, 1954.

PIN, EMILE. *Pratique religieuse et classes sociales dans une paroisse urbaine, Saint-Pothin à Lyon*. Paris: Spes, 1956.

POPE, LISTON. *Millhands and Preachers*. New Haven, Conn.: Yale University Press, 1942.

———. "Religion as a Social Force in America." *Social Action* (May 1953), 2–15.

PORTER, JOHN. *Canadian Social Structure: A Statistical Profile*. Toronto, Ont.: McClelland and Steward, 1967.

———. "The Future of Upward Mobility." *American Sociological Review*, 33 (February 1968), 5–19.

———. *The Vertical Mosaic: An Analysis of Social Class and Power in Canada*. Toronto, Ont.: University of Toronto Press, 1965.

POWDERMAKER, HORTENSE. *After Freedom. A Cultural Study in the Deep South*. New York: The Viking Press, Inc., 1939.

PUTNEY, SNELL, and RUSSELL MIDDLETON. "Dimensions and Correlates of Religious Ideologies." *Social Forces*, 39 (May 1961), 285–290.

———. "Ethical Relativism and Anomia." *American Journal of Sociology*, 67 (January 1962), 430–438.

———. "Rebellion, Conformity, and Parental Religious Ideologies." *Sociometry*, 24 (June 1961), 125–135.

RAAB, EARL, ed. *Religious Conflict in America*. Garden City, N.Y.: Doubleday & Company, Inc., 1964.

RADCLIFFE-BROWN, ALFRED R. *The Andaman Islanders*. Cambridge, England: Cambridge University Press, 1922.

———. *Religion and Society*. London: Royal Anthropological Institute of Great Britain and Ireland, 1945.

———. *Structure and Function in Primitive Society*. New York: The Free Press, 1952.

RADIN, PAUL. *Primitive Religion. Its Nature and Origin*. New York: The Viking Press, Inc., 1937.

RAMSEY, PAUL. *War and the Christian Conscience*. Durham, N.C.: Duke University Press, 1961.

RANDALL, JUDITH. "Witch Doctors and Psychiatry." *Harper's*, 231 (December 1965), 56–61.

RANDALL, JOHN H., and JOHN H. RANDALL, JR. *Religion and the Modern World*. New York: Frederick A. Stokes Company, 1929.

RANDALL, JOHN H., JR. *The Making of the Modern Mind*, rev. ed. Boston, Mass.: Houghton Mifflin Company, 1940.

RANKE, LEOPOLD VON. *History of the Reformation in Germany*. Trans. by Sarah Austin. Ed. by R. A. Johnson. London: Routledge and Kegan Paul, 1905.

RAPOPORT, ROBERT N. *Changing Navaho Religious Values. A Study of Christian Missions to the Rimrock Navahos*. Papers of the Peabody Museum of American Archaeology and Ethnology, Harvard University, Vol. 41. Cambridge: The Peabody Museum, 1954.

RAPPAPORT, ROY A. *Pigs for the Ancestors: Ritual in the Ecology of a New Guinea People*. New Haven, Conn.: Yale University Press, 1968.

———. "Ritual Regulation of Environmental Relations among a New Guinea People." *Ethnology*, 6 (January 1967), 17–30.

RAUSCHENBUSCH, WALTER. *Christianity and the Social Crisis.* New York: The Macmillan Company, 1907.

———. *Christianizing the Social Order.* New York: The Macmillan Company, 1912.

REDFIELD, ROBERT. *The Primitive World and Its Transformations.* Ithaca, N.Y.: Cornell University Press, 1953.

REED, EDWARD, ed. *Pacem In Terris.* An International Convocation on the Requirements of Peace Sponsored by the Center for the Study of Democratic Institutions. New York: Pocket Books, Inc., 1965.

REIMERS, DAVID. *White Protestantism and the Negro.* New York: Oxford University Press, 1965.

REITERMAN, CARL. "Birth Control and Catholics." *Journal for the Scientific Study of Religion*, 4 (Spring 1965), 213–233.

RENAN, ERNEST. *The Future of Science.* Boston, Mass.: Roberts Bros., 1891.

RETTIG, SALOMON and BENJAMIN PASAMANICK. "Moral Value Structure and Social Class." *Sociometry*, 24 (March 1961), 21–35.

RIEFF, PHILIP. *Freud: The Mind of the Moralist.* New York: The Viking Press, Inc., 1959.

———. *The Triumph of the Therapeutic: Uses of Faith After Freud.* New York: Harper and Row, Publishers, 1966.

RIESMAN, DAVID. *Individualism Reconsidered.* New York: The Free Press, 1954.

———, in collaboration with REUEL DENNEY and NATHAN GLAZER. *The Lonely Crowd. A Study of the Changing American Character.* New Haven: Yale University Press, 1950.

RINGER, BENJAMIN B. *The Edge of Friendliness. A Study of Jewish-Gentile Relations.* New York: Basic Books, 1967.

———, and CHARLES Y. GLOCK. "The Political Role of the Church as Defined by Its Parishioners." *Public Opinion Quarterly*, 18 (Winter 1954–55), 337–347.

RIVERS, W. H. R. *The Todas.* London: Macmillan & Co., Ltd., 1906.

ROBERTS, BRYAN R. "Protestant Groups and Coping with Urban Life in Guatemala City." *American Journal of Sociology*, 73 (May 1968), 753–767.

ROBERTS, DAVID E. *Psychotherapy and a Christian View of Man.* New York: Charles Scribner's Sons, 1950.

ROBERTS, WILLIAM H., and others. "Analysis and Faith." *New Republic* (May 1955), 16–22.

ROBERTSON, D. B. *Should Churches Be Taxed?* Philadelphia, Pa.: The Westminster Press, 1968

ROBERTSON, H. M. *Aspects of the Rise of Economic Individualism. A Criticism of Max Weber and His School.* Cambridge, England: Cambridge University Press, 1933.

ROBINSON, JOHN A. T. *Honest to God.* Philadelphia, Pa.: The Westminster Press, 1963.

RODMAN, HYMAN. "Technical Note on Two Rates of Mixed Marriage." *American Sociological Review*, 30 (October 1965), 776–778.

ROGERS, DAVID PRICE. "Some Religious Beliefs of Scientists and the Effect of the Scientific Method." *Review of Religious Research*, 7 (Winter 1966), 70–77.

ROKEACH, MILTON. *The Open and Closed Mind.* New York: Basic Books, 1960.

ROSE, PETER. "Small-Town Jews and Their Neighbors in the United States." *Jewish Journal of Sociology*, 3 (1961), 174–191.

ROSEN, BERNARD C. *Adolescence and Religion. The Jewish Teenager in American Society.* Cambridge, Mass.: Schenkman Publishing Co., 1965.

———. "Race, Ethnicity, and the Achievement Syndrome." *American Sociological Review*, 21 (April 1959), 47–60.

ROSENBERG, STUART A. *The Search for Jewish Identity in America.* Garden City, N.Y.: Doubleday & Company, Inc., 1965.

ROSENSTONE, ROBERT A., ed. *Protest from the Right.* Beverly Hills, Calif.: The Glencoe Press, 1968.

ROSENTHAL, ERICH. "Acculturation Without Assimilation? The Jewish Community in Chicago, Illinois." *American Journal of Sociology,* 66 (November 1960), 275–288.

ROSS, E. A. *Social Control.* New York: The Macmillan Company, 1901.

ROY, RALPH L. *Apostles of Discord. A Study of Organized Bigotry and Disruption on the Fringes of Protestantism.* Boston, Mass.: The Beacon Press, 1953.

———. *Communism and the Churches.* New York: Harcourt, Brace, & World, Inc., 1960.

SALISBURY, W. SEWARD. "Religion and Secularization." *Social Forces,* 36 (March 1958), 197–205.

———. *Religion in American Culture.* Homewood, Ill.: The Dorsey Press, 1964.

SANDERSON, ROSS W. *The Church Serves the Changing City.* New York: Harper and Row, Publishers, Inc., 1955.

SANFORD, NEVITT, ed. *The American College.* New York: John Wiley & Sons, Inc., 1962.

SANUA, VICTOR D. "A Review of Social Science Studies on Jews and Jewish Life in the United States." *Journal for the Scientific Study of Religion,* 4 (Fall 1964), 71–83.

SARKISYANZ, E. *Buddhist Backgrounds of the Burmese Revolution.* The Hague: Nijhoff, 1965.

SARTRE, JEAN-PAUL. *Being and Nothingness: An Essay on Phenomenological Ontology.* Trans. by Hazel E. Barnes. New York: Philosophical Library, 1956.

———. *Nausea.* Trans. by Robert Baldick. Harmondsworth, Md.: Penguin Books, 1965.

———. *No Exit; and Three Other Plays.* Trans. by L. Abel. New York: Vintage Books, 1965.

SAWYER, JACK. "The Altruism Scale: A Measure of Co-operative, Individualistic, and Competitive Interpersonal Orientation." *The American Journal of Sociology,* 71 (January 1966), 407–416.

SCANZONI, JOHN. "A Note on Method for the Church-Sect Typology." *Sociological Analysis,* 26 (Winter 1965), 189–202.

SCHECTER, JERROLD. *The New Faces of Buddha: Buddhism and Political Power in Southeast Asia.* New York: Coward-McCann, Inc., 1967.

SCHELSKY, HELMUTH. "Religionssoziologie und Theologie." *Zeitschrift für evangelische Ethik* (1959), 129–145.

SCHEUER, JOSEPH F., JOSEPH B. SCHUYLER, and FRANK A. SANTOPOLO. "Parish Sociology." *Thought* (Summer 1955), 243–259.

SCHILLING, HAROLD K. *Science and Religion: An Interpretation of Two Communities.* New York: Charles Scribner's Sons, 1962.

SCHLATTER, R. B. "The Problem of Historical Causation in Some Recent Studies of the English Revolution." *Journal of the History of Ideas* (June 1943), 349–367.

———. *The Social Ideas of Religious Leaders, 1660–1688.* London: Humphrey Milford, 1940.

SCHLISSEL, LILLIAN, ed. *Conscience in America. A Documentary History of Conscientious Objection in America, 1757–1967.* New York: E. P. Dutton and Co., 1968.

SCHMIDT, PAUL W. *The Origin and Growth of Religion.* New York: The Dial Press, Inc., 1931.

SCHNEIDER, HERBERT W. *Religion in 20th Century America.* Cambridge, Mass.: Harvard University Press, 1952.

SCHNEIDER, LOUIS, ed. *Religion, Culture, and Society*. New York: John Wiley & Sons, Inc., 1964.

——. "The Role of the Category of Ignorance in Sociological Theory: An Exploratory Statement." *American Sociological Review*, 27 (August 1962), 492–508.

——, and SANFORD M. DORNBUSCH. *Popular Religion: Inspirational Books in America*. Chicago, Ill.: University of Chicago Press, 1958.

SCHROEDER, W. WIDICK, and VICTOR OBENHAUS. *Religion in American Culture. Unity and Diversity in a Midwestern County*. New York: The Free Press, 1964.

SCHUYLER, JOSEPH B. *Northern Parish, A Sociological and Pastoral Study*. Chicago, Ill.: Loyola University Press, 1960.

SCHWER, WILHELM. *Catholic Social Theory*. Trans. by Bartholomew Landheer. Preface by Franz Mueller. St. Louis, Mo.: B. Herder Book Co., 1940.

SECOND VATICAN COUNCIL. *Pastoral Constitution on the Church in the Modern World, December 7, 1965*. National Catholic Welfare Conference, 1966.

SEE, HENRI. "Dans quelle mesure puritains et juifs ont-ils contribué aux progrés du capitalisme moderne?" *Revue Historique*, 155 (1927).

——. *Modern Capitalism*. Trans. by H. B. Vanderblue and G. F. Doriot. New York: Adelphi Co., 1928.

THE SEIKYO PRESS. *Sōka Gakkai*. Tokyo: The Seikyo Press, 1960.

SHEEN, FULTON J. *Peace of Soul*. New York: Whittlesey House, 1949.

SHELDON, ELEANOR B. and WILBERT E. MOORE. *Indicators of Social Change*. New York: Russell Sage Foundation, 1968.

SHERMAN, C. BEZALEL. *The Jew Within American Society: A Study in Ethnic Individuality*. Detroit, Mich.: Wayne State University Press, 1961.

SHESTOV, LEV. *Athens and Jerusalem*. Trans. with an intro. by Bernard Martin. New York: Simon and Schuster, Inc., 1968.

SHILS, EDWARD. "Charisma, Order, and Status." *American Sociological Review*, 30 (April 1965), 199–213.

SHINER, LARRY. "The Concept of Secularization in Empirical Research." *Journal for the Scientific Study of Religion*, 6 (Fall 1967), 207–220.

SHIPPEY, FREDERICK. *Protestantism in Suburban Life*. Nashville, Tenn.: Abingdon Press, 1964.

SHUSTER, GEORGE N. *Catholic Education in a Changing World*. New York: Holt, Rinehart & Winston, Inc., 1967.

SIBLEY, MULFORD Q., and PHILIP E. JACOB. *Conscription of Conscience*. Ithaca, N.Y.: Cornell University Press, 1952.

SIEGMAN, ARON WOLFE. "An Empirical Investigation of the Psychoanalytic Theory of Religious Behavior." *Journal for the Scientific Study of Religion*, 1 (October 1961), 74–78.

SILVERMAN, JULIAN. "Shamans and Acute Schizophrenia." *American Anthropologist*, 69 (February 1967), 21–31.

SILVERT, KALMAN H., ed. *Churches and States: The Religious Institution and Modernization*. New York: American Universities Field Staff, 1967.

SIMMEL, GEORG. "A Contribution to the Sociology of Religion." Trans. by W. W. Elwang. *American Journal of Sociology* (November 1905). Reprinted in *American Journal of Sociology* (May, 1955).

SIMPSON, GEORGE E. "Jamaican Revivalist Cults." *Social and Economic Studies*, 5 (December 1956), whole issue.

——. "The Ras Tafari Movement in Jamaica: A Study of Race and Class Conflict." *Social Forces*, 34 (December 1955), 167–170.

——. *The Shango Cult in Trinidad*. San Juan, P.R.: University of Puerto Rico: Institute of Caribbean Studies, 1965.

——, and J. Milton Yinger. *Racial and Cultural Minorities: An Analysis of*

Prejudice and Discrimination, 3rd ed. New York: Harper and Row, Publishers, Inc., 1965.

SKLARE, MARSHALL. "Assimilation and the Sociologist." *Commentary,* 39 (May 1965), 63–67.

———. "Church and Laity Among Jews." *Annals of the American Academy,* 332 (November 1960), 60–69.

———. *Conservative Judaism: An American Religious Movement.* New York: The Free Press, 1955.

———, ed. *The Jews: Social Patterns of an American Group.* New York: The Free Press, 1958.

———, and JOSEPH GREENBLUM. *Jewish Identity on the Suburban Frontier. A Study of Group Survival in the Open Society.* New York: Basic Books, 1967.

SLATER, PHILIP. *Microcosm: Structural, Psychological and Religious Evolution in Groups.* New York: John Wiley & Sons, Inc., 1966.

SLOTKIN, J. S. *The Peyote Religion: A Study in Indian-White Relations.* New York: The Free Press, 1956.

SMITH, DONALD EUGENE. *Religion and Politics in Burma.* Princeton, N.J.: Princeton University Press, 1965.

———, ed. *South Asian Politics and Religion.* Princeton, N.J.: Princeton University Press, 1966.

SMITH, HOMER W. *Man and His Gods.* Boston, Mass.: Little, Brown and Co., 1952.

SMITH, JAMES OTIS, and GIDEON SJOBERG. "Origins and Career Patterns of Leading Protestant Clergymen." *Social Forces,* 39 (May 1961), 290–296.

SMITH, PRESERVED. *The Age of the Reformation.* New York: Holt, Rinehart & Winston, Inc., 1920.

SMITH, TIMOTHY L. "Historic Waves of Religious Interest in America." *Annals of the American Academy of Political and Social Science,* 332 (November 1960), 9–19.

———. *Revivalism and Social Reform in Mid-Nineteenth Century America.* New York: Abingdon Press, 1957.

SMITH, WILFRED CANTWELL. *The Faith of Other Men.* New York: Mentor Books, 1965.

SMITH, WILLIAM ROBERTSON. *Lectures on the Religion of the Semites,* 3rd ed. London: A. & C. Black, Ltd., 1927.

SOLT, LEO F. *Saints in Arms. Puritanism and Democracy in Cromwell's Army.* Stanford, Calif.: Stanford University Press, 1959.

SOMBART, WERNER. *The Jews and Modern Capitalism.* Trans., with notes, by M. Epstein. London: George Allen & Unwin, Ltd., 1913.

———. *The Quintessence of Capitalism.* Trans. and edited by M. Epstein. London: George Allen & Unwin, Ltd., 1915.

SOROKIN, PITIRIM A. *Social and Cultural Dynamics,* 4 vols. New York: American Book Company, 1937–1941.

———. *The Ways and Power of Love: Types, Factors, and Techniques of Moral Transformation.* Boston, Mass.: The Beacon Press, 1954.

SPANN, J. RICHARD, ed. *The Church and Social Responsibility.* New York: Abingdon-Cokesbury Press, 1953.

SPENCER, HERBERT. *The Principles of Sociology,* 3rd ed. New York: Appleton-Century-Crofts, Inc., 1896.

SPERRY, WILLARD L. *Religion in America.* New York: The Macmillan Company, 1946.

SPILKA, BERNARD, and J. F. REYNOLDS. "Religion and Prejudice: A Factor-Analytic Study." *Review of Religious Research,* 6 (1965), 163–168.

SPINDLER, GEORGE D. "Personality and Peyotism in Menomini Indian Acculturation." *Psychiatry,* 15 (May 1952), 151–159.

SPINKA, MATTHEW. *The Church in Soviet Russia.* New York: Oxford University Press, 1956.

SPIRO, MELFORD E. "The Acculturation of American Ethnic Groups." *American Anthropologist,* 57 (December 1955), 1240–1252.

———. "Buddhism and Economic Action in Burma." *American Anthropologist,* 68 (October 1966), 1163–1173.

———. *Burmese Supernaturalism: A Study in the Explanation and Reduction of Suffering.* Englewood Cliffs, N.J.: Prentice-Hall, Inc., 1967.

SRINIVAS, M. N. *Caste in Modern India.* New York: Asia Publishing House, 1962.

———. *Religion and Society Among the Coorgs of South India.* Oxford: The Clarendon Press, 1952.

STANKIEWICZ, W. J. *Politics and Religion in Seventeenth-Century France.* Berkeley, Calif.: University of California Press, 1960.

STARK, RODNEY. "Class, Radicalism, and Religious Involvement in Great Britain." *American Sociological Review,* 29 (October 1964), 698–706.

———. "On the Incompatibility of Religion and Science: A Survey of American Graduate Students." *Journal for the Scientific Study of Religion,* 3 (Fall 1963), 3–20.

———, and CHARLES Y. GLOCK. *American Piety: The Nature of Religious Commitment.* Berkeley, Calif.: University of California Press, 1968.

STARK, WERNER. *The Sociology of Religion. A Study of Christendom,* 3 vols. New York: Fordham University Press, 1967.

STEINBERG, STEPHEN. "The Anatomy of Jewish Identification: A Historical and Theoretical View." *Review of Religious Research,* 7 (Fall 1965), 1–8.

STELZLE, CHARLES. *The Church and Labor.* Boston, Mass.: Houghton Mifflin Company, 1910.

STINCHCOMBE, ARTHUR L. *Constructing Social Theories.* New York: Harcourt, Brace, and World, Inc., 1968.

STOKES, ANSON P. *Church and State in the United States,* 3 vols. New York: Harper and Row, Publishers, Inc., 1950. (Rev. one-volume ed., with Leo Pfeffer. Harper and Row, Publishers, Inc., 1964.)

STRAUSS, LEO. *Natural Right and History.* Chicago, Ill.: University of Chicago Press, 1953.

STROUP, HERBERT H. *The Jehovah's Witnesses.* New York: Columbia University Press, 1945.

———. *Church and State in Confrontation.* New York: The Seabury Press, 1967.

STURZO, LUIGI. *Church and State.* New York: Longmans, Green & Company, 1939.

SUNDKLER, BENGT G. M. *Bantu Prophets in South Africa,* 2nd ed. Preface by Edgar H. Brookes. New York: Oxford University Press, 1961.

SUZUKI, DAISETZ TEITARO. *Outlines of Mahayana Buddhism.* Prefatory Essay by Alan Watts. New York: Schocken Books, Inc., 1963.

SWANSON, GUY E. *The Birth of the Gods: The Origin of Primitive Beliefs.* Ann Arbor, Mich.: University of Michigan Press, 1960.

———. *Religion and Regime: A Sociological Account of the Reformation.* Ann Arbor, Mich.: University of Michigan Press, 1967.

SWEET, WILLIAM W. *The American Churches. An Interpretation.* New York: Abingdon-Cokesbury Press, 1947.

———. *The Story of Religion in America.* Rev. ed. New York: Harper and Row, Publishers, Inc., 1939.

SWIFT, ARTHUR L., JR. *New Frontiers of Religion.* New York: The Macmillan Company, 1938.

TALMON, YONINA. "Pursuit of the Millennium: The Relation between Religious Change and Social Change." *Archives Européennes de Sociologie,* 3 (1962), 125–148.

TANNENBAUM, EDWARD R. *The Action Française: Die-Hard Reactionaries in Twentieth-Century France.* New York: John Wiley & Sons, Inc., 1962.

TAVUCHIS, NICHOLAS. *Pastors and Immigrants: The Role of a Religious Elite in the Absorption of Norwegian Immigrants.* The Hague: Martinus Nijhoff, 1963.

TAWNEY, R. H. *The Acquisitive Society.* New York: Harcourt, Brace & World, Inc., 1920.

———. *Religion and the Rise of Capitalism.* New York: Harcourt, Brace & World, Inc., 1926.

———. "Religious Thought on Social and Economic Questions in the Sixteenth and Seventeenth Centuries." *The Journal of Political Economy,* 31 (1923), 461–493, 637–674, and 804–825.

TEILHARD DE CHARDIN, PIERRE. *The Phenomenon of Man,* rev. ed. London: William Collins Sons and Company, Ltd., 1965.

THOMAS, NORMAN. *The Conscientious Objector in America.* New York: B. W. Huebsch, Inc., 1923.

THOMTE, REIDAR. *Kierkegaard's Philosophy of Religion.* Princeton, N.J.: Princeton University Press, 1948.

TILLICH, PAUL. *Christianity and the Encounter of the World Religions.* New York: Columbia University Press, 1963.

———. *The Courage to Be.* New Haven, Conn.: Yale University Press, 1952.

———. *The Interpretation of History.* Trans. by N. A. Rasetzki and E. L. Talmey. New York: Charles Scribner's Sons, 1938.

———. *The Shaking of the Foundations.* New York: Charles Scribner's Sons, 1948.

———. *Systematic Theology,* 3 vols. Chicago, Ill.: University of Chicago Press, 1951–1963.

TIMASHEFF, N. S. *Religion in Soviet Russia.* New York: Sheed and Ward, Inc., 1942.

TIRYAKIAN, EDWARD A., ed. *Sociological Theory, Values, and Sociocultural Change. Essays in Honor of Pitirim A. Sorokin,* New York: The Free Press, 1963.

TITIEV, MISCHA. "A Fresh Approach to the Problem of Magic and Religion." *Southwestern Journal of Anthropology,* 16 (1960), 292–298.

TOYNBEE, ARNOLD J. *A Study of History.* Vol. 5. *The Disintegration of Civilizations.* London: Oxford University Press, 1939.

———. *A Study of History.* Vol. 7. *Universal States and Universal Churches.* London: Oxford University Press, 1954.

TRENT, JAMES W., and JENETTE GOLDS. *Catholics in College: Religious Commitment and the Intellectual Life.* Chicago, Ill.: University of Chicago Press, 1967.

TROELTSCH, ERNST. *Gesämmelte Schriften.* Zweiter Band, *Zur religiösen Lage, Religionsphilosophie und Ethik,* 1922. Vierter Band, *Aufsätze zur Geistesgeschichte und Religionssoziologie,* 1925. Tübingen: J. C. B. Mohr (Paul Siebeck).

———. *Protestantism and Progress. A Historical Study of the Relation of Protestantism to the Modern World.* Trans. by W. Montgomery. New York: G. P. Putnam's Sons, 1912.

———. *The Social Teaching of the Christian Churches,* 2 vols. Trans. by Olive Wyon. New York: The Macmillan Company, 1931.

TRUEBLOOD, ELTON. "Vocational Christian Pacifism." *Christianity and Crisis* (November 1941), 2–5.

TUCKER, ROBERT W. *Just War and Vatican Council II: A Critique.* New York: Council on Religion and International Affairs, 1966.

TURNER, WALLACE. *The Mormon Establishment.* Cambridge, Mass.: Houghton Mifflin Company, 1966.

TYLOR, EDWARD B. *Primitive Culture*, 7th ed. New York: Brentano's, Inc., 1924.

UNDERHILL, EVELYN. *Mysticism: A Study in the Nature and Development of Man's Spiritual Consciousness.* New York: Noonday Press, 1955.

UNDERHILL, RUTH M. *Papago Indian Religion.* New York: Columbia University Press, 1946.

------. *Red Man's Religion. Beliefs and Practices of the Indians North of Mexico.* Chicago, Ill.: University of Chicago Press, 1965.

UNDERWOOD, KENNETH W. *Protestant and Catholic: Religious and Social Interaction in an Industrial Community.* Boston, Mass.: The Beacon Press, 1957.

UNITED NATIONS EDUCATIONAL, SCIENTIFIC AND CULTURAL ORGANIZATION. "Sociology of Religions. A Trend Report and Bibliography." *Current Sociology*, 5 (1956).

UNITED STATES BUREAU OF THE CENSUS. "Religion Reported by the Civilian Population of the United States: March, 1957." *Current Population Reports*, Series P-20 (1958).

VAHANIAN, GABRIEL. *The Death of God.* New York: George Braziller, Inc., 1961.

VALLIER, IVAN. "Church, Society, and Labor Resources: An Intra-Denominational Comparison." *American Journal of Sociology*, 68 (July 1962), 21–33.

VAN BUREN, PAUL. *The Secular Meaning of the Gospel.* New York: The Macmillan Company, 1963.

VAN DEN BERGHE, PIERRE L. "Dialectic and Functionalism: Toward a Theoretical Synthesis." *American Sociological Review*, 28 (October 1963), 695–705.

VAN DER VELDT, JAMES H., and R. P. ODENWALD. *Psychiatry and Catholicism.* New York: McGraw-Hill Book Company, Inc., 1952.

VAUGHN, TED R., DOUGLAS H. SMITH, and GIDEON SJOBERG. "The Religious Orientation of American Natural Scientists." *Social Forces*, 44 (June 1966), 519–526.

VERNON, GLENN M. "The Religious 'Nones': A Neglected Category." *Journal for the Scientific Study of Religion*, 7 (Fall 1968), 219–229.

------. *Sociology of Religion.* New York: McGraw-Hill Book Company, Inc., 1962.

VISCHER, LUKAS, ed. *A Documentary History of the Faith and Order Movement, 1927–1963.* St. Louis, Mo.: Bethany Press, 1963.

VOGET, FRED W. "The American Indian in Transition: Reformation and Accommodation." *American Anthropologist*, 58 (April 1956), 249–263.

------. "The American Indian in Transition: Reformation and Status Innovations." *American Journal of Sociology*, 62 (January 1957), 369–378.

VOGT, EVON Z., and THOMAS F. O'DEA. "A Comparative Study of the Role of Values in Social Action in Two Southwestern Communities." *American Sociological Review*, 18 (December 1953), 645–654.

VOGT, EVON Z., and ETHEL M. ALBERT, eds. *People of Rimrock: A Study of Values in Five Cultures.* Cambridge, Mass.: Harvard University Press, 1966.

VOGT, EVON Z., and RAY HYMAN. *Water Witching U.S.A.* Chicago, Ill.: University of Chicago Press, 1959.

VON DER MEHDEN, FRED R. *Religion and Nationalism in Southeast Asia.* Madison, Wis.: University of Wisconsin Press, 1963.

VRIJHOF, P. H. "Was ist Religionssoziologie?" *Kölner Zeitschrift für Soziologie und Sozialpsychologie*, No. 6 (1962), 10–35.

WAARDENBURG, JEAN-JACQUES. *L'Islam dans le miroir de l'Occident.* Paris: Mouton & Cie, 1963.

WACH, JOACHIM. *The Comparative Study of Religions.* New York: Columbia University Press, 1958.

------. *Sociology of Religion.* Chicago, Ill.: University of Chicago Press, 1944.

------. *Types of Religious Experience, Christian and Non-Christian.* Chicago, Ill.: University of Chicago Press, 1951.

WAGNER, HELMUT. "The Protestant Ethic: A Mid-Twentieth Century View." *Sociological Analysis*, 25 (Spring 1964), 34–40.

WAKIN, EDWARD, and JOSEPH F. SCHEUER. *The De-Romanization of the American Catholic Church*. New York: The Macmillan Company, 1966.

WALKER, BROOKS R. *The Christian Fright Peddlers*. Garden City, N.Y.: Doubleday & Company, Inc., 1965.

WALLACE, ANTHONY F. C. *Religion: An Anthropological View*. New York: Random House, Inc., 1966.

———. "Revitalization Movements." *American Anthropologist*, 58 (April 1956), 264–281.

WALLIS, LOUIS. "Sociological Significance of the Bible." *American Journal of Sociology* (January 1907), 532–552.

———. *Sociological Study of the Bible*. Chicago, Ill.: University of Chicago Press, 1912.

WALLIS, WILSON D. *Messiahs: Their Role in Civilization*. Washington, D.C.: American Council on Public Affairs, 1943.

———. *Religion in Primitive Society*. New York: Appleton-Century-Crofts, Inc., 1939.

WALZER, MICHAEL. *The Revolution of the Saints*. Cambridge, Mass.: Harvard University Press, 1965.

WARD, HARRY F. *Democracy and Social Change*. New York: Modern Age Books, 1940.

———. *Our Economic Morality and the Ethic of Jesus*. New York: The Macmillan Company, 1929.

WARDWELL, WALTER I. "Christian Science Healing." *Journal for the Scientific Study of Religion*, 4 (Spring 1965), 175–181.

WARKOV, SEYMOUR, and ANDREW M. GREELEY. "Parochial School Origins and Educational Achievement." *American Sociological Review*, 31 (June 1966), 406–414.

WARNER, W. LLOYD. *American Life: Dream and Reality*. Chicago, Ill.: University of Chicago Press, 1953.

———. *The Family of God: A Symbolic Study of Christian Life in America*. New Haven, Conn.: Yale University Press, 1961.

WARNER, WELLMAN J. *The Wesleyan Movement in the Industrial Revolution*. London: Longmans, Green & Company, 1930.

WATT, W. MONTGOMERY. *Islam and the Integration of Society*. London: Routledge and Kegan Paul, 1961.

WAX, MURRAY. "Ancient Judaism and the Protestant Ethic." *American Journal of Sociology*, 65 (March 1960), 449–455.

WAX, ROSALIE, and MURRAY WAX. "The Magical World View." *Journal for the Scientific Study of Religion*, 1 (Spring 1962), 179–188.

———. "The Vikings and the Rise of Capitalism." *American Journal of Sociology*, 61 (July 1955), 1–10.

WEARMOUTH, ROBERT F. *Methodism and the Working-Class Movements of England, 1800–1850*. London: The Epworth Press, 1937.

WEBB, SAM C. "An Exploratory Investigation of Some Needs Met Through Religious Behavior." *Journal for the Scientific Study of Religion*, 5 (Fall 1965), 51–58.

WEBER, MAX. *Ancient Judaism*. Trans. and ed. by Hans H. Gerth and Don Martindale. New York: The Free Press, 1952.

———. *From Max Weber: Essays in Sociology*. Trans. and ed. by H. H. Gerth and C. Wright Mills. New York: Oxford University Press, 1946.

———. *General Economic History*. Trans. by Frank Knight. New York: Greenberg, Publishers, Inc., 1927.

WEBER, MAX. *The Protestant Ethic and the Spirit of Capitalism*. Trans. by Talcott Parsons. London: George Allen and Unwin, Ltd., 1930.

———. *The Religion of China*. Trans. by Hans H. Gerth. New York: The Free Press, 1951.

———. *The Religion of India*. Trans. and ed. by Hans H. Gerth and Don Martindale. New York: The Free Press, 1958.

———. *The Sociology of Religion*. Trans. by Ephraim Fischoff. Intro. by Talcott Parsons. Boston, Mass.: The Beacon Press, 1963.

———. *The Theory of Social and Economic Organization*. Trans. by A. M. Henderson and Talcott Parsons, ed. with an intro. by Talcott Parsons. New York: Oxford University Press, 1947.

WELBON, GUY RICHARD. *The Buddhist Nirvana and Its Western Interpreters*. Chicago, Ill.: University of Chicago Press, 1968.

WERTHEIM, W. F. "Religious Reform Movements in South and Southeast Asia." *Archives de Sociologie des Religions*, No. 12 (1961), 53–62.

WESLEY, JOHN. *Sermons*. New York, 1868.

WHALEN, WILLIAM J. *Armageddon Around the Corner: A Report on Jehovah's Witnesses*. New York: The John Day Company, Inc., 1962.

WHITAM, FREDERICK L. "Subdimensions of Religiosity and Race Prejudice." *Review of Religious Research*, 3 (Spring 1962), 166–174.

WHITE, ANDREW D. *A History of the Warfare of Science with Theology in Christendom*, 2 vols. New York: Appleton-Century-Crofts, Inc., 1896.

WHITEHEAD, ALFRED N. *Religion in the Making*. New York: The Macmillan Company, 1926.

———. *Science and the Modern World*. New York: The New American Library (Mentor Books), 1948. (First published by Macmillan, 1925.)

WHITING, BEATRICE. *Paiute Sorcery*. New York: Viking Fund, 1950.

WHITING, JOHN W. M., and IRVIN L. CHILD. *Child Training and Personality: A Cross-Cultural Study*. New Haven: Yale University Press, 1953.

WHITLEY, OLIVER R. *Religious Behavior: Where Sociology and Religion Meet*. Englewood Cliffs, N.J.: Prentice-Hall, Inc., 1964.

———. *Trumpet Call to Reformation*. St. Louis, Mo.: Bethany Press, 1959.

WIEHN, ERHARD. *Theorien der Sozialen Schichtung*. München: R. Piper & Co. Verlag, 1968.

WIESE, LEOPOLD VON. *Systematic Sociology*. Adapted and amplified by Howard Becker. New York: John Wiley & Sons, Inc., 1932.

WILENSKY, HAROLD L., and JACK LADINSKY. "From Religious Community to Occupational Group: Structural Assimilation Among Professors, Lawyers, and Engineers." *American Sociological Review*, 32 (August 1967), 541–561.

WILLEMS, EMILIO. *Followers of the New Faith. Culture Change and the Rise of Protestantism in Brazil and Chile*. Nashville, Tennessee: Vanderbilt University Press, 1967.

———. "Validation of Authority in Pentecostal Sects of Chile and Brazil." *Journal for the Scientific Study of Religion*, 6 (Fall 1967), 253–258.

WILLIAMS, GEORGE HUNTSTON. *The Radical Reformation*. London: Weidenfeld and Nicholson, 1962.

WILLIAMS, J. PAUL. "The Nature of Religion." *Journal for the Scientific Study of Religion*, 2 (Fall 1962), 3–14.

WILLIAMS, MELVIN J. *Catholic Social Thought*. New York: The Ronald Press Company, 1950.

WILLIAMS, ROBIN M., JR. *American Society*, rev. ed. New York: Alfred A. Knopf, Inc., 1960.

———. "Religion, Value-Orientations, and Intergroup Conflict." *Journal of Social Issues*, 12 (1956), 12–20.

WILSON, BRYAN R. "The Migrating Sects." *British Journal of Sociology*, 18 (September 1967), 303–317.
———. "The Origins of Christian Science." *The Hibbert Journal*, 57 (January 1959), 161–170.
———, ed. *Patterns of Sectarianism. Organization and Ideology in Social and Religious Movements*. London: William Heinemann, Ltd., 1967.
———. *Religion in Secular Society*. London: C. A. Watts and Co., 1966.
———. *Sects and Society*. London: William Heinemann, Ltd., 1961.
WILSON, CODY. "Extrinsic Religious Values and Prejudice." *Journal of Abnormal and Social Psychology* (March 1960), 286–291.
WILSON, EDMUND. *The Scrolls from the Dead Sea*. New York: Oxford University Press, 1955.
WILSON, JAMES Q., and EDWARD C. BANFIELD. "Public Regardingness as a Value Premise in Voting Behavior." *American Political Science Review*, 58 (1964), 876–887.
WINTER, GIBSON. "Methodological Reflection on 'The Religious Factor'." *Journal for the Scientific Study of Religion*, 2 (Fall 1962), 53–63.
———. *The Suburban Captivity of the Churches*. Garden City, N.Y.: Doubleday & Company, Inc., 1961.
WOLIN, SHELDON S. "Politics and Religion: Luther's Simplistic Imperative." *American Political Science Review*, 50 (March 1956), 24–42.
WOOD, JAMES R., and MAYER N. ZALD. "Aspects of Racial Integration in the Methodist Church: Sources of Resistance to Organizational Policy." *Social Forces*, 45 (December 1966), 255–265.
WOOD, WILLIAM W. *Culture and Personality Aspects of the Pentecostal Holiness Religion*. The Hague: Mouton and Co., 1965.
WOODHOUSE, A. S. P., ed. *Puritanism and Liberty*. Being the Army Debates, 1647–1649. London: J. M. Dent & Sons, Ltd., 1938.
WORKMAN, HERBERT B. *The Dawn of the Reformation*. London: The Epworth Press, 1901.
WORLD COUNCIL OF CHURCHES. *Six Ecumenical Surveys*. Preparatory material for the Second Assembly of the World Council of Churches, 1954. New York: Harper and Row, Publishers, Inc., 1954.
WORSLEY, PETER. *The Trumpet Shall Sound. A Study of "Cargo" Cults in Melanesia*. London: MacGibbon and Kee, 1957.
WRIGHT, ARTHUR F., ed. "Studies in Chinese Thought." Comparative Studies of Cultures and Civilizations, No. 1. Robert Redfield and Milton Singer, eds. *The American Anthropologist* (December 1953).
YANG, C. K. *Religion in Chinese Society*. Berkeley, Calif.: University of California Press, 1961.
YEARBOOK OF AMERICAN CHURCHES. Ed. by Constant H. Jacquet, Jr. New York: Dept. of Publication Services, National Council of Churches of Christ in the U.S.A., 1967.
YINGER, J. MILTON. "Contraculture and Subculture." *American Sociological Review*, 25 (October 1960), 625–635.
———. "The Influence of Anthropology on Sociological Theories of Religion." *American Anthropologist*, 60 (June 1958), 487–496.
———. *A Minority Group in American Society*. New York: McGraw-Hill Book Company, Inc., 1965.
———. "On the Definition of Interfaith Marriage." *Journal for the Scientific Study of Religion*, 7 (1968), 104–107.
———. "Pluralism, Religion and Secularism." *Journal for the Scientific Study of Religion*, 6 (Spring 1967), 17–28.
———. "A Research Note on Interfaith Marriage Statistics." *Journal for the Scientific Study of Religion*, 7 (1968), 97–103.

YINGER, J. MILTON. *Religion in the Struggle for Power. A Study in the Sociology of Religion.* Durham, N.C.: Duke University Press, 1946 (Reprinted, Russell and Russell, 1961).

———. *Sociology Looks at Religion.* New York: The Macmillan Company, 1963.

———. *Toward a Field Theory of Behavior.* New York: McGraw-Hill Book Company, Inc., 1965.

YOUNGER, GEORGE D. *The Church and Urban Renewal.* Philadelphia, Pa.: J. B. Lippincott Company, 1965.

———. "Protestant Piety and the Right Wing." *Social Action* (May 1951), 5–35.

ZAEHNER, R. C. *The Comparison of Religions.* London: Faber and Faber, Ltd., 1958.

ZAHN, GORDON. *German Catholics in Hitler's Wars.* New York: Sheed and Ward, Inc., 1962.

ZAHN, JANE C., ed. *Religion and the Face of America.* Berkeley, Calif.: University of California, 1959.

ZEITLIN, JOSEPH. *Disciples of the Wise.* New York: Bureau of Publications, Teachers College, Columbia University, 1945.

ZINKIN, TAYA. *Caste Today.* London: Oxford University Press, for the Institute of Race Relations, 1962.

ZOLLSCHAN, GEORGE K., and WALTER HIRSCH, eds. *Explorations in Social Change.* Boston, Mass.: Houghton Mifflin Company, 1964.

NAME INDEX

Abbott, Freeland, 435
Abbott, Lyman, 359
Aberle, David, 21, 94, 164, 280, 320, 323, 324, 342
Abrams, Ray, 411, 461, 466
Ackerknecht, Erwin H., 172
Adams, Bert, 116
Adler, Alfred, 186, 201
Adorno, T. W., 456
Ahmann, Mathew, 325, 366
Albert, Ethel, 205–207
Alexander VI, 376
Alland, Alexander, Jr., 151, 152
Allegro, John M., 483
Allen, Russell, 193
Allport, Gordon, 26, 58, 59, 79, 121, 131–33, 153, 179, 193, 206
Almond, Gabriel, 99, 197, 219, 266, 431, 434, 435
Altgeld, John P., 359
Altizer, Thomas, 45, 525
Ambedkar, B. R., 127
Ames, Michael, 404
Anderson, Charles, 240, 428
Anderson, Donald N., 452
Andreski, Stanislav, 394
Aquinas, St. Thomas, 57, 195, 256, 447, 494
Arbousse-Bastide, Paul, 195
Argyle, Michael, 489
Aristotle, 53, 54, 108
Arminius, 50
Augustine, St., 459, 461, 486
Ayal, E. B., 400

Babbie, Earl, 28, 134, 169, 369

Babbitt, Irving, 167
Bainton, Roland, 253, 293, 460
Balandier, Georges, 279, 280, 310
Baldwin, James, 336
Bales, Robert F., 21, 99, 211, 219
Balk, Alfred, 355
Ballou, Robert O., 458
Baltzell, E. Digby, 300, 364
Banfield, Edward C., 450, 451
Banton, Michael, 4, 80, 99
Barber, Bernard, 320, 323
Barnett, H. G., 324
Barr, Donald, 167
Barth, Karl, 370, 492, 521
Barton, Bruce, 361
Barton, Ralph, 103
Bates, E. S., 376, 436
Bates, Frederick, 284
Bateson, Gregory, 103
Baumer, Franklin, 194–96
Baxter, Richard, 384–86
Bea, Augustin, 246
Beatles, The, 157
Becker, Carl, 194
Becker, Howard P., 47, 256, 257, 262, 279, 280
Beecher, Henry Ward, 359
Bell, Daniel, 454
Bellah, Robert, 6, 47, 72, 124, 219, 228, 350, 400, 403–405, 414, 435, 437, 438, 479, 514–16
Bendix, Reinhard, 100, 166, 219, 304, 381, 397, 512
Benedict, Ruth, 52, 152, 204, 206, 215, 348
Bennett, John C., 366, 462, 464, 465, 471, 522

577

Bennigsen, Alexandre, 198
Benyon, E. D., 328, 329
Berelson, Bernard, 450
Berger, Peter, 80, 151, 156, 157, 280, 289,
    455, 456, 510, 519–21, 525
Bergson, Henri, 106, 107, 123, 529
Bernard, L. L., 50
Berne, Eric, 92
Bertalanffy, Ludwig von, 98
Berton, Pierre, 151
Besanceney, Paul, 241
Bhatt, G. S., 259
Bhave, Vinoba, 520
Biggar, Jeanne, 193
Binder, Leonard, 405, 431, 435
Birnbaum, Norman, 92
Black, Hugo, 445
Black, Max, 99
Blake, Eugene Carson, 247
Blanshard, Paul, 495, 496
Boas, Franz, 52
Bobilin, Robert, 458, 459, 470
Boisen, A. T., 122, 154, 178, 200, 303, 304,
    307
Bonhoeffer, Dietrich, 45, 492, 516, 524, 525
Borgia, Cesare, 376
Borgia, Lucrezia, 376
Borhek, J. T., 268
Braden, Charles S., 173, 485
Braden, William, 154, 166, 168, 329
Brailsford, H. N., 272, 297
Brand, Charles, 323
Brandon, S. G. F., 298
Breasted, James, 88
Bredemeier, Harry C., 99, 102
Bressler, Marvin, 67
Brock, Timothy, 122
Brown, H. Rap, 340
Brown, L. B., 131
Brown, Robert M., 246, 247, 366, 495,
    496
Brunner, Edmund de S., 494
Buchman, Frank, 158
Buckley, Walter, 99
Budd, Susan, 196
Buddha, 124, 148, 404, 415
Bultmann, Rudolf, 45, 516, 524, 525
Bunyan, John, 200
Burchinal, Lee, 241
Burke, Kenneth, 90
Burridge, Kenelm, 317, 318
Burrows, Millar, 483

Cahnman, Werner, 241
Calhoun, Robert, 365
Callahan, Daniel, 525
Calvin, John, 127, 256, 357, 358, 378, 382–
    85, 387, 486, 520
Campbell, Ernest, 325, 369
Campbell, Joseph, 220
Camus, Albert, 523, 524, 534
Cantril, Hadley, 158

Caporale, Rocco, 498
Carliner, David, 469
Carlyle, Thomas, 49
Carmichael, Stokely, 332, 333, 340
Carrier, Hervé, 154
Carter, G. W., 453
Carter, Paul, 331, 363, 364
Cartus, F. E., 498
Cattell, R. B., 205, 206
Catton, William R., Jr., 99
Cayton, H. R., 326
Centers, Richard, 285
Chambers, Whittaker, 197
Chancellor, Loren, 241
Chein, Isidor, 117
Child, Irvin, 186, 206, 221
Childs, Marquis, 366
Chmaj, Betty E., 454
Churchill, Winston, 160
Clark, Burton, 66
Clark, Elmer T., 256, 276, 277, 280, 301,
    302, 304
Clark, Kenneth, 340
Clark, S. D., 280, 307, 308
Clark, W. H., 158
Cleaver, Eldridge, 340
Codrington, R. H., 85
Cohen, Arthur, 504
Cohn, Norman, 117, 198, 258, 280, 292,
    293, 301, 339
Cohn, Werner, 32, 276
Coleman, James Samuel, 235, 396
Coleman, James Smoot, 99, 219, 266, 431,
    434, 435
Coleman, John, 280
Collier, K. S., 217
Compton, John, 63
Comte, Auguste, 12, 57, 195, 196, 218, 437
Condorcet, M. J. A., 194
Confucius, 106
Conlin, Joseph, 466
Conot, Robert, 331, 332
Conwell, Russell, 370
Conyers, James, 334
Coser, Lewis, 116, 117
Coulson, Noel, 46, 228, 404, 435
Coulton, G. G., 374
Cox, Harvey, 45, 47, 156, 198, 201, 248,
    366, 493, 494, 525, 526
Cragg, G. R., 231
Cromwell, Oliver, 296, 297
Cross, Frank M., Jr., 483
Crow, Paul, 246
Culver, Dwight, 325
Cumming, Elaine, 517
Cutler, Donald, 1, 87, 92, 159, 165, 201,
    214, 223, 250, 300, 335, 355, 438, 458,
    466, 504, 535

Dahrendorf, Ralf, 99, 100, 114, 115, 117
D'Andrade, R. G., 390
Daniel, V. E., 326, 328

D'Antonio, William, 405, 406, 431
Dator, James A., 169, 170
Davies, A. Powell, 483
Davies, W. D., 482, 483
Davis, A. W., 326, 327
Davis, Kingsley, 16, 85, 90, 92, 93, 99, 100, 109, 129
Decter, Moshe, 198
DeJong, Gordon, 26
Dembitz, Nanette, 469
Demerath, N. J. III, 90, 98, 99, 271, 280, 281, 284, 287, 288, 300, 489
De Quincy, Thomas, 164
Derrett, J. D. M., 355
Desroche, Henri, 198, 200, 400
Dewey, John, 49, 196, 201, 216, 534
Diamont, Alfred, 244
Diderot, Denis, 194
Dierenfeld, Richard, 443, 444
Dittes, James, 32
Dobashi, Fumiko, 173
Dollard, John, 326, 327
Dornbusch, Sanford, 492
Douglas, William O., 445
Douglass, Frederick, 340
Douglass, H. P., 300, 494
Douglass, James, 462, 463
Douglass, Truman B., 300
Drake, St. C., 326
Dreger, R. M., 131
DuBois, W. E. B., 335
Ducasse, C. J., 3
Dunlap, Knight, 9
Durkheim, Emile, 11, 12, 85–88, 101, 105, 116, 125, 183, 196, 204, 221, 429, 437
Durnbaugh, Donald, 268, 272
Dynes, Russell R., 254, 281, 287, 288

Eaton, Joseph, 175
Ebenstein, William, 427
Ebersole, Luke E., 438, 439, 450
Ebisawa, Arimichi, 473
Eckardt, A. Roy, 156
Eckstein, Harry, 466
Eddy, Mary Baker, 174, 176
Edwards, David, 525
Edwards, Harry, 340
Eggan, Fred, 324
Ehrmann, Henry, 479
Eichhorn, Robert, 396
Eisenstadt, S. N., 219, 381, 390–92, 400, 403, 411
Eister, Allan W., 99, 107, 158, 266, 281, 405, 435
Elder, Joseph, 395
Eliade, Mircea, 21, 22, 80, 154, 164, 172, 220
Elinson, Howard, 454
Emerson, Ralph W., 486
Engels, Friedrich, 511
England, R. W., 174, 175
Ennis, Philip, 154

Epstein, B. R., 454
Erickson, Kai, 78, 92, 213, 412, 487
Erikson, Erik, 87
Ernst, Morris L., 197
Espy, R. H. Edwin, 325
Essien-Udom, E. U., 128, 337
Esslin, Martin, 524
Etzioni, Amitai, 476, 504
Etzioni, Eva, 476
Evans-Pritchard, E. E., 47, 48, 72, 85, 94, 172, 221
Evers, Hans-Dieter, 263

Fallding, Harold, 210
Fanfani, Amintore, 381
Fanon, Frantz, 117, 339, 340, 466
Fard, W. D., 328, 336
Farmer, William, 334
Farrakhan, Louis, 338
Faulkner, Joseph, 26
Fauset, A. H., 325, 326, 341
Feld, Sheila, 396, 397
Festinger, Leon, 286, 287
Fetter, George, 210
Feuer, Lewis, 198
Feuerbach, Ludwig, 182
Fichter, Joseph, 2, 27, 28, 67, 517
Finkelstein, Louis, 290, 291, 481
Finney, Charles G., 363
Fiske, Edward B., 469
Fletcher, Joseph, 47
Fletcher, William, 198
Forster, Arnold, 454
Fortas, Abe, 445
Fortes, Meyer, 55, 87, 94, 183, 221
Fox, George, 200
Frank, Jerome, 76, 77
Frankfort, Henri, 88
Frazer, James G., 56, 70–72, 85, 87, 220
Frazier, E. F., 325, 326
Freedman, Mervin, 133
Freeman, L. C., 220
Freeman, Susan Tax, 94
Fremantle, Anne, 463
Freud, Sigmund, 47, 85, 106, 108, 109, 122, 135, 181–89, 200–202, 510, 524
Friedrich, Carl J., 199, 412
Fromm, Erich, 11, 50, 122, 155, 156, 186–89, 201, 472, 534
Fuchs, Lawrence, 450, 496

Gandhi, Mohandas, 333, 467
Gans, Herbert J., 504
Garaudy, Roger, 248
Gardner, B. B., 326, 327
Gardner, Herb, 91
Gardner, M. R., 326, 327
Garrison, W. E., 223, 487
Garvey, Marcus, 312, 335
Gaster, Theodore, 483
Gaudet, Hazel, 450
Gaustad, Edwin, 223, 300

Geertz, Clifford, 13, 14, 80, 81, 90, 152, 228, 405, 484
Geffken, Heinrich, 431
George, Charles, 294
George, Katherine, 294
Gerlach, Luther, 281
Germani, Gino, 219
Gerth, Hans H., 63, 284, 289, 415, 509, 511
Gilkey, Langdon, 46, 526
Gillespie, James M., 59, 131
Glantz, Oscar, 450
Glazer, Nathan, 503, 504
Glenn, Norval, 395–97
Glick, Paul, 241
Glock, Charles Y., 17, 26–28, 34, 44, 117, 134, 172, 239, 248, 270, 305, 369, 423, 451, 490, 494
Gluckman, Max, 117
Goddijn, W., 281
Goffman, Erving, 91
Göhre, Paul, 421
Golds, Jenette, 67
Goldschmidt, Dietrich, 281
Goldschmidt, Walter, 5, 95, 99, 104, 206, 221
Goldsen, Rose, 31
Goldstein, Bernice, 396
Gompers, Samuel, 360
Gooch, G. P., 294, 297
Goode, Erich, 281, 300
Goode, William J., 70, 85, 102, 219, 221, 349, 350
Goodenough, Erwin R., 126, 152, 154, 201
Goodrich, H. B., 68
Goody, Jack, 4
Gordon, Albert, 146, 154
Gordon, Milton, 239, 240, 428, 504
Gorlow, Leon, 122
Gouldner, Alvin, 90, 99, 235
Grafton, T. H., 84
Graham, Billy, 303, 428, 493
Greeley, Andrew, 25, 60, 66–69, 396
Green, R. W., 381
Greenberg, Bradley, 437
Greenberg, Irving, 504
Greenblum, Joseph, 240, 504–506
Greenslade, S. L., 230–32
Gregor, James, 99
Gregory XI, 377
Gregory, D. S., 358
Grose, Peter, 198
Gross, Llewellyn, 90, 99
Grotius, Hugo, 465, 466
Gumplowicz, Ludwig, 116
Guntrip, Henry, 178
Gurian, Waldemar, 199
Gurin, Gerald, 396, 397
Gusfield, Joseph, 477
Gustafson, Paul, 256, 281
Guterman, Norbert, 156, 191
Guttman, Louis, 31

Hagen, E. E., 403, 476, 478
Hager, Don, 117
Hagopian, Elaine, 266
Hall, Richard, 261
Hall, T. C., 385, 487
Haller, William, 296
Hamilton, Charles, 332, 333, 340
Hamilton, Thomas, 521
Hamilton, William, 45, 525
Hammond, Barbara, 229
Hammond, John L., 229
Hammond, Phillip, 258, 268, 271, 280, 369, 519
Handlin, Oscar, 501, 502
Handsome Lake, 324
Harding, Vincent, 335
Harrington, Charles, 517
Harris, Marvin, 283
Harrison, Paul, 235, 494
Hartigan, Richard, 466
Havens, Joseph, 131, 168
Heer, David, 241
Hegel, G. F. von, 57, 509
Heise, David, 529
Heiss, Jerold, 241
Heist, Paul, 133
Hempel, Carl, 99, 101, 105
Heraclitus, 116, 117
Herberg, Will, 240, 428, 438, 491, 497, 501, 502, 504
Hero, Alfred, 456
Herskovitz, M. J., 71, 325
Hill, Christopher, 294
Hiltner, Seward, 178
Himes, Joseph, 116
Himmelfarb, Milton, 441, 445, 446, 504
Hintze, Otto, 512
Hiriyanna, Mysore, 42
Hirsch, Walter, 476
Hitler, Adolf, 199, 343, 365, 412, 521
Hobbes, Thomas, 107, 108, 116
Hobhouse, L. T., 50, 481, 482
Hoffer, Eric, 166, 191, 192
Holt, Arthur E., 359
Holt, John B., 301, 306
Holtom, D. C., 458, 472, 485
Homans, George, 99
Homer, 54
Hopkins, C. H., 359, 364
Hopkins, Raymond, 528
Hori, Ichiro, 169
Horney, Karen, 274
Horton, John, 116
Horton, Robin, 4, 71, 214, 215
Horton, Walter, 522
Houtart, François, 498
Howard, Peter, 158
Howe, Mark D., 431
Howell, F. C., 97
Howell, Leon, 494
Howells, William W., 61, 129, 320, 321, 324

Hoyt, Robert, 250
Hsu, Francis L. K., 74, 77
Hu Shih, 49
Hubert, Henri, 154, 221, 215
Hudson, Winthrop, 223, 487, 489
Hughes, Everett, 286
Humphrey, Hubert H., 238, 424
Hunt, Richard, 26
Hunt, Rolfe, 66
Huss, John, 377, 378
Hutchinson, Anne, 412
Hutchinson, John A., 366
Hutchinson, Paul, 230, 489
Huxley, Aldous, 164, 165
Huxley, Julian, 49, 534, 535
Hyland, Ruth, 395–97
Hyman, Ray, 79
Hynes, Virginia, 281

Ibn Khaldun, 116
Iglehart, Charles W., 459
Ikado, Fujio, 156, 169, 170
Innocent VIII, 375
Isaiah, 130
Israel, Herman, 391

Jackson, Elmore, 468
Jackson, Elton, 284
Jackson, Robert H., 443
Jacob, Philip, 205, 467
James, E. O., 220
James, William, 10, 127, 144, 146, 151, 153, 200, 314
Jefferson, Thomas, 438
Jesus, 45, 482, 483
Joachim of Fiore, 293
John XXIII, 463, 464, 466, 498
Johnson, Arthur, 192, 193
Johnson, Benton, 225, 271, 281, 306, 307, 451, 452
Johnson, Charles S., 274, 326
Johnson, John J., 406
Johnson, Thomas A., 338
Jones, W. Lawson, 301
Jung, Carl G., 135, 179, 186, 187, 190, 201

Kahn, Herman, 462, 463
Kant, Immanuel, 49, 157, 516, 526
Katz, Wilbur, 443
Keene, James, 135
Kelly, W. H., 204
Kemper, Theodore, 396
Kennedy, Diane, 79
Kennedy, John F., 437, 496
Kennedy, John G., 99, 185
Kennedy, Robert, 238
Kennedy, Robert E., Jr., 395
Kierkegaard, Sören, 45, 58, 141, 533
Kiev, Ari, 76, 154, 175
Killian, Lewis, 274, 275
King, Irving, 85
King, Larry, 67

King, Martin Luther, Jr., 330, 333, 334, 340, 341, 371
King, Morton, 16, 27
King, Winston, 64, 139, 141, 142, 153, 172, 228, 434, 484
Kingsley, Charles, 364
Kirkpatrick, Clifford, 58
Kitagawa, Joseph, 169, 170, 220, 228, 246
Klausner, Samuel, 127, 162, 178, 180, 196
Klohr, Olaf, 92
Kluckhohn, Clyde, 18, 76, 78, 94, 101, 121, 152, 172, 204, 206, 207, 213
Kluckhohn, Florence, 205–208, 274
Knapp, Robert H., 68
Koestler, Arthur, 196, 197
Kolarz, Walter, 198
Kornhauser, William, 244, 427
Kramer, Judith, 504
Kritsky, Fred, 442
Kroeber, A. L., 18, 19, 94
Kropotkin, Peter, 117
Kuehnelt-Leddihn, Erik von, 68
Küng, Hans, 499

LaBarre, Weston, 52, 164, 308, 323
Ladinsky, Jack, 243
Lang, Andrew, 85
LaNoue, George R., 446
Lanternari, Vittorio, 117, 277, 281, 310, 317, 323
Larson, Martin, 355
Laski, Harold, 486
Laski, Marghanita, 154
Latourette, Kenneth, 49
Laue, James, 337
Lauer, Quentin, 248
Laumann, Edward O., 239
Lawrence, D. H., 186
Lawrence, Peter, 317, 318
Lawrence, William, 358
Lazarsfeld, Paul, 450
Lazerwitz, Bernard, 223
Learsi, Rufus, 502
Leary, Timothy, 165, 168
Lee, James M., 68
Lee, Robert, 117, 246, 352, 423
Leeming, Bernard, 246
Lemercier-Quelquejay, Chantal, 198
Lenski, Gerhard, 24, 26, 29, 66–68, 100, 133, 239, 240, 242, 243, 270, 284, 369, 396–99, 405, 428, 450, 504
Lerner, Daniel, 403, 476, 478
Leskes, Theodore, 441
Leslie, Charles, 20, 103
Lessa, William, 172, 221, 280, 281
Lesser, Alexander, 320, 321
Leuba, James H., 126, 154
Leventman, Seymour, 504
Levi-Strauss, Claude, 17, 172, 221
Levy, Marion, Jr., 99
Levy, Reuben, 42, 46, 58, 411, 435
Lewin, Kurt, 237

Name Index 582

Munger, Edwin, 453
Müntzer, Thomas, 339, 340
Murdock, George, 220
Murphy, Raymond, 396
Murray, Gilbert, 53, 54, 155, 252, 298
Murray, Henry A., 248
Murray, Thomas, 462
Murvar, Vatro, 411

Nadel, S. F., 47, 81, 99, 215, 221
Naegele, Kaspar, 99
Nagel, Ernest, 98, 99
Nagle, William, 462
Nakamura, Hajime, 485
Narayan, Jayaprakash, 520
Nash, Manning, 404
Nash, Philleo, 324
Needham, Joseph, 73, 75, 123, 349
Nelson, Geoffrey, 279, 280
Neuwien, Reginald, 67
Newell, William, 134, 156, 173
Newman, Jeremiah, 498
Newton, Isaac, 194
Nichols, J. H., 441
Nicholson, J. W., 326
Niebuhr, H. Richard, 223, 230, 248, 267, 298–300, 325, 363, 365, 381, 487
Niebuhr, Reinhold, 1, 8, 11, 45, 87, 141, 142, 199, 218, 231, 281, 360, 365, 366, 370, 419, 492, 521, 530
Nietzsche, Friedrich, 288, 509, 510, 525, 526
Nisbet, Robert A., 352
Nixon, Richard M., 424, 437
Norbeck, Edward, 47, 117
Novak, Michael, 165, 201, 214, 498–500, 524, 526

Obenhaus, Victor, 135
O'Dea, Thomas, 67, 103, 209, 210, 235, 236, 267, 451, 498
Odenwald, Robert, 163, 178
Otto, Rudolf, 126
Outler, Albert C., 178, 180
Overstreet, Bonaro, 454
Overstreet, Harry, 454

Page, Charles, 51
Paine, Thomas, 194
Parenti, Michael, 451
Pareto, Vilfredo, 235, 510
Parker, Edwin, 437
Parsons, Anne, 406
Parsons, Talcott, 5, 18, 21, 32, 79, 94, 99, 100, 104, 125, 141, 146, 207, 210, 211, 213, 219, 381, 388, 510, 512, 516
Pascal, Blaise, 57
Pauck, Wilhelm, 365, 374, 532
Paul VI, 498, 499
Paul, St., 124, 200, 291, 482, 483
Peale, Norman Vincent, 159–63, 173, 175, 176, 493

Pearson, Karl, 194
Peel, Robert, 368
Pelagius, 50
Pellegrin, Roland, 284
Perry, Ralph Barton, 436
Petegorsky, David W., 295–97
Peters, Victor, 268
Peterson, Richard H., 98, 99
Peterson, William, 223
Pettigrew, Thomas, 325, 369
Pfautz, Harold W., 262
Pfeffer, Leo, 431, 441, 442, 447
Phillips, Norman, 453
Photiadis, John, 192, 193
Pike, Frederick, 405, 406, 431
Pike, James, 79, 355, 356
Pitts, Jesse, 99
Pius XII, 163
Plato, 53, 54, 107
Polybius, 106
Pope, Liston, 151, 226, 256, 278, 302, 303, 306, 325, 360
Porter, John, 244, 396
Powderly, Terence, 360
Powdermaker, Hortense, 326, 327
Putney, Snell, 26, 28, 55, 192, 471

Raab, Earl, 117
Radcliffe-Brown, A. R., 21, 75, 90, 99, 125, 221
Radin, Paul, 86, 347
Ramsey, Paul, 462, 464, 465
Randal, Judith, 181
Randall, John H., 201, 484, 485, 532
Randall, John H., Jr., 201, 484, 485, 532
Rappaport, Roy, 12, 94, 350, 351
Rauschenbusch, Walter, 361, 370
Redfield, Robert, 217
Reed, Edward, 462, 463
Reedy, John, 356
Reich, Wilhelm, 186
Reimers, David, 325
Reiss, Paul, 241
Reiterman, Carl, 498
Renan, Ernest, 195
Reynolds, James F., 122, 456
Rieff, Philip, 178, 181, 183, 186, 187, 200, 201, 478
Riesman, David, 181
Ringer, Benjamin, 28, 134, 240, 369, 504
Rivers, W. H. R., 349
Roberts, Bryan, 406, 407
Roberts, David E., 178
Roberts, William, 180
Robertson, D. B., 355
Robertson, H. M., 381, 382
Robinson, John, 45, 46, 201, 525
Rodman, Hyman, 241
Rogers, David P., 60
Rokeach, Milton, 249, 456
Rose, Peter, 504
Rosen, Bernard, 68, 390, 396–98

Rosenberg, Stuart, 502, 504, 505
Rosenstone, Robert, 454
Rosenthal, Erich, 504
Ross, E. A., 106
Rossi, Alice, 67
Rossi, Peter, 66, 67, 69
Rousseau, Jean Jacques, 194, 437, 534
Roy, Ralph L., 438, 454
Rubenstein, Richard, 504, 506
Rusinow, Dennison, 418
Rustin, Bayard, 117
Rustow, Dankwart, 266, 435
Rydenfelt, Sven, 419

Saint-Simon, Henri de, 195
Sampson, Edward, 286
Samuelsson, Kurt, 381, 382
Sanders, Thomas, 271
Sanderson, Ross, 494
Sanford, Nevitt, 133
Sarachandra, E. R., 124, 404
Sarkisyanz, E., 43
Sartre, Jean-Paul, 47, 201, 339, 523, 524, 534
Sawyer, Jack, 28, 55
Scanzani, John, 281
Schachter, Zalman, 504
Schecter, Jerrold, 431
Scheler, Max, 220
Schelsky, Helmuth, 2
Scheuer, Joseph, 495
Schilling, Howard, 62
Schlatter, R. B., 294, 298
Schleiermacher, Friedrich, 492, 516, 521, 525
Schlissel, Lillian, 466
Schroeder, Harold, 122
Schmidt, P. W., 85
Schneider, Herbert, 223, 300, 440, 494
Schneider, Louis, 99, 492
Schopenhauer, Arthur, 106
Schroeder, W. W., 135
Seeman, Melvin, 422, 423
Selznick, Philip, 236
Sewell, William, 396
Shah, Vimal, 396
Sharp, Harry, 395
Sheen, Fulton J., 162, 163
Sheinbaum, Stanley, 463
Sheldon, Charles M., 362
Sheldon, Eleanor, 489
Sherif, Muzafer, 249
Sherman, C, Bezalel, 504
Shestov, Lev, 58
Shils, Edward, 18, 21, 99, 207, 210, 211, 479, 489, 518
Shippey, Frederick, 151
Shuster, George, 66, 68
Sibley, Mulford, 467
Siegman, Aron W., 186
Silberstein, Fred, 422

Sills, David, 235
Silverman, Julian, 152
Silvert, Kalman, 271, 400, 418, 431
Simmel, Georg, 86, 87, 116
Simpson, George E., 90, 152, 172, 193, 274, 312, 313, 326, 502
Singer, Milton, 395
Siriwardane, C. D. S., 263, 419
Sixtus IV, 375
Sjoberg, Gideon, 60
Skinner, Elliott, 528
Sklare, Marshall, 240, 500, 502–506, 517
Slater, Philip, 159, 180
Slotkin, J. S., 164, 323
Smelser, Neal, 211
Smith, Adam, 116, 358
Smith, Donald E., 128, 172, 263, 355, 395, 411, 418, 419, 431, 434, 435, 470, 485
Smith, Douglas, 60
Smith, Homer, 58, 106, 481–483
Smith, Joseph, 527
Smith, Preserved, 64, 293, 355, 374–76, 380, 411
Smith, Timothy, 363
Smith, W. Robertson, 53, 410, 481
Smith, Wilfred C., 220, 470
Snyder, Richard, 116, 117
Socrates, 53
Solt, Leo, 296
Sombart, Werner, 381
Sorel, George, 117
Sorokin, Pitirim A., 219
Spaak, Henri, 463
Spann, J. Richard, 366
Spencer, Herbert, 56, 72, 85, 105, 116
Sperry, W. L., 223, 341, 342, 439, 440, 486, 487, 523
Spilka, Bernard, 122, 193, 456
Spindler, George, 323
Spiro, Melford E., 4, 42, 76, 99, 121, 139, 153, 172, 175, 227, 400, 401, 411
Spuhler, J. N., 97
Srinivas, M. N., 228, 395
Stackhouse, May, 92
Stanner, W. E. H., 343
Stark, Rodney, 26, 27, 34, 44, 59, 145, 149, 154, 172, 232, 239, 248, 270, 305, 420, 451, 490, 494
Stark, Werner, 232, 233, 254–58, 270, 281, 287, 288, 293
Steinberg, Stephen, 504
Stelzle, Charles, 364
Stinchcombe, Arthur, 119
Stokes, Anson Phelps, 431, 433, 434, 440, 447, 448, 461, 497
Stouffer, S. A., 285, 454
Stritch, Samuel, 495
Strodtbeck, F. L., 205–208, 281
Stroup, Herbert, 276, 441
Sturzo, Luigi, 431
Sunday, Billy, 493

Sundkler, Bengt, 277, 310
Sutherland, Harold, 443
Suzuki, D. T., 43, 64, 142, 226
Swanson, G. E., 88, 214, 219, 398
Sweet, W. W., 223, 487
Swift, Arthur, 513
Sykes, Gresham, 167

Talmon, Yonina, 281, 317, 319
Tannenbaum, Edward R., 453
Tavuchis, Nicholas, 248
Tawney, R. H., 374, 379–81
Tax, Sol, 94
Teilhard de Chardin, Pierre, 57, 534
Teune, Henry, 205
Thieu, Nguyen Van, 411
Thoreau, Henry David, 438
Thorner, Isidor, 148, 151, 154
Tillich, Paul, 6, 11, 157, 195, 200, 201, 229, 247, 365, 463, 492, 516, 525
Tiryakian, Edward, 32, 516
Titiev, Mischa, 70, 71
Tocqueville, Alexis de, 455
Toynbee, Arnold, 257, 414
Trent, James, 67
Troeltsch, Ernst, 64, 216, 227–29, 252–57, 262, 273, 291, 374, 379, 381, 383, 391, 530
Trotsky, Leon, 420
Trow, Martin, 235
Trueblood, Elton, 468
Tucker, Robert, 462, 464
Turner, Nat, 320
Turner, Ralph H., 274, 275
Turner, Wallace, 267
Tylor, Edward B., 4, 47, 56, 71, 72, 84, 85, 103, 105, 220

Underhill, Evelyn, 154
Underhill, Ruth, 319
Underwood, Kenneth, 117

Vahanian, Gabriel, 45, 57, 525
Van Buren, Paul, 45, 366, 525
Van den Berghe, Pierre L., 90, 99, 116, 117, 453
Van der Veldt, James, 163, 178
VanDusen, Henry P., 365
Vaughan, Ted, 60
Veblen, Thorstein, 92, 371
Verba, Sidney, 219, 437
Vernon, Glenn, 26, 281, 300, 517
Vernon, Philip, 26, 206
Veroff, Joseph, 396, 397
Vesey, Denmark, 330
Vischer, Lukas, 246
Vitoria, Francisco de, 465
Voget, Fred, 324
Vogt, Evon, 79, 172, 205–207, 209, 210, 221, 280, 281
Voltaire, F. M. A. de, 194

Von der Mehden, Fred, 418, 431

Waardenburg, Jean-Jacques, 228
Wach, Joachim, 2, 10, 144, 153, 216, 220, 227, 259, 288, 413, 517
Wagner, Helmut, 396
Wakin, Edward, 495
Walker, Brooks, 454
Wallace, Anthony, 14, 16, 17, 47, 99, 152, 154, 213, 214, 281, 315–17, 337, 514
Wallace, George, 238, 424
Wallis, Louis, 481
Walzer, Michael, 296, 466
Ward, A. Dudley, 366
Wardwell, Walter, 175
Warkov, Seymour, 69
Warner, W. Lloyd, 113, 114, 437
Warwick, Donald, 69
Washburn, S. L., 97
Washington, Booker T., 335
Watt, Thomas, 205
Watt, W. Montgomery, 228, 257, 435
Watts, Alan, 64
Wax, Murray, 70
Wax, Rosalie, 70
Webb, Sam, 122
Weber, Max, 8, 42, 43, 63, 71, 88, 127, 138, 140, 142, 146–48, 150, 153, 158, 166, 196, 207, 218, 219, 227, 228, 234, 235, 274, 284, 286, 288–91, 294, 307, 350, 351, 374, 379–83, 385–95, 399, 402, 414–16, 470, 475, 481, 484, 509, 511–14, 517–20
Webster, Harold, 133
Weil, Robert, 175
Weiner, Myron, 434
Weizmann, Chaim, 192
Wertheim, W. F., 219
Wesley, John, 225, 357, 358, 370
Westoff, Charles F., 67
Whalen, William, 276
Whitam, Frederick, 193, 454, 493
White, Andrew Dixon, 57, 58
White, Richard, 452
Whitehead, Alfred North, 19, 63
Whiting, Beatrice, 206, 214, 219, 221
Whiting, John W. M., 185, 186, 205, 206, 208, 221
Whitney, John R., 438
Whyte, William, 401
Wiehn, Edward, 100
Wiese, Leopold von, 262
Wilensky, Harold, 243
Wilkins, Roy, 334
Willems, Emilio, 281, 406
William of Occam, 57
Williams, Charles, 360
Williams, George H., 272, 293
Williams, J. Paul, 4
Williams, Robin M., Jr., 116, 118, 204, 491

SUBJECT INDEX

applied to religion, 51, 52, 72, 84, 514–16
Existentialism, 523, 524

Faith, 79, 159, 180, 378, 485, 491, 532
Family, 390
   communality, 239–41
   economic development, 394
Field theory, deprivation, 420–21
   drug use, 164–69
   pacifism, 496–72
   Protestantism, 387–92
   religion, 17–21, 89–92, 118–19, 151–53, 171–72, 250, 292–93
   social change, 388–92, 476–77
   values, 206–207
Freudian theory, 534
   critics, 186–87
   of religion, 85–86, 181–86
Functionalism, 52, 92–99, 119, 182, 185, 206, 502–503
   bibliography on, 99
   definition, 5–11
   developmental type, 95–97
   difficulties with, 100–105
   feedback model, 97–98
   immigration policy, 95–97
   magic, 74–76
   sects, 306–309, 316, 341–45
   theory, 86, 89–94, 129, 189, 250, 531–32
Fundamentalism, 488, 492
   politics, 451–55

Germany, 402, 403, 472
   churches, 355
   theology, 521
Ghost Dance, 320–22, 342
God, 45
   conceptions, 121, 188, 481
   death of, social sources, 214, 524–26
Great Britain, 470
   See also England
Greece, Ancient, religions of, 52–55, 298
Guttman scales, 31, 220, 240, 261

Health, religious interest in, 169, 171–76
   See also Psychiatry
"Healthy-mindedness," religion of, 144
Hinduism, 127–28, 228, 263, 289–90, 419
   church-state relationships, 434
   economic development, 394–95
   education, 65
   moral aspects, 42
   problem of evil, 137–38
   war, 470
History of religions, 21–22, 219–20
Holland, communality in, 240–44, 427–28
Homeostatic processes, 476–77
   in functional theories, 102–103
Hope, importance as a character variable, 286–87
   influence on religion, 305–307, 311–12, 333–35, 337, 344

Humanism, 201, 292
Hutterites, 268

Ideas, role of, 508–14, 527
Independents, in English Civil War, 294–95
India, 479
   See also Hinduism
Indians, American, 313
   religious beliefs, 215
   religious movements, 319–24
Individual needs, religion, 84–86, 121–35, 155–58, 177–90, 232
   sectariansm, 255–56, 301–303
   secular alternatives, 191–93
   variation in religious responses, 136–43
   variation in sources, 130–35
   See also Character
Indonesia, 405
Institutionalization, criteria for measuring, 264
Intermarriage, religious, 239–41, 494–95, 504
"Invisible religion," 32–33, 492
Islam, 65, 266, 419, 435–36, 447, 470
   See also Muhammadanism
Israel, ancient, 519
   influence on American Jews, 505–506
   See also Judaism

Japan, 171–72, 402, 403
   ecumenism in, 246
   "new religions," 169–71, 265, 272–73
   religion and war, 458–59, 470, 472
   religious complexity of, 44
   social change, 478–79
Jehovah's Witnesses, 276, 303–304, 467
Jews, 431–32
   assimilation vs. pluralism, 504–507
   political behavior, 429
   religious views, 503–506
   See also Judaism
Judaism, 289, 298, 300
   Conservative, 500, 502, 503
   early, social change and, 480–82
   moral aspects, 42, 52–55
   Orthodox, 500, 505
   politics, 450–51
   Reform, 501, 502
   science, 58, 63
   as a sect, 268–69
   social change, 500–507
   social stratification, 290–91
   war, 470
Just war, doctrine of, 459–60, 462–65, 469

Labor unions, churches and, 358–60
Latin America, religious influences on development, 405–406
Laymen, Catholic, 499
Levellers, 276, 296–97

religious differentiation, 232
religious radicalism, 296–98
types of relationship with religion, 409–30
universal religions, 412–16, 472–74
use of religion in, 411–12, 437–39, 448–49
varieties of church-state relationship, 431–36
"Positive thinking," 160–62, 166, 492
Positivism, religious aspects of, 12, 194–96, 534
Possession, religious, 151–52
Predestination, 295–96, 378, 383–84, 513
Prejudice and religion, 192–93, 453–56
Presbyterians, in English Civil War, 294–96
Priests, 50, 498, 499, 517–19
Primitive religions, 83–88, 103, 123, 259
    morals, 47–48
    politics, 409–10
    technology, 347–50
Prohibition, effects on social gospel, 364–65
Prophecy, 142–43, 274–75, 518–20
    definition, 146
    ethical, 147–48
    exemplary, 147–48
Prophets, 50, 150, 481, 517–20
Protestantism, capitalism and, 207, 396–99, 406
    distribution of income, 357–62
    ecumenism in, 246–47
    education, 68–69
    politics, 450–51
    science, 64
    social effects of values, 210
    social gospel in, 362–72
Protests, Negro religious, 327, 335–36
    religious support, 282, 315–17
    sectarian, in Christendom, 292–98
    See also Conflict
Psychiatry, religion and, 162, 177–81
    comparative, 152
    See also Health
Psychoanalysis, religion and, 181–90
    as a faith, 200–201
Psychology, approach to religion of, 18
    explanations of religious origins of, 84–86
Puritanism, 416–17, 486
    in English Civil War, 294–96

Quakerism, 267, 271, 468

Radical theology, 523–26
Reformation, 516
    economic aspects, 374–80
    radical sects, 292
Relative natural law, doctrine of, 447, 461
Religion, authoritarian-humanistic contrast of, 187–90

crosscultural measurement of, 32–40
declining influence of, 490–91
definitions, 3–16, 33–34
dimensions, 25–29, 135
effects on education, 68–69
effects on science, 63–65
element in conflict, 92, 117–18
evolution of, 514–16
extrinsic-intrinsic contrast, 193
forms, 10, 16–17, 46–47
functional alternatives, 183, 190–202, 342–43
functions, 1, 6–10, 122–125
group aspects, 19, 86–88
individual aspects, 19, 120–35
individual beliefs, 10–11
joyful aspects, 7–8, 171
levels in a society, 221–22
measurement of, 24–40
non-theistic types, 11–13, 534
objective study, 1–3
persistence of, 172
social integration, 105–14, 253, 376, 412
source of change, 526–30
sources, 7–8, 15–16
structural approach, 33–40
theories of origin, 83–88, 347
ultimate quality, 7, 13, 80–81, 139, 201–202
universality, 104
variation with type of society, 215–18
See also Culture; Economics; Education;
    Evil; Health; Magic; Morals; Politics;
    Psychiatry; Salvation; Science; Social
    change; Social stratification; Society;
    Suffering
Religious change, social change and, 476–80, 508–35
    in early Christianity, 482–85
    in early Judaisim, 480–82
    in United States, 485–506
Religious differentiation, 198, 251–81
    causes of, 226–39
    social differentiation and, 224–26
Religious experience, bibliography on, 153–54
    variables affecting, 145–53
    varieties, 143–55
Religious leaders, 177–78, 217, 233–34, 314, 361, 369, 475, 481
    competition with political leaders, 413–16, 515–16
    dilemma, 234–39, 354, 361, 416–17, 447–48, 460, 464–65, 500
    incomes, 354
    types, 516–20
Religious movements, bridging function of, 273, 343, 389
Religious practice, categories of, 16–17
    sex differences, 133–34
    variations in intensity, 7, 141, 227
Resentment, religious effects of, 288

"Return to religion," 48, 489–90
Revitalization movements, 315–16, 337
Revivalism, 363, 493
Revolution, 424–25
  religious influences on, 297
Ritual, 16–17, 535
Role influences on religion, 133–34
Roman Catholicism, 162–63, 300
  church-state values in United States, 441–42
  economic development, 392, 396–99, 405–406
  ecumenism, 246–47
  educational programs, 65–69, 444–46
  politics, 417–18, 430, 450–51
  sect elements, 270–71
  social change, 484, 494–500
  wealth, 354–55, 376
Russian Orthodox Church, 411–12

Saintliness, 128–29
Salvation, 384, 512–13
  religious roads to, 139–43, 377, 516
Salvation Army, 276, 303, 308
Sanctity, 12
Sangha, 419
Satyagraha, doctrine of, 467, 470
Scales for dimensions of religion, 27–32, 288
  of communality, 239–40
  of ecumenism, 245
Schempp case, 443, 444
Schism. *See* Religious differentiation
Schools, parochial, 65–68, 444–46
  question of religion in United States, 443–46
Science, approach to religion, 38–40, 202, 530–32
  relationships with religion, 56–65, 175–76, 526
  as religion, 11–12, 194–96
  of religion, naming of, 21–22
Scientists, religious views of, 11–12, 60
Secondary elites, social change and, 391
Sects, 252–56, 273–79, 300–309, 427, 474–75
  economic development, 399
  effects, 305–309
  factors supporting, 287–88
  among minorities, 311–17
  Negro, 324–98
  radical, 294–98
  secular, 238–39
  transition to churches, 225–26, 256, 267–73
  types, 273–79
  war, 466–69
Secular alternatives to religion, 190–202, 312
Secularism, 491
Segmentation, structural model of, 425–27

Segregation, effects on Negro religion, 325–26
Seichō no Ie, 275
Shinto, 458, 479
"Sick souls," religion of, 144
Skepticism, 195–96
Slavery, movement to abolish, 363–64
Snake-handling cult, 308
Social change, ecumenism and, 248–49
  religion, 233, 395, 401–407, 476–535
  theories, 388–92, 476–80
Social differentiation, religion and, 224–26, 239–44, 425–30, 481, 515
  See also Religious differentiation; Social stratification
Social gospel, 362–72
Social integration, religion and, 105–14, 253
Social mobility, effects on religion, 233
  religious influences on, 225–26, 306–307
Social movements, types of, 274
Social psychology of religion, 22, 527
Social stratification, religion and, 112, 138, 141–42, 225–26, 282–305
  types of systems, 283–84
  See also Caste systems; Class systems; Minority-majority systems
Social structure, definition, 211–12
  elements supporting drug use, 166
  religion, 170, 203, 211–15, 248, 304, 470–71
  social change, 388–92, 478
  types, 425–30
  See also Society
Socialism, Christian, 365, 387
Socialization, 209, 225–26
  religious effects of variation in, 185–86
Society, 18, 20
  functional prerequisites, 20–21, 94, 103–104
  integration-coercion theory, 115, 117
  problems of order, 107–10
  religion, 211–18, 408–409
  as source of religion, 86–88
  as a system, 20, 94, 476–77
  types, 429
  See also Social structure
Sociology, approach to study of religion of, 14, 18–19, 21–23, 86–88, 141–42, 231, 409, 434
  relation of religion and morals, 50–52
  relation of religion and science, 61–63
Sōka Gakkai, 169–71, 273
Sorcery, sources of belief, 186
South Africa, 429, 453
Southern Christian Leadership Conference, 334, 335, 340
Soviet Union, 478–79
  religion in, 411–12
Status inconsistency, among clergymen, 369

as source of sectarianism, 287–88, 292, 296, 422–23
varieties of, 284–88
Students, religious views, 35–38, 59–60, 131–32
Subculture, religion and, 167
Suffering, 136–39, 169–70
religious significance, 126–30, 289, 357, 414, 481–82, 515
Supernaturalism, 533
definition of religion, 13–15
Supreme Court, 441–45, 454
Sweden, religion and politics, 419

Taoism, 19
Taxation, churches and, 355–56
Technology, magic and, 73–74
religion and, 346–52
Thailand, Buddhism in, 263–64
Theatre of the Absurd, 523, 524
Theologians, 218, 492
contemporary, 520–26
Todas, 349
Totalitarianism, 199
Transcendentalism, 364
Transmigration, 127, 512, 513
Trobriand Islanders, 348
Tsembaga, 350–51
Types of religious organization, 251–81
bibliography of, 280–81
criteria for classifying, 257, 259–62
degree of complexity, 261
See also Church; Cult; Denomination; Ecclesia; Sect

Ulama, 419
"Underground churches," 493, 499
United States, bibliography on religion, 223
Catholicism, 270–71
church and state, 436–49
class and religion, 298–305, 357–62
communality, 240–44
cultural support for Black Power, 322–23

1968 political campaign, 238–39
pluralism, 428–29
radical religion, 493–94
religion and economic behavior, 395–99
religion and political behavior, 449–56
religious change, 484–506, 521–26
religious patterns, 221–23
Universalist religious values, 414–17, 533
political domination, 472–74
sociocultural context, 474–75
states, 433, 447, 449, 461–62
Upper classes, religious inclinations, 138, 141–42, 158, 288–99, 297–98, 357–62

Values, 424
scientific study, 205–11
See also Culture
Vatican, 355, 498
Vatican Council II, 68, 246–47, 464, 495, 497–98
Vicious circles, 316
Vietnam, 411, 417–18
Violence, 333, 339, 466
in religion, 333, 339–40, 416
Voodoo cult, 328

War, as source of religious dilemma, 415–16
internal, 466
religion, 457–75, 505–506
Wealth, distribution of and religion, 352–62
Witchcraft, 76, 78, 213–14
World Council of Churches, 246–47, 449, 464
World Fellowship of Buddhists, 246
Worship, 127, 195

Youth movements, religious elements, 534
Yugoslavia, 426–27

Zorach case, 442
Zuni, 348